Managing Change

Cases and Concepts **Third Edition**

Todd D. Jick
Columbia Business School
Global Leadership Services, Inc.

Maury A. Peiperl
IMD

McGraw-Hill Irwin

MANAGING CHANGE: CASES AND CONCEPTS, THIRD EDITION

Published by McGraw-Hill, a business unit of The McGraw-Hill Companies, Inc., 1221 Avenue of the Americas, New York, NY 10020.

Some ancillaries, including electronic and print components, may not be available to customers outside the United States.

This book is printed on acid-free paper.

3 4 5 6 7 8 9 0 SCI/SCI 1 0 9 8 7 6 5

ISBN 978-0-07-310274-0
MHID 0-07-310274-1

Vice President & Editor-in-Chief: *Brent Gordon*
Publisher: *Paul Ducham*
Marketing Manager: *Curt Reynolds*
Development Editor: *Laura Spell*
Editorial Coordinator: *Jonathan Thornton*
Marketing Manager: *Jaime Halteman*
Project Manager: *Melissa M. Leick*
Design Coordinator: *Brenda A. Rowles*
Cover Designer: *Studio Montage, St. Louis, Missouri*
Cover Image: *© Getty Images/RF*
Buyer: *Nicole Baumgartner*
Compositor: *Glyph International*
Typeface: *10/12 Times Roman*
Printer: *Strategic Content Imaging*

All credits appearing on page or at the end of the book are considered to be an extension of the copyright page.

Library of Congress Cataloging-in-Publication Data

Jick, Todd, 1949-
    Managing change: cases and concepts / Todd D. Jick, Maury A.
Peiperl.—3rd ed.
    p. cm.
    Includes bibliographical references and index.
    ISBN 978-0-07-310274-0 (alk. paper)
    1. Organizational change. 2. Organizational change—Case studies.
I. Peiperl, Maury.   II. Title.
    HD58.8.J53   2010
    658.4'06—dc22

                                                                              2010030324

www.mhhe.com

To our children: Zoe, Adina, Evan, and Julia

Preface to the Third Edition

There may have been a time when change was the exception rather than the rule in business. If there was, most people by now seem to have forgotten it. The pace of change in technology; in products and services; in the flows of money, goods, and information across borders; in needed skills; in networks; in ways of going to market—the constant impermanence in so many aspects of business has brought about, for many, a shift from looking at changes as bounded alterations on a fundamentally permanent background, to looking at all structures and processes—indeed, the background itself—as intrinsically changing; limited in time and destined to evolve—if not to be destroyed and re-created entirely.

Thus businesses and scholars have collectively dedicated millions of hours over several dozen years to figuring out how change works and how to do it well. We have amassed an impressive amount of know-how—research, tools, cases, stories—and created various kinds of training programs and qualifications. A large number of professionals now consider themselves primarily to be change practitioners, in the same way as others consider themselves marketing or finance or IT practitioners. In many places of higher education, courses on change (such as those using this book) have gone from specialized electives to core subjects. In short, managers are better equipped than ever with models and toolkits for understanding change and bringing it about.

Given all that progress, how has the success rate of change management improved in practice? If we look at the record of merger integrations, or at the return on private equity investments (many of them aimed at turning around troubled businesses), or at the outcomes of major change initiatives in corporations and governments, the news is not encouraging. Depending on whose estimates we choose to believe, anywhere from 50 to 80 percent of change efforts fail. It would seem that, despite all the attention paid to the subject, most organizations still do not know how to manage change.

Or perhaps it is more accurate to say that they are missing not so much the knowledge but rather the skills. The gap between understanding and doing has never been greater, not only because we have made far more progress on the former than on the latter, but also because the latter keeps getting more complicated. The presence of multiple, simultaneous changes; the breathtaking speed with which strategies are altered and CEOs turn over; the mind-boggling complexity of global organizations across which mass communication, though blunt, is trivially easy—these are a few of the things that today challenge change practitioners like never before.

On top of this, the audience for change has changed. Most people in most firms have now already been exposed to change—in fact, few of them expect to stay in the same organization over the long term, and they are more willing to challenge change on its merits, or to be cynical about, or ignore outright, change efforts in which their predecessors (or their parents) might have engaged directly (whether or not willingly).

Finally, the criteria on which change is judged are changing as well. Market share and return on equity have not gone away, but a wider universe of stakeholders with broader and longer-term performance criteria now demands the attention of change leaders, and they ignore it at their peril. Successful change that is not sustainable has rarely if ever deserved to be called a success, and now that "sustainable" has developed a more substantial meaning, change agents of many different stripes find their efforts subject to the judgment not only of financial markets, but also of sociopolitical ones.

These issues and others are the subject of new material in this volume. Whether or not their inclusion and, we hope, their eventual teaching leads to improvements in practice—gradually closing the knowing–doing gap mentioned above—will be up to you.

A text on change, then, needs to focus on the issues of its time, as well as those that transcend eras. In a second edition, it is perhaps relatively easy to identify what topics have waxed and waned since the first edition was published, and to change the contents accordingly. In this third edition, however, in making such judgments we have had, in a sense, to cement our position more thoroughly—that is, any topic still remaining after two previous editions must now take on an aura of some permanence, and any removed will equally appear to have suffered the judgment of impermanence.

The tendency may therefore be to include more and more material, in order to avoid the criticism of making rash judgments about deletions that leave a favorite topic or case out, disappointing instructors or other readers. Despite the support and flexibility of our publishers regarding the size of this volume, we have chosen to take a more activist approach to constructing this third edition, replacing much of the previous material. We are confident that in so doing we have given voice to some important new themes and deserving new contributors, as well as providing more current work on some of the existing themes from enduring authors.

Of course, we have retained some of the most popular cases and readings from the first and, in particular, second editions. Six cases—one per module—we have labeled "Change Classics" because they continue to illustrate clearly some of the most important and enduring themes of change. Take the time to compare these stories with some of the more recent examples in the volume and you will be rewarded with a deeper sense of what change means—for indeed, there is much we can all learn by understanding what has actually changed about change management and what, really, has not.

This book would not have been possible without the work of a large number of people. Once again we would like first to thank all those teachers, students, and executives who have used the earlier editions and offered feedback—it has been encouraging, humbling, and above all helpful to read, and we deeply appreciate it. We have incorporated many of your suggestions in the present volume, although it was of course not possible to implement them all. We thank you for your time, your input, and especially your patience over the time it took us to compile this third edition.

We are extremely grateful for the expert help of several very capable assistants and researchers. In addition to those we have already acknowledged in the first and second editions, we would like to thank Afroze Mohammed, Nancy J. Brandwein, Omar Eissa, Sonia Klosé, Julie Poivey, Marianne Rothenbuehler, Kaitlin Semler, and especially Karsten Jonsen. We also acknowledge the excellent work of all those whose writing appears in this volume. We appreciate in particular the help and advice of several new contributors, in particular Peter Killing, Jean-Pierre Lehmann, Vlado Pucik, David Robertson, and Michael Yaziji, as well as our co-case writers and/or protagonists Susan Baskin, Marie Bell, "Kerstin Berger," Archana Raja, Henry Silva, and Chew Ling Tan.

For their support, flexibility, and patience we would like to thank the editorial and marketing team at McGraw-Hill (and its partner companies), including Laura Spell, Lori Bradshaw, Melissa Leick, Deepti Narwat Agarwal, Jaime Halteman, Kelly Odom, Robin Reed, Ryan Blankenship, Allison Belda, and John Biernat. We are pleased to be associated with such a first-rate operation.

Each of us has also personally been through some significant changes since the publication of the second edition. In particular, we have each taken up new professorships—Todd Jick at Columbia and Maury Peiperl at IMD—and we would like to acknowledge the support of our new institutions, and in particular the constant learning—our own, that is!—that takes place in both of these world-class business schools. The students and executives we are privileged to teach there, and others whom we continue to teach or consult with in various parts of the globe, are the constant source of that learning, as well as the inspiration for much of what is contained in these pages.

Finally, we would like to thank our families for their continued support and for their input and feedback over the years. They have added much to our courses and to this volume. Our children in particular continue to prove to us every day that change can only be managed so far, that doing so is more art than science, and that helping others to manage their own changes is really what brings us closest to being true change leaders.

— T.D.J. & M.A.P.

New York, USA and Lausanne, Switzerland

August, 2010

Preface to the Second Edition

A recurring theme of change is how to change what is working well; how to take what is successful and change it enough so that it remains well positioned for the future without losing the essence of what has made it succeed to date. It is a challenge many managers have faced, but far fewer have mastered. It is, in essence, the challenge we face in compiling the second edition of this book, which has for nearly ten years enjoyed gratifyingly wide use and remains the leading text in its field.

But face it we must, for change is changing. Where once managing change was the exception, or the vanguard, now it is the norm. Where once most companies had never faced large-scale change, today most have done so—at least in the major Western economies, and in many others as well. Many firms have now moved beyond these large-scale changes to confront the new challenge of making change work in the longer term. They meet this challenge both by finding ways to better embed the major changes already made, and by making more—usually incremental—changes, often in a constant stream, to address the turbulent business environment.

The study of change, then, must now encompass this accumulated experience. In addition, the increasing effects of globalization and technology require that these forces play a more central role. We have therefore put them front and center, in a substantially revised Module 1, and added a new section, Module 6, to address the subject of continuous change head-on. Along the way we have modified the approaches of several other sections and have replaced nearly three-quarters of the material, including a wider and, of course, more recent set of cases and readings, drawing on many of the leading thinkers in the change arena, and sourcing material from a variety of companies, institutions, and countries.

Some of the best and most popular readings, of course, remain. We have labeled four of the case studies "Change Classics" in honor of both their long-standing popularity and their enduring themes. There is an element of timelessness to these and several other cases and readings; replacing them purely on the basis of their age would have been a disservice to readers, in our view. Two of these cases now have separate updates, which may be used to place the large-scale change from the original case in the context of the longer term.

Thus, while the dates of the contributions run the course of some fifteen years, the balance is toward more recent material. The core themes remain and have been augmented, and the book contains more than enough material for a full-length course on change management. This is no accident, because since the first edition was published, each of us has taught a somewhat different version of the course. From its origins at Harvard Business School it was enhanced and extended, largely concurrently, at both Insead and the London Business School, giving it, we hope, a more pluralistic and global feel. In addition, material was developed from the practical experiences of applying the concepts through The Center for Executive Development in Boston. As instructors, students, and managers dip into these pages, we hope you will agree that all the major themes of change are here—accessible and ready for debate. It is, of course, by applying this material through discussion, by bringing it to life through debates in the classroom and beyond, that the deepest understanding of change can be reached.

This book would not have been possible without the efforts of many people, in addition to all those mentioned in the preface to the first edition. We would first like to acknowledge all those who have used the text and provided feedback. We deeply appreciate the time and effort you put in to provide us your reactions and ideas. We have used many of your suggestions, though it was impossible to use them all. To those who waited longer than they should have to see this volume, thank you for your patience. We hope that you, and others, will continue to give us the benefit of your experience and your counsel.

The compilation of the material was done capably and expeditiously by Alistair Williamson, who took on the job from Brandon Miller, also a very capable assistant. Alistair also helped with drafting, editing, and permissions, and was a model of patience and resourcefulness. Additional assistance was provided by Cheri Grace, Richard Jolly, Valentina Pierantozzi, Rosemary Robertson, Kate Lewis, and especially Jeanne-Marie Hudson.

A number of people helped us compile new cases and updates and deserve our thanks. Their names are on their respective cases, but we would like to acknowledge Francesca Gee, Jennifer Georgia, Morgan Gould, Katharine MacLaverty,

Brandon Miller, Daniel Mueller, Stephen Paine, and especially Nikhil Tandon. For the inclusion of the merger simulation, we thank Alastair and Guy Giffin of Prendo. Their work has dazzled executives in many companies, and we hope you will have the opportunity of seeing it as well.

For their long-standing support and encouragement, not to mention their infinite patience, we would like to thank the editorial team at Irwin/McGraw Hill: John Biernat, Ryan Blankenship, Ellen Cleary, Tammy Higham, Tracy Jensen, Natalie Ruffatto, and Marianne Rutter.

In recent years many MBA students and executives have been the (often unwitting) recipients of early versions of much of this material in our classes and seminars. We thank them for their help in poking holes, finding new angles, and suggesting changes. The material in this volume has benefited immensely from their input.

Finally, we want to thank our wives, Rose and Jennifer, for their encouragement and their input, and our children, Zoe, Adina, Evan, and Julia, for teaching us more about change than probably anyone else. As this course and this book have developed, so have they, and with them our appreciation and understanding of the art of managing change. We hope that they, and you, find the result to your liking. If so, then they, and all the people mentioned here, deserve some of the credit.

T.D.J.

M.A.P.

Boston and London

July 2002

Preface to the First Edition

During the last fifteen years, a wide variety of management topics have interested me, such as: how organizations merge and how they downsize, how individuals handle the stress of organizational life, and how leaders can help organizations through challenging crisis conditions and revitalize. I taught a course about how the quality of organizational life can be improved and another course about the realities of power and politics, focusing on how managers try to influence people in their day-to-day behavior.

What increasingly became clear to me about my interests, research, and teaching was the common thread of CHANGE. In everything I did, and everything I was observing about managers, someone or something was changing. The management challenge was always to figure out a way to create that change or to ease the burden of change, or both.

Moreover, students taking my courses came with dreams and aspirations, and with a burning question: "How can I help organizations to change—for the better?" And, increasingly, another question also emerged as the pace and complexity of change evidenced in daily newspaper stories became overwhelming: "How well will I cope with all the change happening in today's organizations?"

I, thus, decided that it was time for a course, and ultimately this textbook, which addressed the issue of managing and adapting to change. In 1986, I set out to develop ideas, cases, videos, and a logic that would bring the subject of managing change "live and in color" to students facing the daunting challenges of the 1990s and the new century ahead. I originated the Managing Change course at the Harvard Business School in 1988, and over 600 students had taken the course by 1991 and helped me to refine the materials contained in this textbook.

Indeed, over the years, I have dedicated myself to making this subject of managing change a very personal matter. Introducing change in an organization is an exciting and yet formidable venture, and adventure. The lives and well-being of many are affected, including those who are at the cutting edge of driving change. Careers are made and sometimes broken as a result of major organizational change efforts. Managing change taxes the talent, skill, and conviction of an individual. It tests one's ability to understand the complexity of organizations, of corporate culture and politics, and of human psychology. And, inevitably, it hits up against ethical questions and choices.

This book attempts to give you a firsthand look and feel of how organizations change and how you can become a proactive participant in the many changes occurring in organizations today. It is designed to be a realistic preview of the difficulties and the pitfalls, while also suggesting the more successful paths for significant change in large complex organizations.

To achieve these objectives, materials had to be assembled with great care and with an unyielding focus on managerial situations that would be exciting change "puzzles" to try to solve. The cases and the readings contained herein will challenge your imagination and managerial aspirations, provoke you to discover and test your personal values and assumptions, and allow some fun along the way.

I had lots of help in putting all this together. First and foremost, I had the intellectual partnership and creativity of my editor, Barbara Feinberg, who stuck with me from the days of a blank syllabus through the final completion of this book. Barbara gave me, and now gives you, an impeccable eye as to what makes a case "sing" and how to link a series of cases that build more and more "sophistication," as she would call it. She also gave me every bit of confidence and support that an author and teacher would want.

The cases were written and crafted with the help of three research associates over the years. Each of them was subjected to the same ambiguities of weaving a story from a ragtag amalgam of facts and opinions—and from the same burden of dealing with me. The cases in this volume attest to their many skills in helping me to tell fascinating stories and in a well-written way. Their names are on their respective cases, but I want to thank each one individually.

My gratitude goes out to Susan Rosegrant who weathered the last two years of an accelerated, frantic pace; to Lori Ann MacIssac, who went right from Wellesley College into the offices of CEOs with amazing ease; and to Mary Gentile, my first research associate, who set a very high standard for writing, sensitivity, and humility.

Academic colleagues and friends challenged my ideas and offered suggestions throughout the development of the Managing

Change course. Harvard colleagues included Chris Argyris, whose timely and insightful feedback were always intellectually challenging; Mike Beer, with whom I collaborated for a number of years in teaching executives the subject of organizational effectiveness and change; Jack Gabarro, who was a personal role model of what teaching and cases can be; Rosabeth Moss Kanter, who helped me see the relationship of my ideas to the "field," and with whom I collaborated on another book about change, *The Challenge of Organizational Change;* John Kotter, whose instincts and pithy comments about my work were always on the mark; and, finally, Len Schlesinger, who not only helped to bring me to Harvard initially but who also gave me the inspiration to "think big" always.

Others who, through no fault of their own, were subjected to my intellectual quandaries and who often used my cases and found new richness in them: Peter Frost (UBC), Paul Goodman (Carnegie Mellon), Vic Murray (York University), Noel Tichy (University of Michigan), Mike Tushman (Columbia University), and Dave Ulrich (University of Michigan). I also received support and counsel from the Brookline Group, a group that claims responsibility for no one, but which is nurturing to all of us that meet monthly to discuss personal and professional issues. Thanks to all of its members: Lee Bolman, Dave Brown, Tim Hall, Bill Kahn, Phil Mirvis, and Barry Oshry.

Last to thank, but hardly least, is my wife, Rose, who is a dedicated and skillful teacher from whom I have learned, and who is a wonderful spouse from whom I have learned much as well. By chance, the birth of our first child, Zoe, coincided with the birth of the Managing Change course and the arrival of our second child, Adina, coincides with the birth of this textbook. Rose is almost as proud of my course and textbook as she is of our daughters, and that is saying a lot, more than I and the book surely deserve.

The course has "grown up" since its inception and I think has developed nicely. I trust you will agree, and, if you do, all the people listed here deserve some of the credit.

Todd D. Jick

Contents

Introduction

The Challenge of Change

Change is not made without inconvenience, even from worse to better.

Richard Hooker, 1554–1600

An adventure is only an inconvenience rightly understood. An inconvenience is only an adventure wrongly understood.

G. K. Chesterton, 1874–1936

We do not have to change, because staying in business is not compulsory.

W. Edwards Deming, 1900–1993

As the first decade of the new century draws to a close amid some of the most turbulent economic and political times in memory, and when business and political leaders—indeed, many global companies and some entire nations—assert their dedication to change; when "change agent" is a title many proudly claim, it seems propitious to write—or, given how much has changed since the last edition of this volume, to *re*-write—a textbook on how to deal with the phenomenon. It is hardly a new topic of course; human beings have been commenting on change for millennia. These comments, moreover, consistently fall into two broad camps: "it's good," "it's bad." It is also inevitable, and in recent years has been very much in the forefront of the business world's agenda.

W. Edwards Deming's view of change, put more bluntly as "change or die" by management guru Tom Peters, has been the bottom line for countless firms since at least the mid-1970s, as competitive onslaughts ravaged industry after industry. It is hard to overestimate the shock to so many companies, whether they should or should not have been prepared for it, whether they deserved it or not. And, to their credit, many firms chose not to die but embarked on tremendously ambitious change efforts, some of which, and many other more recent examples, are chronicled in this book. There may be much to criticize about many of these efforts, but that criticism should be directed toward doing it better, not denigrating those who pioneered.

Doing it better is the goal of this text. Unfortunately, there is no singular *best* that can be shared. There are no sure-fire instructions that, when scrupulously followed, make change succeed, much less eliminate or solve the problems accompanying any change process. Changing is inherently messy, confusing, and loaded with unpredictability, and no one escapes this fact. At the outset, then, it's important to keep a sense of proportion about change. As an example, a Harvard Business School case was being written about a *Fortune* 100 company in the middle of a major revamping of one division—a soup-to-nuts change effort. It was not a pretty picture, and the firm's public relations chief was extremely nervous about the image being portrayed in the case. The head of the change effort saw it differently. "This is cutting edge," he exclaimed. "This is what cutting edge looks like!"

"Change," in its broadest sense, is a planned or unplanned response to pressures and forces. Hence, there is nothing new about change or the need for it. Technological, environmental, economic, social, regulatory, political, and competitive forces have caused organizations to modify for decades—if not centuries. Change is such a potent issue these days, however, because simultaneous, unpredictable, and turbulent pressures have become the norm. When this is broadened to a global scale, the forces multiply, some might argue, exponentially. Competition intensifies, more complex relations with other firms are established, strategic choices increase, and adaptation is needed for mere survival, let alone long-term success.

Managing change is itself a kind of paradox: Can *change* really *be* managed? The answer depends, first, on the kind of change we are talking about, and second, on what we mean by "manage." In this introduction we first consider what kinds of changes organizations pursue, and what it means to "manage" those changes. We then introduce the issues of when to change, how to enable change, reactions to change, and first-order, second-order, and simultaneous change, all as a prelude to the cases and readings that follow.

TYPES OF CHANGE

Linda Ackerman[1] provides a useful way of categorizing changes common in organizations, each of which varies in scope and depth (see Figure 1). The first type Ackerman suggests is *developmental* change: "The improvement of a skill, method or condition that for some reason does not measure up to current expectation . . . [thus] 'to do better than' or 'do more of' what already exists."[2] This might be considered fine tuning—helping an organization stretch and, thereby, change. Managing such changes is a question of plotting a direct course from A to B, where both beginning and end points are well understood and not very far apart. The next two categories Ackerman proposes are those that we are principally concerned with (at least until Module 6); they are more far-reaching, potentially wrenching, and, therefore, most in need of managing.

Transitional change is introduced in order to help an organization evolve slowly. Current ways of doing things are replaced by something new—for example, a reorganization; a merger; the introduction of new products, services, processes, systems, technologies, and the like. This kind of change involves many transition steps, during which the organization is neither what it once was nor what it aims to become. Such steps may include temporary arrangements, pilots, or phased-in operations, among many others.

---

[1] Linda Ackerman, "Development. Transition or Transformation: The Question of Change in Organizations," *OD Practitioner*. December 1986, pp. 1–8.
[2] Ibid., p. 1.

FIGURE 1   Three Perspectives on Change

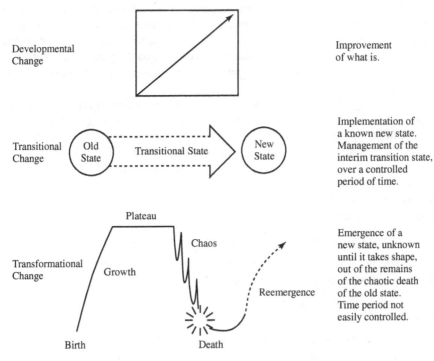

NOTE: Transformation may involve both developmental and transitional change.
        Transitional change may involve developmental change.
        Transformational change in an organization may be managed as a series of transitional changes.

Source: © 2001 Being First, Inc., Linda Ackerman Anderson and Dean Anderson.

The management task is more complex than in developmental change and may include launching several new processes at once, analyzing risk and uncertainty, and looking after the needs of change recipients. Gradually the firm eases into a new picture of itself.

The most radical change Ackerman suggests is *transformational:*

> It is catalyzed by a change in belief and awareness about what is possible and necessary for the organization. . . . It is something akin to letting go of one trapeze in mid-air before a new one swings into view. . . . Unlike transitional change, the new state is usually unknown until it begins to take shape. . . . Most of the variables are not to be controlled, rushed, or short-circuited.[3]

Transformational change does require a leap of faith for the organization, although often it is initiated when other options appear to have failed. It is typified by a radical reconceptualization of the organization's mission, culture, critical success factors, form,

[3] Ibid., p. 2.

leadership, and the like. Here is where it becomes difficult to "manage" in a proactive sense; it may be more important to react quickly to opportunities and threats than it is to develop and execute a detailed change plan. Transformational changes occurred in the automobile and steel industries in the 1980s, in the telecommunications and computer industries in the 1990s, and in the retail and investment banking industries in the 2000s, for example. Other industries, and the companies within them, undoubtedly will require such change in the next decade.

Determining what kind of change an organization requires is clearly vital, for the depth and complexity of implementation grow significantly from developmental (much skill-building training) to transitional (setting up temporary positions, structures) to transformational (developing new beliefs, gaining organization-wide commitment in the face of uncertainty). The level of investment grows accordingly.

One way of assessing the kind of change an organization needs is to ponder the following questions. Given that the organization is under pressure to change its current way of doing things:

1. How far do we want to go? Is that too far—not far enough?

2. Are we contemplating the "path of least resistance" or a direction that is truly needed?

3. What kind of results do we want—short term, longer term?

4. Do we want permanent change—or will that risk inflexibility, making future change more difficult?

5. How much change can the organization absorb? At once? Cumulatively?

6. Can the changes contemplated be presented positively? If not, why not?

7. What happens if we don't change at all?

Woven into the determination of what changes an organization needs is envisioning the future "look and feel" of the organization. The vision may embrace only improvements of what already exists; it may depict a new look that gradually materializes; or it may be a fuzzier image—not clearly distinguishable for the moment but resembling nothing like the current organizational "shape."

WHEN TO CHANGE

Given the pressures and the types of changes possible to institute, when is the decision made to pull the lever—"Let's change now"? Basically, an organization can institute change when things are going well, when results are mixed, or when a full-fledged crisis is upon it.

An organization can anticipate pressures down the road. Considering making changes proactively can be partly a matter of foresight and preparation, but it also can entail the belief that if the organization is not routinely changing itself, it risks complacency and stagnation.

Or, an organization can encounter a problem, not necessarily life-threatening but one deserving attention, and, thus, feel the need to introduce change. It might, for example, consider a reorganization in response to a competitor's new product introduction; it might consider creating a quality program after receiving disturbing customer feedback about its own product or service quality.

Alternatively, an organization faced with a definite threat—alarmingly deteriorating results, the withdrawal of a major account—most probably will institute change, acutely recognizing the need to do so.

Given these general "times" for introducing change, one might assume that the process is easier when the organization is in crisis: The situation is clear to all, survival is on the line; everyone recognizes that the way things have been done won't work anymore. But the very fact of the crisis suggests that at best there has been inattentiveness to its origins; there may be deep organizational problems that deter introducing changes to confront the situation. Thus, one might say, changes really should be made in anticipation of difficulties. But, paradoxically, making changes before "the event" is equally difficult—how can an organization be energized to make changes when the need for them is not universally perceived? How *far* down the road is down the road?

Some argue that one way around this paradox is to manufacture a sense of crisis, rather than wait for the real one to appear. This crafting of urgency presumably elicits a responsiveness to change while not placing the organization at risk. The danger of this approach, of course, is in crying wolf. Claim too many times that survival is at stake, and the organization will greet you with "This, too, shall pass."

When to change, thus, involves an exquisite sense of timing: Have we waited too long or have we started too soon? The challenge is to choose the time when the organization both should make changes and can do so. However, those two dimensions don't always come together—hence, the challenge.

ENABLING CHANGE

Beyond the issues of what kind of change is needed and when it should be introduced, an organization needs to consider how to enable the change to be effective. This is not strictly an implementation matter; rather, it involves yet another group of strategic choices to be contemplated before actual (tactical) implementation occurs.

The first enabling issue is *pace.* How long will it take to design the change plan/program? How quickly should the change unfold? How much accommodation should be made for trial-and-error learning? Is it easier for the organization if the change is introduced quickly or over a longer period? How much time does the organization have, given customer needs, competitive demands, or changes in the environment (i.e., the forces that are driving the change in the first place)?

Related to pace is *scope.* Obviously, this issue stems in large measure from the vision of what change is needed, but there are still choices to be made. Should the change start small and grow, or should it start big? If it is to be piloted—where and with whom? Should the pilot run in an area "loaded for success"? Where is the best climate for experimentation? Where is it more generalizable to the rest of the organization?

If the decision is to start big, issues of *depth* arise. How many changes can be introduced in any one area? The high risk/high reward approach is to simultaneously blitz an organization with a large number of consistent changes to ensure maximum impact.

But there is probably a limit to how much change can be absorbed before resistance is mobilized—actively or, possibly, passively and negatively.

And related to scope is *publicity:* How loud, how long, and to whom should the organization announce change is on the way? There is, on one hand, the hype approach. Out come the speeches, the binders, the newsletters, the banners/buttons/T-shirts. The rationale is that to enable an organization to change there must be many clear reinforcements and motivational cues: everybody has to be excited and committed at the outset.

On the other hand, of course, this approach raises expectations (which may be too high already) and makes the change highly visible and, thus, a target for snipers and naysayers (and legitimate critics as well). Little room for flexible adjustments of the change plan may be left. Thus, there is an argument for a quiet, understated introduction, which controls resistance, allows for mistakes in learning, and moderates expectations. In either approach the issue is publicity, not communication, which is essential, although the degree of explicit information and to whom it is given may vary.

Another enabling change issue is *supporting structures.* What mechanisms does an organization have, or put in place, to further the change effort? Decisions here clearly are linked to pace and scope; but regardless of choices in those areas, some care and nurturing of the change will be needed. How much should be done through normal management processes and how much should be specially created?

Going through routine channels enables the change to be considered part of the normal and expected organizational activities. The risk, of course, is that it might not be perceived as sufficiently important to get adequate attention and dedication. All too many change projects die early because they become too routinized. However, bringing in too many consultants and having too many task forces or off-site gatherings risks making the change effort the only organizational preoccupation.

The final enabling issue is deciding who *drives* the change. The classic approach has a senior staff person or a CEO develop a vision, which in turn is endorsed by top management, and then assigned to middle management to implement. Clearly, this approach depends on gaining top management commitment, but it underplays the need for middle- or bottom-level ownership. A second classic approach is the reverse: The need for change is envisioned from deep down in the organization and implemented upward and outward. A third approach uses an outside consultant as an implementer/facilitator. Many variations and combinations of these are possible.

What seems clear, given the complexities that the challenge of change involves, is that the selection of the change team is pivotal. All too often people are chosen on the basis of their availability, rather than on their ability to comprehend the full ramifications of introducing change.

REACTIONS TO CHANGE

Perhaps the greatest challenge of all comes with the awareness that managing change includes managing the reactions to that change. Unfortunately, change frequently is introduced without considering its psychological effect on others in the organization—particularly those who have not been part of the decision to make the change: those who arrive on Monday to learn "from now on, it's all different." Further, when reactions are taken into account, they often are lumped under "resistance" to change, a pejorative phrase that conjures up stubbornness, obduracy, traditionalists, "just saying no." It seems fair to state, however, that, if the reactions to change are not anticipated—and managed—the change process will be needlessly painful and perhaps unsuccessful.

Traditionally grouped under resistance to change are inertia, habit, and comfort with the known. For most people, change isn't actively sought; some level of routine is preferred. But routine is preferred because it enables some control. Given that change, at its onset at least, involves some ambiguity if not outright confusion, this control is threatened. That is, resistance is frequently a reaction to a loss of control, not necessarily to the change itself. The further away a person is from knowing the rationale for the change and the implications of the change and how the change is to be operationalized, the greater the threat to that person's control over his or her environment. Quite simply, contemplating change in the abstract can evoke fear.

Other forces also may serve to dampen change. Collective interests in preserving the status quo can emerge to mobilize political roadblocks, and a conservative culture—often one built on years of success—may prevent an organization from appreciating the gravity of a problem, the up side of an opportunity, and the creative boldness of a major change.

Change also may be perceived as an indictment of previous decisions and actions. It is difficult for people to change when they have been part of creating the conditions that precipitated the change. Or change can be resisted when there are barriers to being able to respond adequately.

Finally, people are simply more alert to change than they used to be. Given "streamlining," "downsizing," and "restructuring"—all euphemisms for layoffs (itself a euphemism for being fired)—people are more wary of change because of its inferred adverse consequences.

For all these reasons, employees at all levels in organizations psychologically defend against change, and reactions can be both more hostile and less predictable than the phrase "resistance to change" might imply.

Reactions to change are not always in the psychological realm, of course. Legitimate philosophical differences of opinion may exist. The change solution that is designed to treat one problem can create difficulties elsewhere: many changes for the good have led to changes for the worse. People who say, "Wait a minute, maybe we shouldn't" aren't always hopeless reactionaries.

One final point about reacting to change: There are limits to the stress that organizations can absorb—either at a given moment or cumulatively. Organizations, like individuals, can become saturated and, thereby, be either unwilling or unable to integrate new and deeper changes, even if these are acknowledged to be needed.

For one theorist, Herbert Kaufman,[4] there is a predictable pattern to managing change that encompasses resistance. He argues that (1) organizations require change to survive; (2) yet they always face considerable forces of resistance; (3) nevertheless, they do change; (4) but that change is always "dampened" later, with the original inertia

---

[4] Herbert Kaufman, *Limits of Organizational Change* (Tuscaloosa, AL: University of Alabama Press, 1971).

and status quo overtaking the change—leading back to (1), when organizations face the need to change once again. This assessment of a change process underscores the difficulty of instituting and institutionalizing permanent change, and the necessity of looking at change over time.

First-Order, Second-Order and Simultaneous Change

Most of the changes that get written about are the big transitions or transformations—large-scale, planned or partly planned changes that may be termed "First-Order Change." From about 1979 to about 1993 in America, slightly later in Europe, in the late 1990s in Asia, and once again in the late 2000s in a variety of industries across most of the world, untold numbers of business organizations experienced these kinds of shifts. They continue today, and are illustrated by many of the cases in this book.

But major change, high-profile and difficult as it is, is only part of the story. What happens after big change is still very much the stuff of change management. Ongoing changes, developmental or transitional, determine the long-term success of the enterprise. This "rest of the story" is what we term "Second-Order Change," and several of the cases in this volume now come paired with updates that address the continuing change issues faced by these firms. It soon becomes apparent that whether or not we judge a change effort to be successful has everything to do with the time window we apply, and that only some of the changes that succeed in the short term are able to sustain the firm in the long run.

In addition, the new change landscape contains many change efforts occurring simultaneously. There may be the ongoing quality push, now in its final year of rollout. The customer-first program, four years old, is now reaching down to the next-to-last group for implementation. The integrated global organization effort is gearing up, and the "boundaryless" teams reorganization is hot off the press. Thus, one employee could be in the following situation: As a member of a newly formed cross-functional team (part of the "boundaryless" drive), she is envisioning a radically different product development process with major ramifications for R&D, engineering, and operations. As a functional manager, she is simultaneously drawing up implementation plans with a global virtual team for the new, integrated organization. She is also participating in the customer-first effort by intensifying her interactions with key clients. And, she has just learned that, as part of a dramatic shift in strategy, the CEO intends to sell off her division—she may soon be redundant, but she must nonetheless inform her direct reports of their fate. Looking at this person's overall work, we can say *her job* is managing change, not enacting pieces of change programs.

An Integrated Approach

This is precisely the point of *Managing Change*: how to manage change overall, not how to become a particular player in a change program. The learning from this book appears when envisioning, implementing, and receiving change are seen as fundamentally *interrelated* activities.

Thus, the materials—cases and readings—have been chosen and arranged to introduce change as an integrated process. There are modules dedicated to envisioning, implementing, and receiving change, but these are provided to look at the specific issues each entails, not to present them as separate activities. Indeed, it is impossible to determine when "rolling out the vision" ends and implementing it—and, inevitably, further changing it—begins.

Cases in the text represent a wide variety of change situations. Companies range from a few hundred employees to hundreds of thousands, and there are individual profiles as well. Industries run from bottle caps to dot-coms to international airlines. Some change programs are intended to be introduced over a weekend, whereas others are to be phased in over years. There are stunning successes, dismal failures, and everything in between. Every case reveals turbulence, confusion, and not a little pain as organizations and individuals wittingly or unwittingly make choices and trade-offs.

Accompanying many cases are readings, likewise chosen to reflect a broad range of issues. Some readings provide theoretical underpinnings for a case, supporting the action; others challenge the action with alternative viewpoints. Still others provide broader context—views of the changing world, for example, or commentaries on how we look at change; ideas that go well beyond the issues in any particular case. This material comes from popular business magazines as well as from books and professional journals. Beyond demonstrating the range of opinions on the topic of change, the readings also reinforce how pervasive the issue has become.

Each module contains a summary of the major points the cases and readings explore, and three modules contain practical and highly realistic activities. In one module, you are challenged to come up with a vision for a company just formed from two very different competitors. In the next, as part of a team, you must begin to implement a merger reflecting major change for two firms, choosing and sequencing various approaches to get the troops—and the wider set of stakeholders—on board. Finally, you must decide the best way to proceed with a massive downsizing for a once-dominant, far-flung organization.

The people whom you meet throughout the cases in this book are themselves learning how to manage change; in that sense, each situation is really a work in progress. They are your guides through the messy change terrain and will teach you much if you let them. That is, if you allow yourself to experience change as you approach this book, you will discover at the end, that although you have not discerned *the* answer to managing change, you can pose the four questions that count:

1. What is to be changed?
2. How is it to be done?
3. Who is affected?
4. What are the consequences so far?

Those who are managing change with some degree of success—for themselves and for others—recognize that they must continually ask these questions and listen to the answers, then transfer that learning to continually modify their efforts. In fact, this all adds up to the following, as many wise people have noted: Managing change well means, quite simply, managing well.

OUTLINE OF THE BOOK

This book is organized according to a descriptive framework for change. We begin in Module 1 with the ***Forces for Change***—three primary forces that have evolved somewhat, but are nonetheless long-standing and pervasive: the fast pace of innovation and the rapid development of technology, an ever-increasing focus on customers, and the more and more self-evident reality of the global marketplace. Forces that can inhibit change also appear, pointing up the eternal tensions that change managers must face.

Module 2 tracks an evolving change in the arena of change itself, ***Changing the Game: From Vision to Adaptation***. We review the long-accepted necessity of spelling out a vision—a desired future state—but also chronicle the limitations of such a focus in light of the tremendous need for flexibility faced by most organizations (and individuals!) in turbulent markets. All major changes we have observed in an organization have included at least the beginnings of a vision of what will and must change. Still, the "vision thing" is often all too mushy and abstract and fails to motivate people to change or to help sustain change in the longer term. Visions that lead to successful change today do so because they not only inspire and direct toward a common goal but also point the way along a flexible path, responsive to opportunities and constraints that arise.

Implementing Change, the bread-and-butter stuff of the course, follows in Module 3. It is the "how" that everyone seeks to understand. What managers most often bemoan is their frustration—with how long it takes to make change happen, with how to overcome the resistance they encounter, with how to communicate information about the change, and so on. The lengthy list of issues to consider in how to get an organization to change is sampled in this module. And while there are no quick or easy formulas for addressing all of these successfully, you will be able to develop some rules of thumb—some do's and don'ts for dealing with the myriad choices around how change gets implemented.

Before you can be successful, however, at managing change, you must deepen your sensitivity and understanding about how people respond to change. How do people typically react? Is there really a "typical" reaction, or is it different for each person? How can managers make it easier for people to cope with change, particularly when that change may be ongoing? These questions, among others, are the subject of Module 4, ***The Recipients of Change***. They must be considered and understood—although it may be they can never be fully mastered—before one can truly become an agent of long-lasting change.

Module 5, then, is an up-front and personal look at what it means to be that change agent. ***Leading Change: The Personal Side*** is about the change leader's own experience. So far, by developing an understanding of the forces for change, the need for vision and adaptation, and the ways to implement change and sustain it by successfully managing the recipients, you will have strengthened your cognitive abilities to take on this critical managerial task. However, actually being an agent of change is a hefty emotional and personal challenge. This module offers some insights into the frustrations and the joys of being a change agent, from a personal standpoint and in a wide variety of situations, from startups to global service firms to the street markets of South Africa.

If the focus in the first five modules is on large-scale change efforts directed at transforming an organization's fundamental way of operating, and the mindset and behavioral changes commensurate with that challenge, in our final module we look beyond these first-order change situations to consider ***Continuous Change***, the longer-term, second-order challenges that often mean the end of the line for successful turn-arounds, restructurings, and other major change programs. Here we come face to face with the uncertainties of change, the changing features of the firm's environment over which we often have no control. The necessity of knowing what can and cannot be managed, and of learning to work, long-term, with the messy, continuous, unpredictable side of change, is perhaps the ultimate challenge of change leadership.

Thus, our framework and our course begin and end with an appreciation of the challenges—organizational and personal—of managing change. After all, it is the challenge itself that has brought out the best in many managers. How about you?

Forces for Change

INTRODUCTION

The drivers of change are many—too many to list, which is why managing change is more an art than a science. In a given industry, for a given firm, there may be a set of drivers unique enough, despite the substantial experience of those involved, that each approach to change must be worked out anew.

Yet there are recurrent themes in change, and, at the macro level, recurrent forces whose effects can be seen time and again in changes from the smallest feature shift to the largest corporate takeover; from the placement of one well in a Congolese village to the Internet wiring ("wirelessing"?) of the entire Asian subcontinent. This module explores perhaps the largest three such forces: innovation (technological and otherwise), customer focus, and globalization. In addition, we consider the social role of business, clearly one of the most important issues for business in an era when many global enterprises are more powerful than most national governments. In the process we review four quite different case studies and, along with them, three very different models for approaching change, along with several commentaries on the changing state of business and of our world.

Innovation

It is now well understood that technology, central though it may be to productivity, progress, and value-creation, only ever confers a temporary advantage. Firms that were in the vanguard of new technology only a year or two ago now find themselves threatened with decline if they fail to stay innovative and entrepreneurial. The same is true of those in many more traditional product markets. It is the production and application of new ideas—that is, innovation, technological and otherwise—that count in the long term. The LEGO group, an icon of creative play toys for generations, finds in the first case in this module that, although diversification can drive growth and technology can be an aid to progress, these things alone do not make for long-term success. In 2004 the company is struggling for its survival, and the irony of the situation is that it is the very innovation and creativity it is known for fostering in children that so elude it in its search for a way forward.

In the reading that follows, "The 12 Different Ways for Companies to Innovate," Mohanbir Sawhney, Robert C. Wolcott, and Inigo Arroniz describe how most companies limit their view of innovation to known product lines and markets, and therefore end up pursuing the same avenues of change as their competitors, finding little or no advantage in so doing. They encourage firms to take a broader, more systemic view of innovation and provide a model, the 12-dimensional "Innovation Radar," to enable the process.

Customer Focus

Most of the first-order, large-scale changes that took place in the late 1980s and early 1990s had their roots in a rededication to serving the customer (and in certain industries and regions of the world, such changes were still only just catching on at the beginning of the new millennium). Many firms had become so large and set in their ways that they lost the ability to take the point of view of those who made them successful in the first place. Painful restructurings ensued, and many corporate leaders (those who managed to survive the changes) vowed never again to take their customers for granted. In the current era of continuous change, customer focus remains a basic touchstone of business success.

A striking example of a large, complex—and successful—change is found in the next case in this module, the classic "Changing the Culture at British Airways." During a decade, the airline went from "awful" to "awesome," with stunning statistics to back up that assessment—all driven by a single-minded focus on customer service. All the issues that will be examined in depth throughout subsequent modules are here: what "vision" drove the changes; how they were led, implemented, sustained, and modified; how people responded, and what challenges the airline was to face in the future.

The accompanying reading, the classic change article "Re-Energizing the Mature Organization," reinforces the BA case substantially as well as presenting more generic recommendations for established firms. The model developed by its authors, Richard W. Beatty and David O. Ulrich, charts a path for large organizations in need of first-order change, and just begins to address the somewhat different question of the second-order change, the ongoing "encore," which will be addressed specifically in Module 6.

Globalization

Globalization can no longer be called a coming trend that will reshape much of business. It must, rather, be recognized as a fact—as a force that has already done so. Still, globalization is perhaps the least understood of the three major forces for change. This is not because it is unrecognized—the events of recent years have proven its power—but because no one is entirely certain how it works. The crossing of borders—first by goods, then by capital, and latterly by services and, to some extent, labor—has had profound effects on business. But globalization's effects are political and cultural as well as economic, and global expansion is not without risk for companies. Those from richer and more productive countries must take into account the needs of those in less developed areas, lest they find themselves the target of resistance—either passive or active—to the free-market capitalism that sustains them. Those with cultural norms far different from countries where they would do business must continually decide how far to adjust, even whether to institute long-term changes to their socioeconomic systems.

Still, the unprecedented global connectedness offered by the Internet and other communications vehicles provides instant, cross-border information—often, knowledge of opportunities that would previously have been unavailable. Such knowledge in turn drives innovation and entrepreneurship, as well as cross-border demand for goods and services. But global business entails considerable risks, not least of which is incomplete knowledge of the risks themselves.

The third case in this module, "Nestlé's Globe (A)," is the story of a multilocal company struggling with how global it really wants to be. The case reviews how, faced with more centralized competitors with higher margins, Nestlé's CEO and board decide to implement a standardized, worldwide information system for keeping track of all operational data on a daily basis. Because this project will affect everyone in the firm, especially the frontline businesses based in each country, the CEO and CFO ask one of Nestlé's market leaders to take charge of the effort. The challenges Chris Johnson faces—particularly in asking his former peers in the markets to give up significant autonomy while accepting real threats to their P&Ls—are a microcosm of issues confronting globalizing firms everywhere, and an illustration of the human dilemmas of cross-border leadership.

Kathleen Eisenhardt explains the strategic implications of globalization in the article "Has Strategy Changed?" Although she says that the strategy should be "simple," she recognizes the complexity of the environment in which an organization operates. To find the simplicity that uniquely fits its own product or service offering and its global network, a company needs to organize in such a way that the knowledge and motivation of its people, rather than the brilliant designs of its leaders, determine at any moment the work that actually takes place. The organizational and temporal nature of strategy in global firms suggests, according to Eisenhardt, that modularity and flexibility are more important than the idea of sustainable advantage—a thing managers cannot know really exists "except in retrospect."

"These are scary times for managers in big companies," write Clayton M. Christensen and Michael Overdorf in "Meeting the Challenge of Disruptive Change," referring to the impact of the forces laid out in this module and deriving an approach that could be applied to each of the case studies we have seen so far. Disruptive innovations, the authors point out, "create an entirely new market through the introduction of a new kind of product or service." They see sustaining success as a function of being able to adapt, not only individually and to new products or approaches, but organizationally and to entirely new business models. Since disruptive innovations occur rarely and unpredictably, they cannot be planned for—and it is at times like these that it becomes apparent that an organization's processes, resources, and values may not be nearly as flexible or adaptable as its leaders would like to believe.

The business imperatives of globalization with all their human implications are, however, only half the story of change in today's world. It is also essential to consider the human imperatives of globalization, with all their implications for business. The final case in this module, "Glaxo SmithKline and AIDS Drugs in South Africa," illustrates the latter, in one of the most high-profile dilemmas of the modern age—often, but incompletely, stated as "lives versus profits."

The Glaxo case is complemented by a *Reason* magazine feature, "Re-Thinking the Social Responsibility of Business," in which two prominent executives and the late economist Milton Friedman debate both the basics and the finer points of this highly salient topic. There are lessons here for everyone, from the staunchest capitalist to the most strident socialist.

We end this module with a reading that has little to do directly with business, but everything to do with change and the future of the planet. In "The Collapse and Transformation of Our World," Duncan Taylor and Graeme Taylor make it clear that sustainability is incompatible with the path humanity has taken thus far, and that in the very near future either integration or disintegration must be our path. This "biggest picture" view is an important backdrop to our discussions of change, both here and throughout subsequent modules.

Case

Innovation at the Lego Group (A)

When Jørgen Vig Knudstorp was appointed president and CEO of the LEGO Group in October 2004, the company was in deep trouble. Competition was on the increase, the toy industry was evolving in ways that did not favor the LEGO Group, and the company was on the verge of bankruptcy (*refer to **Exhibit 1** for LEGO revenues and net income*). Further, Knudstorp felt the company had lost its way and had no clear idea of who it was nor what products it should offer. It was clear to everyone that changes were needed.

Knudstorp and several other colleagues had in early 2004 formulated a new business strategy for the company. Their plan had three phases. First, they had to improve the company's cash flow and eliminate its debt; much of this, they announced, would be accomplished by selling off non-core assets, reducing operational complexity

Source: Research Associate Rob Crawford and Professor David Robertson prepared this case as a basis for class discussion rather than to illustrate either effective or ineffective handling of a business situation.

and outsourcing some manufacturing. Second, to increase profit margins, they had to revitalize their product lines. This would be trickier, particularly in light of the cuts that would have to be made. Finally, the company had to grow organically, to invent new ways of creating value. By the end of 2005, they had accomplished the major goals of the first phase, and it was time to begin the second and third phases. A requirement for these phases was to re-invent innovation in the company—the challenge was, how?

HISTORY

Established in 1932 by Ole Kirk Christiansen, the LEGO Group at first crafted wooden toys in the founder's carpenter shop in Billund, Denmark. LEGO was a shortened form of the Danish phrase, "leg godt" (play well).[1] Over the next 15 years, Christiansen built a business based on offering high quality products that encouraged creative play. He designed his toys to captivate the imagination of the local children; through building, they were supposed to develop a sense of pride in accomplishment and learn while playing.

[1] It was only years later that Christiansen learned that, in Latin, LEGO means "I put together."

EXHIBIT 1   **Revenues and Net Income of the LEGO Group (in billions of Danish krone)**

Source: Company information

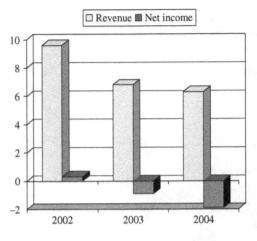

In 1947, convinced that he had found the ideal new material for his growing company, Christiansen bought his first plastic injection-molding machine. The eventual result was LEGO's iconic product, the plastic brick with eight studs, which the company patented in 1958. It became the focus of a tight-knit community of devoted enthusiasts, with their own newsletters, competitions and even conventions. It was this legacy—for quality, creative play, community and experimentation—that Christiansen passed on to his sons, who continued to own and run the company.

GROWTH

For the next 20 years, the LEGO Group grew slowly and steadily, reaching approximately 1 billion Danish kroner (DKK) in sales in 1978.[2] During those years, the LEGO play experience was based on free-form play: Children constructed worlds of their own choosing; they did not follow

[2] The exchange rate in 2004 was about DKK 6 = $1, and DKK 7.5 = €1.

elaborate instructions or systematic blueprints. Over the next 10 years the company operated on an increasingly global scale, growing sales to DKK 5 billion in 1988. Growth slowed in the mid-1990s, including a loss of DKK 300 million in 1998, despite expansion into several new categories that were more than "just toys" such as books, TV, watches, etc. But in 2000 the company began a period of explosive growth as it saw sales increase with licensed products, including LEGO based on popular intellectual properties (such as the Star Wars™ movies) and growth driven by a steep increase in the value of the US dollar (vs. Euro).

The sales growth begun in 2000 was the result of the aggressive expansion in the range of play experiences that the LEGO Group offered. No longer content with offering building sets, the company had expanded into computer games, clothing, amusement parks and movies. To accomplish this expansion, it hired many designers of a "new breed" from design schools, whose ideas went beyond modeling with the traditional bricks. With the support and encouragement of their management, these new designers challenged and pushed back the boundaries that had previously defined what a LEGO product was.

For example, in 1999 Lucasfilm Ltd. convinced Christiansen's grandson, Kjeld, to create a partnership based on the *Star Wars™* films. The result was a series of elaborate kits, each representing machines and characters from the Star Wars™ universe *(refer to **Exhibit 2** for examples of*

EXHIBIT 2   **Examples of LEGO Star Wars™ Toys**

Source: Company information

LEGO Star Wars™ toys). The LEGO Star Wars™ kits were very controversial within the company: For the first time, the LEGO Group introduced "modern" weapons into its universe, which had never been part of any LEGO toy (hitherto the weapons in LEGO sets were pirate guns, swords, and the like). The LEGO Star Wars™ also offered a different play experience—they came with complicated sets of instructions and produced fragile models rather than active playthings, another first for the LEGO Group. This new type of play, which fostered a "right way of doing things" mentality regarding the play experience, made many of LEGO's longtime designers uneasy. The trend toward models based on licensed characters continued in 2001 with the introduction of the first series of LEGO Harry Potter™ building sets.

Another new direction in play experience was represented by the narrative-based product series called "Bionicle." Bionicle, whose name combined biological with chronicle, were embedded in an evolving multimedia story. This narrative, renewed regularly, was supported by books, cartoons, movies and later a website. Each new episode introduced new characters and contexts in which the characters interacted, similar in some ways to Pokémon™ (*refer to **Exhibit 3** for examples of Bionicle toys*). This move to toy sets driven by story telling was seen as a major growth driver.

The sudden infusions of cash from the Star Wars™ and Harry Potter™ kits, coupled with the ability to push back the boundaries of what a LEGO play experience was, allowed designers to experiment in increasingly diverse directions. The LEGO Group, some believed, should become a "family lifestyle" company with a greatly expanded portfolio of products, from entertainment experiences—

such as the LEGOLAND amusement parks—to fashionable clothes and computer games. Between 1996 and 2002, three new LEGOLAND parks (in addition to the original park near the LEGO Group's headquarters) were opened in the US and Europe, at a cost of nearly DKK 1.5 billion each. LEGO Mindstorms, a sophisticated building set with motors, sensors and a programmable "brain," was introduced in 1998 and targeted an older audience. Some designers even argued that the LEGO brick was passé, and that it was only a matter of time before the LEGO Group would go virtual, providing play experiences predominantly through CDs and the internet.

This expansion in the range of offerings not only affected the identity of the LEGO Group but also altered its cost structure. The LEGO Star Wars™ building sets and other customized toys demanded the creation of new, specialized elements. Each new element had to have its own mold, production method and inventory, which added to the fixed cost of the company. As the range of elements expanded, the costs did as well.[3]

THE CRISIS

In 2003 the risks inherent in this growth strategy became frighteningly real. The LEGO Star Wars™ and LEGO Harry Potter™ kits, while successful in years with a new movie, proved cyclical and sold less in years without a successful film. In 2003 there was neither a Star Wars™ nor Harry Potter™ film. The US

[3] In the LEGO Group, the word "element" is used to describe a unique geometric shape. An element may have many different colors or decorations on it; each unique color-shape combination is called a "component."

EXHIBIT 3 **Examples of Bionicle Toys**

Source: Company information

dollar began declining from its 2002 peak, LEGOLAND parks were draining earnings, and the fixed costs of supporting a staggering 12,500 different components remained high. In 2003 and 2004 the company saw its biggest losses ever (refer to Exhibit 1).

As its troubles became apparent and the management team began searching for solutions, they realized that the toy industry was changing dramatically in at least four ways. First, electronic games—video-game consoles, hand-held games, websites and even mobile phones—were reducing the demand for traditional toys. No one knew how far the market would fall, though many forecast that electronics would essentially replace old-fashioned mechanical toys in the coming years. Moreover, with children preferring to enter multimedia fantasy worlds at about the age of eight, they were losing interest in traditional toys at an earlier age, which shaved as much as four years off the projected duration of traditional toy play. Second, the retail sector was consolidating into mega-stores—such as Wal-Mart and Carrefour—which had an increasingly large share of total toy sales. This represented a decisive power shift in favor of the retailers and away from the manufacturers, which in the 1960s had been able to impose their product lines on customers.[4] In this new retail environment, toy manufacturers had to compete with each other for shelf space, often accepting marketing dictates from retail outlets or producing toys for them under license. Third, because of the new retail environment and the outsourcing of manufacturing to Asia, the toy industry faced strong downward pressure on prices. And, as the US dollar gradually declined against the Danish krone, LEGO products became relatively more expensive in the company's most important market. Finally, the LEGO Group began to see cheaper, look-alike bricks that were virtually interchangeable with LEGO elements. These toys began to take market share away from LEGO building sets—the competitors were not only cheaper than the LEGO Group but also faster, bringing products to market before LEGO could. The LEGO Group took these competitors to court in many countries, arguing that the LEGO brick was an iconic form that should be covered by trademark protection (which does not expire), not patent protection (which had expired in all major markets). The courts disagreed, leaving markets open for lower-priced competition.

In 2003 the LEGO Group lost nearly DKK 1 billion and its cash dwindled dangerously low. This was the largest loss in the history of the company, a sign that many observers believed indicated bankruptcy and perhaps even the breakup and sale of the company. The losses for 2004 were projected to nearly double (refer to Exhibit 1). It was at this point that Knudstorp, who had developed a plan to save the company, was appointed president and CEO. He was only 35 years old.

THE NEW PLAN: SHARED VISION

With a PhD in economics, Knudstorp began his career at McKinsey & Co. He worked there for three years, then joined the LEGO Group as director of strategic development in 2001. As the LEGO Group slid into the most serious crisis in its history, Knudstorp and his team began to formulate a plan to save the company. It was a very tough problem. On the one hand, the company's previous leaders had already tried to "innovate" and by any measure had produced an impressive set of new, revenue-generating products and play experiences. However, too many of these were not profitable. What, he wondered, could they do differently? Given the challenges facing the company— limited cash, increasing price pressure, powerful retailers, high fixed costs and, in particular, the shift away from traditional

---

[4] See Misha Petrovic and Gary G. Hamilton, "Making Global Markets," in *Wal-Mart: The Face of Twentieth Century Capitalism*, Nelson Lichtenstein (ed.). The New Press, 2005, p. 119.

play and the consolidation of retail-outlet power—it was unclear what options remained for them.

Knudstorp and his team titled their new plan "Shared Vision." Knudstorp characterized it not as a new strategy, but as "an action plan for survival" that built on LEGO's traditional strengths. The plan had three parts. The first phase, "Stabilize for Survival," to be carried out in 2004 and 2005, focused on reducing costs, eliminating debt and returning the company to profitability. The second phase, "Profit from the Core," to be carried out in 2006 and 2007, aimed to improve the profitability and growth of the company by revitalizing the core product lines and transforming the business platform (e.g., through outsourcing of manufacturing and strengthening the IT platform). The final phase, "Achieving Vision," scheduled for 2008 and 2009, focused on developing innovative new play experiences to profitably grow the company.

The LEGO Group immediately began the effort to reduce debt and cut costs. In 2004 it announced a decision to investigate outsourcing of the majority of its plastic brick manufacturing to external suppliers or its own factories in low cost countries, an effort that despite a target of reducing the overall workforce by more than 50% was done in collaboration with LEGO blue collar employees. In 2006, LEGO announced that 80 percent of manufacturing would relocate to low cost countries in Eastern Europe and Mexico. To reduce debt and generate some much-needed cash, the LEGO Group sold a 70% share of the four LEGOLANDs to the Blackstone Group for $456 million. To reduce complexity and manufacturing costs, it began reducing the inventory of LEGO components.

Knudstorp and his team knew that reducing the number of components would be controversial in LEGO's design community and could potentially hurt the company's performance. Some designers argued that it would hinder creative expression and reduce the number of products on the market, which would lower revenues. Yet a reduction in components would simplify manufacturing operations, trim inventories, reduce cost of obsolescence, reduce mold investment cost dramatically and unburden the distribution systems. The team tasked with the effort believed that many of the components were unnecessary and hurt the company's profitability. For example, the chef figurine had seven different facial expressions, each represented by a separate component; only one, the team reasoned, should suffice. Reducing the current number of 12,500 components by as much as 50%, the team speculated, would force the designers to focus.

CLARIFYING THE GROUP'S IDENTITY

As the company executed the first phase of Shared Vision, Knudstorp began to think about the next phases. Successfully revitalizing the core product lines and inventing new ones would require a better sense of what LEGO stood for. Knudstorp believed that LEGO had lost a "crisp sense" of its identity. The LEGO brand, he felt, had been stretched almost beyond recognition. More focus was needed to prevent the company from repeating its mistakes. He explained:

> Every year we started at least five major new initiatives: TV, film, huge theme parks. We expanded so fast that it was harder and harder to execute anything properly. . . . If an initiative

failed, we would just drop it and start something else.

The end result, he said, "was a loss of confidence" in the company's direction and abilities: It was unsure of what to do and its execution was weak.

"What," Knudstorp asked, "makes us unique? Why are we here?" While Knudstorp posed this question to his inner circle, it also sparked a debate throughout the company. "If there is a quick answer to these questions," he said, "we know what we were doing. If not, then the brand is too vague." After intense discussion, both within the company and through focus groups with customers, the answer emerged: The core assets of the LEGO Group were: (1) the brick, which was instantly recognizable; (2) the building system, which amounted to a platform for innovation; (3) an emotionally appealing brand, perhaps the world's best for children; and (4) the unusually devoted LEGO community. According to Knudstorp:

> In essence, we saw ourselves as a unique niche player in the toy industry. We would never become the biggest, but being the best is good enough. Our products should transmit the joy of building, generate pride in creation, and help to equip children for the future through playful learning and education, in other words make children the builders of tomorrow.

From this base, they formulated the company's next strategic direction. They decided that any new product family from the LEGO Group had to be true to this identity; a new play experience should be "obviously LEGO, but never seen before." While this did not rule out the extension of the LEGO brand into new media and experiences, it did mean a return to the iconic brick as a focal point.

PHASE 2: PROFIT FROM THE CORE

By the end of 2005 the LEGO Group was out of immediate trouble. Although sales were flat due to the elimination of some products, the company was in a solid cash position, costs were down 35% and it was debt free. As Phase 2 of Shared Vision began, the company turned its focus toward revitalizing its product lines and restoring profitability. The product groups were called upon to demonstrate profitable results. They were also asked to start thinking of how they would implement the third phase of the Shared Vision—new ideas for organic growth—that was scheduled to begin in 2008. One product line that needed revitalization was LEGO City.

Long one of the traditional and best-selling product lines of the company, LEGO City[5] sales had been declining since 2000. Some believed that the product line should be phased out. Its share of the company's gross revenues had dwindled from over 15% to about half that figure in 2003. In 2004 LEGO City marketing director Birthe Jensen asked her team to reassess where they were going. Their products, Jensen concluded, were not differentiated enough and had become overly simplified, that is, dumbed down for easy assembly. Moreover, they appeared undistinguished and unrealistic, somehow lacking focus or relevance. "We were doing space stations and race tracks," she recalled, "but not things that children saw every day." To move ahead, Jensen and her team decided they would develop more realistic products, with convincing details, for a limited number of products with which children had direct experience. "We would make

---

[5] This product line had gone under various names, including LEGO Land and World City.

EXHIBIT 4   Examples of LEGO City Toys

Source: Company information

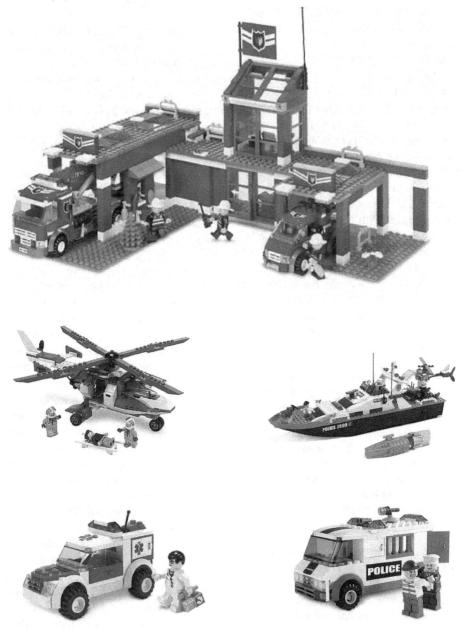

fire engines that look real," she explained (*refer to **Exhibit 4** for examples of LEGO City toys*). But the team, like the rest of the LEGO Group, had to contend with a reduced product line necessitated by the reduction in complexity.

FUTURE CHALLENGES

At the end of 2005, with the company on a solid financial footing, Knudstorp and the management team considered what to do next. Sales had fallen by 35% in the previous two years, and the company was still adjusting to the dramatic cutback in personnel. The reduction in LEGO components was also being felt, inside and outside the company. Designers complained that their creativity was being reduced, and some passionate users complained when their favorite components or figures were eliminated. The team wondered how LEGO's designers would react to a reduction in the number of components available to them. If the toys were constructed only from the components available, would the cut in manufacturing, supply chain and inventory costs be worth the loss of creativity?

Knudstorp and his team also realized that they needed to improve development effectiveness. It was important to develop not just breakthrough new toy ideas but also the next generation of Bionicle, Exoforce, LEGO City, Harry Potter™, Star Wars™ and other toys. How could the product development process be sped up and improved? The company had implemented a stage-gate process in 1995, called the LEGO Development Process (LDP), to improve the flow of products to market. Over the past nine years, the LDP had evolved into a cumbersome bureaucratic mechanism. For a product to advance, elaborate checklists had to be filled out, and each person understood the requirements differently. According to Per Hjuler, vice president of product and marketing development, "At first it worked well, but then it got too dense." It also remained a sequential, linear process:

Designers would brainstorm, then engineers took over. Next, it went to the manufacturing groups, and finally the marketers got it. Getting something to market took about 36 months.

And, as the process slowed down, the success rate dropped. By 2003, according to Hjuler, "only one or two" of ten new product ideas actually made it to market. How could they improve the process both to make it faster and to increase the success rate?

In addition to being slow, the product development process suffered from a lack of success in developing and bringing to market radically new ideas. In an effort to address this, LEGO had created a Concept Lab, whose charter was to develop revolutionary breakthrough products. Set up as a cost center, the Lab was seen as a free resource to development teams, and Concept Lab personnel often became involved in the development of more incremental product concepts. This diversion of personnel, coupled with the difficulty of navigating ideas through the LEGO Group's cumbersome development process, hindered the productivity of the Concept Lab.

Another opportunity for improvement was in the area of licensing. While the company was aggressively lowering its internal product range and complexity, it agreed that there was still an opportunity to generate income by licensing the LEGO brands to external partners. These partners could produce books, movies, computer games, T-shirts and other products around brands such as Bionicle, Exoforce and LEGO Star Wars.™ The company also wished to explore whether it could augment its internal development team with outside inventors. But in both cases, it needed to ensure that the products generated were consistent with the brand image of each product line, and were delivered to the market at the same time as the products they were designed to complement.

EXHIBIT 5   Screenshots of the LEGO Factory Website and LEGO Digital Designer

Source: Company information

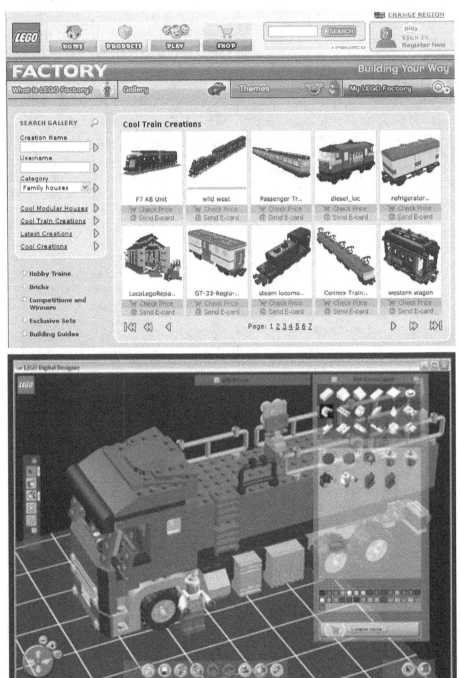

Based on its research, the company also knew that it had a unique asset that it had not been leveraging—its passionate customer base. For example, LEGO had recently released a computer-aided design tool called LEGO Digital Designer, which allowed users to create new LEGO toys virtually. After building a virtual toy a user could check the price of the new creation, upload it to the LEGO website, and order exactly the pieces needed to build it. The new service, called LEGO Factory, also allowed users to purchase other users' creations. While the logistics of the packing and shipping of these kits was still under development, the company saw great potential in the service and wondered how it could grow the idea more. (*Refer to* **Exhibit 5** *for screenshots of the LEGO Factory website and the LEGO Digital Designer design environment.*)

Another opportunity to leverage the company's customer base was for the development of the toys themselves. For example, in the previous generation of LEGO Mindstorms, users had hacked the code for the programmable brick and developed other programming languages that many in the community felt were better. Should the company prevent this from happening in the future, or should it develop its next generation of LEGO Mindstorms as an open source product?

Reading

The 12 Different Ways for Companies to Innovate

Mohanbir Sawhney, Robert C. Wolcott, and Inigo Arroniz

Faced with slow growth, commoditization and global competition, many CEOs view innovation as critical to corporate success. William Ford Jr., chairman and CEO of Ford Motor Co., recently announced that, "[f]rom this point onward, innovation will be the compass by which the company sets its direction" and that Ford "will adopt innovation as its core business strategy going forward."[1] Echoing those comments, Jeffrey Immelt, chairman and CEO of General Electric Co., has talked about the "Innovation Imperative," a belief that innovation is central to the success of a company and the only reason to invest in its future.[2] Thus GE is pursuing around 100 "imagination breakthrough" projects to drive growth though innovation. And Steve Ballmer, Microsoft Corp.'s CEO, stated recently that "innovation is the only way that Microsoft can keep customers happy and competitors at bay."[3]

---

[1] "Bill Ford: Innovation Key to Ford's Future; Commitment to Hybrids to Grow," Sept. 21, 2005, http://media.ford.com

Source: Reprinted from *Sloan Management Review*, vol. 47, no. 3, Spring 2006, pp. 74–81, by permission of the publisher.

[2] J. Immelt, "The Innovation Imperative" (2004 Robert S. Hatfield Fellow in Economic Education lecture at Cornell University, Ithaca, New York, April 15, 2004).

[3] C. Nobel, "Ballmer: Microsoft's Priority Is Innovation," Oct. 19, 2005, www.eweek.com

But what exactly is innovation? Although the subject has risen to the top of the CEO agenda, many companies have a mistakenly narrow view of it. They might see innovation only as synonymous with new product development or traditional research and development. But such myopia can lead to the systematic erosion of competitive advantage, resulting in firms within an industry looking more similar to each other over time.[4] Best practices get copied, encouraged by benchmarking. Consequently, companies within an industry tend to pursue the same customers with similar offerings, using undifferentiated capabilities and processes. And they tend to innovate along the same dimensions. In technology-based industries, for example, most firms focus on product R&D. In the chemical or oil and gas industries, the emphasis is on process innovations. And consumer packaged-goods manufacturers tend to concentrate on branding and distribution. But if all firms in an industry are seeking opportunities in the same places, they tend to come up with the same innovations. Thus, viewing innovation too narrowly blinds companies to opportunities and leaves them vulnerable to competitors with broader perspectives.

In actuality, "business innovation" is far broader in scope than product or technological innovation, as evidenced by some of the most successful companies in a wide range of industries. Starbucks Corp., for example, got consumers to pay $4 for a cup of latte, not because of better-tasting coffee but because the company was able to create a customer experience referred to as "the third place"—a communal meeting space between home and work where people can unwind, chat and connect with each other. Dell Inc. has become the world's most successful personal computer manufacturer, not through R&D investments but by making PCs easier to use, bringing products to market more quickly and innovating on processes like supply-chain management, manufacturing and direct selling. And Google has become a multibillion-dollar goliath not because it has the best search engine, but because it pioneered "paid search"—the powerful concept that vendors would be willing to pay Google to match consumers with relevant offerings as a byproduct of free searches the consumers conduct.

Conversely, technological innovation in the laboratory does not necessarily translate into customer value. For instance, high-definition television is a radically new innovation from a technological perspective, requiring new recording, transmission and receiving equipment, communication frequencies and programming. But the result—an incremental improvement in picture sharpness—is of limited value to the general consumer. One of the most technologically advanced computers ever created was the NeXT Cube, developed by Steve Jobs' company NeXT Computer, Inc. The product featured a host of technological advances, including clickable embedded graphics and audio within e-mail, object-oriented programming, magneto-optical storage and an innovative operating system. But the NeXT Cube was a commercial flop. Few compatible software applications were available, and consumers balked at the prospect of switching to a radically new system.

[4] Organization-theory researchers have shown that firms competing in the same markets begin to look increasingly similar through a process referred to as "isomorphism." See, for instance, M.T. Hannan and J. Freemen, *Organizational Ecology* (Cambridge, Mass.: Harvard University Press, 1989).

DEFINING BUSINESS INNOVATION

To avoid innovation myopia, we propose anchoring the discussion on the customer outcomes that result from innovation, and we suggest that managers think holistically in terms of all possible dimensions through which their organizations can innovate. Accordingly, we define business innovation as the creation of substantial new value for customers and the firm by creatively changing one or more dimensions of the business system. This definition leads to the following three important characterizations.

BUSINESS INNOVATION IS ABOUT NEW *VALUE*, NOT NEW *THINGS*

Innovation is relevant only if it creates value for customers—and therefore for the firms. Thus creating "new things" is neither necessary nor sufficient for business innovation.[5] Customers are the ones who decide the worth of an innovation by voting with their wallets. It makes no difference how innovative a company thinks it is. What matters is whether customers will pay.

BUSINESS INNOVATION COMES IN MANY FLAVORS

Innovation can take place on any dimension of a business system. The Home Depot Inc., for example, innovated by

[5] Joseph Schumpeter's seminal work in this area identifies "new combinations" of existing things as fundamental to the definition and accomplishment of innovation. See J. Schumpeter, *The Theory of Economic Development* (Cambridge, Mass.: Harvard University Press, 1934).

targeting "do it yourselfers," an underserved customer segment. JetBlue Airways Corp. has succeeded in the U.S. domestic airline market by offering a better customer experience that includes live satellite television, leather seats and fashionably clad flight attendants. And Cisco Systems Inc. has improved its margins through process innovations, such as the company's ability to close its quarterly financial accounts on the same day that its quarter ends.

BUSINESS INNOVATION IS SYSTEMIC

Successful business innovation requires the careful consideration of all aspects of a business. A great product with a lousy distribution channel will fail just as spectacularly as a terrific new technology that lacks a valuable end-user application. Thus, when innovating, a company must consider all dimensions of its business system.

A 360-DEGREE VIEW

The question then immediately arises: How many possible dimensions of business innovation are there, and how do they relate to each other? For three years, we have examined that issue in depth with a group of leading companies, including Motorola, Chamberlain Group ADT, Sony, MicroSoft and ConocoPhilips. Based on discussions with managers leading innovation efforts at these companies and a comprehensive survey of the academic literature on the topic, we have developed, validated and applied a new framework called the "innovation radar." This tool presents and relates all of the dimensions through which a firm can look for opportunities to innovate. Much like a map,

The Innovation Radar

The innovation radar displays the 12 dimensions of business innovation, anchored by the offerings a company creates, the customers it serves, the processes it employs and the points of presence it uses to take its offerings to market.

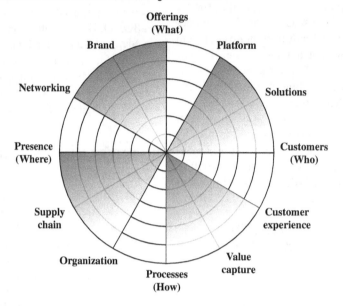

the innovation radar consists of four key dimensions that serve as business anchors: (1) the offerings a company creates, (2) the customers it serves, (3) the processes it employs and (4) the points of presence it uses to take its offerings to market. Between these four anchors, we embed eight other dimensions of the business system that can serve as avenues of pursuit. Thus, the innovation radar contains a total of 12 key dimensions. (See "The Innovation Radar," above and "The 12 Dimensions of Business Innovation," p. 19.)

Offerings   Offerings are a firm's products and services. Innovation along this dimension requires the creation of new products and services that are valued by customers. Consider the Procter & Gamble Company's Crest SpinBrush. Introduced in 2001, the product became the world's best-selling electric toothbrush by 2002. A simple design and the use of disposable AA batteries translated into ease of use, portability and affordability. Moreover, Procter & Gamble's no-frills approach enabled the SpinBrush to be priced at around $5, substantially chapter than competing products.

Platform   A platform is a set of common components, assembly methods or technologies that serve as building blocks for a portfolio of products or services. Platform innovation involves exploiting the "power of commonality"—using modularity to create a diverse set of derivative offerings more quickly and cheaply than if they were stand-alone items. Innovations along this dimension are frequently overlooked even though their power to create value can be considerable. Platform innovation, for

The 12 Dimensions of Business Innovation

Dimension	Definition	Examples
Offerings	Develop innovative new products or services.	• Gillette Mach3Turbo razor • Apple iPod music player and iTunes music service
Platform	Use common components or building blocks to create derivative offerings.	• General Motors OnStar telematics platform • Disney animated movies
Solutions	Create integrated and customized offerings that solve end-to-end customer problems.	• UPS logistics services Supply Chain Solutions • DuPont Building Innovations for construction
Customers	Discover unmet customer needs or identify underserved customer segments.	• Enterprise Rent-A-Car focus on replacement car renters • Green Mountain Energy focus on "green power"
Customer Experience	Redesign customer interactions across all touch points and all moments of contact.	• Washington Mutual Occasio retail banking concept • Cabela's "store as entertainment experience" concept
Value Capture	Redefine how company gets paid or create innovative new revenue streams.	• Google paid search • Blockbuster revenue-sharing with movie distributors
Processes	Redesign core operating processes to improve efficiency and effectiveness.	• Toyota Production System for operations • General Electric Design for Six Sigma (DFSS)
Organization	Change form, function or activity scope of the firm.	• Cisco partner-centric networked virtual organization • Procter & Gamble front-back hybrid organization for customer focus
Supply Chain	Think differently about sourcing and fulfillment.	• Moen ProjectNet for collaborative design with suppliers • General Motors Celta use of integrated supply and online sales
Presence	Create new distribution channels or innovative points of presence, including the places where offerings can be bought or used by customers.	• Starbucks music CD sales in coffee stores • Diebold Remote Teller System for banking
Networking	Create network-centric intelligent and integrated offerings.	• Otis Remote Elevator Monitoring service • U.S. Department of Defense Network Centric Warfare
Brand	Leverage a brand into new domains.	• Virgin Group "branded venture capital" • Yahoo! as a lifestyle brand

example, has allowed Nissan Motor Co. to resurrect its fortunes in the automotive industry. The company has relied on a common set of components to develop a line of cars and sport utility vehicles with markedly different styles, performance and market positioning. Nissan uses essentially the same small engine block (a 3.5-liter V6) to power its upscale models of a midsize sedan (Altima), large sedan (Maxima), luxury sedans (Infiniti G and M series), minivan (Quest) and sports coupe (350Z). Clever modifications of the common engine allow the production of anywhere between 245 and 300 horsepower, creating enough distinctiveness between the vehicles while gaining efficiency advantages.

Solutions A solution is a customized, integrated combination of products, services and information that solves a customer problem. Solution innovation creates value for customers through the breadth of assortment and the depth of integration of the different elements. An example here is Deere & Co., which has combined an array of products and services (including mobile computers, a Global Positioning System-based tracking system and software) to provide an end-to-end solution to farmers who need to improve their sowing, tilling and harvesting, as well as manage the business aspects of their operations more effectively.

Customers are the individuals or organizations that use or consume a company's offerings to satisfy certain needs. To innovate along this dimension, the company can discover new customer segments or uncover unmet (and sometimes unarticulated) needs. Virgin Mobile USA was able to successfully enter the U.S. cellular services market late by focusing on consumers under 30 years old—an

underserved segment. To attract that demographic, Virgin offered a compelling value proposition: simplified pricing, no contractual commitments, entertainment features, stylish phones and the irreverence of the Virgin brand. Within three years of its 2002 launch, Virgin had attracted several million subscribers in the highly competitive market.

Customer Experience This dimension considers everything a customer sees, hears, feels and otherwise experiences while interacting with a company at all moments. To innovate here, the company needs to rethink the interface between the organization and its customers. Consider how the global design firm IDEO, headquartered in Palo Alto, California, has helped health care provider Kaiser Permanent to redesign the customer experience provided to patients.[6] Kaiser has created more comfortable waiting rooms, lobbies with clearer directions and larger exam rooms with space for three or more people and curtains for privacy. Kaiser understands that patients not only need good medical care but also need to have better experiences before, during and after their treatments.

Value Capture refers to the mechanism that a company uses to recapture the value it creates. To innovate along this dimension, the company can discover untapped revenue streams, develop novel pricing systems and otherwise expand its ability to capture value from interactions with customers and partners. Edmunds.com, the popular automotive Web site, is a case in point. The company generates revenues from an array of sources, including

---

[6] B. Nussbaum, "The Power of Design," *Business Week*, May 17, 2004, 86.

advertising; licensing of its tools and content to partners like *The New York Times* and America Online; referrals to insurance, warranty and financing partners; and data on customer buying behavior that are collected through its Web site and sold to third parties. These various revenue streams have significantly increased Edmunds' average sales per visitor.

Processes are the configurations of business activities used to conduct internal operations. To innovate along this dimension, a company can redesign its processes for greater efficiency, higher quality or faster cycle time. Such changes might involve relocating a process or decoupling its front end from its back end. That's the basis of the success of many information technology services firms in India, including companies like Wipro Infotech and Infosys Technologies Ltd. that have created enormous value by perfecting the model of delivering business processes as an outsourced service from a remote location. To accomplish this, each process is decomposed into its constituent elements so that cross-functional teams in multiple countries can perform the work, and the project is coordinated through the use of well-defined protocols. The benefits are flexibility and speed to market, access to a competitive pool of talent (the highly educated and relatively low-cost Indian knowledge worker) and the freedom to redirect resources to core strategic activities.

Organization is the way in which a company structures itself, its partnerships and its employee roles and responsibilities. Organizational innovation often involves rethinking the scope of the firm's activities as well as redefining the roles, responsibilities and incentives of different business units and individuals. Thomson

Financial, a New York City-based provider of information and technology applications for the financial services industry, transformed its organization by structuring around customer segments instead of products. In this way, Thomson was able to align its operational capabilities and sales organization with customer needs, enabling the company to create offerings like Thomson ONE, an integrated workflow solution for specific segments of financial services professionals.

Supply Chain A supply chain is the sequence of activities and agents that moves goods, services and information from source to delivery of products and services. To innovate in this dimension, a company can streamline the flow of information through the supply chain, change its structure or enhance the collaboration of its participants. Consider how the apparel retailer Zara in La Coruña, Spain, was able to create a fast and flexible supply chain by making counterintuitive choices in sourcing, design, manufacturing and logistics. Unlike its competitors, Zara does not fully outsource its production. Instead it retains half in-house, allowing it to locate its manufacturing facilities closer to its markets to cut product lead times. Zara eschews economies of scale by making small lots and launching a plethora of designs, allowing it to refresh its designs almost weekly. The company also ships garments on hangers, a practice that requires more warehouse space but allows new designs to be displayed more quickly. Thanks to such practices, Zara has decreased the design-to-retail cycle to as short as 15 days and is able to sell most merchandise at full price.

Presence Points of presence are the channels of distribution that a company employs to take offerings to market and the places where its offerings can be bought or used by customers. Innovation in this dimension involves creating new points of presence or using existing ones in creative ways. That's what Titan Industries Ltd. did when it entered the Indian market with stylish quartz wristwatches in the 1980s. Initially, Titan was locked out of the market because the traditional watch retailing channels were controlled by a competitor. But the company took a fresh look at the industry and asked itself the following fundamental question: Must watches be sold at watch stores? In answering that, Titan found that target customers also shopped at jewelry, appliance and consumer electronics stores. So the company pioneered the concept of selling watches through free-standing kiosks placed within other retail stores. For service and repair, Titan established a nationwide aftersales network through which customers could get their watches fixed. Such innovations have enabled Titan not only to enter the Indian market but also to become the industry leader.

Networking A company and its products and services are connected to customers through a network that can sometimes become part of the firm's competitive advantage. Innovations in this dimension consist of enhancements to the network that increase the value of the company's offerings. Consider how Mexican industrial giant CEMEX was able to redefine its offerings in the ready-to-pour concrete business. Traditionally, CEMEX offered a three-hour delivery window for ready-to-pour concrete with a 48-hour advance ordering requirement. But construction is an unpredictable business. Over half of CEMEX's customers would cancel orders at the last minute, causing logistical problems for the company and financial penalties for customers. To address that,

CEMEX installed an integrated network consisting of GPS systems and computers in its fleet of trucks, a satellite communication system that links each plant and a global Internet portal for tracking the status of orders worldwide. This network now allows CEMEX to offer a 20-minute time window for delivering ready-to-pour concrete, and the company also benefits from better fleet utilization and lower operating costs.

Brand are the symbols, words or marks through which a company communicates a promise to customers. To innovate in this dimension, the company leverages or extends its brand in creative ways. London-based easyGroup has been a leader in this respect. Founded by Stelios Haji-Ioannou, easyGroup owns the "easy" brand and has licensed it to a range of businesses. The core promises of the brand are good value and simplicity, which have now been extended to more than a dozen industries through various offerings such as easyJet, easyCar, easyInternetcafé, easyMoney, easyCinema, easyHotel and easyWatch.

PUTTING THE INNOVATION RADAR TO WORK

The various examples of Nissan, Virgin, Edmunds.com and others help illustrate the many possible avenues of innovation, but companies can reap greater value by thinking of those dimensions as intertwined within a business system. Consider Apple Computer Inc. Its famously successful iPod is more than a nifty product. It is also an elegant solution for customers (simple, integrated buying and consumption of digital music), content owners (secure pay-per-song model for legal music downloads) and its manufacturer (the discovery of new growth markets).

Innovation Profiles of Four Leading Latin-American Banks

Benchmarking the innovation radars of competitors can reveal the relative strengths and weaknesses of each company.

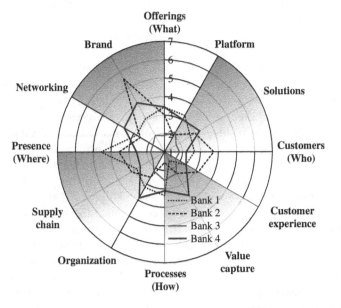

With respect to the innovation radar, Apple attacked not only the offerings and platform dimensions but also the supply chain (content owners), presence (portability of a customer's *entire* collection of music, photos and videos), networking (connecting with Mac or Windows computers), value capture (iTunes), customer experience (the complete iPod experience) and brand (extending the Apple brand).

In our current research, we are investigating how companies can use the innovation radar to construct a strategic approach to innovation. Specifically, the radar could help a firm determine how its current innovation strategy stacks up against its competitors. Using that information, the company could then identify opportunities and prioritize on which dimensions to focus its efforts. For example, we have worked with a top global bank to benchmark its innovation profile against that of its top three competitors in a major Latin American country. (See "Innovation Profiles of Four Leading Latin American Banks," on this page.) Such analyses can reveal the strengths and weaknesses of each company as well as any promising opportunities, particularly those overlooked by the industry as a whole.[7]

[7] The challenge is figuring out which of the radar dimensions might mean the most to customers and why. Customer value is often not apparent when a company is attempting to innovate in areas traditionally neglected by an industry. There might be few precedents to validate the firm's beliefs and assumptions, and customers are often unable to provide helpful feedback regarding a new direction. However, it is this uncertainty that provides significant opportunity. Researchers have discovered numerous practical insights regarding conquering the inherent risk involved in innovation. See, in particular, R.G. McGrath and I. MacMillan, *The Entrepreneurial Mindset: Strategies for Continuously Creating Opportunity in an Age of Uncertainty* (Boston: Harvard Business School Press, 2000); and S.H. Thomke, *Experimentation Matters: Unlocking the Potential of New Technologies for Innovation* Boston: Harvard Business School Press, 2003).

Traditionally, most firms' innovation strategies are the result of simple inertia ("this is what we've always innovated on") or industry convention ("this is how everyone innovates"). But when a company identifies and pursues neglected innovation dimensions, it can change the basis of competition and leave other firms at a distinct disadvantage because each dimension requires a different set of capabilities that cannot be developed or acquired overnight. And innovating along one dimension often influences choices with respect to other dimensions. Brand innovation, for example, might require concurrent innovations along the dimensions of customer experience, offerings and presence. As such, selecting and acting on dimensions that define a firm's innovation strategy requires a deliberate, portfolio-based approach that must be communicated clearly within the company as well as to external constituents. All of that takes considerable effort and time. So, for instance, when Enterprise Rent-A-Car Co. began placing rental car locations in the neighborhoods where people lived and worked rather than at airports (thus innovating along the dimensions of customers and presence), entrenched competitors Hertz Corp. and Avis Corp. found it difficult to respond.

As we continue to expand our database of radar profiles, we will be able to test a broad set of hypotheses. For example, our research to date supports the notion that successful innovation strategies tend to focus on a few high-impact dimensions, rather than attempting a shotgun approach along many dimensions at once. Ultimately, the innovation radar could guide the way companies manage the increasingly complex business systems through which they add value, enabling innovation beyond products and technologies. In doing so, the framework could become an important tool for corporate executives, entrepreneurs and venture capitalists—anyone seeking growth through innovation.

Change Classic

Changing the Culture at British Airways

I remember going to parties in the late 1970s, and if you wanted to have a civilized conversation, you didn't actually say that you worked for British Airways, because it got you talking about people's last travel experience, which was usually an unpleasant one. It's staggering how much the airline's image has changed since then, and, in comparison, how proud staff are of working for BA today.

—*British Airways employee, Spring 1990*

I recently flew business class on British Airways for the first time in about 10 years. What has happened over that time is amazing. I can't tell you how my memory of British Airways as a company and the experience I had 10 years ago contrasts with today. The improvement in service is truly remarkable.

—British Airways customer, Fall 1989

In June 1990, British Airways (BA) reported its third consecutive year of record profits, £345 million before taxes, firmly establishing the rejuvenated carrier as one of the world's most profitable airlines. The impressive financial results were one indication that BA had convincingly shed its historic "bloody awful" image. In October 1989, one respected American publication referred to it as "bloody awesome,"[1] a description most would not have thought possible after pretax losses totalling more than £240 million in 1981 and 1982. Productivity had risen more than 67 percent during the 1980s.[2] Passengers reacted very favorably to the changes. After suffering through years of poor market perception during the 1970s and before, BA garnered four Airline of the Year awards during the 1980s, as voted by the readers of *First Executive Travel*. In 1990

the leading American aviation magazine, *Air Transport World*, selected BA as the winner of its Passenger Service Award. In the span of a decade, British Airways had radically improved its financial strength, convinced its workforce of the paramount importance of customer service, and dramatically improved its perception in the market. Culminating in the privatization of 1987, the carrier had undergone fundamental change through a series of important messages and events. With unprecedented success under its belt, management faced an increasingly perplexing problem: how to maintain momentum and recapture the focus that would allow them to meet new challenges.

CRISIS OF 1981

Record profits must have seemed distant in 1981. On September 10 of that year, chief executive Roy Watts issued a special bulletin to British Airways staff:

> British Airways is facing the worst crisis in its history . . . unless we take swift and remedial action we are heading for a loss of at least £100 million in the present financial year. We face the prospect that by next April we shall have piled up losses of close to £250 million in two years. Even as I write to you, our money is draining at the rate of nearly £200 a minute.
>
> No business can survive losses on this scale. Unless we take decisive action now, there is a real possibility that British Airways will go out of

[1] "From 'Bloody Awful' to Bloody Awesome," *Business Week*, October 9, 1989, p. 97.
[2] As measured by available ton-kilometers (ATKs) per employee, or the payload capacity of BA's aircraft multiplied by kilometers flown, the industry standard for productivity. BA's ATKs per employee were 145,000 in 1980 and 243,000 in 1989.

Source: This case was prepared by Research Associate James Leahy (under the supervision of Professor John P. Kotter) for the basis of class discussion rather than to illustrate either effective or ineffective handling of an administrative situation.

Copyright © 1990 by the President and Fellows of Harvard College. Harvard Business School case 9-491-009. Reprinted by permission of Harvard Business School.

business for lack of money. We have to cut our costs sharply, and we have to cut them fast. We have no more choice, and no more time.[3]

Just two years earlier, an optimistic British government had announced its plan to privatize British Airways through a sale of shares to the investing public. Although airline management recognized that its staff of 58,000 was too large, they expected increased passenger volumes and improved staff productivity to help them avoid complicated and costly employee reductions. While the 1978–1979 plan forecasted passenger traffic growth at 8 to 10 percent, an unexpected recession left BA struggling to survive on volumes that instead decreased by more than 4 percent. A diverse and aging fleet, increased fuel costs, and the high staffing costs forced the government and BA to put privatization on hold indefinitely. With the airline technically bankrupt, BA management and the government would have to wait before the public would be ready to embrace the ailing airline. (See Exhibit 1.)

THE BA CULTURE, 1960–1980

British Airways stumbled into its 1979 state of inefficiency in large part because of its history and culture. In August 1971, the Civil Aviation Act became law, setting the stage for the British Airways Board to assume control of two state-run airlines, British European Airways (BEA) and British Overseas Airways Corporation (BOAC), under the name British Airways. In theory, the board was to control policy over British Airways, but in practice, BEA

and BOAC remained autonomous, each with its own chairman, board, and chief executive. In 1974, BOAC and BEA finally issued one consolidated financial report. In 1976, Sir Frank (later Lord) McFadzean replaced the group division with a structure based on functional divisions to officially integrate the divisions into one airline. Still, a distinct split within British Airways persisted throughout the 1970s and into the mid-1980s.

After World War II, BEA helped pioneer European civil aviation. As a pioneer, it concerned itself more with building an airline infrastructure than it did with profit. As a 20-year veteran and company director noted, "The BEA culture was very much driven by building something that did not exist. They had built that in 15 years, up until 1960. Almost single-handedly they opened up air transport in Europe after the war. That had been about getting the thing established. The marketplace was taking care of itself. They wanted to get the network to work, to get stations opened up."

BOAC had also done its share of pioneering, making history on May 2, 1952, by sending its first jet airliner on a trip from London to Johannesburg, officially initiating jet passenger service. Such innovation was not without cost, however, and BOAC found itself mired in financial woes throughout the two decades following the war. As Chairman Sir Matthew Slattery explained in 1962, "The Corporation has had to pay a heavy price for pioneering advanced technologies."[4]

For most who were involved with BEA and BOAC in the 1950s and 1960s, success had less to do with net income and more to do with "flying the British flag." Having inherited numerous war veterans, both airlines had been injected with a military

---

[3] Alison Corke, *British Airways: Path to Profitability* (London: Pan Books, 1986), p. 82.

[4] Ibid., p. 39.

EXHIBIT 1 **British Airways' Results, 1977–1990**

Year ended March 31	1977	1978	1979	1980	1981	1982	1983	1984	1985	1986	1987	1988	1989	1990
Turnover (revenues) in £ billions	1.25	1.36	1.64	1.92	2.06	2.24	2.50	2.51	2.94	3.15	3.26	3.76	4.26	4.84
Operating profit in £ millions (airline only)	96	57	76	17	(102)	5	169	274	303	205	183	241	340	402
Pretax profit in £ millions	96	54	90	20	(140)	(114)	74	185	191	195	162	228	268	345
Net profit in £ millions	35	52	77	11	(145)	(545)	89	216	174	181	152	151	175	245
Revenue per passenger kilometer (pence)	2.98	3.24	3.28	3.35	3.74	4.20	4.89	5.57	5.87	5.80	6.00	5.82	5.96	6.37
Number of employees (000s)	54	55	56	56	54	48	40	36	37	39	40	43	49	50
ATK per employee (000s)	121	123	135	145	154	158	182	199	213	221	222	236	243	247

mentality. These values combined with the years BEA and BOAC existed as government agencies to shape the way British Airways would view profit through the 1970s. As former Director of Human Resources Nick Georgiades said of the military and civil service history, "Put those two together and you had an organization that believed its job was simply to get an aircraft into the air on time and to get it down on time."[5]

While government support reinforced the operational culture, a deceiving string of profitable years in the 1970s made it even easier for British Airways to neglect its increasing inefficiencies. Between 1972 and 1980, BA earned a profit before interest and tax in each year except for one. "This was significant, not least because as long as the airline was returning profits, it was not easy to persuade the work force, or the management for that matter, that fundamental changes were vital."[6] Minimizing cost to the state became the standard by which BA measured itself. As one senior manager noted, "Productivity was not an issue. People were operating effectively, not necessarily efficiently. There were a lot of people doing other people's jobs, and there were a lot of people checking on people doing other people's jobs." As a civil service agency, the airline was allowed to become inefficient because the thinking in state-run operations was, "If you're providing service at no cost to the taxpayer, then you're doing quite well."

A lack of economies of scale and strong residual loyalties upon the merger further complicated the historical disregard for efficiency by BEA and BOAC. Until Sir Frank McFadzean's reorganization in 1976, British Airways had labored under several separate organizations (BOAC; BEA European, Regional, Scottish, and Channel) so that the desired benefits of consolidation had been squandered. Despite operating under the same banner, the organization consisted more or less of separate airlines, carrying the associated costs of such a structure. Even after the reorganization, divisional loyalties prevented the carrier from attaining a common focus. "The 1974 amalgamation of BOAC with the domestic and European divisions of BEA had produced a hybrid racked with management demarcation squabbles. The competitive advantages sought through the merger had been hopelessly defeated by the lack of a unifying corporate culture."[7] A BA director summed up how distracting the merger proved: "There wasn't enough management time devoted to managing the changing environment because it was all focused inwardly on resolving industrial relations problems, on resolving organizational conflicts. How do you bring these very, very different cultures together?"

Productivity at BA in the 1970s was strikingly bad, especially in contrast to other leading foreign airlines. BA's productivity[8] for the three years ending March 31, 1974, 1975, and 1976, had never exceeded 59 percent of that of the average of the other eight foreign airline leaders. Service suffered as well. One human resources senior manager recalled the "awful" service during her early years in passenger services: "I remember 10 years ago standing at the gate handing out boxes of food to people as they got on the aircraft. That's how we dealt with service." With increasing competition and rising costs of labor in Britain in the late 1970s, the lack of productivity

---

[5] Ibid., p. 116.
[6] Company document.

[7] Duncan Campbell-Smith, *The British Airways Story: Struggle for Take-Off* (London: Coronet Books, 1986), p. 10.
[8] In terms of available ton-kilometers per employee, taken from annual reports.

and poor service was becoming increasingly harmful. By the summer of 1979, the number of employees had climbed to a peak of 58,000. The problems became dangerous when Britain's worst recession in 50 years reduced passenger numbers and raised fuel costs substantially.

LORD KING TAKES THE REINS

Sir John (later Lord) King was appointed chairman in February 1981, just a half-year before Roy Watts' unambiguously grim assessment of BA's financial state. King brought to British Airways a successful history of business ventures and strong ties to both the government and business communities. Despite having no formal engineering qualifications, King formed Ferrybridge Industries in 1945, a company that found an unexploited niche in the ball-bearing industry. Later renamed the Pollard Ball and Roller Bearing Co. Ltd., King's company was highly successful until he sold it in 1969. In 1970 he joined Babcock International, and as chairman led them through a successful restructuring during the 1970s. King's connections were legendary. Handpicked by Margaret Thatcher to run BA, King's close friends included Lord Hanson of Hanson Trust and the Princess of Wales' family. He also knew personally Presidents Ronald Reagan and Jimmy Carter. King's respect and connections proved helpful both in recruiting and in his dealings with the British government.

One director spoke of the significance of King's appointment. "British Airways needed a chairman who didn't need a job. We needed someone who could see that the only way to do this sort of thing was radically, and who would be aware enough

of how you bring that about." In his first annual report, King predicted hard times for the troubled carrier. "I would have been comforted by the thought that the worst was behind us. There is no certainty that this is so." Upon Watts' announcement in September 1981, he and King launched their Survival plan, "tough, unpalatable and immediate measures" to stem the spiraling losses and save the airline from bankruptcy. The radical steps included reducing staff numbers from 52,000 to 43,000, a 20 percent decrease, in just nine months, freezing pay increases for a year, and closing 16 routes, eight on-line stations, and two engineering bases. It also dictated halting cargo-only services and selling the fleet, and inflicting massive cuts upon offices, administrative services, and staff clubs.

In June 1982, BA management appended the Survival plan to accommodate the reduction of another 7,000 staff, which would eventually bring the total employees down from about 42,000 to nearly 35,000. BA accomplished its reductions through voluntary measures, offering such generous severance that it ended up with more volunteers than necessary. In total, the airline dished out some £150 million in severance pay. Between 1981 and 1983, BA reduced its staff by about a quarter.

About the time of the Survival plan revision, King brought in Gordon Dunlop, a Scottish accountant described by one journalist as "imaginative, dynamic, and extremely hardworking," euphemistically known on Fleet Street as "forceful," and considered by King as simply "outstanding."[9] As CFO, Dunlop's contribution to the recovery years was significant. When the results for the year ending March 31, 1982, were announced in October, he and

[9] Campbell-Smith (1986), p. 46.

the board ensured that 1982 would be a watershed year in BA's turnaround. Using creative financing, Dunlop wrote down £100 million for redundancy costs, £208 million for the value of the fleet (which would ease depreciation in future years), and even an additional £98 million for the 7,000 redundancies that had yet to be effected. For the year, the loss before taxes amounted to £114 million. After taxes and extraordinary items, it totaled a staggering £545 million.

Even King might have admitted that the worst was behind them after such a report. The chairman immediately turned his attention to changing the airline's image and further building his turnaround team. On September 13, 1982, King relieved Foote, Cone & Belding of its 36-year-old advertising account with BA, replacing it with Saatchi & Saatchi. One of the biggest account changes in British history, it was King's way of making a clear statement that the BA direction had changed. In April 1983, British Airways launched its "Manhattan Landing" campaign. King and his staff sent BA management personal invitations to gather employees and tune in to the inaugural six-minute commercial. Overseas, each BA office was sent a copy of the commercial on videocassette, and many held cocktail parties to celebrate the new thrust. "Manhattan Landing" dramatically portrayed the whole island of Manhattan being lifted from North America and whirled over the Atlantic before awestruck witnesses in the United Kingdom. After the initial airing, a massive campaign was run with a 90-second version of the commercial. The ad marked the beginning of a broader campaign, "The World's Favourite Airline," reflecting BA's status as carrier of the most passengers internationally. With the financial picture finally brightening, BA raised its advertising budget for 1983–1984 to £31 million, compared with £19 million the previous year, signaling a clear commitment to changing the corporate image.

COLIN MARSHALL BECOMES CHIEF EXECUTIVE

In the midst of the Saatchi & Saatchi launch, King recruited Mr. (later Sir) Colin Marshall, who proved to be perhaps the single most important person in the changes at British Airways. Appointed chief executive in February 1983, Marshall brought to the airline a unique résumé. He began his career as a management trainee with Hertz in the United States. After working his way up the Hertz hierarchy in North America, Marshall accepted a job in 1964 to run rival Avis' operations in Europe. By 1976, the British-born businessman had risen to chief executive of Avis. In 1981, he returned to the United Kingdom as deputy chief executive and board member of Sears Holdings. Fulfilling one of his ultimate career ambitions, he took over as chief executive of British Airways in early 1983. Although he had no direct experience in airline management, Marshall brought with him two tremendous advantages. First, he understood customer service, and second, he had worked with a set of customers quite similar to the airline travel segment during his car rental days.

Marshall made customer service a personal crusade from the day he entered BA. One executive reported, "It was really Marshall focusing almost on nothing else. The one thing that had overriding attention the first three years he was here was customer service, customer service, customer service—nothing else. That was the only thing he was interested in, and it's not an exaggeration to say that was his exclusive focus." Another senior manager added, "He has certainly put an enabling culture in place to allow customer service to come out, where rather than people waiting to be told what to do to do things better, it's an environment where people feel they can actually come out with ideas, that they will be listened to, and feel they are much more a part of the success of the company." Not just a strong verbal communicator, Marshall became an active role model in the terminals, spending time with staff during morning and evenings. He combined these actions with a number of important events to drive home the customer service message.

CORPORATE CELEBRATIONS, 1983–1987

If Marshall was the most important player in emphasizing customer service, then the Putting People First (PPF) program was the most important event. BA introduced PPF to frontline staff in December 1983 and continued it through June 1984. Run by the Danish firm Time Manager International, each PPF program cycle lasted two days and included 150 participants. The program was so warmly received that non-front-line employees eventually asked to be included, and a one-day "PPF II" program facilitated the participation of all BA employees through June 1985. Approximately 40,000 BA employees went through the PPF programs. The program urged participants to examine their interactions with other people, including family, friends, and, by association, customers. Its acceptance and impact was extraordinary, due primarily to the honesty of its message, the excellence of its delivery, and the strong support of management.

Employees agreed almost unanimously that the program's message was sincere and free from manipulation, due in some measure to the fact that BA separated itself from the program's design. The program emphasized positive relations with people in general, focusing in large part on non-work-related relationships. Implied in the positive relationship message was an emphasis on customer service, but the program was careful to aim for the benefit of employees as individuals first.

Employees expressed their pleasure on being treated with respect and relief that change was on the horizon. As one frontline ticket agent veteran said, "I found it fascinating—very, very enjoyable. I thought it was very good for British Airways. It made people aware. I don't think people give enough thought to people's reaction to each other. . . . It was hard hitting. It was made something really special. When you were there, you were treated extremely well. You were treated as a VIP, and people really enjoyed that. It was reverse roles, really, to the job we do." A senior manager spoke of the confidence it promoted in the changes: "It was quite a revelation, and I thought it was absolutely wonderful. I couldn't believe BA had finally woken and realized where its bread was buttered. There were a lot of cynics at the time, but for people like myself it was really great to suddenly realize you were working for an airline that had the guts to change, and that it's probably somewhere where you want to stay."

Although occasionally an employee felt uncomfortable with the "rah-rah" nature of the program, feeling it perhaps "too American," in general PPF managed to eliminate cynicism. The excellence in presentation helped signify a sincerity to the message. One senior manager expressed this consistency in saying, "There was a match between the message and the delivery. You can't get away with saying putting people first is important, if in the process of delivering that message you don't put people first." Employees were sent personal invitations, thousands were flown in from around the world, and a strong effort was made to prepare tasteful meals and treat everyone with respect. Just as important, BA released every employee for the program, and expected everyone to attend. Grade differences became irrelevant during PPF, as managers and staff members were treated equally and interacted freely. Moreover, a senior director came to conclude every single PPF session with a question-and-answer session. Colin Marshall himself frequently attended these closing sessions, answering employee concerns in a manner most felt to be extraordinarily frank. The commitment shown by management helped BA avoid the fate suffered by British Rail in its subsequent attempt at a similar program. The British Rail program suffered a limited budget, a lack of commitment by management and interest by staff, and a high degree of cynicism. Reports surfaced that employees felt the program was a public relations exercise for the outside world, rather than a learning experience for staff.

About the time PPF concluded in 1985, BA launched a program for managers only, called, appropriately, Managing People First (MPF). A five-day residential program for 25 managers at a time, MPF stressed the importance of, among other topics, trust, leadership, vision, and feedback. On a smaller scale, MPF stirred up issues long neglected at BA. One senior manager of engineering said, "It was almost as if I were touched on the head. . . . I don't think I even considered culture before MPF. Afterward I began to think about what makes people tick. Why do people do what they

do? Why do people come to work? Why do people do things for some people that they won't do for others?" Some participants claimed the course led them to put more emphasis on feedback. One reported initiating regular meetings with staff every two weeks, in contrast to before the program when he met with staff members only as problems arose.

As Marshall and his team challenged the way people thought at BA, they also encouraged changes in more visible ways. In December 1984, BA unveiled its new fleet livery at Heathrow Airport. Preparations for the show were carefully planned and elaborate. The plane was delivered to the hangar-turned-theater under secrecy of night, and hired audio and video technicians put together a dramatic presentation. On the first night of the show, a darkened coach brought guests from an off-site hotel to an undisclosed part of the city and through a tunnel. The guests, including dignitaries, high-ranking travel executives, and trade union representatives, were left uninformed of their whereabouts. To their surprise, as the show began, an aircraft moved through the fog and laser lights decorating the stage and turned, revealing the new look of the British Airways fleet. A similar presentation continued four times a day for eight weeks for all staff to see. On its heels, in May 1985, British Airways unveiled its new uniforms, designed by Roland Klein. With new leadership, strong communication from the top, increased acceptance by the public, and a new physical image, few on the BA staff could deny in 1985 that his or her working life had turned a corner from its condition in 1980.

Management attempted to maintain the momentum of its successful programs. Following PPF and MPF, they put on a fairly successful corporatewide program in 1985 called "A Day in the Life" and another less significant program in 1987 called "To Be the Best." Inevitably, interest diminished and cynicism grew with successive programs. BA also implemented an "Awards for Excellence" program to recognize outstanding contributions, and a "Brainwaves" program to encourage employee input. Colin Marshall regularly communicated to staff through video. While the programs enjoyed some success, not many employees felt "touched on the head" by any successor program to PPF and MPF.

PRIVATIZATION

The financial crisis of 1981 rendered irrelevant the 1979 announcement of privatization by the British government until BA's return to profitability in 1983. Unfortunately for BA, a number of complicated events delayed the selling of shares to the public for almost four more years. On April 1, 1984, the government passed legislation that made BA a public limited company. Still, the transport minister maintained control of the shares. Before a public sale, BA first had to weather an antitrust suit against it and a number of other airlines by the out-of-business Laker airline chief Freddie Laker. They were also confronted by complicated diplomatic difficulties with the United States concerning U.K.-U.S. flight regulations, and increased fears of terrorism. Finally, they faced a challenge at home by British Caledonian over routes, a challenge that ironically turned out to be the final ingredient in the cultural revolution.

In 1984, British Caledonian management persuaded some influential regulators, civil servants, and ministers that the government should award the smaller airline some of BA's routes for the sake of competition. In July the Civil Aviation Authority

(CAA) produced its report recommending the changes. Arguing that substitution was a poor excuse for competition, Lord King led BA into a fierce political battle. Against the odds, King managed to extract a non-threatening compromise. An October government policy report recommended increased competition but rejected forced transfers from BA to British Caledonian. Instead, it approved of a mutually agreed transfer between BA and BCal by which BCal attained BA's Saudi Arabia routes and BA attained BCal's South American routes. Perhaps just as important as the results, King led BA through a battle that both bound staff together and identified their cause with his board. Over 26,000 British Airways employees signed a petition against the route transfers. Thousands sent letters to their MPs and ministers. King's battle may have been the final stake in the heart of the lingering divisions that existed from the BEA and BOAC merger more than a decade earlier. The organization had been offered a uniting motive and a leader with whom to identify. As BA's legal director offered, King "took his jacket off, and he had a most fantastic punchout with [the government] about keeping the route rights. He got the whole of this organization behind him because they could see that he was fighting for them."

With its CAA review, diplomatic concerns with the United States, and Freddie Laker legal battle finally resolved, BA was ready for privatization in 1986. In September of that year, newly appointed Secretary of State for Transport John Moore announced the intention to sell shares to the public in early 1987. With the offer 11 times oversubscribed, the public clearly displayed its approval of the changed British Airways.

After privatization, King and Marshall made globalization a major thrust. In 1987,

BA took a 26 percent stake in Galileo, an advanced computer reservation system also supported by KLM Dutch Airlines and Swissair. That same year, BA arranged a partnership with United Airlines, allowing each carrier to extend its route coverage without stretching its resources. In early 1988, British Airways finally outmuscled Scandinavian Airlines System (SAS) to acquire British Caledonian. Finally, in December 1989, BA concluded a deal with Sabena World Airlines through which it secured a 20 percent stake in the Belgian carrier. Combined, the steps bolstered British Airways' global power and prepared it for what analysts expected to be a post-1992 European marketplace in which only the strongest carriers would survive. They also put an exclamation point on an evolving shift from a strongly British, engineering, and operationally driven culture to one that emphasized global marketing through customer service.

REACTION AT BA

Although not unanimously, by 1990 staff and management at BA felt that the culture at the airline had changed for the better since the 1970s. There was near-complete agreement on the positive feelings generated by success.

> The general atmosphere of the company is a much more positive one. There is an attitude of "we can change things, we are better than our competitors." I'm not certain if there's a relationship which is that a good culture leads to a successful company, but there is certainly the converse of that, that a successful company leads to a better culture. We are a more successful company now, and as a result of that it's easier to have a positive culture. (Senior Manager, Marketing)

> I think the core difference is that when I joined this was a transport business. And I now work for a service industry. (Senior Manager, formerly of Cabin Services)

> You start to think not just as an engineering department, where all my concerns are just about airplanes and the technical aspects. My concerns have developed into what the operation requires of me, and the operation is flight crew, cabin crew operations, ground operations. . . . What do I need to do to help British Airways to compete aggressively against all the other operators? (Senior Manager, Engineering)

> Fifteen years ago, you just did one thing, and only went so far with the job, and the next bloke would do his bit. Now, I can go and do the lot, whatever I need to do. I don't call someone else to do the job. Now, you just get on with it. A job that could have taken eight hours is done in two hours. (Veteran engineer)

> In the late 1970s, it was very controlled, a lot of rules and regulations. It stifled initiative. . . . We've become very free, and that's nice. There's not so much personal restriction. You can now talk to your boss. When I first started, it was definitely officers and rank. Now you've got more access to managers. (Ticketing supervisor)

> In terms of both its superficial identity, its self-confidence, and also the basic service and product, there's an enormous difference to 10 or 11 years ago. Its management is perceived as more professional and its business is perceived to be more competent and effective. (Executive, Human Resources)

CHALLENGES FOR THE 1990S

Despite the enormous change in the culture over the 1980s, BA still faced huge challenges. Management and staff agreed that, while the new culture fostered a strong commitment to service, a much higher morale, and a better market image, certain pockets within BA still needed to institutionalize change.

> I like it much better now, but I think it's still got a long way to go. . . . The trust and the belief in this organization is not quite there. We can see the problems, but we still don't have any input. . . . We waste so much time waiting for spares, waiting for airplanes. . . . We still think of ourselves as little areas. The five shifts here are five little outfits. We still don't quite think of ourselves as British Airways. (Veteran engineer)

> I don't think the culture change by any means has taken place as much as the public perceives. I think a lot has been done, but I don't feel it has become the norm. There is in places a lack of recognition of emotional labor, and the management and leadership requirements of emotional labor. I suspect we've gone a long way compared to many organizations, but it would be very easy to lose it. Eight years is a relatively short period of time to establish that, particularly when the economic pressure comes back on. (Executive, Human Resources)

> If you all pull together, then you get more out of it. The problem is getting everyone pulling together. You never get 100%, obviously, but I suppose if you get 80% pulling together, then you're not doing too bad. There will

always be a percentage that won't be pulling together. (Veteran engineer)

Ironically, attacking those pockets was more difficult because of the strong impact of the 1983–1985 corporate celebrations. Employees as a group were changed by those celebrations, and to some degree by successive programs, but excessive repetition risked rebellion. Management had to make a judgment of whether the communication programs of the 1980s were worn out.

> I think that the fundamental message has not changed over the last decade. We're restating old values. When the message was first heard, people did listen and read and absorb, because it was new, and it was radically different from the previous decade. So they had an incentive. The difference is there is no longer the incentive. First, because it's old news. Second, because there is a degree of cynicism about the sincerity. (Senior Manager, Passenger Services)

> You go on a million courses to see how wonderful you are and how wonderful British Airways is, and you get back to work and nothing changes. . . . The larger you are, it has to be more and more impersonal. You are always going to find that the lower levels feel so far removed from the upper levels that pulling together is almost an impossibility. (Veteran ticket agent)

> You can't go on selling the same old socks. In terms of messages and themes and something to focus the company around, it's a bit difficult to repackage in another way, and put all the sort of support mechanisms around it that we did in the 1980s, and do it all again in a way that captures the imagination in the 1990s. (Executive, Marketing and Operations)

Increasing costs complicated the effort to fine-tune the cultural changes. In the mid- and late-1980s there was a gradual drift toward higher ratings and higher pay scales. Added to that was an increase in sheer numbers, due to the 1987 merger with British Caledonian and the loss of focus.

> When this all started five years ago, the idea was to cut out levels of management, and they did one night— the night of the long knives, they called it. Forty managers, hundreds of years of experience were chopped. We've doubled those managers now. (Ticket supervisor)

> We're trying to get our cost base down. We're trying to find out why it is that as we try to grow, somehow or other our costs rise faster than our revenue generation. How do you manage all those issues, get them under control, as well as keeping the people in the business focused upon delivering quality consistently over time? (Executive, Marketing and Operations)

BA also faced both a loss of focus and a contradictory new message. The apparent contradiction between cutting costs and driving customer service may have been the most difficult challenge of all.

> During the early- and mid-1980s period, there were some specific challenges for us to overcome, and they are less obvious now than they have been in the past. (Executive, Internal Business Consulting)

> The real challenge in a people culture and a service culture is when the pressure's on. How do you manage change which requires you to get more productivity or more cost-efficiency or

> whatever, but still maintain a degree of trust, a respect for the individual, which I still think underpins service? (Executive, Human Resources)

> Today, there is the unrelenting almost fanaticism about being able to deliver customer service. It's the thing staff remember above all else. And the frustration they talk about now is in terms of their ability to deliver that customer service and some of the difficulties that we as a company are having in trading off still needing consistent customer service, but also needing to do it at a cost. We're struggling with a way of putting that message across to the work force that doesn't some way get returned to us as "you don't care about service anymore" because we've generated that single focus over the last seven or eight years. (Executive, Marketing and Operations)

In less than 10 years, British Airways had lifted itself out of bankruptcy to become one of the world's most respected airlines. The financial crisis of 1981 and the drive to ready itself for privatization had given the people of BA a focus that led to many changes. Still, there were obviously parts of the organization in which new beliefs were not institutionalized by the tornado of change. And in looking for a new focus, management dealt with the seemingly unattractive alternative of trying to get staff to identify with an issue as glamorless as cost-cutting. Yet, without increasing the value the culture placed on productivity and profits, while maintaining or increasing the value placed on customer service, King and Marshall could not guarantee BA's continued success in an increasingly competitive global marketplace.

Reading

Re-energizing the Mature Organization

Richard W. Beatty
Professor of Industrial Relations and Human Resources, Institute of Management and Labor Relations, Rutgers University

David O. Ulrich
Professor, School of Business, University of Michigan

Globalization, reduced technology cycles, shifting demographics, changing expectations among workers and customers, and restructuring of capital markets made the 1980s a "white water decade," rapidly introducing changes for both public and private organizations.

The greater the forces for change, the greater the competitive pressure, the greater the demand for change. This seemingly endless cycle of competition-change can become a vicious circle if executives cannot discover novel ways to compete.

Traditional ways of competing have reached a level of parity in which businesses cannot easily distinguish themselves solely on the basis of technology, products, or price. The ability of an organization to conceptualize and manage change—to compete from the inside out by increasing its capacity for change—may represent that novel way to compete. The universal challenge of change is to learn how organizations and employees can change faster than changing business conditions to become more competitive. That is, to change faster on the inside than the organization is changing on the outside.

Source: Reprinted by permission of publisher, from *Organizational Dynamics,* Summer/1991 © 1991. American Management Association, New York. All rights reserved.

This need to understand and manage change is salient, particularly for mature firms where the long-established norms of stability and security must be replaced with new values, such as speed, simplicity, unparalleled customer service, and a self-confident, empowered work force. The purpose of this article is to explore how mature firms can be re-energized. To do this, we will describe the unique challenges of creating change in mature firms, detail principles that can be used to guide change, and identify leadership and work activities required to accomplish change.

THE CHALLENGE OF CHANGE AND THE ORGANIZATION LIFE-CYCLE

Organizations evolve through a life-cycle, with each evolving stage raising change challenges. We shall use an hourglass to portray the process of organizational life-cycles and change challenges.

As illustrated in Figure 1, organizations in their entrepreneurial stage focus on the definition and development of new products and markets. During this life-stage, the change challenge is primarily one of defining and

FIGURE 1   **Organization life cycle and change challenge**

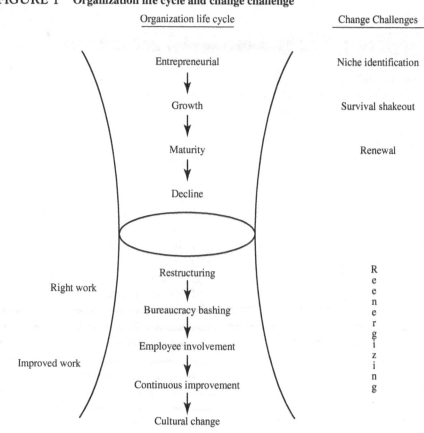

learning how to penetrate a market or niche. Managers who translate ideas into customer value overcome this *niche challenge* and proceed to the growth stage.

In the laundry equipment industry, for example, the entrepreneurial stage developed in the early 1900s, when over 60 appliance makers entered the market to provide more automated equipment for doing laundry. These autonomous (and often small) appliance makers served local markets with their specialized machines.

During the growth stage, businesses proliferate. This evolutionary stage could become corporate nirvana—if it persists.

Unfortunately, as more firms enter a market, meeting the change challenge becomes necessary for survival. Over time, small firms frequently join together to form large firms; firms that cannot compete either merge or go out of business. Between 1960 and 1985, a major shakeout occurred in the North American appliance market. From over 60 major appliance makers, the market shrank to five major companies that, together, held over 80 percent of the market. Each of these five major appliance makers faced and overcame the shakeout change challenge.

As organizations overcome the niche and shakeout challenges, they develop standard operating procedures. This third evolutionary stage is maturity. Organizations in the mature stage face a significant renewal change challenge. The presence of established norms that once helped accomplish past success may lead to complacency, and managers may become too dependent on these for future success. These calcified norms then become irrevocable patterns of behavior that eventually lead to structural inertia, as would be evidenced in the way they affect structure, systems, and processes. Not only do they create inertia but the insulation they provide leads to an avoidance of challenges that can lead to success.

In the appliance industry in the late 1980s, renewal became a major agenda. For example, Whirlpool changed its century-old functional organization into business units and formed a joint venture with Phillips to enter markets outside North America. General Electric spent over $1 billion refurbishing plants, technologies, and management systems. These efforts at renewal, still under way, will predict which firms will emerge as winners in the new century. Organizations that fail the renewal change challenge enter a period of decline, during which they slowly lose market share to firms that have renewed.

In many ways, the renewal change challenge is more onerous than the niche identification or shakeout challenges. To overcome the niche and shakeout challenges, managers in successful organizations were able to focus on customers and develop products and technologies to meet customer needs. During the maturity phase, product and technological parity is likely to emerge. Competitors offer customers similar product features at comparable costs. Given a technological and financial parity, managers facing a renewal challenge must identify additional capabilities to meet customer needs. They must learn to compete through competencies; they must develop the ability to compete from the inside out—to build internal organizational processes that meet external customer requirements.

ORGANIZATIONAL MINDSETS AND LIFE-CYCLES

Perhaps the greatest effort involved in overcoming the renewal challenge is to change the mindset of employees at all levels of an organization. The mindset represents a shared way of thinking and behaving within an organization. Mindsets are reflected in "accepted behaviors and attitudes"—customer service at Nordstrom, quality at Ford, and speed, simplicity, and self-confidence at General Electric. Mindsets are often institutionalized in vision, value, and mission.

It takes time for mindsets to be instilled. By the time an organization becomes mature, it has likely established a relatively fixed mindset. Employees self-select into the organization because of its particular set of norms. They are rewarded by promotions, salary increases, and enhanced job responsibility when they embody the mindset. Mindsets become very powerful means of gaining unity and focus. Students of Japanese service organizations have argued that this unity of mindset becomes a means of gaining competitiveness. The mindset provides a common focus and, therefore, increases the intensity of work done.

In mature organizations, a shared mindset can be a liability, and its intensity may hinder the ability to change. Since employees come to accept, adopt, and associate with the mindset of a mature company, the renewal process requires letting go. To accomplish renewal, traditional control measures must be replaced with an empowered work force that is more self-directed, self-managed, and self-controlled, thus reducing the need not only for strong competencies in managerial control but for large numbers of managers and supervisors as well. Thus, a truly empowered work force is one that acts out of commitment to purpose without the traditional boundaries and narrow mindsets of mature organizations. In Figure 1, the more open end of the hourglass represents the more open and flexible organizations; the closed end of the hourglass represents the constraints of mature organizations. The hourglass analogy shows this movement from more open and flexible (top of hourglass) to closed and inflexible (center). In this model, renewal becomes the change challenge that allows a firm to go through the "neck" of the hourglass and rediscover a vitality and energy that move the mature firm out of the decline trap and into a revived state of activity.

PRINCIPLES OF RENEWAL

Responding to the renewal challenge is difficult at best and unlikely in most cases. Few organizations successfully accomplish renewal from within. Rather than renew, organizations that perpetuate out-moded mindsets become prey to consolidations, acquisitions, or mergers—external pressures that *impose* renewal. We propose that the probability of renewal of mature organizations increases if four principles are understood and practiced. If managers recognize these principles, they may be able to help overcome the renewal challenge.

1. *Mature organizations renew by instilling a customer perspective and focusing on customer demands.* To begin to overcome the renewal challenge, a company and all its employees must be completely devoted to gaining a sustained competitive advantage. Competitive advantage comes from understanding and meeting customer needs in unique ways.

One of the most difficult challenges of renewal is the ability to recognize whether existing mindsets and practices are inconsistent with current customer requirements. When the mindset within an organization becomes a way of life, embedded in employee work habits, it is even more difficult to acknowledge or change. By examining the organization from a customer perspective, employees may better understand the internal processes and practices that reinforce existing mindsets. Hewlett-Packard, one of the first organizations to adopt such a practice as a part of its renewal effort, did this by incorporating internal and external customer satisfaction into its performance appraisal system.

A more detailed example of this practice is provided by a company that, in working through the renewal challenge, experienced at first mixed results. While employees enjoyed participating in innovative self-managed work teams and preparing vision statements, over a period each new activity that appeared promising fizzled, and employees went back to business as usual. To encourage and advance renewal, a workshop was held in which the employees were asked to examine their organization and four of its major competitors, pretending they were buyers of the product. As customers, they talked about why they would pick one supplier over another. They explored the images each of the five companies communicated and examined reasons why customers picked one competitor over another. After performing this analysis, they were able to articulate, from a customer's perspective, the perceived mindsets residing within each of the five competing organizations.

Having done this customer assessment of the competitors, the employees were able to decipher and enunciate the mindset within their own company and distinguish how their company's mindset differed from those of their competitors.

Becoming devoted to customers comes from employees spending less time thinking about internal company policies and practices and more time interacting with and worrying about their next customers. Companies that compete through service seek creative and extensive ways to involve customers in all activities. Customers may become involved in product design, in reviewing vision statements, in attending and making presentations at training and development sessions, and in doing employee reviews. The more interaction there is between customers and employees, the more a customer perspective is instilled within the organization. By taking an active role in meeting customer needs, employees in mature organizations may begin the conquest of the renewal change challenge. They can in effect change their performance expectations from meeting demands vertically dictated, to focusing horizontally on the process requirements in order to meet internal and external customer requirements. When meeting customer needs becomes more important to the organization than preserving political boundaries, employees will be more willing to renew themselves and their company. There are several reasons for this, including the freedom from autocratic directions created by

giving autonomy to those whose services are dependent upon it.

Mature companies seeking to renew have engaged in a variety of activities to ensure customer commitment. At Hewlett-Packard, engineers who design products spend months meeting with customers in focus groups, in laboratories, and in application settings to ensure that new products meet customer requirements. When the minivan was first announced at Chrysler, several senior executives were not supportive of the concept. They believed the vehicle was neither a truck nor a passenger car and would have no market. However, after extensive meetings with customers, the executives became convinced that this vehicle created an entire new niche.

At an oil service company, sales personnel were trained to interview and work with customers to identify their needs, rather than sell products. As these sales personnel spent time with customers and became aware of their current and future needs, the oil service company experienced dramatic market share growth.

The principle of customer-centered activity is consistent with the extensive work on quality done by a number of management researchers over the years. It encourages employees to define their value as a function of customer requirements, rather than personal gain. It replaces old practices with new ones that add value to customers. It refocuses attention outside to change inside—that is, toward the ultimate and the next customer.

2. *Mature organizations renew by increasing their capacity for change.* Most individuals have internal clocks, or biorhythms, that determine when we wake up, when we need to eat, and how quickly we make decisions. Like individuals, most organizations have

internal clocks that determine how quickly decisions are made and activities are completed. These internal clocks affect how long it takes organizations to move from idea to definition, to action. It has been argued that a major challenge for organizations is to reduce their cycle time, which means to change the internal clock and timing on how decisions are made. For mature organizations to experience renewal, their internal clocks must be adjusted. Cycle lengths must be reduced and the capacity for change increased.

Typically, the internal clocks of mature organizations have not been calibrated for changing erratic and unpredictable business conditions. To enact and increase a capacity for change, managers need to work on alignment, symbiosis, and reflexiveness.

"Alignment" refers to the extent to which different organization activities are focused on common goals. When organizations have a sense of alignment, their strategy, structure, and systems can move more readily toward consistent and shared goals.

Aligned organizations have a greater capacity for change, because less time is spent building commitment, and more energy and time are spent accomplishing work. To calibrate alignment, a number of organizations have sponsored "congruence" workshops where the degree of congruence between organizational activities is assessed.

"Symbiosis" refers to the extent to which organizations are able to remove boundaries inside and outside an organization.

General Electric CEO Jack Welch describes any organizational boundary as a "toll-gate." Any time individuals or products must cross a boundary, an economic, emotional, and time toll is paid. When organizations have extensive boundaries, tolls can be direct and indirect expenses. Direct boundary costs result in higher prices to customers, because of extra costs in producing the product. Indirect boundary costs occur from each boundary increasing the time required to accomplish tasks. Boundaries, and the tolls required for crossing, set an organization's internal clock and impair capacity for change. Decreasing cycle time and creating symbiosis mean reducing boundaries and increasing capacity for change and action. The Ford Taurus has become a classic example of reducing boundaries and increasing capacity for change. By forming and assigning a cross-functional team responsible for the complete design and delivery of the Taurus, Ford removed boundaries between departments. The time from concept to production for the Taurus was 50 percent less than established internal clocks.

To ensure that a capacity for change continues over time, individuals must become reflexive and have the ability to continue to learn and adapt over time. "Reflexiveness" is the ability to learn from previous actions. Organizations increase their capacity for change when time is spent reflecting on past activities and learning from them.

The capacity for change principle expedites renewal. When individuals and systems inside an organization can so change their internal clocks that decisions move quicker from concept to action, renewal occurs more frequently. In this way, organizational cycles differ from individual biorhythms: Cycle times are not genetic and intractable but learned and adjustable. By adjusting cycles, the capacity for change increases, which may lead to renewal of mature organizations.

3. *Mature organizations renew by altering both the hardware and software within the organization.* Management activities within an organization may be dissected into hardware and software. Management hardware represents issues, such as strategy, structure, and systems. These domains of activity are malleable and measurable and can be heralded with high visibility—for example, timely announcements about new strategies, structures, or systems. Also, like computer hardware, unless they are connected to appropriate software they are useless. In the organization, software represents employee behavior and mindset. These less visible domains of organizational activity are difficult to adjust or measure, but they often determine the extent to which renewal occurs.

Most renewal efforts begin by changing hardware—putting in a new strategy, structure, or system. These hardware efforts help mature organizations to turn around or change economic indicators. They do not, however, assure transformation; this comes only when new hardware is supported by appropriate software. Organizational renewal efforts that focus extensively or exclusively on strategy, structure, and systems engage in numerous discussions and debates. These discussions are necessary but are not sufficient to make any difference. At times, in fact, these discussions consume so much energy and resources that too few resources are left to make sure that employee behavior and mindset match the changes. Just as many companies have storage rooms filled with unused hardware, many organizations have binders of strategy, structure, and system changes that were never implemented.

For renewal in mature organizations, changing strategy and structure is not enough. Adjusting and encouraging individual employee behavior and working on changing the mindset are also critical. In one organization attempting to examine and modify software, the focus was not on strategy, structure, and systems but on work activities. Groups of employees met in audit workshops to identify work activities as done by suppliers for customers, then to examine each set of work activities to eliminate whatever did not add value to customers and to improve whatever did. The key to the success of these work audit workshops was that participants would leave with work inspected and modified in a positive manner. As a result of the workshops, participants have changed some of the existing behaviors and beliefs within the business.

For organizations seeking to increase the probability of renewal, new mindsets must be created that will be shared by all employees, customers, and suppliers. For suppliers, this commonly is a shared perspective that leverages competitive advantage. Xerox, between 1980 and 1988, reduced its number of suppliers from over 3,000 to 300. By focusing attention and certifying qualified suppliers, Xerox has built a shared mindset among its supplier network. Ford Motor Company has done similar work with suppliers. A team of Ford executives must accredit each Ford supplier on a number of dimensions of quality, delivery, and service. Without passing the accreditation test, the supplier cannot work with Ford. By maintaining this policy, Ford builds its vision and values into its supplier network, and Ford suppliers mesh their vision and values with Ford. These types of activities build the software that reinforces the hardware, or system changes that eventually lead to renewal.

4. *Mature organizations renew by creating empowered employees who act as leaders at all levels of the organization.* Shared leadership implies that individuals have responsibility and accountability for activities within their domain. Individuals become leaders by having influence and control over the factors that affect their work performance.

Organizations that renew have leaders stationed throughout the hierarchy regardless of position or title. Employees are trusted and empowered to act on issues that affect their work performance. Leaders have the obligation of articulating and stating a vision and of ensuring that the vision will be implemented. Leadership can come either from bringing new leaders into the organization or building competencies into existing leadership positions.

When Michael Blumenthal became chairman of Burroughs, he changed 23 of the top 24 managers within his first year. His assessment was that the current leadership team was so weighed down with traditional vision and values that they could not develop a new leadership capability, capacity for change, and competitiveness. Blumenthal could change the top echelon of his organization, but he could not replace the 1,000 secondary leaders throughout the organization. These leaders needed to be developed to induce a renewal within the company.

Primary and secondary leaders must be able to communicate the new mindset, articulating the vision and values in ways that are not only readily understandable and acceptable to all employees but that are inspirational, also. In other words, the employees must believe that it is worth giving extraordinary effort to make the vision a reality.

In addition to communication, leaders are expected to possess the competencies members perceive as necessary to lead the organization to the heights of its vision. Although some of these competencies may be functional, others are clearly the management of human resources, especially the effective use of measures both positive and negative following the actions of all employees. While the use of alternative reward strategies has become extremely popular in the last few years, leaders should be able to confront employees who are unwilling to perform at levels necessary for making a substantive contribution to competitive advantage.

Finally, leaders must be credible. Members must be able to trust in the word of their leaders; if they cannot, they will be unwilling to accept the vision or the values—and certainly unwilling to marshal the level of energy necessary to accomplish higher and higher levels of performance. The credibility of leadership cannot be overestimated when trying to energize the organization's human resource.

In brief, we have proposed four principles that can increase the probability of renewal for a mature organization. By understanding these four principles, managers may engage in a series of activities that make this renewal possible.

LEADERSHIP AND WORK ACTIVITIES

Having identified a need for mature organizations to overcome a renewal challenge, and a set of principles on which renewal is based, we can identify specific leadership and work activities which accomplish this effort. Generally, the process for re-energizing mature organizations follows the five steps shown in Figure 2, although these may not always be in sequence as some steps may occur simultaneously.

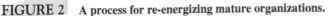

FIGURE 2   **A process for re-energizing mature organizations.**

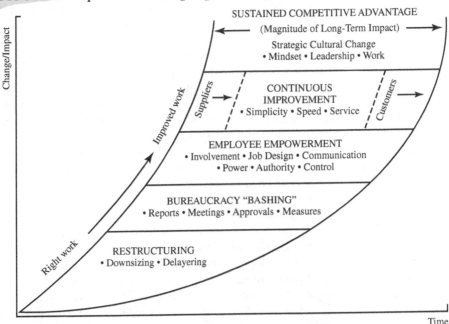

STAGE I: RESTRUCTURING

Organizational renewal generally begins with a turnaround effort focused on restructuring by downsizing or delayering, or both. Through head-count reduction, organizations attempt to become "lean and mean," recognizing that they had become "fat" by not strategically managing performance at all levels. Organizations continue to improve global measures of productivity (sales or other measures of performance per employee) by reducing the number of employees.

At General Electric, staff reductions removed approximately 25 percent of the work force between 1982 and 1988. This reduction came from retirements, reorganizations, consolidations, plant closings, and greater spans of control. Such a head-count reduction can save organizations billions of dollars and initiate renewal. At J. I. Case, the implement manufacturer,

well over 90 percent of the top management group was replaced as the organization faced a substantial change in how it was to do business in a highly competitive global environment.

The leadership requirement during restructuring is clear: Have courage to make difficult decisions fairly and boldly. No one likes to take away jobs. It will not lead to great popularity or emotional attachment of employees. However, leaders who face a renewal change challenge must act. They must implement a process that ensures equity and due cause to employees. By so doing, leaders start the renewal process by turning around an organization through restructuring.

STAGE 2: BUREAUCRACY BASHING

"Bureaucracy bashing" follows restructuring. In this stage, attempts are made to get rid of unnecessary reports, approvals, meetings, measures, policies, procedures, or other work activities that create backlogs. By focusing on bureaucracy reduction, employees throughout the organization experience changes in how they do their work. Often, sources of employee work frustration come from being constrained by bureaucratic procedures and not being able to see or feel the impact of their work. Bureaucratic policies and processes that consume energy and build frustration may have been developed in older work settings, causing more harm than good; these need to be examined and replaced.

In the restructuring stage, mindsets of corporate loyalty are shattered. Employees who believed in lifelong employment and job security may be angered by restructuring activities. Many companies that go through the restructuring phase eliminate corporate loyalty but fail to replace the employee contract with the firm. As a result, employees feel that their contract with the firm is one-way and short-term. They are giving their psychological commitment to the firm, but only for short-term monetary gains. To resolve this imbalance, employees may reduce their commitment. Executives must learn to sustain employee commitment by replacing loyalty with some other means of employee attachment.

In one company, employee contracts based on loyalty were replaced with opportunity. The chief executive of this company was honest with employees. He told them that there were no guarantees. Job loyalty, as known in stable work settings, could no longer be an economically viable alternative. However, he promised each employee that loyalty would be replaced by opportunity. He personally promised each employee that the organization would guarantee that each of them had the opportunity to develop his or her talents, to participate in key management actions, and to feel that they belonged to a part of a winning team. To guarantee this opportunity, bureaucracy had to be removed. Employees were able to identify the bureaucratic blockages in their jobs, to discuss these blockages with their bosses and peers, and to suggest how they could be removed. By so doing, employees could feel and see the value of opportunity in their work.

The bureaucracy bashing stage is necessary because, even though the head count may have reduced costs, the workload still remains, and adjustments must be made to meet the work volume requirements with the reduced head count.

At General Electric, Jack Welch has talked about reducing the work force by 25 percent but not reducing work. As a result, employees are faced with the burden of doing 25 percent more work, which over a period may lead to malaise and lower productivity. Unnecessary, non-value-added work must be removed to gain parity between employees and their workload.

To get rid of bureaucracy requires getting rid of work that adds little value to customers. Continuous improvement programs that focus on meeting needs of internal and external customers may be desired to yield higher quality, speed, and greater simplicity in how all suppliers service the organization.

A process developed by one of the authors and shown in Figure 3 focuses on bureaucracy "busting." A work audit is conducted using two questions: (1) To what extent does this work activity add value to customers? and (2) To what extent are these activities performed as effectively as possible?

FIGURE 3   **Developing a customer focus in bureaucracy bashing.**

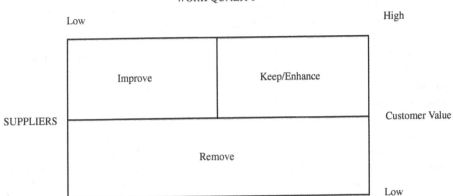

The first question is answered by inviting customers to share their views on the value added by work activities performed by the supplier. This dialogue between suppliers and customers may occur exclusively within a company (internal supplier/customer discussions) or between a firm and its external customers. One company began inviting customers to training programs in an effort to understand customer needs and to ensure that work activities proposed within the company met customer requirements. Activities which add little value to customers were removed. This two-step process attempts to determine the "right" of the organization to leverage its competitive advantage and that of its customers.

Activities that add great value to customers become subject to the second question. This question is answered by developing an improved process to perform the work. Auditing work processes encourages specific analysis to ensure that quality in work activities is improved.

However, leaders must first model the bureaucracy busting they advocate. They must be willing to let go of work systems that were implemented but that have added

little or no value to the processes' next or ultimate customer. Reports or procedures that may be seen as bureaucratic blockages to employees must be identified, and leaders must be willing to concede their pet projects for the sake of removing blockages. Leaders must demonstrate flexibility and listen to all reasonable requests (as long as they add value to customers and fall within legal and ethical boundaries). Finally, leaders need to encourage and reinforce risk taking among employees who initiate bureaucracy busting activities. A single equation predicts the propensity for risk taking. We see risk taking as a function of the will to win, divided by fear of failure. If the numerator is high, by selecting and developing committed employees, then leaders have the responsibility of reducing the fear of failure quotient.

STAGE 3: EMPLOYEE EMPOWERMENT STAGE

Bureaucracies empower top managers. Bureaucracy busting empowers employees. Removing barriers between employees and managers builds openness and dialogue in ongoing management processes and begins to change the nature of the organization. Self-directed teams, employee involvement processes, and dialogue should be built into the fabric of the organization. Without employee involvement and a fundamental new approach to management, costs may be reduced, productivity increased, and bureaucracy eliminated—but the results will not be long lasting if employees are not empowered for organizational improvement.

Many work activities encourage employee involvement. In a Japanese firm, newer professional employees have the opportunity and obligation to make the first drafts of important business proposals. By asking new employees to make these first drafts, the firm helps employees learn more about the overall business, feel empowered to have an impact on the business, and build relationships with colleagues in preparing the proposals. PepsiCo has involved and empowered all employees by announcing profit sharing for all. Federal Express has institutionalized employee involvement by guaranteeing employees access to the senior management meeting held each Wednesday. Employee complaints may be directed to this forum by employees without fear of any retributions by their immediate bosses. IBM assures employee involvement by allowing employees to work through a corporate ombudsman, who can represent the employees' views to management without fear of reprisal or having to undergo subordinate appraisals. Amoco has initiated an extensive employee involvement program, where employees are formed into teams to discuss ways to improve work and to get subordinate appraisals of their managers. These examples of employee involvement mark a fundamental change from the traditional work contract of hierarchical

mature organizations to a more fluid, flexible, mutual work environment.

Traditional models of power and authority came from position and status. Power and authority in a renewing organization should come from relationships, trust, and expertise. Empowerment is a movement away from leader and expert problem solving to a system where everyone is continuously involved in improving the organization in order to leverage its competitive advantage through speed, simplicity, and service. Leaders must learn that sharing power builds a capacity to change, commitment, and competitiveness.

STAGE 4: CONTINUOUS IMPROVEMENTS

Employee empowerment builds employee commitment. This initial commitment must be translated into long-term processes so employee involvement is not tied to any one individual but is part of a system.

Continuous improvement efforts began in mature companies by focusing on error detection and error prevention. In these efforts, statistical tools—for example, flow charting, Pareto analysis, histograms, studies of variance, and operational definitions—were used to ensure that errors could be taken out of work procedures.

The continuous improvement required for this stage includes, but also goes beyond, this error focus. Continuous improvement is changing not only the technical tools of management but also the fundamental approaches to management. The continuous improvement philosophy overcomes the practice. The focus on continuous improvement must be upon the "right" work that was identified through restructuring and bureaucracy bashing. The philosophy must be one of service to customers through speed and simplicity in work processes. As this philosophy is understood throughout an organization, it becomes the rallying cry, ensuring an ongoing commitment to improve work processes.

Generating this philosophy becomes the major leadership requirement at this stage. The leader must manage through principles. The leader must articulate and communicate the principles that will govern the organization. These principles must be sensitive to each of the previous stages—restructuring for productivity, bureaucracy busting for flexibility, and employee involvement for empowerment. By instilling a philosophy of management that can then be practiced according to the specific needs of the business, leaders are able to set a direction, motivate, and steer a company through renewal.

STAGE 5: CULTURAL CHANGE

The final stage of renewal is really an outgrowth of the other four. Fundamental cultural change means that employees' mindset—the way they think about their work—is shifted. Employees do not feel part of a "mature" company, but they see themselves as having faced and overcome the renewal change challenge. They feel the enthusiasm and commitment of trying new approaches to work and, as a result, they bring more desirable changes into the organization.

We would agree with many others who have studied these issues that accomplishing cultural change takes many years. Our rule of thumb is that, for mature organizations, the cycle time for creating fundamental cultural change is twice the cycle time it takes for introducing a new technology. Some technologies change more rapidly than others—say, for example, genetic engineering as opposed to utilities. In more rapidly changing technologies, there is more receptivity to cultural change. These

organizations seem to have a more external focus. In industries with slow changing technologies, the cycle time for cultural change is extended, since these industries probably have a greater structural inertia. The latter are more internally and vertically focused.

In the re-energized organization, every leader would be judged by his ability to persevere, and how strong an advocate he is of the new culture. But it is also necessary that he exhibits tolerance since culture changes require time to take effect. More importantly a leader must constantly and demonstratively be a model and a cheerleader of the culture he hopes to implement.

At General Electric, Jack Welch has committed the entire company to a cultural change. He constantly talks about his commitment—to financial analysts, to investors, to shareholders, to employees, and to public forums. He has defined a set of principles and has frequently asked managers to spend time implementing these principles. Welch also has asked his managers to provide him with feedback on his personal behavior. At GE he has become the nucleus of encouraging employees to commit energy and time to understanding and adopting the new work culture.

In short, the five stages in Figure 2 indicate a sequence for adopting changes to re-energize a mature organization. By first defining the right work to do, then finding ways to improve that work, companies may make simple, short-term changes that can have major, long-term impact. These five stages are based on the four principles we have identified.

MAKING IT HAPPEN

We have put forward a very simple argument in this paper: Mature organizations must face and overcome the renewal change challenge; they must change; they must redefine how work is done and re-create work cultures consistent with changing customer demands.

How do we anticipate that these changes will occur? It will happen because organizations and leaders at all levels have developed a new vision of strategy and culture. Organizations are becoming far more strategic, far more purposeful, and far more customer oriented. It will happen also because of new tools that are focusing more and more closely upon performance and that are raising difficult questions about the value of work and of the customer requirements within the organization.

Most mature organizations will sooner or later have to face the renewal change challenge. They will then have to find ways to change their culture; their vision will have to actually be translated into specific actions, and managers must be prepared to help employees improve, to observe their progress, and to give them feedback. Employees also must seek responsibilities,

strive for continuous improvement, and change the organization's culture by making each effort add value to its customers and investors strategically and continuously.

The role of the leader is to challenge the value of each process for its contribution to customers and investors, encourage a shared vision and values, and enable employees to act by encouraging greater customer and cost consciousness, adaptability, initiative, accountability, and teamwork. To accomplish these goals, managers must model the way and immediately recognize the contributions of employees as they take risks in changing established work habits and attempt to continuously improve and enhance their contributions.

If the renewal change challenge can be overcome, an organization may move through the neck of the hourglass (see Figure 1). At the other side of the hourglass is the ability to become re-energized and meet customer needs through innovative, resourceful, and bold customer-focused initiatives.

Case

Nestlé's Globe Program (A)

The Early Months

Journalists ask what is the legacy that I want to leave at Nestlé. A large part of my answer is the successful implementation of the Globe Program. Ensuring the success of this program is the most important thing that I can do for Nestlé.

—*Peter Brabeck, Vice Chairman and CEO, Nestlé SA*

In April 2000 Chris Johnson, a 39-year-old American manager running Nestlé's business in Taiwan, received a phone call from Mike Garrett, his boss, telling him that he

had been chosen to head up a major Nestlé initiative called the GLOBE Program. (GLOBE was short for "Global Business Excellence.") Details were not clear, but it was apparent that this program was intended to transform Nestlé from a "collection of independent fiefdoms" into an integrated global company, capable of showing a common face to customers and suppliers around the world. GLOBE would be the largest program Nestlé had ever undertaken.

Chris would move from Taiwan to Nestlé's head office in Vevey, Switzerland, where he would report to Mario Corti, the creator of the GLOBE project and Nestlé's executive vice president of finance and administration.

At the same time, Chris would also become the youngest member of Nestlé's "group management," the team of nine senior managers at the top of the company. His new title, "deputy executive vice president," would last for the duration of his assignment as the head of GLOBE. Chris's elevation to the top team was seen as a deliberate breaking of the status quo, signaling to the Nestlé world the importance of GLOBE.

NESTLÉ IN THE YEAR 2000

Nestlé was the world's largest food and beverage company, with approximately 230,000 employees producing more than 8,000 products in 81 countries. Total revenue for the year 2000 was expected to be in the region of SFr 80 billion, and profit around SFr 5 to 6 billion. Less than 2% of

Source: Professor Peter Killing prepared this case as a basis for class discussion rather than to illustrate either effective or ineffective handling of a business situation.

the company's revenues and profits were generated in Switzerland.

Peter Brabeck took over as CEO of Nestlé in mid-1997, and under his direction the company had performed well. Nestlé's share price had almost doubled since he became CEO, and if the targets for the year 2000 were met, profit would have increased by more than 30% during his tenure. With a healthy stable of well-recognized brands such as Nestlé, Nescafé, Nestea, Buitoni, Kit Kat, Friskies and Perrier, no one saw anything but more growth for Nestlé.

However, although Nestlé's growth rate was the envy of many of its peers, its profitability was below average in the food and beverage business. One analysis,[1] for example, showed that in 2000 Nestlé's margins were lower than those of competitors such as Coca-Cola, Pepsi, General Mills, Hershey, Kellogg, Heinz and Campbell's soup. Areas of particular concern were sales overhead, which for 14 of Nestlé's competitors averaged 5.8% of sales and in Nestlé's case was 8.4%, and administrative overhead, for which the competitors' average was 6.2% and the Nestlé figure was 8.3%. This combined difference of 4.7% of sales represented billions of Swiss francs, and in the words of Schroder SalomonSmithBarney, "If Nestlé could reduce its sales and administration overheads to match industry averages, group EBIT would rise by a staggering 39%."[2]

Shortly after becoming CEO, Brabeck initiated a program titled MH 97. It was focused on reducing Nestlé's manufacturing costs by rationalizing its almost 500 factories, and encouraging more of what Nestlé called intermarket supply, which meant that markets in a given country

[1] Nestlé SA, Global leverage, SchroderSalomon SmithBarney, 3 October 2001.
[2] Ibid., p. 3.

were supplied from factories in adjacent countries. The result would be fewer, larger, more efficient factories. By 2000 MH 97 was making good progress as factory employment, number of factories and manufacturing costs were all declining.

THE NESTLÉ ORGANIZATION

Profit and loss responsibility in Nestlé rested primarily with its market heads, the executives who ran Nestlé's 80 or so geographic markets around the world. These managers were rewarded on the basis of results in their local market. Each market head reported to one of three zone managers (Europe, the Americas and "AOA," which stood for Asia, Oceania and Africa), and the zone managers reported to Brabeck. Running alongside this organization, but without profit responsibility, were half a dozen strategic business units that oversaw product areas such as beverages, dairy products and infant nutrition.

Brabeck had clear priorities for Nestlé. The first was to create a more integrated, coordinated organization. As he put it, "Nestlé is a federation of independent markets" that he wanted to combine into one company that could act effectively vis-à-vis the marketplace and suppliers. GLOBE would play a key role in this, as it would allow Nestlé to know, at the touch of a computer key, how much it sold, product by product, to international customers like Carrefour and Wal-Mart; how many units of products such as Kit Kat chocolate bars it sold through different channels (supermarkets, fast-food operators, food service, vending machines, etc); and how much it bought, globally, from key suppliers.

Brabeck also wanted to make Nestlé a faster-moving company. As he said to a Nestlé gathering:

My friends, we are still walking with slippers, but I want us to train together, so that we put on, as a first step, tennis shoes. Then we will train even more so that some day we will be able to put on racing shoes. . . . I would rather have an 80% solution now, than a 100% solution in five years. Perfection is not the target—we use it as an excuse for not moving faster.

Although GLOBE would be the largest SAP roll-out in the world to date, Brabeck was adamant that GLOBE was not to be an IT exercise:

I want this to be very clear. With GLOBE we will create common business processes, standardized data, and a common IT infrastructure—but do not think this is an IT initiative. We are going to fundamentally change the way we run this company.

Brabeck's comments were very much in line with the first of Nestlé's General Principles, which stated that systems were "necessary and useful but should never be an end in themselves." These principles (*refer to* Exhibit 1) were jointly created by Brabeck and his predecessor, Helmut Maucher. These fundamental concepts played an important role in his thinking and he referred to them often.

LATE APRIL: CHRIS JOHNSON IN VEVEY

In late April Chris met with Brabeck and Corti in Vevey to discuss his new position and learn what he could about the GLOBE program. When told that SAP, the German enterprise software company, had been chosen to supply the software that Nestlé would need to implement the GLOBE program, Chris pointed out that he knew nothing of SAP and not much

---

Exhibit 1

Nestlé's General Principles

1. Nestlé is more people and product oriented than systems oriented. Systems are necessary and useful but should never be an end in themselves.

2. Nestlé is committed to create value for its shareholders. However, Nestlé does not favor short-term profit and shareholder value maximization at the expense of long-term successful business development. But Nestlé remains conscious of the need to generate a reasonable profit each year.

3. Nestlé is as decentralized as possible, within the limits imposed by basic policy and strategy decisions, as well as the group-wide need for co-ordination and management development.

4. Nestlé is committed to the concept of continuous improvement of its activities, thus avoiding more dramatic one-time changes as much as possible.

Source: The Basic Nestlé Management and Leadership Principles

---

about IT.[3] The reply was that that was fine: the program was to be run by a business manager, not an IT specialist. Years earlier Nestlé had introduced IMPACT, a program somewhat similar to GLOBE, but of a much smaller scale and scope, under the direction of a senior IT manager. It had struggled for more than a decade without creating any tangible benefits.

Corti explained the three primary objectives of the GLOBE program:

1. **To create a common set of "best practice" business processes that would be used throughout Nestlé.** GLOBE was to bring all of the far-flung Nestlé organizations up to a common set of best practices. "We accept that each local market may need to behave a little differently from others when dealing with their local customers," Chris was told, "but when it comes to back office

functions, things like purchasing, invoicing, dealing with distributors, there is surely a best way of doing things. We want to install best practice across the whole company."

2. **To create a standard set of Nestlé data.** Under the GLOBE program, all Nestlé data would be standardized and become a "corporate asset." To create standardized data, each supplier, each raw material, each product and each customer would have the same number applied to it throughout the entire Nestlé world. This would allow a global picture to be created of how much Nestlé bought from a particular company, sold to a particular company, and so on.

3. **To create a standard information systems infrastructure.** As a part of GLOBE, Nestlé would standardize its computer hardware and software, signing global purchasing agreements with suppliers such as SAP, Microsoft,

[3] Nestlé reportedly spent more than $250 million for the GLOBE SAP license.

Dell and others. There would also be far fewer Nestlé data centers—down from the current total of 100 or so to perhaps 4. The end result would be lower costs on a global basis, and easier communication across markets.

Chris also learned during this first meeting that Brabeck and Corti wanted to have the GLOBE processes, data and systems implemented in Nestlé's key markets by the end of 2003. These 14 markets (plus Nestlé's water business) accounted for 73% of Nestlé turnover, 360 factories and approximately 127,000 employees. The timing of GLOBE's implementation was important because the major financial benefits of the program were expected to come from coordinated cross-border purchasing, which could only begin when Nestlé's data codes for purchased products became standardized within regions and then globally.

Before leaving Vevey, Chris signaled that he was ready and willing to take on the job and would move to Vevey in July. In his final meeting with Corti, Chris was given a sheet of paper with a few boxes drawn on it—the beginning of a possible GLOBE organization chart—and about a dozen names of people that Corti thought would be a good team nucleus. Some of them worked in the IT department in Vevey, reporting to Corti, and some were in the markets.

BACK IN TAIWAN

Back in Taiwan, Chris began to prepare for his new job. He quickly decided that he needed to create a core team of perhaps half a dozen people to get the program started. He concluded that he would need with him in Vevey at least one person from each of Nestlé's three zones, and at the

same time ensure that he had at least one person from the following areas: communications, sales and marketing, technical and supply chain, finance and administration, and IT.

He commented:

I have been with Nestlé for a long time, and know a lot of people. So I started making phone calls. It was not important that the core team would consist of people I already knew, but they had to have a good reputation among people I trusted. At the same time I checked out the people on the list that Mario had given me. Most of them did not check out well. They were either close to retirement, had been involved in the IMPACT program, or simply were not respected by the people in the markets. Some were Mario's direct reports.

What I had to decide was how much this mattered—we were talking of 10 or 12 people out of an organization that I thought might total 250 once it really got going—and the last thing I wanted to do was get into a fight with my new boss, the originator of the program, before I had even started working for him. My sense was that these people really wanted to be part of GLOBE—and Mario would get a lot of complaints if they were not.

While mulling these issues over, Chris started putting together a list of the principles that should govern his activities while leading GLOBE. He explained these as follows:

Pragmatic: "This is a Nestlé core value and it makes me and everyone else feel comfortable to have it listed first. What it means is that we will only go ahead with things that make sense—we will stay clear of initiatives that are theoretically appealing but practically not much use."

Business Benefit Driven: "This is perhaps obvious, but I need to reinforce the notion that we are doing this for the businesses—not for the IT department, for example. It is easy to get sucked into wanting to be on the cutting edge of IT—have the fastest servers, the latest software, and so on—but that is not the point. If it does not have clear benefit for the business, we must not do it."

Market Involvement: "The Nestlé market organizations are the ultimate users of whatever we create, so they have to be involved—whether it is in standardizing data, determining best practices, or whatever. This cannot be a project staffed exclusively by people at the Center."

Speed: "Peter Brabeck has made increasing the speed at which Nestlé does things one of his priorities. I fully agree, and we will *not* have this project come in late."

Communication: "No one knows what GLOBE is. One of our priorities must be to explain to people what GLOBE entails and why we are doing it. Everyone has to understand the business logic. It is not enough to say that we are doing this because Peter Brabeck and Mario Corti think we should."

Our Best People: "This is the issue I face with Mario. Should I try and create the GLOBE team using Nestlé's best people—creating an elite group? That's always dangerous, but without the best people Nestlé has to offer, I do not see how I can make a success of this. Plenty of SAP-based projects

less ambitious than this one have failed."[4]

Chris continued:

"The GLOBE team will consist of a small core of people permanently attached to the program, plus consultants from SAP and PwC [PricewaterhouseCoopers], and a lot of people we will bring in from the markets for periods ranging between 3 and 12 months. I want to have this group in its own building in Vevey, with no closed offices, no reserved parking spots, only a few titles indicating rank (invented titles that are not comparable in the Nestlé world), and with everyone— including secretaries—with high bonus potential, well beyond normal Nestlé levels. In short, I would like to create a totally different environment than there is at head office."

THE MARKET HEADS' CONFERENCE

In May, Chris would be going back to Vevey for the Market Managers' Conference, a major event held every 18 months. During this event, Brabeck would unveil GLOBE, and Chris's new position would be announced.

Chris would also be meeting with Corti to discuss his staffing plans for GLOBE. He wondered how he should handle this, especially since he had learned that one of the people on Corti's list, whom Chris definitely did not want (after checking with the head of the market in which the person was working), had apparently been promised a position in the GLOBE organization.

---

[4] Chris had recently read a front-page article in the *Wall Street Journal* describing how problems with an SAP launch in the fall of 1999 had led Hershey Foods to be unable to deliver candy to its distributors in time for Halloween. Hershey's stock price fell more than 8% the day the news was announced.

Reading

Has Strategy Changed?

The powerful forces of globalization are fundamentally changing the nature and dimensions of strategy.

Kathleen M. Eisenhardt

Has strategy changed in the wake of the recent economic frenzy and subsequent downturn? Is the New Economy finished? Has the Old Economy returned? At this point, most managers understand what the advent of the Internet implies—operating efficiency for most companies, a terrific channel for some and a fundamentally new business opportunity for only a few. So is it back to "strategy as usual"?

The answer is no. While many executives were focused on the implications of the Internet, a more powerful force was quietly transforming the economic playing field. Globalization. Massive in scope, deep in impact—and ironically, almost unmanaged—globalization is the increasingly deep interrelationship among countries, companies and individuals. The connections may be cultural, as in the case of global brands like Sony, or environmental, as in global climate change and overfishing of the oceans. The connections may be technical, as in the case

The author is grateful for the wisdom, counsel and creativity of Chris Bingham, Shona Brown, Charlie Galunic, Jeff Martin, Filipe Santos and Don Sull in helping to shape the ideas expressed.

of the Web and wireless communication, or financial, as in the linking of major stock exchanges and the proliferation of NAFTA-like trade agreements. Globalization, not the Internet, is the fundamental driver of the real New Economy.

INSTABILITY

Density of connections throughout the world affects corporations by amplifying instability. Even small events in one location can affect events in another, in often oblique and nonlinear fashion. Cold weather means increased coal usage in England that can trigger acid rain in Ukraine. Economies of scale at a smattering of Australian wineries can affect life in rural France. AIDS activists in South Africa can threaten the profits of the pharmaceuticals industry. The scale and pace of change are particularly challenging to predict. Wall Street expected that a correction would follow dot-com mania, but no one anticipated the correction's magnitude and speed.

The international power structure, or lack of one, further amplifies instability. For almost five decades, the geopolitics of the post-World War II era were shaped by the two principal Cold War combatants. Today, although the United States is dominant and the European Union is asserting a more unified point of view, free trade and transparent markets are the forces shaping commerce, not any one nation. The Internet speeds communication. Invention spreads almost overnight. Yet no one is in charge. In the era of globalization, it is not obvious whether major political leaders, such as British Prime Minister Tony Blair, or business leaders, such as AOL Time Warner's Steve Case, have much economic clout. Perhaps both types will take a back seat to some single-issue global crusader. Adding to the instability is a strong and often thoughtful backlash to globalization among an unlikely coalition of trade unionists, environmentalists and cultural nationalists.

At the same time, industries with strong network effects (for example, telecommunications), in which standards can take hold rapidly, and industries such as software, which depend on the economics of information rather than the economics of things, have further destabilized the predictable world of business. Globalization, together with those forces, has created a new economic playing field. The play on that field is high-velocity with strikingly nonlinear instability, unpredictability and ambiguity. No wonder that the principal theme of the January 2002 gathering of the economic and political elite at the World Economic Forum in New York City was designated as "coping with fragility."

NEW ECONOMICS, NEW STRATEGY

Does the new economic playing field imply throwing out traditional economics? No, but it does suggest that the belief in equilibrium and the naïve understanding of (or perhaps lack of interest in) the internal working of corporations that characterize traditional economics render its paradigms less germane. Rather, a new economics—or more accurately, an *old* new economics pioneered by Frank Knight, Friedrich Hayek and Joseph Schumpeter—is coming into its own. This latter form of economics is entrepreneurial in its riveted focus on disequilibrium, the capture of fleeting opportunities and the relentless cycle of wealth creation and destruction.

The new economic playing field also suggests a fresh view of strategy. During conversations on our collective work, Donald N. Sull of Harvard Business School struck upon a military analogy that graphically conveys the point. Military leaders often fight traditional wars in the map room by locating defensible positions and then fortifying them. In the same way, executives plan their strategic positions and defend them with carefully intertwined activity systems.

Sometimes a traditional war is fought in the storeroom, with leaders amassing stockpiles of specific weapons such as tanks and then deploying them wherever the battle may be. Similarly, executives may formulate resource-based strategy and then leverage their related core competencies in many markets.

But as we know, there are wars in which the enemy is difficult to engage, battle dynamics fluctuate, and the terrain is treacherous and unknown. Here, the strategy of choice is guerilla warfare—moving quickly, taking advantage of opportunity and rapidly cutting losses. That kind of entrepreneurial strategy always makes sense for underdog companies because they lack resources and position. But in unstable, unpredictable and ambiguous terrain like the new economic playing field, entrepreneurial strategy is attractive for large companies as well. The fundamental precept that "strategy is about being different" continues to be true. But what constitutes that strategy has changed. The new strategic watchwords are simplicity, organization and timing.

STRATEGY IS SIMPLE

First and foremost, strategy on the new economic playing field has to be simple. Complicated, intertwined activity systems or elaborately planned leveraging of core competencies make sense in slower and more-linear situations. On the new high-velocity playing field, they are cumbersome and glacially slow. Managers now must jump into uncertain situations because that is where the opportunities are most abundant. They must capture and exploit promising opportunities or drop them rapidly if they fail to develop. Counterintuitively, complicated markets demand simple, back-to-basics strategy.

Simple strategy means using one or two critical strategic processes and the handful of unique rules that guide them. The critical processes are those that put the corporation into the flow of the most promising opportunities and therefore will differ company to company. For consumer-products giant Colgate-Palmolive, global product management is a key strategic process. Product managers follow a few simple precepts, such as "maintain the brand" and "keep relative product positioning stable." But within those rules, Colgate mangers around the globe have considerable freedom. For example, while maintaining the defined brand image of toothpaste and its relative positioning against other Colgate dental-care products, managers can alter the flavor, change the packaging, create locally tailored advertising, tinker with the ingredients, shift

prices and more. Within a few parameters, managers move as they see fit.

Another example is Netherlands-based Ispat International, one of the fastest-growing steel companies in the world. Throughout the 1990s, the Ispat strategy was centered on the acquisition process and a few simple guidelines for two aspects of that process: first, which acquisition opportunities to pick (state-owned companies, companies in which costs could be reduced, companies with direct-reduction or electric-arc technologies); second, how to integrate the acquisitions (always retain existing top managers, insist on daily meetings and reporting). But within the guidelines, Ispat managers could buy companies from Germany to Kazakhstan and run them in accordance with the changing flow of opportunities.

In contrast, complicated and richly resourced strategies often do not work. Take Pandesic, the joint venture for e-commerce services that Intel and SAP launched in 1997 and that folded in 2000. Too much effort went into a strategic plan that was overly complex and difficult to revise. Too many people were assigned to execute the plan. Pandesic executives had too many resources and an overly defined strategic position. What they did not have was simplicity. As the real market opportunity unfolded, they needed a simple focus in order to adjust flexibly.

STRATEGY IS ORGANIZATIONAL

Programming the strategy from the top and then figuring out an organization to implement it may work in slow-moving markets. It's the signature approach of strategists who simplistically think of organizations in terms of control and alignment of management incentives. In high-velocity markets, that approach won't work. In such circumstances, strategy consists of choosing an excellent team, picking the right roles for team members and then letting their moves emerge. It's like basketball. Los Angeles Lakers' coach Phil Jackson does not mastermind the moves of Kobe Bryant and Shaquille O'Neal. Rather, he puts the right personnel in a triangle offense and lets them play. To the uninformed, the moves seem to flow from an elaborate playbook, but the astute fan understands that the organization itself is the strategy.

For companies, organizational strategy is the unique mapping (often termed patching) of modular businesses onto specific market opportunities. Think Velcro. Organizational strategy is firm and clear at any point in time but also is able to change quickly. A prime example: Hewlett-Packard's wildly successful strategy in the mid-1980s to mid-1990s, which led to domination of the global printer industry.

H-P executives focused their business-unit teams—whether in Spain, Italy, Idaho, Colorado or Singapore—on clearly defined product and market targets. The teams' assignment was to "take the hill." They were guided by a few simple rules—for example, never spend money on an activity if someone else can do it. But the real key to the strategy was organizational. The quarterly realignment of the businesses against the shifting pattern of emerging, colliding, splitting and declining market and product opportunities defined the H-P strategy. As the markets changed, H-P executives added businesses, such as scanners and printer cartridges. They spilt off businesses, including removing the deskjet business from LaserJets. Sometimes they combined businesses (the dot-matrix and network-printing businesses). Occasionally, they

exited a business. The repatching of businesses was rarely reported in the media, becaue the moves were usually small and even routine. Nonetheless, the frequent realignment of business units was the central feature of H-P's enormously successful printer strategy.

More subtly, organizational strategy involves choosing the business scale, not just the focus, that is uniquely suited to the velocity of each market. Dell managers operate their businesses at the scale of about $1 billion. As businesses grow beyond that size, they are broken into smaller modules. Microsoft managers often operate their businesses at the scale of about 200 programmers.

The Economist magazine embodies a particularly strategic use of modularity and scale. From the outside, the weekly publication's strategy seems to be to leverage a core competence in writing and to position itself as a magazine for the sophisticated reader. From the inside, the strategy is the organization. Editors at *The Economist* give their writers unusually large swaths of territory and considerable freedom in choosing what to cover. The organizational strategy not only gives writers greater scope to develop stories, it enables senior editors to hire fewer (and, presumably, better) writers and compensate them more, both with money and with unfettered, interesting work. The resulting product is more creative than that of other news magazines and has the greater depth that appeals particularly to the upmarket reader.

STRATEGY IS TEMPORAL

Finally, strategy is temporal. In traditional strategy, time is not part of the strategic equation. After all, markets are assumed to move slowly and predictably, if at all. In contrast, time is crucial on the new high-velocity playing field. The easiest way to think about temporal strategy is through understanding the concept of corporate genes. A corporation's unique mix of genes is its combined products, brand, technology, manufacturing capabilities, geographic locations and so on. Managers using temporal strategy conduct a kind of genetic engineering, pursuing a series of unique strategic moves in which one or more genes are changed. They may introduce a new technology, change a brand, enter a new country or drop a manufacturing competence. They are constantly splicing in new genes or cutting out others to engineer genetic evolution.

The best temporal strategies also exhibit a pattern that occurs in the natural world of earthquakes and tropical storms: the inverse power law. That is, small events are common, mid-size events occur occasionally, and large events are rare. Good temporal strategies are unique combinations of small, incremental changes plus mid-size changes and large, radical changes. Most of the time, temporal strategy should feature safe, small changes that elaborate on aspects of the core business. But temporal strategy needs to include medium-scale moves occasionally and, even more occasionally, large-scale moves that reinvent significant portions of the corporation. This also means that the dichotomy of "stick to the core" versus "creative destruction" is a false one. Effective managers pursue both approaches.

EBay offers an excellent example of temporal strategy. The Internet star was launched as a Web site where traders of collectibles could congregate and trade. It morphed into an auction, added other kinds of merchandise (such as cars and fine art), branched beyond the auction format to fixed-price markets and expanded into numerous countries. It became what the business-to-business exchange was to have been. Most often, eBay's changes were small. Occasionally they were large. There was always a mix of large and small changes, with varying emphasis on changing the genes of country, merchandise, business model or auction format. EBay managers also sometimes added rhythm to their temporal strategy by pacing the evolution more rapidly or more slowly as the opportunity for advantage dictated. As a result, eBay managers evolved their businesses through varying moves—and created the Internet's most durable star.

SUSTAINABLE COMPETITIVE ADVANTAGE?

Is sustained competitive advantage still relevant? Sometimes long-term competitive advantage and its attendant creation of wealth can occur on the new economic playing field. More often, they cannot. The more salient point is, however, that the duration of competitive advantage is unpredictable. It may last 10 minutes, 10 months or 10 years. So although most executives would like sustained advantage, they are forced to operate as if it does not exist. The challenge is, therefore, not so much achieving sustainable advantage as it is coping with not knowing whether such an advantage actually exists—except in retrospect.

Strategy is still about being different. But today, the way in which strategy is different is itself different. Globalization is rearranging the turf. The speed of play on the field is lightning fast. The scale and pace of change are unpredictable. The economics of disequilibrium and information have moved to center stage. As a result, the recipe for effective strategy must now focus on unique strategic processes with simple rules, on the modular patching of businesses to fleeting market opportunities and on evolutionary timing for ongoing strategic moves. In other words, we are not back to "strategy as usual." Whether we like it or not, strategy has changed.

Reading

Meeting the Challenge of Disruptive Change

Clayton M. Christensen

Michael Overdorf

These are scary times for managers in big companies. Even before the Internet and globalization, their track record for dealing with major, disruptive change was not good. Out of hundreds of department stores, for example, only one—Dayton Hudson—became a leader in discount retailing. Not one of the minicomputer companies succeeded in the personal computer business. Medical and business schools are struggling—and failing—to change their curricula fast enough to train the types of doctors and managers their markets need. The list could go on.

It's not that managers in big companies can't see disruptive changes coming. Usually they can. Nor do they lack resources to confront them. Most big companies have talented managers and specialists, strong product portfolios, first-rate technological know-how, and deep pockets. What managers lack is a habit of thinking about their organization's capabilities as carefully as

Source: *Harvard Business Review,* March–April 2000. Reprinted with permission. Copyright © 2000 by the Harvard Business School Publishing Corporation; all rights reserved.

they think about individual people's capabilities.

One of the hallmarks of a great manager is the ability to identify the right person for the right job and to train employees to succeed at the jobs they're given. But unfortunately, most managers assume that if each person working on a project is well matched to the job, then the organization in which they work will be, too. Often that is not the case. One could put two sets of identically capable people to work in different organizations, and what they accomplished would be significantly different. That's because organizations themselves—independent of the people and other resources in them—have capabilities. To succeed consistently, good managers need to be skilled not just in assessing people but also in assessing the abilities and disabilities of their organization as a whole.

This article offers managers a framework to help them understand what their organizations are capable of accomplishing. It will show them how their company's disabilities become more sharply defined even as its core capabilities grow. It will give them a way to recognize different kinds of change and make appropriate organizational responses to the opportunities that arise from each. And it will offer some bottom-line advice that runs counter to much that's assumed in our can-do business culture: If an organization faces major change—a disruptive innovation, perhaps—the worst possible approach may be to make drastic adjustments to the existing organization. In trying to transform an enterprise, managers can destroy the very capabilities that sustain it.

Before rushing into the breach, managers must understand precisely what types of change the existing organization is capable and incapable of handling. To help them do that, we'll first take a systematic look at how to recognize a company's core capabilities on an organizational level and then examine how these capabilities migrate as companies grow and mature.

WHERE CAPABILITIES RESIDE

Our research suggests that three factors affect what an organization can and cannot do: its resources, its processes, and its values. When thinking about what sorts of innovations their organization will be able to embrace, managers need to assess how each of these factors might affect their organization's capacity to change.

RESOURCES

When they ask the question, "What can this company do?" the place most managers look for the answer is in its resources—both the tangible ones like people, equipment, technologies, and cash, and the less tangible ones like product designs, information, brands, and relationships with suppliers, distributors, and customers. Without doubt, access to abundant, high-quality resources increases an organization's chances of coping with change. But resource analysis doesn't come close to telling the whole story.

PROCESSES

The second factor that affects what a company can and cannot do is its processes. By processes, we mean the patterns of interaction, coordination, communication, and decision making employees use to transform resources into products and services of greater worth. Such examples as the processes that govern product development, manufacturing, and budgeting come immediately to mind. Some processes are formal, in the sense that they are explicitly defined and documented. Others are informal: They are routines or ways of working that evolve over time. The former tend to be more visible, the latter less visible.

One of the dilemmas of management is that processes, by their very nature, are set up so that employees perform tasks in a consistent way, time after time. They are *meant* not to change or, if they must change, to change through tightly controlled procedures. When people use a process to do the task it was designed for, it is likely to perform efficiently. But when the same process is used to tackle a very different task, it is likely to perform sluggishly. Companies focused on developing and winning Food and Drug Administration (FDA) approval for new drug compounds, for example, often prove inept at developing and winning approval for medical devices because the second task entails very different ways of working. In fact, a process that creates the capability to execute one task concurrently defines disabilities in executing other tasks.[1]

The most important capabilities and concurrent disabilities aren't necessarily embodied in the most visible processes, like logistics, development, manufacturing, or customer service. In fact, they are more likely to be in the less visible, background processes that support decisions about where to invest resources—those that define how market research is habitually done, how such analysis is translated into financial projections, how plans and budgets are negotiated internally, and so on. It is in those processes that many organizations' most serious disabilities in coping with change reside.

VALUES

The third factor that affects what an organization can and cannot do is its values. Sometimes the phrase "corporate values" carries an ethical connotation: One thinks of the principles that ensure patient well-being for Johnson & Johnson or that guide decisions about employee safety at Alcoa. But within our framework, "values" has a broader meaning. We define an organization's values as the standards by which employees set priorities that enable them to judge whether an order is attractive or unattractive, whether a customer is more important or less important, whether an idea for a new product is attractive or marginal, and so on. Prioritization decisions are made by employees at every level. Among salespeople, they consist of on-the-spot, day-to-day decisions about which products to push

with customers and which to deemphasize. At the executive tiers, they often take the form of decisions to invest, or not, in new products, services, and processes.

The larger and more complex a company becomes, the more important it is for senior managers to train employees throughout the organization to make independent decisions about priorities that are consistent with the strategic direction and the business model of the company. A key metric of good management, in fact, is whether such clear, consistent values have permeated the organization.

But consistent, broadly understood values also define what an organization cannot do. A company's values reflect its cost structure or its business model because those define the rules its employees must follow for the company to prosper. If, for example, a company's overhead costs require it to achieve gross profit margins of 40 percent, then a value or decision rule will have evolved that encourages middle managers to kill ideas that promise gross margins below 40 percent. Such an organization would be incapable of commercializing projects targeting low-margin markets—such as those in e-commerce—even though another organization's values, driven by a very different cost structure, might facilitate the success of the same project.

Different companies, of course, embody different values. But we want to focus on two sets of values in particular that tend to evolve in most companies in very predictable ways. The inexorable evolution of these two values is what makes companies progressively less capable of addressing disruptive change successfully.

As in the previous example, the first value dictates the way the company judges acceptable gross margins. As companies add features and functions to their

---

[1] See Dorothy Leonard-Barton, "Core Capabilities and Core Rigidities: A Paradox in Managing New Product Development," *Strategic Management Journal*, Summer 1992, pp. 111–136.

products and services, trying to capture more attractive customers in premium tiers of their markets, they often add overhead cost. As a result, gross margins that were once attractive become unattractive. For instance, Toyota entered the North American market with the Corolla model, which targeted the lower end of the market. As that segment became crowded with look-alike models from Honda, Mazda, and Nissan, competition drove down profit margins. To improve its margins, Toyota then developed more sophisticated cars targeted at higher tiers. The process of developing cars like the Camry and the Lexus added costs to Toyota's operation. It subsequently decided to exit the lower end of the market; the margins had become unacceptable because the company's cost structure, and consequently its values, had changed.

In a departure from that pattern, Toyota recently introduced the Echo model, hoping to rejoin the entry-level tier with a $10,000 car. It is one thing for Toyota's senior management to decide to launch this new model. It's another for the many people in the Toyota system—including its dealers—to agree that selling more cars at lower margins is a better way to boost profits and equity values than selling more Camrys, Avalons, and Lexuses. Only time will tell whether Toyota can manage this down-market move. To be successful with the Echo, Toyota's management will have to swim against a very strong current—the current of its own corporate values.

The second value relates to how big a business opportunity has to be before it can be interesting. Because a company's stock price represents the discounted present value of its projected earnings stream, most managers feel compelled not just to maintain growth but to maintain a constant rate of growth. For a $40 million company to grow 25 percent, for instance, it needs to find $10 million in new business the next year. But a $40 billion company needs to find $10 billion in new business the next year to grow at that same rate. It follows that an opportunity that excites a small company isn't big enough to be interesting to a large company. One of the bittersweet results of success, in fact, is that as companies become large, they lose the ability to enter small, emerging markets. This disability is not caused by a change in the resources within the companies—their resources typically are vast. Rather, it's caused by an evolution in values.

The problem is magnified when companies suddenly become much bigger through mergers or acquisitions. Executives and Wall Street financiers who engineer megamergers between already-huge pharmaceutical companies, for example, need to take this effect into account. Although their merged research organizations might have more resources to throw at new product development, their commercial organizations will probably have lost their appetites for all but the biggest blockbuster drugs. This constitutes a very real disability in managing innovation. The same problem crops up in high-tech industries as well. In many ways, Hewlett-Packard's recent decision to split itself into two companies is rooted in its recognition of this problem.

THE MIGRATION OF CAPABILITIES

In the start-up stages of an organization, much of what gets done is attributable to resources—people, in particular. The addition or departure of a few key people can profoundly influence its success.

Over time, however, the locus of the organization's capabilities shifts toward its processes and values. As people address recurrent tasks, processes become defined. And as the business model takes shape and it becomes clear which types of business need to be accorded highest priority, values coalesce. In fact, one reason that many soaring young companies flame out after an initial public offering (IPO) based on a single hot product is that their initial success is grounded in resources—often the founding engineers—and they fail to develop processes that can create a sequence of hot products.

Avid Technology, a producer of digital-editing systems for television, is an apt case in point. Avid's well-received technology removed tedium from the video-editing process. On the back of its star product, Avid's stock rose from $16 a share at its 1993 IPO to $49 in mid-1995. However, the strains of being a one-trick pony soon emerged, as Avid faced a saturated market, rising inventories and receivables, increased competition, and shareholder lawsuits. Customers loved the product, but Avid's lack of effective processes for consistently developing new products and for controlling quality, delivery, and service ultimately tripped the company and sent its stock back down.

By contrast, at highly successful firms such as McKinsey & Company, the processes and values have become so powerful that it almost doesn't matter which people get assigned to which project teams. Hundreds of MBAs join the firm every year, and almost as many leave. But the company is able to crank out high-quality work year after year because its core capabilities are rooted in its processes and values rather than in its resources.

When a company's processes and values are being formed in its early and middle years, the founder typically has a profound impact. The founder usually has strong opinions about how employees should do their work and what the organization's priorities need to be. If the founder's judgments are flawed, of course, the company will likely fail. But if they're sound, employees will experience for themselves the validity of the founder's problem-solving and decision-making methods. Thus processes become defined. Likewise, if the company becomes financially successful by allocating resources according to criteria that reflect the founder's priorities, the company's values coalesce around those criteria.

As successful companies mature, employees gradually come to assume that the processes and priorities they've used so successfully so often are the right way to do their work. Once that happens and employees begin to follow processes and decide priorities by assumption rather than by conscious choice, those processes and values come to constitute the organization's culture.[2] As companies grow from a few employees to hundreds and thousands of them, the challenge of getting all employees to agree on what needs to be done and how can be daunting for even the best managers. Culture is a powerful management tool in those situations. It enables employees to act autonomously but causes them to act consistently.

Hence, the factors that define an organization's capabilities and disabilities evolve over time: They start in resources; then move to visible, articulated processes and values; and migrate finally to culture. As long as the organization continues to face the same sorts of problems that its processes and values were designed to address,

[2] Our description of the development of an organization's culture draws heavily from Edgar Schein's research, as first laid out in his book *Organizational Culture and Leadership* (San Francisco: Jossey-Bass, 1985).

managing the organization can be straight-forward. But because those factors also define what an organization cannot do, they constitute disabilities when the problems facing the company change fundamentally. When the organization's capabilities reside primarily in its people, changing capabilities to address the new problems is relatively simple. But when the capabilities have come to reside in processes and values, and especially when they have become embedded in culture, change can be extraordinarily difficult. (See Exhibit 1, "Digital's Dilemma.")

SUSTAINING VERSUS DISRUPTIVE INNOVATION

Successful companies, no matter what the source of their capabilities, are pretty good at responding to evolutionary changes in their markets—what in *The Innovator's Dilemma* (Harvard Business School, 1997), Clayton Christensen referred to as *sustaining innovation.* Where they run into trouble is in handling or initiating revolutionary changes in their markets, or dealing with *disruptive innovation.*

Sustaining technologies are innovations that make a product or service perform better in ways that customers in the mainstream market already value. Compaq's early adoption of Intel's 32-bit 386 microprocessor instead of the 16-bit 286 chip was a sustaining innovation. So was Merrill Lynch's introduction of its Cash Management Account, which allowed customers to write checks against their equity accounts. Those were breakthrough innovations that sustained the best customers of these companies by providing something better than had previously been available.

Disruptive innovations create an entirely new market through the introduction of a new kind of product or service, one that's actually worse, initially, as judged by the performance metrics that mainstream customers value. Charles Schwab's initial entry as a bare-bones discount broker was a disruptive innovation relative to the offerings of full-service brokers like Merrill Lynch. Merrill Lynch's best customers wanted more than Schwab-like services. Early personal computers were a disruptive innovation relative to mainframes and minicomputers. PCs were not powerful enough to run the computing applications that existed at the time they were introduced. These innovations were disruptive in that they didn't address the next-generation needs of leading customers in existing markets. They had other attributes, of course, that enabled new market applications to emerge—and the disruptive innovations improved so rapidly that they ultimately could address the needs of customers in the mainstream of the market as well.

Sustaining innovations are nearly always developed and introduced by established industry leaders. But those same companies never introduce—or cope well with—disruptive innovations. Why? Our resources-processes-values framework holds the answer. Industry leaders are organized to develop and introduce sustaining technologies. Month after month, year after year, they launch new and improved products to gain an edge over the competition. They do so by developing processes for evaluating the technological potential of sustaining innovations and for assessing their customers' needs for alternatives. Investment in sustaining technology also fits in with the values of leading companies in that they promise higher margins from better products sold to leading-edge customers.

Exhibit 1

Digital's Dilemma

A lot of business thinkers have analyzed Digital Equipment Corporation's abrupt fall from grace. Most have concluded that Digital simply read the market very badly. But if we look at the company's fate through the lens of our framework, a different picture emerges.

Digital was a spectacularly successful maker of minicomputers from the 1960s through the 1980s. One might have been tempted to assert, when personal computers first appeared in the market around 1980, that Digital's core capability was in building computers. But if that was the case, why did the company stumble?

Clearly, Digital had the resources to succeed in personal computers (PCs). Its engineers routinely designed computers that were far more sophisticated than PCs. The company had plenty of cash, a great brand, good technology, and so on. But it did not have the processes to succeed in the personal computer business. Minicomputer companies designed most of the key components of their computers internally and then integrated those components into proprietary configurations. Designing a new product platform took two to three years. Digital manufactured most of its own components and assembled them in a batch mode. It sold directly to corporate engineering organizations. Those processes worked extremely well in the minicomputer business.

PC makers, by contrast, outsourced most components from the best suppliers around the globe. New computer designs, made up of modular components, had to be completed in six to 12 months. The computers were manufactured in high-volume assembly lines and sold through retailers to consumers and businesses. None of these processes existed within Digital. In other words, although the people working at the company had the ability to design, build, and sell personal computers profitably, they were working in an organization that was incapable of doing so because its processes had been designed and had evolved to do other tasks well.

Similarly, because of its overhead costs, Digital had to adopt a set of values that dictated, "If it generates 50 percent gross margins or more, it's good business. If it generates less than 40 percent margins, it's not worth doing." Management had to ensure that all employees gave priority to projects according to these criteria or the company couldn't make money. Because PCs generated lower margins, they did not fit with Digital's values. The company's criteria for setting priorities always placed higher-performance minicomputers ahead of personal computers in the resource-allocation process.

Digital could have created a different organization that would have honed the different processes and values required to succeed in PCs—as IBM did. But Digital's mainstream organization was simply incapable of succeeding at the job.

Disruptive innovations occur so intermittently that no company has a routine process for handling them. Furthermore, because disruptive products nearly always promise lower profit margins per unit sold and are not attractive to the company's best customers, they're inconsistent with the established company's values. Merrill Lynch had the resources—the people, money, and technology—required to succeed at the sustaining innovations (Cash Management Account) and the disruptive innovations (bare-bones discount brokering) that it has confronted in recent history. But its processes and values supported only the sustaining innovation: They became disabilities when the company needed to understand and confront the discount online brokerage businesses.

The reason, therefore, that large companies often surrender emerging growth markets is that smaller, disruptive companies are actually more capable of pursuing them. Start-ups lack resources, but that doesn't matter. Their values can embrace small markets, and their cost structures can accommodate low margins. Their market research and resource allocation processes allow managers to proceed intuitively; every decision need not be backed by careful research and analysis. All these advantages add up to the ability to embrace and even initiate disruptive change. But how can a large company develop those capabilities?

CREATING CAPABILITIES TO COPE WITH CHANGE

Despite beliefs spawned by popular change-management and reengineering programs, processes are not nearly as flexible or adaptable as resources are—and

values are even less so. So whether addressing sustaining or disruptive innovations, when an organization needs new processes and values—because it needs new capabilities—managers must create a new organizational space where those capabilities can be developed. There are three possible ways to do that. Managers can:

- Create new organizational structures within corporate boundaries in which new processes can be developed.

- Spin out an independent organization from the existing organization and develop within it the new processes and values required to solve the new problem.

- Acquire a different organization whose processes and values closely match the requirements of the new task.

CREATING NEW CAPABILITIES INTERNALLY

When a company's capabilities reside in its processes, and when new challenges require new processes—that is, when they require different people or groups in a company to interact differently and at a different pace than they habitually have done—managers need to pull the relevant people out of the existing organization and draw a new boundary around a new group. Often, organizational boundaries were first drawn to facilitate the operation of existing processes, and they impede the creation of new processes. New team boundaries facilitate new patterns of working together that ultimately can coalesce as new processes. In *Revolutionizing Product Development* (New York: Free Press, 1992), Steven Wheelwright and Kim Clark referred to these structures as "heavyweight teams."

These teams are entirely dedicated to the new challenge, team members are physically located together, and each member is charged with assuming personal responsibility for the success of the entire project. At Chrysler, for example, the boundaries of the groups within its product development organization historically had been defined by components: power train, electrical systems, and so on. But to accelerate auto development, Chrysler needed to focus not on components but on automobile platforms—the minivan, small car, Jeep, and truck, for example—so it created heavyweight teams. Although these organizational units aren't as good at focusing on component design, they facilitated the definition of new processes that were much faster and more efficient in integrating various subsystems into new car designs. Companies as diverse as Medtronic for its cardiac pacemakers, IBM for its disk drives, and Eli Lilly for its blockbuster drug Zyprexa have used heavyweight teams as vehicles for creating new processes so they could develop better products faster.

CREATING CAPABILITIES THROUGH A SPINOUT ORGANIZATION

When the mainstream organization's values would render it incapable of allocating resources to an innovation project, the company should spin it out as a new venture. Large organizations cannot be expected to allocate the critical financial and human resources needed to build a strong position in small, emerging markets. And it is very difficult for a company whose cost structure is tailored to compete in high-end markets to be profitable in low-end markets as well. Spinouts are very much in vogue among managers in old-line companies struggling with the question of how to address the Internet.

But that's not always appropriate. When a disruptive innovation requires a different cost structure in order to be profitable and competitive, or when the current size of the opportunity is insignificant relative to the growth needs of the mainstream organization, then—and only then—is a spinout organization required.

Hewlett-Packard's (HP's) laser-printer division in Boise, Idaho, was hugely successful, enjoying high margins and a reputation for superior product quality. Unfortunately, its ink-jet project, which represented a disruptive innovation, languished inside the mainstream HP printer business. Although the processes for developing the two types of printers were basically the same, there was a difference in values. To thrive in the ink-jet market, HP needed to be comfortable with lower gross margins and a smaller market than its laser printers commanded, and it needed to be willing to embrace relatively lower performance standards. It was not until HP's managers decided to transfer the unit to a separate division in Vancouver, British Columbia, with the goal of competing head-to-head with its own laser business, that the ink-jet business finally became successful.

How separate does such an effort need to be? A new physical location isn't always necessary. The primary requirement is that the project not be forced to compete for resources with projects in the mainstream organization. As we have seen, projects that are inconsistent with a company's mainstream values will naturally be accorded lowest priority. Whether the independent organization is physically separate is less important than its independence from the normal decision-making criteria in the resource allocation process. Exhibit 2, "Fitting the Tool to the Task," goes into more detail about what kind of innovation challenge is best met by which organizational structure.

Exhibit 2

Fitting the Tool to the Task

Suppose that an organization needs to react to or initiate an innovation. The matrix illustrated below can help managers understand what kind of team should work on the project and what organizational structure that team needs to work within. The vertical axis asks the manager to measure the extent to which the organization's existing processes are suited to getting the new job done effectively. The horizontal axis asks managers to assess whether the organization's values will permit the company to allocate the resources the new initiative needs.

In region A, the project is a good fit with the company's processes and values, so no new capabilities are called for. A functional or a lightweight team can tackle the project within the existing organizational structure. A functional team works on function-specific issues, then passes the project on to the next function. A lightweight team is cross-functional, but team members stay under the control of their respective functional managers.

In region B, the project is a good fit with the company's values but not with its processes. It presents the organization with new types of problems and therefore requires new types of interactions and coordination among groups and individuals. The team, like the team in region A, is working on a sustaining rather than a disruptive innovation.

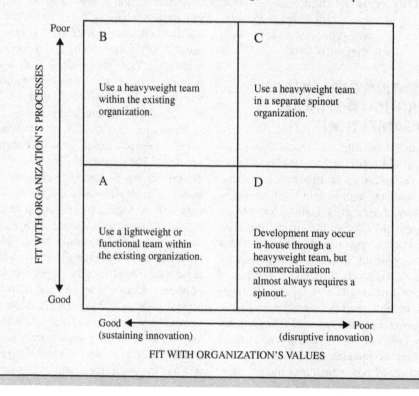

	Poor		
	B		C
	Use a heavyweight team within the existing organization.		Use a heavyweight team in a separate spinout organization.
	A		D
	Use a lightweight or functional team within the existing organization.		Development may occur in-house through a heavyweight team, but commercialization almost always requires a spinout.

FIT WITH ORGANIZATION'S PROCESSES

Good ← (sustaining innovation) → Poor (disruptive innovation)

FIT WITH ORGANIZATION'S VALUES

In this case, a heavyweight team is a good bet, but the project can be executed within the mainstream company. A heavyweight team—whose members work solely on the project and are expected to behave like general managers, shouldering responsibilities for the project's success—is designed so that new processes and new ways of working together can emerge.

In region C, the manager faces a disruptive change that doesn't fit the organization's existing processes or values. To ensure success, the manager should create a spinout organization and commission a heavyweight development team to tackle the challenge. The spinout will allow the project to be governed by different values—a different cost structure, for example, with lower profit margins. The heavyweight team (as in region B) will ensure that new processes can emerge.

Similarly, in region D, when a manager faces a disruptive change that fits the organization's current processes but doesn't fit its values, the key to success almost always lies in commissioning a heavyweight development team to work in a spinout. Development may occasionally happen successfully in-house, but successful commercialization will require a spinout.

Unfortunately, most companies employ a one-size-fits-all organizing strategy, using lightweight or functional teams for programs of every size and character. But such teams are tools for exploiting established capabilities. And among those few companies that have accepted the heavyweight gospel, many have attempted to organize *all* their development teams in a heavyweight fashion. Ideally, each company should tailor the team structure and organizational location to the process and values required by each project.

Managers think that developing a new operation necessarily means abandoning the old one, and they're loath to do that since it works perfectly well for what it was designed to do. But when disruptive change appears on the horizon, managers need to assemble the capabilities to confront that change before it affects the mainstream business. They actually need to run two businesses in tandem—one whose processes are tuned to the existing business model and another that is geared toward the new model. Merrill Lynch, for example, has accomplished an impressive global expansion of its institutional financial services through careful execution of its existing planning, acquisition, and partnership processes. Now, however, faced with the online world, the company is required to plan, acquire, and form partnerships more rapidly. Does this mean Merrill Lynch should change the processes that have worked so well in its traditional investment-banking business? Doing so would be disastrous, if we consider the question through the lens of our framework. Instead, Merrill should retain the old processes when working with the existing business (there are probably a few billion dollars still to be made under the old business model!) and create additional processes to deal with the new class of problems.

One word of warning: in our studies of this challenge, we have never seen a company succeed in addressing a change that disrupts its mainstream values without the personal, attentive oversight of the

CEO—precisely because of the power of values in shaping the normal resource allocation process. Only the CEO can ensure that the organization gets the required resources and is free to create processes and values that are appropriate to the new challenge. CEOs who view spinouts as a tool to get disruptive threats off their personal agendas are almost certain to meet with failure. We have seen no exceptions to this rule.

CREATING CAPABILITIES THROUGH ACQUISITIONS

Just as innovating managers need to make separate assessments of the capabilities and disabilities that reside in their company's resources, processes, and values, so must they do the same with acquisitions when seeking to buy capabilities. Companies that successfully gain new capabilities through acquisitions are those that know where those capabilities reside in the acquisition and assimilate them accordingly. Acquiring managers begin by asking, "What created the value that I just paid so dearly for? Did I justify the price because of the acquisition's resources? Or was a substantial portion of its worth created by processes and values?"

If the capabilities being purchased are embedded in an acquired company's processes and values, then the last thing the acquiring manager should do is integrate the acquisition into the parent organization. Integration will vaporize the processes and values of the acquired firm. Once the acquisition's managers are forced to adopt the buyer's way of doing business, its capabilities will disappear. A better strategy is to let the business stand alone and to infuse the parent's resources into the acquired company's processes and values. This approach truly constitutes the acquisition of new capabilities.

If, however, the acquired company's resources were the reason for its success and the primary rationale for the acquisition, then integrating it into the parent can make a lot of sense. Essentially, that means plugging the acquired people, products, technology, and customers into the parent's processes as a way of leveraging the parent's existing capabilities.

The perils of the ongoing Daimler-Chrysler merger can be better understood in this light. Chrysler had few resources that could be considered unique. Its recent success in the market was rooted in its processes—particularly in its processes for designing products and integrating the efforts of its subsystem suppliers. What is the best way for Daimler to leverage Chrysler's capabilities? Wall Street is pressuring management to consolidate the two organizations to cut costs. But if the two companies are integrated, the very processes that made Chrysler such an attractive acquisition will likely be compromised.

The situation is reminiscent of IBM's 1984 acquisition of the telecommunications company Rolm. There wasn't anything in Rolm's pool of resources that IBM didn't already have. Rather, it was Rolm's processes for developing and finding new markets for PBX products that mattered. Initially, IBM recognized the value in preserving the informal and unconventional culture of the Rolm organization, which stood in stark contrast to IBM's methodical style. However, in 1987 IBM terminated Rolm's subsidiary status and decided to fully integrate the company into its own corporate structure. IBM's managers soon learned the folly of that decision. When they tried to push Rolm's resources—its products and its customers—through the processes that had been honed in the large-computer business, the Rolm business stumbled badly. And it was impossible for a computer company whose values had been whetted on profit margins of 18 percent to get excited about products with much lower profit margins. IBM's integration of Rolm destroyed the very source of the deal's original worth. DaimlerChrysler, bowing to the investment community's drumbeat for efficiency savings, now stands on the edge of the same precipice. Often, it seems, financial analysts have a better intuition about the value of resources than they do about the value of processes.

By contrast, Cisco Systems' acquisitions process has worked well because, we would argue, it has kept resources, processes, and values in the right perspective. Between 1993 and 1997, it primarily acquired small companies that were less than two years old, early-stage organizations whose market value was built primarily upon their resources, particularly their engineers and products. Cisco plugged those resources into its own effective development, logistics, manufacturing, and marketing processes and threw away whatever nascent processes and values came with the acquisitions because those weren't what it had paid for. On a couple of occasions when the company acquired a larger, more mature organization—notably its 1996 acquisition of StrataCom—Cisco did not integrate. Rather, it let StrataCom stand alone and infused Cisco's substantial resources into StrataCom's organization to help it grow more rapidly.[3]

[3] See Charles A. Holloway, Stephen C. Wheelwright, and Nicole Tempest, "Cisco Systems, Inc.: Post-Acquisition Manufacturing Integration," a case published jointly by Stanford Business School and Harvard Business School, 1998.

Managers whose organizations are confronting change must first determine whether they have the resources required to succeed. They then need to ask a separate question: Does the organization have the processes and values it needs to succeed in this new situation? Asking this second question is not as instinctive for most managers because the processes by which work is done and the values by which employees make their decisions have served them well in the past. What we hope this framework introduces into managers' thinking is the idea that the very capabilities that make their organizations effective also define their disabilities. In that regard, a little time spent soul searching for honest answers to the following questions will pay off handsomely: Are the processes by which work habitually gets done in the organization appropriate for this new problem? And will the values of the organization cause this initiative to get high priority or to languish?

If the answers to those questions are no, it's okay. Understanding a problem is the most crucial step in solving it. Wishful thinking about these issues can set teams that need to innovate on a course fraught with roadblocks, second-guessing, and frustration. The reason that innovation often seems to be so difficult for established companies is that they employ highly capable people and then set them to work within organizational structures whose processes and values weren't designed for the task at hand. Ensuring that capable people are ensconced in capable organizations is a major responsibility of management in a transformational age such as ours.

Case

GlaxoSmithKline and AIDS Drugs in South Africa (A)

The Fight for Lives and Profits

Cape Town, South Africa, October 2000: Zackie Achmat could barely conceal his excitement when he arrived at Cape Town International Airport from Bangkok and strolled past customs agents with his suitcase full of illegal drugs. Buried beneath his folded clothes were 3,000 tablets of fluconazole, the only drug known to treat the potentially fatal inflammation of the brain that afflicts people with AIDS. Once past customs, Achmat held a press conference flaunting what he had done and claiming that the need for AIDS drugs took priority over patent rights.

Dr Jean-Pierre Garnier, the CEO of GlaxoSmithKline (GSK), was concerned about the developments in South Africa. Garnier, who was awarded the Legion d'Honneur by the French government in 1997, had been successful in getting GSK recognized as one of the pharma industry's most altruistic companies.

Four months later—in February 2001—Oxfam, a highly respectable NGO, singled out GSK as the target for its new campaign, "Cut the Cost." The goal was to hit where it would hurt the most—GSK's share price. TAC, a South African AIDS-focused NGO, warned GSK and other pharmaceutical companies that it would launch more campaigns, animal rights activists threatened to go after the pharmaceutical conglomerate; and Médecins Sans Frontières (MSF) also launched a campaign, "Access to Essential Medicines," demanding a 95% price cut on all medicines in Africa.

BACKGROUND

DISCOVERY OF AIDS IN THE US

Acquired Immune Deficiency Syndrome (AIDS) was first discovered in the early 1980s in the US. Scientists found that the virus was transmitted through the exchange of body fluids: blood transfusions, sharing contaminated needles, sexual contact (both homosexual and heterosexual), and through perinatality (from mother to child during childbirth).

HIV spreads in the body by targeting cells that normally clear foreign pathogens. As the HIV-infected cells replicate themselves, the immune system is compromised and patients die from AIDS-related secondary diseases.

During the 1980s, AIDS spread quickly in the US. In the first 10 years 200,000 people tested positive for HIV/AIDS and with no effective medical treatment many people died within 10 years of being infected. By 1987, as many as 127 countries around the world had reported cases.

By the mid-1990s, the infection rate in the US had peaked: It dropped from 80,000 diagnosed cases in 1993 to 21,700 in 2000. However, globally the disease was spiraling out of control and in 2000 over 20 million people had died and another 40 million were living with the disease. In Africa alone 25 million people were infected with HIV/AIDS, of which 55% were women.

AIDS Drugs

In 1986 the U.S. Food and Drug Administration (FDA) approved the first AIDS drug—an antiviral medication, known as AZT, produced by GSK.

In the mid-1990s doctors began to treat patients with a combination of drugs, known as HAART (Highly Active Antiretroviral Therapy), which attacked the virus from several different angles.[1] Even if the HIV virus developed resistance to one drug it would still be susceptible to the others. The HAART method was successful: in 70% to 80% of the patients these drugs were able to lower the virus levels to undetectable. But the HAART method was extremely expensive—in 1996 a one-year treatment cost $60,000 for a patient in the US. A few years later the price had come down, but was still a dizzying $10,000 to $15,000 a year.

Nearly two decades after AIDS was first discovered successful treatments were available, but there was still no cure for the disease.

---

[1] HAART could also produce severe side effects (stroke, toxication, heart attack, development of diabetes and certain forms of cancers) in some patients. In addition, the number of drugs involved (sometimes up to 20 pills a day) and the fact that some needed to be taken with water, others on a full stomach and in accordance with a very strict schedule made the treatment very complex.

HIV/AIDS IN SOUTH AFRICA

South Africa had the highest HIV-positive population in the world: In 2000 five million people were infected with HIV/AIDS (20% of the population). Sadly, the high-risk behavior continued and healthcare officials predicted that by 2010 as many as seven and a half million people could be infected with HIV/AIDS, many of whom would be between 15 and 29 years of age.

During apartheid, male workers were forced to work in locations far away from their families for up to 11 months per year. The areas around the cities and mines developed into slums, where prostitution was common and where opportunities for risky sexual behavior were great. As a result, many women contracted the virus from their husbands. Due to the nature of spreading, AIDS often infected both parents in a family and estimations were made that by 2015 30% of all children in South Africa would be AIDS orphans.

HIV/AIDS was a complex issue in South Africa. Having lived under severe oppression during apartheid most South Africans no longer wanted to be controlled. Advocating the use of condoms was said to be a "genocidal plot" and people joked that AIDS stood for "Afrikaner Invention to Deprive us of Sex." In 1999 Thabo Mbeki was elected president after Nelson Mandela, and even before he took office he made several controversial comments about AIDS. Mbeki claimed that the toxicity of the anti-retroviral drug AZT was a more serious health concern than AIDS itself. He also questioned the link between HIV and AIDS. Sue Roberts, a head nurse at Johannesburg's Helen Joseph Hospital, remarked:

> Some patients dropped out of our program because the president was saying HIV doesn't cause AIDS and

they thought his opinion should be worth something.

Although AIDS drugs had increased life expectancy and quality of life for many AIDS patients in industrialized countries, a positive HIV test was almost always a death sentence for a South African. In 1998, the average income was about $2,000 a year and a one-year treatment with HAART cost $14,000; the medicine was unattainable for most people. Roberts said:

> Those who can't afford to buy the drugs at a private pharmacy—they just sit at home and die.

Thousands of children who could be prevented from contracting the virus from their mothers with a few doses of drugs were also condemned to death. Dr Iwan Bekker, head of pediatrics at a South African hospital, stated:

> When a baby gets bad, we won't admit it for a second time, but we will tell the mother to take it home and let it die.

THE PHARMACEUTICAL INDUSTRY

The Most Profitable Industry in the World

The pharma industry was one of the most profitable industries in the world with annual revenues of around $400 billion and an average ROE of 20%. It was a heavily research-focused industry and pharma often claimed it took 10 to15 years to bring a new drug to the market at a cost of around $800 million.

The biggest producers of AIDS drugs worldwide were GlaxoSmithKline, Merck, Pfizer and Boehringer Ingelheim. In countries such as Brazil, Thailand, Malaysia and India local companies also started to produce generic AIDS drugs.

PHARMA TRADE REGULATIONS

TRIPS[2] (trade-related aspects of intellectual property rights) came into effect on 1 January 1995 and developed, developing and "least developed" countries were given 1, 5 and 10 years respectively to implement the agreement.[3]

The pharma industry lobbied hard for the passage of the TRIPS Agreement, which stated that the domestic legislation of GATT members should cover: IP protection of pharmaceutical and biotechnology products; banning the production of cheaper products of a patented drug by generic manufacturers, and recognition of 20 years of monopoly rights for both the manufacturing and marketing of patented drugs.

TRIPS did allow some exceptions with regard to the patent, such as parallel importation and compulsory licensing[4] when there was a medical emergency. However, due to the economic and political realities, the safeguards were usually hard to implement. US Trade Representatives often threatened countries with trade sanctions if they tried to use the safeguards.

Critics of the TRIPS agreement stated that by setting unreasonably high IP protections, the agreement prioritized corporate interests over human rights. In countries such as India where the patent regime was not yet in place (or was not recognized) manufacturers made generic

---

[2] TRIPS is administered by the World Trade Organization (WTO) through the TRIPS council.
[3] For countries where there were no patent laws in place for technology (such as pharmaceuticals) a 10-year implementation period was granted.
[4] Parallel importation is the importation of drugs from another country where they are sold for a lower price. Compulsory licensing gives the right to a government to temporarily override a patent by forcing the patent holder to license the product to a generic producer.

versions of patented drugs, which sold for around 2% of the price of a patented drug.

PHARMA LOBBY GROUPS

PhRMA

Pharmaceutical Research Manufacturers of America (PhRMA), based in Washington DC, was the pharma industry's main industry trade group. GSK, Pfizer, Boehringer Ingelheim and Merck were among the many members of PhRMA.

According to Oxfam, PhRMA contributed almost $20 million to the 2000 presidential campaign and spent around $120 million every year for lobbying activities.

GLAXOSMITHKLINE—A GLOBAL GIANT

In 2000 Glaxo Wellcome and SmithKline Beecham merged and formed GlaxoSmith Kline. The result was the largest pharmaceutical company in the world with sales of $30 billion and a profit before tax of $10 billion. GSK was the largest AIDS drug producer in the world[5] with many drugs under patent. The company also controlled 40% of the profitable US AIDS drugs market. Its AIDS drugs generated $2 billion in sales in 2000. For GSK the South African market was considered "relatively large" compared to other markets in Africa, even though it only represented 1% of global sales.

THE CHALLENGE

GSK was facing a difficult situation in South Africa. It had a pending lawsuit against the government and it was being attacked by NGOs on all fronts. Prices and patent protection were at risk, as was the firm's reputation, profits and share price.

LAWSUIT AGAINST THE SOUTH AFRICAN GOVERNMENT

In 1998 GSK and another 41 pharmaceutical companies, among them Boehringer-Ingelheim, Bristol-Meyers Squibb, Merck, Roche and Eli Lilly, filed a lawsuit against the South African government. The lawsuit centered around the Medicines and Related Substances Control Amendment of 1997 which was introduced to the South African Parliament by the then President, Nelson Mandela. The Amendment allowed the government to import generic drugs or give out compulsory licenses in case of a national emergency. The government argued that the measure was necessary in order for the country to get access to drugs that the people could afford.

At the beginning of 2001[6] a doctor from MSF commented:

> The pharmaceutical companies have already won a major victory whatever the outcome of the court case. They have been able to keep cheaper generic drugs out of Africa for three years, while they sell their drugs and make a huge profit at the expense of millions of AIDS sufferers across the continent.[7]

GSK IS ATTACKED ON ALL FRONTS

Many foreign NGOs were present in South Africa as it was seen as a market where they could get their voices heard. Oxfam

---

[5] GSK AIDS drugs included among others Epivir and Epivir-HBV, Agenerase, Combivir, Retrovir, Ziagen, Lexiva. In addition, GSK were testing several others as well as an HIV vaccine.

[6] The lawsuit was supposed to be brought before the court in March that year.

[7] Julien Macken, "Cipla Launches AIDS drugs price battle." *Australian Financial Review*, 13 February, 2001.

had officially launched its "Cut the Cost" campaign against GSK, but it was not the only headache for the pharma giant—other NGOs were also on the offensive.

Oxfam's "Cut the Cost" Campaign

Oxfam International was founded in the UK in 1942 as a charity organization. Since then it had become one of the world's most important and respected NGOs.

Oxfam retaliated against the pending lawsuit by launching the "Cut the Cost" campaign on 12 February 2001, demanding that GSK withdraw the lawsuit against the South African government. The campaign was a protest against all pharmaceutical companies charging excessive prices in developing countries. It aimed to raise the public profile of the problem, destroy GSK's reputation and thus damage the company's share price. The campaign was also aimed to target something bigger that was, according to Oxfam, the core of the problem—the TRIPS agreement. Oxfam claimed that the agreement had been made by Pharma (through lobbying) for Pharma.

Oxfam recognized that patents were used to recoup R&D costs; however, in some cases drugs were more expensive in developing countries than in industrialized ones. For example, the price of GSK's Lamivudine (used in AIDS treatment) was on average 20% higher in Africa than in industrial markets.

GSK's programs to make drugs more accessible had been criticized by Oxfam, which claimed that the amounts supplied or the time frame of the commitment had not been defined.

TAC Defiance Campaigns

TAC was launched in 1998 in South Africa. After its campaign against Pfizer in 2000, Achmat,[8] TAC's chairman, commented:

> This is a challenge to Pfizer and the entire profiteering industry to sue TAC. The organization will also prepare to challenge the patents of GlaxoSmithKline, Bristol-Meyers Squibb, Boehringer Ingelheim, Merck, Abbott and Roche to anti-retroviral drugs.[9]

Médecins Sans Frontières (Doctors without Borders)

MSF, which had won the Nobel Peace Prize in 1999, argued that the globalization of markets and the trade system, which set the rules for how products were sold, was unacceptable for medicines. "Access to Essential Medicines" was an MSF campaign whose goal was to encourage generic drug competition, voluntary discounts on branded drugs, global procurement and local production in order to increase access to specific medicines. One of the target diseases in the campaign was HIV/AIDS. MSF demanded that prices of AIDS drugs should be cut by 95% at the start of 2001, stating that the pharmaceutical companies had not done enough and that they should live up to their promises.

MSF also confirmed that they supported Oxfam in its "Cut the Cost" campaign.

---

[8] Being HIV positive Achmat risked his own life by not taking antiretroviral drugs as long as they were not made available to the public. In 2004 he gave in to pressure from the AIDS/HIV community and Nelson Mandela, who had pleaded with him to take the medication as he would do no good if he were dead (Achmat had been seriously ill with an AIDS-related disease) and started to take antiretroviral drugs.

[9] "Defying the Drug Cartel" (Interview). *Multinational Monitor.* January 1, 2001.

Act UP

Act UP, an American AIDS NGO founded in New York in 1987, was perhaps the most radical of the various foreign AIDS/HIV NGOs active in Africa. On 5 March 2001, Act UP was holding a day of worldwide demonstrations in solidarity with the South African NGOs in their fight against the lawsuit filed against the South African government. Outside South Africa, demonstrations were also scheduled to take place in the US, Canada, Brazil, Australia, France, Germany, Italy, the Philippines, and Thailand. Act UP's John Bell remarked:

> It is not 1997 anymore. World opinion has changed and we no longer write off the lives of millions infected with HIV worldwide. And broad access to generics is the cornerstone of bringing medication in reach of these people. Those of us living with HIV in the United States are standing with South African people with HIV to fight for the lives of its 4.2 million people who are infected.

DARK CLOUDS

Patents and the profits they created were the lifeblood of pharma companies. They argued that to cover their huge research and development costs patents were necessary. Now the patents were being challenged and GSK's brand name was being tarnished.

Price Pressure

In early 2001 GSK declined a voluntary licensing offer from the generic drug manufacturer Cipla for the South African market. Phil Thomson, a spokesman for GSK, said:

> Patent protection is fundamental to continued research and development in

these areas. We have to aim to protect our patents across the developing world.[10]

Pharma feared that prices would also be undermined in industrial markets if they gave in to pressure in markets such as South Africa. Healthcare costs were soaring in almost every industrialized country around the globe and the issue of expensive healthcare was already a hot topic everywhere. An institutional investor commented on why GSK fought so hard to keep its patents sacred:

> Their nightmare is that AIDS drugs will turn up for 10 cents a packet on the streets of San Francisco.[11]

Licensing and parallel import were heavily criticized by pharma. A former GSK executive commented:

> The companies are sensitive about a pattern starting to develop where countries use generics.[12]

Pharma companies often argued that due to the complexity of AIDS drugs it was hard to maintain effective treatment in developing countries and scientists claimed that in the long run the medications could lose their effect if not taken correctly, as the virus could mutate. The pharma industry also argued that it was not enough to just give away free drugs; political and social issues also needed to be addressed and taken care of. NGOs such as MSF, however, argued that in most large cities in the developing countries the conditions

[10] "Patents, profits, and AIDS care." *Christian Science Monitor*, 28 February, 2001.
[11] David Pilling, "Patents and patients." *Financial Times*, 17 February, 2001.
[12] Mark Schoofs, "Glaxo enters fight in Ghana on AIDS drug." *The Wall Street Journal*, December 1, 2000.

and the equipment were sufficient to give good quality treatment if only tests and drugs were available. A doctor from MSF in South Africa stated:

> The only limiting factor for us is price.[13]

GSK could have afforded to give its drugs away in Africa as the market only represented 1% of total sales. However, if prices were drastically lowered in these markets it would send a message to customers in markets such as the US and Europe that they were being overcharged.

Reputation of Brand

Oxfam had warned GSK that it risked doing severe damage to its reputation if it did not do more to help poor people get access to affordable, life-saving medicines. One institutional investor confirmed this, saying that the "Cut the Cost" campaign by Oxfam in South Africa could potentially damage GSK's brand and its share price.

The pharmaceutical industry argued that with drug donations it was doing what it could to help developing countries and that it already donated more than one-third of what the US healthcare assistance gave to the developing countries. GSK was, for example, taking part in a program aimed at accelerating access to AIDS treatments in developing countries. Garnier stated that Oxfam and other NGOs had failed to recognize drug donations and price discount programs.

It was now March; one month had passed since Oxfam had launched its "Cut the Cost" campaign and the lawsuit was to be brought up in court.

In the same month GSK cut prices by as much as 90% in Africa.[14] Garnier said that the price of the three AIDS drugs (Trizivir, Ziagen and Agenerase) would be reduced to sell at cost in 63 of the world's poorest countries, including sub-Saharan Africa:

> We are not naïve about the fact that compared to the means in these countries, everything is overpriced, even the generics. [15]

In addition, GSK said that it would continue to offer a preferential price on its drug Combivir (a mix of AZT and 3TC) to governments, charities and NGOs in developing countries. The company was also negotiating price cuts for large corporations having AIDS programs in affected regions. NGOs argued that even if promises had been made, little action had been taken. Garnier replied:

> We're not surprised. You can't simply use those drugs in an open environment because there are a whole lot of practical issues to overcome from establishing distribution channels to ensuring compliance with a complex medical regimen. But the ball is more in their camp than ours.[16]

GSK had reduced prices but held on to its position that it would not engage in discussions with Cipla, which had shown interest in selling generic versions of GSK's AIDS drugs in South Africa.

---

[13] Deborah Spar & Nicolas Bartlett, "Life, Death and Property Rights: Pharmaceutical Industry Faces AIDS in Africa," *Harvard Business School*, February 25, 2003.

[14] "Glaxo to widen access to cheap AIDS drugs." *Reuters News*, 21 February, 2001.
[15] Rachel Zimmermann, "Glaxo plans another price cut in AIDS drugs to poor countries." *Wall Street Journal*, 11 June, 2001.
[16] Rachel Zimmermann, "Glaxo plans another price cut in AIDS drugs to poor countries." *Wall Street Journal*, 11 June, 2001.

Nelson Mandela, among others, felt that it was not enough to reduce prices and he commented on the pending lawsuit:

> The pharmaceuticals are exploiting the situation that exists in countries like South Africa because they charge exorbitant prices, which are beyond the capacity of the ordinary HIV/AIDS person. The government is perfectly entitled, in facing that situation, to import generic drugs and it is a gross error for the companies, for the pharmaceuticals, to take the government to court.[17]

Even with all the price cuts offered, GSK was still getting hammered in the press. The outcome of the court case against the South African government was uncertain. The well-established global patent protection system that was responsible for drug creation in the first place was under threat. Garnier was frustrated and in an interview in the Guardian he expressed his concerns:

> Why is there a disagreement here? The disagreement is because there is an economic war going on. This is a great opportunity for the Indian and Brazilian generic companies to conquer the world. If they could just get rid of our patents then the whole developing world would open up to them. So there is an economic war. There are a couple of pirate companies who want to undermine the patent system and they have found the best horse of Troy to come in against the patent. This is the first time there is a genuine risk that intellectual property would disappear in the developing world. I'm saying the poorest countries of the world—and there is a list prepared by WHO—they should be able to disregard patents. That's what I am for, in all the diseases that constitute healthcare crises for those countries. What I don't agree is that patents would be disregarded in China, in India and so forth and those companies would be able to prosper by pirating our discoveries made in Europe and the US and therefore we'd be shut out of 80% of the world population. That is not fair. If the patents go away in those countries it's the end of the pharmaceutical industry, as we know it.[18]

Meanwhile, millions of HIV-positive South Africans were waiting impatiently.

---

[17] Samanta Sen, "Health, South Africa: Battle won, but not war says aids activists." *Inter Press Service*, 19 April, 2001.

[18] "Jean Pierre Garnier, Head of Glaxo, he will drop the prices of his drugs to the poorest countries." *The Guardian*, 18 February, 2003.

Reading

Rethinking the Social Responsibility of Business

*A **Reason** debate featuring Milton Friedman, Whole Foods' John Mackey, and Cypress Semiconductor's T. J. Rodgers*

Thirty-five years ago, Milton Friedman wrote a famous article for *The New York Times Magazine* whose title aptly summed up its main point: "The Social Responsibility of Business Is to Increase Its Profits." The future Nobel laureate in economics had no patience for capitalists who claimed that "business is not concerned 'merely' with profit but also with promoting desirable 'social' ends; that business has a 'social conscience' and takes seriously its responsibilities for providing employment, eliminating discrimination, avoiding pollution and whatever else may be the catchwords of the contemporary crop of reformers."

Friedman wrote that such people are "preaching pure and unadulterated socialism. Businessmen who talk this way are unwitting puppets of the intellectual forces that have been undermining the basis of a free society these past decades."

John Mackey, the founder and CEO of Whole Foods, is one businessman who disagrees with Friedman. A self-described ardent libertarian whose conversation is peppered with references to Ludwig von Mises and Abraham Maslow, Austrian economics and astrology, Mackey believes Friedman's view is too narrow a

description of his and many other businesses' activities. As important, he argues that Friedman's take woefully undersells the humanitarian dimension of capitalism.

In the debate that follows, Mackey lays out his personal vision of the social responsibility of business. Friedman responds, as does T. J. Rodgers, the founder and CEO of Cypress Semiconductor and the chief spokesman of what might be called the tough love school of laissez faire. Dubbed "one of America's toughest bosses" by *Fortune*, Rodgers argues that corporations add far more to society by maximizing "long-term shareholder value" than they do by donating time and money to charity.

PUTTING CUSTOMERS AHEAD OF INVESTORS

John Mackey

In 1970 Milton Friedman wrote that "there is one and only one social responsibility of business—to use its resources and engage in activities designed to increase its profits so long as it stays within the rules of the game, which is to say, engages in open and free competition without deception or fraud." That's the orthodox view among free market economists: that the only social responsibility a law-abiding business has is to maximize profits for the shareholders.

I strongly disagree. I'm a businessman and a free market libertarian, but I believe that the enlightened corporation should try to create value for *all* of its constituencies. From an investor's perspective, the purpose of the business is to maximize profits. But that's not the purpose for other stakeholders—for customers, employees, suppliers, and the community. Each of those groups will define the purpose of the business in terms of its own needs and desires, and each perspective is valid and legitimate.

My argument should not be mistaken for a hostility to profit. I believe I know something about creating shareholder value. When I co-founded Whole Foods Market 27 years ago, we began with $45,000 in capital; we only had $250,000 in sales our first year. During the last 12 months we had sales of more than $4.6 billion, net profits of more than $160 million, and a market capitalization over $8 billion.

But we have not achieved our tremendous increase in shareholder value by making shareholder value the primary purpose of our business. In my marriage, my wife's happiness is an end in itself, not merely a means to my own happiness; love leads me to put my wife's happiness first, but in doing so I also make myself happier. Similarly, the most successful businesses put the customer first, ahead of the investors. In the profit-centered business, customer happiness is merely a means to an end: maximizing profits. In the customer-centered business, customer happiness is an end in itself, and will be pursued with greater interest, passion, and empathy than the profit-centered business is capable of.

Not that we're only concerned with customers. At Whole Foods, we measure our success by how much value we can create for all six of our most important stakeholders: customers, team members (employees), investors, vendors, communities, and the environment.

There is, of course, no magical formula to calculate how much value each stakeholder should receive from the company. It is a dynamic process that evolves with the competitive marketplace. No stakeholder remains satisfied for long. It is the function of company leadership to develop solutions that continually work for the common good.

Many thinking people will readily accept my arguments that caring about customers and employees is good business. But they might draw the line at believing a company has any responsibility to its community and environment. To donate time and capital to philanthropy, they will argue, is to steal from the investors. After all, the corporation's assets legally belong to the investors, don't they? Management has a fiduciary responsibility to maximize shareholder value; therefore, any activities that don't maximize shareholder value are violations of this duty. If you feel altruism towards other people, you should exercise that altruism with your own money, not with the assets of a corporation that doesn't belong to you.

This position sounds reasonable. A company's assets do belong to the investors, and its management does have a duty to manage those assets responsibly. In my view, the argument is not *wrong* so much as it is too narrow.

First, there can be little doubt that a certain amount of corporate philanthropy is simply good business and works for the long-term benefit of the investors. For example: In addition to the many thousands of small donations each Whole Foods store makes each year, we also hold five 5% Days throughout the year.

On those days, we donate 5 percent of a store's total sales to a nonprofit organization. While our stores select worthwhile organizations to support, they also tend to focus on groups that have large membership lists, which are contacted and encouraged to shop our store that day to support the organization. This usually brings hundreds of new or lapsed customers into our stores, many of whom then become regular shoppers. So a 5% Day not only allows us to support worthwhile causes, but is an excellent marketing strategy that has benefited Whole Foods investors immensely.

That said, I believe such programs would be completely justifiable even if they produced no profits and no P.R. This is because I believe the entrepreneurs, not the current investors in a company's stock, have the right and responsibility to define the purpose of the company. It is the entrepreneurs who create a company, who bring all the factors of production together and coordinate it into viable business. It is the entrepreneurs who set the company strategy and who negotiate the terms of trade with all of the voluntarily cooperating stakeholders—including the investors. At Whole Foods we "hired" our original investors. They didn't hire us.

We first announced that we would donate 5 percent of the company's net profits to philanthropy when we drafted our mission statement, back in 1985. Our policy has therefore been in place for over 20 years, and it predates our IPO by seven years. All seven of the private investors at the time we created the policy voted for it when they served on our board of directors. When we took in venture capital money back in 1989, none of the venture firms objected to the policy. In addition, in almost 14 years as a publicly traded company, almost no investors have ever raised objections to the policy. How can Whole Foods' philanthropy be "theft" from the current investors if the original owners of the company unanimously approved the policy and all subsequent investors made their investments after the policy was in effect and well publicized?

The shareholders of a public company own their stock voluntarily. If they don't agree with the philosophy of the business, they can always sell their investment, just as the customers and employees can exit their relationships with the company if they don't like the terms of trade. If that is unacceptable to them, they always have the legal right to submit a resolution at our annual shareholders meeting to change the company's philanthropic philosophy. A number of our company policies have been changed over the years through successful shareholder resolutions.

Another objection to the Whole Foods philosophy is where to draw the line. If donating 5 percent of profits is good, wouldn't 10 percent be even better? Why not donate 100 percent of our profits to the betterment of society? But the fact that Whole Foods has responsibilities to our community doesn't mean that we don't have any responsibilities to our investors. It's a question of finding the appropriate balance and trying to create value for all of our stakeholders. Is 5 percent the "right amount" to donate to the community? I don't think there is a right answer to this question, except that I believe 0 percent is too little. It is an arbitrary percentage that the co-founders of the company decided was a reasonable amount and which was approved by the owners of the company at the time we made the decision. Corporate philanthropy is a good thing, but it requires the legitimacy of investor approval. In my experience, most investors understand that it can be beneficial to both the corporation and the larger society.

That doesn't answer the question of *why* we give money to the community stakeholder. For that, you should turn to one of the fathers of free-market economics, Adam Smith. *The Wealth of Nations* was a tremendous achievement, but economists would be well served to read Smith's other great book, *The Theory of Moral Sentiments*. There he explains that human nature isn't just about self-interest. It also includes sympathy, empathy, friendship, love, and the desire for social approval. As motives for human behavior, these are at least as important as self-interest. For many people, they are more important.

When we are small children we are egocentric, concerned only about our own needs and desires. As we mature, most people grow beyond this egocentrism and begin to care about others—their families, friends, communities, and countries. Our capacity to love can expand even further: to loving people from different races, religions, and countries—potentially to unlimited love for all people and even for other sentient creatures. This is our potential as human beings, to take joy in the flourishing of people everywhere. Whole Foods gives money to our communities because we care about them and feel a responsibility to help them flourish as well as possible.

The business model that Whole Foods has embraced could represent a new form of capitalism, one that more consciously works for the common good instead of depending solely on the "invisible hand" to generate positive results for society. The "brand" of capitalism is in terrible shape throughout the world, and corporations are widely seen as selfish, greedy, and uncaring. This is both unfortunate and unnecessary, and could be changed if businesses and economists widely adopted the business model that I have outlined here.

To extend our love and care beyond our narrow self-interest is antithetical to neither our human nature nor our financial success. Rather, it leads to the further fulfillment of both. Why do we not encourage this in our theories of business and economics? Why do we restrict our theories to such a pessimistic and crabby view of human nature? What are we afraid of?

MAKING PHILANTHROPY OUT OF OBSCENITY

Milton Friedman

By pursuing his own interest [an individual] frequently promotes that of the society more effectually than when he really intends to promote it. I have never known much good done by those who affected to trade for the public good.

—Adam Smith, *The Wealth of Nations*

The differences between John Mackey and me regarding the social responsibility of business are for the most part rhetorical. Strip off the camouflage, and it turns out we are in essential agreement. Moreover, his company, Whole Foods Market, behaves in accordance with the principles I spelled out in my 1970 *New York Times Magazine* article.

With respect to his company, it could hardly be otherwise. It has done well in a highly competitive industry. Had it devoted any significant fraction of its resources to exercising a social responsibility unrelated to the bottom line, it would be out of business by now or would have been taken over.

Here is how Mackey himself describes his firm's activities:

1. The most successful businesses put the customer first, instead of the investors [which clearly means that this is the way to put the investors first].
2. There can be little doubt that a certain amount of corporate philanthropy is simply good business and works for the long-term benefit of the investors.

Compare this to what I wrote in 1970:

Of course, in practice the doctrine of social responsibility is frequently a cloak for actions that are justified on other grounds rather than a reason for those actions.

To illustrate, it may well be in the long run interest of a corporation that is a major employer in a small community to devote resources to providing amenities to that community or to improving its government. . . .

In each of these . . . cases, there is a strong temptation to rationalize these actions as an exercise of "social responsibility." In the present climate of opinion, with its widespread aversion to "capitalism," "profits," the "soulless corporation" and so on, this is one way for a corporation to generate goodwill as a by-product of expenditures that are entirely justified in its own self-interest.

It would be inconsistent of me to call on corporate executives to refrain from this hypocritical window-dressing because it harms the foundations of a free society. That would be to call on them to exercise a "social responsibility"! If our institutions and the attitudes of the public make it in their self-interest to cloak their actions in this way, I cannot summon much indignation to denounce them.

I believe Mackey's flat statement that "corporate philanthropy is a good thing" is flatly wrong. Consider the decision by the founders of Whole Foods to donate 5 percent of net profits to philanthropy. They were clearly within their rights in doing so. They were spending their own money, using 5 percent of one part of their wealth to establish, thanks to corporate tax provisions, the equivalent of a 501c(3) charitable foundation, though with no mission statement, no separate by-laws, and no provision for deciding on the beneficiaries. But what reason is there to suppose that the stream of profit distributed in this way would do more good for society than investing that stream of profit in the enterprise itself or paying it out as dividends and letting the stockholders dispose of it? The practice makes sense only because of our obscene tax laws, whereby a stockholder can make a larger gift for a given after-tax cost if the corporation makes the gift on his behalf than if he makes the gift directly. That is a good reason for eliminating the corporate tax or for eliminating the deductibility of corporate charity, but it is not a justification for corporate charity.

Whole Foods Market's contribution to society—and as a customer I can testify that it is an important one—is to enhance the pleasure of shopping for food. Whole Foods has no special competence in deciding how charity should be distributed. Any funds devoted to the latter would surely have contributed more to society if they had been devoted to improving still further the former.

Finally, I shall try to explain why my statement that "the social responsibility of business [is] to increase its profits" and Mackey's statement that "the enlightened corporation should try to create value for all of its constituencies" are equivalent.

Note first that I refer to *social* responsibility, not financial, or accounting, or legal. It is social precisely to allow for the constituencies to which Mackey refers. Maximizing profits is an end from the private point of view; it is a means from the social point of view. A system based on private property and free markets is a sophisticated means of enabling people to cooperate in their economic activities without compulsion; it enables separated knowledge to assure that each resource is used for its most valued use, and is combined with other resources in the most efficient way.

Of course, this is abstract and idealized. The world is not ideal. There are all sorts of deviations from the perfect market—many, if not most, I suspect, due to government interventions. But with all its defects, the current largely free-market, private-property world seems to me vastly preferable to a world in which a large fraction of resources is used and distributed by 501c(3)s and their corporate counterparts.

PUT PROFITS FIRST

T. J. Rodgers

John Mackey's article attacking corporate profit maximization could not have been written by "a free market libertarian," as claimed. Indeed, if the examples he cites had not identified him as the author, one could easily assume the piece was written by Ralph Nader. A more accurate title for his article is "How Business and Profit Making Fit Into My Overarching Philosophy of Altruism."

Mackey spouts nonsense about how his company hired his original investors, not vice versa. If Whole Foods ever falls on persistent hard times—perhaps when the Luddites are no longer able to hold back the genetic food revolution using junk science and fear—he will quickly find out who has hired whom, as his investors fire him.

Mackey does make one point that is consistent with, but not supportive of, free market capitalism. He knows that shareholders own his stock voluntarily. If they don't like the policies of his company, they can always vote to change those policies with a shareholder resolution or simply sell the stock and buy that of another company more aligned with their objectives. Thus, he informs his shareholders of his objectives and lets them make a choice on which stock to buy. So far, so good.

It is also simply good business for a company to cater to its customers, train and retain its employees, build long-term positive relationships with its suppliers, and become a good citizen in its community, including performing some philanthropic activity. When Milton Friedman says a company should stay "within the rules of the game" and operate "without deception or fraud," he means it should deal with all its various constituencies properly in order to maximize long-term shareholder value. He does not mean that a company should put every last nickel on the bottom line every quarter, regardless of the long-term consequences.

My company, Cypress Semiconductor, has won the trophy for the Second Harvest Food Bank competition for the most food donated per employee in Silicon Valley for the last 13 consecutive years (1 million pounds of food in 2004). The contest creates competition among our divisions, leading to employee involvement, company food drives, internal social events with admissions "paid for" by food donations, and so forth. It is a big employee morale builder, a way to attract new employees, good P.R. for the company, and a significant benefit to the community—all of which makes Cypress a better place to work and invest in. Indeed, Mackey's own proud example of Whole Foods' community involvement programs also made a profit.

But Mackey's subordination of his profession as a businessman to altruistic ideals shows up as he attempts to negate the empirically demonstrated social benefit of "self-interest" by defining it narrowly as "increasing short-term profits." Why is it that when Whole Foods gives money to a worthy cause, it serves a high moral objective, while a company that provides a good return to small investors—who simply put their money into their own retirement funds or a children's college fund—is somehow selfish? It's the philosophy that is objectionable here, not the specific actions. If Mackey wants to run a hybrid business/charity whose mission is fully disclosed to his shareholders—and if those shareholder-owners want to support that mission—so be it. But I balk at the proposition that a company's "stakeholders" (a term often used by collectivists to justify unreasonable demands) should be allowed to control the property of the shareholders. It seems Mackey's philosophy is more accurately described by Karl Marx: "From each according to his ability" (the shareholders surrender money and assets); "to each according to his needs" (the charities, social interest groups, and environmentalists get what they want). That's not free market capitalism.

Then there is the arrogant proposition that if other corporations would simply emulate the higher corporate life form defined by Whole Foods, the world would be better off. After all, Mackey says corporations are viewed as "selfish, greedy, and uncaring." I, for one, consider free market capitalism to be a high calling, even without the infusion of altruism practiced by Whole Foods.

If one goes beyond the sensationalistic journalism surrounding the Enron-like debacles, one discovers that only about 10 to 20 public corporations have been justifiably accused of serious wrongdoing. That's about 0.1 percent of America's 17,500 public companies. What's the failure rate of the publications that demean business? (Consider the *New York Times* scandal involving manufactured stories.) What's the percentage of U.S. presidents who have been forced or almost forced from office? (It's 10 times higher than the failure rate of corporations.) What percentage of our congressmen have spent time in jail? The fact is that despite some well-publicized failures, most corporations are run with the highest ethical standards—and the public knows it. Public opinion polls demonstrate that fact by routinely ranking businessmen above journalists and politicians in esteem.

I am proud of what the semiconductor industry does—relentlessly cutting the cost of a transistor from $3 in 1960 to *three-millionths* of a dollar today. Mackey would be keeping his business records with hordes of accountants on paper ledgers if our industry didn't exist. He would have to charge his poorest customers more for their food, pay his valued employees less, and cut his philanthropy programs if the semiconductor industry had not focused so relentlessly on increasing its profits, cutting his costs in the process. Of course, if the U.S. semiconductor industry had been less cost-competitive due to its own philanthropy, the food industry simply would have bought cheaper computers made from Japanese and Korean silicon chips (which happened anyway). Layoffs in the nonunion semiconductor industry were actually good news to Whole Foods' unionized grocery store clerks. Where was Mackey's sense of altruism when unemployed semiconductor workers needed it? Of course, that rhetorical question is foolish, since he did exactly the right thing by ruthlessly reducing his recordkeeping costs so as to maximize his profits.

I am proud to be a free market capitalist. And I resent the fact that Mackey's philosophy demeans me as an egocentric child because I have refused on moral grounds to embrace the philosophies of collectivism and altruism that have caused so much human misery, however tempting the sales pitch for them sounds.

PROFIT IS THE MEANS, NOT END

John Mackey

Let me begin my response to Milton Friedman by noting that he is one of my personal heroes. His contributions to economic thought and the fight for freedom are without parallel, and it is an honor to have him critique my article.

Friedman says "the differences between John Mackey and me regarding the social responsibility of business are for the most part rhetorical." But are we essentially in agreement? I don't think so. We are thinking about business in entirely different ways.

Friedman is thinking only in terms of maximizing profits for the investors. If putting customers first helps maximize profits for the investors, then it is acceptable. If some corporate philanthropy creates goodwill and helps a company "cloak" its self-interested goals of maximizing profits, then it is acceptable (although Friedman also believes it is "hypocritical"). In contrast to Friedman,

I do not believe maximizing profits for the investors is the only acceptable justification for all corporate actions. The investors are not the only people who matter. Corporations can exist for purposes other than simply maximizing profits.

As for who decides what the purpose of any particular business is, I made an important argument that Friedman doesn't address: "I believe the entrepreneurs, not the current investors in a company's stock, have the right and responsibility to define the purpose of the company." Whole Foods Market was not created solely to maximize profits for its investors, but to create value for all of its stakeholders. I believe there are thousands of other businesses similar to Whole Foods (Medtronic, REI, and Starbucks, for example) that were created by entrepreneurs with goals beyond maximizing profits, and that these goals are neither "hypocritical" nor "cloaking devices" but are intrinsic to the purpose of the business.

I will concede that many other businesses, such as T. J. Rodgers' Cypress Semiconductor, have been created by entrepreneurs whose sole purpose for the business is to maximize profits for their investors. Does Cypress therefore have any social responsibility besides maximizing profits if it follows the laws of society? No, it doesn't. Rodgers apparently created it solely to maximize profits, and therefore all of Friedman's arguments about business social responsibility become completely valid. Business social responsibility should not be coerced; it is a voluntary decision that the entrepreneurial leadership of every company must make on its own. Friedman is right to argue that profit making is intrinsically valuable for society, but I believe he is mistaken that all businesses have only this purpose.

While Friedman believes that taking care of customers, employees, and business philanthropy are means to the end of increasing investor profits, I take the exact opposite view: Making high profits is the means to the end of fulfilling Whole Foods' core business mission. We want to improve the health and well-being of everyone on the planet through higher-quality foods and better nutrition, and we can't fulfill this mission unless we are highly profitable. High profits are necessary to fuel our growth across the United States and the world. Just as people cannot live without eating, so a business cannot live without profits. But most people don't live to eat, and neither must a business live just to make profits.

Toward the end of his critique Friedman says his statement that "the social responsibility of business [is] to increase its profits" and my statement that "the enlightened corporation should try to create value for all of its constituencies" are "equivalent." He argues that maximizing profits is a private end achieved through social means because it supports a society based on private property and free markets. If our two statements are equivalent, if we really mean the same thing, then I know which statement has the superior "marketing power." Mine does.

Both capitalism and corporations are misunderstood, mistrusted, and disliked around the world because of statements like Friedman's on social responsibility. His comment is used by the enemies of capitalism to argue that capitalism is greedy, selfish, and uncaring. It is right up there with William Vanderbilt's "the public be damned" and former G.M. Chairman Charlie Wilson's declaration that "what's good for the country is good for General Motors, and vice versa." If we are truly interested in spreading capitalism throughout the world (I certainly am), we need to do a better job marketing it. I believe if economists and business people consistently communicated and acted on my message that "the enlightened corporation should try to create value for all of its constituencies," we would see most of the resistance to capitalism disappear.

Friedman also understands that Whole Foods makes an important contribution to society besides simply maximizing profits for our investors, which is to "enhance the pleasure of shopping for food." This is why we put "satisfying and delighting our customers" as a core value whenever we talk about the purpose of our business. Why don't Friedman and other economists consistently teach this idea? Why don't they talk more about all the valuable contributions that business makes in creating value for its customers, for its employees, and for its communities? Why talk only about maximizing profits for the investors? Doing so harms the brand of capitalism.

As for Whole Foods' philanthropy, who does have "special competence" in this area? Does the government? Do individuals? Libertarians generally would agree that most bureaucratic government solutions to social problems cause more harm than good and that government help is seldom the answer. Neither do individuals have any special competence in charity. By Friedman's logic, individuals shouldn't donate any money to help others but should instead keep all their money invested in businesses, where it will create more social value.

The truth is that there is no way to calculate whether money invested in business or money invested in helping to solve social problems will create more value. Businesses exist within real communities and have real effects, both good and bad, on those communities. Like individuals living in communities, businesses make valuable social contributions by providing goods and services and employment. But just as individuals can feel a responsibility to provide some philanthropic support for the communities in which they live, so too can a business. The responsibility of business toward the community is not infinite, but neither is it zero. Each enlightened business must find the proper balance between all of its constituencies: customers, employees, investors, suppliers, and communities.

While I respect Milton Friedman's thoughtful response, I do not feel the same way about T. J. Rodgers' critique. It is obvious to me that Rodgers didn't carefully read my article, think deeply about my arguments, or attempt to craft an intelligent response. Instead he launches various ad hominem attacks on me, my company, and our customers. According to Rodgers, my business philosophy is similar to those of Ralph Nader and Karl Marx; Whole Foods Market and our customers are a bunch of Luddites engaging in junk science and fear mongering; and our unionized grocery clerks don't care about layoffs of workers in Rodgers' own semiconductor industry.

For the record: I don't agree with the philosophies of Ralph Nader or Karl Marx; Whole Foods Market doesn't engage in junk science or fear mongering, and neither do 99 percent of our customers or vendors; and of Whole Foods' 36,000 employees, exactly zero of them belong to unions, and we are in fact sorry about layoffs in his industry.

When Rodgers isn't engaging in ad hominem attacks, he seems to be arguing against a leftist, socialist, and collectivist perspective that may exist in his own mind but does not appear in my article. Contrary to Rodgers' claim, Whole Foods is running not a "hybrid business/charity" but an enormously profitable business that has created tremendous shareholder value.

Of all the food retailers in the *Fortune 500* (including Wal-Mart), we have the highest profits as a percentage of sales, as well as the highest return on invested capital, sales per square foot, same-store sales, and growth rate. We are currently doubling in size every three and a half years. The bottom line is that Whole Foods stakeholder business philosophy works and has produced tremendous value for all of our stakeholders, including our investors.

In contrast, Cypress Semiconductor has struggled to be profitable for many years now, and their balance sheet shows negative retained earnings of over $408 million. This means that in its entire 23-year history, Cypress has lost far more money for its investors than it has made. Instead of calling my business philosophy Marxist, perhaps it is time for Rodgers to rethink his own.

Rodgers says with passion, "I am proud of what the semiconductor industry does—relentlessly cutting the cost of a transistor from $3 in 1960 to *three-millionths* of a dollar today." Rodgers is entitled to be proud. What a wonderful accomplishment this is, and the semiconductor industry has indeed made all our lives better. Then why not consistently communicate this message as the purpose of his business, instead of talking all the time about maximizing profits and shareholder value? Like medicine, law, and education, business has noble purposes: to provide goods and services that improve its customers' lives, to provide jobs and meaningful work for employees, to create wealth and prosperity for its investors, and to be a responsible and caring citizen.

Businesses such as Whole Foods have multiple stakeholders and therefore have multiple responsibilities. But the fact that we have responsibilities to stakeholders besides investors does not give those other stakeholders any "property rights" in the company, contrary to Rodgers' fears. The investors still own the business, are entitled to the residual profits, and can fire the management if they wish. A doctor has an ethical responsibility to try to heal her patients, but that responsibility doesn't mean her patients are entitled to receive a share of the profits from her practice.

Rodgers probably will never agree with my business philosophy, but it doesn't really matter. The ideas I'm articulating result in a more robust business model than the profit-maximization model that it competes against, because they encourage and tap into more powerful motivations than self-interest alone. These ideas will triumph over time, not by persuading intellectuals and economists through argument but by winning the competitive test of the marketplace. Someday businesses like Whole Foods, which adhere to a stakeholder model of deeper business purpose, will dominate the economic landscape. Wait and see.

Reading

The Collapse and Transformation of Our World

Duncan M. Taylor
University of Victoria, Canada

Graeme M. Taylor
BEST Futures Project, Australia

TERRORISM WILL NOT DESTROY GLOBAL CIVILIZATION; OUR CIVILIZATION WILL DESTROY ITSELF

The world as we know it is coming to an end. Industrial civilization will soon collapse because of a fatal flaw: it is designed to grow constantly within a finite planet. *[Diagram 1]* Our economic system has reached its global limits of growth and is now unsustainable. Humanity is currently using 25% more renewable resources

each year than the biosphere is producing (World Wildlife Fund 2006). This is deficit spending, which means that we are now consuming the biophysical foundations of our civilization. *[Diagram 2]* The pace of environmental destruction is likely to accelerate: between the year 2006 and 2050 the world population is projected to increase from 6 billion to 8.9 billion (United Nations 2004), while world consumption is projected to almost quadruple (Poncet 2006).

While world population, per capita consumption and expectations are increasing, resources are declining. On every continent water tables are dropping,

DIAGRAM 1   Our expansionist economic model was developed at a time when there were unexplored frontiers and natural resources seemed limitless.

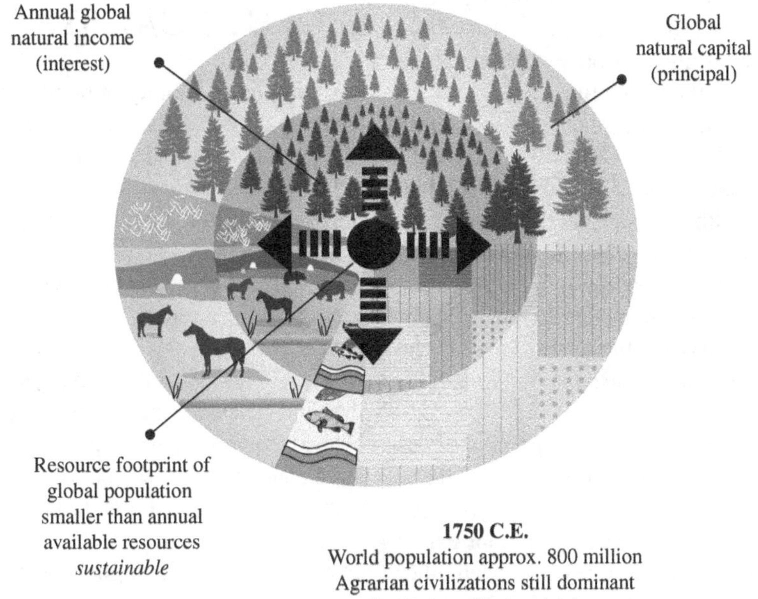

Annual global
natural income
(interest)

Global
natural capital
(principal)

Resource footprint of
global population
smaller than annual
available resources
sustainable

1750 C.E.
World population approx. 800 million
Agrarian civilizations still dominant
Beginning of Industrial Age

DIAGRAM 2   Globalization marks the end of unexplored terrestrial frontiers. An economic system based on limitless growth is no longer viable.

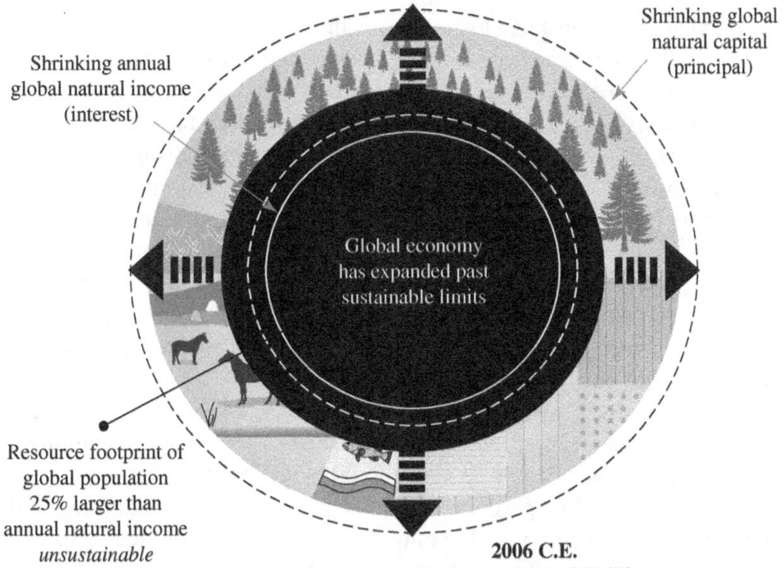

Shrinking annual
global natural income
(interest)

Shrinking global
natural capital
(principal)

Global economy
has expanded past
sustainable limits

Resource footprint of
global population
25% larger than
annual natural income
unsustainable

2006 C.E.
World population 6.5 billion
Global industrial economy
Consumer culture

forests are disappearing, major fisheries are degrading, topsoil is eroding, oil and mineral discoveries are becoming rarer, and the air is being polluted. If present trends continue, global warming alone may cause the extinction of 25% of all existing animal and plant species within 50 years (Tidwell 2006).

Our health and survival is dependent on the health and survival of the complex ecosystems that support life on our planet. Already we are beginning to witness the cascading collapse of interconnected ecosystems (Bright 2000). As a result the foundations of industrial civilization have also begun to collapse.

Environmental and demographic trends alone indicate that the frequency, severity and scale of crises will escalate over the next two decades. These regional crises will progressively interact with each other to create global crises. A failing world economy will affect increasing numbers of people, who will begin to question the values and institutions of the current world order. At this point humanity will reach a bifurcation point: our unsustainable global civilization will either transform itself into a sustainable global civilization, or it will enter a prolonged period of escalating crises marked by the collapse of vital ecosystems, conflicts over disappearing resources, population decline, political fragmentation, and economic and social regression.

One way or the other the world as we know it will soon end.

In the next sections we will examine three issues: why global industrial civilization is unsustainable; what the requirements are for a sustainable civilization; and how we can help a peaceful and sustainable global civilization evolve out of the coming collapse of our social and natural worlds.

SOCIAL SYSTEMS ARE DEPENDENT ON BIOPHYSICAL SYSTEMS

The long-term viability of human societies is utterly dependent on the long-term viability of the biophysical systems that support them. Consequently, the long-term sustainability of human systems requires the maintenance and restoration of ecosystem integrity, resilience, and biodiversity. Industrial economies are unsustainable because they are based on a mechanistic worldview: reality is made up of discrete objects rather than interrelated systems. As a result they convert "natural capital" into manufactured and financial capital without taking into account environmental costs. *[Diagram 3]*

Industrial civilization will continue to destroy its own life support systems because its economic system is based upon continuous material growth, and continuous material growth involves the constant degradation of biophysical systems.

Driving our unsustainable global economy is an unsustainable culture. The consumer culture creates false needs for power, status and wealth instead of satisfying real needs for meaning, community and survival. Consumer society creates the illusion of scarcity in the rich world, where people try to satisfy their emotional and spiritual needs through consuming things, and real scarcity in the poor world, where the resources do not exist to meet basic human needs for food, shelter, health and education.

Because real human needs cannot be satisfied by a consumer culture, people will never feel that they have enough and there will never be an end to the destruction of the environment. However, our most basic need is to survive, and without a liveable environment we will not survive.

DIAGRAM 3   Orthodox economics dismisses social and environmental costs as "externalities." This means that values such as health and well-being are not included in economic modelling, planning or accounting.

Will Economists Realize that
Fresh Air and Water Have Value?
Money is not the real bottom line

A culture based on greed is not just morally wrong, it is unsustainable.

TECHNOLOGICAL SOLUTIONS CANNOT FIX SOCIAL PROBLEMS

Every developing country in the world is counting on technological breakthroughs and increased production to provide them with the standards of living of industrialized countries. It can't be done. The resources of four more Planet Earths would be needed for everyone on the planet to have an American life style. *[Diagram 4]* Despite this fact, in almost every country advertising is urging people to live like Americans. The people of the world are being sold an impossible dream.

Although modern industrial development has improved the living standards of much of the world's population, all further plans for meeting the needs of humanity through increasing the consumption of natural resources are unrealistic, given that the carrying capacity of the biosphere is already in decline. In the coming decades the global economy will have not more but fewer resources at its disposal. *[Diagram 5]* It will not be enough to reduce the rate of destructive growth if we wish to avoid the total collapse of human civilization: the process of destruction has to be reversed and the environment restored.

Moreover, in order to meet the minimal needs of a growing global population, resources will have to be redistributed. Ecosystems will only be preserved when humans enjoy peace and basic prosperity,

DIAGRAM 4   The per capita ecological footprint is a tool for measuring the average annual resource consumption and waste output of individuals. (World Wildlife Fund 2006)

= 1.8 ha.   Each person's fair earthshare in 2003.

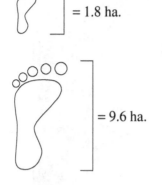

= 9.6 ha.   The average footprint of U.S. citizens in 2003.

Human economies will only survive over the long-term if they are able to function within the carrying capacity of planet Earth.

The resources of 4 more planets would be needed for everyone in the world to live like Americans. The globalization of the American consumer society is not possible.

DIAGRAM 5   The problem is that average per capita footprints are increasing each year, not decreasing.

2.2 ha. =
Average per capita global footprint in 2003

= 1.8 ha.
Fair earthshare in 2003 with a world population of 6 billion

20% reduction needed in 2003

The annual per capita ecological deficit was approximately 25% in 2003.

The global per capita footprint needs to be reduced now if human economies are to be sustainable.

2.2 ha. =
Average per capita global footprint in 2003

= 1.25 ha.
Estimated fair earthshare in 2050 with a world population of 9 billion

43% reduction from 2003 consumption needed by 2050

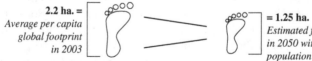

since desperately poor people are often compelled to scavenge their environments and fight over scarce resources in their efforts to survive. It will not be possible to create a sustainable planet unless the disparities between rich and poor are greatly reduced. However, at present global inequality is steadily increasing (Milanovic 2005).

Many people hoped that the introduction of information technologies would reduce the need for natural resources and human labour. Instead profits have been increased through increasing the intensity of production. Smokestack industries have not disappeared; they have simply been transferred from high-wage to low-wage countries.

New technologies may delay the collapse of industrial civilization, but they will not prevent it. While technological advances will reduce waste and improve efficiencies, they will not change the values and social structures that promote unsustainable exploitation, inequality, greed and war.

OUR UNSUSTAINABLE GLOBAL CIVILIZATION CANNOT BE MADE SUSTAINABLE

It will be argued that the collapse of contemporary civilization will not happen because governments and businesses will eventually act to avert the developing crises. The reality is that the politicians and business leaders that govern our world will not and can not reallocate the resources of their countries and corporations in order to develop a peaceful, equitable and sustainable global system.

All the material resources and scientific knowledge needed to resolve the major problems on the planet have been available for decades, but the will to change the political and economic priorities of society

has not. As a result increasing global wealth has been accompanied by increasing global poverty. Although many leaders have good intentions, their efforts to implement change are constrained by the existing system, whose worldview, values and structures oppose the development of new priorities such as the reduction of consumption and the redistribution of wealth.

We can be certain that politicians and business leaders will increasingly respond to the collapse of vital ecosystems and the rising cost of scarce resources through implementing policies for "sustainable development." However, to date most of these policies have been designed to sustain growth (quantitative expansion) rather than to develop sustainability (qualitative transformation). Attempts to adjust the existing system without making fundamental changes will not work because all growth-based development is ultimately unsustainable (Daly 2005).

Humanity has no choice: if global civilization is to survive, it must evolve into a completely new type of societal system. A consumer society cannot be transformed into a conserver society without structural change.

A CIVILIZATION WILL ONLY BE SUSTAINABLE IF IT CAN SATISFY HUMANITY'S REAL NEEDS

In the 1987 Brundtland Report, sustainability was defined as "meeting the needs of the present without compromising the ability of future generations to meet their own needs" (World Commission on Environment and Development 1987: 1). Sustainable development has also been defined as "improving the quality of human life while living within the carrying capacity of supporting ecosystems" (World Conservation Union et al. 1991: 10). Human needs are more than simply material needs for food, shelter and safety: they are also needs for health and wholeness, for meaning and belonging, for relationship to one's community and biophysical context.

Advertising sells the illusion that qualitative needs can be satisfied by quantitative consumption. Because most emotional and spiritual needs cannot be met by acquiring things, people continue to consume in vain efforts to find comfort and satisfaction.

For this reason industrial civilization is not only environmentally unsustainable but socially unsustainable: it creates emotional scarcity in the overdeveloped world and material scarcity in the underdeveloped world. In the rich world mental illnesses and addictions are widespread, and communities and families are fragile. Globally, the rich nations are plagued by obesity while poor nations are plagued by hunger; more research is done on developing cosmetics for the rich than on discovering cures for the diseases of the poor; and many of the best scientists are developing new weapons for countries that can already destroy all life on the planet.

The self-destructive behaviours of industrial civilization prevent it from meeting real needs. Complex human societies will only survive if the current unhealthy and unsustainable global economy is replaced with a sustainable economy based on the maintenance of social, physical and biophysical health and wholeness.

Human society will only be able to end scarcity, and international competition over limited resources, when it is able to satisfy the minimal physical, emotional, mental, and spiritual needs of all the humans on the planet. This means that we need to replace an unsustainable system that is designed to increase the quantity of things, with a sustainable system that is designed to improve the quality of people's lives. And, in turn, because basic human rights and a quality of life cannot be achieved in a degraded and toxic environment, these goals will only be met by also meeting the needs of the planet's biophysical systems and protecting their millions of life forms.

HUMAN NEEDS INCLUDE NEEDS FOR COMMUNITY, MEANING, IDENTITY, AND JUSTICE

As industrial civilization expands, it consumes and degrades not only natural resources, but also other civilizations and cultures. When it comes in contact with traditional agrarian or tribal societies, the force and attraction of its superior power and wealth begin to break down the economies, values, and social institutions of the older societies.

Rapid urbanization has been accompanied by soaring rates of poverty, crime, and addiction. While industrial civilization has provided personal freedom to more people than ever before, the price has often been the loss of community and meaning.

Identity and resource conflicts only occur when people believe that their needs are not being met or are being threatened. People compete and fight over material goods when they fear material scarcity, and people compete and fight over religious, ethnic and national issues when they fear the loss of cultural identities.

Industrial civilization perpetuates conflict by perpetuating fear and alienation:

it pits the individual good against the common good and material needs against emotional needs. In order to eliminate war and preserve the environment, a sustainable global system will have to meet the full range of human spiritual, social, material, and biophysical needs, including our needs for meaning, identity, and justice. While current social structures facilitate competition, inequality, injustice, and conflict, sustainable structures will need to facilitate cooperation, equality, justice, and peaceful conflict resolution.

A SUSTAINABLE GLOBAL CIVILIZATION MUST VALUE INTERDEPENDENCE AND DIVERSITY

Two mass extinctions are taking place on our planet. Our current civilization is not only destroying species, it is also destroying cultures. There were 6000 languages spoken on Earth in the year 2000. Half of these will have disappeared by 2050 (Davis 2001). With the extinction of each ancient culture, humanity will lose a unique perspective along with knowledge accumulated over thousands of years.

Individual species risk extinction when they lose critical habitat and genetic diversity, and with these the ability to adapt to environmental stressors. Since human knowledge and behaviours are primarily transmitted through culture rather than genes, the loss of cultural diversity similarly threatens the survival of complex societies.

Not only are healthy species genetically diverse, but healthy ecosystems are composed of a wide variety of interdependent species. The diversity increases the system's resilience, which is its ability to manage fluctuations and change. Systemic resilience is lost with the destruction of both human cultural diversity as well as ecosystem biodiversity, increasing the likelihood of widespread social and biophysical collapse (Berkes et al. 2003).

The cultural requirements of a sustainable global societal system are similar to the biological requirements of a sustainable ecosystem: values and institutions must foster wholeness, interdependence, diversity, and resilience.

Industrial civilization globalizes inequality and concentrates power at the expense of local autonomy, community, and diversity. As the many varieties of human civilizations and societies become undifferentiated parts of an expanding societal monoculture, the system loses checks and balances. The result is an increasingly closely connected but unstable world system: new crises can rapidly spread throughout the system's political and economic structures. Over the next decades the number and complexity of large crises will grow, eventually producing uncontrollable fluctuations and the potential for total system failure.

VIABLE SOCIETIES WILL REQUIRE MORE EFFICIENT AND LESS BUREAUCRATIC SOCIAL STRUCTURES

In the past many successful societies have expanded to the point where their resources could no longer maintain their increasingly complex social structures. When easily accessed resources were exhausted, they were forced to seek out ever more distant and expensive resources.

Eventually the political, economic, and military cost of acquiring new resources reached an unsustainable point and the societies collapsed. Our industrial civilization, with its bureaucratic structures and expansionist economy, is following the same unsustainable trajectory of other great civilizations (Tainter 1988).

The majority of industrial countries are democratic and capitalist to varying degrees. However, whether they have democratic or totalitarian governments and market or planned economies, all industrial societies are composed of interconnected layers of centralized structures supported by large regulatory institutions. These bureaucratic structures are necessary because industrial society is a system of minority rule.

The competing nations, institutions, and corporations in industrial societies have social structures that distribute power and wealth unevenly within and between countries. Elites in every country and institution collect information, make decisions, and then enforce compliance through regulations and sanctions. Because this societal system is based on inequality, it can only be maintained through complex financial and regulatory bureaucracies and repressive military, police, and judicial systems.

In order to meet the real needs of humanity in a sustainable fashion, human societies must eliminate unnecessary waste, including the enormous cost of regulation and repression. Currently much of the world's economy is engaged in unproductive activities connected with the control of power and wealth. A sustainable economy will have to reallocate human and natural resources away from socially dysfunctional activities and towards activities that promote health and wholeness.

Although a sustainable global societal system will be more advanced (i.e. more differentiated and complex) than industrial civilization, it will not be able to support larger bureaucratic structures. If complex societies are to survive, humanity must develop new economic structures that utilize energy and resources more efficiently, and new political structures that more efficiently process information and allocate tasks and resources.

SUSTAINABLE SOCIETIES MUST BE DECENTRALIZED AND SELF-REGULATING

Industrial civilization has an inefficient structure that wastes the creative potential of most of humanity. The concentration of information and decision-making at a few powerful centres creates bottlenecks in which critical parts of the social network are overloaded while most of the system is underutilized.

The practical alternative to centralized decision-making is decentralized decision-making. In order to function more efficiently, political and economic structures will have to be transformed from being primarily centralized to being primarily decentralized, and from being primarily focused on the production of quantities of goods for trade to being primarily focused on improving the local quality of life.

A decentralized network can improve efficiency by giving all its parts the ability to respond flexibly and autonomously to local conditions. The need for energy and resources can be reduced by having most social and environmental needs met at the local level with local resources (Madron & Jopling 2003).

Although most needs can be met at a local level, not all functions can or should be devolved: for example, regional issues need to be dealt with at a regional level and global issues need to be dealt with at a global level. Indeed, national and international environmental and human rights standards are necessary as buffers to guard against any infringement of these rights at the local or regional levels. A decentralized network will require a holarchical structure that supports the appropriate distribution of power and resources and the appropriate self-regulation of each node and level.

In reality we have not yet made the transition from an industrial economy to an information economy. The world is still dominated by mechanistic—not systemic—values and structures. The principal use for new technologies has been and will be to reinforce existing unsustainable political and economic institutions. Information technologies will not become an integral part of a new societal system until sustainable holarchical social structures begin to form in the midst of the collapse of industrial civilization.

SUSTAINABLE SOCIETIES REQUIRE INTEGRAL WORLDVIEWS

Most national governments have highly centralized forms of political decision making. These not only restrict access to information, power and resources, but also make it difficult for most people to participate in political and economic decision-making. Although most industrial countries are democracies, most people have little say in the day-to-day decisions made in their workplaces or communities.

To the extent that people can participate in the political process, many do not because they are poorly informed and motivated. A major cause of public apathy is that knowledge in industrial civilization is fragmented, specialized, and controlled. Life in the consumer society is morally and intellectually contradictory, and this confusion is corrosive and disempowering. Because the consumer worldview represents the commodification of both humans and the natural world, it promotes the illusion of a separate self that exists independently of both the larger human and biophysical communities (Sivaraksa 2002). On the other hand, more local and decentralized communities help to foster a greater sense of caring both for other humans and for the local environment (Norberg-Hodge 2002).

However, a decentralized societal network will only function if every part at every level is capable of appropriate self-regulation and self-organization. Self-regulation is only possible if the system gives all its nodes the ability to control their own lives, communities, and natural environments.

People and communities will need greater access to the theoretical and practical tools required for self-direction, self-regulation, self-organization, and constructive action. For this to occur, the dominant industrial model must give way to an integral model that recognizes the inextricable interconnectedness of both human and biophysical systems and the environmental limitations placed on human activities. A fragmenting worldview must be replaced with an integrating worldview, since people can only control their lives when their understanding of reality permits them to act effectively in the real world.

A sustainable society will need values and social structures that support the relatively egalitarian distribution of power, information and resources to every part of the system. The shift from a primarily centralized societal system to a primarily decentralized societal system is the shift from partial democracy to participatory democracy.

ENTERING THE BIFURCATION: CIVILIZATION WILL EITHER COLLAPSE OR TRANSFORM

There are only three possibilities for the future of civilization:

a. Cascading environmental crises will rapidly escalate, producing uncontrollable economic and political crises. At some point these crises will cause the catastrophic collapse of the societal system. This process may produce irreversible damage to social and biophysical systems.

b. Political and business leaders will proactively respond to the growing crises through supporting environmentally friendly technologies, introducing policies for sustainable development and preventing political unrest. These efforts will slow the rate of environmental destruction and help to extend the life of industrial civilization. However, attempts to improve the system without redesigning its unsustainable structure will ultimately fail. Over time efforts to manage crises will consume more and more scarce resources and industrial civilization will collapse.

c. As regional and global crises increase and the world economy begins to fail, the ability of existing political and economic structures to influence and control people will weaken. Growing numbers of people will question the values of contemporary civilization and start to organize alternative structures. Maintaining and restoring large areas of the earth's biosphere will become an international priority. At this point a successful transformation to a sustainable societal system is possible if new values and technologies have already developed an appropriate worldview—one capable of organizing functional new social structures. Should this happen, the collapse of contemporary civilization will become a springboard for the evolution of a sustainable civilization.

Our B.E.S.T (Biosocial Evolutionary Systems Theory) Model suggests that we are beginning a period of major societal and biophysical transformation. *[Diagram 6]* Since World War II there has been a dramatic accumulation and concentration of wealth as well as the rapid conversion of natural capital to manufactured and financial capital. With this has also come the emergence of greater vulnerability, due to the increasing number of interconnections that link that wealth and those that control and maintain it. This growing connectedness leads to increasing rigidity and brittleness as the system becomes ever more tightly bound together. This has reduced resilience and the capacity of the system to absorb change, thus increasing the threat of abrupt change.

As we enter the backloop of reorganization, we shall witness a collapse of existing structures and accumulated

DIAGRAM 6

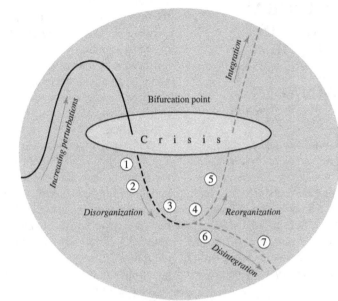

The springboard effect helps systems reorganize

① People lose faith in the industrial system as crises worsen

② Human and economic resources are released from the system

③ Support increases for both inclusive (sustainable) and exclusive (ethnocentric) solutions

④ If sustainable solutions are supported, constructive reorganization begins

⑤ The reorganization of the global system accelerates
or

⑥ If ethnocentric values and structures dominate, conflicts over scarce resources intensify

⑦ Global civilization disintegrates

connections, and the release of bound-up knowledge and capital (Gunderson & Holling 2002). On the one hand, this collapse will inevitably initiate a reversion to "lower" levels of response in the form of "blood and belonging" and "us/them" forms of fear-based security reactions. On the other hand, the creative aspect of this backloop destruction is bound up with the release of knowledge and the appearance of new or latent elements which can then be re-associated in novel and unexpected ways to trigger re-growth and reorganization into fundamentally new forms of learning and innovative social patterns.

THE EMERGENCE OF AN INTEGRAL WORLDVIEW IS CRITICAL FOR THE CREATION OF A SUSTAINABLE SOCIETAL SYSTEM

For the first time in history, humanity shares a common concern: industrial civilization will not survive a catastrophic collapse of our environment. As a result, humanity shares a common challenge: to ensure that the emerging elements of a sustainable global system are sufficiently self-organized to be able to successfully transform the existing system and prevent catastrophic collapse.

Evolution is an unpredictable process that involves the emergence of previously unknown properties that take hold and spread because they are more relevant and functional than previously existing attributes (Laszlo 1987). While we know that industrial civilization is no longer viable,

we do not know all the new properties that will evolve during the transformation of the current global system to a sustainable system. We can be sure that the process of transformation cannot be dictated by any center: evolution is an organic process and a sustainable, decentralized, and empowered societal system can only develop in a process of self-creation and self-organization.

A new paradigm began to develop over a hundred years ago with the discovery of force fields and relativity theory. Important emerging elements of the new integral society are now everywhere. Some examples are quantum mechanics, computer networks, feminism, ecology, conflict resolution, the peace movement, nongovernmental organizations and the International Criminal Court.

However, the emerging property that will be critical for the creation of a sustainable global societal system is an integral worldview (Wilber 1998), as it will provide the organizing pattern around which sustainable social institutions can be formed. *[Diagram 7]* The articulation of

DIAGRAM 7

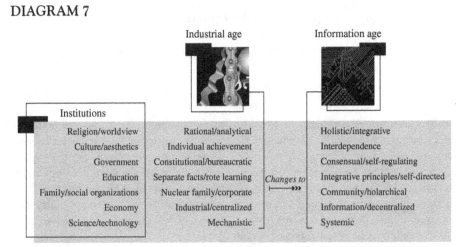

Institutions	Industrial age	Information age
Religion/worldview	Rational/analytical	Holistic/integrative
Culture/aesthetics	Individual achievement	Interdependence
Government	Constitutional/bureaucratic	Consensual/self-regulating
Education	Separate facts/rote learning	Integrative principles/self-directed
Family/social organizations	Nuclear family/corporate	Community/holarchical
Economy	Industrial/centralized	Information/decentralized
Science/technology	Mechanistic	Systemic

Changes to ▸▸▸

The Universal Culture Pattern   The Evolving Culture Pattern this holonic, systems-based worldview will assist with the development and integration of emerging theories, values, and organizations. Many people have contributed to the science behind an integral worldview; we are writing this article in order to help it emerge as a coherent perspective.

PEACEFUL TRANSFORMATION WILL ONLY OCCUR IF THE NEW STRUCTURES INCLUDE AND TRANSCEND THE OLD

The process of changing global values and structures will inevitably be difficult, uneven, and protracted. The driving forces behind change will be, on the one hand, increasing resource shortages and collapsing ecosystems, and, on the other, the emergence of sustainable technologies and an integral worldview. Different ethnopolitical groups and organizations will support or oppose change depending on their values, interests, and understandings.

In order to make a successful transformation to a viable global system people must be educated about our common need: if we wish to survive, all human societies must become sustainable. The key to successful conflict resolution is maximizing cooperation around common interests while minimizing competition over scarce resources and differing values (Cloke 2001).

Resistance to change occurs when people believe that they have more to lose than to gain. The expansion of industrial society is still being resisted by many agrarian and pre-agrarian societies because they fear the loss of meaning and

community. A successful transformation to a sustainable civilization must include and transcend older societal systems through retaining the positive aspects of the older societies while meeting a wider range of needs. Although ruling elites and societal inertia will inevitably oppose change, much opposition can be avoided through promoting values of diversity and inclusiveness.

The cure for a dying planet cannot be the replacement of one monoculture by another; instead we need to create a global system that promotes and protects both cultural diversity and biodiversity. In order to support resilience, a viable global system should include a variety of sustainable societal systems from simple (e.g. hunter-gatherer economies) to complex (e.g. information-based economies).

ORGANIZING FOR CHANGE

People in every country need to know that while systemic change is inevitable, destructive outcomes are not. Positive change is possible if concerned people unite around a common vision of a peaceful and sustainable planet. The Earth Charter calls for international agreement to "help build a sustainable world based on respect for nature, universal human rights, economic justice and a culture of peace" (Earth Charter Initiative 2000: 1).

A global movement needs to be mobilized to secure international agreements on the following points:

1. Because our planet has finite resources, there are limits to growth. If the global economy continues to exceed sustainable limits it will destroy its biophysical foundations and collapse.

DIAGRAM 8

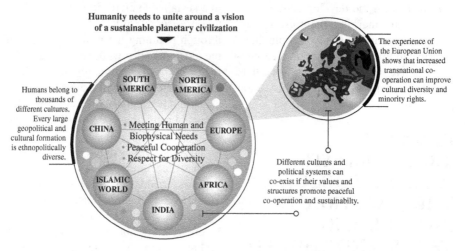

Humanity needs to unite around a vision of a sustainable planetary civilization

Humans belong to thousands of different cultures. Every large geopolitical and cultural formation is ethnopolitically diverse.

SOUTH AMERICA

NORTH AMERICA

CHINA

EUROPE

ISLAMIC WORLD

AFRICA

INDIA

• Meeting Human and Biophysical Needs
• Peaceful Cooperation
• Respect for Diversity

The experience of the European Union shows that increased transnational co-operation can improve cultural diversity and minority rights.

Different cultures and political systems can co-exist if their values and structures promote peaceful co-operation and sustainabilty.

2. Our collective survival depends on human economies becoming sustainable.

3. Essential human and biophysical needs must be met in order for human economies to be sustainable.

4. Resources must be redistributed to meet essential human and biophysical needs.

5. Cultural and genetic diversity is essential for health and wholeness.

6. In order for different cultures and societal systems to coexist, their values and structures must promote peaceful co-operation and sustainability. *[Diagram 8]*

References

Berkes, Fikret and Johan Colding and Carl Folke, eds. (2003). *Navigating Social-Ecological Systems: Building Resilience for Complexity and Change.* Cambridge: Cambridge University.

Bright, Chris. (2000). "Anticipating Environmental Surprise." In Linda Starke, ed., *State of the World 2000.* New York: W.W. Norton & Company. Pp. 26–39.

Cloke, Kenneth. (2001). *Mediating Dangerously.* San Francisco: Jossey-Bass Publishers.

Daly, Herman. (2005). "Economics in a Full World." *Scientific American.* 293(3): 100–107.

Davis, Wade. (2001). *Light at the Edge of the World.* Vancouver: Douglas & McIntyre Press.

Earth Charter Initiative (2000). *The Earth Charter.* Available at <http://www.earthcharter.org/files/charter/charter.pdf>, accessed on December 15, 2004.

Gunderson, Lance and C. S. Holling. (2002). *Panarchy: Understanding Transformations in Human and Natural Systems.* Washington: Island Press.

Laszlo, Ervin. (1987). *Evolution: The Grand Synthesis.* Boston: Shambhala Publications.

Madron, Roy and John Jopling. (2003). *Gaian Democracies: Redefining Globalisation and People Power.* Totnes: Green Books.

Milanovic, Branko. (2005). *Worlds Apart.* Princeton: Princeton University Press.

Norberg-Hodge, Helena. (2002). "The Pressure to Moderize and Globalize." In Jerry Mander and Edward Goldsmith, eds., *The Case Against the Global Economy.* San Francisco: Sierra Books. Pp. 33–46.

Poncet, Sandra. (2006). *The Long Term Prospects of the World Economy: Horizon 2050.* Available at <http://www.cepii.fr>, accessed on December 7, 2006.

Sivaraksa, Sulak. (2002). "Alternatives to Consumerism." In Alan Badiner, ed., *Mindfulness in the Marketplace— Compassionate Responses to Consumerism.* San Francisco: Parallax Press. P. 135.

Tainter, Joseph. (1988). *The Collapse of Complex Societies.* Melbourne: Cambridge University Press.

Tidwell, John. (2006). "Global Warming Capable of Sparking Mass Species Extinctions." Posted online at *Conservation International.* Available at <http://www.conservation.org>, accessed on April 11, 2006.

United Nations Department of Economic and Social Affairs. (2006). *World Population Prospects: the 2004 Revision Population Database.* Available at <http://www.un.org/esa/population/unpop.htm, accessed on December 19, 2006.

Wilber, Ken. (1998). *The Marriage of Sense and Soul.* New York: Random House.

World Commission on Environment and Development. (1987). *Report of the World Commission on Environment and Development.* Available at <http://www.un.org/documents/ga/res/42/ares42–187.htm>, accessed on August 15, 2004.

World Conservation Union, United Nations Environment Program & World Wide Fund For Nature. (1991). *Caring for the Earth.* Available at <http://coombs.anu.edu.au/~vern/caring/caring.html>, accessed on August 15, 2004.

World Wildlife Fund. (2006). *Living Planet Report 2006.* P. 1. Available at <http://www.panda.org>, accessed on December 19, 2006.

Module Two

Changing the Game (from Vision to Adaptation)

INTRODUCTION

To make change successful, some picture of the desired future state—a vision—is essential. Visions, of course, are about change, about achieving or becoming something better. There is much to be said about vision, and much of this module is devoted to saying it. But the dynamic nature of most of the changes in business in recent years means that, more than anything, visions need to be adaptable, and adaptation itself may be even more important than vision.

A 1998 study of chief executives in Europe asked what skills and characteristics these top managers saw as essential to their own performance, versus that of their successors in five to ten years' time. "Vision" was number two for the then-CEOs, but only number five, as they saw it, for their successors of today. Highest of all in the successor column was "adaptability in new situations" (AESC, 1998). This assessment has been more than borne out by the succeeding turbulence across markets and regions in the ensuing decade. In fact, if there is one aspect of change that seems to be changing the most, it is the necessity for leaders not only to plan and motivate, but to constantly seek new knowledge about forces beyond their control that will require them to adjust their plans, and to find new ways of influencing others to adapt accordingly, often in mid-execution.

Still, "visions," "visionaries," and "envisioning" are concepts everyone agrees are essential to change; indeed, common sense tells us that a change must be "seen," its direction in some way charted, before anything happens. Someone, or a group of people, must be authorized—explicitly or implicitly—to come up with that vision. In the words of Dennis Hightower, the protagonist of a case in Module 5, "If you don't know where you're going, any road will take you there."

At the same time, vision is a vexing idea, frustratingly difficult to pin down. Noted one CEO in a study that remains the basis for much important work on goal-setting, "I've come to believe that we need a vision to guide us, but I can't seem to get my hands on what 'vision' is" (Collins and Porras, 1991, p. 31). This is hardly surprising. "Vision" in the non-business world reverberates with contradictions, denoting at the same time dreams and impracticability, as well as unusual competence in discernment or perception. Definitions of vision within the business environment also are elusive. Collins and Porras investigated "visionary" organizations and concluded that "vision is an overarching concept under which a variety of concepts are subsumed." They divided vision into two components, guiding philosophy and tangible image: "Guiding philosophy is deep and serene; tangible image is bold, exciting, and emotionally charged" (Collins and Porras, 1991, pp. 32, 42).

In considering how the game of change management has changed, we would argue that while tangible image is important, it is guiding philosophy—culture and values, as others have put it (including Clayton Christensen and Michael Overdorf in Module 1)—that allows organizations to sustain and develop themselves (that is, to change by adapting) over time. This is fundamentally because tangible images, difficult as they may be to conceive and propagate successfully, are more and more subject to alteration as the forces of technology and innovation, globalization, and customer preference act on their markets. A guiding philosophy from which members of an organization can make local decisions on how to respond to challenges and opportunities is thus more important than a shared picture of what the organization wishes to become.

Thus, while it is still important to consider visionary thinking, it is not the *sine qua non* it once was. No matter how compelling the vision and how dynamic the leadership style of the visionary, the true test of an organization's ability to change lies in its ability to adapt to market forces, to be flexible and innovative in the face of a turbulent environment. The cases and readings in this module have been chosen to introduce the terrain that vision and adaptation occupy, working their way from the former to the latter.

OVERVIEW OF CASES AND READINGS

The module begins with a brief introductory exercise, "Yinscape and Yangsearch," which deals with the merger of two Internet companies, one in India and the other in California. Each company has consistently viewed the other as the enemy, and industry analysts are skeptical about whether the merger can succeed. Using the information in the case, you are to prepare a 10-minute "vision" speech to deliver to the first official meeting of Yinscape and Yangsearch's top officers.

On the surface, the need for a vision seems obvious in this situation: the merger is just "beginning." Yet there is considerable baggage to be taken into consideration. At the end of the session, you will hear what the CEO did, and what happened to the merged companies in their first year.

"The Vision Thing," a reading, synthesizes various research and other ideas on vision; it lays out what a good vision looks like and what approaches can be taken to develop one. One essential requirement of good visions, according to the reading, is that they be "stable but flexible."

The classic change case "Bob Galvin and Motorola, Inc. (A)" takes visioning into the territory of renewing (revitalizing, reenergizing) a company; this is frequently called "revisioning." Galvin's challenge, among others, is raised in the book's introduction: *when* change should be initiated. Motorola, at the time of the case, is performing well, and, as a consequence, the need for change, particularly of the sort Galvin considers, is not apparent. Thus, unlike in "Yinscape and Yangsearch," when a vision seems appropriate because something is beginning, in this case the role of visioning is murkier. In a provocative accompanying reading, "From Bogged Down to Fired Up: Inspiring Organizational Change," Bert Spector argues for a concept he calls "diffusing dissatisfaction" as a way to prepare an organization for change. A question that can be asked when contemplating Galvin's situation, however, is: How does one *inspire dissatisfaction*?

Of the seismic changes wrought on Wall Street in the financial crisis of 2008, perhaps none was more poignant than the forced sale of Merrill Lynch, the fiercely independent brokerage firm whose entry into investment banking in the early 1980s had set the stage for its eventual downfall. The case "Merrill Lynch: Evolution, Revolution and Sale, 1996–2008" chronicles the last decade of this financial icon, and the leadership of three very different CEOs in three very different market situations. How vision can clash with the need for adaptation is evident at every step, as is the challenge of dealing with forces outside of one's control.

One of this book's quintessential readings, "An Improvisational Model for Change Management: The Case of Groupware Technologies," uses two powerful metaphors—the different approaches of European and Trukese navigators, and the improvisational-style jazz band—to articulate a change model that is particularly well suited to the turbulence found in contemporary business. Authors Wanda J. Orlikowski and J. Debra Hofman recognize three types of change: anticipated, emergent, and opportunity-based. Their improvisational model argues that change—in particular technological change—in organizations "is an iterative series of different changes, many unpredictable at the start, that evolve from practical experience with the new technologies." The experience of Zeta, a $100 million software company, is presented to illustrate the improvisational model at work. Its implications, however, run far beyond the world of technology and inform nearly every example within these pages.

The final case in this module, "Charlotte Beers at Ogilvy & Mather Worldwide (A)," describes the CEO's efforts to craft a new vision with the senior management team of the world's sixth-largest advertising agency. David Ogilvy, the firm's legendary founder, had retired in 1975, and in the nearly 20 years since that time, Ogilvy & Mather had begun to lose sight of what it stood for. Soon after taking the reins in 1992, Beers identified a group of top executives whom she described as "thirsty for change" and invited them to join her in reinventing the agency.

The module ends with an article by Gary Hamel and Liisa Välikangas, "The Quest for Resilience." Their contention is that strategic resilience—"the capacity to change before the case for change becomes desperately obvious"—is what differentiates the successful companies of the future from those of the present and the past. Their argument is only strengthened by the spiraling instability in corporate performance in the few years since the article was written. And in response to one of the most frequently heard warnings about change programs, Hamel has argued before against the assumption that people are resistant to change: "There's a huge quest for novelty which we haven't unleashed in most organizations" (*CEO*, 1999). How to unleash—and harness—this energy in a productive way is the subject of the next module.

References

Association of Executive Search Consultants (AESC) (1998). *Chief Executives in the NewEurope.* Brussels: AESC Europe.

CEO Magazine (1999). Gary Hamel, interviewed by Jennifer Marie Reese. PriceWaterhouseCoopers, May.

Collins, James C., and Jerry I. Porras (1991). "Organizational Vision and Visionary Organizations." *California Management Review* (Fall), pp. 30–53.

Case

Yinscape and Yangsearch

It is the end of September and the joint chairman and CEO of India's Yinscape Corporation, with the support of his board and a wealthy private investor, has just taken control of the American Yangsearch Company. Both Internet firms are ten years old, and both offer specialized business-to-business Internet services using similar technologies. Both are pioneers in their market segment. However, their products are very different and technologically incompatible. Assuming no major client losses, the new company will be number two in this Internet sector by market share, with the market leader still in a dominant position, based in the U.K.

and led by a brilliant, high-profile and aggressive entrepreneur.

Yinscape attempted a friendly takeover last summer, but was fended off by Yangsearch's board. The eventual takeover has taken a lot of effort and has been under intense scrutiny, partly by regulators but mostly by financial and industry analysts, the majority of whom have yet to decide whether this deal is a good thing or not. Their main concern is that putting together two "number twos" does not necessarily create a winner, particularly given the many differences between the two firms. The chairman and CEO has promised to sort things out by next summer, tripling earnings and merging the two companies' cultures, product ranges, and systems to put the new joint company in a position to challenge the dominant player for market leadership. It is unlikely that analysts will be forgiving if these promises are broken.

Source: *This case was prepared by Professor Maury Peiperl as the basis for class discussion. It is based in part on the case "Yincom and Yangnet" from the second edition of this volume. © 2010 by IMD. Reprinted with permission.*

Both companies have clearly defined cultures based in no small part on the personalities of their founders. These cultures are fiercely defended, and each company has traditionally viewed the other as "the enemy." But there the similarities end. Yinscape, based in Mumbai, employs 250 people and has a strongly centralized, performance-based culture. Its sales focus has allowed it to build a network of large international clients that it continues to service to a high level. Such a structure, however, makes it vulnerable should one of its small number of clients decide to move its business elsewhere. Its professionalism has ensured a strong relationship with analysts that helped considerably in its ability to raise the capital for this takeover.

Yangsearch, in contrast, is based in Silicon Valley (California) and employs 400 people. It is highly decentralized in structure, retaining the entrepreneurial spirit engendered by its founders. It focuses on developing cutting-edge products and is highly creative, not just in its products but also in its business philosophy. The main emphasis is on relationships within the firm, which are strong and very sociable. The client base is diverse in location and line of business, but is mainly made up of small companies. Cash flow has been a problem from the start, but the belief among employees in the superiority of their products has seen them through every crisis so far.

The chairman and CEO is determined that the new company will succeed. Having just surfaced from months of grinding financial and due diligence negotiations, he sees his main challenge as beginning to develop a vision and a strategy for the new company.

Reading

The Vision Thing (A)

The "vision thing" has become a major preoccupation in the past decade in both the corporate and the political areas. Arguably, this demand for "a vision" from our leaders has served to overwork and trivialize—perhaps even distort—what real visions are and why they are necessary. It is true that the concept of vision is elusive; there are many definitions, none of which is precise. It is, in fact, almost easier to say what a vision isn't. Despite this imprecision, however, a vision is considered fundamental for helping a firm, quite literally, *visualize* its future.

When that future includes change, particularly of the transformational sort, having a vision of the new direction in advance of actually making the changes is indispensable. According to one study, "We found that no effort to produce strategic change was successful without a new vision."[1]

Source: Harvard Business School Case No. 9-490-019, Copyright 1989 by the President and Fellows of Harvard College. All rights reserved. This case was prepared by Professor Todd D. Jick. HBS Cases are developed solely for class discussion and do not necessarily illustrate effective or ineffective management.

[1] L. A. Bennigson and H. Swartz, "The CEO's Change Agenda," *Planning Review* 15(3): May–June 1987, p. 13.

But visions are difficult to craft and often remain paper exercises. All too few achieve their purpose of helping an organization to meet its goals and to stimulate change. What is a "good" vision? How do effective visions get created? What do successful visionary leaders do? And how can those without formal authority influence the conceptualizing of an organization's vision? In addressing these questions, this note will help managers think about the use of vision and envisioning in the change process.

WHAT IS A VISION?

A vision is an attempt to *articulate* what a desired future for a company would look like. It can be likened to "an organizational dream—it stretches the imagination and motivates people to rethink what is possible."[2] Martin Luther King, Jr.'s, most famous speech is literally labeled "I Have a Dream," because in it he elucidated his vision of a nonracist America.

Visions are *big* pictures. They are new terrains, descriptions of a time and place that are happy and successful. In that sense, they are idyllic, perhaps even "impossible dreams." But when the time and place are understandable (e.g., "one happy family") people can and do respond. We know some of the things that one happy family implies: we don't beat up on each other, we try to cooperate, and so on.

According to one observer, a vision has two fundamental elements:

One is to provide a conceptual framework for understanding the

organization's purpose—the vision includes a roadmap. The second important element is the emotional appeal: the part of the vision that has a motivational pull with which people can identify.[3]

A vision is not the same as a mission, which is a brief explanation of the organization's purpose. A vision is not the same as strategic objectives, the specific measurable performance goals. A vision is not the same as a philosophy, the values and belief system underlying a company. Yet, a vision must be consistent with mission, strategy, and philosophy. A vision is both much more than and much less than these elements. It is much less than these elements because visions tend to be evocative, rather than precise. And yet in its simplicity and evocativeness, a vision can have a more profound influence on real behavior than binders full of strategic plans with detailed documentation.

Indeed, the true value of a vision is to guide behavior. Tom Peters tells the story of the Raychem worker on the night shift who notices something amiss with the packing labels on the last few boxes going onto a truck. No supervisor is around. No one else seems to have noticed and, in fact, senior employees have already passed on the order "as is." The worker could just let it go, and no one would have known about the problem.

But he stopped the line! With the company's vision of zero defects and the best quality products ringing in his consciousness, the worker took the initiative to catch the problem. He could have let things go by, with no negative personal consequences. But he didn't because the dream and spirit of Raychem's vision led

[2] W. P. Belgard, K. K. Fisher, and S. R. Rayner, "Vision, Opportunity, and Tenacity: Three Informal Processes That Influence Transformation." In *Corporate Transformation*, R. Kilmann and T. Covin, eds. (San Francisco: Jossey-Bass, 1988), p. 135.

[3] N. Tichy and M. Devanna, *The Transformational Leader* (New York: John Wiley, 1986), p. 130.

him to make a different calculus and a different choice. Behavior was changing at Raychem on account of a new vision.

How does this happen? When are visions effective? Why did this employee change his habitual behavior? Many characteristics of good visions can be identified. Good visions are:

- Clear, concise, easily understandable.

- Memorable.

- Exciting and inspiring.

- Challenging.

- Excellence centered.

- Stable, but flexible.

- Implementable and tangible.

Consider the following example:

Liza Foley has an ideal and unique image of the future for the organization she leads. Foley is the president and chief executive officer of Canton Industrial Corporation of Canton, Illinois, [which] occupies the old International Harvester facility that was shut down in 1984, putting 250 people out of work in a town with a population of 14,000 in the guts of the rust belt.…

[Bought with private funds and the help of the city] there were 42 people working initially there. A year and a half later there were 200. It was also the only publicly held, women-owned and operated manufacturing facility in the United States. We asked Foley what motivated her to buy the company and take such a risk, and she replied: "I saw what closing a plant did to the community. And I also saw that there was a great deal of desire. People were anxious to get to work. And that was challenging.… I have a clear sense of purpose and vision of where I want to go.…

For the organization, I want to take this to a $100 million company in less than five years. I want to make acquisitions…that will allow us to service some of our key customers from several locations. I want to make Canton, Illinois, the mailbox capital of the world. I can see a little sign as you enter the town: Welcome to Canton, the Mailbox Capital of the World.… I'd like to think that we are starting the resurgence of the rust belt.[4]

This particular example seems to meet many of the criteria above. It inspired people, it elicited an image of excellence, and it challenged people to new heights.

A vision is sometimes even captured by a slogan, although this is very risky because of the shallowness of such sloganeering. But the following seems to have been a successful use of a slogan to symbolize and embody a vision of creativity and innovation:

A software company executive replaced the firm's slogan, "We Can Do Anything," with one he thought better typified his vision, "The Technical Edge."… As he mulled over phrases that might recapture the old vision in fresh language, he considered, "Think Young," but then he realized that the phrase might offend some older employees. Then it struck him: "Outrageous Thinking." He might have to fine-tune it, but it did express what he wanted from his people.… A week after his meditation, the software executive pinned a button to his jacket: "Outrageous Thinking Keeps Us

[4] J. Kouzes and B. Posner, *The Leadership Challenge* (San Francisco: Jossey-Bass, 1988), pp. 92–93. (It later transpired, unfortunately, that Foley, though a visionary, was not all she appeared to be. See Matt O'Connor, "Canton's Dream Becomes Scandal," *Chicago Tribune*, December 6, 1987, p. C1.)

Ahead." Soon, the slogan fired up even the senior staff, who seemed to enjoy this call to youthful exuberance.[5]

A slogan thus sometimes becomes the vehicle for communicating and symbolizing a new vision. And yet, there is always a fine line between an empty slogan and an inspirational vision and guide. This particular embodiment of a vision seemed to work; many others fail.

What is it about a vision that grabs people? First, people like to feel proud that they are part of something larger than their career or family, and the corporate vision tends to mobilize this source of personal motivation. Second, having a vision of the future highlights the contrast with today's reality. This creates a structural tension between today and tomorrow that seeks a resolution.

Another reason visions have become so important is because, with increasing turbulence in organizations, people are seeking some sort of anchor or certainty as a mooring. In providing a direction and a focus, an organization can more easily converge on the necessary actions. For example, when Johnson & Johnson experienced the Tylenol poisonings, it responded very quickly and with consensus because its longstanding credo, which clearly placed the needs of the customer above all else, served as a worldwide guide for action.

Vision statements tend to incorporate four elements: (1) customer orientation, (2) employee focus, (3) organizational competencies, and (4) standards of excellence. These elements help the organization do the "right thing." They specify the key success factors in satisfying the customer

(e.g., service, quality, delivery); the values and principles that employees stand for and rally behind; the organizational capabilities that have distinguished its performance in the past and provide a foundation for the future; and finally, a demanding standard of excellence that appeals to the pride and desire of all associated with the organization. Thus, visions always seem to include such superlatives as world class, lowest cost, fastest.

HOW VISIONS ARE CREATED: THE VISIONING PROCESS

Visions have been created in organizations in very different ways. Some are very personal experiences of creativity and inspiration. Some are products of elaborate information-gathering processes. Some are developed at a workshop or off-site with key players. Some are even word-smithed by public relations or advertising staff. The most typical are: (a) CEO/leader developed, (b) CEO–senior team developed, and (c) bottom-up developed.

A study by Warren Bennis of 90 top leaders highlighted the central role they played in developing visions for their organizations.[6] Although obviously this is never purely a solo endeavor, the impression is that these leaders all had compelling visions and dreams about their companies. The classic examples are Steve Jobs at Apple, Harry Gray at United Technologies, Mitch Kapor at Lotus, and Jack Welch at General Electric. These people are typically described as self-styled visionaries. Bennis concluded that the successful visionary CEO does the following:

[5] C. Hickman and M. A. Silva, *Creating Excellence* (New York: New American Library, 1984), p. 167.

[6] Ibid., pp. 160–161.

- Searches for ideas, concepts, and ways of thinking until clear vision crystallizes.

- Articulates the vision into an easy-to-grasp philosophy that integrates strategic direction and cultural values.

- Motivates company employees to embrace the vision through constant persuasion and by setting an example of hard work.

- Makes contact with employees at all levels in the organization, attempting to understand their concerns and the impact the vision has on them.

- Acts in a warm, supportive, expressive way, always communicating that "We're all in this together, like a family."

- Translates the vision into a reason for being for each employee by continually relating the vision to individual cares, concerns, and work.

- Concentrates on the major strengths within the organization that will ensure the success of the vision.

- Remains at the center of the action, positioned as the prime shaper of the vision.

- Looks for ways to improve, augment, or further develop the vision by carefully observing changes inside and outside the organization.

- Measures the ultimate success of the organization in terms of its ability to fulfill the vision.

These various actions place the visionary leader in a very visible and powerful position in the development of a vision. It assumes that this leadership is *the* key. Indeed, inspiring a shared vision is often listed as a key leadership success factor.

Yet managers say that inspiration is most difficult to apply and only 10 percent think of themselves as inspiring.[7] Maybe managers are selling themselves short, or glorifying those enviable individuals who have that certain something called "charisma." Managers who are successful in providing a vision, however, do some very simple things, which more than 10 percent are certainly capable of doing: they (1) appeal to a common purpose, (2) communicate expressively, and (3) sincerely believe in what they are saying.[8]

Other leaders view the process in much more collaborative fashion and, thus, craft an immediate partnership with their senior staff. They view vision creation as less inspiration and more perspiration.

LEADER-SENIOR TEAM VISIONING

This collaborative vision process is described and epitomized by Michael Blumenthal, former CEO of Unisys. When Blumenthal was chairman of Burroughs, he recalled how he went about shaping a vision for that company:

> I gathered six or eight people around me and we talked about everything, and were very open. I'm very open and I listened to them, and I traveled around and talked to a lot of people, and then eventually I tried to enunciate what it was that we learned and I suggested this is what we are going to do. And then people reacted to it and at the end I said, okay.[9]

This informal gathering of thoughts and testing for reaction is one approach

[7] Kouzes and Posner, 1988, p. 109.
[8] Ibid., p. 113.
[9] Tichy and Devanna, 1986, p. 137.

in building a vision with a senior management team. But there are more and more companies that do this in a more structured and systematic format—using the help of inside or outside facilitators.

For example, after Contel Texocom's executive management team drew up a vision statement, it had the statement inscribed on a banner, which each team member signed. Next, the executive group met with the company's entire management, with members explaining what the statement meant to them. Managers were invited to sign the banner as well. Anyone who decided to sign the banner became a "sponsor." That is, potential "enrollees" could select any name appearing on the banner (other than direct supervisor) and arrange a one-on-one meeting with that person, during which the vision and its meaning would be discussed. That process was voluntary and nonhierarchical.

BOTTOM-UP VISIONING

Finally, the third prototype involves more bottom-up or middle-up involvement. It can be done again through formal channels or through informal influence processes.

For example, there are various techniques used with middle managers to stimulate them to "dream" a vision of the future. In one design, managers are asked to write an article about their company that they would like to see in an issue of *Business Week* five years hence. What would they like to be able to read about their company? How would the company be described in ways different than it was today? Then the articles are read to each other and commonalities and differences are discussed. Ultimately, the group might agree on one scenario, or a few, which would then be presented to senior management.

With this bottom-up approach, visions are only effective insofar as they are meaningful and motivating to those that have to implement them. Thus, it is better to solicit or be responsive to those in the middle particularly. Otherwise, there will be resistance or apathy, and the vision will be an unrealized dream or an empty slogan.

However, those who are neither the leader nor in an organization that formally structures an opportunity are not doomed to passive acceptance. It is possible to participate as a "vision influencer," rather than a "vision driver." These influencers are typically persons with limited hierarchical power (e.g., lower-level managers and staff) but they can influence key executives. They not only can generate ideas but also can gather support for a future transformation through their ability to influence still other people.[10]

What do effective influencers do? One study describes their actions:

> They create a vision of the potential future state of the transformed organization, they take advantage of every opportunity to discuss their vision, and they tenaciously support processes that facilitate the implementation of the vision while discouraging processes that inhibit it.[11]

Thus, change influencers can develop their own vision and opportunistically find occasions to discuss and gain support for it, whether through formal meetings or chance water cooler encounters. With a vision and opportunity comes one other key element, tenacity. Influencers must be dogged and dedicated, willing to make

---

[10] Belgard, Fisher, and Rayner, 1988, p. 133.
[11] Ibid.

their case as strongly as possible, personally modeling the behaviors they are promoting, and being flexible and politically astute wherever needed. Specific actions might include: conversations in parking lots, informal networking and lobbying, phone calls, and occasional blank stares.

The premise of this kind of approach is that those down in the organization may have a better "feel" for what is needed to revitalize, reshape, or transform an organization. After all, they are the ones closest to the customers, the products, and the services.

Indeed, those without the formal authority to create or authorize a vision are often the most frustrated. They constantly complain that the top-down visions are unclear, inadequate, or misguided. They become weary from trying to figure it out or unsuccessfully challenging the top people, and they yearn for the empowerment that would give them an easier say in the visioning process.

HAVING VISIONS THAT "TAKE"

Whichever approach is used, certain steps must be taken. A vision ultimately must be deemed strategically sound. It certainly must have widespread support to be made real and translatable into behavior. It continually must be reinforced through words, symbols, and actions or else it will be viewed as temporary or insincere. Respected individuals, wherever they reside in an organization, must personally embody the vision by how they spend their time; whom they surround themselves with; and, of course, what they say.

The creation of a compelling vision that guides behavior and change is never easy. Perhaps no complaint is more common in

today's fast-moving and turbulent environment than "We just don't have a clear vision of where we're headed." In part, this is common because the path to the future, much less the "best" future, has become increasingly less obvious. But it's also true that managers have not given enough attention to the *process* of crafting and gaining commitment to a vision. It's not just having a vision—the "right" one, of course—that counts, but also having one that is well accepted and can be translated into an actual behavior.

Many organizations may find themselves in a situation similar to one I recently observed. A large international unit of a major Fortune 500 company brought together its top 25 managers to ponder their strategy and direction. Their vision, established three years earlier, focused on their global impact, the rekindling of some of the basics of their business, and the dedication of longstanding employees. They captured this in a well-communicated phrase, which seemed simple and compelling enough: "Redirect the Ship." In their discussion about the current state of the business, everyone nodded when the phrase was used. It seemed like it continued to serve as a guide to decisions and behavior. But then, one manager suggested it was time for a new vision because the ship had been redirected. The business had moved in the new strategic direction and the new behaviors were well in evidence. Another manager, however, disagreed and argued that the ship indeed had not yet been redirected enough. Then a third voice emerged quizzically and stated, "I don't even know what 're-directing the ship' means!" Sure enough, the group was split in thirds. Was it time for a new vision, a reaffirmation of the old vision, or a clarification of what the vision meant?

The "vision thing" had reared its ugly head again. The organization would have to grapple with all the issues raised in this note. Ultimately, this crossroads would test how well the vision had been created in the first place, how well it had been adhered to, and how an organization can use a vision to provide direction when change is needed again.

Change Classic

Bob Galvin and Motorola, Inc. (A)

On April 24, 1983, the biennial meeting of the top 153 officers of Motorola, Inc. was drawing to a close, and Bob Galvin, chairman and chief executive officer (CEO) of the $4 billion company, was about to offer his concluding comments. The theme of the two-day session had been "Managing Change," an appropriate topic, since the 55-year-old producer of electronics equipment had experienced a year of 15 percent growth—or half a billion dollars between 1982 and 1983. Galvin knew that the message he had in mind was surprising in light of the company's apparent success.

Increasingly as he "walked the halls" of the corporation, Galvin had heard more and more complaints. Managers were upset by longer product development cycles, by too many layers in the management structure, and by ponderous, inflexible decision approval processes. Galvin interpreted these frequently heard complaints in the context of a rapidly changing competitive environment. He recognized the growing threat from Japanese manufacturers to key Motorola products, such as cellular

Source: Harvard Business School Case No. 9-487-062. Copyright 1987 by the President and Fellows of Harvard College. All rights reserved. This case was prepared by Professor Todd D. Jick. HBS Cases are developed solely for class discussion and do not necessarily illustrate effective or ineffective management.

telephones and semiconductors. And much to the annoyance of his senior managers, he often asserted, "We haven't even begun to compete internationally yet."

Galvin believed that the firm's current inability to respond quickly and flexibly to the changing needs of the customer could prove fatal in the coming global competitive crisis. Still, he kept asking himself whether he, as chief executive officer, could make the kinds of changes Motorola needed. If he did nothing else in his last years before retirement, he wanted to reposition Motorola on the path toward renewed competitiveness. He knew this would be all the more difficult because many of his managers did not recognize the problems he saw. As he approached the speaker's podium, Galvin reflected that "I suppose I've been preparing for this speech for the last 45 years."

MOTOROLA, INC.

Galvin Manufacturing Company was founded by Paul V. Galvin, Bob Galvin's father, in 1928. The Chicago-based firm's earliest products were alternating electrical current converters and automobile radios. Paul Galvin dubbed the car radio he developed the "Motorola"—from motor and victrola—and in 1947, this became the company's name as well.

From their firm's modest beginning with less than $1,500 in working capital and equipment, Paul Galvin and his brother, Joe, tried to create a humane and democratic work environment for their employees: Everyone, from Paul Galvin himself to the newest production-line employee, was addressed on a first-name basis; the Galvins had replaced the typical time clock in the plant with an employee honor system; and by 1947, Paul Galvin established a profit-sharing program for the 2,000 workers the firm then employed. As a result of such efforts, Motorola remained union free.

Over the years, Motorola extended its product base to include home radios, phonographs, televisions, and transistors and semiconductor components. By 1983, however, under Bob Galvin's leadership, the firm had sold many of its consumer electronic businesses and developed other markets based on new technology. By then, the firm was composed of five geographically dispersed sectors or groups:

1. *The Semiconductor Products Sector,* with 1982 net sales of $1.3 billion, produced such products as microprocessors, memory chips, and integrated circuits.

2. *The Communications Sector,* with 1982 net sales of $1.5 billion, produced such products as two-way radios, paging devices, and cellular telephones.

3. *The Information Systems Group (ISG),* with 1982 net sales of $485 million, produced an integrated line of data transmission and distributed data processing systems.

4. *The Automotive and Industrial Electronics Group (AIEG)* and *The Government Electronics Group (GEG)* had combined 1982 net sales of $564 million. AIEG produced such products as fuel-injection systems, electronic engine controls and instrumentation, and electronic appliance controls. GEG conducted research in satellite communications technology.

This product-focused organizational structure grew out of Paul and Bob Galvin's emphasis on the customers' interests and their concern that a large, centralized organization might not be responsive enough to those interests. Over the years, Motorola had gradually decentralized. In the 1950s Paul Galvin formed divisions; in the early 1960s Bob Galvin established product lines with product managers who managed specific marketing and engineering areas, but who purchased the centralized manufacturing and sales functions. By the 1980s, the groups and sectors structure was in place, along with a multilayered matrix system of management. At the close of 1982 Motorola had approximately 75,000 employees, with operations in 15 foreign countries as well as the United States.

BOB GALVIN

Bob Galvin joined the firm as a stock clerk in 1944, without completing his college degree. He worked in a variety of positions until 1948 when he became executive vice president. He became president in 1956, and chairman/CEO in 1964.

Galvin was an equitable and accessible manager. His leadership style was rooted in humility and an abiding respect for his father's values. He often quoted Paul Galvin when explaining a decision he had made, and in assessing his own influence at Motorola, he pointed to the "privilege" of his long service with the firm, as well as to the "mantle" he had received from his father: "I am fortunate to carry some of his reputation, in addition to what I've earned myself." He was a serious and thoughtful man who defined his role as "leading the institution: I try to be a good listener, to look for the unattended, the void, the exception that my associates are too busy to see."

Over the years he had championed not only various reorganizational efforts and product/market shifts but a variety of participatory management, executive education, and strategic planning programs. In the 1970s, Motorola developed the Participative Management Program (PMP) as a means to enhance productivity and employee involvement in the firm. PMP divided employees into small groups that met to discuss problems and potential improvements in their area of responsibility. Each group sent one member to report its ideas to the group one level up, which thereby enhanced communication in all directions. PMP efforts were also tied to a bonus incentive program.

Galvin's style and the Motorola culture were clearly people oriented. High value was placed on senior service and in fact, no employee with more than 10 years' service could be fired without approval from Galvin himself. John Mitchell, Motorola's president, commented: "Bob *is* the culture here."

Some Motorola managers, however, criticized Motorola's "low demand environment," a tone set by Galvin himself. He devoted significant attention to the development of a strong managerial succession at Motorola and consequently was quite confident in Motorola's senior managers—his "family," as he called them. He felt convinced that if he but pointed out a problem to his officers, they would certainly be motivated and capable of resolving it appropriately. From time to time he gave a speech on leadership as he perceived it (Exhibit 1) including the following excerpt:

> Again, we see the paradox of the leader—a finite person with an apparent infinite influence.

Exhibit 1
Speech by Bob Galvin on Leadership

I would like to share with you a special selective view of leadership. It finds its expression in a series of paradoxes.

We know so much about leadership, yet we know too little. We can define it in general, but find it hard to particularize. We recognize it when obvious, but it is not always obvious why. We practice leadership, which implies we are still preparing for the real thing.

It is neither necessary to impress on you an elaborate definition of leadership nor is this an appropriate time to characterize its many styles. Let it suffice that we acknowledge that no leader is worthy of the title absent creative and judgmental intelligence, courage, heart, spirit, integrity, and vision applied to the accomplishment of a purposeful result through the efforts of followers and the leader. Rather, I elect to share with you some observations on a further series of paradoxes that reveal themselves as we analyze leadership.

When one is vested with the role of the leader, he inherits more freedom. The power of leadership endows him with rights to a greater range of self-determination of his own destiny. It is he who may determine the what or the how and the when or the where of important events. Yet, as with all rights, there is a commensurate, balancing group of responsibilities that impose upon his freedom. The leader cannot avoid the act of determining the what or the who or the where. He cannot avoid being prepared to make these determinations. He cannot avoid being prepared to make these terminations. He cannot avoid seeing to their implementation. He cannot avoid living with the consequences of his decision on others and the demands these consequences impose on him. Only time will prove the merit of his stewardship. Because he is driven to pass this test of time, he will be obliged often to serve others more than himself. This obligation will more and more circumscribe his destiny. So those who assume true leadership will wonder from time to time if the apparent freedom of the leader adds a greater measure of independence, or whether the dependence of others on him restricts his own freedom.

For one to lead implies that others follow. But, is the leader a breed apart, or is he, rather, the better follower? Leadership casts the leader in many such roles:

- Observer—of the work his associates perform.
- Sensor—of attitudes, feelings, and trends.
- Listener—to ideas, suggestions, and complaints.
- Student—of advisors, inside and out of his situation.
- Product of experience—both his and others'.
- Mimic—of other leaders who have earned his respect.

Is he not the better follower, as he learns more quickly and surely from the past, selects the correct advice and trends, chooses the simpler work patterns and combines the best of other leaders? Is it not good leadership to know when not to follow an aimless path?

The paradox again: To lead well presumes the ability to follow smartly.

Because a leader is human and fallible, his leadership is in one sense finite—constrained by mortality and human imperfections. In another sense, the leader's influence is almost limitless. He can spread hope, lend courage, kindle confidence, impart knowledge, give heart, instill spirit, elevate standards, display vision, set direction, and call for action today and each tomorrow. The frequency with which one can perform these leadership functions seems without measure. His effectiveness and personal resources, rather than attenuating with use, amplify as he reuses and extends his skills.

Like the tree whose shadow falls where the tree is not, the consequence of the leader's act radiates beyond his fondest perception.

Again, we see the paradox of the leader—a finite person with an apparent infinite influence.

continued

Exhibit 1 continued

A leader is decisive—is called on to make many critical choices, and can thrive on the power and attention of that decision-making role. Yet, the leader of leaders moves progressively away from that role.

Yes, he or she can be decisive and command as required. Yet that leader's prime responsibility is not to decide or direct, but to create and maintain an evocative situation, stimulating an atmosphere of objective participation, keeping the goal in sight, recognizing valid consensus, inviting unequivocal recommendation, and finally vesting increasingly in others the privilege to learn through their own decisions.

A wiser man puts it thus:

We measure the effectiveness of the true leader, not in terms of the leadership he exercises, but in terms of the leadership he evokes; not in terms of his power over others but in terms of the power he releases in others; not in terms of the goals he sets and the directions he gives, but in terms of the plans of action others work out for themselves with his help; not in terms of decisions made, events completed and the inevitable success and growth that follow from such released energy, but in terms of growth in competence, sense of responsibility and in personal satisfactions among many participants.

Under this kind of leadership it may not always be clear at any given moment just who is leading. Nor is this important. What is important is that others are learning to lead well.

The complement to that paradox is that the growth that such leadership stimulates generates an ever-growing institution and an ever-increasing number of critical choices, more than enough of which fall squarely back on the shoulders of the leader who trained and willingly shared decision-making with others.

And there are others which, if not paradoxes, at least are incongruities. Have we not witnessed some who have claimed leadership yet never fully achieved it? Have we not observed others who have shunned leadership only to have it thrust upon them?

Each of us here is at once part leader and part follower as we play our roles in life. Fortunately, there is a spark of leadership quality in many men and women, and, most fortunately, the flame of future leadership burns brightly in many who matriculate here. It is this wellspring from which we will draw and which gives us confidence for the continued advance of society.

On this day, you may feel a sense of relief that you have borne your final test. Walter Lippman, for one, would not long have let you cherish this illusion. He once observed:

The final test of a leader is that he leaves behind in others the conviction and will to carry on.

This, for a few of the best of you here who would be leaders, may be the most personal paradox and crucial test of all.

A leader is decisive—is called on to make many critical choices, and can thrive on the power and attention of that decision-making role. Yet, the leader of leaders moves progressively away from that role.

Yes, he or she can be decisive and command as required. Yet that leader's prime responsibility is not to decide or direct, but to create and maintain an evocative situation, stimulating an atmosphere of objective participation, keeping the goal in sight, recognizing valid consensus, inviting unequivocal recommendation, and finally vesting increasingly in others the privilege to learn through their own decisions.

Galvin hoped to encourage this "privilege to learn through their own decisions" through the variety of innovative programs that Motorola adopted.

MOTOROLA IN 1983

Galvin believed, in the spring of 1983, that Motorola was poised on the edge of a new competitive era. The company had just come through a recession in the semiconductor industry which had caused an 8 percent downturn in earnings between 1980 and 1982. Difficult as that period had been, however, Motorola's losses had been far less severe than those of competitors like Texas Instruments and Intel. "Motorola did see their profits slip by 6 percent during the worst year of the recession. But their archrivals, TI and Intel, experienced a 49 percent and 72 percent drop, respectively."[1] (See Exhibit 2.) Galvin wanted to build on Motorola's strengths at a time when performance was beginning to look strong again. Although the first quarter

[1] James O'Toole, "Second Annual NM Vanguard Award," *New Management* 3(2): Fall 1985, p. 5.

was a bit slow, sales seemed to be on the upswing as Motorola faced the summer of 1983, and Galvin saw the national economy and his firm gearing up for rapid growth in the next few years. He recognized this growth as a blessing and a threat.

Increases in sales and earnings were welcome, of course, as was the accompanying confidence within the firm. However, rapid expansion brought new structural and managerial challenges and exacerbated existing deficiencies. In addition, confidence could engender a dangerous complacency that made change all the more difficult. Finally, Galvin was all too cognizant of the cyclical nature of the semiconductor and computer industries and the growing threat of Japanese competition in both the communications and the semiconductor sectors of the business.

Galvin was also looking internally. One of Galvin's favored management techniques was walking the halls of the organization, listening to the ideas and the complaints of Motorola's employees, especially the middle managers. Galvin believed these managers were in touch with "real world" implementation issues that higher-level managers might miss because of their need to oversee so many different functions and systems. Galvin was a strong believer in open communications, and he encouraged employees at all levels to sit down with him in the company cafeteria at lunch, or to catch him in the halls of the firm to share their ideas and their criticisms.

STRUCTURAL ISSUES

The issues he heard about in spring 1983 were disturbingly consistent with concerns that had been building throughout the 1970s. Galvin identified them as

EXHIBIT 2 Motorola Financial Information, 1979–1982

Four-Year Financial Summary: Motorola, Inc., and Consolidated Subsidiaries, Years Ended December 31

	1982	1981	1980	1979
	Operating Results (in millions of dollars)			
Net sales	$3,786	$3,570	$3,284	$2,879
Manufacturing and other administrative costs of sales	2,269	2,066	1,895	1,672
Selling, general, and administrative expenses	1,013	985	877	756
Depreciation and amortization of plant and equipment	244	205	173	132
Interest expense, net	48	35	43	27
Special charge	—	—	13	10
Total costs and other expenses	3,574	3,311	3,002	2,597
Earnings before income taxes and extraordinary gain	212	259	282	282
Income taxes	42	77	90	111
Net earnings before extraordinary gain	170	182	192	171
Net earnings as a percent of sales	4.5%	5.1%	5.8%	5.9%
Extraordinary gain	8	—	—	—
Net earnings	$178	$182	$192	$171

Sector Performance, 1979–1982

Information by Industry Segment and Geographic Region: Information about the Company's operations in different industry segments for the years ended December 31 is summarized below (in millions of dollars):

	Net Sales				Operating Profit			
	1979	1980	1981	1982	1979	1980	1981	1982
Semiconductor products	$992	$1,222	$1,278	$1,298	$170	$186	$131	
Communications products	1,272	1,252	1,422	1,527	139	144	162	$97
Information systems products	NA	279	358	485	NA	34	42	31
Other products	655	683	718	564	14	26	50	44
Adjustments and eliminations	(61)	(60)	(82)	(88)	(3)	2	(4)	(7)
Industry totals	$2,713	$3,098	$3,335	$3,786	$259	$274	$251	307

"structural concerns." Employees complained of the problems engendered by the sheer size and complexity of Motorola's matrix organization. Objective and methodology conflicts routinely developed between Motorola's customer-oriented functional managers (in sales or distribution, for example) and their product line managers. Although traditionally Galvin had always stressed the importance of staying close to the customer and the customer's needs, the complexity of the firm's products often caused product line managers to be more technology driven than market driven in their planning and managing processes.

No single manager was clearly responsible for a particular project through all its cycles, from its origin in customer discussions through design, development, testing, and production and into sales. Consequently, project deadlines set by engineers carried little weight with the production staff, and the needs of the sales and distribution managers were poorly integrated into the realities of the manufacturing area. Galvin was alarmed by the ever-lengthening product development cycles.

Motorola's lines of authority were as often dotted as solid, and spans of control were narrow. As the company grew and its products multiplied, management layers increased as well. One company study, completed in 1983, reported nine to twelve layers between first-line managers and the executive level, with an average span of control over five people or fewer. Thirty percent managed three or fewer people. Individuals were struggling to preserve their turf and budget and to maintain internal performance standards. Long-term competitive strategy and customer needs were obscured by short-term incentives, and employees felt both overmanaged and underdirected.

Top management's efforts to energize the firm and to enhance creative cooperation translated into programs like PMP, with their step-by-step procedures and committee-based processes. Such programs involved employees at all levels and kept critical issues before them, but some managers worried that their format was too mechanistic and that they enabled employees to comply with the letter, rather than the spirit, of the programs.

Finally, Motorola's chief executive office was structured as a triumvirate, with Bob Galvin as chairman, William Weisz as vice chairman, and John Mitchell as president. Galvin defined their respective responsibilities as follows: "John Mitchell is running the business; Bill Weisz is managing the company; and my job is to lead the institution. And in a way, they are all the same thing." Galvin saw the chief executive office as a model of democratic practice and open communications for the firm. However, this tripartite structure was one of the other complaints that circulated among Motorola's managers. Mitchell explained: "They call us the three bears, and they ask, 'Why can't you be single in voice, style, and direction?'"

Galvin reviewed the concerns he gathered from Motorola's managers; from his son, Chris, who worked in the Communications Sector; and from his own observations. Taken alone, he believed they were cause for concern. When he also considered the rapid growth Motorola appeared to face as the economy emerged from the last two years of recession, and the growing competitive threat from Japan, Galvin became convinced that it was time for action.

JAPANESE COMPETITION

Motorola was one of the world's leading producers of two-way radios, cellular telephone systems, semiconductors, and microprocessor chips, and Japan was competing in and threatening each of these markets. The firm faced Japanese market practices such as "dumping" (selling product at less than "fair value" as a way to increase market share quickly) and "targeting" (the cooperative efforts of a group of Japanese firms, supported by Japanese law, to break into and capture a particular international market, such as computer memory chips). In response to these challenges, Galvin worked with federal foreign relations and trade committees, attempting to fight "unfair" trade practices and protectionism.

Galvin also knew, however, that he had to make changes closer to home, within Motorola. Galvin thought that effective competition with the Japanese meant not only modifications in federal trade regulations but Motorola's investment in R&D, enhanced productivity, and quality control. He believed the means to this end were through the company's employees. This was consistent with the kind of thinking behind PMP, 10 years earlier.

As Galvin considered his company's current condition and challenges, he felt a great sense of personal urgency. He was 61 years old, nearing retirement, and he wanted to leave a strong and healthy company to his family of managers. And although he wasn't certain how to implement a process of "renewal" at Motorola, he was quite confident of the need. He remembered his father's advice to "just get in motion" when action was required, confident that he would find his way.

MOTOROLA BIENNIAL OFFICERS' MEETING, APRIL 1983

Galvin came to the Officers' Meeting[2] with his mind full of a recent trip to Japan. He had been impressed by the commitment

of the industry employees he saw there and with the cutting-edge production technology the Japanese firms utilized. On the long plane ride back to the United States, Galvin had been reading the current management best-seller, *In Search of Excellence*. Its authors, Tom Peters and Robert Waterman, advocated simpler organizational structures with direct ties to the consumer.

With all these observations, conclusions, and influences in his mind, Galvin felt an uncanny, undeniable immediacy in his senior officers' discussion of their efforts to manage change. Every time an individual complained of too many layers of command, Galvin winced, "There it is again." Each time an officer mentioned the absence of realistic and convincing deadlines that made sense across departments, Galvin sighed, "There it is again." He knew he needed no more evidence. He was sure of his message and of its significance.

As the meeting drew to a close, his staff expected Galvin's usual clear, concise concluding summary. Instead he stood up and issued a challenge. He called upon his senior managers to take a fresh look at their organizations and to consider structural changes—smaller, more focused business units. He wanted to decrease the many layers of management and to bring management closer to the product and the market. Galvin spoke with ease and conviction: "My message was spontaneous in tone and mood, but it had been building out of years of experience. I had been hearing this message from my middle managers and I'm a good listener."

In his speech, Galvin stressed Motorola's

> ...constant thrust for renewal. Renewal is the most driving word in this corporation for me, the continual search for ways to get things done better.

[2] "Officers" refers to both business officers and officers of the corporation (appointed and elected vice presidents). Elected officers are elected by the board of directors, and appointed officers must be approved by the chief executive officer.

As I walk the halls, I keep my ears open and I keep picking up signals. A middle manager might tell me that he can't understand how the business did because we keep aggregating our results into one big number. Or another might tell me he thinks he has a good idea but he can't get the authority to get it done.

I see a welling up of the evidence of need and today I think the window is open. So I decided to express my concern and my conviction to you, confident that you share my insights and that together we will find our way to an organized effort of change. When we come together in two years, we will report and share the changes made and the lessons learned.

Galvin had not discussed this presentation with Weisz or Mitchell beforehand. Nor had he explicitly addressed with his Human Resources staff the issue of structural reorganization as the key method of a change at Motorola. He was confident that he knew his audience, his "constituency," and that they would welcome his challenge.

As Galvin concluded, however, and managers stood and began to move out of the room, the buzzing conversations were colored by surprise and confusion more than eagerness. Suddenly the firm's rising sales were a problem. Was this just another PMP pep talk? Was Galvin serious about restructuring the organization? Who would be responsible for this? Even Galvin's wife, Mary, turned to him later that evening and asked: "What exactly did you have in mind, Bob?"

That was Friday evening. On Monday morning, the calls started coming in to Galvin's office, to Joe Miraglia, corporate vice president and director of Human Resources, and passed back and forth between the various senior managers. Rumors were spreading: people wanted to know what had Galvin been reading, and with whom had he been talking? One senior manager jested that perhaps Galvin was miffed that Motorola had not been mentioned enough by the authors of *In Search of Excellence*. But everyone wanted to know: What did Galvin mean and was he serious?

RESPONSES TO GALVIN'S CHALLENGE

THE CHIEF EXECUTIVE OFFICE

Responses to Galvin's surprise speech varied according to each individual's position and the implications of this challenge for his or her responsibilities. William Weisz, vice chairman, and John Mitchell, president, for example, did not expect the timing and form of Galvin's presentation. The message itself, however, felt familiar. It coincided with both a long-term trend in Motorola toward decentralization and with Galvin's constant concern for the customer's needs. Mitchell commented:

> Bob Galvin's style is to make strong statements like "the implied solution to the problems of the matrix is to divide the company into small businesses." This took people aback. It sounded simplistic and it sounded like it would start right away.

Both Mitchell and Weisz could place Galvin's comments into a context, knowing and trusting the CEO as they did, and although they might not have chosen the timing and the particular solution Galvin proposed, they agreed with his diagnosis of Motorola's ills. As Galvin explained, "The vice chairman came on board with me on this issue in the spirit of faith and of insight. The president was preoccupied with running the business, but he came on as well."

OPERATING OFFICERS

For many of the top sector and group officers at Motorola there was an initial hesitancy about Galvin's unexpected spontaneous challenge, according to Robert Schaffer, an external consultant who interviewed these officers. Although they recognized that Galvin was earnest, they asked themselves some questions before considering what their response would be and how serious an effort was involved. Was this another in a string of innovations that arose from the visionary Galvin? Was this a commitment by all three chief executive officers or something Galvin alone would pursue as a reflection of his frustration? Would the head of any unit take this as a commitment to action? Did Galvin already have answers or was he willing and ready to open up the issue for questions?

Many of the firm's top officers did not share Galvin's sense of urgency about Motorola's competitive position. The company had a tradition of market strength and of technological leadership. Employees felt secure there; the culture placed a premium on commitment and length of service. And in the spring of 1983, the outlook was particularly good for semiconductor products. For despite the threat posed by Japanese competitors, the company had grown by half a billion dollars in the last year and it was still moving. One vice president in the Semiconductor Products Sector explained that Galvin's biggest problem in selling his change agenda was the "status quo: Managers here are scientists. They see themselves and the sector as renegades on the leading edge of technology, but when it comes to management and productivity measures, they stick with 'what worked before.'"

Perhaps managerial resistance to Galvin's challenge was all the more prevalent because no one was quite sure what he was proposing. Was this a major and radical call to action or only a proposal for new executive training? Many believed it was the latter and, thus, even those managers who shared Galvin's concern for Motorola's competitive position were doubtful that more educational programs would make a difference. If, on the other hand, Galvin was ordering a concrete structural change (an action that would be uncharacteristically directive), then he needed to be more precise. In the meantime, many managers simply waited for the thing to blow over.

HUMAN RESOURCES

In the ensuing days, while top management struggled to understand what Galvin had meant in his speech and what implications it had for them, Galvin himself met with Joe Miraglia, vice president of Human Resources at Motorola, whom he considered his "professional pivot point" within the organization; Galvin took the Human Resources function very seriously. The two promptly set about developing the vision the chief executive officer had introduced. Although Miraglia did not question Galvin's identification of problems in the organization, he commented:

> Bob's idea was to create smaller business units more functionally integrated at lower levels. We in Human Resources disagreed; structure was not the sole answer. We didn't want this to be seen as just a structural solution imposed from above by "those who know better."

Miraglia believed Galvin's vision had to be developed and that his influence had to be focused more clearly.

Nevertheless, Miraglia and his staff within the sectors supported Galvin's basic assumptions. Phil Nienstedt, manager of Human Resources Programs for Semiconductor Products, explained:

> Business had been good in 1983, but it was something of a false prosperity as the company came off the leaner recession years. The company was growing with little control or discipline. Galvin was hitting some hot buttons in the Officers' Meeting when he said we needed to focus on the customer, to develop flexibility, smaller business entities, wider spans, less levels, fewer inefficiencies. The Human Resources staff had discussed these issues with Joe Miraglia before. But Bob Galvin was vague and unclear as to what he wanted to do about these things. I think he did this intentionally, to be provocative, to get people thinking and wondering. The problem with this kind of change, however, is that short-term objectives, like getting the work out the door, get in the way of addressing this kind of long-term problem.

Dick Wintermantel, director of Organization and Human Resources in the Semiconductor Products Sector, pointed to another inhibitor to change:

> It's difficult for managers to make changes at Motorola and many times this difficulty relates to core cultural values that served the company well on its way *up* the growth curve, but which may be dysfunctional now. For example, respect for senior service may run counter to competitive staffing needs. Once you have 10 years of service, you're treated with employment *and* job security. We are constrained to redeploy people even if there are strategic and competitive reasons to do so.

Always responding to the customer's request for new products can result in thousands of products and no coherent and efficient organization. A mentality of "we can do it ourselves" runs counter to the alliances necessary for penetrating off-shore markets and resources. And, finally, a mistrust of "systems" and "bureaucracy" can obstruct the development of necessary cost reduction systems or worldwide communications systems.

Although the HR team shared Galvin's sense of urgency and his belief in the necessity for change, they questioned both his structural focus and some aspects of the culture he had built. Miraglia explained: "Bob Galvin is confident that if his senior line managers agree with him, they will be able to assemble the infrastructure necessary to make change happen." The HR staff believed that neither managerial agreement nor an effective change process would be easy to come by.

Reading

From Bogged Down to Fired Up: Inspiring Organizational Change

Bert A. Spector
Northeastern University

My point is simply this—managing organizational change is a topic [all] business needs to examine and understand because fundamental change will be the order of the day for the foreseeable future.[1]

The statement above, made by the president of Southwestern Bell, reflects a growing consensus among business leaders concerning the demands that will be placed upon them and their organizations in the coming decades. That consensus has two distinct dimensions:

- Massive organizational change is inevitable given the volatile nature of our competitive environment.

- Adaptive, flexible organizations will enjoy a distinct competitive advantage over rigid, static ones.

Scholars, too, have been paying attention to the dynamics of large-scale organizational change. How do organizations change? More specifically, how can our understanding of organizational change inform the actions of managers who want to transform their own organizations?

A key question for scholars concerns the initial stage of the change effort; that is, how do managers create a state of organizational *readiness* for change? Organizations are bureaucracies, and as such, Renato Mazzolini says, they tend almost naturally to resist change.[2] Barry Staw explains at least some components of that resistance less in terms of bureaucratic organizational structure than in terms of individual behavior. Organizational members become committed to a course of action and then escalate that commitment out of a sense of self-justification.[3] In order to overcome such resistance to change, extraordinary pressures must be brought to bear on organizations and individuals.

The need for this pressure has long been recognized by students of organizational change. Michael Beer, for instance, notes that organizational arrangements experience pressure to change only when they no longer allow the organization to respond to new competitive or

---

[1] Z. E. Barnes. "Change in the Bell System." *Academy of Management Executive* 1 (February): 1987, p. 43.

Source: From *Sloan Management Review*, Summer 1989.

[2] R. Mazzolini, "Strategy: A Bureaucratic and Political Process." In *Competitive Strategic Management*, R. B. Lamb, ed. (Englewood Cliffs, NJ: Prentice Hall), 1984.

[3] B. M. Staw, "The Escalation of Commitment to a Course of Action," *Academy of Management Review* 6: 1981, 577–587.

environmental conditions.[4] Dissatisfaction with the status quo, in other words, fuels organizational change.

But the literature on change tends to focus exclusively on how such pressures are experienced and acted upon by top managers or unit leaders. "*Top management* [emphasis added] seems to be groping for a solution to its problems," writes Larry Greiner of the opening stages of organizational change.[5] Wendell French and Cecil Bell agree: "Initially, in successful organization development efforts, there is strong pressure for improvement, at least on *top management* [emphasis added] of an organization or one of its subunits, from both inside and outside the organization."[6] Noel Tichy and Dave Ulrich elaborate on this view: "The *dominant group* [emphasis added] in the organization must experience a dissatisfaction with the status quo."[7] Those dissatisfied leaders, in turn, mobilize commitment to a new vision and translate that vision into practice by institutionalizing reinforcements for a new organizational culture.

A recent study of organizational change and revitalization conducted by the author with colleagues Michael Beer and Russell Eisenstat suggests that the dissatisfaction of top leaders may well be *necessary* in order to initiate an organizationwide change process, but that dissatisfaction alone is

hardly *sufficient* to bring about and sustain real change.

CHANGING ORGANIZATIONS

Our study targeted six companies engaged in a process of organizational revitalization; these firms were attempting to fundamentally redefine the relationship between individual employees and the corporation in order to make the organization more competitive. We selected six companies that would provide a range of organizational forms—centralized and decentralized—as well as of industries—smokestack manufacturing, financial services, consumer electronics, and information systems.

The research methodology included extensive field interviews and observations conducted over a four-year period. We spent five to six weeks, and in some instances longer, in each company. We started by interviewing human resource executives and then visited various plants, branches, and divisions. In all locations, we interviewed key line managers, employees at all levels, human resource staff, union leaders if there were any, and consultants. Finally, we interviewed top corporate executives. Later we made follow-up visits to get longitudinal data on the change process.

When the fieldwork was completed, we ranked the six companies on an effectiveness dimension: How innovative were their changes, and to what extent had innovations permeated the organization? We ranked each individual unit visited, as well as the corporations as a whole. Data from the questionnaires distributed to organizational members after the field research was factored into the judgments of effectiveness.

What became clear to us was that organizational leaders do not change

[4] M. Beer, *Organization Change and Development: A Systems View* (New York: Scott, Foresman, 1980).

[5] L. E. Greiner. "Patterns of Organization Change." *Harvard Business Review* (May–June) 1967, p. 122.

[6] W. L. French, and C. H. Bell, Jr., *Organization Development*, 3d ed. (Englewood Cliffs, NJ: Prentice Hall, 1984), p. 216.

[7] N. Tichy, and D. Ulrich, "Revitalizing Organizations: The Leadership Role." In *Managing Organizational Transitions*, J. R. Kimberly and R. E. Quinn, eds. (Homewood, IL: Richard D. Irwin, 1984), p. 245.

organizations. What they do is to oversee and orchestrate a process in which line managers up and down the organization attempt to change their own operating units. Plant managers seek increased worker commitment to enhance productivity and quality as well as shopfloor flexibility. Divisional leaders encourage general managers to do more collaboration and problem solving. Unit leaders try to instill employees with more aggressiveness and responsiveness. While leaders may be convinced of the need for change based on their own dissatisfaction with the status quo, that dissatisfaction is not enough. They must find ways of sharing it with the members of the organization who will actually institute new ways of thinking and acting.

This distinction between a dissatisfied leader and a leader who *diffuses dissatisfaction throughout the organization* is more than a simple refinement of the existing theory of organizational change. Overlooking the diffusion step can be (and often is) profoundly debilitating. When leaders jump directly from being dissatisfied to imposing new operating models, they fail to generate any real commitment to change. Employees greet new organizational and behavioral models with resistance or, at best, half-hearted compliance. Change programs get bogged down, and leaders become frustrated by employees' failure to perceive the dire and seemingly obvious need for change.

STRATEGIES FOR DIFFUSING DISSATISFACTION

In the successful change efforts that we observed, the top leader's desire for change was inevitably followed by interventions that diffused his or her dissatisfaction. The

interventions can be sorted into four generic types:

- Sharing competitive information.

- Pointing to shortcomings in individual, on-the-job behaviors.

- Offering models that suggest not just where the company ought to be headed but also how far it is from that goal.

- Mandating dissatisfaction.

SHARING COMPETITIVE INFORMATION

The most common method for diffusing dissatisfaction was the dissemination of information. Usually the information consisted of details about the company or unit's competitive position. For the most part, this information had previously been available *only* to top management.

Information sharing of this kind is a symbolic way of equalizing power, overcoming conflict, and building trust.[8] It also spreads dissatisfaction. The case of Scranton Steel's Youngstown plant illustrates this use of information sharing.[9]

As the competitive crisis within the steel industry in general and at Scranton Steel in particular mounted, plant manager Fred Howard started sharing competitive information throughout the plant. "If you look at the newsletters we're sending out now," he said, "quite frankly there's information in there that in the past wouldn't have been given to all our employees. On a case-by-case basis, we've

---

[8] This use of information sharing as opposed to information hoarding has been discussed in R. R. Blake et al., *Managing Intergroup Conflict in Industry* (Houston, TX: Gulf, 1964); and in R. E. Walton and R. McKersie, *A Behavioral Theory of Labor Negotiations* (New York: McGraw-Hill, 1965).

[9] Company names were disguised.

given departments actual profit information on their products. Ten years ago, this wouldn't even have been considered."[10]

What was the impact of this information sharing? One of the key stakeholders was the local United Steelworkers' union. Because of the existing contract, little change could occur in the way work was organized on the shop floor without the union's okay. The local union president *did* support Howard's call to change, reporting that Howard's willingness to share information—"to open the books to the union"—convinced him that the plant faced a severe competitive crisis. The information made union leaders, as well as rank-and-file workers, aware that maintaining the status quo would result in extensive layoffs, if not a plant closing. Thus, as dissatisfaction spread beyond the plant manager's office into the union hall, union leaders and the employees they represented began working closely with management on a wide variety of labor innovations.

The information sharing we observed was sometimes less rooted in specific competitive data than was the case at Youngstown. When Hugh Dorsey assumed control of the Fairweather Corporation, he presented not competitive data but an organizational diagnosis, and not by quietly disseminating information throughout the organization—he took his blunt, prodding diagnosis to the press. Dorsey talked freely to national and local reporters about his belief that poor management had undermined Fairweather's competitive position.

Similarly, when Henry Lester became president of US Financial, he frequently used the press as a platform. Almost immediately after becoming president, he announced on the pages of a national

business magazine his intention of turning US Financial's "cautious and conservative style into a more streamlined and venturesome enterprise that stresses a market-oriented strategy and strategic planning." His use of the press as a bully pulpit from which to spread his message through the ranks of the organization continued throughout his tenure; he later used *Business Week* to complain about the risk-averse, noninnovative culture that he claimed permeated upper management.

Based on our research, these two approaches to information sharing are not equally effective. Most managers at Fairweather and US Financial reported being aware that their leaders' public statements indicated a high level of dissatisfaction. But they also reported feeling resentful toward these highly public and extremely critical comments. "These are matters that should not be aired in public," stated one of Dorsey's direct reports. Said another, "Dorsey talks about 'tough love' when he makes these statements. Well, as far as I can see, there's no 'love' here. Just a lot of 'tough.'" These managers and others like them remained in the organization, but top management's approach may well have caused them to resist or to comply only minimally with proposed changes.

CREATING BEHAVIORAL DISSATISFACTION

Sharing competitive information is intended to unfreeze attitudes and shake up the status quo. But organizational change has a micro as well as a macro perspective; it also focuses on individual managers' on-the-job behaviors and styles.

The field of organizational development has long recognized and employed such individually oriented interventions, ranging from T-groups and team building

---

[10] Unless otherwise noted, all quotes were collected as part of the field research.

to more systematic ways of analyzing, categorizing, and transforming managerial behavior. Half the companies in our study used specific strategies to change individual behavior; interventions were designed to create dissatisfaction with the way managers were currently behaving.

Shortly after becoming president of US Financial, for instance, Henry Lester introduced attitude surveys that would be given regularly throughout the organization. The main tool was an employee opinion survey administered annually to about half the company's employees. It included a core group of about 50 questions designed to elicit a "general satisfaction level"; each division could add its own questions to meet specific needs. The results were broken down by units and given to unit managers, who were expected to conduct feedback sessions with employees and to "contract" for some specific actions to address issues raised by the survey.

Both Scranton Steel and Fairweather relied heavily on team building as part of their change process. At Scranton Steel, it occurred at the plant level as a follow-up to local union-management agreements. Immediately following an agreement to work toward improved quality of worklife and productivity, there was an off-site session attended by top plant management and local union leadership. Specifics of the change process were worked out at that session, but participants from both union and management reported that the meeting was more important from the perspective of team development. External facilitators helped participants from both sides confront behavioral impediments to future collaboration. Said Howard, "If I could isolate one important step in getting us on the right footing, it would be the off-site. To me, that was a major turning point. When the meeting ended, it was clear to me just how similar our goals and ends really were. The process of getting away was an absolutely necessary step."

Fairweather's experience with team building was not nearly as successful. Immediately after assuming the presidency, Hugh Dorsey adopted an explicit strategy for building dissatisfaction with managerial behavior. He arranged for his managers to be taken off-site in groups of 25 to 30; for five days they were put through a rigorous behavioral workshop that included self-assessment, lectures, team-building exercises, role playing, skits, and outdoor "survival" exercises all designed to point out shortcomings in current behavior and foster the new behaviors desired by Dorsey.

The actual impact of this behavioral intervention was evidently somewhat limited. Participants openly wondered about its relevance to their work lives. Organizers worried that they had never successfully followed up on the insights and commitments made at the off-site sessions. And Dorsey himself, although still a supporter of this type of intervention, conceded that the resulting change had been too small and had occurred too slowly to help save the company from its declining competitive position.

How can we account for the apparently significant differences in the impact of interventions aimed at creating dissatisfaction with behaviors? The key variable in the examples here seems to be the degree to which the dissatisfaction resulted from actual on-the-job behaviors or was imposed upon managers by the leader. US Financial's use of attitude surveys did seem to have some immediate impact. The company's own internal research could formally track improved attitudes and informally point to improved bottom-line performance in divisions that used the surveys rigorously. And the dissatisfaction reported in those surveys was produced, at least indirectly, by how managers actually behaved on the job. However, the positive impact proved to be transitory. Little evidence could be found regarding any real long-term changes in on-the-job behaviors.

Scranton Steel's team building proved more successful. Remember, though, that it occurred in this context: Managers *had* to behave in new ways as they began working with union representatives to solve real business problems. The literature on plant-level change where unions are involved indicates that Youngstown's example is far from unique.[11] When managers work with unions in new ways, some training mechanism is required to confront, indeed change, traditional modes of behavior.

Fairweather's experience with team building was the least successful intervention. Whereas US Financial's attitude survey related directly to performance behaviors, and team building at Scranton Steel followed up union-management agreements that required changing old patterns of adversarial behavior, Dorsey's intervention seemed (to many participants) to be rooted less concretely in the needs of the business. The off-site sessions followed Dorsey's own assessment that his company needed to foster more collaboration among employees if they were to compete more successfully. Participants were not so sure. Some used words like "weird" and "crazy," while others dismissed the whole exercise as brainwashing. "You

guys are trying to _____ with our minds" was the blunt assessment of one disgruntled participant. A key organizer admitted that participants found it difficult to take what they had learned back to their day-to-day work situation.

The changes promoted at Fairweather's off-site sessions, in other words, seemed to meet the needs of one individual—Hugh Dorsey—rather than to address the demands of the business. Thus, they could easily be dismissed.

USING MODELS TO PRODUCE DISSATISFACTION

Scholars and managers alike stress that successful models encourage change to occur. They provide a vision of the future, and they can also help spread dissatisfaction with the status quo.[12]

Scranton Steel, for instance, used internal subunit models to build dissatisfaction. Almost immediately after a union contract made collaborative quality-of-worklife efforts possible, Scranton Steel's head of labor relations began working with consultants on a process to ensure successful implementation. The consultants suggested using a survey to identify plants where implementation was most likely to succeed. These plants would already be close to the new model: a high level of union-management cooperation, managers whose problem-solving style had already become more participative, and generally positive working conditions.

The survey identified two possible plants, but the process had a more far-reaching impact than that. Information

[11] See, for example: J. M. Rosow, ed. *Teamwork: Joint Labor Management Programs in America* (New York: Pergamon Press, 1986).

[12] See, for example: Beer, 1980; Tichy and Ulrich, 1984; and G. Barczak et al., "Managing Large-Scale Organizational Change," *Organizational Dynamics*, Autumn 1987, pp. 22–35.

about these sites got back to the nondesignated plants; as managers at the firm's two largest plants realized they had not even been considered, and as word spread that the new chairman had endorsed joint union-management efforts in the strongest possible terms, anxieties began to arise. A member of the task force created to oversee implementation recalled, "Plant managers were saying to us, 'If we're not ready, what do we need to do to get ready?'" Key line managers began to demand a process that would move them toward revitalization. Holding some plants up as models of readiness, in other words, created dissatisfaction in many of the organization's other plants.

MANDATING DISSATISFACTION

When Don Singer, the newly named chairman of Scranton Steel, announced at an executive meeting what changes he considered necessary, one member of his management team objected. "You're talking about participative management—about collaborating with the union, information sharing, cooperative problem solving. But it won't be so easy. There's a *lot* of history to overcome." Singer listened while the executive finished this cautionary speech. He then pointed his finger directly at the executive and said, "Things are going to change around here. This is a way of life. And if things don't change," he added, "I won't be the first to go." Hugh Dorsey delivered virtually the same message: you must change according to my diagnosis of what needs to be done or leave the organization.

It would be difficult to pinpoint the precise impact of such a threat. In both cases, it was used only once. (This may be a case of "once is enough," since intimidating messages spread quickly.) Nevertheless,

judging from the reports of managers, these mandates seemed to create compliance more than commitment. At Scranton Steel, the manager to whom the warning was delivered reacted by repressing any further public objections and reluctantly going along with the effort. He never agreed to an interview for the research project, so I cannot offer any direct insight into his thought processes. But subordinates and superiors alike agreed about his lack of enthusiasm and commitment. The chairman took to referring to the individual as his "internal resister."

Occasionally, the individuals to whom warnings were issued were replaced at a later stage of the change process. But while they were with the company, they almost never wholeheartedly accepted the leader's diagnosis. Top-down commands and threats violate the notion of free choice; doubters don't feel they "own" the choice to adopt new patterns of behavior.

At least one mandate proved much more effective. Duluth Products, the most successful "change" company in our sample, used models designed to create dissatisfaction, as well as a kind of threat, though not one aimed directly at individuals. After some early successes at job restructuring, participative management, and gain-sharing plans in small, relatively isolated plants, chief operating officer John Watson simply mandated dissatisfaction with the status quo throughout the organization. He made no explicit threats to job security. Instead, he announced that future corporate investments would go only to plants that undertook similar innovations. If plant managers did not yet share Watson's dissatisfaction with the status quo, Watson would provide them with a new source of dissatisfaction: you will lose corporate investment and support if you maintain the status quo.

DIFFUSING DISSATISFACTION—A KEY CONCERN

While this article has identified four distinct strategies for diffusing dissatisfaction, it is clear that not all applications of those strategies are equally effective in promoting change. Table 1 lays out the intervention strategies employed by three of the companies in our research sample: the leading change company (Duluth Products), the lagging company (US Financial), and a middle-level company (Scranton Steel). Although overall success in transforming organizations rests on far more than the initial intervention strategy, the evidence is nonetheless revealing on several points:

- First, no single intervention alone is sufficient to diffuse dissatisfaction properly.

- Second, pointing to individual behaviors early in the change process is not necessarily associated with success. Successful transformations aim to change the organizational context in which individual behaviors occur, rather than the behaviors themselves. Individual behavioral changes result from contextual interventions, not from direct assaults on those behaviors.

- Third, consistent with much previous literature on organizational change, models can show both where the organization is headed and how great a gap exists between the reality and the goal. The use of models seems to be a key element in diffusion strategies.

- Fourth, some sort of forcing strategy also seems to be a key element, although, as noted earlier, some forcing strategies are more effective than others.

It is commonplace to see dissatisfied leaders who attempt to impose change on organizational members who are not ready—and yet this pattern is inevitably disastrous. Of our six case studies, five started with a dissatisfied leader who imposed change programs. In each instance, little real change occurred. We need to add a new step to our understanding of how change unfolds: The leader with a "felt need" for change must diffuse dissatisfaction before lasting change can occur.

TABLE 1   **Dissatisfaction Diffusion Interventions**

Company	Sharing Competitive Information	Pointing to Individual Behavior	Using Original Models	Mandating Dissatisfaction
Leading company (Duluth Products)	X		X	X
Middle company (Scranton Steel)	X	X	X	X
Lagging company (US Financial)	X	X		

Case

Merrill Lynch

Evolution, Revolution and Sale, 1996–2008

Todd D. Jick
Professor, Columbia Business School

INTRODUCTION

Merrill Lynch was founded in 1914 when Wall Street bond salesman Charles Merrill teamed up with friend Edmund Lynch to open an underwriting firm. By reaching out to investors—ranging from retired shopkeepers to small business owners and widows with nest eggs—Merrill Lynch gained renown for "bringing Wall Street to Main Street." Its growing ranks of brokers—numbering 17,000 by 2008—were nicknamed "the thundering herd," in a nod to the company's iconic bull logo.[1] Yet, Merrill Lynch itself was long personified as a nurturing, benevolent entity, so-called "Mother Merrill," who spared no expense in taking care of either her clients or her employees. The company became known as a place where loyalty was amply rewarded, where an employee's child was

[1] http://premium.hoovers.com/subscribe/co/factsheet.xhtml?ID=10990

Acknowledgments *Nancy J. Brandwein and Omar Eissa MBA '10 provided research and writing assistance for this case.*

This case was prepared as a basis for class discussion rather than to illustrate either effective or ineffective handling of a business situation.

likely to be handed a job.[2] Many say this collegial culture contributed to the company's ability to withstand the Depression, the crash of 1987 and the terrorist attacks of 9/11.

Yet, this organizational culture and its business model and brand, strong as they were, did not enable the company to withstand the fall 2008 financial crisis. Before that time, Merrill Lynch was a multinational corporation with nearly $2 trillion in private, institutional and government client assets. It operated in 40 countries and provided financial services in two segments: the Global Markets and Investment Banking Group and Global Investment Management Units. All of these features made it an important strategic asset for Bank of America, which announced its merger with Merrill Lynch on September 15, 2008. As many company histories might reveal, the journey of Merrill Lynch was marked by evolutions and revolutions, changes by degree and profound transformation. This précis looks at the different routes taken to transform Merrill Lynch by its CEOs

[2] Smith, Randall, "O'Neal Out as Merrill Reels From Loss; Startled Board Ditches A Famously Aloof CEO; The Revenge of Mother," *Wall Street Journal*, October 29, 2007, p. A1. Thornton, Emily, "THE NEW MERRILL LYNCH Stan O'Neal has made the firm leaner and meaner. Now, he's betting big on trading and other risky ventures," *Business Week*, May 5, 2003. Iss. 3831, pp. 80–85.

in its last decade: David H. Komansky, E. Stanley (Stan) O'Neal, and the last CEO to preside over Merrill Lynch as an independent entity, John Thain.

THE KOMANSKY YEARS (1996–2003)

The appointment of David H. Komansky as Merrill Lynch's CEO in 1996 can be seen as the first significant departure from 80-plus years of company tradition. Like all CEOs before him, Komansky came up through the brokerage side and was a self-admitted "back-slapping, gregarious person." Yet, he was the first Jew to run a company that had been called "the Catholic firm" of Wall Street. This move was hailed as an entrance into a new phase of meritocracy and diversity necessary to tackle the global marketplace. And tackle it, Komansky did. "Five years from today, there will be 6, 8, 10 of the most truly global financial services firms, and we intend to be one of them," he said, and he set a goal of deriving 50% of the company's revenues from abroad, compared to 25% in 1996.[3] With his deal-making prowess, Komansky went on an acquiring spree. In less than a decade Merrill made 19 acquisitions, many of which were in developing Asian economies.[4] Komansky is credited for completing former CEO Daniel Tully's transformation of Merrill from a domestic retail brokerage giant to a global investment banking powerhouse:

> I had the opportunity to see it [Merrill Lynch] metamorphize from a pure retail

stock and bond operation to a globally integrated financial firm. It was a constant case of evolving, and it had an esprit de corps and familiar feeling valued by a lot of people. It could take on any challenge.[5]

Yet, toward the end of Komansky's tenure, the company was bloated and foundering. While revenues soared at a 15% annualized rate, expenses rose in tandem. By 2000, the best year in investment banking history, Merrill's underwriting and advisory business only managed a $200 million profit.[6] A full three-quarters of the company's bottom line came from low-margin, equity-related business. According to some, the company was lavishing too much money on the famed thundering herd for too little return.[7] In addition, the company had been slow to get on the Internet bandwagon, leaving firms like Charles Schwab to snag low margin clients at lower cost. With the market crash of 2000, it was revealed just how bad things were, and rumors swirled that Merrill Lynch was ripe for a takeover attempt.[8]

THE O'NEAL ERA (2003–2007)

There was no takeover, but there was a "revolution" within Merrill Lynch, fomented by the retiring Komansky's successor, E. Stanley O'Neal. Known for his

---

[3] Truell, Peter, "Komansky, an Old Retail Broker, Takes the World Stage," *New York Times*, December 20, 1996, p. D1.
[4] Thornton, Emily, "Shaking Up Merrill," *Businessweek Online*, November 12, 2001, http://www.businessweek.com/print/magazine/content/01-46/b3757068.htm?chan=mz

[5] Anderson, Jenny, "Shrinking the Culture Gap at Merrill," *New York Times*, October 23, 2005, p. 3.1.
[6] Rynecki, David, "Putting the Muscle Back in the Bull," *Fortune*, April 5, 2004. Vol. 149, Iss. 7, p. 162+.
[7] Horwood, Clive, "How Stan O'Neal transformed Merrill Lynch," *Euromoney*, July 2006, p. 1+.
[8] Rynecki, David, "Putting the Muscle Back in the Bull."

cost-cutting abilities in the brokerage division, where he had fired 2,000 brokers, sending profit margins up by five percentage points, O'Neal became president under Komansky in July of 2001 and CEO in 2003.[9] In just his first three years, he took the company through more cultural change than it had gone through in the previous five decades. Former CEO Daniel Tully, who presided over Merrill from 1992 to 1996, commented:

> [Mr. O'Neal] forgot what Mother Merrill stood for and just disavowed the past. We had a great thing going for us, with the so-called backslapping type of people that we are. We were tough taskmasters but not mean-spirited.[10]

However, according to O'Neal, none of this mattered:

> People say all these things about me. They say I'm a bean counter. I'm not. I spend so little time thinking about numbers, they wouldn't believe it. But if people want to say that I can't do anything about it. I have a job to do, and it has nothing to do with worrying about what people say about me.[11]

O'Neal was the very opposite of Komansky in almost every respect. The first African American to run a major investment bank, he had never been a broker and was described as "aloof," "a loner," and a "bean counter," but also as brilliant and utterly objective. A defining moment in his tenure came right after the 9/11 terrorist attacks, when shaken Merrill employees were forced to evacuate their World Financial Center offices. O'Neal

did not wait for the literal dust to subside before announcing his dramatic restructuring plan. For this he was lambasted in the press and reviled by employees.

Yet, his quick cost-cutting actions brought the company back to profitability.[12] Deeming the old Mother Merrill culture passé, O'Neal cut 24,000 jobs and closed 300 field offices. He froze pay, cut bonuses and took away perks to which employees had become accustomed. In the retail business, he began segmenting customers, diverting those with low account balances to impersonal call centers, coddling only the richest clients. As a result, Merrill became the leanest and most profitable of any such firm in the U.S. Profit margins soared to 28%, and the company made more money per broker than either Goldman Sachs or Citigroup.[13]

At the same time that O'Neal was cutting, segmenting and rearranging, he was pushing the company into new and riskier territories. Shortly after he assumed the CEO mantle, he told investors that he wanted to build "a new kind of financial services firm" that provided a greater range of services but with far fewer people and a constant focus on profitability. He initiated a cutthroat Darwinian ethos that could be described as survival of the riskiest—encouraging managers to take risks, and giving them only six months to a year to show they could succeed. Scuttlebutt was that O'Neal wanted to turn Merrill into another Goldman Sachs.[14] The company continued to increase its exposure in collateralized debt obligations, known as CDOs, complex debt instruments and subprime mortgages. At first, this strategy was a boon, delivering what

[9] Thornton, Emily, "The New Merrill Lynch."
[10] Smith, Randall, "O'Neal Out as Merrill Reels From Loss."
[11] Rynecki, David, "Putting the Muscle Back in the Bull."
[12] Ibid.
[13] Thornton, Emily, "Shaking Up Merrill."
[14] Thornton, Emily, "The New Merrill Lynch."

The New York Times called "high-octane, high-risk returns." Then, in July 2007, there was a global credit crunch, spurred by a steep downturn in the value of subprime mortgages, which was, in turn, caused by the high default rate among less creditworthy borrowers. According to Winthrop H. Smith, Jr., a former Merrill executive who spent 28 years at the firm and whose father was a founding partner:

> Under Stan's watch, Merrill Lynch has written down $10 billion. This is someone who has tinkered with the culture of a successful firm. Merrill Lynch is in need of a real leader.[15]

When Merrill took an $8.4 billion write-down in the third quarter of 2007 and suffered $2.4 billion in losses, the length of O'Neal's term was the subject of much speculation. Then, when the board learned that O'Neal had made unauthorized merger overtures to Wachovia, his ouster was assured. It didn't help that over the years O'Neal had alienated and pushed out many senior managers, his allies among them, leaving himself quite alone at the top during the crisis. He was forced to resign in October 2007.[16]

THE BRIEF REIGN OF THAIN

O'Neal's forced resignation put Merrill Lynch at a crucial juncture. As an analyst at RCM Capital Management said, "The board needs to decide whether the business model was good and the company just needs better execution, or the business model itself needs to be changed.[17] In other words, the company could continue O'Neal's attempt to model the firm after Goldman Sachs and seek out new investment opportunities or go back to the company's retail brokerage roots.[18] The board appointed the first CEO from outside the company, John Thain, a former Goldman Sachs executive of 20 years, but someone with no prior retail brokerage experience. He had most recently been CEO of the New York Stock Exchange (NYSE), with a glowing reputation for having pushed the NYSE into the future. Thain readied the Exchange for the global digital marketplace at a time when morale was at an all-time low. In an interview in 2007 about his view of his new firm Thain said:

> This is a people business, and whether it's on the wealth management side or on the investment banking side or on the trading side, in the end the main asset is people. And so making sure that you're paying attention to people, making sure that you're sensitive to the culture, making sure that the organization is working together as a team is critical to its long-term success.[19]

A former Goldman colleague said, "John loves to take things apart and fix

[15] Anderson, Jenny and Thomas Jr., Landon, "Big Risk, and a Big Loss," *New York Times*, October 25, 2007, p. C1.
[16] Thomas Jr., Landon and Anderson, Jenny, "A Risk-Taker's Reign at Merrill Ends With a Swift, Messy Fall," *New York Times*, October 29, 2007, p. A1.

[17] Rosenbush, Steve, "What Merrill Needs in a New CEO," *BusinessWeek Online*, Oct. 31, 2007.
[18] Rosenbush, Steve, "What Merrill Needs in a New CEO," *BusinessWeek Online*, October 31, 2007 http://www.businessweek.com/print/bwdaily/dnflash/content/oct2007/db200771030_94196.htm
[19] Bartiromo, Maria, "John Thain on his new job as CEO of Merrill Lynch," *BusinessWeek*, November 26, 2007. Iss. 4060, p. 25 .

them. He understands risk."[20] In fact, Thain's nickname was "Mr. Fix-it." Yet, in an interview with a *BusinessWeek* reporter shortly after he was named CEO of Merrill, Thain implied he would neither rush to dismantle nor to acquire, but said simply, "The company will focus on developing the business it has."[21] In the retail brokerage business, so tied to Merrill's roots and old culture, Thain left Bob McCann in place to rule over the thundering herd.[22] McCann was a longtime Merrill veteran, known for his Irish-Catholic glad-handing, of whom a colleague said "[he] connects with people."[23]

From the start, Thain had to resolve many questions. Would it be best to instill a Goldman-like business model and a Goldman-like culture in troubled Merrill? But hadn't O'Neal himself tried to push Merrill to be more than an investment banking and retail brokerage firm, similar to Goldman? Hadn't this led to much of its trouble? And what about the Mother Merrill which had once existed? Ex-Merrill executives such as Win Smith, who was removed by O'Neal, predicted that Thain would "... take time to understand the old culture and what made it so good ... because he understands the power of culture, which Stan did not."[24] And former Merrill chairman Dan Tully said of Thain,

"Let's give him a chance," even as he said, in the same breath, "Charlie Merrill would turn over in his grave if he knew we hired someone from Goldman Sachs."[25]

In that early interview with CNBC's Maria Bartiromo in the November 2007 *BusinessWeek*, the cautious, measured Thain emerged, making comments such as:

I'm not at all sure that I want to change it (the wealth management business). I first have to learn about it. It is the leading wealth management franchise in the world.

I think that phrase (Mother Merrill) had a negative connotation in the past, and I don't think about it that way. I don't know if they think about it that way.

The Board is looking for leadership. The Board is looking for strategy and direction. The Board is looking to unify the company. And it's also looking to focus on some specific concerns—risk management, and of course, the fixed income area. And also to further develop the senior management team.[26]

All eyes were on Thain. The next chapter of Merrill Lynch's story had begun to be written. Would it be a further evolution or another revolution?

THAIN'S BUMPY RIDE

At the outset, Thain set clear goals for himself and the organization. He vowed to establish a new leadership team, repair the firm's failed risk function, and raise capital to replace huge losses on mortgage securities. Within weeks of his appointment,

[20] Goldstein, Matthew and Thornton, Emily, "He Fixed the NYSE. Can He Fix Merrill?; John Thain won kudos for turning around the Big Board. Now he faces a bigger challenge cleaning up the subprime mess at the investment bank," *BusinessWeek*, November 26, 2007. Iss. 4060, p. 28.
[21] Bartiromo, Maria, "John Thain on his new job as CEO of Merrill Lynch," *BusinessWeek*, Nov 26, 2007.
[22] Ibid.
[23] Anderson, Jenny, "Shrinking the Culture Gap at Merrill."
[24] Ibid.

[25] Farrell, Greg, "Merrill Lynch hires NYSE chief as CEO: Going outside to find leader is a first for the company," *USA Today*, November 15, 2007, p. B1.
[26] Bartiromo, Maria, "John Thain on his new job as CEO of Merrill Lynch."

Thain lured a cadre of former colleagues from Goldman Sachs and the NYSE to run various parts of the business. Nelson Chai of NYSE was appointed CFO. Margaret Tutwiler, also of the NYSE, was appointed Head of Communications. High-profile recruits from Goldman Sachs included Peter Krause to run Strategy, Tom Montag as Head of Sales and Trading and Noel Donohoe as Co-Chief Risk Officer, all reporting directly to the CEO.[27] In particular, regarding the newly formed risk function, Thain said:

> Noel's appointment and the new reporting structure of risk management emphasize the importance of this area to me and to Merrill Lynch. Noel's many years of market risk and product control experience will make an important addition to our risk management function and is complementary to the firm's existing team.[28]

Having made significant structural and personnel changes, the firm focused on repairing its balance sheet. At the close of 2007, additional losses forced Thain to raise equity from a group of sovereign wealth and private equity funds. But the new fiscal year brought an even more challenging environment. In March 2008, Wall Street woke up to news that Bear Stearns, a firm with a storied history, was being sold to JPMorgan Chase for $2 per share—with government assistance—essentially wiping out shareholders. As markets tumbled, Merrill Lynch employees and shareholders found themselves facing a similarly dire situation. After three consecutive quarters of staggering writedowns, seeking to end the cycle of losses and dilutions, Thain arranged a fire sale of nearly $30 billion of CDOs, at the price of 22 cents on the dollar, to the Lone Star fund. Merrill booked the transaction as a sale, which some said was optimistic if Lone Star decided to send the CDOs back, leaving Merrill holding only the down payment.[29]

Thain explained the reasoning behind the transaction this way:

> If you look at our business in the second quarter, the work of 60,000 employees generated $7.5 billion in revenues and almost $2 billion in pre-tax income, but all of the efforts of all those people were wiped out by the declines in asset values . . . These assets that we sold accounted for about 70% of all the losses we've taken over the last twelve months. So when we had the opportunity to sell them . . . and to raise capital at the same time, we took advantage of that opportunity because it's a great risk reduction trade, it puts us in a much better position to manage our business going forward and with the new capital, we are very well capitalized.[30]

Many criticized this move. Since Merrill financed 75% of the transaction with its own balance sheet, many analysts believed the firm had not reduced much of its exposure at all. Moreover, other investment banks, such as Lehman Brothers, who were holding similar assets on their balance sheets at significantly higher market values, were forced to mark them to down to Thain's 22 cents valuation.

[27] Merrill Lynch press releases (Donohoe January 17, 2008; Montag April 28, 2008; Krause May 5, 2008).
[28] http://www.ml.com/index.asp?id=7695_7696_8149_88278_88282_89140 [This is a press release entitled, "Merrill Lynch Appoints Noel B. Donohoe Co-Chief Risk Officer"].
[29] http://www.nytimes.com/2008/08/01/business/01norris.html
[30] http://www.youtube.com/watch?v=uLT 1 eEfCQVM

Thain had taken bold steps in his first year at the helm—raising over $27 billion in capital in five separate offerings. He integrated and elevated the firm's risk functions and tied business unit compensation to the profitability of the firm as a whole. With risky exposures (at least seemingly) down significantly, the firm was thought to be "well-capitalized," and with new leadership in place, Merrill Lynch seemed poised to withstand tough markets.

THE SALE, AND END, OF MERRILL LYNCH

On Friday, September 12, 2008 Thain was invited to secret weekend meetings at the New York Federal Reserve where it was revealed that if no buyers emerged, Lehman Brothers, the 138-year-old investment firm, would face bankruptcy when the markets opened Monday morning. It was widely believed that Bank of America (BofA) and Barclay's were the only serious bidders. When the U.S. Treasury refused to provide any backstop similar to that provided in the Bear Stearns transaction, both Barclay's and Bank of America declined the Lehman acquisition. As the Lehman bankruptcy became imminent, Thain, fearing a systemic lack of confidence and the onslaught of short-sellers, picked up the phone, called Ken Lewis of Bank of America and asked if he would be interested in a transaction. Lewis flew up from Charlotte, North Carolina immediately.[31] As Lewis recalled, "It didn't take but about two seconds to see the strategic implications—the positive

implications . . . [Merrill Lynch] has created the best wealth management company in the world and we acknowledge that.[32] This was the same Ken Lewis who had said almost a year before the deal, "I've had all the fun I can stand in investment banking at the moment. To get bigger is not something I want to do."[33] Yet, at the time of the deal, Lewis seemed to be the only one who wasn't questioning its viability. Business columnist Jack Flack parsed the Bank of America press release announcing the deal as meaning one thing for the company: adding Merrill Lynch would finally get us the respect we deserve. By merging Merrill's investment bank with Bank of America's existing operations, the huge Charlotte-based bank would be instantly catapulted into the "league tables" for both debt and equity underwriting.[34]

On Monday morning, September 15, concurrently with the announcement of Lehman's demise, Thain and Lewis appeared in a press conference announcing the sale of Merrill Lynch to Bank of America in an all-stock transaction, valuing the firm at nearly $50 billion on the date of the announcement. The two executives stressed the strategic rationale behind the deal, with Merrill gaining access to a massive balance sheet and Bank of America attaining Merrill's prized wealth-management franchise, lucrative clients and international footprint. Soon after the deal was announced, Bank of America issued a press release confirming that John

---

[31] Craig, Susanne, McCracken, Jeffrey, Lucchetti, Aaron and Kate Kelly, "How Wall Street Unraveled in a September Weekend," Posted to: Thecharlotteobserver.com on December 30, 2008.

[32] September 15, 2008. Deal Announcement Press Conference.

[33] White, Ben, "Investment Shock for BofA," *The Financial Times*, October 19, 2007, p.1.

[34] Barrett, Megan, "Ken Lewis, Hot or Not?" Portfolio.com, September 15, 2008 or http://www.portfolio.com/executives/features/2008/09/15/Ken-Lewis-Hot-or-Not

Thain would join the combined company as Head of Investment Banking, Commercial Banking and Wealth Management, reporting directly to Ken Lewis. In announcing the deal, Thain said:

> The deal that we have with Bank of America is a strategic one that makes a huge amount of strategic sense—the combination of their strength in the US on the commercial banking side and on the retail banking side combined with our strength in wealth management and global investment banking makes a tremendous amount of sense . . . The combined entity is probably the world's strongest financial institution. We will have great financial strength. We will have a global reach. If you look across the different businesses we are number one or number two across almost every business that we will be in. Whether it's commercial banking, retail banking, investment banking, wealth management, we will be the leading financial institution in the world.
>
> There really won't be any cuts necessarily in fixed income or commodities because there's a commitment to continue to expand both . . . but there will be redundancies in the combined companies. Most of those redundancies really come on the infrastructure side. In places like IT, operations, finance, where there is an overlap of corporate functions . . . Between the two companies, it will be thousands of jobs.[35]

As the next months unfolded, Merrill Lynch's past and present executives either fled the merged company or dug their heels in, resisting changes. Year-end bonuses awarded to Merrill Lynch executives by John Thain were publicly exposed and

challenged by the media and U.S. congressional committees overseeing financial bailouts to firms such as the Bank of America. And Bank of America began to institute changes to many sacred Merrill Lynch traditions including ending Broker Sales Award Incentives such as elaborate travel and entertainment events. Among Merrill employees, there was fear, uncertainty and anger about the future. Some of it was attributed to John Thain's actions and some to Bank of America. Whatever emotions emerged, one fact would not change. Merrill Lynch's 93-year history as an independent company and iconic American brand was coming to a close.

At the final shareholders' meeting approving the transaction, on December 5, 2008, Winthrop H. Smith, Jr., delivered an emotional speech to shareholders and employees. Here is a brief excerpt:

> At this point I want to make it very clear that I support the merger with Bank of America, and I am thankful for John Thain's clear and decisive leadership at that moment of crisis this fall. I am encouraged by the respect that Ken Lewis says he has for our great franchise and for the many thousands of fine professionals who are still part of the Merrill Lynch team. I do hope Ken and his colleagues at Bank of America will allow the firm that they bought to thrive under its new ownership, and that they will appreciate the strong culture that made Merrill what it was by 2001 and will also appreciate the many fine people who hung in and are still with Merrill Lynch, including members of my own family.
>
> All of us want this new organization to succeed and become preeminent. We all know that what has occurred is the given reality and it is time to move forward. However, before we do, some things need to be said for the record.

[35] http://www.youtube.com/watch?v=S12Jpz M791U

. . .

Today is not the result of the sub-prime mess or synthetic CDOs. They are the symptoms. This is the story of failed leadership and the failure of the Board of Directors to understand what was happening to this great company, and its failure to take action soon enough. I stand here today and say shame to both the current as well as the former Directors who allowed this former CEO [O'Neal] to wreak havoc on this great company. . . . Shame, shame, shame for allowing one man to consciously unwind a culture and rip out the soul of this great firm. Shame on them for allowing this former CEO to retire with a $160 million retirement package and shame on them for not resigning themselves. . . .

But I must give the Devil his due. I applaud the Board for selecting John Thain. John inherited a mess, but he did so many of the right things. He reached out to the past; he reached out to the people of Merrill Lynch around the world and showed them his humanity as well as his intelligence. John had the intellect, the experience, the humility, the common sense and the integrity to pull it off had not the markets melted down this past fall. Then he had the wisdom, as Kenny Rogers sang, to know when to fold them so that Merrill did not go the way of Lehman.

We thank you John not only for what you tried to do and what you did do. We thank you because we know you knew what Mother Merrill really stood for. As a competitor at Goldman Sachs you respected our past and our present and you were serious about restoring our valued principles once you became our leader.

Having led the battle to save Merrill Lynch, Thain's next task would be to manage the aftermath of the deal. The months after the consummation of the transaction were marked by public relations disasters that called both the viability of the deal and Thain's credibility into question. Shortly after the deal closed, Bank of America announced severe cutbacks in the brokerage unit, cutting back training and monitoring expenses. This enraged the highly independent brokerage force.[36] By December 2008 a formidable clash of cultures had developed leading to the high-level defections of Greg Fleming, the Merrill Lynch president and deal architect slated to run Global Commercial and Investment Banking for the combined firm, and Bob McCann, long time veteran and head of Merrill's prized brokerage unit.[37] With his leadership in question, Thain reported dramatic losses to close the fourth quarter of 2008. Reeling from losses, Bank of America's board was forced to seek a bailout from the US Treasury. With the media swirling, Lewis claimed to know nothing of the mounting losses at Merrill as tensions between Thain and Lewis escalated.

During the first weeks of 2009, Thain was plagued by allegations, not denied by Bank of America, that he had accelerated bonus payments to Merrill executives to skirt Bank of America approval, squandered $1.2 million on lavish renovations of his executive suite, and misled Bank of America about the financial outlook of Merrill Lynch's business. Headlines across the financial and mainstream press reviled the ex-Mr. Fix-it as the new face of Wall Street excess.

[36] Philbin, Brett, "Merrill Lynch Global Wealth Management Cutting Branch Support Staff," Dow Jones Newswires, Feb. 9, 2009.
[37] Anonymous, "Merrill-BofA left reeling after Fleming, McCann quit in one week," *Euroweek*, January 9, 2009.

The tension culminated on January 22, 2009, in a meeting with Lewis that reportedly lasted less than 15 minutes, in which in no uncertain terms, John Thain was ousted from the combined company. Thain's departure was perhaps the final symbol that Merrill Lynch would no longer exist. Just as it had brokered many deals of companies that would become absorbed in others, Merrill Lynch would now become absorbed into Bank of America.

Reading

An Improvisational Model for Change Management

The Case of Groupware Technologies

Wanda J. Orlikowski

J. Debra Hofman

In her discussion of technology design, Lucy Suchman refers to two different approaches to open sea navigation—the European and the Trukese:

> The European navigator begins with a plan—a course—which he has charted according to certain universal principles, and he carries out his voyage by relating his every move to that plan. His effort throughout his voyage is directed to remaining "on course." If unexpected events occur, he must first alter the plan, then respond accordingly. The Trukese navigator begins with an objective rather than a plan. He sets off toward the objective and responds to conditions as they arise in an *ad hoc* fashion. He utilizes information provided by the wind, the waves, the tide and current, the fauna, the stars, the clouds, the sound of the water on the side of the boat, and he steers accordingly. His effort is directed to doing whatever is necessary to reach the objective.[1]

Like Suchman, we too find this contrast in approaches instructive and use it here to motivate our discussion of managing technological change. In particular, we suggest that how people think about managing change in organizations most often resembles the European approach to navigation. That is, they believe they need to start with a plan for the change, charted according to certain general organizational principles, and that they need to relate their actions

[1] Berreman (1966, p. 347), as cited in L. Suchman, *Plans and Situated Actions: The Problem of Human-Machine Communication* (Cambridge, England: Cambridge University Press, 1987), p. vii.

Source: From Sloan Management Review, Winter 1997.

to that plan, ensuring throughout that the change remains on course.

However, when we examine how change occurs in practice, we find that it much more closely resembles the voyage of the Trukese. That is, people end up responding to conditions as they arise, often in an ad hoc fashion, doing whatever is necessary to implement change. In a manner similar to Argyris and Schön's contrast between espoused theories and theories-in-use, we suggest that there is a discrepancy between how people think about technological change and how they implement it.[2] Moreover, we suggest that this discrepancy significantly contributes to the difficulties and challenges that contemporary organizations face as they attempt to introduce and effectively implement technology-based change.

Traditional ways of thinking about technological change have their roots in Lewin's three-stage change model of "unfreezing," "change," and "refreezing."[3] According to this model, the organization prepares for change, implements the change, and then strives to regain stability as soon as possible. Such a model, which treats change as an event to be managed during a specified period,[4] may have been appropriate for organizations that were relatively stable and bounded and whose functionality was sufficiently fixed to allow for detailed specification. Today, however, given more turbulent, flexible, and uncertain organizational and environmental conditions, such a model is becoming less appropriate—hence, the discrepancy.

This discrepancy is particularly pronounced when the technology being implemented is open-ended and customizable, as in the case of the new information technologies that are known as groupware.[5] Groupware technologies provide electronic networks that support communication, coordination, and collaboration through facilities such as information exchange, shared repositories, discussion forums, and messaging. Such technologies are typically designed with an open architecture that is adaptable by end users, allowing them to customize existing features and create new applications.[6] Rather than automating a predefined sequence of operations and transactions, these technologies tend to be general-purpose tools that are used in different ways across various organizational activities and contexts. Organizations need the experience of using groupware technologies in particular ways and in particular contexts to better understand how they may be most useful in practice. In such a technological context, the traditional change model is thus particularly discrepant.

[2] C. Argyris and D. A. Schön, *Organizational Learning* (Reading, MA: Addison Wesley, 1978).
[3] K. Lewin, "Group Decision and Social Change," in E. Newcombe and R. Harley, eds., *Readings in Social Psychology* (New York: Henry Holt, 1952), pp. 459–473; and T. K. Kwon and R. W. Zmud, "Unifying the Fragmented Models of Information Systems Implementation," in R. J. Boland, Jr., and R. A. Hirschheim, eds., *Critical Issues in Information Systems Research* (New York: John Wiley, 1987), pp. 227–251.
[4] A. M. Pettigrew, *The Awakening Giant* (Oxford, England: Blackwell Publishers,1985).

[5] Not all groupware technologies are flexible and customizable (e.g., fixed-function e-mail systems). We are interested here only in those that are (e.g., Lotus Notes).
[6] D. Dejean and S. B. Dejean, *Lotus/Notes at Work* (New York: Lotus Books, 1991); and T. W. Malone, K. Y. Lai, and C. Fry, "Experiments with OVAL: A Radically Tailorable Tool for Cooperative Work" (*Proceedings of the Third Conference on Computer-Supported Cooperative Work,* (Toronto, Canada: November 1992), pp. 289–297).

The discrepancy is also evident when organizations use information technologies to attempt unprecedented, complex changes such as global integration or distributed knowledge management. A primary example is the attempt by many companies to redefine and integrate global value chain activities that were previously managed independently. While there is typically some understanding up-front of the magnitude of such a change, the depth and complexity of the interactions among these activities is fully understood only as the changes are implemented. For many organizations, such initiatives represent a new ball game, not only because they haven't played the game before but because most of the rules are still evolving. In a world with uncertain rules, the traditional model for devising and executing a game plan is very difficult to enact. And, as recent strategy research has suggested, planning in such circumstances is more effective as an ongoing endeavor, reflecting the changing, unfolding environments with which organizations interact.[7]

In many situations, therefore, predefining the technological changes to be implemented and accurately predicting their organizational impact is infeasible. Hence, the models of planned change that often inform implementation of new technologies are less than effective. We suggest that what would be more appropriate is a way of thinking about change that reflects the unprecedented, uncertain, open-ended, complex, and flexible nature of the technologies and organizational initiatives involved. Such a model would

[7] H. Mintzberg, "The Fall and Rise of Strategic Planning," *Harvard Business Review* 73, (January–February 1994), 107–114; and R. G. McGrath and I. C. MacMillan, "Discovery-Driven Planning," *Harvard Business Review* 73 (July–August): 1995, 44–54.

enable organizations to systematically absorb, respond to, and even leverage unexpected events, evolving technological capabilities, emerging practices, and unanticipated outcomes. Such a model for managing change would accommodate—indeed, encourage—ongoing and iterative experimentation, use, and learning. Such a model sees change management more as an ongoing improvisation than a staged event. Here we propose such an alternative model and describe a case study of groupware implementation in a customer support organization to illustrate the value of the model in practice. We conclude by discussing the conditions under which such an improvisational model may be a powerful way to manage the implementation and use of new technologies.

AN IMPROVISATIONAL MODEL FOR MANAGING CHANGE

The improvisational model for managing technological change is based on research we have done on the implementation and use of open-ended information technologies. The model rests on two major assumptions that differentiate it from traditional models of change: First, the changes associated with technology implementations constitute an ongoing process rather than an event with an end point after which the organization can expect to return to a reasonably steady state. Second, all the technological and organizational changes made during the ongoing process cannot, by definition, be anticipated ahead of time.

Given these assumptions, our improvisational change model recognizes three different types of change: anticipated, emergent, and opportunity-based.

FIGURE 1 An improvisational model of change management over time.

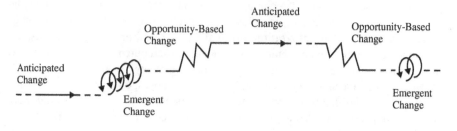

These change types are elaborations on Mintzberg's distinction between deliberate and emergent strategies.[8] Here, we distinguish between *anticipated* changes—changes that are planned ahead of time and occur as intended—and *emergent* changes—changes that arise spontaneously from local innovation and that are not originally anticipated or intended. An example of an anticipated change is the implementation of e-mail software that accomplishes its intended aim to facilitate increased, quicker communication among organizational members. An example of an emergent change is the use of the e-mail network as an informal grapevine disseminating rumors throughout an organization. This use of e-mail is typically not planned or anticipated when the network is implemented but often emerges tacitly over time in particular organizational contexts.

We further differentiate these two types of changes from *opportunity-based* changes—changes that are not anticipated ahead of time but are introduced purposefully and intentionally during the change process in response to an unexpected opportunity, event, or breakdown. For example, as companies gain experience with the World Wide Web, they are finding opportunities to apply and leverage its capabilities in ways that they did not anticipate

or plan before the introduction of the Web. Both anticipated and opportunity-based changes involve deliberate action, in contrast to emergent changes that arise spontaneously and usually tacitly from people's practices with the technology over time.[9]

The three types of change build on each other iteratively over time (see Figure 1). While there is no predefined sequence in which the different types of change occur, the deployment of new technology often entails an initial anticipated organizational change associated with the installation of the new hardware and software. Over time, however, use of the new technology will typically involve a series of opportunity-based, emergent, and further anticipated changes, the order of which cannot be determined in advance because the changes interact with each other in response to outcomes, events, and conditions arising through experimentation and use.

One way of thinking about this model of change is to consider the analogy of a jazz band. While members of a jazz band, unlike members of a symphony orchestra, do not decide in advance exactly what notes each is going to play, they do decide ahead of time what musical composition

[8] H. Mintzberg, "Crafting Strategy," *Harvard Business Review* 65 (July–August): 1987, 66–75.

[9] W. J. Orlikowski, "Improvising Organizational Transformation over Time: A Situated Change Perspective," *Information Systems Research* 7 (March): 1996, 63–92.

will form the basis of their performance. Once the performance begins, each player is free to explore and innovate, departing from the original composition. Yet the performance works because all members are playing within the same rhythmic structure and have a shared understanding of the rules of this musical genre. What they are doing is improvising—enacting an ongoing series of local innovations that embellish the original structure, respond to spontaneous departures and unexpected opportunities, and iterate and build on each other over time. Using our earlier terminology, the jazz musicians are engaging in anticipated, opportunity-based, and emergent action during the course of their performance to create an effective, creative response to local conditions.

Similarly, an improvisational model for managing technological change in organizations is not a predefined program of change charted by management ahead of time. Rather, it recognizes that technological change is an iterative series of different changes, many unpredictable at the start, that evolve from practical experience with the new technologies. Using such a model to manage change requires a set of processes and mechanisms to recognize the different types of change as they occur and to respond effectively to them. The illustrative case we present next suggests that when an organization is open to the capabilities offered by a new technological platform and willing to embrace an improvisational change model, it can achieve innovative organizational changes.

THE CASE OF ZETA

Zeta is one of the top fifty software companies in the United States, with $100 million in revenues and about 1,000 employees. It produces and sells a range of powerful software products that provide capabilities such as decision support, executive information, and marketing analysis. Zeta is headquartered in the Midwest, with sales and client-service field offices throughout the world.

Specialists in the customer service department (CSD) at Zeta provide technical support via telephone to clients, consultants, value-added resellers, Zeta client-service representatives in the field, and other Zeta employees who use the products. This technical support is often quite complex. Specialists typically devote several hours of research to each problem, often searching through reference material, attempting to replicate the problem, and reviewing program source code. Some incidents require interaction with members of other departments such as quality assurance, documentation, and product development. The CSD employs approximately fifty specialists and is headed by a director and two managers.

In 1992, the CSD purchased the Lotus Notes groupware technology within which it developed a new incident tracking support system (ITSS) to help it log customer calls and keep a history of progress toward resolving the customers' problems. Following a successful pilot of the new system, the CSD decided to commit to the Notes platform and to deploy ITSS throughout its department. The acquisition of new technology to facilitate customer call tracking was motivated by a number of factors. The existing tracking system was a homegrown system that had been developed when the department was much smaller and Zeta's product portfolio much narrower. The system was not real-time, entry of calls was haphazard, information accuracy was a concern, and performance was slow and unreliable. It provided little assistance for reusing prior solutions and no support for the management of resources in the department. The volume and complexity of calls to the CSD had increased in recent years due to the introduction of new products, the expanded sophistication of existing products, and the extended range of operating platforms supported. Such shifts had made replacement of the tracking system a priority, as the CSD managers were particularly concerned that the homegrown system provided no ability to track calls, query the status of particular calls, understand the workload, balance resources, identify issues and problems before they became crises, and obtain up-to-date and accurate documentation on work in progress and work completed. In addition, calls would occasionally be lost, as the slips of paper on which they were recorded would get mislaid or inadvertently thrown away.

INTRODUCTION OF ITSS

The initial introduction of the new ITSS system was accompanied by anticipated changes in the nature of both the specialists' and managers' work. In contrast to the previous system, which had been designed to capture only a brief description of the problem and its final resolution, ITSS was designed to allow specialists to document every step they took in resolving a particular incident. That is, it was designed to enable the capture of the full history of an incident. As specialists began to use ITSS this way, the focus of their work shifted from primarily research—solving problems—to both research and documentation—solving problems and documenting work in progress.

The ITSS database quickly began to grow as each specialist documented his or her resolution process in detail. While documenting calls took time, it also saved time by providing a rich database of information that could be searched for potential resolutions. Moreover, this new database of information served as an unexpected, informal learning mechanism by giving the specialists exposure to a wide range of problems and solutions. As one specialist noted: "If it is quiet, I will check on my fellow colleagues to see what . . . kind of calls they get, so I might learn something from them . . . just in case something might ring a bell when someone else calls." At the same time, however, using the ITSS database as a sole source of information did pose some risk, because there were no guarantees of the accuracy of the information. To minimize this risk, the specialists tacitly developed informal quality indicators to help them distinguish between reliable and unreliable data. For example, resolutions that were comprehensively documented, documented by certain individuals, or verified by the customer were considered reliable sources of information.

In addition to these changes in specialists' work, the CSD managers' use of the new system improved their ability to control the department's resources. Specialists' use of ITSS to document calls provided managers with detailed workload information, which was used to justify increased headcount and adjust work schedules and shift assignments on a dynamic and as-needed basis. ITSS also supplied managers with more accurate information on specialists' work process—for example, the particular steps followed to research and resolve a problem, the areas in which specialists sought advice or were stalled, and the quality of their resolutions. As managers began to rely on the ITSS data to evaluate specialists' performance, they expanded the criteria they used to do this evaluation. For example, quality of work-in-progress documentation was included as an explicit evaluation criterion, and documentation skills became a factor in the hiring process.

STRUCTURAL CHANGES

As the CSD gained experience with and better understood the capabilities of the groupware technology, the managers introduced a change in the structure of the department to further leverage these capabilities. This change had not been planned prior to the implementation of ITSS, but the growing reliance on ITSS and an appreciation of the capabilities of the groupware technology created an opportunity for the CSD to redistribute call loads. In particular, the CSD established "first-line" and "second-line" support levels, with junior specialists assigned to the first line, and senior specialists to the second line. The CSD created partnerships between the less experienced junior specialists and the more experienced senior specialists. Front-line specialists now took all incoming calls, resolved as many as they could, and then electronically transferred calls to their second-line partners when they were overloaded or had especially difficult calls. In addition to handling calls transferred to them, senior specialists were expected to proactively monitor their front-line partners' progress on calls and to provide assistance.

While this partnership idea was conceptually sound, it regularly broke down in practice. Junior specialists were often reluctant to hand off calls, fearing that such transfers would reflect poorly on their competence or that they would be overloading their more senior partners. Senior specialists, in turn, were usually too busy resolving complex incidents to spend much time monitoring their junior partners' call status or progress. In

response to this unanticipated breakdown in the partnership idea, the CSD managers introduced another opportunity-based structural change. They created a new intermediary role that was filled by a senior specialist who mediated between the first and second lines, regularly monitored junior specialists' call loads and work in progress, and dynamically reassigned calls as appropriate. The new intermediary role served as a buffer between the junior and senior specialists, facilitating the transfer of calls and relieving senior specialists of the responsibility to constantly monitor their frontline partners. With these structural changes, the CSD in effect changed the prior undifferentiated, fixed division of labor within the department to a dynamic distribution of work reflecting different levels of experience, various areas of expertise, and shifting workloads. In response to the new distribution of work, managers adjusted their evaluation criteria to reflect the changed responsibilities and roles within the CSD.

Another change that emerged over time was a shift in the nature of collaboration within the CSD from a primarily reactive mode to a more proactive one. Because all specialists now had access to the database of calls in the department, they began to go through one anothers' calls to see which ones they could help with, rather than waiting to be asked if they had a solution to a particular problem (which is how they had solicited and received help in the past). This shift from solicited to unsolicited assistance was facilitated by the capabilities of the groupware technology, the complex nature of the work, existing evaluation criteria that stressed teamwork, and the longstanding cooperative and collegial culture in the CSD. Several specialists commented: "Everyone realizes that we all have a certain piece of the puzzle. . . . I may have one critical piece, and Jenny may have another piece. . . . If we all work separately, we're never going to get the puzzle together. But by everybody working together, we have the entire puzzle"; "Here I don't care who grabs credit for my work. . . . This support department does well because we're a team, not because we're all individuals."[10] Managers responded to this shift in work practices by adjusting specialists' evaluation criteria to specifically consider unsolicited help. As one manager explained: "When I'm looking at incidents, I'll see what help other people have offered, and that does give me another indication of how well they're working as a team."

LATER CHANGES

After approximately one year of using ITSS, the CSD implemented two further organizational changes around the groupware technology. Both had been anticipated in the initial planning for ITSS, although the exact timing for their implementation had been left unspecified. First, the ITSS application was installed in three overseas support offices, with copies of all the ITSS databases replicated regularly across the four support sites (United States, United Kingdom, Australia, and Europe). This provided all support specialists with a more extensive knowledge base on which to search for possibly helpful resolutions. The use of ITSS in all the support offices further allowed specialists to transfer calls across offices, essentially enacting a global support department within Zeta.

[10] W. J. Orlikowski, "Evolving with Notes: Organizational Change around Groupware Technology," MIT Sloan School of Management, Cambridge, MA, 1995. Working Paper 3823.

Second, the CSD funded the development of a number of bug-tracking systems that were implemented within groupware and deployed in Zeta's departments of product development, product management, and quality assurance. These bug-tracking applications were linked into ITSS and enabled specialists to enter any bugs they had discovered in their problem resolution activities directly into the relevant product's bug-tracking system. Specialists could now also directly query the status of particular bugs and even change their priority if customer calls indicated that such an escalation was needed. Specialists in particular found this change invaluable. For the other departments, the link with ITSS allowed users such as product managers and developers to access the ITSS records and trace the particular incidents that had uncovered certain bugs or specific use problems. Only the developers had some reservations about the introduction of the bug-tracking application—reservations that were associated with the severe time constraints under which they worked to produce new releases of Zeta products.

In addition to the improved coordination and integration achieved with other departments and offices, the CSD also realized further opportunity-based innovations and emergent changes within its own practices. For example, as the number of incidents in ITSS grew, some senior specialists began to realize that they could use the information in the system to help train newcomers. By extracting certain records from the ITSS database, the specialists created a training database of sample problems with which newly hired specialists could work. Using the communication capabilities of the groupware technology, these senior specialists could monitor their trainees' progress through the sample database and intervene to educate when necessary. As one senior specialist noted: "We can kind of keep up to the minute on their progress. . . . If they're on the wrong track, we can intercept them and say, 'Go check this, go look at that.' But it's not like we have to actually sit with them and review things. It's sort of an online, interactive thing." As a result of this new training mechanism, the time for new specialists to begin taking customer calls was reduced from eight weeks to about five.

Another change was related to access control. An ongoing issue for the CSD was who (if anybody) outside the CSD should have access to the ITSS database with its customer call information and specialists' work-in-progress documentation. This issue was not anticipated before the acquisition of the technology. While the managers were worried about how to respond to the increasing demand for access to ITSS as the database became more valuable and word about its content spread throughout the company, they continued to handle each access request as it came up. Over time, they used a variety of control mechanisms ranging from giving limited access to some "trusted" individuals, generating summary reports of selected ITSS information for others, and refusing any access to still others. As one manager explained, only after some time did they realize that their various *ad hoc* responses to different access requests amounted to, in essence, a set of rules and procedures about access control. Through local responses to various requests and situations over time, an implicit access control policy for the use of ITSS evolved and emerged.

ZETA'S CHANGE MODEL

Along with the introduction of the new technology and the development of the ITSS application, the CSD first implemented some planned organizational changes, expanding the specialists' work to include work-in-progress documentation and adjusting the managers' work to take advantage of the real-time access to workload information. (Figure 2 represents the change model around the groupware technology that Zeta followed in its CSD.) The changes were anticipated before introducing the new technology. As specialists and managers began to work in new ways with the technology, a number of changes emerged in practice, such as the specialists' developing norms to determine the quality and value of prior resolutions, and the managers' paying attention to documentation skills in hiring and evaluation decisions.

Building on these anticipated and emergent changes, the CSD introduced a set of opportunity-based changes, creating junior-senior specialist partnerships to

FIGURE 2   **Zeta's improvisational management of change over time.**

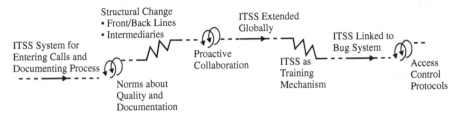

take advantage of the shared database and communication capabilities of the technology, and then adding the new intermediary role in response to the unexpected problems with partnership and work reassignment. The CSD did not anticipate these changes at the start, nor did the changes emerge spontaneously in working with the new technology. Rather, the CSD conceived of and implemented the changes *in situ* and in response to the opportunities and issues that arose as it gained experience and better understood the new technology and their particular use of it. This change process around the groupware technology continued through the second year at Zeta when some anticipated organizational changes were followed by both emergent and opportunity-based changes associated with unfolding events and the learning and experience gained by using the new technology in practice.

Overall, what we see here is an iterative and ongoing series of anticipated, emergent, and opportunity-based changes that allowed Zeta to learn from practical experience, respond to unexpected outcomes and capabilities, and adapt both the technology and the organization as appropriate. In effect, Zeta's change model cycles through anticipated, emergent, and opportunity-based organizational changes over time. It is a change model that explicitly recognizes the inevitability, legitimacy, and value of ongoing learning and change in practice.

ENABLING CONDITIONS

Clearly, there were certain aspects of the Zeta organization that enabled it to effectively adopt an improvisational change model to implement and use the groupware technology. Our research at Zeta and other companies suggests that at least two sets of enabling conditions are critical: aligning key dimensions of the change process and dedicating resources to provide ongoing support for the change process. We consider each in turn.

ALIGNING KEY CHANGE DIMENSIONS

An important influence on the effectiveness of any change process is the interdependent relationship among three dimensions: the technology, the organizational context (including culture, structure, roles, and responsibilities), and the change model used to manage change (see Figure 3). Ideally, the interaction among these three dimensions is compatible or, at a minimum, not in opposition.

First, consider the relation of the change model and the technology being implemented. When the technology has been designed to operate like a "black box," allowing little adaptation by users, an improvisational approach may not be more effective than the traditional approach to technology implementation. Similarly, when the technology is well established and its impacts are reasonably well understood, a traditional planned change approach may be effective. However, when the technology being implemented is new

FIGURE 3   **Aligning the change model, the technology, and the organization.**

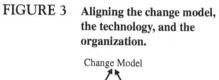
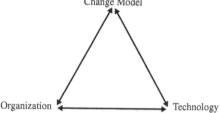

and unprecedented and, additionally, is open ended and customizable, an improvisational model providing the flexibility for organizations to adapt and learn through use becomes more appropriate. Such is the case, we believe, with the groupware technologies available today.

Second, the relation of the change model to organizational context is also relevant. A flexible change model, while likely to be problematic in a rigid, control-oriented, or bureaucratic culture, is well suited to an informal, cooperative culture such as the one at the CSD. In another study, we examined the MidCo organization's successful adoption and implementation of CASE (computer-aided software engineering) tools within its information systems organization.[11] While MidCo, a multinational chemical products company with revenues of more than $1.5 billion, was a relatively traditional organization in many ways, key aspects of its culture—a commitment to total quality management, a focus on organizational learning and employee empowerment, as well as a long-term outlook—were particularly compatible with the improvisational model it used to manage ongoing organizational changes around the new software development technology.

Finally, there is the important relationship between the technology and the organizational context. At Zeta, the CSD's cooperative, team-oriented culture was compatible with the collaborative nature of the new groupware technology. Indeed, the CSD's existing culture allowed it to take advantage of the opportunity for improved collaboration that the groupware technology afforded. Moreover, when existing roles, responsibilities, and evaluation criteria became less salient, the CSD managers expanded or adjusted them to reflect new uses of the technology. Compare these change efforts to those of Alpha, a professional services firm that introduced the Notes groupware technology to leverage knowledge sharing and to coordinate distributed activities.[12] While the physical deployment of groupware grew very rapidly, anticipated benefits were realized much more slowly. Key to the reluctance to use groupware for knowledge sharing was a perceived incompatibility between the collaborative nature of the technology and the individualistic and competitive nature of the organization. Like many professional services firms, Alpha rewarded individual rather than team performance and promoted employees based on "up or out" evaluation criteria. In such an environment, knowledge sharing via a global Notes network was seen to threaten status, distinctive competence, and power. In contrast to Zeta, managers at Alpha did not adjust policies, roles, incentives, and evaluation criteria to better align their organization with the intended use and capabilities of the technology they had invested in.

DEDICATING RESOURCES FOR ONGOING SUPPORT

An ongoing change process requires dedicated support over time to adapt both the organization and the technology to

---

[11] M. J. Gallivan, J. D. Hofman, and W. J. Orlikowski, "Implementing Radical Change: Gradual Versus Rapid Pace," *Proceedings of the Fifteenth International Conference on Information Systems,* December 1994, 14–17, pp. 325–339.

[12] W. J. Orlikowski, "Learning from Notes: Organizational Issues in Groupware Implementation," *Proceedings of the Third Conference on Computer-Supported Cooperative Work,* (Toronto, Canada, November 1992, pp. 362–369).

changing organizational conditions, use practices, and technological capabilities. Opportunity-based change, in particular, depends on the ability of the organization to notice and recognize opportunities, issues, breakdowns, and unexpected outcomes as they arise. This requires attention on the part of appropriate individuals in the organization to track technology use over time and to initiate organizational and technological adjustments that will mitigate or take advantage of the identified problems and opportunities.

At Zeta, the managers and technologists played this role, incorporating it into their other responsibilities. So, for example, the managers adjusted the structure of their department by introducing first-line/second-line partnerships to facilitate a dynamic division of labor and then made further adaptations by introducing an intermediary role to overcome some unanticipated difficulties associated with the initial change. Similarly, the technologists working with the CSD incorporated enhancements to the ITSS system as they realized ways to improve ease of use and access time. The CSD's commitment to noticing and responding to appropriate changes did not end after the implementation of the technology. The managers clearly realized that the change process they had embarked upon with the use of groupware was ongoing. As one manager noted, "We've had ITSS for two years. I'm surprised that the enthusiasm hasn't gone away. . . . I think it's because it's been changed on a regular basis. . . . Knowing that [the changes are going to get implemented] keeps you wanting to think about it and keep going."

Ongoing change in the use of groupware technology also requires ongoing adjustments to the technology itself as users learn and gain experience with the new technology's capabilities over time. Without dedicated technology support to implement these adaptations and innovations, the continued experimentation and learning in use central to an improvisational change model may be stalled or thwarted. At Zeta, a dedicated technology group supported the CSD's use of groupware and ITSS. Initially consisting of one developer, this group grew over time as groupware use expanded. After two years, the group included four full-time technologists who provided technology support for the various systems that had been deployed within Zeta via the Notes platform. The group also maintained strong ties with all their users through regular meetings and communications. This dedicated, ongoing technical support ensured that the technology would continue to be updated, adjusted, and expanded as appropriate.

The value of ongoing support to enable ongoing organizational and technological change was similarly important in another organization we studied, the R&D division of a large Japanese manufacturing firm.[13] A newly formed product development team within the R&D division installed a groupware technology, the Usenet news system (a computer conferencing system). Similar to the CSD at Zeta, the team's use of this new technology also iterated among anticipated, emergent, and opportunity-based changes over time. Here, a small group of users who had previously used the groupware technology took on the responsibility to manage and support its ongoing use for themselves and their colleagues. They tracked technology usage and project events as they unfolded, responded as

[13] W. J. Orlikowski, J. Yates, K. Okamura, and M. Fujimoto, "Shaping Electronic Communication: The Metastructuring of Technology in Use," *Organization Science*, vol. 6, July–August 1995, pp. 423–444.

appropriate with adjustments to communication policies and technology functionality, and proactively made changes to the team's use of the conferencing system to leverage opportunities as they arose.

CONCLUSION

Global, responsive, team-based, networked—these are the watchwords for organizations today. As managers redesign and reinvent organizations in a new image, many are turning to information technologies to enable more flexible processes, greater knowledge sharing, and global integration. At the same time, effectively implementing the organizational changes associated with these technologies remains difficult in a turbulent, complex, and uncertain environment. We believe that a significant factor contributing to these challenges is the growing discrepancy between the way people think about technological change and the way they actually implement it.

We propose that people's assumptions about technology-based change and the way it is supposed to happen are based on models that are no longer appropriate. Traditional models for managing technology-based change treat change as a sequential series of predefined steps that are bounded within a specified time. With these models as a guide, it makes sense to define—as the European navigator does—a plan of action in advance of the change and track events against the plan, striving throughout the change to remain on track. Deviations from the intended course—the anticipated versus the actual—then require explanation, the subtle (or sometimes not-so-subtle) implication being that there has been some failure, some inadequacy in planning, that has led to this deviation.

Indeed, many organizational mechanisms such as budgeting and resource planning are based on these notions. The problem is that change as it actually occurs today more closely resembles the voyage of the Trukese navigator, and the models and mechanisms most commonly used to think about and manage change do not effectively support this experience of change.

We have offered here an improvisational change model as a different way of thinking about managing the introduction and ongoing use of information technologies to support the more flexible, complex, and integrated structures and processes demanded in organizations today. In contrast to traditional models of technological change, this improvisational model recognizes that change is typically an ongoing process made up of opportunities and challenges that are not necessarily predictable at the start. It defines a process that iterates among three types of change—anticipated, emergent, and opportunity-based—and that allows the organization to experiment and learn as it uses the technology over time. Most important, it offers a systematic approach with which to understand and better manage the realities of technology-based change in today's organizations.

Because such a model requires a tolerance for flexibility and uncertainty, adopting it implies that managers relinquish what is often an implicit paradigm of "command and control."[14] An improvisational model, however, is not anarchy, and neither is it a matter of "muddling through." We are not implying that planning is unnecessary or should be abandoned. We are suggesting, instead, that a plan is a guide rather than a blueprint and

[14] S. Zuboff, *In the Age of the Smart Machine* (New York: Basic Books, 1988).

that deviations from the plan, rather than being seen as a symptom of failure, are to be expected and actively managed.[15]

Rather than predefining each step and then controlling events to fit the plan, management creates an environment that facilitates improvisation. In such an environment, management provides, supports, and nurtures the expectations, norms, and resources that guide the ongoing change process. Malone refers to such a style of managing as "cultivation."[16] Consider again the jazz band. While each band member is free to improvise during the performance, the result is typically not discordant. Rather, it is harmonious because each player operates within an overall framework, conforms to a shared set of values and norms, and has access to a known repertoire of rules and resources. Similarly, while many changes at Zeta's CSD were not planned, they were compatible with the overall objectives and intentions of the department's members, their shared norms and team orientation, and the designs and capabilities of the technology.

Effectively executing an improvisational change model also requires aligning the technology and the organizational context with the change model. Such alignment does not happen automatically: It requires explicit, ongoing examination and adjustment, where and when necessary, of the technology and the organization.

As such, mechanisms and resources allocated to ongoing support of the change process are critical. Tracking and noticing events and issues as they unfold is a responsibility that appropriate members of the organization need to own. Along with the responsibility, these organizational members require the authority, credibility, influence, and resources to implement the ongoing changes. Creating the environment; aligning the technology, context, and change model; and distributing the appropriate responsibility and resources are critically important in the effective use of an improvisational model, particularly as they represent a significant (and therefore challenging) departure from the standard practice in effect in many organizations.

An improvisational model of change, however, does not apply to all situations. As we have noted, it is most appropriate for open-ended, customizable technologies or for complex, unprecedented change. In addition, as one reviewer noted, "Jazz is not everyone's 'cup of tea.' . . . Some people are incapable of playing jazz, much less able to listen to what they consider to be 'noise.'" We noted above that some cultures do not support experimentation and learning. As a result, they are probably not receptive to an improvisational model and are less likely to succeed with it. As these organizations attempt to implement new organizational forms, however, they too may find an improvisational model to be a particularly valuable approach to managing technological change in the twenty-first century.

---

[15] Suchman (1987).
[16] T. W. Malone, informal conversation, 1996.

Case

Charlotte Beers at Ogilvy & Mather Worldwide (A)

It was December 1993, and during the past year and a half, Charlotte Beers had found little time for reflection. Since taking over as CEO and chairman of Ogilvy & Mather (O&M) Worldwide in 1992, Beers had focused all her efforts on charting a new course for the world's sixth-largest advertising agency. The process of crafting a vision with her senior management team had been—by all accounts—painful, messy, and chaotic. Beers, however, was pleased with the results. Ogilvy & Mather was now committed to becoming "the agency most valued by those who most value brands."

During the past year, the agency had regained, expanded, or won several major accounts. Confidence and energy appeared to be returning to a company the press had labeled "beleaguered" only two years earlier. Yet, Beers sensed that the change effort was still fragile. "Brand Stewardship," the agency's philosophy for building brands, was not well understood below the top tier of executives who had worked with Beers to develop the concept. Internal communication efforts to 272 worldwide offices were under way, as were plans to adjust O&M's structures and systems to a new set of priorities. Not the least of the challenges before her was

ensuring collaboration between offices on multinational brand campaigns. The words of Kelly O'Dea, her Worldwide Client Service president, still rang in her ears. "We can't lose momentum. Most change efforts fail after the initial success. This could be the prologue, Charlotte . . . or it could be the whole book."

OGILVY & MATHER

In 1948, David Ogilvy, a 38-year-old Englishman, sold his small tobacco farm in Pennsylvania and invested his entire savings to start his own advertising agency. The agency, based in New York, had financial backing from two London agencies, Mather & Crowther and S.H. Benson. "I had no clients, no credentials, and only $6,000 in the bank," Ogilvy would later write in his autobiography, "[but] I managed to create a series of campaigns which, almost overnight, made Ogilvy & Mather famous."[1]

Ogilvy's initial ads—for Rolls-Royce, Schweppes, and Hathaway Shirts—were based on a marketing philosophy that Ogilvy had begun developing as a door-to-door salesman in the 1930s, and later, as a pollster for George Gallup. Ogilvy believed that effective advertising created an indelible image of the product in consumers' minds and, furthermore, that campaigns should always be intelligent, stylish, and "first class." Most of all,

Source: This case was prepared by Research Associate Nicole Steckler (under the supervision of Professor Herminia Ibarra).

[1] David Ogilvy, *Blood, Beer, and Advertising* (London: Hamish Hamilton, 1977).

however, David Ogilvy believed that advertising must sell. "We sell—or else" became his credo for the agency. In 1950, Ogilvy's campaign for Hathaway featured a distinguished man with a black eye patch, an idea that increased sales by 160 percent and ran for 25 years. Other famous campaigns included Maxwell House's "Good to the Last Drop" launched in 1958 and American Express's "Don't Leave Home Without It," which debuted in 1962.

GENTLEMEN WITH BRAINS

David Ogilvy imbued his agency's culture with the same "first class" focus that he demanded of creative work. Employees were "gentlemen with brains," treating clients, consumers, and one another with respect. "The consumer is not a moron," admonished Ogilvy. In a distinctly British way, collegiality and politeness were highly valued: "We abhor ruthlessness. We like people with gentle manners and see no conflict between adherence to high professional standards in our work and human kindness in our dealings with others."[2]

At Ogilvy's agency, gentility did not mean blandness. Ogilvy took pride in his agency's "streak of unorthodoxy." He smoked a pipe, refused to fly, and peppered his speeches with literary references and acerbic wit. He once advised a young account executive, "Develop your eccentricities early, and no one will think you're going senile later in life." In a constant stream of letters, he made his dislikes clear: "I despise toadies who suck up to their bosses. . . . I am revolted by pseudo-academic jargon like *attitudinal, paradigms,* and *sub-optimal.*" He also exhorted his staff to achieve brilliance through "obsessive curiosity, guts under pressure, inspiring enthusiasm, and

resilience in adversity." No one at Ogilvy & Mather ever forgot the full-page announcement he placed in the *New York Times:* "Wanted: Trumpeter Swans who combine personal genius with inspiring leadership. If you are one of these rare birds, write to me in inviolable secrecy."

In 1965, Ogilvy & Mather merged with its partner agencies in Britain to form Ogilvy & Mather International.[3] "Our aim," wrote David Ogilvy, "is to be One Agency Indivisible; the same advertising disciplines, the same principles of management, the same striving for excellence." Each office was carpeted in the same regal Ogilvy red. Individual offices, however, were run independently by local presidents who exercised a great deal of autonomy.

David Ogilvy retired in 1975. Succeeding the legendary founder proved daunting. "The next four chairmen," commented one longtime executive, "did not have his presence. David is quirky; they were straightforward, middle-of-the-road, New York." Ogilvy's successors focused on extending the network of offices internationally and building direct response, marketing research, and sales promotion capabilities. Revenues soared in the 1970s, culminating in record double-digit gains in the mid-1980s (see Exhibit 1). The advertising industry boomed, and Ogilvy & Mather led the pack. Nowhere was the agency's reputation greater than at its New York office, heralded in 1986 by the press as "the class act of Madison Avenue."

ADVERTISING INDUSTRY CHANGES

The booming economy of the 1980s shielded the advertising industry from the intensifying pressures of global competition.

---

[2] David Ogilvy, *Confessions of an Advertising Man* (New York: Atheneum, 1963).

[3] *Dictionary of Company Histories,* 1986.

EXHIBIT 1 Ogilvy & Mather
Selected Financial and Organization Data

Source: Ogilvy Group Annual Report, 1988.

1984–1988					
	1984	**1985**	**1986**	**1987**	**1988**
Revenues (in thousands)	$428,604	$490,486	$560,132	$738,508	$838,090
Net income (in thousands)	25,838	30,247	26,995	29,757	32,950
Operating profit (in thousands)	49,191	45,350	47,764	57,933	65,922

Source: *Advertising Age.*

1989–1993[a]					
	1989	**1990**	**1991**	**1992**	**1993**
Total annual billings (in thousands)[b]	$4,089,000	$4,563,700	$5,271,000	$5,205,700	$5,814,100
Revenue (in thousands)	592,600	653,700	757,600	754,800	740,000
Percent change in net income[c]	NA	4.7	-2.8	1.9	5.3
Operating margin	NA	6.4	4.1	4.9	7.6

[a] Financial information for 1989–1993 is not comparable to 1984–1988 due to the restructuring of the company following sale to WPP Group, plc. It is the policy of WPP Group, plc, not to release revenue and net income information about its subsidiaries.
[b] Represents an estimate by *Advertising Age* of the total value of all advertising and direct marketing campaigns run in a given year.
[c] The percent increase or decrease is given from an undisclosed sum at base year 1989.

Companies fought for consumer attention through marketing, and advertising billings grew—on average, between 10 percent and 15 percent per annum. Brand manufacturers—challenged by the growth of quality generic products and the diverse tastes of a fragmented mass market—created multiple line extensions and relied on agencies' creative powers to differentiate them. As business globalized, so did agencies. Responding to clients' demands for global communications and a range of integrated services, agencies expanded rapidly, many merging to achieve economies of scale as "mega-agencies" with millions in revenues worldwide.

After the stock market crash of 1987, companies reconsidered the value added by large advertising budgets. Increasingly, many chose to shift resources from expensive mass media and print campaigns toward direct mail, cable, telemarketing, and sales promotion. Fixed fees began to replace the agencies' historical 15 percent commission on billings. Longstanding client-agency relations were severed as companies sought the best bargains. Viewed by some as ad factories selling a commodity product, the mega-agencies were challenged by new, "boutique" creative shops. The globalization of media and pressures for cost efficiencies encouraged companies to consolidate product lines and to sell them in more markets worldwide. They, in turn, directed agencies to transport their brands around the world. The advertising agency of the 1990s—often a loose federation of hundreds of independent firms—was asked to launch simultaneous brand campaigns in North America, Europe, and the emerging markets of Asia, Latin America, and Africa.

ORGANIZATIONAL STRUCTURE

By 1991, Ogilvy's 270 offices comprised four regions. The North American offices were the most autonomous, with office presidents reporting directly to the Worldwide CEO. Outside North America, presidents of local offices—sometimes majority stakeholders (see Exhibit 2)—reported to country presidents, who in turn reported to regional chairmen. Europe was coordinated centrally, but—with significant European multinational clients and a tradition of high creativity—the region maintained its autonomy from New York. To establish a presence in Latin America, Ogilvy obtained minority ownership in locally owned agencies and formed partnerships with local firms. The last region to be fully formed was Asia/Pacific, with the addition of Australia, India, and Southeast Asia in 1991 (see Exhibit 3 for organization chart).

Between and across regions, "worldwide management supervisors" (WMSs) coordinated the requirements of multinational clients such as American Express and Unilever. WMSs served as the point of contact among multiple parties: client headquarters, clients' local subsidiaries, and the appropriate Ogilvy local offices. They were also responsible for forming and managing the core multidisciplinary account team. More important, they facilitated the exchange of information throughout the network, attempting to ensure strategic unity and avoid operating at cross purposes.

Over time, Ogilvy & Mather came to pride itself as "the most local of the internationals, the most international of the locals." Local delivery channels and the need for consumer acceptance of multinational products required specialized local knowledge and relationships. Local and global clients also served as magnets for each other: Without local accounts, country offices were unable to build sufficient critical mass to service multinational clients well; without multinational accounts to draw top talent, the agency was less attractive to local clients.

With a "light center and strong regions," most creative and operating decisions were made locally. The role of Worldwide Headquarters in New York, staffed by 100 employees, was limited largely to ensuring consistency in financial reporting and corporate communications. Key capital allocation and executive staffing decisions were made by the O&M Worldwide

EXHIBIT 2 Percentage of Regional Offices Owned by O&M Worldwide

	Number of offices	100 Percent	>50 Percent	<50 Percent	0 Percent
North America	40	80	20	0	0
Europe	97	63	24	8	5
Asia/Pacific	66	57	36	7	0
Latin America	48	25	6	21	48

EXHIBIT 3   Ogilvy & Mather
Worldwide Organization Chart, 1991

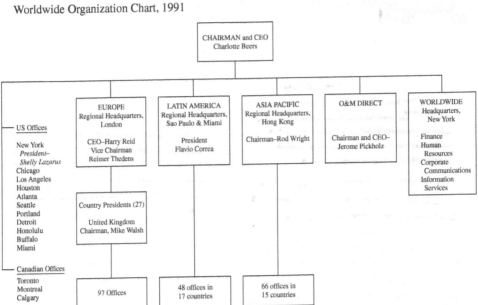

board of directors, which included regional chairmen and presidents of the most powerful countries and offices such as France, Germany, the United Kingdom, New York, and Los Angeles.

The Ogilvy offices represented four core disciplines: sales promotion, public relations, advertising, and direct marketing.[4] Sales promotion developed point-of-purchase materials such as in-store displays and flyers. Public relations offices worked to promote clients' corporate reputation and product visibility. Advertising focused on mass marketing, establishing the core of a client's brand image through the development and production of television commercials, print campaigns, and billboards. Direct Marketing created

[4] The number of Ogilvy offices by discipline in 1994 were as follows: 83 in advertising, 60 in direct response, 12 in promotional, 23 in public relations, and 92 in other areas, including highly specialized market research firms.

and delivered targeted advertising—from mail-order catalogs to coupons and television infomercials—designed to solicit a direct response from consumers. While the other three resided within the regional structure, O&M Direct was an independent subsidiary. In the late 1980s, the Ogilvy board of directors decided to focus on advertising and direct marketing, the firm's chief competitive strengths. Unlike advertising, Direct's business in the 1980s remained chiefly local, but expanded explosively. By 1991, O&M Direct had received numerous industry accolades and was ranked the largest direct marketing company in the world.

"BELEAGUERED" OGILVY & MATHER

As clients demanded lower costs and greater service, Ogilvy & Mather—like many large agencies at the time—was slow to make adjustments. In 1988,

Ogilvy was ranked the sixth-largest advertising firm in the world. As one executive remembered:

> Everything was going well. All we had to do was wake up in the morning and we were plus 15 percent. So why did we need to change? Our vision was "just keep doing the same thing, better." We failed either to recognize or acknowledge what were the first real indications that life around here was about to change fundamentally.

In May 1989, WPP Group plc, a leading marketing services company, acquired Ogilvy & Mather for $864 million.[5] WPP, led by Harvard Business School–trained Martin Sorrell, had purchased the J. Walter Thompson agency for $550 million two years earlier.[6] The takeover was hostile, with agency executives—including CEO Kenneth Roman—opposed. "It was a shock," explained one long-time executive. "We were a proud company with a constant stock market growth, the masters of our destiny. Suddenly, we were raided." Within months of the takeover, CEO Roman resigned. "Ken had absolutely nothing in common with WPP. There was a lack of trust, an air of conflict, adversaries, and invasion," remembered another. A number of top creative and account executives followed Roman, leaving Ogilvy & Mather for other agencies.[7]

Graham Phillips, a 24-year Ogilvy veteran, was appointed Roman's successor. One executive who worked with Phillips described him as "a brilliant account guy and a very good manager who identified our need to become a total communications company. But few would describe him as an inspirational leader."

In 1989, the agency lost major advertising assignments from Unilever and Shell. In 1990, Seagram's Coolers and Nutrasweet withdrew their multinational accounts.[8] Account losses in 1991 proved particularly damaging to the New York office, the agency's center and standard bearer. "If New York thrives, the world thrives. If New York fails, the world fails," went a familiar company adage. New York's client defections were explained by one executive as a failure in leadership: "The office was run by czars with big accounts. People got used to a highly political way of working and work deteriorated." In 1991, Campbell Soup withdrew $25 million in business, Roy Rogers $15 million, and American Express—the account for which Ogilvy had won "Print Campaign of the Decade"—pulled out $60 million.[9] "Losing American Express had symbolism far beyond what the actual business losses were," recalled one Ogilvy executive. "People who were loyal Ogilvy employees, believers for years, disengaged. They threw up their hands and said, 'This place is falling apart.'"

Despite declines in revenue, the agency found itself unable to adapt to clients' changing demands. Budgets were not reduced at local offices, even as large clients pushed Ogilvy to streamline and centralize their accounts. "We were a high-cost operation in a low-cost world. There was a lack of financial discipline, a lack of focus on cost, and a lack of structured decision making on business issues," noted one executive. Another faulted the firm's

---

[5] Christie Dugas, "The Death of Ogilvy and an Era," *Newsday*, May 17, 1989.
[6] Ibid.
[7] "Change Comes to Fabled Ogilvy," *New York Times*, April 12, 1992.

[8] Kevin McCormack, "Beers Succeeds Phillips at O&M Worldwide," *Adweek*, April 13, 1992, p. 2.
[9] "Operation Winback," *Advertising Age*, February 1993.

tradition of local autonomy and failure to institute systems for managing collaboration: "We were spending a lot of money at the creative center without cutting back locally—building costs at both ends."

Recalling the atmosphere at the time, another executive concluded, "A shaken confidence permeated the whole company. We talked about change and what we needed to do ad nauseam, but nothing was happening. We tried to work within the old framework when the old ways of working were irrelevant."

At the end of 1991, Phillips stepped down as CEO, telling the press: "I have taken Ogilvy through a very difficult period in the industry. I had to let go people whom I had worked with for 27 years, and that wears you down." In April, Charlotte Beers was appointed CEO and chairman of Ogilvy & Mather Worldwide, the first outsider ever to lead the company.

CHARLOTTE BEERS

The daughter of a cowboy, Beers grew up in Texas, where she began her career as a research analyst for the Mars Company. In 1969, she moved to Chicago as an account executive with J. Walter Thompson. Once there, she cultivated success with clients Sears, Kraft, and Gillette, combining a southern Texan charm with sharp business acumen. Beers rose quickly to senior vice president for Client Services.

At Thompson, Beers was known for her passionate interest—unusual in account executives—in the philosophy of marketing. Commented Beers, "I try never to discuss with clients only the stuff of business. I focus on advertising as well as on the ideas." Once described on a performance evaluation as "completely fearless," Beers earned a reputation for her ability to win over clients. Colleagues retold the story of how Beers impressed a roomful of Sears executives in the early 1970's by taking apart, then reassembling, a Sears power drill without skipping a beat in her pitch for a new advertising campaign.

In 1979, Beers became COO of the Chicago agency Tatham-Laird & Kudner (TLK). Her success in winning the mid-sized agency several new brands with Proctor & Gamble helped turn the firm around. Accounts with Ralston-Purina and Stouffer Foods followed. Beers was elected CEO in 1982 and chairman of the board in 1986. In 1987, she became the first woman ever named chairman of the American Association of Advertising Agencies. One year later, she led TLK through a merger with the international agency Eurocome-RSCG. Tatham's billings had tripled during Beers' tenure, to $325 million.

BEERS TAKES OVER

Beers' appointment, recalled O&M veterans, created initial apprehension. Commented one executive, "She was from a smaller agency in Chicago and had not managed multiple offices. O&M is a worldwide company, and she had never worked outside the United States. And, she was not from Ogilvy." Added another, "This is an organization that rejects outsiders."

Her approach quickly made an impression with Ogilvy insiders. "It was clear from day one that Charlotte would be a different kind of leader. Full of life. Eyes open and clearly proud of the brand she was now to lead. Here was somebody who could look around and see the risks, but wasn't afraid to turn the corner even though it was dark out," said one executive. "We had leaders before, who said all the right things, were terribly nice, did a good job, but they didn't inspire. Charlotte has an ability to inspire—Charlotte has presence." Commented another executive, "She is delightfully informal, but you always know that she means business." Within two months of her appointment, Beers dismissed a top-level executive who had failed to instigate necessary changes.

ACTIVATE THE ASSETS

"When I took over," recalled Beers, "all the press reports talked about 'beleaguered' Ogilvy. My job was to remove 'beleaguered' from our name." In her first six weeks, Beers sent a "Hello" video to all 7,000 of Ogilvy's employees. It began:

> Everybody wants to know my nine-point plan for success and I can't tell you that I know yet what it is. I'm building my own expectations and dreams for the agency—but I need a core of people who have lived in this company and who have similar dreams to help me. That's going to happen fast, because we are rudderless without it. David [Ogilvy] gave us a great deal to build on, but I don't think it's there for us to go backward. It's there to go forward.

Beers concluded that people had lost sight of Ogilvy's still impressive assets—its vast network of offices worldwide, its creative talent, and its distinguished list of multinational clients. "We must," she told senior executives, "activate the assets we already have." In her second month at Ogilvy, Beers observed a major client presentation by the heads of five O&M offices:

> It was a fabulous piece of thinking. We had committed enormous resources. But in the end, they didn't tell the clients why it would work. When the client said, "We'll get back to you," they didn't demand an immediate

response, so I intervened: "You saw a remarkable presentation, and I think you need to comment." Ogilvy had gotten so far from its base that talented people lacked the confidence to speak up.

For Beers, her early interactions with a key client symbolized the state of the company.

"He kept retelling the tale of New York's downfall: how we blew a major account in Europe and how our groups fought among one another. The fourth time I heard this story," remembered Beers, "I interrupted: 'That's never going to happen again, so let's not talk about it any more. Let's talk about what we can accomplish together.'"

Beers spent much of her first months at Ogilvy talking to investors and clients. For Wall Street, she focused on the quality of Ogilvy's advertising. "I refused to do a typical analyst report," she said. "When the Wall Street analysts asked me why I showed them our ads, I told them it was to give them reason to believe the numbers would happen again and again." Clients voiced other concerns. "I met with 50 clients in six months," recalled Beers, "and found there was a lot of affection for Ogilvy. Yet, they were also very candid. Clients stunned me by rating us below other agencies in our insight into the consumer." Beers shared these perceptions with senior managers: "Clients view our people as uninvolved, distant, and reserved. We have organized ourselves into fiefdoms, and that has taken its toll. Each department—Creative, Account, Media, and Research—are often working as separate entities. It's been a long time since we've had some famous advertising."

To restore confidence both internally and externally, Beers maintained that the agency needed a clear direction. "I think it's fair to say Ogilvy had no clear sense of what it stood for. I wanted to give people something that would release their passion, that would knit them together. I wanted the extraneous discarded. I wanted a rallying point on what really matters."

For Beers, what mattered was brands. "She is intensely client- and brand-focused," explained one executive. "You can't go into her office with financial minutiae. You get about two seconds of attention." Beers believed that clients wanted an agency that understood the complexity of managing the emotional as well as the logical relationship between a consumer and a product. "I became confident that I knew what clients wanted and what Ogilvy's strengths were. It was my job to be the bridge." Beers, however, was as yet unsure what form that bridge would take or how it would get built. One of her early challenges was to decide whom to ask for help in charting this new course:

> I knew I needed their involvement, and that I would be asking people to do much more than they had been, without the benefits of titles and status. I avoided calling on people on the basis of their titles. I watched the way they conducted business. I looked to see what they found valuable. I wanted people who felt the way I did about brands. I was looking for kindred spirits.

THE "THIRSTY FOR CHANGE" GROUP

Over the next few months, Beers solicited ideas for change from her senior managers, asking them to give candid evaluations of disciplines and regions, as well as of one another. In a style that managers would describe as "quintessential Charlotte," Beers chose to meet with executives one-on-one and assigned them tasks without regard to their disciplinary backgrounds. She commented, "I was slow to pull an executive committee together. I didn't know who could do it. It was a clumsy period, and I was account executive on everything—everything came to me." At first, some found the lack of structure unnerving. Noted one executive, "People weren't quite sure what their roles were. It caused discomfort. We began to wonder, 'Where do I fit? Who is whose boss?'" Another added, "She was purposely vague in hopes that people would stretch themselves to new configurations." Several executives, though cautious, found Beers' talk of change inspiring and responded with their ideas.

By May 1992, Beers had identified a group whom she described as "thirsty for change." Some were top executives heading regions or key offices; others were creative and account directors who caught her eye as potential allies. Her selection criterion was "people who got it"—those who agreed on the importance of change. All had been vocal about their desire to move Ogilvy forward. She sent a memo inviting them to a meeting in Vienna, Austria, that month:

HIGHLY CONFIDENTIAL

Date: May 19,1992
From: Charlotte Beers
To: LUIS BASSAT, President, Bassat, Ogilvy & Mather, Spain
BILL HAMILTON, Creative Director, O&M New York
SHELLY LAZARUS, President, O&M New York
KELLY O'DEA, Worldwide Client Service Director, Ford and AT&T, London
ROBYN PUTTER, President and Creative Director, O&M South Africa

HARRY REID, CEO, O&M
  Europe, London
REIMER THEDENS, Vice
  Chairman, O&M Europe,
  Frankfurt
MIKE WALSH, President, O&M
  United Kingdom, London
ROD WRIGHT, Chairman, O&M
  Asia/Pacific, Hong Kong

Will you please join me . . . in reinventing our beloved agency? I choose
you because you seem to be truth-
tellers, impatient with the state we're
in and capable of leading this revised,
refreshed agency. We want to end up
with a vision for the agency we can
state . . . and excite throughout the
company. Bring some basics to Vienna,
like where we are today and where
we'd like to be in terms of our clients
and competition. But beyond the basics,
bring your dreams for this great brand.

BRAND STEWARDSHIP

The Vienna meeting, recalled Beers, "put
a diversity of talents in a climate of disruption." Having never met before for such
a purpose, members were both tentative
with each other and elated to share their
perspectives. Two common values provided an initial glue: "We agreed to take
no more baby steps. And it seemed clear
that brands were what we were going to
be about."

Beers asked Rod Wright, who had led
the Asia/Pacific region through a vision
formulation process, to organize and facilitate the meeting. Wright proposed a conceptual framework, based on the McKinsey
"7-S" model,[10] to guide discussion of the
firm's strengths and weaknesses. He also

hoped to generate debate. "We don't have
passionate arguments in this company. We
avoid conflict, and debates go off line.
When you use a framework, it's easier to
depersonalize the discussion."

Reactions to the discussion ranged from
confusion to disinterest. "It was theoretical mumbo-jumbo," commented one participant. "I tend to be far more pragmatic
and tactical." Added another, "I don't have
much patience for the theoretical bent. I
wanted to get on with it." Wright admitted, "They rolled their eyes and said, 'You
mean we've got to do all that?'" Beers
agreed: "The B-school approach had to
be translated." As the discussion unfolded,
the group discovered that their personalities, priorities, and views on specific action implications diverged widely.

One debate concerned priorities for
change. Shelly Lazarus diagnosed a firm-
wide morale problem. She argued for
restoring confidence with a pragmatic
focus on bottom-line client results and
counseled against spending much energy
on structural changes. Mike Walsh agreed
but insisted that the group take time to articulate clearly its vision and values. But
Kelly O'Dea had become frustrated with
Ogilvy's geographical fragmentation and
argued that anything short of major structural changes would be insufficient.

Participants were also divided on
whether the emerging brand focus was an
end or a starting point. The "creatives" in
the group[11]—Luis Bassat, Bill Hamilton,
and Robyn Putter—flanked by Beers,
Lazarus, and Walsh, were interested primarily in finding an effective vehicle for
communicating O&M's distinctive competency. An eloquent statement, they felt,

---

[10] Wright's model included 10 issue categories:
shared values, structures, stakeholders, staff,
skills, strategy, suggestions, solutions, service
systems, and a shared vision.

[11] Within advertising and direct marketing,
"creatives" develop the art and copy for each
media outlet of a brand campaign.

would sell clients and inspire employees. The others—O'Dea, Wright, Harry Reid, and Reimer Thedens—wanted a vision that provided guidelines for an internal transformation. Summarized Wright, "One school of thought was looking for a line which encapsulates what we do: our creative credo. The other was looking for a strategy, a business mission to guide how we run the company."

Yet another discussion concerned the route to competitive advantage. Bassat, Putter, and Hamilton, commented one participant, felt that Ogilvy had lost sight of the creative product in its rush to worry about finances: "We'd become too commercial." A recommitment to better, more imaginative advertising, they believed, would differentiate the firm from its competitors. Reid and Thedens, architects of a massive reengineering effort in Europe, insisted on financial discipline and tighter operations throughout the company as the only means of survival in the lean operating environment of the 1990's. Wright and Thedens added the O&M Direct perspective. Convinced that media advertising by itself was becoming a commodity product, each pressed for a commitment to brand building through a broader, more integrated range of communication services.

At the close of the meeting, remembered one attendee, "There was a great deal of cynicism. 'Was this just another chat session?' we asked ourselves. But we also had a sense that Charlotte felt right. She fit."

In August 1992, the group reassembled at the English resort Chewton Glen. Members presented Beers with their respective lists of priorities requiring immediate attention. Taken together, there were 22 "to do" items, ranging from "examine the process by which we develop and present creative ideas" to "improve our delivery of services across geographical divisions."

Beers recalled, "No one can focus on 22 things! I was so depressed, I stayed up all night and wrote a new list." She delivered her thoughts the next day:

> I think we have hit bottom and are poised for recovery. Poised but not assured. Our job is to give direction for change. So here is where I start. For 1993, we have three—and only three—strategies. They are:
>
> 1. *Client security.* Let's focus our energy, resources and passion on our present clients. It takes three years to replace the revenue from a lost client. Under strategy one, there's a very important corollary: We must focus particularly on multinational clients. This is where we have our greatest opportunity for growth and where our attitudes, structure, and lack of focus have been obstacles.
> 2. *Better work, more often.* Without it, you can forget the rest. Our work is not good enough. Maybe it will never be, but that's OK—better to be so relentless about our work that we are never satisfied. You tell me there's nothing wrong with our credo, "We Sell, or Else," but you also say we need some fresh thinking on how to get there. We must have creative strategies that make the brand the central focus.
> 3. *Financial discipline.* This has been a subject of high concentration but not very productively so. We simply have not managed our own resources very well, and that must change.

These 1993 strategies were linked to the emerging vision by a declaration: "The purpose of our business is to build our clients' brands." One participant recalled, "The idea of brand stewardship was still embryonic. Charlotte clearly understood it in her own mind but was just learning how to communicate it. She used us as guinea pigs to refine her thinking." But some expressed concern: "There was no disagreement that the 1993 strategy was correct. It was fine for the short term but we needed a long-term strategy."

Through the fall of 1992, group members worked to communicate the strategy—dubbed the "Chewton Glen Declaration"—to the next level of managers. Beers directed her energy toward clients, working vigorously to win new and lost accounts. She spoke about the emotional power of brands, warning them of the abuse inflicted by agencies and brand managers who failed to understand the consumer's relationship with their products. Ogilvy & Mather, Beers told clients, was uniquely positioned to steward their brands' growth and development. Clients were intrigued. By October, O&M boasted two major successes: Jaguar Motor cars' entire U.S. account and the return of American Express's $60 million worldwide account.[12] The press hailed, "Ogilvy & Mather is back on track."

WORLDWIDE CLIENT SERVICE

The Chewton Glen mandate to focus on multinationals heightened the need for better global coordination. Although Ogilvy had pioneered multinational account service in the 1970s, the firm in the 1990s remained "segregated into geographic and discipline fiefdoms" that hampered the development and delivery of brand campaigns worldwide. Noted O'Dea, "What most clients began to seek was the best combination of global efficiencies and local sensitivity, but we were not set up to facilitate that. We had the local strength, but international people were commandos

[12] "Operation Winback," *Advertising Age*, February 1993.

with passports and begging bowls, totally dependent on the goodwill of local agencies and their own personal charisma."

In the fall of 1992, Beers asked O'Dea to head a new organization, Worldwide Client Service, that would "tap the best brains from anywhere in the world for each account." O'Dea envisioned dozens of virtual organizations, each focused on a multinational client, with multiple "centers" located wherever their respective clients maintained international headquarters. Under WCS, members of multinational account teams became "dual citizens," reporting both to their local office presidents and to WCS supervisors. One WCS director noted, "International people coordinating multinational accounts used to be regarded by the local offices as staff. We thought we were line; the clients treated us like line; but internally, we had no real authority. What WCS did was give us teeth by giving us line responsibility for our accounts—tenure, profits, growth, and evaluation of local offices."

WCS brand teams were structured to mirror their clients' organizations. Some WCS directors served largely as consultants, while others ran highly centralized operations, with a core team responsible for the entire creative and client development process. "We had to reinvent ourselves in the client's footprint," remarked the WCS account director for Kimberly-Clark. His counterpart at Unilever agreed but noted that current trends favored centralization. "Speed, cost efficiency, and centralization are our clients' priorities. What matters is not just having good ideas, but getting those ideas to as many markets as possible, as fast as possible."

By 1993, O'Dea began to travel the world presenting the possibilities of transnational teams without borders. "Good sell-ins had to be done. Office heads had to understand that there were no choices—global accounts had to be managed horizontally. We'd be dead if we didn't do it," said Reid.

TOOLS FOR BRAND STEWARDSHIP

"The first six months were high excitement, high energy, and a steep learning curve," said Beers. "That was followed by 12 months of disappointment and frustration. It didn't look as if we were getting anywhere." In December 1992, Beers asked Robyn Putter and Luis Bassat, two of the firm's top creative talents, for help in developing the emerging notion of "Brand Stewardship." They answered: "If we are to be successful, we must 'audit' our brands. We must ask the kinds of questions that will systematically uncover the emotional subtleties and nuances by which brands live." Beers took their insight directly to existing and prospective clients. One manager remembered:

> Clients immediately bought into Brand Stewardship. That created pressure to go public with it before we had every "i" dotted and "t" crossed. We didn't have a codified process, but Charlotte would talk to clients and we'd have to do it. Clients came to O&M offices saying, "I want a brand audit." And, our offices responded with, 'What's a brand audit?' One client asked us for permission to use the term. We had to move quickly, or risk losing ownership of the idea.

Beers responded by asking a group of executives to elaborate the notion of a brand audit. Led by Walsh, they produced a series of questions designed to unveil the emotional as well as the logical significance of a product in the users' lives:

"What memories or associations does the brand bring to mind? What specific feelings and emotions do you experience in connection with using this brand? What does this brand do for you in your life that other brands cannot?" The insights gathered from these questions—which became the brand audit—would, in Beers' words, "guide each brand team to the rock-bottom truth of the brand." Focusing on two of Ogilvy's global brands—Jaguar and Dove—Beers' working group struggled to articulate in a few words and images each brand's unique "genetic fingerprint." The result was O&M's first BrandPrints™:

- A Jaguar is a copy of absolutely nothing—just like its owners.

- Dove stands for attainable miracles.

CRAFTING A VISION

As the "technology" of brand stewardship developed, the senior team continued to wrestle with the formulation of a vision statement. Some argued, "We have the vision—it's Brand Stewardship." Others maintained that Brand Stewardship was but a tool to be used in attaining a yet undefined, future state. Further, as O'Dea explained, "Nearly everyone had had some contact with Brand Stewardship and WCS but they viewed them as separate and isolated actions without a strategic context."

The solution to the impasse, for some, was to include a larger group in the vision formulation. "We needed to decide collectively what we were going to be. If you have 30 people deciding and 30 people who have bought into the vision, then they have no reason not to go out and do it," reasoned Wright. Walsh agreed: "You get the 30 most influential people in the company to open their veins together—which hasn't happened in a very long time." Others, including Beers, worried about losing control of the end result. Advocates for a larger group prevailed, and the entire O&M Worldwide board of directors along with eight other local presidents attended the next meeting in July 1993 at the Doral Arrowwood, a conference center in Westchester, New York.

The purpose of the meeting, explained one of the organizers, was to get final agreement on the vision and where Brand Stewardship fit in. Feedback from clients on Brand Stewardship and WCS was used to guide the initial discussion. Participants' recollections of the three-day event ranged from "ghastly" to "painful" and "dreadful." Noted Lazarus, "It seemed an endless stream of theoretical models. Everyone was frustrated and grumpy."

The turning point, Beers recalled, took place at the end of a grueling first day, when one person voiced what many were thinking: "He said, 'There's nothing new here. I don't see how Brand Stewardship can be unique to Ogilvy.' This was very helpful. One of the negatives at Ogilvy is all the real debates unfold outside the meeting room." The next morning, Beers addressed the group: "Certainly, the individual pieces of this thinking are not new. But to practice it would be remarkable. I have heard that in any change effort, one-third are supporters, one-third are resisters, and one-third are apathetic. I'm in the first group. Where are you?"

With Beers' challenge precipitating consensus, attendees split into groups to tackle four categories of action implications. One group, which included Beers, was charged with crafting the specific wording of the vision. A second began to develop a statement of shared values that would integrate traditional Ogilvy

principles with the emerging values of the new philosophy. "That was hard to agree on," recalled Wright. "At issue was how much of the past do we want to take forward." The third group worked on a strategy for communicating the vision to all levels and offices throughout the company. Plans for a Brand Stewardship handbook, regional conferences, and a training program were launched. A fourth group was asked to begin thinking about how to realign titles, structures, systems, and incentives to support the new vision.

After heated brainstorming and drawing freely from the other three groups to test and refine their thinking, Walsh remembered that, finally, "There it was: 'To be the agency most valued by those who most value brands.'" Summing up the meeting, one attendee said, "There had been an amazing amount of distraction, irrelevance, and digression. I didn't think we could pull it together, but we did." (See Exhibit 4 for the final version of the Vision and Values statement.)

MOVING FORWARD

Through the fall of 1993, Beers and her senior team worked relentlessly to spread the message of Brand Stewardship throughout the agency. It was a slow, sometimes arduous, process. By the end of the year, they had identified several issues that they felt required immediate attention.

SPREADING THE GOSPEL

Compared to clients' enthusiasm, reactions to Brand Stewardship within the agency were initially tepid. Across disciplines, employees below the most senior level lacked experience with, and knowledge of how to use, the principles

EXHIBIT 4   **Statement of Vision and Values, 1993**

To our people, our clients, and our friends–

The winds of change are blowing through Ogilvy & Mather. We are raising the sights of everybody in the company to a sweeping new vision:

TO BE THE AGENCY MOST VALUED
BY THOSE WHO MOST VALUE BRANDS

Not that we have ever been unmindful of the importance of brands. Quite the contrary; our new thrust gets a big boost from ingrained Ogilvy & Mather strengths. Its roots lie in the teachings of David Ogilvy that reverberate through our halls. We have always aimed to create great campaigns with the spark to ignite sales and the staying power to build enduring brands.

> *What's new is a restructuring of resources, an arsenal of modern techniques, and an intensity of focus that add up to a major advance in the way we do business. We call it BRAND STEWARDSHIP–the art of creating, building, and energizing profitable brands.*

The new techniques and procedures of Brand Stewardship have already proved their value for many important brands. As I write they are being put to work for others. In March we will launch them formally–in print, on tape, and throughout the Oglvy & Mather network.

This will affect the working habits of every professional in the agency, to the benefit, I am convinced, of every brand we work for. I predict that it will bring out the best in all of you–creatively and in every other aspect of your work–and add a lot to the pleasure and satisfaction you get out of your jobs.

As a first formal step the Board of Directors is putting forward the new statement of Shared Values on the next page. You may notice that several of the points are taken from principles that have guided the company since its start–principles that were most recently set on paper in 1990 when David Ogilvy brought our Corporate Culture up to date.

Thus the Shared Values perform two functions: they *expand* our culture to reflect inexorable change, and in the same breath they *reinforce* its timeless standards.

All vital cultures–national, artistic, corporate–tend to evolve as conditions change, preserving valuable old characteristics as new ones come into the spotlight. In just that way these Shared Values now take their place at the forefront of the dynamic culture of Ogilvy & Mather.

Charlotte

Charlotte Beers
Chairman, Ogilvy & Mather Worldwide

continued

EXHIBIT 4 *continued*

The market in which we compete is not a static one. To progress toward our new Vision will demand restless challenge and frequent change. The values we share, however—the way we do things day-to-day—will remain constant.

We work not for ourselves, not for the company, not even for a client. We work for Brands.

———•———

We work with the client, as Brand Teams. These Teams represent the collective skills of our clients and ourselves. On their performance, our client will judge the whole agency.

———•———

We encourage individuals, entrepreneurs, inventive mavericks: with such members, teams thrive. We have no time for prima donnas and politicians.

———•———

We value candor, curiosity, originality, intellectual rigor, perseverance, brains–and civility. We see no conflict between a commitment to the highest professional standards in our work and to human kindness in our dealings with each other.

———•———

We prefer the discipline of knowledge to the anarchy of ignorance. We pursue knowledge the way a pig pursues truffles.

———•———

We prize both analytical and creative skills. Without the first, you can't know where to go; without the second, you won't be able to get there.

———•———

The line between confidence and arrogance is a fine one. We watch it obsessively.

———•———

We respect the intelligence of our audiences:
"The consumer is not a moron."

We expect our clients to hold us accountable for our Stewardship of their Brands. Only if we have built, nourished, and developed prosperous Brands, only if we have made them more valuable both to their users and their owners, may we judge ourselves successful.

of Brand Stewardship. O'Dea remarked, "Brand Stewardship has not seeped into everyday practice. Only a minority of the O&M population truly understands and embraces it. Others are aware of Brand Stewardship, but not deeply proficient. Many are still not true believers."

Account executives who misunderstood the concept were at a loss when their clients demanded it. Planners expressed confusion about how to use Brand Stewardship to develop a creative strategy.[13] Recalled one executive, "People didn't understand such basic things as the difference between a BrandPrint™ and an advertising strategy."

Greater familiarity with the process did not always mitigate opposition. Admitted Beers, "We didn't always have much internal support. It did not sound like anything new." Another problem was that a brand audit might suggest a change of advertising strategy. "Doing an audit on existing business can be seen as an indictment of what we have been doing," noted one executive. Lazarus concluded:

> It will only be internalized throughout the organization with experience. I did a Brand Stewardship presentation recently with some of our account people. The client was mesmerized. They wanted the chairman of the company to see the presentation. Now, that had an effect on the people who were with me. I can bet you that when they make the next presentation, Brand Stewardship will be their focal point.

Perhaps the greatest resistance came from the creative side. "We've got to get

greater buy-in from the creative people," noted Walsh. Their initial reactions ranged from viewing the BrandPrint™ as an infringement on their artistic license—"I didn't believe in recipe approaches. They can lead to formulaic solutions," said one early convert—to the tolerant skepticism reported by another: "The creatives tell me, 'If it helps you get new business, that's great, but why are you in my office talking about this? I have a deadline and don't see what this has to do with creating advertising.' But you can't develop a good BrandPrint™ without cross-functional involvement."

Others questioned the relevance of Brand Stewardship for O&M Direct. While it was clear to Beers that Brand Stewardship clarified the rewards to clients from integrating advertising and direct marketing, some were slow to see this potential. Dispelling the popular notion that direct encourages short-term sales while advertising builds brands over the long term, Thedens argued, "You can't send a message by mail that contradicts what you show on television. Both disciplines sell and both build the brand."

One executive concluded that the biggest problem was insufficient communication: "Anyone who heard it firsthand from Charlotte bought in. From the moment she opens her mouth to talk about brands, you know she has a depth of understanding that few people have. The problem is that, until recently, she has been the only missionary." Although the senior team had started "taking the show on the road," Walsh felt they were too few for the magnitude of the task: "The same six or seven people keep getting reshuffled. The result is that follow-through is not good."

O'Dea, however, pointed out that the new missionaries had different tribes to

---

[13] Account executives managed the agency's contact with clients, bringing in new accounts and coordinating information flow between other functions and the client. Planners worked with account executives to establish creative marketing strategies.

convert. He emphasized the importance of translating the vision into a new role for each employee:

> We need to move beyond a vision that is useful to the top 5 percent of account and creative people, to one that has meaning for everyone at Ogilvy. The Information Systems staff should see themselves as brand stewards, because without information technology, we can't respond with appropriate speed. I want the Media people to say, "I will not buy airtime on these T.V. shows because they don't fit the BrandPrint™." Creatives at O&M Direct developing coupon designs must be as true to the BrandPrint as creatives in advertising. Everyone must see themselves as co-stewards of the vision.

LOCAL/GLOBAL TENSIONS

Success in 1993 in winning several large multinational accounts created further challenges for the embryonic WCS. Their goal of helping clients to develop a consistent brand image globally created tension in the firm's traditional balance of power. WCS pressed local agencies to give priority to brands with high global development potential over local accounts. For local agencies, however, local accounts often provided the most stable revenue stream and greatest profit. Further, in their zeal to exercise their newfound "line" responsibility, WCS supervisors were viewed at times as overstepping the bounds of their authority.

While tension had always existed between the centers and the local markets, the increasingly centralized brand campaigns exacerbated conflicts. "Local agencies were used to always giving the client what they wanted," explained one WCS supervisor. "I had to start telling them to stop over-servicing the client."

Some balked. Local expertise had always been one of Ogilvy's greatest competitive strengths. As one senior executive explained, "Certain local offices have not responded well to some of the advertising created centrally. One downside of global work is that it can end up being middle-of-the-road. When this happens, it's bad for an office's creative image locally."

But with costs escalating both centrally and locally, many felt that "the local barons" had to be reigned in. "How do we help our clients globalize," asked Walsh, "when our local management will conspire to keep them geographically oriented?"

For smaller agencies, issues of creative pride and autonomy were especially salient. Under the new system, the central WCS team developed the BrandPrint™ and advertising campaign with input from local offices. Local offices then tailored execution to regional markets. But while large offices usually served as the center for at least one global account, smaller offices, explained one WCS director, "are more often on the receiving end now. They begin to feel like post boxes. How do you attract good people to smaller offices if they never get to run big accounts?"

Beers felt that maintaining flexibility was key. "Some of our competitors— McCann Erickson is a good example—are excellent at running highly centralized campaigns. For us to view WCS that way would be a mistake. WCS should build upon, not diminish, our local strength." Creative and execution roles, she explained further, should shift according to the locus of the best ideas or relevant resources:

> I want to continue to cultivate the tension between local and center. The easiest thing would be to have far more dominance centrally. It is more efficient, and the clients like it, because

they invariably wish they had more control at the center. The reality is that nothing substitutes for full-blown, local agencies where the people are talented enough to articulate the heart of the brand, to interpret it in a sophisticated way, and—if necessary—to change it. If you have messengers or outlets, you will never execute well. The best ideas have unique, local modifications. One brand campaign we tested, for example, was an absolute win around the world, except in Asia, where the humor did not translate well. Our creative director in Asia worked with the idea, and it became the print campaign we use globally.

Also on her mind was the brewing controversy about how to split fees and allocate costs between WCS and local offices. Agency compensation on large accounts consisted frequently of fixed fees that were negotiated up front. With new clients, it could be difficult to estimate the range of Ogilvy services needed and the extent of local adaptation that would be required. Agencies in more distant markets were asked to contribute—sometimes without compensation—when the need for additional local work was discovered. Local presidents complained that, although WCS accounts pulled their people away from local accounts with clear-cut billable time, their portion of multinational fees was small. WCS, on the other hand, maintained that they were being forced to absorb more than their fair share of local costs.

Beers recounted one specific incident that unfolded in December. "Kelly told me that one of our offices had refused to do any more work for a client, because they did not have any fees. I said to him, 'I think you ought to talk to them about our new way of working and how much promise there is in it. Give them more

information. If they still can't see their way, have them come to me.' You ask for collaboration," she concluded, "but occasionally you act autocratically."

As conflicts continued to erupt, senior management was divided on the solution. "We have highly individual personalities running our offices. With 272 worldwide," one account director observed, "it's been like herding cats." Debate swirled around the degree of management structure required. Lazarus advocated commonsense resolutions between the global account director and local agency presidents:

> In our business, the quality of the work that gets done all comes down to the people who are doing it, not to bureaucratic structures. If you create the right environment and you have the right people, you don't need a whole structure.

Others, O'Dea and his WCS corps included, insisted that organizational changes were necessary to make Brand Stewardship a reality agency-wide. Walsh agreed: "What we don't have is a structure, working practices, remuneration, praise of people—all based on Brand Stewardship." Referring to the trademark Ogilvy color, Beers offered her perspective:

> We have to make Ogilvy "redder." The finances should follow our goal of killing geography as a barrier to serving the brand.... Let's get the emotional content high and the structure will follow. We have people in the company who would prefer it the other way, but I want to get it done in my lifetime. So much of what happens at Ogilvy is cerebral, thoughtful and slow. We can't afford to move at a "grey" pace.

At the end of 1993, yet another issue had come to the fore. With large multinational accounts, some WCS heads controlled billings that easily surpassed those of many countries in the network. The agency, however, had always accorded the greatest prestige and biggest bonuses to presidents of local offices, countries, and regional chairmen. Brand Stewardship now required top-notch brand stewards and organizations centered around products and processes rather than Ogilvy office locations. "I ask people to collaborate, but I don't pay them for it. This company has never asked its feudal chiefs to consider the sum," observed Beers. She pondered how to attract the best and the brightest to WCS posts, knowing she would be asking them to leave the safety of turf to head brand-focused, virtual organizations.

The "thirsty for change" veterans believed another hurdle would be learning to work better as a team. Said Lazarus, "I don't think we make a lot of group decisions. We talk about it, but decisions tend to get made by Charlotte and by the specific individuals who are affected." But implementation revived many of the debates of the first Vienna meeting. "I think we are all still very guarded," explained Walsh. "As each meeting goes by, it's a bit like a lump of ice slowly melting—our edges getting smoother all the time." Lazarus hoped that team members would grow "comfortable enough to disagree openly with one another." Battling a culture she had once described as "grotesquely polite" was still on Beers' list of priorities as she considered the group she had assembled to help carry the change forward.

In December 1993, Charlotte Beers assessed the year's progress: "Clients love Brand Stewardship. Competitors are trying to copy it. And internally, we lack consensus." She wondered what course of action in 1994 would provide the best stewardship of the Ogilvy brand.

Reading

The Quest for Resilience

Gary Hamel and Liisa Välikangas

Call it the resilience gap. The world is becoming turbulent faster than organizations are becoming resilient. The evidence is all around us. Big companies are failing more frequently. Of the 20 largest U.S. bankruptcies in the past two decades, ten occurred in the last two years. Corporate earnings are more erratic. Over the past four decades, year-to-year volatility in the earnings growth rate of S&P 500 companies has increased by nearly 50%—despite vigorous efforts to "manage" earnings. Performance slumps are proliferating. In each of the years from 1973 to 1977, an average of 37 *Fortune* 500 companies were entering or in the midst of a 50%, five-year decline in net income; from 1993 to 1997, smack in the middle of the longest economic boom in modern times, the average number of companies suffering through such an earnings contraction more than doubled, to 84 each year.

Even perennially successful companies are finding it more difficult to deliver consistently superior returns. In their 1994 best-seller *Built to Last*, Jim Collins and Jerry Porras singled out 18 "visionary" companies that had consistently outperformed their peers between 1950 and 1990. But over the last ten years, just six of these companies managed to outperform the Dow Jones Industrial Average. The other twelve—a group that includes companies like Disney, Motorola, Ford, Nordstrom, Sony, and Hewlett-Packard—have apparently gone from great to merely OK. Any way you cut it, success has never been so fragile.

In less turbulent times, established companies could rely on the flywheel of momentum to sustain their success. Some, like AT&T and American Airlines, were insulated from competition by regulatory protection and oligopolistic practices. Others, like General Motors and Coca-Cola, enjoyed a relatively stable product paradigm—for more than a century, cars have had four wheels and a combustion engine and consumers have sipped caffeine-laced soft drinks. Still others, like McDonald's and Intel, built formidable first-mover advantages. And in capital-intensive industries like petroleum and aerospace, high entry barriers protected incumbents.

The fact that success has become less persistent strongly suggests that momentum is not the force it once was. To be sure, there is still enormous value in having a coterie of loyal customers, a well-known brand, deep industry know-how, preferential access to distribution channels, proprietary physical assets, and a robust patent portfolio. But that value has steadily dissipated as the enemies of momentum have multiplied. Technological discontinuities, regulatory upheavals, geopolitical shocks, industry deverticalization and disintermediation, abrupt shifts in consumer tastes, and hordes of nontraditional competitors—these are just a few of the forces undermining the advantages of incumbency.

In the past, executives had the luxury of assuming that business models were more or less immortal. Companies always had to work to get better, of course, but they seldom had to get different—not at their core, not in their essence. Today, getting different is the imperative. It's the challenge facing Coca-Cola as it struggles to raise its "share of throat" in noncarbonated beverages. It's the task that bedevils McDonald's as it tries to rekindle growth in a world of burger-weary customers. It's the hurdle for Sun Microsystems as it searches for ways to protect its high-margin server business from the Linux onslaught. And it's an imperative for the big pharmaceutical companies as they confront declining R&D yields, escalating price pressure, and the growing threat from generic drugs. For all these companies, and for yours, continued success no longer hinges on momentum. Rather, it rides on resilience—on the ability to dynamically reinvent business models and strategies as circumstances change.

Strategic resilience is not about responding to a onetime crisis. It's not about rebounding from a setback. It's about continuously anticipating and adjusting to deep, secular trends that can permanently impair the earning power of a core business. It's about having the capacity to change before the case for change becomes desperately obvious.

ZERO TRAUMA

Successful companies, particularly those that have enjoyed a relatively benign environment, find it extraordinarily difficult

Revolution, Renewal, and Resilience: A Glossary for Turbulent Times

What's the probability that your company will significantly outperform the world economy over the next few years? What's the chance that your company will deliver substantially better returns than the industry average? What are the odds that change, in all its guises, will bring your company considerably more upside than downside? Confidence in the future of your business—or of any business—depends on the extent to which it has mastered three essential forms of innovation.

REVOLUTION

In most industries it's the revolutionaries—like JetBlue, Amgen, Costco, University of Phoenix, eBay, and Dell—that have created most of the new wealth over the last decade. Whether newcomer or old timer, a company needs an unconventional strategy to produce unconventional financial returns. Industry revolution is creative destruction. It is innovation with respect to industry rules.

RENEWAL

Newcomers have one important advantage over incumbents—a clean slate. To reinvent its industry, an incumbent must first reinvent itself. Strategic renewal is creative reconstruction. It requires innovation with respect to one's traditional business model.

RESILIENCE

It usually takes a performance crisis to prompt the work of renewal. Rather than go from success to success, most companies go from success to failure and then, after a long, hard climb, back to success. Resilience refers to a capacity for continuous reconstruction. It requires innovation with respect to those organizational values, processes, and behaviors that systematically favor perpetuation over innovation.

to reinvent their business models. When confronted by paradigm-busting turbulence, they often experience a deep and prolonged reversal of fortune. Consider IBM. Between 1990 and 1993, the company went from making $6 billion to losing nearly $8 billion. It wasn't until 1997 that its earnings reached their previous high. Such a protracted earnings slump typically provokes a leadership change, and in many cases the new CEO—be it Gerstner at IBM or Ghosn at Nissan or Bravo at Burberry—produces a successful, if wrenching, turnaround. However celebrated, a turnaround is a testament to a company's lack of resilience. A turnaround is transformation tragically delayed.

Imagine a ratio where the numerator measures the magnitude and frequency of strategic transformation and the denominator reflects the time, expense, and emotional energy required to effect that transformation. Any company that hopes to stay relevant in a topsy-turvy world has no choice but to grow the numerator. The real trick is to steadily reduce the denominator at the same time. To thrive in turbulent times, companies must become as efficient at renewal as they are at producing today's products and services. Renewal must be the natural consequence of an organization's innate resilience.

The quest for resilience can't start with an inventory of best practices. Today's best practices are manifestly inadequate. Instead, it must begin with an aspiration: zero trauma. The goal is a strategy that is forever morphing, forever conforming itself to emerging opportunities and incipient trends. The goal is an organization that is constantly making its future rather than defending its past. The goal is a company where revolutionary change happens in lightning-quick, evolutionary steps—with no calamitous surprises, no convulsive reorganizations, no colossal write-offs, and no indiscriminate, across-the-board layoffs. In a truly resilient organization, there is plenty of excitement, but there is no trauma.

Sound impossible? A few decades ago, many would have laughed at the notion of "zero defects." If you were driving a Ford Pinto or a Chevy Vega, or making those sorry automobiles, the very term would have sounded absurd. But today we live in a world where Six Sigma, 3.4 defects per million, is widely viewed as an achievable goal. So why shouldn't we commit ourselves to zero trauma? Defects cost money, but so do outdated strategies, missed opportunities, and belated restructuring programs. Today, many of society's most important institutions, including its largest commercial organizations, are not resilient. But no law says they must remain so. It is precisely because resilience is such a valuable goal that we must commit ourselves to making it an attainable one. (See the box "Why Resilience Matters.")

Any organization that hopes to become resilient must address four challenges:

The Cognitive Challenge: A company must become entirely free of denial, nostalgia, and arrogance. It must be deeply conscious of what's changing and perpetually willing to consider how those changes are likely to affect its current success.

The Strategic Challenge: Resilience requires alternatives as well as awareness—the ability to create a plethora of new options as compelling alternatives to dying strategies.

The Political Challenge: An organization must be able to divert resources from yesterday's products and programs to tomorrow's. This doesn't mean funding flights of fancy; it means building an ability to support a broad portfolio of breakout experiments with the necessary capital and talent.

The Ideological Challenge: Few organizations question the doctrine of optimization. But optimizing a business model that is slowly becoming irrelevant can't secure a company's future. If renewal is to become continuous and opportunity-driven, rather than episodic and crisis-driven, companies will need to embrace a creed that extends beyond operational excellence and flawless execution.

Few organizations, if any, can claim to have mastered these four challenges. While there is no simple recipe for building a resilient organization, a decade of research on innovation and renewal allows us to suggest a few starting points.

CONQUERING DENIAL

Every business is successful until it's not. What's amazing is how often top management is surprised when "not" happens. This astonishment, this belated recognition of dramatically changed circumstances, virtually guarantees that the work of renewal will be significantly, perhaps dangerously, postponed.

Why the surprise? Is it that the world is not only changing but changing in ways that simply cannot be anticipated—that it is *shockingly* turbulent? Perhaps, but even

Why Resilience Matters

Some might argue that there is no reason to be concerned with the resilience of any particular company as long as there is unfettered competition, a well-functioning market for corporate ownership, a public policy regime that doesn't protect failing companies from their own stupidity, and a population of start-ups eager to exploit the sloth of incumbents. In this view, competition acts as a spur to perpetual revitalization. A company that fails to adjust to its changing environment soon loses its relevance, its customers, and, ultimately, the support of its stakeholders. Whether it slowly goes out of business or gets acquired, the company's human and financial capital gets reallocated in a way that raises the marginal return on those assets.

This view of the resilience problem has the virtue of being conceptually simple. It is also simpleminded. While competition, new entrants, takeovers, and bankruptcies are effective as purgatives for managerial incompetence, these forces cannot be relied on to address the resilience problem efficiently and completely. There are several reasons why.

First, and most obvious, thousands of important institutions lie outside the market for corporate control, from privately owned companies like Cargill to public-sector agencies like Britain's National Health Service to nonprofits like the Red Cross. Some of these institutions have competitors; many don't. None of them can be easily "taken over." A lack of resilience may go uncorrected for a considerable period of time, while constituents remain underserved and society's resources are squandered.

Second, competition, acquisitions, and bankruptcies are relatively crude mechanisms for reallocating resources from poorly managed companies to well-managed ones. Let's start with the most draconian of these alternatives—bankruptcy. When a firm fails, much of its accumulated intellectual capital disintegrates as teams disperse. It often takes months or years for labor markets to redeploy displaced human assets. Takeovers are a more efficient reallocation mechanism, yet they, too, are a poor substitute for organizational resilience. Executives in underperforming companies, eager to protect their privileges and prerogatives, will typically resist the idea of a takeover until all other survival options have been exhausted. Even then, they are likely to significantly underestimate the extent of institutional decay—a misjudgment that is often shared by the acquiring company. Whether it be Compaq's acquisition of a stumbling Digital Equipment Corporation or Ford's takeover of the deeply troubled Jaguar, acquisitions often prove to be belated, and therefore expensive, responses to institutional decline.

And what about competition, the endless warfare between large and small, old and young? Some believe that as long as a society is capable of creating new organizations, it can afford to be unconcerned about the resilience of old institutions. In this ecological view of resilience, the population of start-ups constitutes a portfolio of experiments, most of which will fail but a few of which will turn into successful businesses.

In this view, institutions are essentially disposable. The young eat the old. Leaving aside for the moment the question of whether institutional longevity has a value in and of itself, there is a reason to question this "who needs dumb, old incumbents when you have all these cool start-ups" line of reasoning. Young companies are generally less efficient than older companies— they are at an earlier point on the road from disorderly innovation to disciplined optimization. An economy composed entirely of start-ups would be grossly inefficient. Moreover, start-ups typically depend on established companies for funding, managerial talent, and market access. Classically, Microsoft's early success was critically dependent on its ability to harness IBM's brand and distribution power. Start-ups are thus not so much an alternative to established incumbents, as an insurance policy against the costs imposed on society by those incumbents that prove themselves to be unimaginative and slow to change. As is true in so many other situations, avoiding disaster is better than making a claim against an insurance policy once disaster has struck. Silicon Valley and other entrepreneurial hot spots are a boon, but they are no more than a partial solution to the problem of nonadaptive incumbents.

To the question, Can a company die an untimely death? an economist would answer no. Barring government intervention or some act of God, an organization fails when it deserves to fail, that is, when it has proven itself to be consistently unsuccessful in meeting the expectations of its stakeholders. There are, of course, cases in which one can reasonably say that an organization "deserves" to die. Two come immediately to mind: when an organization has fulfilled its original purpose or when changing circumstances have rendered the organization's core purpose invalid or no longer useful. (For example, with the collapse of Soviet-sponsored communism in Eastern Europe, some have questioned the continued usefulness of NATO.)

But there are cases in which organizational death should be regarded as premature in that it robs society of a future benefit. Longevity is important because time enables complexity. It took millions of years for biological evolution to produce the complex structures of the mammalian eye and millions more for it to develop the human brain and higher consciousness. Likewise, it takes years, sometimes decades, for an organization to elaborate a simple idea into a robust operational model. Imagine for a moment that Dell, currently the world's most successful computer maker, had died in infancy. It is at least possible that the world would not now possess the exemplary "build-to-order" business model Dell so successfully constructed over the past decade—a model that has spurred supply chain innovation in a host of other industries. This is not an argument for insulating a company from its environment; it is, however, a reason to imbue organizations with the capacity to dynamically adjust their strategies as they work to fulfill their long-term missions.

There is a final, noneconomic, reason to care about institutional longevity, and therefore resilience. Institutions are vessels into which we as human beings pour our energies, our passions, and our wisdom. Given this, it is not surprising that we often hope to be survived by the organizations we serve. For if our genes constitute the legacy of our individual, biological selves, our institutions constitute the legacy of our collective, purposeful selves. Like our children, they are our progeny. It is no wonder that we hope they will do well and be well treated by our successors. This hope for the future implies a reciprocal responsibility—that we be good stewards of the institutions we have inherited from our forebears. The best way of honoring an institutional legacy is to extend it, and the best way to extend it is to improve the organization's capacity for continual renewal.

Once more, though, we must be careful. A noble past doesn't entitle an institution to an illustrious future. Institutions deserve to endure only if they are capable of withstanding the onslaught of new institutions. A society's freedom to create new institutions is thus a critical insurance policy against its inability to recreate old ones. Where this freedom has been abridged as in, say, Japan, managers in incumbent institutions are able to dodge their responsibility for organizational renewal.

"unexpected" shocks can often be anticipated if one is paying close attention. Consider the recent tech sector meltdown—an event that sent many networking and computer suppliers into a tailspin and led to billions of dollars in write-downs.

Three body blows knocked the stuffing out of IT spending: The telecom sector, traditionally a big buyer of networking gear, imploded under the pressure of a massive debt load; a horde of dot-com customers ran out of cash and stopped buying computer equipment; and large corporate customers slashed IT budgets as the economy went into recession. Is it fair to expect IT vendors to have anticipated this perfect storm? Yes.

They knew, for example, that the vast majority of their dot-com customers were burning through cash at a ferocious rate but had no visible earnings. The same was true for many of the fledgling telecom outfits that were buying equipment using vendor financing. These companies were building fiber-optic networks far faster than they could be utilized. With bandwidth increasing more rapidly than demand, it was only a matter of time before plummeting prices would drive many of these debt-heavy companies to the wall. There were other warning signs. In 1990, U.S. companies spent 19% of their capital budgets on information technology. By 2000, they were devoting 59% of their capital spending to IT. In other words, IT had tripled its share of capital budgets—this during the longest capital-spending boom in U.S. history. Anyone looking at the data in 2000 should have been asking, Will capital spending keep growing at a double-digit pace? And is it likely that IT spending will continue to grow so fast? Logically, the answer to both questions had to be no. Things that can't go on forever usually don't. IT vendors should

have anticipated a major pullback in their revenue growth and started "war gaming" postboom options well before demand collapsed.

It is unfair, of course, to single out one industry. What happened to a few flat-footed IT companies can happen to any company—and often does. More than likely, Motorola was startled by Nokia's quick sprint to global leadership in the mobile phone business; executives at the Gap probably received a jolt when, in early 2001, their company's growth engine suddenly went into reverse; and CNN's management team was undoubtedly surprised by the Fox News Channel's rapid climb up the ratings ladder.

But they, like those in the IT sector, should have been able to see the future's broad outline—to anticipate the point at which a growth curve suddenly flattens out or a business model runs out of steam. The fact that serious performance shortfalls so often come as a surprise suggests that executives frequently take refuge in denial. Greg Blonder, former chief technical adviser at AT&T, admitted as much in a November 2002 *Barron's* article: "In the early 1990s, AT&T management argued internally that the steady upward curve of Internet usage would somehow collapse. The idea that it might actually overshadow traditional telephone service was simply unthinkable. But the trend could not be stopped—or even slowed—by wishful thinking and clever marketing. One by one, the props that held up the long-distance business collapsed." For AT&T, as for many other companies, the future was less unknowable than it was unthinkable, less inscrutable than unpalatable.

Denial puts the work of renewal on hold, and with each passing month, the cost goes up. To be resilient, an organization must dramatically reduce the time it takes to go from "that can't be true" to "we must face the world as it is." So what does it take to break through the hard carapace of denial? Three things.

First, senior managers must make a habit of visiting the places where change happens first. Ask yourself how often in the last year you have put yourself in a position where you had the chance to see change close-up—where you weren't reading about change in a business magazine, hearing about it from a consultant, or getting a warmed-over report from an employee, but were experiencing it first-hand. Have you visited a nanotechnology lab? Have you spent a few nights hanging out in London's trendiest clubs? Have you spent an afternoon talking to fervent environmentalists or antiglobalization activists? Have you had an honest, what-do-you-care-about conversation with anyone under 18? It's easy to discount second-hand data; it's hard to ignore what you've experienced for yourself. And if you have managed to rub up against what's changing, how much time have you spent thinking through the second- and third-order consequences of what you've witnessed? As the rate of change increases, so must the personal energy you devote to understanding change.

Second, you have to filter out the filterers. Most likely, there are people in your organization who are plugged tightly in to the future and understand well the not-so-sanguine implications for your company's business model. You have to find these people. You have to make sure their views are not censored by the custodians of convention and their access is not blocked by those who believe they are paid to protect you from unpleasant truths. You should be wary of anyone who has a vested interest in your continued ignorance, who fears that a full understanding of what's changing

would expose his own failure to anticipate it or the inadequacy of his response.

There are many ways to circumvent the courtiers and the self-protecting bureaucrats. Talk to potential customers who aren't buying from you. Go out for drinks and dinner with your most free-thinking employees. Establish a shadow executive committee whose members are, on average, 20 years younger than the "real" executive committee. Give this group of 30-somethings the chance to review capital budgets, ad campaigns, acquisition plans, and divisional strategies—and to present their views directly to the board. Another strategy is to periodically review the proposals that never made it to the top—those that got spiked by divisional VPs and unit managers. Often it's what doesn't get sponsored that turns out to be most in tune with what's changing, even though the proposals may be out of tune with prevailing orthodoxies.

Finally, you have to face up to the inevitability of strategy decay. On occasion, Bill Gates has been heard to remark that Microsoft is always two or three years away from failure. Hyperbole, perhaps, but the message to his organization is clear: Change will render irrelevant at least some of what Microsoft is doing today—and it will do so sooner rather than later. While it's easy to admit that nothing lasts forever, it is rather more difficult to admit that a dearly beloved strategy is rapidly going from ripe to rotten.

Strategies decay for four reasons. Over time they get *replicated*; they lose their distinctiveness and, therefore, their power to produce above-average returns. Ford's introduction of the Explorer may have established the SUV category, but today nearly every carmaker—from Cadillac to Nissan to Porsche—has a high-standing, gas-guzzling monster in its product line.

No wonder Ford's profitability has recently taken a hit. With a veritable army of consultants hawking best practices and a bevy of business journalists working to uncover the secrets of high-performing companies, great ideas get replicated faster than ever. And when strategies converge, margins collapse.

Good strategies also get *supplanted* by better strategies. Whether it's made-to-order PCs à la Dell, flat-pack furniture from IKEA, or downloadable music via KaZaA, innovation often undermines the earning power of traditional business models. One company's creativity is another's destruction. And in an increasingly connected economy, where ideas and capital travel at light speed, there's every reason to believe that new strategies will become old strategies ever more quickly.

Strategies get *exhausted* as markets become saturated, customers get bored, or optimization programs reach the point of diminishing returns. One example: In 1995, there were approximately 91 million active mobile phones in the world. Today, there are more than 1 billion. Nokia rode this growth curve more adeptly than any of its rivals. At one point its market value was three-and-a-half times that of its closest competitor. But the number of mobile phones in the world is not going to increase by 1,000% again, and Nokia's growth curve has already started to flatten out. Today, new markets can take off like a rocket. But the faster they grow, the sooner they reach the point where growth begins to decelerate. Ultimately, every strategy exhausts its fuel supply.

Finally, strategies get *eviscerated*. The Internet may not have changed everything, but it has dramatically accelerated the migration of power from producers to consumers. Customers are using their newfound power like a knife, carving big chunks out of once-fat margins. Nowhere has this been more evident than in the travel business, where travelers are using the Net to wrangle the lowest possible prices out of airlines and hotel companies. You know all those e-business efficiencies your company has been reaping? It's going to end up giving most of those productivity gains back to customers in the form of lower prices or better products and services at the same price. Increasingly it's your customers, not your competitors, who have you—and your margins—by the throat.

An accurate and honest appraisal of strategy decay is a powerful antidote to denial. (See the box "Anticipating Strategy Decay" for a list of diagnostic questions.) It is also the only way to know whether renewal is proceeding fast enough to fully offset the declining economic effectiveness of today's strategies.

VALUING VARIETY

Life is the most resilient thing on the planet. It has survived meteor showers, seismic upheavals, and radical climate shifts. And yet it does not plan, it does not forecast, and, except when manifested in human beings, it possesses no foresight. So what is the essential thing that life teaches us about resilience? Just this: Variety matters. Genetic variety, within and across species, is nature's insurance policy against the unexpected. A high degree of biological diversity ensures that no matter what particular future unfolds, there will be at least some organisms that are well-suited to the new circumstances.

Evolutionary biologists aren't the only ones who understand the value of variety. As any systems theorist will tell you, the larger the variety of actions available to a

Anticipating Strategy Decay

Business strategies decay in four ways—by being replicated, supplanted, exhausted, or eviscerated. And across the board, the pace of strategy decay is accelerating. The following questions, and the metrics they imply, make up a panel of warning lights that can alert executives to incipient decline.

The fact that renewal so often lags decay suggests that corporate leaders regularly miss, or deny, the signs of strategy decay. A diligent, honest, and frequent review of these questions can help to remedy this situation.

REPLICATION

Is our strategy losing its distinctiveness?

Does our strategy defy industry norms in any important ways?

Do we possess any competitive advantages that are truly unique?

Is our financial performance becoming less exceptional and more average?

SUPPLANTATION

Is our strategy in danger of being superseded?

Are there discontinuities (social, technical, or political) that could significantly reduce the economic power of our current business model?

Are there nascent business models that might render ours irrelevant?

Do we have strategies in place to co-opt or neutralize these forces of change?

EXHAUSTION

Is our strategy reaching the point of exhaustion?

Is the pace of improvement in key performance metrics (cost per unit or marketing expense per new customer, for example) slowing down?

Are our markets getting saturated; are our customers becoming more fickle?

Is our company's growth rate decelerating, or about to start doing so?

EVISCERATION

Is increasing customer power eviscerating our margins?

To what extent do our margins depend on customer ignorance or inertia?

How quickly, and in what ways, are customers gaining additional bargaining power?

Do our productivity improvements fall to the bottom line, or are we forced to give them back to customers in the form of lower prices or better products and services at the same price?

---

system, the larger the variety of perturbations it is able to accommodate. Put simply, if the range of strategic alternatives your company is exploring is significantly narrower than the breadth of change in the environment, your business is going to be a victim of turbulence. Resilience depends on variety.

Big companies are used to making big bets—Disney's theme park outside Paris, Motorola's satellite-phone venture Iridium, HP's acquisition of Compaq, and GM's gamble on hydrogen-powered cars are but a few examples. Sometimes these bets pay off; often they don't. When audacious strategies fail, companies often react by imposing draconian cost-cutting measures. But neither profligacy nor privation leads to resilience. Most companies would be better off if they made fewer billion-dollar bets and a whole lot more $10,000 or $20,000 bets—some of which will, in time, justify more substantial commitments. They should steer clear of grand, imperial strategies and devote themselves instead to launching a swarm of low-risk experiments, or, as our colleague Amy Muller calls them, stratlets.

The arithmetic is clear: It takes thousands of ideas to produce dozens of promising stratlets to yield a few outsize successes. Yet only a handful of companies have committed themselves to broad-based, small-scale strategic experimentation. Whirlpool is one. The world's leading manufacturer of domestic appliances, Whirlpool competes in an industry that is both cyclical and mature. Growth is a function of housing starts and product replacement cycles. Customers tend to repair rather than replace their old appliances, particularly in tough times. Megaretailers like Best Buy squeeze margins mercilessly. Customers exhibit little brand loyalty. The result is zero-sum competition, steadily declining real prices, and low growth. Not content with this sorry state of affairs, Dave Whitwam, Whirlpool's chairman, set out in 1999 to make innovation a core competence at the company. He knew the only way to counter the forces that threatened Whirlpool's growth and profitability was to generate a wide assortment of genuinely novel strategic options.

Over the subsequent three years, the company involved roughly 10,000 of its 65,000 employees in the search for breakthroughs. In training sessions and workshops, these employees generated some 7,000 ideas, which spawned 300 small-scale experiments. From this cornucopia came a stream of new products and businesses—from Gladiator Garage Works, a line of modular storage units designed to reduce garage clutter; to Briva, a sink that features a small, high-speed dishwasher; to Gator Pak, an all-in-one food and entertainment center designed for tailgate parties.

Having institutionalized its experimentation process, Whirlpool now actively manages a broad pipeline of ideas, experiments, and major projects from across the company. Senior executives pay close attention to a set of measures—an innovation dashboard—that tracks the number of ideas moving through the pipeline, the percentage of those ideas that are truly new, and the potential financial impact of each one. Whirlpool's leadership team is learning just how much variety it must engender at the front end of the pipeline, in terms of nascent ideas and first-stage experiments, to produce the earnings impact it's looking for at the back end.

Experiments should go beyond just products. While virtually every company has some type of new-product pipeline, few have a process for continually generating, launching, and tracking novel strategy experiments in the areas of pricing, distribution, advertising, and customer service. Instead, many companies have created innovation ghettos—incubators, venture funds, business development functions, and skunk works—to pursue ideas outside the core. Cut off from the resources, competencies, and customers of the main business, most of these units produce little in the way of shareholder wealth, and many simply wither away.

The isolation—and distrust—of strategic experimentation is a leftover from the industrial age, when variety was often seen as the enemy. A variance, whether from a quality standard, a production schedule, or a budget, was viewed as a bad thing—which it often was. But in many companies, the aversion to unplanned variability has metastasized into a general antipathy toward the nonconforming and the deviant. This infatuation with conformance severely hinders the quest for resilience.

Our experience suggests that a reasonably large company or business unit—having $5 billion to $10 billion in revenues, say—should generate at least 100 groundbreaking experiments every year, with each one absorbing between $10,000 and $20,000 in first-stage investment funds. Such variety need not come at the expense of focus. Starting in the mid-1990s, Nokia pursued a strategy defined by three clear goals—to "humanize" technology (via the user interface, product design, and aesthetics); to enable "virtual presence" (where the phone becomes an all-purpose messaging and data access device); and to deliver "seamless solutions" (by bundling infrastructure, software, and handsets in a total package for telecom operators). Each of these "strategy themes" spawned dozens of breakthrough projects. It is a broadly shared sense of direction, rather than a tightly circumscribed definition of served market or an allegiance to one particular business model, that reins in superfluous variety.

Of course, most billion-dollar opportunities don't start out as sure things—they start out as highly debatable propositions. For example, who would have predicted, in December 1995, when eBay was only three months old, that the on-line auctioneer would have a market value of $27 billion in the spring of 2003—two years after the dot-com crash? Sure, eBay is an exception. Success is always an exception. To find those exceptions, you must gather and sort through hundreds of new strategic options and then test the promising ones through low-cost, well-designed experiments—building prototypes, running computer simulations, interviewing progressive customers, and the like. There is simply no other way to reconnoiter the future. Most experiments *will* fail. The issue is not how many times you fail, but the value of your successes when compared with your failures. What counts is how the portfolio performs, rather than whether any particular experiment pans out.

LIBERATING RESOURCES

Facing up to denial and fostering new ideas are great first steps. But they'll get you nowhere if you can't free up the resources to support a broad array of strategy experiments within the core business. As every manager knows, reallocating resources is an intensely political process. Resilience requires, however, that it become less so.

Institutions falter when they invest too much in "what is" and too little in "what could be." There are many ways companies overinvest in the status quo: They devote too much marketing energy to existing customer segments while ignoring new ones; they pour too many development dollars into incremental product enhancements while underfunding breakthrough projects; they lavish resources on existing distribution channels while starving new go-to-market strategies. But whatever the manifestation, the root cause is always the same: Legacy strategies have powerful constituencies; embryonic strategies do not.

In most organizations, a manager's power correlates directly with the resources he or she controls—to lose resources is to lose stature and influence. Moreover, personal success often turns solely on the performance of one's own unit or program. It is hardly surprising, then, that unit executives and program managers typically resist any attempt to reallocate "their" capital and talent to new initiatives—no matter how attractive those new initiatives may be. Of course, it's unseemly to appear too parochial, so managers often hide their motives behind the facade of an ostensibly prudent business argument. New projects are deemed "untested," "risky," or a "diversion." If such ruses are successful, and they often are, those seeking resources for new strategic options are forced to meet a higher burden of proof than are those who want to allocate additional investment dollars to existing programs. Ironically, unit managers seldom have to defend the risk they are taking when they pour good money into a slowly decaying strategy or overfund an activity that is already producing diminishing returns.

The fact is, novelty implies nothing about risk. Risk is a function of uncertainty, multiplied by the size of one's financial exposure. Newness is a function of the extent to which an idea defies precedent and convention. The Starbucks debit card, which allows regular customers to purchase their daily fix of caffeine without fumbling through their pockets for cash, was undoubtedly an innovation for the quick-serve restaurant industry. Yet it's not at all clear that it was risky. The card offers customers a solid benefit, and it relies on proven technology. Indeed, it was an immediate hit. Within 60 days of its launch, convenience-minded customers had snapped up 2.3 million cards and provided Starbucks with a $32 million cash float.

A persistent failure to distinguish between new ideas and risky ideas reinforces companies' tendency to overinvest in the past. So too does the general reluctance of corporate executives to shift resources from one business unit to another. A detailed study of diversified companies by business professors Hyun-Han Shin and René Stulz found that the allocation of investment funds across business units was mostly uncorrelated with the relative attractiveness of investment opportunities within those units. Instead, a business unit's investment budget was largely a function of its own cash flow and, secondarily, the cash flow of the firm as a whole. It seems that top-level executives, removed as they are from day-to-day operations, find it difficult to form a well-grounded view of unit-level, or subunit-level, opportunities and are therefore wary of reallocating resources from one unit to another.

Now, we're not suggesting that a highly profitable and growing business should be looted to fund some dim-witted diversification scheme. Yet if a company systematically favors existing programs over new initiatives, if the forces of preservation regularly trounce the forces of experimentation, it will soon find itself overinvesting in moribund strategies and outdated programs. Allocational rigidities are the enemy of resilience.

Just as biology can teach us something about variety, markets can teach us something about what it takes to liberate resources from the prison of precedent. The evidence of the past century leaves little room for doubt: Market-based economies outperform those that are centrally planned. It's not that markets are infallible. Like human beings, they are vulnerable to mania and despair. But, on average, markets are better than hierarchies at getting the right resources behind the right opportunities at the right time. Unlike hierarchies, markets are apolitical and unsentimental; they don't care whose ox gets gored. The average company, though, operates more like a socialist state than an unfettered market. A hierarchy may be an effective mechanism for applying resources, but it is an imperfect device for allocating resources. Specifically, the market for capital and talent that exists within companies is a whole lot less efficient than the market for talent and capital that exists between companies.

In fact, a company can be operationally efficient and strategically inefficient. It can maximize the efficiency of its existing programs and processes and yet fail to find and fund the unconventional ideas and initiatives that might yield an even higher return. While companies have many ways of assessing operational efficiency, most firms are clueless when it comes to strategic efficiency. How can corporate leaders be sure that the current set of initiatives represents the highest value use of talent and capital if the company hasn't generated and examined a large population of alternatives? And how can executives be certain that the right resources are lined up behind the right opportunities if capital and talent aren't free to move to high-return projects or businesses? The simple answer is, they can't.

When there is a dearth of novel strategic options, or when allocational rigidities lock up talent and cash in existing programs and businesses, managers are allowed to "buy" resources at a discount, meaning that they don't have to compete for resources against a wide array of alternatives. Requiring that every project and business earn its cost of capital doesn't correct this anomaly. It is perfectly possible for a company to earn its cost of capital and still fail to put its capital and talent to the most valuable uses.

To be resilient, businesses must minimize their propensity to overfund legacy strategies. At one large company, top management took an important step in this direction by earmarking 10% of its $1 billion-a-year capital budget for projects that were truly innovative. To qualify, a project had to have the potential to substantially change customer expectations or industry economics. Moreover, the CEO announced his intention to increase this percentage over time. He reasoned that if divisional executives were not funding breakout projects, the company was never going to achieve breakout results. The risk of this approach was mitigated by a requirement that each division develop a broad portfolio of experiments, rather than bet on one big idea.

Freeing up cash is one thing. Getting it into the right hands is another. Consider, for a moment, the options facing a politically disenfranchised employee who hopes to win funding for a small-scale strategy experiment. One option is to push the idea up the chain of command to the point where it can be considered as part of the formal planning process. This requires four things: a boss who doesn't peremptorily reject the idea as eccentric or out of scope; an idea that is, at first blush, "big" enough to warrant senior management's attention; executives who are willing to divert funds from existing programs in favor of the unconventional idea; and an innovator who has the business acumen, charisma, and political cunning to make all this happen. That makes for long odds.

What the prospective innovator needs is a second option: access to many, many potential investors—analogous to the multitude of investors to which a company can appeal when it is seeking to raise funds. How might this be accomplished? In large organizations there are hundreds, perhaps thousands, of individuals who control a budget of some sort—from facilities managers to sales managers to customer service managers to office managers and beyond. Imagine if each of these individuals were a potential source of funding for internal innovators. Imagine that each could occasionally play the role of angel investor by providing seed funding for ideas aimed at transforming the core business in ways large and small. What if everyone who managed a budget were allowed to invest 1% or 3% or 5% of that budget in strategy experiments? Investors within a particular department or region could form syndicates to take on slightly bigger risks or diversify their investment portfolios. To the extent that a portfolio produced a positive return, in terms of new revenues or big cost savings, a small bonus would go back to those who had provided the funds and served as sponsors and mentors. Perhaps investors with the best track records would be given the chance to invest more of their budgets in breakout projects. Thus liberated, capital would flow to the most intriguing possibilities, unfettered by executives' protectionist tendencies.

When it comes to renewal, human skills are even more critical than cash. So if a market for capital is important, a market for talent is essential. Whatever their location, individuals throughout a company need to be aware of all the new projects that are looking for talent. Distance, across business unit boundaries or national borders, should not diminish this visibility. Employees need a simple way to nominate themselves for project teams. And if a project team is eager to hire a particular person, no barriers should stand in the way of a transfer. Indeed, the project team should have a substantial amount of freedom in negotiating the terms of any transfer. As long as the overall project risk is kept within bounds, it should be up to the team to decide how much to pay for talent.

Executives shouldn't be too worried about protecting employees from the downside of a failed project. Over time, the most highly sought-after employees will have the chance to work on multiple projects, spreading their personal risk. However, it is important to ensure that successful projects generate meaningful returns, both financial and professional, for those involved, and that dedication to the cause of experimentation is always positively recognized. But irrespective of the financial rewards, ambitious employees will soon discover that transformational projects typically offer transformational opportunities for personal growth.

EMBRACING PARADOX

The final barrier to resilience is ideological. The modern corporation is a shrine to a single, 100-year-old ideal—optimization. From "scientific management" to "operations research" to "reengineering" to "enterprise resource planning" to "Six Sigma," the goal has never changed: Do more, better, faster, and cheaper. Make no mistake, the ideology of optimization, and its elaboration into values, metrics, and processes, has created enormous material wealth. The ability to produce millions of gadgets, handle millions of transactions, or deliver a service to millions of customers is one of the most impressive achievements of humankind. But it is no longer enough.

The creed of optimization is perfectly summed up by McDonald's in its famous slogan, "Billions Served." The problem comes when some of those billions want to be served something else, something different, something new. As an ideal, optimization is sufficient only as long as there's no fundamental change in what has to be optimized. But if you work for a record company that needs to find a profitable on-line business model, or for an airline struggling to outmaneuver Southwest, or for a hospital trying to deliver quality care despite drastic budget cuts, or for a department store chain getting pummeled by discount retailers, or for an impoverished school district intent on curbing its dropout rate, or for any other organization where more of the same is no longer enough, then optimization is a wholly inadequate ideal.

An accelerating pace of change demands an accelerating pace of strategic evolution, which can be achieved only if a company cares as much about resilience as it does about optimization. This is currently not the case. Oh sure, companies have been working to improve their operational resilience—their ability to respond to the ups and downs of the business cycle or to quickly rebalance their product mix—but few have committed themselves to systematically tackling the challenge of strategic resilience. Quite the opposite, in fact. In recent years, most companies have been in retrenchment mode, working to resize their cost bases to accommodate a deflationary economy and unprecedented competitive pressure. But retrenchment can't revitalize a moribund business model, and great execution can't reverse the process of strategy decay.

It's not that optimization is wrong; it's that it so seldom has to defend itself against an equally muscular rival. Diligence, focus, and exactitude are reinforced every day, in a hundred ways—through training programs, benchmarking, improvement routines, and measurement systems. But

where is the reinforcement for strategic variety, wide-scale experimentation, and rapid resource redeployment? How have these ideals been instantiated in employee training, performance metrics, and management processes? Mostly, they haven't been. That's why the forces of optimization are so seldom interrupted in their slow march to irrelevance.

When you run to catch a cab, your heart rate accelerates—*automatically*. When you stand up in front of an audience to speak, your adrenal glands start pumping—*spontaneously*. When you catch sight of someone alluring, your pupils dilate—*reflexively*. Automatic, spontaneous, reflexive. These words describe the way your body's autonomic systems respond to changes in your circumstances. They do not describe the way large organizations respond to changes in their circumstances. Resilience will become something like an autonomic process only when companies dedicate as much energy to laying the groundwork for perpetual renewal as they have to building the foundations for operational efficiency.

In struggling to embrace the inherent paradox between the relentless pursuit of efficiency and the restless exploration of new strategic options, managers can learn something from constitutional democracies, particularly the United States. Over more than two centuries, America has proven itself to be far more resilient than the companies it has spawned. At the heart of the American experiment is a paradox—unity and diversity—a single nation peopled by all nations. To be sure, it's not easy to steer a course between divisive sectarianism and totalitarian conformity. But the fact that America has managed to do this, despite some sad lapses, should give courage to managers trying to square the demands of penny-pinching efficiency and break-the-rules innovation. Maybe, just maybe, all those accountants and engineers, never great fans of paradox, can learn to love the heretics and the dreamers.

THE ULTIMATE ADVANTAGE

Perhaps there are still some who believe that large organizations can never be truly resilient, that the goal of "zero trauma" is nothing more than a chimera. We believe they are wrong. Yes, size often shelters a company from the need to confront harsh truths. But why can't size also provide a shelter for new ideas? Size often confers an inappropriate sense of invincibility that leads to foolhardy risk-taking. But why can't size also confer a sense of possibility that encourages widespread experimentation? Size often implies inertia, but why can't it also imply persistence? The problem isn't size, but success. Companies get big because they do well. Size is a barrier to resilience only if those who inhabit large organizations fall prey to the delusion that success is self-perpetuating.

Battlefield commanders talk about "getting inside the enemy's decision cycle." If you can retrieve, interpret, and act upon battlefield intelligence faster than your adversary, they contend, you will be perpetually on the offensive, acting rather than reacting. In an analogous way, one can think about getting inside a competitor's "renewal cycle." Any company that can make sense of its environment, generate strategic options, and realign its resources faster than its rivals will enjoy a decisive advantage. This is the essence of resilience. And it will prove to be the ultimate competitive advantage in the age of turbulence—when companies are being challenged to change more profoundly, and more rapidly, than ever before.

Implementing Change

INTRODUCTION

Implementation is the "how" of the change process. It is the initial "How do we get the organization to change?" It is the "Here is how we will go about changing." It is the monitoring question "How are we doing?" And that involves "How are people responding to the change?" These four hows should continually interrelate.

How to get an organization to change entails choosing among a range of techniques, most of which are familiar and used for other purposes: speeches, seminars, off-sites, training, newsletters, and the like. What transforms these into change vehicles is the message they carry: With these devices, here is how we will go about changing. If you were given the "Motorola (C)" case, you will recall that Bob Galvin's call to action eventually resulted in a program called the "Organizational Effectiveness Process" (OEP). At first it was unclear what OEP was—perhaps another ingredient in the firm's "alphabet soup." In this example, as in many others, it was yet to be made clear that the program would actually be used as a model for change.

Crucial to such a message is its consistency, which runs from perception to reality. The former may arise, usually in the negative—inconsistency—when one group believes that it is doing all the changing, and business as usual occurs elsewhere. This may be an artifact of the implementation processes, whereby certain changes are made in one area before another. Real consistency is more difficult to achieve, and again this can be illustrated negatively. Cross-functional teams are increasingly being used as change vehicles, charged in many cases with designing and implementing processes with large ramifications for a company. Yet all too often functional (and other) constraints inhibit their work. The message and the ability to enact are inconsistent, and this inconsistency, if unchecked, will derail the change effort.

Discovering such problems means that the change process must be monitored; monitoring, of course, also means determining what is going *right*. Monitoring, however, is not the same as measuring concrete results. Change programs intended to improve productivity, increase quality, speed up product development, and so on, which is to say most of the efforts explored in this text, include numerical goals—a 20 percent increase in X by time Y. Such goals are essential. Change efforts are expensive, either in direct resource outlay or in the time and productivity loss associated with disrupted routines, particularly at the outset. Measuring progress in concrete terms helps justify this expense and encourages those enacting the change. But there is often a tendency, or at least a temptation, to confound achieving the numerical goal with making the deeper and inherently less measurable changes in thinking and behavior that most change efforts intend.

A manufacturing quality effort, for example, invariably includes statistical standards for producing (ultimately) defect-free products. Progress toward achieving these standards can be measured, and increments toward reaching them are to be celebrated along the way. But while this progress is being made, competitors may be redefining or expanding the *concept* of quality to include, for example, total customer satisfaction—one *component* of which is (ultimately) defect-free products. If a firm is not paying attention to how its employees are understanding quality per se, and if the focus has been only on achieving a numerical goal, it can end up in the unhappy position of winning a battle and losing the war.

Monitoring a change effort, while it includes tracking concrete goal achievement, entails asking broader questions and listening to the answers—How are we doing? How are people responding to the effort?—beyond the numbers. Depending on factors like the size of the organization, this can be an informal process or a formal one. To be effective, however, monitoring must be perceived as helping the effort, not as an implied threat—looking over employees' shoulders to see whether things are being done right. Most important, built into any monitoring process must be the willingness to revisit the first two hows: how to get the organization to change and how to convey the change message within those methods. As such, what is built into any overall implementation effort that hopes to succeed is the potential of changing the change program itself.

CASES AND READINGS

The module opens with a classic case, "Peter Browning and Continental White Cap (A)," one that introduces new elements into the implementation challenge, which can be summed up as "Where to begin?" In this situation, the decision to "push for real, measurable change in the division's [White Cap's] culture and performance" comes from the corporate level; at the same time, however, nothing is to be done to disrupt that culture's "tradition of employee loyalty," which is a direct result of the family-style culture itself. Leading the change effort is Browning, who not only comes from another part of the organization but has, in his previous assignment, instituted a "drastic and accelerated change program," which he referred to as "radical surgery." Finally, since the division has led its market for fifty years and is deemed a "jewel" by corporate, it—not surprisingly—does not perceive the need for real, measurable change in its culture and performance!

"Implementing Change" is the reading that accompanies the Peter Browning case. A synthesis of some of the most useful approaches and metrics to change implementation, this article contains, among other things, the now-famous "Ten Commandments" of implementing change, a useful set of fundamental criteria against which to evaluate the change efforts of the individuals and organizations spotlighted in this module and elsewhere. (But lest it not be clear, the authors firmly believe that implementing change is more art than science, and the term "Ten Commandments" is used more tongue-in-cheek than to suggest any universal truth.)

In the Browning case, we see a traditional old-line manufacturing concern coping with external threats and challenges, though still from a strong position in its traditional market—at least for the moment. The pressure intensifies as we move to "Marconi plc (A)," the case of Britain's one-time leading industrial and telecommunications firm, now faced with a major crisis and a "change or die" situation. New chief executive Mike Parton has to figure out how to get "both good management and great leadership" at a time when many in the firm "are in denial" about what is happening to their business. Parton holds a leadership conference to begin to address key issues and to create a unified, focused management team. How the conference unfolds, and whether it will generate enough momentum to save the firm, will be subjects for discussion.

"Organizational Frame Bending: Principles for Managing Reorientation" goes deeply into the distinct challenges of managing large-scale planned change and the difficulties inherent in sustaining the effort when the implementation process is expected to be long. In the authors' model, a reorientation is defined as a strategic change (one that addresses fundamental changes in the organization) that is anticipatory in nature. In a few cases, such as that of Oticon (see below), change leaders have the relative luxury of the time necessary to drive changes in their organization *before* being forced to do so by external forces and events. This luxury is not available to all leaders or organizations, however. In "Leading Culture Change at Seagram," we encounter Seagram's president and CEO, Edgar Bronfman Jr., at a time when Seagram's core markets are maturing and eroding. One response has been to transform Seagram into a portfolio of businesses in industries very different from the core business—most notably the entertainment industry, through the acquisition of MCA Inc. Seagram had also begun a major reengineering effort in 1994, the goals of which included the identification of future growth opportunities. As the reengineering progressed, however, it became increasingly clear that the culture and work processes that had guided Seagram for more than seventy years would have to undergo a distinct shift.

"Leading Culture Change at Seagram" raises tough questions about how to help the members of an organization "unlearn" an old culture while internalizing the values of the emergent culture. Accompanying this case is the provocatively titled article, "Why Change Programs Don't Produce Change." Arguing for bottom-up, grass-roots change and "task alignment," the authors assert that "the most effective way to change behavior . . . is to put people into a new organizational context." It is a fundamentally different model for implementing change—one that has less to do with changing minds and more to do with changing work.

To provide a hands-on grasp of implementation dilemmas, and to put some of these principles to the test, we now introduce an online simulation called "Merger Plan." Your team will take the role of the implementation manager of a newly announced merger between two banks. Your task is, first, to decide the parameters of the merger implementation (branch consolidations, HR and IT systems linkages, layoffs, rollout schedule, and the like), and, second, to influence a set of key stakeholders to support the merger and the implementation plan. A variety of choices and communication options is available, and as important as the choice of a tactic is the sequencing of them all. Stakeholder analysis and communication are central. Although the activity may be structured as a competition (the team earning the highest return, adjusted for stakeholder support, wins), the dynamics within each team are powerful, and can hint at what struggles must be overcome to get people to change. Even the most cohesive team will find navigating the complexity of the underlying relationships in the simulation a challenge.

In "Oticon: Building a Flexible World-Class Organization (A)," Lars Kolind is brought into the struggling Denmark-based hearing aid manufacturer after it loses its position as market leader and falls to third place. Kolind acts quickly and dramatically, and Oticon returns to profitability in just six months. A year later, on January 1, 1990, Kolind challenges his employees to "think the unthinkable" and describes his vision of an organization with no paper and no walls. A key element of his approach is to change everything at once, including moving to a new, open-plan building and abolishing all departments and titles. These bold strokes attract a lot of attention, and appear to result in dramatic increases in performance, after an initial drop. Still, Kolind, like the rest of us, will eventually have to face an important question: Is there such a thing as *too much* change?

In "Changing the Deal While Keeping the People," Denise Rousseau addresses the issue of implementing change from the point of view of the psychological contract—the unwritten expectations between employer and employee about everything from job security to the evolution of work roles and the openness of communication channels. When business changes, particularly in uncertain markets, the psychological contract often has to change, and a firm's ability to achieve such a change has everything to do with the nature of the relationship already existing between the company and its people. The article describes two approaches to change—accommodation and transformation—and shows how trust and commitment may be extended, sustained, or lost in the process.

The final case in the module, Ayudha Allianz CP, describes the transformation of the German insurance company Allianz' life insurance business in Thailand. CEO Wilf Blackburn has to learn an entirely new culture and work system, steeped in hierarchy and entrenched relationships. Over three years, beginning with "radical surgery," continuing through slow and painstaking rebuilding of relationships and trust, and moving eventually on to big celebrations, Blackburn leads the near-failing business to a position of leadership. Still, the personal cost to many of the firm's agents and former agents is high. This latter point underscores the importance of understanding the people who *receive* change. They are the focus of Module 4.

Change Classic

Peter Browning and Continental White Cap (A)

On April 1, 1984, Peter Browning assumed the position of vice president and operating officer of Continental White Cap, a Chicago-based division of the Continental Group, Inc. Having completed a successful five-year turnaround of Continental's troubled Bondware Division, Browning found this new assignment at White Cap to be a very different type of challenge. He was taking over the most successful of Continental's nine divisions—"the jewel in the Continental crown," as one Continental executive described it. White Cap was the market leader in the production and distribution of vacuum-sealed metal closures for glass jars.

Browning's charge, though, was to revitalize and reposition the division to remain preeminent in the face of threatened, but not yet fully realized, changes in the competitive environment. Sales were stable and costs were up. Recent years had brought changes in the market: One competitor in particular was utilizing price cuts for the first time to build market share, and the introduction of plastic packaging to many of White Cap's traditional customers threatened sales. White Cap had not yet developed a plastic closure or the ability to seal plastic containers. After more

Source: Harvard Business School Case No. 9-486-090, Copyright 1986 President and Fellows of Harvard College. All rights reserved. This case was prepared by Professor Todd D. Jick. HBS Cases are developed solely for class discussion and do not necessarily illustrate effective or ineffective management.

than 50 years of traditional management and close control by White Cap's founding family, corporate headquarters decided it was time to bring in a proven, enthusiastic young manager to push the business toward a leaner, more efficient, and more flexible operation—one capable of responding to the evolving market conditions.

From the very start, Browning recognized two major obstacles that he would have to address. First, few managers or employees at White Cap acknowledged the need for change. Business results for more than 50 years had been quite impressive and, when dips were experienced, they were perceived as cyclical and transient. Second, White Cap had a family-style culture characterized by long-term loyalty from its employees, longstanding traditions of job security, liberal benefits, and paternalistic management. Attempts to alter these traditions would not be welcome.

Reflecting on his new assignment at White Cap, Browning recalled that at Bondware he had walked into a failing business where he "had nothing to lose." Now he was entering "a successful business with absolutely everything to lose." One White Cap manager observed: "White Cap will be the testing period for Peter Browning in the eyes of Continental." Browning's success in reframing the business would be critical for his future in corporate leadership there. Browning thought about the stern words of caution he had received from his boss, Dick Hofmann, executive vice president of the Continental Group: "White Cap needs changes, but just don't break it while you're trying to fix it. Continental can't afford to lose White Cap."

WHITE CAP BACKGROUND

In 1926, William P. White ("old W.P.") and his two brothers started the White Cap Company in an old box factory on Goose Island, located in the Chicago River. From the beginning, the White Cap Company was active in many areas: in closure production and distribution, in new product development, and in the design of cap-making and capping machinery. Thus, White Cap promoted itself as not only a source of quality closures but also providers of a "Total System" of engineering and R&D support and service to the food industry. It claimed the latest in closure technology—for example, in 1954, White Cap pioneered the twist-off style of closure, and, in the late 1960s, it developed the popular "P.T." (press-on/twist-off) style of cap. It also took pride in its capping equipment and field operations service. White Cap's customers were producers of ketchup, juices, baby foods, preserves, pickles, and other perishable foods.

In 1956, the Continental Can Company bought White Cap, and, in 1984, the Continental Group, Inc., went from public to private as it was merged into KMI Continental, Inc., a subsidiary of Peter Kiewit Sons, a private construction company. The White Cap Company became Continental White Cap, the most profitable of the parent firm's nine divisions—each of which produced different types of containers and packaging.

Despite the sale of White Cap in 1956, the White family continued to manage the organization, and its traditional company culture persisted. As the manager of human resources at the Chicago plants expressed it: "I really think that many employees felt that White Cap bought Continental Can, instead of the other way around." W. P. White, the company founder, and later his son, Bob, inspired and encouraged a strong sense of family among their employees, many of whom lived in the Polish community immediately surrounding the main plant. Once hired, employees tended to remain and to bring in their friends and relatives as well. At the two Chicago plants in 1985, 51.2 percent of the employees were over 40 years old and 30 percent were over 50.

The Whites themselves acted as patrons, or father figures. Legends recounted their willingness to lend money to an hourly worker with unexpected medical bills, or their insistence, in a bad financial year, on borrowing the money for Christmas bonuses. In exchange for hard work and commitment, employees received good salaries, job security, and the feeling that they were part of a "winner." In an area as heavily unionized as Chicago, these rewards were potent enough to keep White Cap nearly union-free. Only the lithographers—a small and relatively autonomous group—were unionized.

White Cap was rife with rituals, ceremonies, and traditions. In the early days of the company, Mrs. W. P. White would prepare and serve lunch every day for the company employees in the Goose Island facility. Over the years, White Cap continued to provide a free family-style hot lunch for all salaried employees and free soup, beverage, and ice cream for the hourly workers.

A press department manager, a White Capper for 28 years, explained:

> For work in a manufacturing setting,
> you couldn't do better than White Cap.

White Cap isn't the real world; when the economy is hurting, White Cap isn't. White Cap always lived up to the ideal that "our people are important to us." They sponsored a huge family picnic every year for all White Cappers and friends. When they first instituted the second shift in the factory, they lined up cabs to take late workers home after their shift. They sponsored golf outings and an "old-timers' softball team." People generally felt that nothing's going to happen to us as long as we've got a White there.

But in 1982, Bob White stepped down and turned the management over to Art Lawson, who became vice president and executive officer. Lawson, 63 years old, was an old-time White Capper, and many saw him as simply a proxy for the Whites. Even Lawson would say that he saw himself as a caretaker manager, maintaining things as they had always been.

At about this time, price competition began to heat up in the closure industry. White Cap had been the market leader for over 50 years, but customers were beginning to take the Total System for granted. There were by then five significant manufacturers in the national marketplace and 70 worldwide who offered the twist-off cap. Competitors like National Can Company were beginning to slash prices, aware that the very advantage White Cap had maintained in the market (i.e., its R&D and full service) made it difficult for it to compete effectively with drastic price cutting.

Just at this time, plastic containers—requiring plastic closures—began to be available (see Exhibit 1). In 1982, the Food and Drug Administration (FDA) had approved the use of a particular plastic substance as an appropriate oxygen barrier for food containers. Subsequently, the American Can Company's Gamma™ bottle, a squeezable plastic container, was adopted by the Heinz Company for its ketchup and by Hunt for its barbecue sauce. (White Cap had held 100 percent of the ketchup business worldwide.) Welch's jams and jellies also adopted this new technology, and the reasons were typical:

> Welch's expects the new packaging to help revitalize a relatively flat product category, having conducted research indicating that their customers are willing to pay more for the convenience of the squeezable plastic bottle.[1]

Another major White Cap account had announced plans to introduce a new juice line in plastic containers for the spring of 1986, as well. Without a competitive plastic closure, White Cap would continue to lose customers. Senior White Cap management, however, had been reluctant to allow R&D to commercialize plastics developments because such plastics threats in the past had never materialized.

In 1984, two years after Bob White had left, Peter Browning was named vice president and operating officer, reporting to Art Lawson. He took over a division with $175 million in gross sales, 1,450 employees (of whom 480 were salaried), 12 sales offices, and 4 plants (2 in Chicago, Illinois; 1 in Hayward, California; and 1 in Hazleton, Pennsylvania).

PETER BROWNING'S BACKGROUND

I'm Peter Browning and I'm 43 years of age. I have four children—three girls, 20, 16, and 12, and a 7-year-old son.

---

[1] Melissa Larson, "Dispensing Closures Revitalize Flat Markets," *Packaging*, August 1985, p. 25.

EXHIBIT 1   **Changes in the Container Industry**

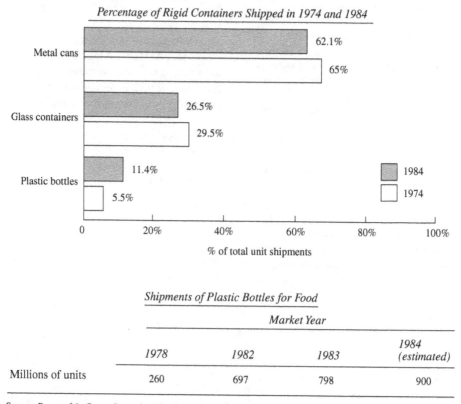

Percentage of Rigid Containers Shipped in 1974 and 1984

% of total unit shipments

Shipments of Plastic Bottles for Food

	Market Year			
	1978	*1982*	*1983*	*1984 (estimated)*
Millions of units	260	697	798	900

Sources: Bureau of the Census, International Trade Association, Can Manufacturers' Institute, and *U.S. Industrial Outlook* 1985.

My undergraduate degree is in history, and, while at White Cap, I earned my MBA through the Executive Program at the University of Chicago. I have been with Continental for 20 years.

This was Peter Browning's characteristic opening each time he presented himself and his ideas to a new audience. On first impression, Browning appeared youthful, charming, and intellectually and socially curious. Various employees and managers described him alternately as "Mr. Energy," "ambitious," "direct," "the most powerful boss I've had," and "the quintessential old-time politician, shaking hands and kissing babies." His speeches to management and staff were peppered with inspirational aphorisms and historical, often military, metaphors, repeated as refrains and rallying cries.

In spring 1985, the Continental Group arranged for each of the nine divisional managers to be interviewed by industrial psychologists. The psychologist's report on Browning stated:

His intellectual ability is in the very superior range.... He is a hard-driving individual for whom success in an organization is extremely important.... Further, he is completely open in communicating the strategy he has conceived, the goals he has chosen, and the ongoing success of the organization against those goals. He cares about people, is sensitive to them, and makes every effort to motivate them.... His own values and beliefs are so strong and well-defined that his primary means of motivation is the instilling of enthusiasm and energy in others to think and believe as he does. By and large he is successful at this, but there are those who have to be motivated from their own values and beliefs, which may be different but which may nonetheless lead to productive action. These people are apt to be confused, overwhelmed, and left behind by his style.[2]

Browning's career began with White Cap and Continental Can in 1964 when he took a position as sales representative in Detroit. He continued in marketing with White Cap for nine years and then in other Continental divisions until 1979. At that time, he returned to Chicago to become vice president and general manager of Continental's Bondware Division. Once in the area again, Browning was able to touch base with old contacts from White Cap and to observe firsthand the challenges they faced.

At Bondware (producers of waxed paper cups for hot and cold beverages and food), Browning took over a business that had lost $24 million in five years (1975–1979) and that Continental could not even sell. Browning adopted a drastic and accelerated change program, employing what he called "radical surgery" to reduce employees by half (from 1,200 to 600), to eliminate an entire product line, to close four out of six manufacturing sites, and to turn the business around in five years.

[2] Alexander B. Platt, Platt & Associates, Inc., May 2, 1985.

BROWNING IS REASSIGNED

Early in 1984, Browning received his reassignment orders from the executive officers of the Continental Group (Stamford, Connecticut). They wanted definite changes in the way the White Cap Division did business, and they believed Browning—fresh from his success with Bondware and a veteran of White Cap himself—was surely the person to make those changes.

Continental's executive officers had several major concerns about White Cap. First of all, they saw a competitive onslaught brewing that they believed White Cap's managers did not recognize. They believed the business instincts of White Cap's management had been dulled by a tradition of uncontested market leadership. The majority of White Cap's managers had been with the firm for over 25 years, and most of them had little intention of moving beyond White Cap, or even beyond their current positions. They were accustomed to Bob White's multilayered, formal, and restrained management style—a style that inhibited cross-communication and that one manager dubbed "management without confrontation." Some of them were startled, even offended, by the price-slashing tactics practiced by White Cap's most recent competitors, and they spoke wistfully of an earlier, more "gentlemanly" market style.

Continental's executive officers were also concerned that White Cap's long-time success, coupled with the benevolent paternalism of the White family management, had led to a padded administrative staff. They instructed Browning to communicate a sense of impending crisis and urgency to the White Cap staff, even as he reduced the salary and administrative costs which

Continental perceived as inflated. Furthermore, he was to do all this without threatening White Cap's image in the marketplace or its tradition of employee loyalty.

Browning recognized that corporate attitudes toward White Cap were colored by a history of less than open and cooperative relations with Bob White:

> Bob White engendered and preserved the image of White Cap as an enigma, a mystery. He had an obsession with keeping Continental at arm's length, and he used the leverage of his stock and his years of experience to preserve his independence from corporate headquarters. After all, Bob never wanted to leave White Cap or go further.

This kind of mystery, coupled with White Cap's continued success, engendered doubts, envy, and misconceptions at the corporate level.

A former Continental Group manager elaborated:

> White Cap has always been seen as a prima donna by the Continental Group. I'm not convinced that there aren't some in Connecticut who might want to see White Cap stumble. They have always looked at the salary and administrative costs at 13 percent of net sales, compared with a 3–4 percent ratio in other divisions, and concluded that White Cap was fat.

Perhaps the demand for cost cuts was fueled by the fact that the Continental Group was going through its own period of "radical surgery" at this time. Since 1984, when Peter Kiewit Sons acquired the company, corporate headquarters had "sold off $1.6 billion worth of insurance, paper products businesses, gas pipelines, and oil and gas reserves" and had cut corporate staff

from 500 to 40.[3] The corporate climate was calling for swift, effective action.

TAKING CHARGE

In the first month of his new position, Browning turned his attention to three issues. To begin, he felt he had to make some gesture or take some stand with regard to Bob White. White was very much alive in the hearts and minds of White Cap's employees, and, although retired, he still lived in the Chicago area. Although White represented many of the values and the style that Browning hoped to change, he was also a key to the White Cap pride and morale that Browning had to preserve.

In addition, Bob White's successor, Art Lawson, was another link to White Cap's past, and his strong presence in the marketplace represented continuity in White Cap's customer relations. Since corporate headquarters was determined to maintain an untroubled public image throughout White Cap's transition, they brought Browning in reporting to Lawson—the division's vice president and executive officer and a person Browning had known for over 20 years (see Exhibit 2). Browning knew he had to give some strong messages about new directions if he was to shake up the comfortable division, but he had to do this from below Lawson and in spite of White's heritage.

A second challenge facing Browning was White Cap's marketing department. At a time when major, long-term customers in mature markets were faced with the attraction of an emerging plastic-packaging technology and were beginning to take the White Cap Total System for granted, Browning found a marketing and sales organization that, according to him, "simply administered

---

[3] Allan Dodds Frank, "More Takeover Carnage?" *Forbes*, August 12, 1985, p. 40.

EXHIBIT 2   **Organization Chart, April 1984**

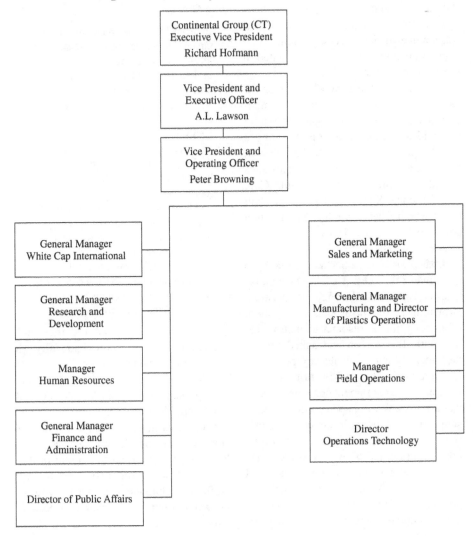

existing programs." It was not spending constructive time with the customers who had built the business, nor was it aggressively addressing new competitive issues.

Jim Stark had been the director of marketing for the previous five years. He had a fine track record with White Cap customers and, as an individual, maintained many strong relationships in the field. Customers knew him well and relied on him. He had been with the company for 30 years and had been a regional sales manager before his transfer to marketing.

In this prior position, Stark's strength had clearly been his ability to deal with the customers, as opposed to his people-managing skills. Despite his strong outside presentation and selling ability, his internal relationships with his marketing staff and with the field sales force had apparently soured over the years. Team spirit was not in evidence. Stark complained that he didn't receive the support he needed to make changes in marketing.

Stark's boss, the general manager for sales and marketing and a highly competent sales professional, urged Browning to avoid any sudden personnel changes and "to give Stark a chance." Moreover, relieving a manager of his responsibilities would be unprecedented at White Cap. Yet, for some, Stark was like "a baseball coach who has been with the team through some slow seasons and was no longer able to turn around his image."

Browning also inherited a manager of human resources, Tom Green, whose role and capabilities he began to question. Browning had always been a proponent of a strong human resources function. He met with Tom Green and asked him to help identify and evaluate key personnel throughout the division in terms of promotion and reassignment decisions. Green was a veteran White Capper, with 20 years' seniority and 5 years in his current position. Older managers were very comfortable with him and he was well liked. He offered few surprises to employees and helped maintain all the traditional and popular benefit policies and practices that they had come to expect from White Cap.

Browning soon recognized a problem with Green:

> In reviewing the personnel files with Green, I found he had few constructive ideas to offer. He seemed to do a lot of delegating and to spend a lot of time reading the *Wall Street Journal.* And a lot of managers seemed to work around him. I found myself getting involved in decisions that he should have been taking care of, such as deciding whether a departing secretary in another department needed to be replaced or not.
>
> One possibility was to replace Green with the human resources manager from Bondware who had helped me with the changes I had made there. But Green was also a valuable information source and someone who could be a nonthreatening conduit to and from White Cap employees.

Peter Browning pondered these initial choices and decisions carefully. He wanted to rejuvenate White Cap and yet not demoralize its loyal work force and management. Browning knew that Dick Hofmann, his boss, expected him to push for real, measurable change in the division's culture and performance. What was less clear was how far he should push—and how fast—in order to succeed. Even Hofmann acknowledged that Browning's assignment put him "smack dab between a rock and a hard place."

Reading
Implementing Change

When people think about change, they often picture designing a bold new change strategy—complete with stirring vision—that will lead an organization into a brave new future. And, in fact, this crafting of a visionary strategy is a pivotal part of the process of change. But even more challenging—and harder to get a grasp on—is what follows the strategy and the vision: the implementation process itself. When it comes to the daily, nitty-gritty, tactical, and operational decision making of change, the implementor is the one who makes or breaks the program's success.

Of course, the implementor doesn't act alone. Change succeeds when an entire organization participates in the effort. An organization can be divided into three broad action roles: *change strategists, change implementors,* and *change recipients;* and each of these roles plays a different key part in the change process. Change strategists, simply put, are responsible for the early work: identifying the need for change, creating a vision of the desired outcome, deciding what change is feasible, and choosing who should sponsor and defend it. And change recipients represent the largest group of people who must adopt, and adapt to, the change. These are the institutionalizers, and their behavior determines whether a change will stick.

Source: Harvard Business School Case No. 4-491-114, Copyright 1991 President and Fellows of Harvard College. All rights reserved. This case was prepared by Professor Todd D. Jick. HBS Cases are developed solely for class discussion and do not necessarily illustrate effective or ineffective management.

But change implementors are the ones who "make it happen," managing the day-to-day process of change. The implementors' task is to help shape, enable, orchestrate, and facilitate successful progress. Depending on the extent of the "vision" they are given, they can develop the implementation plan, or shepherd through programs handed down to them. Simultaneously, they must respond to demands from above while attempting to win the cooperation of those below.

What is the experience of implementing change really like? Here is how the chief executive officer of a major U.S. airline describes managing multiple changes during the tempestuous period of the late 1980s:

> It beat any Indiana Jones movie! It started out with a real nice beginning. Then suddenly we got one disaster after another. The boulder just missed us, and we got the snake in the cockpit of the airplane—that's what it's all about! You've got to be down in the mud and the blood and the beer.

This vivid description captures a sense of the drama involved in wrestling with complex, real-time issues day after day in a changing environment. Because today's companies are composed of and affected by so many different individuals and constituencies—each with their own hopes, dreams, and fears—and because these companies operate in a global environment—with all the regulations, competition, and complexity that implies—implementing change may, indeed, require the dexterity, alertness, and agility of an Indiana Jones.

It sounds exciting, but is it doable? As this brief description implies, implementors face a daunting task. They often feel that they have insufficient authority to make change happen entirely on their own, and that they fail to receive the support from above to move forward. At the same time, the more the "recipients" balk at the decisions implementors make, the more frustrating the task becomes. This middle role in the change process is a challenging one, indeed.

COMMON PITFALLS OF IMPLEMENTATION

Real-life stories of corporate change rarely measure up to the tidy experiences related in books. The echo of well-intentioned and enthusiastic advice fades as the hard work of change begins. No matter how much effort companies invest in preparation and workshops—not to mention pep rallies, banners, and pins—organizations are invariably insufficiently prepared for the difficulties of implementing change. The responsibility for this situation lies in several areas.

Both the popular press and academic literature tend to consider organizational change as a step-by-step process leading to success. Although recent writings have grown more sophisticated, many treatises on organizational change fail to concede that difficulties lie along the way.

This unrealistic portrayal of the change process can be dangerous. Already organizations are inclined to push faster, spend less, and stop earlier than the process requires. Such inclinations are further strengthened by an illusion of control. By making change seem like a bounded, defined, and discrete process with guidelines for success, many authors mislead managers, who find that the reality is far more daunting than they expected. They

feel deceived; instead of a controllable process, they discover chaos.

This kind of frustration is part of the terrain of change. In fact, while the literature often portrays an organization's quest for change as being like a brisk march along a well-marked path, those in the middle of change are more likely to describe their journey as a laborious crawl toward an elusive, flickering goal, with many wrong turns and missed opportunities along the way. Only rarely does a company know exactly where it's going or how it should get there.

Those who make change must also grapple with unexpected forces both inside and outside the organization. No matter how carefully these implementors prepare for change, and no matter how realistic and committed they are, there will always be factors outside their control that may have a profound impact on the success of the change process. These external, uncontrollable, and powerful forces are not to be underestimated, and they are one reason some have questioned the manageability of change at all. Shifts in government regulations, union activism, competitive assaults, product delays, mergers and acquisitions, and political and international crises are all a reality of corporate life today, and managers cannot expect to implement their plans free of such interruptions.

Studies examining the most common pitfalls of implementation document just these kinds of frustration. In one study of strategic business units in 93 medium- and large-sized firms, respondents were asked to reflect on the implementation of a recent strategic decision.[1] The survey results showed seven implementation problems that occurred in at least 60 percent of the responding firms, as follows:

[1] Larry Alexander, "Successfully Implementing Strategic Decisions," *Long Range Planning* 18 (3): 1985, pp. 91–97.

1. Implementation took more time than originally allocated (76 percent).

2. Major problems surfaced during implementation that had not been identified beforehand (74 percent).

3. Coordination of implementation activities (e.g., by task forces, committees, superiors) was not effective enough (66 percent).

4. Competing activities and crises distracted attention from implementing this strategic decision (64 percent).

5. Capabilities (skills and abilities) of employees involved with the implementation were not sufficient (63 percent).

6. Training and instruction given to lower-level employees were not adequate (62 percent).

7. Uncontrollable factors in the external environment (e.g., competitive, economic, governmental) had an adverse impact on implementation (60 percent).

While these seven points are undoubtedly among the most pervasive problems, the list goes on and on. Other frequent implementation shortcomings include failing to win adequate support for change; failing to define expectations and goals clearly; neglecting to involve all those who will be affected by change; and dismissing complaints outright, instead of taking the time to judge their possible validity.

TACTICAL IMPLEMENTATION STEPS

In order to avoid such pitfalls, students and managers frequently call for a checklist for implementing change—a list of do's and don'ts that will guide them on their way.

Unfortunately, managing change does not adhere to a simple, step-by-step process. There is no ironclad list or easy recipe for implementation success. In fact, the more we have studied change, and the more we brush up against its effects, the more humble we have become about dictating the "best" way to do it. Behavioral scientists, themselves, disagree on a number of fundamental implementation issues. One book attempting to pull together the best in practice recognized discord among its contributors on such basic questions as whether there is a logical sequence to the change process; whether change "agents" can lead an organization through a process that cannot be explained ahead of time; even whether change can be planned at all.[2]

But even though there are no easy answers, students and managers can still learn from the experiences of others. Over the last two decades, the growing body of work examining the change process has produced a number of implementation checklists. Although the following list is my own, it embraces many of the major prescriptions contained in the planned change literature—a kind of "Ten Commandments" for implementing successful organizational change (see Figure 1).

As already mentioned, no guidelines provide a recipe for success, and this list is no different. Instead, managers and students should view these commandments as an inventory of ingredients at their disposal. Through a conscientious process of testing, adjusting, and testing again, implementors may find the right combination of ingredients in the right proportion to fit the change needs of their particular organizations.

[2] Allan Mohrman, S. Mohrman, G. Ledford, T. Cummings, and E. Lawler, eds., *Large-Scale Organizational Change* (San Francisco: Jossey-Bass, 1989).

FIGURE 1   The Ten Commandments of Implementing Change

THE TEN COMMANDMENTS

1. Analyze the organization and its need for change.
2. Create a shared vision and common direction.
3. Separate from the past.
4. Create a sense of urgency.
5. Support a strong leader role.
6. Line up political sponsorship.
7. Craft an implementation plan.
8. Develop enabling structures.
9. Communicate, involve people, and be honest.
10. Reinforce and institutionalize change.

TEN COMMANDMENTS FOR IMPLEMENTING CHANGE

1. ANALYZE THE ORGANIZATION AND ITS NEED FOR CHANGE

Change strategists and implementors should understand an organization's operations, how it functions in its environment, what its strengths and weaknesses are, and how it will be affected by proposed changes to craft an effective implementation plan. If this initial analysis is not sound, no amount of implementation knowhow will help the organization achieve its goals.

As part of this process, changemakers also should study the company's history of change. While failures in the past do not doom later change efforts, one observer suggests that companies with historic barriers to change are likely to continue this pattern of resistance.[3] If a

company already has a track record of opposing change, more care should be taken to design a gradual nonthreatening and, preferably, participative implementation process, including the following tactics:

- Explain change plans fully.

- Skillfully present plans.

- Make information readily available.

- Make sure plans include benefits for end users and for the corporation.

- Spend extra time talking.

- Ask for additional feedback from the work force.

- Start small and simple.

- Arrange for a quick, positive, visible payoff.

- Publicize successes.

At this early stage of the change process, implementors may also want to systematically examine the forces for and against change (see Figure 2). Change will not occur unless the forces driving it are stronger than those resisting it. By lifting these forces, managers have a way to determine their organizations' readiness

---

[3] Murray M. Dalziel and Stephen C. Schoonover, *Changing Ways: A Practical Tool for Implementing Change within Organizations* (New York: American Management Association, 1988).

FIGURE 2   Force Field Analysis

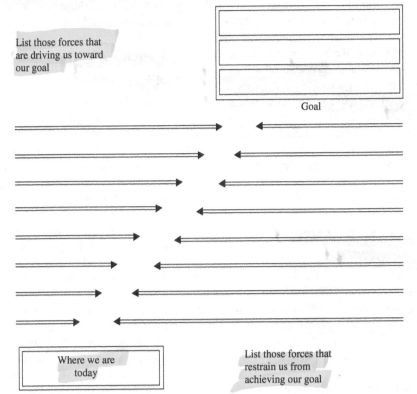

List those forces that
are driving us toward
our goal

Goal

Where we are
today

List those forces that
restrain us from
achieving our goal

for change. If the forces against change appear dominant, implementors should consider what additional forces they can muster—for example, in the form of committed followers, or of better proof of the need for change—before launching a change plan.

2. CREATE A SHARED VISION AND COMMON DIRECTION

One of the first steps in engineering change is to unite an organization behind a central vision. This vision should reflect the philosophy and values of the organization, and should help it to articulate what it hopes to become. A successful vision serves to guide behavior, and to aid an organization in achieving its goals.

While the crafting of the vision is a classic strategists' task, the way that this vision is presented to an organization also can have a strong impact on its implementation. Employees at all levels of the organization will want to know the business rationale behind the vision, the expected organizational benefits, and the personal ramifications—whether positive or negative. In particular, implementors should "translate" the vision so that all employees will understand its implications for their own jobs.

3. SEPARATE FROM THE PAST

Disengaging from the past is critical to awakening to a new reality. It is difficult for an organization to embrace a new vision of the future until it has isolated the structures and routines that no longer work, and vowed to move beyond them.

However, while it is unquestionably important to make a break from the past in order to change, it is also important to hang onto and reinforce those aspects of the organization that bring value to the new vision. That is, some sort of stability—heritage, tradition, or anchor—is needed to provide continuity amid change. As the changes at many companies multiply, arguably this past-within-the-future becomes even more essential.

4. CREATE A SENSE OF URGENCY

Convincing an organization that change is necessary isn't that difficult when a company is teetering on the brink of bankruptcy, or foundering in the marketplace. But when the need for action is not generally understood, a change leader should generate a sense of urgency without appearing to be fabricating an emergency, or crying wolf. This sense of urgency is essential to rallying an organization behind change.

From an implementation standpoint, this commandment requires a deft touch. While strategists may see very real threats that require deep and rapid action, implementors—usually middle managers—may see something else, in two senses. This group may believe that the need isn't as drastic as strategists think, and that, instead of deep change, perhaps more modest alterations will work. Alternatively, implementors may see, from their perspective, that the situation is even worse than the strategists have described. In either case, implementors may be forced to adopt a pace of change that is either faster or slower than they believe necessary. The

best protection against this is direct and frequent communication between implementors and strategists.

5. SUPPORT A STRONG LEADER ROLE

An organization should not undertake something as challenging as large-scale change without a leader to guide, drive, and inspire it. This change advocate plays a critical role in creating a company vision, motivating company employees to embrace that vision, and crafting an organizational structure that consistently rewards those who strive toward the realization of the vision. It should be noted, however, that this leadership role may not be held by one person alone. As the environments in which companies are changing become increasingly complex, and as the implementation of change becomes more demanding, many organizations are now turning to change leader teams. Such teams can have the advantage of combining multiple skills—for example, pairing a charismatic visionary with someone skilled at designing a strong and effective implementation plan.

6. LINE UP POLITICAL SPONSORSHIP

Leadership, alone, cannot bring about large-scale change. To succeed, a change effort must have broad-based support throughout an organization. This support should include not only the managers or change implementors but also the recipients, whose acceptance of any change is necessary for its success.

One way for strategists and implementors to begin winning support for change is to actively seek the backing of the informal leaders of the organization—beginning with those who are most receptive. In addition, they should demonstrate strong personal support for the change effort, and make it clear that the program is a high priority by allocating ample resources to do the job.

In winning sponsorship, it is not necessary to get unanimous support: participation can be representative, not universal. Of more importance is determining precisely whose sponsorship is critical to the change program's success. To help do this, one behavioral scientist suggests that implementors develop a "commitment plan" encompassing the following elements[4]:

- Identify target individuals or groups whose commitment is needed.

- Define the critical mass needed to ensure the effectiveness of the change.

- Develop a plan for getting the commitment of the critical mass.

- Create a monitoring system to assess the progress.

As part of this overall strategy, implementors may want to plot a commitment chart to help secure the minimum level of support necessary for a change program to proceed (see Figure 3).

7. CRAFT AN IMPLEMENTATION PLAN

While a vision may guide and inspire during the change process, an organization also needs more nuts-and-bolts advice on what to do and when and how to do it. This change plan maps out the effort, specifying everything from where the first meetings should be held to the date by which the company hopes to achieve its change goals.

In most cases, the implementation plan is best kept simple: An overly ambitious or too detailed plan can be more demoralizing than it is helpful. This is also the time to consider how many changes an organization can tackle at once. Because the risk of employee burnout is so real during major transformations, the change should be broken into staggered steps in order not to overburden workers with multiple demands.

At the same time, the plan should include specific goals and should detail clear responsibilities for each of the various roles—strategists, implementors, and recipients. Input from all levels of the organization will help to achieve this "role-oriented" focus. A plan devised solely by strategists is far less likely to reflect the realities of what the organization can accomplish than one that involves all three action roles from the start.

Like most other aspects of the change process, the implementation plan should be kept flexible, a kind of "living" document that is open to revision. Too much and too rigid planning can lead to paralysis, indecision, and collapse. Organizations that are locked in a rigid change "schedule" of planned goals and events may find themselves following a path that no longer meets their evolving needs, much less those of the world around them.

8. DEVELOP ENABLING STRUCTURES

Altering the status quo and creating new mechanisms for implementing change can be a critical precursor to any organizational transformation. These mechanisms may be part of the existing corporate structure or may be established as a free

[4] Richard Beckhard and Reuben T. Harris, *Organizational Transitions*, 2nd ed. (Reading, MA: Addison-Wesley, 1987).

FIGURE 3   Commitment Charting

To make a commitment chart, list the "Key Players," all the members or groups who are part of the critical mass—those whose commitment is absolutely essential—in the left-hand column on the vertical axis of the chart. Across the top, list the degrees of commitment: "No Commitment," "Let It Happen," "Help It Happen," and "Make It Happen," and draw vertical lines to make columns.

For each member or group in the left-hand column, place an "O" in the box that indicates the minimum commitment you must have for the change to occur. Do not try to get as much as you can; settle for the least you need.

Then study each of the people and groups as they are *now* and, using your best judgment, put an "X" in the box that represents their *present* degree of commitment.

Where the "O" and "X" are in the same box, circle them and breathe a sigh of relief; there is no work to do to get the necessary commitment.

Where the "O" and "X" are *not* in the same box, draw an arrow connecting them. This gives you a map of the work to be done (though not how to do it) to get the necessary commitment.

Sample Commitment Chart

Key Players	No Commitment	Let It Happen	Help It Happen	Make It Happen
1.		X ————————————————→		O
2.		X ————→	O	
3.		X ————————————————→		O
4.		O ←————	X	
5.			XO	
6.	X ————→	O		
7.		X ————————————————→		O
8.		XO		
9.	X ————————————————————→		O	
10.			O ←————————	X

Source: This information appears in Richard Beckhard and Reuben T. Harris, *Organization Transitions*, 2nd ed. (Reading, MA: Addison-Wesley, 1987), pp. 94–95.

standing organization. Enabling structures designed to facilitate and spotlight change range from the practical—such as setting up pilot tests, off-site workshops, training programs, and new reward systems—to the symbolic—such as rearranging the organization's physical space.

The more complex and large-scale the change, the more important it becomes that these enabling interventions be well thought out and consistent with each other. A series of choices among tactical options is thereby needed. This includes whether to use a pilot test or to go pan-organization; whether to be as participative throughout the process as the goals might warrant; whether to change certain systems sequentially or simultaneously;

whether to reject the old or accentuate the new; whether to use a "programmatic approach" or to have each unit develop its own interpretation; and whether to drive change bottom-up or top-down.

9. COMMUNICATE, INVOLVE PEOPLE, AND BE HONEST

When possible, change leaders should communicate openly, and should seek out the involvement and trust of people throughout their organizations. Full involvement, communication, and disclosure are not called for in every change situation; but these approaches can be potent tools for overcoming resistance and giving employees a personal stake in the outcome of a transformation.

Effective communication is critical from the very start. Even the way in which the change program is first introduced to the workforce can set the stage for either cooperation or rejection. The following list describes some criteria designed to increase an organization's understanding and commitment to change, reduce confusion and resistance, and prepare employees for both the positive and the negative effects of change.[5]

In general, a constructive change announcement:

- Is brief and concise.

- Describes where the organization is now, where it needs to go, and how it will get to the desired state.

- Identifies who will implement and who will be affected by the change.

- Addresses timing and pacing issues regarding implementation.

- Explains the change's success criteria, the intended evaluation procedures, and the related rewards.

[5] O.D. Resources, Inc., *Change Planning Guide*, Atlanta, GA, 1985.

- Identifies key things that will not be changing.

- Predicts some of the negative aspects that targets should anticipate.

- Conveys the sponsor's commitment to the change.

- Explains how people will be kept informed throughout the change process.

- Is presented in such a manner that it capitalizes on the diversity of the communication styles of the audience.

Too often, "communication" translates into a unilateral directive. But real communication requires a dialogue among the different change roles. By listening and responding to concerns, resistance, and feedback from all levels, implementors gain a broader understanding of what the change means to different parts of the organization and how it will affect them.

10. REINFORCE AND INSTITUTIONALIZE THE CHANGE

Throughout the pursuit of change, managers and leaders should make it a top priority to prove their commitment to the transformation process, to reward risk taking, and to incorporate new behaviors into the day-to-day operations of the organization. By reinforcing the new culture, they affirm its importance and hasten its acceptance.

This final commandment is made even more demanding by the fact that what many organizations are seeking today is not a single, discrete change but a continuous process of change. Given this reality, to speak of "institutionalizing" the change may be partially missing the point. Instead, what many companies really want is to institutionalize the *journey*, rather than the change. In other words, instead of achieving one specific change, organizations hope to create cultures and environments that recognize and thrive on the continuing necessity of change.

BOTH A SCIENCE AND AN ART

As already mentioned, these commandments are not the only tactics that the planned change literature has advocated. But they do provide a useful blueprint for organizations embarking on change, as well as a way to evaluate a change effort in progress. By going through this list, students and managers can begin to put together their own strategies for implementing change.

But no list is enough. Implementation is also a process of asking questions like these: Are we addressing the real needs of the company, or taking the easy way out? How shared is the vision? How do we preserve anchors to the past while moving to the future? Does everyone need to feel the same sense of urgency? Can change recipients, particularly those far down in the hierarchy, have an impact? How do we handle those who oppose the change? When should progress be visible? How do we integrate special projects to mainstream operations? When is it wise, or best, to share bad news? And now that we've gotten this far, is this the direction we still want to go?

Questions like these help to keep an organization focused and flexible, and to remind managers that implementing change is an ongoing process of discovery. In addition, it is, perhaps, most important for students and managers to remember that implementation is a mix of art and science. *How* a manager implements change can be almost as important as *what* the change is. In fact, implementation has less to do with obeying "commandments" and more to do with responding to the various "voices" within the organization, to the requirements of a particular situation, and to the reality that change may never be a discrete phenomenon or a closed book.

Case

Marconi plc (A)

February 2000—Our mission is to make Marconi one of the world's leading Telecommunications and Information Management companies in the most dynamic and exciting market sectors of the 21st century. We will do this by following the example of our founder, the young entrepreneur who—through his innovation and determination—gave the communications industry its voice.

We will achieve this by building a culture in which we will all share in the success of the new Marconi. In this spirit, we will mark our birth (in

November) with a grant of 1000 share options to participating employees.
When we double the share price, your shares, will be yours free.

—Lord Simpson, CEO, Marconi[1]

January 2002—Some of our managers are in denial—they don't feel
responsible for the current business situation. They attribute our problems
to analysts—whose comments, they believe, first pushed the share price
up and then caused it to go down—and to those senior executives who
decided to acquire new companies, which placed such a huge debt burden
on Marconi.

I think some of the employees feel that if they just keep quiet now
and go about their business, as they have done previously, the world will
forget and leave the company alone.

—Mike Parton, CEO, Marconi

In January 2002, Mike Parton, who only four months earlier had become CEO of Marconi, put the finishing touches on the plans for his first leadership conference. In a few days he was to address the top 100 managers at Marconi. The future of Marconi—perhaps its very survival—hung in the balance, after what had been an extraordinary two-year roller-coaster ride.

Parton was appointed CEO of the troubled telecommunications company after his predecessor, Lord Simpson, was forced to resign along with the company's chairman, Sir Roger Hurn. He took control of a company that had reported two quarters

Source: This case was written by Nikhil Tandon,
Research Associate, under the supervision
of Prof. Todd Jick and Prof. Maury Peiperl,
as a basis of class discussion rather than to
illustrate effective or ineffective handling of an
administrative situation. Copyright © 2002 by
London Business School. Case CS-02-013.

[1] To the employees, in the letter accompanying
the folder containing Marconi's values ("The
Marconi Way"), and details of a new media
campaign, "Marconi's Finest Hour."

of losses and was heavily burdened in debt that stood at £4.4 billion. In his first four months at the helm he had brought the debt down to £3.5 billion; made over 16 percent of Marconi's workforce (8,000 employees) redundant; sold off noncore businesses worth £1 billion (businesses that employed 9,000 people); and made a plan to reduce another 4,000 jobs, resulting in savings of a further £200 million per annum.

Parton knew how important the conference would be for enlisting the support of the company's top 100 managers for Marconi's turnaround. At the same time he wondered how ready the organization was for change by each and every individual. He wondered whether the recently agreed values—called "The Marconi Way"—would provide a road map or would elicit cynicism. Most important, he wondered whether the top 100 managers would be ready to take the organization forward. "We can't do it the same old way. . . . We will have to make a clear break from the past," he reflected at the time. "I will need both good management and great leadership."

BACKGROUND HISTORY

The year is 1901. The time is 12:30 pm on December 12. A man in a makeshift radio room on Signal Hill, in St. John's, Newfoundland, is listening intently through an earphone. The young Italian inventor, Guglielmo Marconi, waits. . . . and finally hears a faint sound: the Morse code signal for the letter "S." The 150-meter copper aerial—attached to a kite at one end and his "wireless" receiver at the other—has brought in the distinctive clicks of the "dot-dot-dot." They have traveled more than 2,000 km—and constitute the first transatlantic wireless signal.

(http://www.marconi.com).

In 1897 Marconi registered his company as the Wireless Telegraph and Signal Company. The company was renamed Marconi's Wireless Telegraph Company Limited in 1900. The English Electric Company acquired Marconi's Wireless Telegraph Company in 1946.

The English Electric Company merged with the General Electric Company (GEC) in 1968. Thus Marconi came to be a subsidiary of GEC.

THE WEINSTOCK ERA, 1963 TO 1996

Arnold (later Lord) Weinstock was appointed managing director of GEC in 1963. Weinstock was an ardent believer in the philosophy of "putting his eggs in many baskets." This philosophy was a driving force in the conservative acquisition and diversification strategy he pursued for three decades at the helm of GEC. During this period, GEC developed into a huge conglomerate with interests in businesses as diverse as heavy and light engineering (nuclear engineering, industrial appliances, telecommunications, power generation, and transportation), defense and medical electronics, and consumer durables.

> Weinstock was not a man of extravagant tastes. He bought a stud farm in Ireland to indulge his passion for racehorses, but ran it as carefully as he would have done any minor subsidiary of the GEC group—(he) even created a pension fund for the grooms and trainers, which must have been almost unique in the hand-to-mouth world of racing.[2]

Weinstock ran a tightly controlled ship. All major decisions were centralized. He was known for studying the monthly financial reports from the various divisions with great care and asking detailed questions on any deviations from budgets or planned forecasts. In GEC folklore, managers summoned by Weinstock to the head office usually expected to have their finances micromanaged rather than to have the bigger-picture strategy issues addressed.

In the words of a manager:

> The tight control and centralized decision-making process resulted

[2] "Lights Out at Marconi, but This Time It's for Good," http://www.vnunet.com.

in a bureaucratic and risk-averse organization which was unresponsive ("like a utility company or a public sector undertaking"). Weinstock in turn reinforced the risk averse and conservative behavior by being extremely conservative in the way he managed GEC.

With his motto, "Cash is King," Weinstock ensured that GEC had substantial cash reserves in the bank. In addition he was extremely cost conscious. It was said that Weinstock would patrol offices late at night turning out any lights left burning by careless staff.

However, GEC underperformed the market (FTSE All-Share Index) during all but four years between 1981 and 1996—the last 15 years of Weinstock's reign. The investor community was unhappy with Weinstock's conservative approach and the relative underperformance of GEC shares.

In July 1996, Lord Weinstock stood down as managing director of GEC, 33 years after taking the reins, and became Chairman Emeritus. He remained proud of what he had accomplished. During his stewardship GEC had grown from a company with annual revenues of £100 million in 1960 to £11 billion in 1996. He left a company with a sound financial and market standing in its existing businesses, and £1.0 billion in cash.

THE SIMPSON ERA, 1996–2000

Weinstock's replacement, George (later Lord) Simpson was appointed to the Board of GEC, and took over as managing director in September 1996. Simpson had already secured his place in British corporate history as someone who reinvented companies. He had orchestrated the sale of Rover to BMW, and then as the CEO of Lucas had engineered its merger with the Varity Group in the United States. At GEC, he inherited a conglomerate that had fallen out of favor with investors in the 1990s who preferred more focused companies.

Simpson quickly set about restructuring the Weinstock legacy to create a business focused on fewer sectors but with greater growth prospects. He also sought to reduce the company's dependence on joint venture partnerships. (More than 40 percent of the company's revenue in 1997 came from joint ventures with management control shared between GEC and its partners.)

In order to strengthen this management team, Simpson brought in John Mayo as his chief financial officer (CFO)—a former banker with SG Warburg. Mayo had a reputation for major corporate restructuring. While at SG Warburg he had helped mastermind the creation of the FTSE-100 pharmaceutical firm Zeneca, which was spun out of another U.K. industrial conglomerate, ICI.

At a strategic review presentation in July 1997, Simpson stated that his emphasis would be on "people, customers and growth, while maintaining strict cost focus." He had taken several actions in his first 12 months:

To improve performance:

- Restructured the main board.

- Strengthened the senior management team.

- Attended to loss-making businesses.

- Launched a culture change program.

To simplify the organizational structure and refocus the business:

- Reorganized the company into five operating units (see Exhibit 1).

- Accelerated and extended a disposals program.

EXHIBIT 1   Restructuring and Refocusing at GEC/Marconi

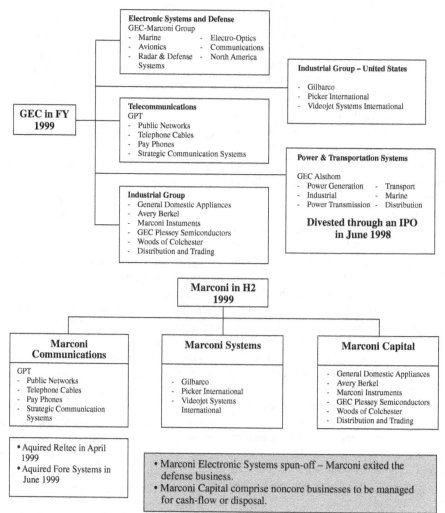

• Identified investment and development potential within each business group.

• Refocused on defense/aerospace, telecommunications, and industrial electronics.

To invest for growth:

• Increased and redirected R&D spending.

• Identified acquisition targets to build market/segment leadership positions.

In the 1997 Annual Report Simpson wrote:

> GEC will position (itself) away from disparate industrial grouping with heavy joint venture emphasis to a tightly focused and more GEC-managed international group whose activities will center around market/segment leadership positions where our electronics expertise and systems integration capability can be better exploited.

EXHIBIT 1   **Restructuring and Refocusing at GEC/Marconi**—*continued*

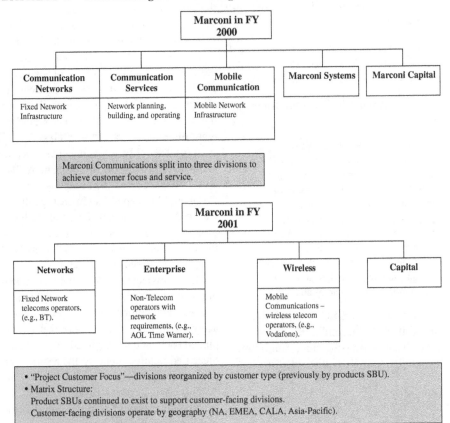

In December 1998, GEC reached the seminal moment in this restructuring process. The separation of GEC's well-known defense electronics business and its merger with British Aerospace was announced. The core of the remaining businesses within GEC was based on telecommunications equipment, where the company had a market leadership position in Europe and a business that held the best prospects for rapid growth. Although the restructuring had been in progress for some time, it was the spin-off of the defense electronics business that shook the organization and sent the clear message to the organization that things would "not be the same again."

The company thus refocused toward being a telecommunications equipment company.

With a strong presence in Europe but a narrow product focus, GEC began to pursue an acquisition strategy to expand internationally and broaden its product range to become an "end-to-end" supplier of networking equipment. The company acquired a number of telecommunications equipment manufacturers. These acquisitions were funded by a combination of cash and debt. The two major acquisitions made by GEC were:

• Reltec Corporation, a New York Stock Exchange (NYSE)–listed supplier of access equipment to many of North America's largest incumbent telecom operators, for US$2.1 billion, in April 1999.

- Fore Systems, a NASDAQ-listed supplier of enterprise networking equipment, for US$4.5 billion, in June 1999.

In the 1999 Annual Report Lord Simpson wrote:

> Our future will be digital. We will lead the race to capture, manage and communicate information. We will ride the rising tide of demand for data transmission. We will be a leading global player in communications and IT. And, we will do this because: we act fast, we are global, and we are leaders. To exploit the opportunities we see ahead we have reorganized into three key divisions: Communications, Systems and Capital.

In November 1999, GEC renamed and rebranded itself "Marconi" after the inventor of wireless transmission, Guglielmo Marconi, to symbolize this new direction.

CREATION OF VALUES—"THE MARCONI WAY"

In late 1999, John Mayo and Rob Meakin, the HR director, launched an initiative to define a set of values that would form the basis of the "new" Marconi. They themselves talked with more than 100 senior managers across the company and asked some fundamental questions:

- What was it really like working at Marconi?

- What were the values people held most strongly?

- How well did the values guide their day-to-day actions?

Focus groups worked at identifying values that were desired in the "new" Marconi. They also identified certain embedded values, which the employees cherished.

In addition, a team undertook a study of the vision, mission, and values of Marconi's competitors and high-performing peers in comparable industries, in order to challenge themselves to create values that would be real differentiators and best-in-class.

A draft set of beliefs and values was prepared and a process of consulting more than 1,000 people across the company was undertaken. Mayo and Meakin ensured that at least one of them attended each of the focus group meetings. Over the next few months, the draft was refined and finally evolved into "The Marconi Way" (Exhibit 2).

Senior managers in Marconi were introduced to the Marconi Way in Atlanta at a management conference in February 2000. They identified key behaviors that underpinned each value and agreed to start being measured against them by their superiors, peers, and direct reports in a 360° appraisal.

The management expected that the Marconi Way would help the organization move past its GEC heritage into the new future. To reinforce the values to the employees, each employee was given a pack containing details of the Marconi Way and the new "This Could Be Your Finest Hour" advertising campaign launching Marconi (Exhibit 3). A letter accompanying the pack also outlined details of 1,000 nil-cost options awarded to every employee, which would vest at a share price of £16.03. Essentially, the employees were given a target to double the value of the firm in three to five years from the quoted price of £8.015. The option plan had the desired impact on the workforce: As one manager recalled, "Little cards appeared on people's desks with £16.03 written on them. People were truly focused on the share price and motivated to achieve the target."

EXHIBIT 2 The Marconi Way

The Marconi Way is a set of shared beliefs, which drives us forward and binds us together as a leading edge, global business.

Our beliefs set standards and expectations—for our customers and stakeholders, to bring the best out of every individual.

- Real People

- Passion and Pride

- Radical Outlook

- High Velocity

- Special Delivery

The Marconi Way is about Real People with Passion and Pride, with Radical Outlook learning fast and working together to deliver long-term success for our customers worldwide.

"Real People" Means:

Straight talkers, people who say what they mean and mean what they say. It's about creating relationships—with customers and colleagues—based on trust and respect—valuing diversity.

It's about recognizing people for who they are and not what they are.

The success of Marconi is built on confidence—facing up to challenge and uncertainty, driving change. That's because people are encouraged to express themselves and reach their full potential.

"Real People" behaviors include:

1. Acting with integrity and honesty in dealing with people, at all times.
2. Straight talking—saying what you mean and meaning what you say.
3. Valuing diversity by recognizing differences, listening to individuals, and treating people with respect.
4. Creating a working environment in which discussion of all issues, even controversial ones, is encouraged.
5. Displaying a genuine interest and empathy for others—in all working relationships—at all levels, with customers, suppliers, partners, and the local community.
6. Encouraging, challenging, and responding constructively to suggestions and criticism.
7. Involving people to achieve their full potential.
8. Being aware of overload, its impact on performance and individual well-being.
9. Working toward shared goals with no hidden agenda.

"Passion and Pride" Means:

Marconi people show by their actions that they care passionately about success—for customers, colleagues, communities, all our stakeholders worldwide. People take pride in our achievements and focus on ways to build a stronger future and a global reputation.

Individuals are self-motivated and enthuse others by showing a desire to succeed. Marconi people take responsibility, own problems, find better ways, and overcome.

EXHIBIT 2   **The Marconi Way**—*continued*

"Passion and Pride" behaviors include:

1. Generating a spirit of "Can do, will do," in dealings with people.
2. Behaving in an entrepreneurial manner and encouraging others to act like owners rather than employees.
3. Caring passionately about success—others enthusing about the company, colleagues, customers, and partners.
4. Going the extra mile to help create a positive, stimulating, and high-performing work environment.
5. Recognizing accomplishments by others and celebrating success.
6. Working by example—taking initiative, promoting a desire to exceed standards and expectations.
7. Demonstrating a high level of personal commitment to goals and corporate objectives—not passing the buck.
8. Maintaining a high level of morale and enthusiasm about Marconi.
9. Acting as an ambassador and advocate for the company in dealings with people outside Marconi.

"Radical Outlook" Means:

Marconi will be at the forefront of new markets, new technologies, and new thinking.

We challenge the norm by thinking radically and acting creatively; each individual makes the difference by finding new things to do and better ways to do them.

We encourage a culture of breakthrough thinking because global success depends on our ability to push the boundaries, to find smarter technologies and better solutions—faster.

"Radical Outlook" behaviors include:

1. Actively promoting innovation and creative thinking—to challenge the status quo.
2. Looking for solutions across Marconi without regard to organizational barriers—building networks and collaboration to achieve breakthrough.
3. Recognizing the ideas of others and supporting them in driving ideas forward.
4. Seeking to develop individual capabilities and contributions to radical thinking.
5. Creating the necessary time, and sharing the tools and techniques, to increase creative thinking in the team.
6. Actively seeking alternative views and encouraging "out-of-box" thinking.
7. Building a climate in which people are motivated to find new and better ways—where there's no such thing as a bad idea.
8. Recognizing innovative thinking in others and celebrating team breakthroughs.
9. Approaching problems with curiosity and an open mind.
10. Providing innovative solutions to add value to customers and partners.
11. Accepting and managing risk, rather than avoiding it.

"High Velocity" Means:

Marconi innovates, breaks through, and keeps close to the edge. Marconi people learn fast, and find better and faster ways to get ideas to the market place.

Customers win with Marconi because we listen carefully, check on expectations and act with speed and precision.

EXHIBIT 2   The Marconi Way—*continued*

More is achieved, more problems are solved and more opportunities are created, every hour of every day, because we are faster to think and faster to act.

"High Velocity" behaviors include:

1. Acting decisively, even with incomplete information.
2. Setting a clear and positive direction, and communicating this through your area of responsibility.
3. Delegating responsibility and authority effectively.
4. Being flexible and adaptable; demonstrating an ability to stop and start, fast.
5. Seeking to identify constraints and to work collaboratively with others to remove them.
6. Constantly seeking to improve processes and addressing organizational barriers, in order to focus on priority tasks and projects.
7. Anticipating future demands and trends and incorporating them into planning activities.
8. Recognizing and rewarding people who exceed expectations on delivery and quality.
9. Creating a learning environment where people are coached to get things right the first time, reviewing success as well as failures.
10. Seeking to eliminate unnecessary activities and bureaucracy.
11. Conveying a sense of urgency and driving issues to closure.
12. Communicating relevant information and sharing knowledge.

"Special Delivery" Means:

Marconi people take responsibility, to deliver each time, every time. That's because every commitment is special—whether for a customer, the shareholders, the team, colleagues, or our communities.

Marconi people share what they know and what they are best at doing—building teamwork and team spirit, and enabling better delivery than any competitor can achieve.

The bottom line is that customers know they can rely on Marconi because customers' needs and expectations are special to us.

"Special Delivery" behaviors include:

1. Taking ownership of delivery, making commitments personal, and welcoming feedback and measurement.
2. Being an advocate for customers at all times—whether internal or external.
3. Displaying a "whatever it takes" mentality to achieve win-win with customer relationships.
4. Setting aggressive yet realistic targets and delivering each time, every time.
5. Motivating and supporting others to deliver results by creating an atmosphere of openness, trust, and shared learning.
6. Being proactive; always seeking to anticipate needs and exceed expectations.
7. Adding personal value in working relationships and succeeding in being the customer's "first choice."
8. Having a non-defeatist attitude to meeting and exceeding customer requirements.
9. Having a consistent track record of delivery on commitments.
10. Fostering an environment that promotes continuous improvement and quality outcomes.

EXHIBIT 3 This Is Marconi's Finest Hour

Guglielmo Marconi's Finest Hour Inspired a Century of Innovation.

Guglielmo Marconi sent the first wireless message over 100 years ago. Yet it's a moment in time that inspires us today, because it shows us that technology can empower people to do amazing things. It reminds us that it is our legacy to help our customers achieve their own moments of greatness. Simply put, Guglielmo Marconi's finest hour remains a part of everything we do, every day.

Our Finest Hour Is Happening This Very Minute.

Today marks a new era at Marconi. It's a time of global expansion, and new partnerships to better serve our customers. All of us must take advantage of this momentum. Work together to push the boundaries of technology. Expand our customers' horizons and, in turn, take Marconi into the twenty-first century.

Helping Customers Achieve Their Finest Hour Will Be Our Mission. Every Day.

There is no higher goal than to help each of our customers succeed. To do this, each one of us must think outside the box. Overcome adversity. Defy the odds. Listen to our customers' problems and discover smarter solutions. Become a true partner in their Vision. It will take breakthrough thinking every day to help our customers achieve their finest hour. Fortunately, that's what we do best.

Our Finest Hour Today Is Just One of Many More to Come.

It's an exciting period in Marconi's history, our finest hour to date—but it's only the beginning. A new century of innovation awaits us, with new opportunities for excellence. Together we'll discover those future moments of greatness.

Just Think. This Could Be Your Finest Hour.

Being a part of Marconi means you're a part of history in the making. It means you have the potential to contribute something special, every day. But this message of empowerment isn't just our corporate philosophy. From this moment on, it is our promise to our current customers, potential customers, partners, and investors. It's a powerful message. We've taken full force of the world via a global marketing effort. Shortly, through magazines and newspapers, with television to follow, we will declare emphatically that, with Marconi's help, anyone can indeed achieve their finest hour. People will look to us to deliver innovative solutions. They will ask us for smarter thinking. So now's the time to ask: When will your finest hour be?

THE EMERGING CRISIS, SEPTEMBER 2000–AUGUST 2001

The first half of 2000 saw rapid growth of business and good earnings reports and the stock traded at an all time high of £12.50 by mid-August 2000. Marconi was a FTSE favorite and considered the "go-go share." The company had launched the "Finest Hour" advertisement campaign to raise awareness of its unique position and capabilities in the minds of current and future stakeholders and customers worldwide.

But for Simpson and Marconi, 2001 was a year to forget (see Exhibit 4). The U.S. market for telecommunications equipment—representing nearly half of the global market—slowed down sharply as the dot-com bubble burst and many new entrants in the deregulated telecom services market began to fail. Demand in the European market initially remained robust, although many of the largest carriers suffered the negative effects of having to pay enormous fees for third-generation mobile-phone licenses. All of this meant that Marconi's customers delayed investment in new network infrastructure and equipment. The slowdown hit the company hard. In these challenging market conditions, some of the companies that Simpson had bought were struggling to provide expected revenue gains.

In the first quarter of 2001, many of Marconi's North American peers, such as Lucent, Nortel, and Cisco, flagged that sales and profits would be below market expectations and announced massive layoffs as the U.S. market faltered. Marconi, however, believed that it could dodge the bullets, based on its strong position in Europe and its leading position in certain key networking technologies. As late as May 16, Simpson told shareholders, "We anticipate the market will recover around the end of the calendar year, initially led by the established European operators. We believe we can achieve growth for the full year, as a result of our relative strength supplying these operators."

Simpson and Mayo faced serious questions from the institutional investors who had lost faith in the growth prospects of the telecom equipment industry in general, and in Marconi's strategy to become a global end-to-end supplier. After the close of the London Stock Exchange on July 4, 2001, Marconi confirmed the worst fears of the market, announcing that the financial year's sales were expected to be 15 percent and the operating profit before

exceptional items 50 percent below market expectations. The share price reacted to the warning and went into a freefall. Trading in Marconi shares opened on the morning of Thursday July 5, 2001, at £1.25, down 50 percent from the day before. After the surprise profit warning, Mayo was asked to resign.

On September 4, 2001, Marconi announced a trading update for the first half of its financial year, pointing to an operating loss and confirming a further 2,000 job losses (taking the total job cuts announced in the year to 10,000) and restructuring. As part of the announcement, the chairman, Sir Roger Hurn, and Simpson himself resigned from the board and the company. Derek Bonham, the senior nonexecutive director, became the interim chairman, and the board appointed Mike Parton, then head of the group's telecommunications products division, to be the new CEO. Marconi was relegated from the FTSE-100 index of the U.K.'s most valuable companies in mid-September 2001, the ultimate indignity for a once blue-chip company.

THE NEW MANAGEMENT TEAM

In the wake of this fast-moving tailspin, Bonham and Parton faced a huge set of challenges when they took over on September 4, 2001. Parton had been the CEO of Marconi Communications Limited since 1998, and in the prior 15 years had held a wide variety of positions in finance and senior management in the telecommunications industry.

Parton moved quickly, and announced his short-term action plan: to sell a host of non-core businesses, to pare Marconi down to its core operations, and to make necessary job cuts. He set a target of

EXHIBIT 4   **Marconi plc.**
Financial Summary

	1990	1991	1992	1993
	(million pounds)			
Sales—prior disposals	8,786	9,482	9,435	9,410
Sales—from continuing operations	5,807	6,569	6,403	6,284
EBIT—prior disposals	1,036	812	863	863
EBIT—from continuing operations	1,036	812	863	863
EPS—prior disposals (p)	25.4	18.4	19.9	19.7
EPS—from continuing operations	25.4	18.4	19.9	19.7
Excluding goodwill and amortization	n/a	n/a	n/a	n/a
Basic	n/a	n/a	n/a	n/a
Ordinary dividend	249	250	260	281
Dividend per share (p)	9.25	9.25	9.60	10.30
Retained profit/(Loss)—prior disposals	433	247	277	255
Retained profit/(Loss)—from continuing operations	433	247	277	255
Goodwill—prior disposals	—	—	—	—
Goodwill—in continuing operations	n/a	n/a	n/a	n/a
Fixed assets—prior disposals	1,080	999	953	926
Fixed assets—in continuing operations	n/a	n/a	n/a	n/a
Investments—prior disposals	718	769	802	970
Investments—continuing operations	n/a	n/a	n/a	n/a
Inventories—prior disposals	1,504	1,362	1,223	1,195
Inventories—continuing operations	n/a	n/a	n/a	n/a
Debtors—prior disposals	1,847	1,663	1,507	1,572
Debtors—continuing operations	n/a	n/a	n/a	n/a
Net monetary funds/(debt)—prior disposals	396	377	801	1,216
Net monetary funds/(debt)—continuing operations	n/a	n/a	n/a	n/a
Liabilities—prior disposals	(2,981)	(2,442)	(2,303)	(2,510)
Liabilities—continuing operations	n/a	n/a	n/a	n/a

1994	1995	1996	1997	1998	1999	2000	2001
				(million pounds)			
9,701	10,330	10,990	11,147	11,101	n/a	n/a	n/a
6,513	6,552	4,479	4,554	4,162	4,090	5,724	6,942
866	891	981	707	1,055	n/a	n/a	n/a
866	891	587	391	555	448	(115)	110
19.8	20.6	22.6	14.7	24.4	n/a	n/a	n/a
19.8	20.6	22.6	n/a	n/a	n/a	n/a	n/a
n/a	n/a	9.4	9.0	11.1	13.0	16.9	17.0
n/a	n/a	15.2	14.3	17.2	22.4	19.4	−9.8
296	312	345	365	311	348	142	148
10.82	11.37	12.51	13.15	11.43	13.00	5.20	5.35
244	252	278	62	198	n/a	n/a	n/a
244	252	72	34	169	259	380	(419)
—	—	—	—	1,781	3,281	n/a	n/a
n/a	n/a	424	456	485	1,220	4,397	5,395
919	913	1,122	1,049	871	982	n/a	n/a
n/a	n/a	658	578	398	470	758	1,142
980	977	988	870	1,166	1,471	n/a	n/a
n/a	n/a	1,069	1,037	1,024	1,223	1,626	591
1,149	1,175	1,197	1,114	940	1,052	n/a	n/a
n/a	n/a	721	668	548	616	946	1,721
1,681	1,752	1,910	1,744	1,726	1,953	n/a	n/a
n/a	n/a	721	668	548	616	946	1,721
1,352	1,323	1,152	1,086	1,184	484	n/a	n/a
n/a	n/a	547	862	1,035	624	(2,145)	(3,167)
(2,495)	(2,546)	(3,048)	(2,998)	(2,753)	(3,142)	n/a	n/a
n/a	n/a	(1,647)	(1,912)	(2,026)	(2,161)	(3,186)	(3,753)

reducing the debt burden from the crippling £4.4 billion as of March 31, 2001, to £2.7–£3.2 billion by March 2002 and to £2.5 billion after that.

Between September and December, Parton brought the debt down to £3.5 billion by selling non-core businesses and through bond buy-backs.

JANUARY 2002: ISSUES FACING PARTON

Parton increasingly saw the need to focus on the basics of the business—employee confidence, the business model, business processes, leadership capabilities, and underlying culture and values. Each of these was under careful review.

1. SHATTERED CONFIDENCE

Up until mid-2000, confidence in the future among the Marconi employees was strong. This confidence was not only internally felt but was also projected externally in the media campaign with the theme. "This Could Be Your Finest Hour."

Suddenly shattered in late 2000, morale was very low by the end of 2001. The future seemed uncertain and mostly negative. The daily press continued to be unyielding in its dramatic headlines and coverage such as:

> "Slump in Marconi's Sales Raises Questions about Its Survival." (*WSJ Europe,* November 14, 2001)

> "Marconi plans 4,000 more job cuts as core business sales slump by 37%." (*The Independent,* January 16, 2002)

> "Marconi's Performance Raises Doubts." (*WSJ Europe,* January 16, 2002)

> "Marconi on borrowed time—but still defiant." (*The Guardian,* January 16, 2002)

> "That shrinking feeling." (*Financial Times,* January 16, 2002)

Nevertheless, the responsibility to move the company forward was not universally felt. Parton in fact was concerned that some employees were "in denial." He said,

> They don't feel responsible for the current situation . . . Some middle managers feel that if they keep quiet and go about their business as they had done previously, the world will forget and leave the company alone.

2. THE BUSINESS MODEL

The Marconi strategy between 1997 and 2001 was dictated by the ambition to be one of the top three telecom equipment companies in the world. The objective was to be an "end to end" supplier to its customers for the full range of services. This strategy was the driving force for the acquisitions made by Simpson.

The strategy review undertaken by Parton challenged these assumptions and questioned the sustainability of such a broad business model, particularly in light of the changed market conditions. However, given the success the organization saw between 1999 and 2000, many managers felt that the end-to-end concept was sound and workable. Parton knew he would face opposition from the ranks if he were to retreat from some market segments. He commented:

> I am living with the myth that we have to be an "end to end" supplier. I have to get people to understand that we do not have to be present in all segments of the market. We have to make hard and big decisions—tactical and strategic—to lead the company through a difficult time. Change is all about unlearning and relearning, isn't it?

3. BUSINESS PROCESSES

GEC and then Marconi underwent a series of acquisitions and disposals between 1997 and 2000. However, little effort was made to integrate the acquired businesses and their processes into Marconi. The end result was a company that had diverse systems and processes, and poorly managed information and intelligence in a rapidly changing and highly competitive industry. In Parton's words:

> What I am looking for is a stable and predictable business. At the moment we have a lot of processes that are broken. We have many companies with different processes that are not integrated. What we need is rational analysis and not decision based on intuition.

4. LEADERSHIP

Managers at GEC and later Marconi were led by CEOs considered stalwarts of British industry, first Weinstock and then Simpson. These were respected leaders who nevertheless left the company under heavy criticism. As the new CEO in a crisis situation, Parton was under close internal as well as external scrutiny. In fact, his whole team was under a microscope. Parton was concerned that the managers lacked a comprehensive "tool kit" for how to manage during a crisis and to motivate their people. He commented:

> Great leadership is exemplified by taking everyone along with you, but this will be especially difficult in the coming year, because the "new dawn" for the industry is too far away to see at the moment.

5. CULTURE AND VALUES

After the huge fanfare of creating and launching the Marconi Way, other efforts to induce culture change in terms of structure, systems, and processes did not take such a high profile. Further, the systems to support culture change, such as 360-degree appraisals and employee workshops based on the values, had not been fully rolled out.

For Parton, the Marconi Way values were clearly associated with a more positive era for the company and the previous management team. However, he felt that these values still seemed sound and reflective of the values of a large percentage of the population. He struggled with how to reinforce the values and communicate them in a crisis:

> I am not trying to do a complete culture change. I want to change the top 108 leaders who in turn influence their 1,200 reports. In due course the change desired will permeate down to the 28,000 employees. However, this change has to be measurable and quantifiable. And it's OK if we lose some of the top 100 managers who do not fall in line in the process.
>
> At this stage I do not want to stand on the soapbox and say—"Here is the Marconi Way—. . . now go and live that way." In fact, the Marconi Way is a mixture of what we already are and what we need to be to succeed in the future. For example, we are very much "real people" and we do operate with "pride and passion." We have very low employee turnover compared to the rest of the industry. However, "radical outlook" and "special delivery" will be a key to our future, and we are by no means there yet. . . .
>
> We are telling people to get the debt down, but I do not know how to link it to the values. You can't say—get the debt down with "high velocity." I am trying to figure out how to link this turnaround with the Marconi Way.

Parton saw the leadership conference as an opportunity to begin addressing these issues and help to create a unified, focused management team. In the meantime, trading results for the company's third quarter showed continued difficult market conditions, and an operating loss in the core communications business of £130 million.

HIGHLIGHTS OF THE LEADERSHIP CONFERENCE

Parton spoke at the beginning and at the end of the two-day conference. In between, there were presentations by external advisors and many opportunities for participants to discuss the key issues in discussion groups.

PARTON'S OPENING SPEECH: THE BUSINESS SITUATION AND PRIORITIES

In his opening speech, Parton focused on the immediate priorities to get Marconi back on an even keel:

- To pay the bills—that is, to reduce operating expenses to £1 billion per annum.

- To ensure that Marconi would generate enough cash to sustain itself as a viable business.

- To have an appropriate capital structure—by disposing of non-core businesses, buying back bonds, and renewing bank facilities.

- To grow the business profitably through differentiation of the product portfolio and service.

He expected everyone to leave the conference with a clear understanding of:

- Company direction.

- Efforts to reduce the cost base.

- Developing a platform for growth.

- Leading the people through the crisis.

Regarding the Marconi Way, Parton said:

> We need to do something about how to reinforce and communicate this going forward. After all, the values are for bad times as well as good.

THE CHANGE CURVE

An external consultant introduced a framework for addressing the question of how the managers and their direct reports were coping with the emotions of change. He presented a framework called "the change curve" showing how people typically react to change in stages. (See Figure 1.)

The audience was polled (using keypads for anonymity) about the stage they felt they were in individually and the stage they felt the employees were in. The results were as shown in Figure 2. On another question, "Have you considered leaving Marconi in the last three months?" 62 percent of the participants answered yes.

WORKSHOP

Parton divided the delegates into breakout groups and asked each for their suggestions to help people commit to change. The aim of the session was to help people talk through some of the emotions they had felt at the company's change of circumstances and to "exorcise some demons." Some common themes that emerged across the various groups were:

- The executive team needed to be more visible to middle managers and employees.

FIGURE 1

FIGURE 2

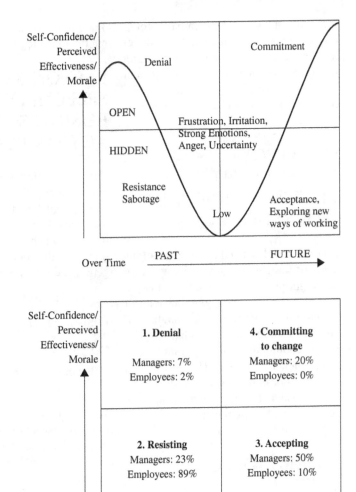

- "Stop living for the next quarter. Develop a long-term strategy."

- The multiple changes in the organizational structure created a lot of confusion: Some managers did not know whom they reported to or were unclear about their responsibilities.

- Need for more communication from Parton on the strategy so that they

would have a clear view of what was to be done.

INVESTOR RELATIONS— AN EXTERNAL VIEW

A consultant from a firm specializing in investor relations talked about what the investment community thought of

Marconi and what the company could do to improve its image and build shareholder value. He ended by explaining that there was enormous upside potential for investors (including the people in the room, all of whom had substantial options packages).

STRATEGY CONSULTANT: PRESENTATION AND WORKSHOP

A consultant discussed the findings of his study of Marconi's strategy. He was very forthright in telling the managers that, in his assessment of the buying behavior of the customers, Marconi's past strategy of becoming an end-to-end global supplier of telecommunications equipment was "fundamentally flawed." He forecast that Marconi's position in some product areas was unsustainable. The group debated the findings and their implications, with many suggestions for action.

WORKSHOP: COST CUTTING

Parton set the scene for the final workshop by challenging the managers to come up with radical actions to reduce Marconi's cost base by £200 million by September 2002.

All ideas generated were captured regardless of the fact that they may not have had unanimous support. Some ideas raised had large-scale radical implications—like closing certain businesses or selling important assets. The suggestions were highly consistent across groups.

At the end of the workshop there was a presentation by one of the executive team members who announced a draft plan for 4,000 redundancies to be completed during the following financial year.

PARTON'S CLOSING SPEECH: LEADERSHIP, BUSINESS PROCESSES, ACTION PLAN

The last session was a presentation by Parton titled, "Leadership—Getting the Basics Right." Parton summed up the key messages from each speaker and the list of actions the managers had agreed to as a group. He then outlined what he meant by getting the basics right, as follows:

- Building from the ground up.

- Simplicity and robustness in execution.

- Delivering relentlessly on commitments.

- Establishing a platform for growth.

Parton went on to outline the specific actions and behaviors he expected of each of his managers to improve the way they managed and led their people, and what they in turn could expect from him.

Behaviors expected of Marconi leaders:

- Be highly capable and respected for their contribution.

- Say with clarity and honesty what they think and feel.

- Challenge the status quo, to improve business performance.

- Be confident and expect to succeed.

- Be team players, fully aligned behind the company's goals.

- Be ambassadors for the company, internally and externally.

- Be good managers, consistently achieving results.

- Be great leaders, leading by example and living our shared values.

What Marconi leaders could expect from Parton:

- A role model: "I am not asking you to do anything I am not going to do myself."

- Clear objectives for the company.

- A personal interest in the performance and development of every person at the leadership conference.

- Ensure that every one of the top 100 leaders had his or her own Personal Development Plan and opportunities to satisfy development needs.

- Communicate with the leaders and involve them in decision making.

- Performance measurement: "Are we doing what we said we will do?"

Parton insisted that he would want total commitment from the leaders in order to achieve the objectives:

> We have an exceptional challenge. We need an exceptional team working exceptionally well together, and we are that *team*. We want leaders who are 100 percent committed. If you are not with me, come to me and I will help you exit the business.

CONFERENCE CLOSING

Unlike the earlier management conferences, the conference ended quietly. Parton's message, style, and intent were quite clear to everyone: "Get back to basics." There was no applause as Parton finished speaking, but the message clearly got through to the attendees. There were lots of private discussions as they departed, and many made plans to get together and discuss issues.

Reading

Organizational Frame Bending

Principles for Managing Reorientation

David A. Nadler

Michael L. Tushman

One of the hallmarks of business in the past decade has been the attempts by

Source: *Academy of Management Executive*, 1989, vol. 3, no. 3, pp. 194–204.

large organizations to manage large-scale planned change. In some cases—AT&T, Chrysler, and Apple, for example—the efforts have been dramatic and have captured public attention. Other cases, such as Corning Glass, Xerox, Citicorp, and GTE, have received less attention, but the changes have been no less profound.

The concept of planned organizational change is not new; but this most recent generation of changes is somewhat different from what has gone before. First, they typically are initiated by the leaders of organizations, rather than consultants or human resource specialists (although they have played significant roles in some cases). Second, they are closely linked to strategic business issues, not just questions of organizational process or style. Third, most of the changes can be traced directly to external factors, such as new sources of competition, new technology, deregulation or legal initiatives, maturation of product sets, changes in ownership, or shifts in fundamental market structure. Fourth, these changes affect the entire organization (whether it be a corporation or a business unit), rather than individual SBUs (strategic business units) or departments. Fifth, they are profound for the organization and its members because they usually influence organizational values regarding employees, customers, competition, or products. As a result of the past decade's changes, there are now more large visible examples than ever before of successful planned organizational change.

Our work has brought us into contact with a number of examples of these changes.[1] In general, they have been changes that encompass the whole organization, have occurred over a number of years, and have involved fundamental

[1] This article is based on observations of approximately 25 organizations in which we have done work over the past five years, and specifically our very close work with the most senior levels of management in planning and implementing significant, multiyear strategic-level changes in six particular organizations.

shifts in the way the organization thinks about its business, itself, and how it is managed. Our experience has included changes that both internal and external observers rate as successes, some that have been described as failures, and some that are still going on.

Our purpose in this article is to share some insights, generalizations, and hunches about large-scale organizational changes, working from our perspective of close observations. We begin by reviewing some basic concepts of organization and change that have shaped the way we think about and observe these events. Next, we briefly describe an approach to differentiating among various types of organization change. Finally, we devote the rest of the article to our concept of "frame bending"—a particular kind of large-scale change found in complex organizations.

BASIC CONCEPTS OF ORGANIZATION AND CHANGE

THINKING ABOUT ORGANIZATIONS

We view organizations as complex systems that, in the context of an environment, an available set of resources, and a history, produce output. To illustrate, we have developed a model that consists of two major elements (see Exhibit 1). The first is *strategy*, the pattern of decisions that emerges over time about how resources will be deployed in response to environmental opportunities and threats. The second is *organization,* the mechanism that is developed to turn strategy into output. Organization includes four core components: work, people, formal structures and processes, and informal structures and

EXHIBIT 1   Organizational Model

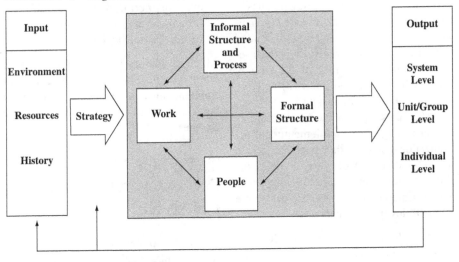

processes. The fundamental dynamic is *congruence* among these elements. Effectiveness is greatest when a firm's strategy is consistent with environmental conditions and there is internal consistency, or fit, among the four organizational components. Our model emphasizes that there is no one best way to organize. Rather, the most effective way of organizing is determined by the nature of the strategy as well as the work, the individuals who are members of the organization, and the informal processes and structures (including culture) that have grown up over time.[2]

While our model implies that congruence of organizational components is a desirable state, it is, in fact, a double-edged sword. In the short term, congruence seems to be related to effectiveness and performance. A system with high

congruence, however, can be resistant to change. It develops ways of insulating itself from outside influences and may be unable to respond to new situations.[3]

ORGANIZATIONAL CHANGE

From time to time, organizations are faced with the need to modify themselves. The change may involve one or more elements of the organizational system, or it may involve a realignment of the whole system, affecting all the key elements—strategy, work, people, and formal and informal processes and structures. A central problem is how to maintain congruence in the system while implementing change, or how to help the organization move to a

[2] See D. A. Nadler and M. L. Tushman, "A Diagnostic Model for Organization Behavior," in E. E. Lawler and L. W. Porter, eds., *Perspectives on Behavior in Organizations* (New York: McGraw-Hill, 1977); and D. A. Nadler and M. L. Tushman, "A Model for Organizational Diagnosis," *Organizational Dynamics*, Autumn 1980.

[3] See M. L. Tushman, W. Newman, and E. Romanelli, "Convergence and Upheaval: Managing the Unsteady Pace of Organizational Evolution," *California Management Review*, Fall 1986, pp. 29–44. Also see M. L. Tushman and E. Romanelli, "Organizational Evolution: A Metamorphosis Model of Convergence and Reorientation," in B. L. Staw and L. L. Cummings, eds., *Research in Organizational Behavior* (Greenwich, CT: JAI Press, 1985), p. 17.

whole new configuration and a whole new definition of congruence. Critical issues in managing such changes include (1) managing the political dynamics associated with the change, (2) motivating constructive behavior in the face of the anxiety created by the change, and (3) actively managing the transition state.[4]

While these approaches have been useful for managers and implementors of organizational change, they have limitations when applied to large-scale, complex organizational changes. Specifically, these larger-scale changes entail at least some of the following characteristics:

- *Multiple transitions.* Rather than being confined to one transition, complex changes often involve many different transitions. Some may be explicitly related; others are not.

- *Incomplete transitions.* Many of the transitions that are initiated do not get completed. Events overtake them, or subsequent changes subsume them.

- *Uncertain future states.* It is difficult to predict or define exactly what a future state will be; there are many unknowns that limit the ability to describe it. Even when a future state can be described, there is a high probability that events will change the nature of that state before it is achieved.

- *Transitions over long periods.* Many large-scale organization changes take long periods to implement—in some cases, as much as three to seven years.

The dynamics of managing change over this period of time are different from those of managing a quick change with a discrete beginning and end.

All these factors lead to the conclusion that the basic concepts of transition management must be extended to deal with the additional issues posed by large-scale changes.[5]

TYPES OF ORGANIZATIONAL CHANGE

As a first step toward understanding large-scale organizational change, we have developed a way of thinking about the different types of change that organizations face. Change can be considered in two dimensions. The first is the scope of the change—that is, subsystems of the organization versus the entire system. Changes that focus on individual components, with the goal of maintaining or regaining congruence, are *incremental* changes. For example, adapting reward systems to changing labor market conditions is an incremental, systems-enhancing change. Changes that address the whole organization, including strategy, are *strategic* changes. These changes frequently involve breaking out of a current pattern of congruence and helping an organization develop a completely new configuration. Incremental changes are made within the context, or frame, of the current set of organizational strategies and components. They do not address

---

[4] R. Beckhard and R. T. Harris, *Organizational Transitions* (Reading, MA: Addison-Wesley, 1977); K. Lewin, "Frontiers in Group Dynamics," *Human Relations* 1 (1947), pp. 5–41; and D. A. Nadler, "Managing Organizational Change: An Integrative Perspective," *Journal of Applied Behavioral Science* 17 (1981): pp. 191–211.

[5] See Beckhard and Harris, 1977; W. G. Bennis, K. D. Benne, and R. Chin, *The Planning of Change* (New York: Holt, Rinehart & Winston, 1961); and W. G. Bennis and B. Nanus, *Leadership: The Strategies for Taking Charge* (New York: Harper & Row, 1985).

fundamental changes in the definition of the business, shifts of power, alterations in culture, and similar issues. Strategic changes change that frame, either reshaping it, bending it, or, in extreme cases, breaking it. For example, when John Sculley took the reins from Steven Jobs at Apple Computer, or when Lee Iacocca took over at Chrysler, systemwide changes followed.

The second dimension of change concerns the positioning of the change in relation to key external events. Some changes are clearly in response to an event or series of events. These are called *reactive* changes. Other changes are initiated, not in response to events but in anticipation of external events that may occur. These are called *anticipatory* changes. (The relationship between the dimensions can best be described using the illustrations shown in Exhibit 2.) Four classes of change are the result:

- *Tuning.* This is incremental change made in anticipation of future events. It seeks ways to increase efficiency but does not occur in response to any immediate problem.

- *Adaptation.* This is incremental change that is made in response to external

events. Actions of a competitor, changes in market needs, new technology, and so on require a response from an organization, but not one that involves fundamental change throughout the organization.

- *Reorientation.* This is strategic change, made with the luxury of time afforded by having anticipated the external events that may ultimately require change. These changes do involve fundamental redirection of the organization and are frequently put in terms that emphasize continuity with the past (particularly values of the past). Because the emphasis is on bringing about major change without a sharp break with the existing organization frame, we describe these as frame-bending changes. For example, the sweeping changes initiated by Paul O'Neil and Fred Federholf at ALCOA were frame-bending changes in that they were not driven by performance crisis (i.e., they were proactive) and they built on ALCOA's past, even though they involved widespread organization change.

- *Re-creation.* This is strategic change necessitated by external events, usually

EXHIBIT 2   **Types of Organizational Change**

	Incremental	*Strategic*
Anticipatory	**Tuning**	**Reorientation**
Reactive	**Adaptation**	**Re-creation**

ones that threaten the very existence of the organization. Such changes require a radical departure from the past and include shifts in senior leadership, values, strategy, culture, and so forth. Consequently, we call these *frame-breaking* changes. Examples of these reactive, systemwide changes abound, and include those at National Cash Register, U.S. Steel, AT&T, GM, ICI, and SAS.

Building on this classification scheme, these different types of change can be described in terms of their intensity (Exhibit 3). Intensity relates to the severity of the change and, in particular, the degree of shock, trauma, or discontinuity created throughout the organization. Strategic changes are obviously more intense than incremental changes, which can frequently be implemented without altering an organization's basic management processes. Reactive changes are more intense than anticipatory changes, because of the

necessity of packing substantial activity into a short time without the opportunity to prepare people to deal with the trauma. There is also less room for error and correction.

Relative intensity is further affected by organizational complexity. Organizations become more difficult to change as they increase in complexity—complexity determined by (1) the size of the organization in terms of employees and (2) the diversity of the organization in terms of the number of different businesses, geographic dispersion, and so on. Smaller organizations with a few highly related businesses are easier places in which to implement changes than are larger, highly diverse organizations.

If we put these concepts together, we get a map of the difficulty of organizational change (see Exhibit 4). The least difficult changes are those that are low intensity and take place in fairly noncomplex settings. The most difficult changes are those that are high intensity (strategic) and take place

EXHIBIT 3   Relative Intensity of Different Types of Change

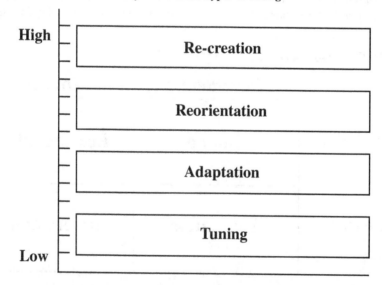

EXHIBIT 4   **Types of Change Management**

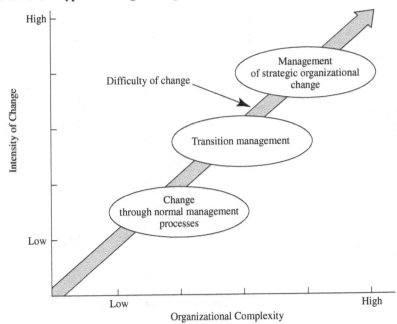

in highly complex settings. Our focus is on strategic organizational change. Re-creations are the most risky and traumatic form of change, and our assumption is that managers would rather avoid the costs and risks associated with them. The challenge, then, is to effectively initiate and implement reorientations, or frame-bending change, in complex organizations.

OBSERVATIONS OF EFFECTIVE ORGANIZATIONAL FRAME BENDING

In the last section, we identified the activities and elements that characterize effective organizational re-creation. The principles have been organized into four clusters for discussion purposes, and we will refer to them as *principles of effective*

frame bending. First, there are those principles associated with *initiating change.* Next, there is a set of principles having to do with how the reorientation is defined, or the *content of change,* and another set having to do with *leading change.* Finally, there are principles associated with *achieving change,* relating to the activities that are required to implement, sustain, and complete reorientations over long periods. The clusters and principles are displayed in Exhibit 5.

THE DIAGNOSIS PRINCIPLE

Managing organizational reorientation involves managing the *what* as well as the *how.* The *what* concerns the content of the change: what strategies and elements of organization will have to be changed to enable the organization effectively to anticipate, respond to, and even shape the challenges to come. While much of the

EXHIBIT 5   Principles of Effective Frame Bending

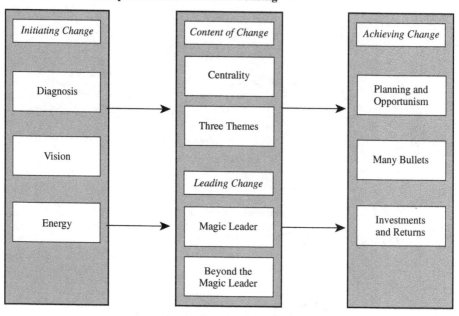

focus of this perspective is on the process of managing reorientations, the content is nevertheless critically important.

Identification of the appropriate strategic and organizational changes comes from diagnostic thinking—analyzing the organization in its environment, understanding its strengths and weaknesses, and analyzing the implications of anticipated changes. Diagnosis typically involves the collection, integration, and analysis of data about the organization and its environment. It involves assessment of the organization usually based on some underlying model of organizational effectiveness.

Effective reorientations are characterized by solid diagnostic thinking. In these cases, managers have spent time understanding the potential *environmental challenges and forces,* be they technological, regulatory, competitive, or otherwise. They have worked to identify the *critical success factors* associated with achieving effective

anticipation or response. They have looked hard at the *organizational strengths and weaknesses,* thus gaining a systematic view on what has to change and why.

In contrast, the less effective reorientation suffers from a lack of diagnosis and the quick adoption of "solutions in search of problems," which often comes about through *organizational mimicry.* In these cases, the senior management of one organization observes how "model" organizations (the referents vary—they could be industry leaders, generally respected companies, and so on) are responding to or anticipating change and they then copy what the model is doing. What they fail to grasp is that the model organization typically has done diagnostic work and has identified a set of changes unique to its own conditions. Because the management of the model organization has participated in the diagnostic work, it has both the understanding and the commitment that results from the process. Thus, mimicking organizations not only adopt strategies that are not designed for the problems or challenges they face, but do so in a manner that leads to low commitment to change. Little wonder that they tend to fail.[6]

THE VISION PRINCIPLE

An effective reorientation involves movement from one state to another. The most effective reorientations include a fully developed description of the desired future state. Since the nature of the change is usually both very broad and profound, this description is more than a statement of objectives or goals; it is a *vision* of what the organization hopes to be once it achieves the reorientation. This vision may range from a set of principles or values all the way to detailed papers outlining specific strategic objectives, operating modes, organizational structures, and so on. In most cases, it addresses values as well as performance. Overall, most visions touch in some way on each of the following points:

- *Rationale.* A description of why the vision is needed, or why the change is required.

- *Stakeholders.* A discussion of the organization's stakeholders and what it seeks to provide for them.

- *Values.* A description of the core values and/or beliefs that drive the organization of the change.

- *Performance objectives.* A definition of what will characterize effective performance of the organization (and in some

cases individuals) once the change has been achieved.

- *Organizational structure or processes.* How the organization will be structured or will work to achieve the vision.

- *Operating style.* A discussion of some of the specific elements of how people in the organization (particularly managers) will operate and interact with one another. In some cases, this is an attempt to describe the required culture in operational terms.

Visions are developed for a number of different purposes. They are directional, signaling where the reorientation is headed. They are symbolic, providing a point for rallying and identification. They are educational, helping individuals to understand the events around them. Finally, they are energizing.

In this context, effective visions seem to be ones that are credible, are responsive to the current (or anticipated) problems, and provide a balance of specificity and ambiguity. Effective visions also have a balance of new and old or sustaining ideas, values, or perspectives. In contrast to re-creations (in which a break with the past is often necessary and appropriate), effective visions for reorientations often are crafted to have "resonance"—to meld with themes from the organization's past.

Effective reorientations tend to have visions that are responsive to the issues raised in diagnosis and meet many of the criteria listed above. Less effective reorientations either have no vision or have visions that are flawed, are the result of mimicry, or have been developed in a way that does not facilitate the creation of understanding and/or commitment.[7]

---

[6] See P. A. Goodman and associates, *Change in Organizations: New Perspectives on Theory, Research, and Practice* (San Francisco: Jossey-Bass, 1982); and E. E. Lawler, D. A. Nadler, and C. Cammann, *Organizational Assessment* (New York: John Wiley, 1980).

[7] J. M. Burns, *Leadership* (New York: Harper & Row, 1978); and Goodman and associates, 1982.

A final note on vision. The question of whether or not to make a vision public has been faced in a number of reorientations. While the issue is important, no definitive answer has yet been identified. Clearly, the vision needs to be made public at some point. The directional, energizing, and educational goals of the vision cannot be met if it is kept secret. On the other hand, there are many cases of premature articulation of vision leading to negative consequences. In what some have called the "rush to plexiglass," certain companies have developed vision statements and immediately distributed them throughout the company, using posters, documents, plaques, pins, plexiglass "tombstones," and so on. When the vision is poorly thought out, when it is not clear how the vision will be achieved, or (perhaps most importantly) when the vision is very much at odds with current management behavior, employees tend to greet such statements with justified skepticism; the net result is a loss of management credibility. In some cases, this problem has been dealt with by clearly positioning the vision as aspirational and recognizing that this is not the way the organization functions today.

THE ENERGY PRINCIPLE

One of the great strengths of organizations is that they contain tremendous forces for stability. They are able to withstand threats and challenges to the established order. The flip side of this characteristic is that organizations (and particularly successful ones) can be inherently resistant to change, particularly change that undermines strongly held values and beliefs. Energy must be created to get change initiated and executed.

Organizational reorientation presents a particular dilemma. In a crisis situation (e.g., the Tylenol poisoning case, the Union Carbide disaster at Bhopal, or deregulation at AT&T) the clear, present danger of organizational failure creates the energy needed to make change happen. Reorientation, by definition, is different because it involves changes in anticipation of the events that may make it necessary. The need for change may be apparent only to a small number of people. For the majority of people in the organization—and sometimes this includes much of senior management—the need for change is often not clear.[8]

Effective reorientations seem to be initiated by specific efforts to create energy. Most often this involves some effort—usually by leaders—to create a *sense of urgency*, and somehow to communicate and convey that sense of urgency throughout the organization. In some cases, a sense of urgency can be created by presenting information that shatters widespread assumptions about the current situation. But this tactic addresses the intellectual inertia. Urgency and energy are emotional issues, and experience indicates that people and organizations develop the energy to change when faced with real *pain*.

The larger and more intense the change, the more extreme the pain needed to mobilize individuals to consider doing things differently. There are a number of different ways in which pain can be created. Most of them involve employees participating in the process of data collection, discovery, and comparison of their organization against accepted benchmarks (frequently competitors). Some reorientations have been started by getting senior managers to spend time with customers, use competitive

[8] See Bennis et al., 1961; Lewin, 1947; and J. M. Pennings and associates, *Organizational Strategy and Change* (San Francisco: Jossey-Bass, 1985).

products or services, or visit companies that are competitive analogs (the now familiar "trip to Japan"). Since individuals have a unique capacity for denial, multiple intense exposures may be necessary to create the required depth of emotional reaction.

The problem is that pain can create energy that is counterproductive. The consequences of pain can be dysfunctional behavior as well as functionally directed action. Negative information can lead to certain defensive reactions, such as denial, flight, or withdrawal. To the extent that the organization is characterized by pathology, the creation of pain or urgency may stimulate maladaptive responses. Therefore, the challenge is to develop methods of creating pain that will create energy and catalyze action.

Successful reorientations involve the creation of a sense of urgency right at the limits of tolerance—just at the point where responses border on defensive. At the same time, efforts are made to track dysfunctional or pathological responses and find ways to redirect the energy in positive ways. In many less-effective reorientations, sufficient energy has not been generated early or broadly enough. This is particularly true in very large organizations that have the capacity to absorb or buffer pain.

The next two principles assume that change has been initiated, and focus on the content of the change. These will be followed by two principles regarding the role of leadership in reorientation.

THE CENTRALITY PRINCIPLE

For a change to engage the entire organization, it must be clearly and obviously linked to the core strategic issues of the firm. The positioning and labeling of the reorientation are critical. Successful

long-term changes are positioned as strategic imperatives that are compelling to members of the organization. Usually, the connection is so clear and has so much validity that the relationship of the change to company health and survival is obvious. For example, the emphasis on quality and customer service at Xerox and ALCOA were clearly linked to their enhanced competitiveness. Where changes are not seen as central to the survival, health, or growth of the organization, they tend to be transient, existing only so long as the perceived interest of senior management lasts. For a change to "catch," employees have to see a clear connection with core organizational and individual imperatives.

To the degree the change is central, it raises another dilemma. If the organization has been successful and has built some degree of congruence over the years, employees may resist wholesale changes. In many successful long-term changes, managers worked to make sure that the core themes of the change (and the vision) had organizational resonance—that is, that they seemed related to and consistent with some of the historical core values of the organization.

But how can one find themes with strategic centrality in an organization of great diversity? It appears to be more difficult to find such themes across widely diverse businesses in large organizations. Success comes most often when generic themes, such as quality, competitiveness, or innovation, can be positioned across the businesses and then related with specificity to each particular operation's situation.[9]

[9] See M. Kets de Vries and D. Miller, "Neurotic Style and Organizational Pathology," *Strategic Management Journal* 5 (1984), pp. 35–55; and N. M. Tichy and M. A. Devanna, *The Transformational Leader* (New York: John Wiley, 1986).

THE THREE-THEME PRINCIPLE

While a strategic change may involve a large number of specific activities, most managers of change find it necessary to identify *themes* to communicate and conceptualize the changes. Themes provide a language through which employees can understand and find patterns in what is happening around them. At the same time, however, they seem to be capable of integrating only a limited number of themes in the midst of all of the other transactions that make up daily life. Employees are bombarded with programs, messages, and directives. In many situations, individuals cope by figuring out which messages they can safely ignore. Usually, more are ignored than not. Successful long-term changes are characterized by a careful self-discipline that limits the number of major themes an organization gives its employees. As a general rule, managers of a change can only initiate and sustain approximately three key themes during any particular period of time.

The challenge in this area is to create enough themes to get people truly energized, while limiting the total number of themes. The toughest part is to decide not to initiate a new program—which by itself has great merit—because of the risk of diluting the other themes.

Most successful reorientations are characterized by consistency of themes over time. It is consistency that appears to be most significant in getting people to believe that a theme is credible. The problem, then, is how to maintain consistency while simultaneously shaping themes to match changing conditions.[10]

[10] See D. A. Nadler and M. L. Tushman, *Strategic Organization Design* (Glenview, IL: Scott, Foresman, 1988); J. B. Quinn, *Strategies for Change: Logical Incrementalism* (Homewood, IL: Richard D. Irwin, 1980); and J. B. Quinn and K. Cameron, eds., *Paradox and Transformation* (Cambridge, MA: Ballinger, 1988).

THE MAGIC LEADER PRINCIPLE

Another important component of a successful reorientation is an individual leader who serves as a focal point for the change, whose presence has some special "feel" or "magic." Large-scale organizational change requires active and visible leadership to help articulate the change and to capture and mobilize the hearts and minds of the people in the organization. This kind of leadership relies on special effects created throughout the organization by the individual leader and, thus, this type of individual can be thought of as a *magic leader*. These leaders display the following characteristics:

- *Distinctive behaviors.* Magic leaders engage in three distinctive types of behavior that encourage employees to act in ways consistent with the desired change. The first is *envisioning*—creating an engaging and inspirational vision of a future state. Next is *energizing*—creating or stimulating energy through personal demonstration, rewards, and punishments, and setting high standards. Finally, there is *enabling*—helping to create the processes, resources, or structures that enable employees to do the things they have been motivated to do. The most successful large-scale change leaders exhibit elements of all three of these types of behavior.

- *Ability to create a sense of urgency.* The magic leader seems to be critical in creating a sense of urgency so essential to organizational changes. The leader is a key player in the creation and management of pain.

- *Guardianship of themes.* The leader is the guardian of the themes of the change. He or she is the one individual who can make sure the themes survive. Successful change managers exhibit great tenacity (or even stubbornness) in the articulation of themes over a period of years, in both good times and bad.

- A *mix of styles.* Magic leaders also display an interesting mix of management styles. On one hand, they appear to be directive and uncompromising in furthering their objectives for change. On the other hand, they seem to welcome participation and spend time getting people involved in shaping the change process. This combination of autocratic and democratic tendencies appears to be critical to their effectiveness.

The dilemma here is that, while the individual magic leader is essential to successful reorientation, continued dependence on him or her can lead to disaster. The change can become too personalized; nothing happens unless that individual assumes personal sponsorship, and the next levels of management may become disenfranchised. Furthermore, when the leader makes mistakes (as he or she inevitably does) the magic may fade. The magic leader finds it difficult to live up to the fantasies that subordinates create. Thus, the challenge is to fulfill the need for the leader at the very time when the organization needs to grow beyond the leader.[11]

THE LEADERSHIP-IS-NOT-ENOUGH PRINCIPLE

While magic leadership is necessary, it cannot, by itself, sustain a large-scale change. Success depends on a broader base of support built with other individuals who act first as followers, second as helpers, and finally as co-owners of the change.

The expansion of the leadership of change beyond the magic leader requires efforts in two directions. The first complements the magic leader with leadership that focuses on the necessary elements of management control, or instrumental leadership.

The second broadens the base of leadership beyond one or two individuals. The most common way to achieve this is through the executive team of the organization. Successful changes are characterized by a large investment in the executive team, both as individuals and as a group. This team needs to share and own the vision, to become over time more visible as champions, and to come to grips collectively with the task of managing today's business while also managing the change to position tomorrow's business. In addition to the executive team, leadership can be expanded through the development and involvement of senior management and by efforts to develop leadership throughout the organization.[12]

The first seven principles have focused on how to initiate change, how to define the content of change, and the role of leadership. The final three principles have to do with the problem of sustaining change and achieving reorientation over time.

THE PLANNING-AND-OPPORTUNISM PRINCIPLE

Profound organizational reorientation does not occur by accident. Rather, it is the result of intensive planning. On the other hand, it is naive to believe that reorientation in the face of uncertainty can occur by mechanistically executing a detailed operating plan. Successful reorientations

---

[11] See D. A. Nadler and M. L. Tushman, *Beyond the Charismatic Leader: Leadership and Organizational Change* (New York: Delta Consulting Group, 1987); and Tichy and Devanna, 1986.

[12] D. A. Nadler and M. L. Tushman, *Managing Strategic Organizational Change* (New York: Delta Consulting Group, 1986); and Nadler and Tushman, 1987.

involve a mix of planning and unplanned opportunistic action.

The argument for planning flows naturally out of many of the principles that have already been articulated. Diagnosis, the development of vision, the creation of energy, and the crafting of the content of the change all require in-depth thinking and planning. The system's nature and complexity of organizations also require that significant changes with multiple components be sequenced and linked together. A number of successful reorientations have involved six months to two years of planning prior to any public action.

At the same time, there is a valid argument for the inherent limitations of planning. By definition, reorientations involve planning in the face of uncertainty. The architect of change does not know for sure what will occur environmentally in the future. Typically, unforeseen events—both positive and negative—will occur and have a profound impact on the reorientation. Some of these events are themselves consequences of the reorientation efforts—products of its success or failure at different stages. Each event may present an opportunity; to ignore them because "they are not in the plan" would be foolish.

As a consequence, effective reorientations seem to be guided by a process of iterative planning; that is, the plans are revised frequently as new events and opportunities present themselves. This reflects the fact that planned organizational change involves a good deal of learning and that this learning can and should shape the development of the vision and reorientation itself. Thus the planned sequence of activity is balanced with what might be called *bounded opportunism.* However, it does not make sense nor is it effective to respond to every problem, event, or opportunity. Some potential courses of action may simply be inconsistent with the intent of the change or may drain energy from the core effort. It is within certain boundaries, then, that the effective architect of reorientation is opportunistic and modifies plans over time.[13]

THE MANY-BULLETS PRINCIPLE

The nature of organizational stability and resistance to change was discussed earlier. It clearly has implications for initiating change, but it also has ramifications for achieving change.

Organizations are typically resistant to change. Changes in one component of a system that do not "fit" are frequently isolated and stamped out, much as the human body fights a foreign organism. In these cases, the forces for congruence are forces that work for stability. Similarly, individual behavior in organizations is frequently overdetermined. If an individual's patterns of activity were examined, one would see that there are multiple forces shaping it— for example, the design of the work, the activities of supervisors, the immediate social system, the rewards, the organizational structure, the selection system that attracted and chose the individual, and the physical setting. Indeed, there are frequently more factors reinforcing a pattern of behavior than are necessary. As a result, changing those patterns will require more than a modification of a single element of the environment.

Effective reorientations recognize the intractability of organizational and individual behavior and thus make use of many "bullets"—as many different devices to change behavior as possible, incorporating intentionally redundant activities. They thus involve planned changes in strategy,

[13] See Quinn, 1980; and Tushman et al., 1986.

the definition of work, structure, informal process, and individual skills—along with attitudes and perceptions.

In effective reorientations, managers use all available points of leverage to bring about change. Underlying the Many-Bullets Principle is the assumption that the organization ultimately must come to grips with the need to adjust its infrastructure to be consistent with, and supportive of, the change. As all the other work is being done, there is the less glamorous but still critical work of building the structures to enable and reinforce the changes. This is tough, detailed, and sometimes tedious work, but it is crucial. Things that need to be addressed include:

- Standards and measures of performance.

- Rewards and incentives.

- Planning processes.

- Budgeting and resource allocation methods.

- Information systems.

The problem here is one of timing. The work cannot get too far ahead of the change, yet it cannot lag too far behind. Successful managers make skillful use of these levers to support and in some cases drive the change over time.[14]

THE INVESTMENT-AND-RETURNS PRINCIPLE

The final principle concerns the amount of effort and resources that are required to achieve a truly effective reorientation as well as the long time span that is usually required to realize the results of those efforts. There

---

[14] See Nadler and Tushman, 1987; and Pennings and associates, 1987.

---

are two sub-points to this principle—one concerning investments (the *no-free-lunch* hypothesis) and one concerning returns (the *check-is-in-the-mail* hypothesis).

The No-Free-Lunch Hypothesis

Large-scale, significant organizational change requires significant investment of time, effort, and money. While change may yield significant positive results, it is not without its costs.

Successful changes are characterized by a willingness on the part of the changers to invest significant resources. The most scarce resource appears to be senior management time. Organizations engaging in large-scale change find it necessary to get senior managers involved in a range of activities—senior team meetings, presentations, attendance at special events, education, and training—all of which are necessary to perform the functions of leadership in the change. This broadening of ownership also requires a significant investment of time, particularly of the senior team. Less successful changes often prove to be those in which the investments of time were delayed or avoided because senior managers felt so overloaded with change activity that they could not do their work. In successful reorientations, senior managers saw change as an integral part of their work.

The dilemma here is that while the senior team's investment of time is essential, it may also cut into time that the team needs to spend being leaders for the rest of the organization. This could lead to charges that the senior team is too insular, too absorbed in its own process. The challenge is to manage the balance of these two demands.

The Check-Is-in-the-Mail Hypothesis

Organizational reorientation takes time. In particular, as the complexity of the organization increases, so does the time required for change. Each level of the organization engaged in the change takes its own time to understand, accept, integrate, and subsequently own and lead change. In many changes, it becomes important to sell and resell the change throughout many levels of the organization. Each level has to go through its own process of comprehending the change and coming to terms with it.

Organizations go through predictable states as they deal with a change and a set of themes:

- *Awareness.* People within the organization first become aware of the need to change and the dimensions of the change. They work to come to grips with this need and to understand what the change is all about.

- *Experimentation.* Small-scale efforts are made to experiment with the changes in a bounded and manageable setting. Efforts are made to see whether the change will really work in "our unique setting."

- *Understanding.* The experimentation leads to increased understanding of the change, its consequences and implications. At this point, employees begin to realize the scope of the change and what it may involve.

- *Commitment.* The leadership faces up to the decisions to change and makes a significant and visible commitment to take action.

- *Education.* Employees spend time acquiring the skills and information needed to implement the change. This may involve training or other transfers of skills.

- *Application to leveraged issues.* The new approach, perspective, and skills are applied to key issues or specific situations where there is leverage. This

is done consciously, and even a bit awkwardly.

- *Integration into ongoing behavior.* The new changed behavior starts to become a way of life. Employees naturally (and unconsciously) are working in new ways.

Obviously, a change rarely follows the steps exactly as described above. Moreover, different levels of the organization may go through the stages at their own pace. But at some time, each part of the organization must come to grips with each of these issues in some way.

As a result, experience indicates that large-scale reorientations generally take from three to seven years in complex organizations. The efforts may entail false starts, derailments, and the necessity to start over in some places. In addition, significant payoffs may not be seen for at least two years. Again, there is a dilemma. People need to be persuaded to invest personally in the change before there is any evidence that it will pay off, either for the organization or for them personally. Their motivation is essential to success, but proven success is essential to their motivation. The challenge is to demonstrate (through experiments, personal example, or through "face validity") that the change will ultimately pay off.[15]

CONCLUSION

This article has focused on the factors that characterize the most successful attempts at frame bending—large-scale, long-term organizational reorientation. But it would be a mistake to conclude without commenting on the very important, critical, and central aspects of organizational life and how these affect change.

[15] See Quinn, 1980; Quinn and Cameron, 1988; and Tichy and Devanna, 1986.

Two elements are tightly intertwined with the implementation of organizational change—*power politics* and *pathology*. All organizations are political systems, and changes occur within the context of both individual and group aspirations. Thus, strategic changes become enmeshed in issues that are ideological ("What type of company should we be?") as well as issues that are personal ("What's going to be the impact on my career?"). These are not aberrations; they are a normal part of organizational life. However, they will be magnified by and indeed may "play themselves out" through the change. It is difficult to provide general guidance for dealing with this, since the issues vary greatly. However, the successful change manager works at understanding these dynamics, predicting their impact on the change and vice versa, and shaping the situation to make constructive use of them.[16]

[16] See Kets de Vries and Miller, 1984; and Tichy and Devanna, 1986.

Not all organizational life is adaptive. Organizations, like people, have their dark sides—their destructive or maladaptive responses to situations. Organizations develop stylized responses to problems and situations. These responses may be elicited by the intensity of a strategic change. An organization that engages in collective despair may become more despairing. Again, it is the leader who must understand the organizational pathology and confront it.

We have attempted here to share some initial views on a particular subset of organizational change: reorientations. Our belief is that reorientations are a particularly significant kind of change. While reorientations require sustained senior management attention, they are more likely to succeed than re-creations.

More and more organizations face the need for such change as competitive pressures increase. This article is a further step in trying to understand this need and to provide guidance to those who are called upon to lead these organizations.

Case

Leading Culture Change at Seagram

Edgar Bronfman, Jr., president and CEO of Joseph E. Seagram Sons, Inc., told 200 senior managers in February 1995 that his vision for Seagram was to be the "best managed beverage company."

> I have a vision and a belief that we will be best managed. We will be focused on growth; we will be fast and flexible,

Source: This case was prepared by The Center for Executive Development, 1996, with permission of Seagram.

customer and consumer oriented. We will honor and reward teamwork; we will lead, not control. We will be willing to learn. We will develop, train and motivate our people. We will be honest with ourselves and each other. We will manage based on the values we articulate and share.

Bronfman's statement was made in the midst of major change and transformation at Seagram. The company was attempting to increase profits through global expansion, reengineering, and diversification. Seagram recognized, however, that it could not ultimately succeed without changing its culture and work processes. The key to this was the creation of "Seagram Values" later that year. Despite initial skepticism by many employees that this was nothing more than the "flavor of the month," Bronfman was determined to prove that values "will not go away" and those who live the values "will be rewarded."

Indeed, throughout the following years, the values played an increasingly central role in implementing and shaping Seagram's priorities and new culture. It was to be a distinct shift away from a once proud and successful culture based on individualism, entrepreneurship, authority, functional pride, and personal relationships. These characteristics, however, were considered to be no longer effective. Instead, the new culture was heralded with values such as teamwork, innovation, and customer focus.

Having codified the values and begun to communicate them corporate-wide, Seagram's leaders faced a series of challenges to ensure that the new culture would be implemented, and sustained: How would people be rewarded for values-based behavior? How would the evaluation process be conducted? Who should be trained in values? And overall, how would values be institutionalized into everyday behavior?

REINVENTING SEAGRAM

NEW BUSINESS AND PERFORMANCE CHALLENGES

The Seagram Company, founded in 1924 with a single distillery in Canada, had been a major player in the beverage industry for more than 70 years. Seagram developed a loyal consumer following with premier products and premier brands such as Crown Royal, Chivas Regal, Glenlivet, and Mum Champagne. Primarily operating in North America and Europe, Seagram successfully positioned itself in these growth markets for decades. It grew to 14,000 employees.

Over the years, Seagram had a history of diversification outside of its core businesses. For example in the 1960s and 1970s, it owned a major oil company, and in 1982, Seagram purchased 25 percent of DuPont. By the late 1980s, with Seagram's markets maturing, Seagram began to diversify again. In 1988 it acquired both Martell S.A. (cognac) and Tropicana Products (fruit juice and juice beverages). These were the first of many steps taken in recognition of the maturing and eroding of Seagram's core markets.

Indeed, by 1992 the operating income growth of Seagram's core spirits and wine business had stalled. The entire $16 billion industry faced harsh new realities: the "new sobriety" of the 1990s, increased taxes on liquor, the early 1990s recession, increased government regulation, and social criticism of spirits marketing. Liquor sales spiraled down, and it was predicted that the decline would continue for several years.

Bronfman and the Seagram executives recognized the need for strategic repositioning and a redefinition of the company's competitive advantage. Bronfman declared over and over that Seagram would "not be able to achieve business results with business as usual." Thus Seagram:

• Expanded its spirits business into China and other countries in Asia Pacific. (Indeed the acquisition of Martell had opened the Asian market for Seagram.)

• Acquired the global fruit juice business from Dole Food Company, Inc.

- Redeemed 156 million of its DuPont shares for $8.8 billion.

- Purchased 80 percent of the entertainment company MCA Inc. (including Universal Studios and theme parks) from Matsushita Electric Industrial Co., Ltd., for $5.7 billion (adding 15,000 employees).

Seagram's success for the late 1990s and beyond would derive from this very different portfolio of businesses and a far more global enterprise. And its young, vibrant, and visionary CEO had visibly taken significant risks and made major new bets for the company. To succeed would require aggressive development of their brands, products, and people to exploit their new businesses and improve old ones. But as the plans for reinventing Seagram were fashioned, it became more and more clear that Seagram had to change every aspect of the way it was managed. Indeed, it was then that Bronfman set the goal of being the "best-managed" company, and a growth goal of 15 percent per year—both highly aggressive targets.

REENGINEERING THE COMPANY

Toward that end, Seagram began a major reengineering effort in 1994. The goal was not only to more effectively manage Seagram's business processes and reduce costs, but also to identify future growth opportunities. The reengineering task involved hundreds of employees throughout Seagram, organized into teams to redesign and streamline key business processes such as: Business Planning, Management Information Systems (MIS), Finance, Customer Fulfillment, Marketing, and Manufacturing. A top priority of these teams was to find out what customers wanted and how to bring growth back to Seagram.

Under the leadership of senior executives, this effort quickly engulfed the energies of people across the company. With a mix of enthusiasm and trepidation, the business processes were subjected to careful scrutiny and a wide variety of efficiencies and cost savings were identified. In addition, by examining the best practices of other companies and determining the true needs of their customers, Seagram began to break out of its internally directed culture. After six to nine months of self-examination, the opportunities for improvement were huge.

Yet, there was also increasing recognition that significant barriers to progress existed. The new processes required numerous changes in how people behaved and interacted with each other—indeed, a new culture. Seagram would have to unlearn its old culture typified by silos, risk aversion, hierarchy, and limited communication. And it would have to learn how to be more innovative, cooperative, communicative, and customer-focused.

VALUES—THE MISSING LINK

Bronfman personally articulated that processes would only change if behavior changed—and to change behavior required a new set of underlying values. He was convinced that "living the values would allow them to behave in ways that *were* new and better at Seagram." And as he told one group of managers,

Performance is not "fine" right now; otherwise we would already be growing 15 percent a year. If we were doing fine and living the values, there wouldn't be the level of frustration there is at Seagram. . . . Values drive behavior,

behavior drives our processes, and our processes will drive results.

Bronfman personally drafted ten governing values to present to his top 200 managers for discussion, debate, and revision at a management meeting in February 1995. This began a nine-month process of creating the corporate values. Supported by the Center for Executive Development (CED), Seagram engaged in an intensive top-down and bottom-up process to reach agreement on the right wording and the right implementation.

Thus, the output of the management conference was refined and redrafted by the top 15 executives. This in turn was reviewed and critiqued by over 300 employees through eight- to ten-person focus groups. These employees represented a vertical cross-section of the entire company—all businesses, all functions, all levels were represented. Moreover, they represented a cross-cultural mix of nationalities from Asia, Europe, North America, and South America. Indeed, important variations in interpretation were found across different cultures, and new wording was developed to minimize culturally unclear or irrelevant concepts. Some individuals did feel, however, that a corporation did not have the right to set values for people to believe in.

Not only were the employees asked to give feedback on the values draft, but also to identify behavioral examples of the values in action, and to make suggestions about how to introduce and communicate the values. The employee version was much simpler, shorter, and easier to understand by all levels and all cultural backgrounds. These inputs were then fed back to the top executives who once again redrafted the values.

With this draft, the company appeared ready to finalize the values: Consumer & Customer Focus, Respect, Integrity, Teamwork, Innovation, and Quality (see Exhibit 1 for values definitions). Along with the values, there also was a summary of "Values in Action," a checklist of behavioral examples for living the values (see Exhibit 2). There was a strong view that the values had to be measurable in order to be enacted.

INTRODUCING THE VALUES

A plan was developed to introduce the values to Seagram's beverage company (MCA/Universal would enter the values process later) which included: (1) a personalized communication cascade, (2) a 360-degree feedback process for the senior executives, and (3) a training program for equipping the top 1,200 managers.

When it came to communicating the values, focus group participants had sent a strong message that "this should not be just another program of the month. No hype, no t-shirts, no hats, and no video conference with Bronfman announcing the values to the whole company." In the spirit of the values, Seagram senior management heeded the advice of their "customers" (i.e., their employees) and decided to try a new technique—a cascade of personal communication meetings. Each manager met with his or her direct reports to discuss the values and what it meant to live them in their specific business environment. The communication plan was led by Bronfman, who held a two-hour meeting with his direct reports to discuss the values. Next, the top 15 executives met with their direct reports who, in turn, met with their direct reports, and so on, to discuss the values, until all employees at Seagram had participated in a "cascade" meeting.

EXHIBIT 1

The Seagram Values

As Seagram Employees We Commit to the Following Values:

Consumer and customer focus:

Everything we do is dedicated to the satisfaction of present and future consumers and customers.

Respect:

We treat everyone with dignity, and we value different backgrounds, cultures, and viewpoints.

Integrity:

We are honest, consistent and professional in every aspect of our behavior.

We communicate openly and directly.

Teamwork:

We work and communicate across functions, levels, geographies, and business units to build our global Seagram family.

We are each accountable for our behavior and performance.

Innovation:

We challenge ourselves by embracing innovation and creativity, not only in our brands, but also in all aspects of our work.

We learn from both our successes and failures.

Quality:

We deliver the quality and craftsmanship that our consumers and customers demand—in all we do—with our products, our services and our people.

By living these values:

We will achieve our growth objectives, and we will make Seagram the company preferred by consumers, customers, employees, shareholders, and communities.

EXHIBIT 2

Seagram Values in Action

Consumer and customer focus	☑ We demonstrate through our actions that consumers and customers have top priority in our daily work. ☑ We treat each person we deal with as a customer. ☑ We work continually to understand our consumer and customer's requirements and anticipate future needs.
Respect	☑ We seek ideas and contributions from people, regardless of their level. ☑ We have a climate where issues are openly discussed and resolved. ☑ We have a balance between our professional and private commitments.
Integrity	☑ We deliver what we promise. ☑ We disclose facts even when the news is bad. ☑ We make decisions based on what's best for the company, rather than personal gain.
Teamwork	☑ We share across borders, across affiliates and across functions to learn from one another. ☑ We work together to achieve consistent, shared goals. ☑ We consider the impact our activities have on other areas of Seagram.
Innovation	☑ We create an atmosphere where continuous improvement and creative thinking are encouraged. ☑ We look for new ways to remove layers of bureaucracy to enable speed and action. ☑ We have patience with new ventures and recognize there will be failures.
Quality	☑ We produce results that consistently meet or exceed the standards of performance our consumers and customers expect. ☑ We consistently improve our processes to better serve our customers. ☑ We get the job done accurately and on time.

Second, focus group participants had also said, "people are waiting to see if management is really serious about living the new values themselves." As a result, a 360-degree feedback tool based on the six values was developed. The survey questions were directly derived by asking focus group participants to identify key behaviors required for living the values (see Exhibit 3 for a sample page). Historically, Seagram managers provided little feedback except through an annual top-down review. Given their lack of experience and lack of trust, the 360-degree process was carefully implemented, using the help of professional coaches; a third-party data processor; and clearly defined developmental, not evaluative, purposes. Initially, Bronfman himself and the top 15 executives participated in the 360-degree feedback process. Next, the top 200 senior managers were evaluated and personally coached during the training program. Each manager was encouraged to share the findings with those who gave them feedback and develop an action plan for improvement in modeling the values.

Finally, the third ingredient for introducing the values was training. To this end, Seagram, assisted by CED, designed two values training programs: "Leading With Values" and "The Seagram Challenge." The first program targeted Seagram's top 200, while the second program was designed for approximately 1,000 middle managers. The two programs focused on the six values, best practice applications in other companies, and how to live the values at Seagram on a daily basis. Each program included mini-case studies of Seagram situations in which the values were put to a test. Participants were encouraged to develop personal action plans and recommendations for the company.

DEEPENING THE NEW CULTURE

Together, these three steps helped to launch Seagram's culture change. After the values were created, Seagram executives faced numerous issues in ensuring that the values would indeed be reinforced and institutionalized. These issues were most typically crystallized at the concluding day of each values training program. On these Fridays, participants spent a full morning in dialogue with one or two senior Seagram leaders. The common themes of the Friday sessions—and the challenges for senior management to resolve—are summarized below:

1. "WHAT SHOULD BE DONE WITH THE VARIOUS RECOMMENDATIONS FOR ACTION RAISED BY PARTICIPANTS IN THE PROGRAMS?"

At the close of each training program, participants presented recommendations for action to a senior executive. However, there was no clear mechanism for implementation and follow-up. Participants could take some actions, while others required senior management support. Participants often wondered aloud, "What will be done with all these good ideas?"

2. "ARE WE GOING TO PUNISH THE VALUES VIOLATORS?"

If management was serious about the values, many argued, the values "violators" should be demoted or fired. Many pointed to a dramatic diagram that Bronfman often referenced—a 2 × 2 portraying

EXHIBIT 3   Sample 360-degree Feedback Report

Value Total	**Total**	**4.14**
	Supervisor	4.57
	Peers	3.96
	Direct Reports	4.21
	Self	4.71
6. This executive is approachable and friendly.	**Total**	**4.67**
	Supervisor	5
	Peers	4.75
	Direct Reports	4.5
	Self	5
1. This executive seeks ideas from people regardless of their level in the organization.	**Total**	**4.44**
	Supervisor	4
	Peers	4.5
	Direct Reports	4.5
	Self	4
3. This executive is careful to consider another person's idea before accepting or rejecting it.	**Total**	**4.11**
	Supervisor	4
	Peers	4.5
	Direct Reports	4.5
	Self	4
4. This executive explains issues and answers questions when communicating.	**Total**	**4.11**
	Supervisor	4
	Peers	3.75
	Direct Reports	4.5
	Self	5
5. This executive treats people fairly when they make a mistake.	**Total**	**4.11**
	Supervisor	5
	Peers	3.75
	Direct Reports	4.25
	Self	5
2. This executive supports people in their efforts to balance professional time with their private lives.	**Total**	**3.78**
	Supervisor	5
	Peers	3.75
	Direct Reports	3.5
	Self	5
7. This executive provides periodic feedback to tell others where they stand in terms of performance.	**Total**	**3.78**
	Supervisor	5
	Peers	3.5
	Direct Reports	3.75
	Self	4

EXHIBIT 4

The Personal Consequences Were Made Very Clear

SUCCESS AND HOW WE ACHIEVE IT

	Inappropriate Values	Appropriate Values
Make the Numbers	Type I Former Heroes	Type II New Heroes
Miss the Numbers	Type IV Newly Unemployed Executives	Type III Potential Heroes

How Results Are Obtained

values (high versus low) on one axis and results (high versus low) on the other (see Exhibit 4). It labeled those who violated the values while still getting good results as "former heroes." But, many asked, wouldn't punishing such people violate the value of "respect"? And how much time should people be afforded to change? Some wanted the 360-degree process to move from developmental to evaluative purposes so that low scorers would be "penalized" in their annual reviews.

3. "HOW WILL WE RECOGNIZE AND REWARD THE VALUES CHAMPIONS?"

Managers often stated that people who behaved consistently in line with the values should be recognized and rewarded. Some argued that those who "lived" the values should be given financial bonuses and/or recognition. But others said that people should not be paid *extra* to live the values—it was expected of everyone. In any case, participants pointed to the performance management and incentive system and looked for changes.

4. "WHAT SHOULD BE DONE WITH THE NEW EMPLOYEES (15,000) WHO HAVE BEEN ACQUIRED FROM MCA/UNIVERSAL?"

With the values having been created and the training conducted with Seagram's managers, the question increasingly arose as to how to integrate the new employees acquired from MCA/Universal. Some argued that they were a totally different company and culture, and should develop their own values. Some felt that having been acquired, they should be expected to subscribe to the values developed by the parent. Still others said that this was not a high-priority issue.

5. "HOW DO WE SUSTAIN THE MOMENTUM AND ATTENTION ON VALUES?" AND "WHAT SHOULD BE DONE TO INSTITUTIONALIZE THE VALUES DEEPER AND WIDER ACROSS SEAGRAM?"

By the Friday session when enthusiasm reached its peak, participants searched for ways to sustain the interest. They asked about (a) training that extended beyond the top 1,200 to the 15,000, (b) opportunities for "alumni" gatherings, and (c) communication support to keep the spotlight on values. No clear plans for any of these were set.

LEADERSHIP RESPONSE

The next phase of the Seagram culture change journey was beginning. And there was a full plate of challenges—and no shortage of opinions about what should be done. It was time to set out the next steps.

Reading

Why Change Programs Don't Produce Change

Michael Beer

Russell A. Eisenstat

Bert Spector

In the mid-1980s, the new CEO of a major international bank—call it U.S. Financial—announced a companywide change effort. Deregulation was posing serious competitive challenges—challenges to which the bank's traditional hierarchical organization was ill suited to respond. The only solution was to change fundamentally how the company operated. And the place to begin was at the top.

The CEO held a retreat with his top 15 executives, where they painstakingly reviewed the bank's purpose and culture. He published a mission statement and hired a new vice president for human resources from a company well known for its excellence in managing people.

And in a quick succession of moves, he established companywide programs to push change down through the organization: a new organizational structure, a performance appraisal system, a pay-for-performance compensation plan, training programs to turn managers into "change agents," and quarterly attitude surveys to chart the progress of the change effort.

As much as these steps sound like a textbook case in organizational transformation, there was one big problem. Two years after the CEO launched the change program, virtually nothing in the way of actual changes in organizational behavior had occurred. What had gone wrong?

The answer is "everything." Every one of the assumptions the CEO made—about who should lead the change effort, what needed changing, and how to go about doing it—was wrong. U.S. Financial's story reflects a common problem. Faced with changing markets and increased competition, more and more companies are struggling to reestablish their dominance; regain market share; and, in some cases, ensure their survival. Many have come to understand that the key to competitive success is to transform the way they function. They are reducing reliance on managerial authority, formal rules and procedures, and narrow divisions of work. And they are creating teams, sharing information, and delegating responsibility and accountability far down the hierarchy. In effect, companies are moving from the hierarchical and bureaucratic model of organization that has characterized corporations since World War II to what we call the "task-driven organization," where what has to be done governs who works with whom and who leads.

But while senior managers understand the necessity of change to cope with new competitive realities, they often misunderstand what it takes to bring it about. They tend to share two assumptions with the CEO of U.S. Financial: that promulgating companywide programs—mission statements, "corporate culture" programs, training courses, quality circles, and new pay-for-performance systems—will transform organizations, and that employee behavior is changed by altering a company's formal structure and systems.

In a four-year study of organizational change at six large corporations (see Exhibit 1, "Tracking Corporate Change"; the names are fictitious), we found that exactly the opposite is true: The greatest obstacle to revitalization is the idea that it comes about through companywide change programs, particularly when a corporate staff group, such as human resources, sponsors them. We call this "the fallacy of programmatic change." Just as important, formal organization structure and systems cannot lead a corporate renewal process.

While in some companies, wave after wave of programs rolled across the landscape with little positive impact, in others, more successful transformations did take place. They usually started at the periphery of the corporation in a few plants and divisions far from corporate headquarters. And they were led by the general managers of those units, not by the CEO or corporate staff people.

The general managers did not focus on formal structures and systems; they created ad hoc organizational arrangements to solve concrete business problems. By aligning employee roles, responsibilities, and relationships to address the organization's most important competitive task—a process we call "task alignment"—they focused energy for change on the work itself, not on abstractions such as "participation" or "culture." Unlike the CEO at U.S. Financial, they didn't employ massive training programs or rely on speeches and mission statements. Instead, we say that general managers carefully developed the change process through a sequence of six basic managerial interventions.

Once general managers understand the logic of this sequence, they don't have to wait for senior management to start a process of organizational revitalization. There is a lot they can do even without support from the top. Of course, having a CEO or other senior managers who are committed to change does make a difference—and when it comes to changing an entire organization, such support is essential. But top management's role in the change process is very different from that which the CEO played at U.S. Financial.

Grass-roots change presents senior managers with a paradox: directing a "nondirective" change process. The most effective senior managers in our study recognized their limited power to mandate

EXHIBIT 1 Tracking Corporate Change

Which strategies for corporate change work, and which do not? We sought the answers in a comprehensive study of 12 large companies where top management was attempting to revitalize the corporation. Based on preliminary research, we identified six for in-depth analysis: five manufacturing companies and one large international bank. All had revenues between $4 billion and $10 billion. We studied 26 plants and divisions in these six companies and conducted hundreds of interviews with human resource managers; line managers engaged in change efforts at plants, branches, or business units; workers and union leaders; and, finally, top management.

Based on this material, we ranked the six companies according to the success with which they had managed the revitalization effort. Were there significant improvements in interfunctional coordination, decision making, work organization, and concern for people? Research has shown that, in the long term, the quality of these four factors will influence performance. We did not define success in terms of improved financial performance because, in the short run, corporate financial performance is influenced by many situational factors unrelated to the change process.

To corroborate our rankings of the companies, we also administered a standardized questionnaire in each company to understand how employees viewed the unfolding change process. Respondents rated their companies on a scale of 1 to 5. A score of 3 meant that no change had taken place; a score below 3 meant that, in the employee's judgment, the organization had actually gotten worse. As the table suggests, with one exception—the company we call Livingston Electronics—employees' perceptions of how much their companies had changed were identical to ours. And Livingston's relatively high standard deviation (which measures the degree of consensus among employees about the outcome of the change effort) indicates that within the company there was considerable disagreement as to just how successful revitalization had been.

Researchers and Employees—Similar Conclusions

	Extent of Revitalization		
	Ranked by Researchers	**Ranked by Employees**	
Company		**Average**	**Standard Deviation**
General Products	1	4.04	0.35
Fairweather	2	3.58	0.45
Livingston Electronics	3	3.61	0.76
Scranton Steel	4	3.30	0.65
Continental Steel	5	2.96	0.83
U.S. Financial	6	2.78	1.07

corporate renewal from the top. Instead, they defined their roles as creating a climate for change, then spreading the lessons of both successes and failures. Put another way, they specified the general direction in which the company should move without insisting on specific solutions.

In the early phases of a companywide change process, any senior manager can play this role. Once grass-roots change reaches a critical mass, however, the CEO has to be ready to transform his or her own work unit as well—the top team composed of key business heads and corporate staff heads. At this point, the company's structure and systems must be put into alignment with the new management practices that have developed at the periphery. Otherwise, the tension between dynamic units and static top management will cause the change process to break down.

We believe that an approach to change based on task alignment, starting at the periphery and moving steadily toward the corporate core, is the most effective way to achieve enduring organizational change. This is not to say that change can *never* start at the top, but it is uncommon and too risky as a deliberate strategy. Change is about learning. It is a rare CEO who knows in advance the fine-grained details of organizational change that the many diverse units of a large corporation demand. Moreover, most of today's senior executives developed in an era in which top-down hierarchy was the primary means for organizing and managing. They must learn from innovative approaches coming from younger unit managers closer to the action.

THE FALLACY OF PROGRAMMATIC CHANGE

Most change programs don't work because they are guided by a theory of change that is fundamentally flawed. The common belief is that the place to begin is with the knowledge and attitudes of individuals. Changes in attitudes, the theory goes, lead to changes in individual behavior. And changes in individual behavior, repeated by many people, will result in

organizational change. According to this model, change is like a conversion experience. Once people "get religion," changes in their behavior will surely follow.

This theory gets the change process exactly backward. In fact, individual behavior is powerfully shaped by the organizational roles that people play. The most effective way to change behavior, therefore, is to put people into a new organizational context, which imposes new roles, responsibilities, and relationships on them. This creates a situation that, in a sense, "forces" new attitudes and behaviors on people. (See Exhibit 2, "Contrasting Assumptions about Change.")

One way to think about this challenge is in terms of three interrelated factors required for corporate revitalization. *Coordination* or teamwork is especially important if an organization is to discover and act on cost, quality, and product development opportunities. The production and sale of innovative, high-quality, low-cost products (or services) depend on close coordination among marketing, product design, and manufacturing departments, as well as between labor and management. High levels of *commitment* are essential for the effort, initiative, and cooperation that coordinated action demands. New *competencies,* such as knowledge of the business as a whole, analytical skills, and interpersonal skills, are necessary if people are to identify and solve problems as a team. If any of these elements is missing, the change process will break down.

The problem with most companywide change programs is that they address only one or, at best, two of these factors. Just because a company issues a philosophy statement about teamwork doesn't mean its employees necessarily know what teams to form or how to function within them to improve coordination. A corporate

EXHIBIT 2 Contrasting Assumptions about Change

Programmatic Change	Task Alignment
Problems in behavior are a function of individual knowledge, attitudes, and beliefs.	Individual knowledge, attitudes, and beliefs are shaped by recurring patterns of behavioral interactions.
The primary target of renewal should be the content of attitudes and ideas; actual behavior should be secondary.	The primary target of renewal should be behavior; attitudes and ideas should be secondary.
Behavior can be isolated and changed individually.	Problems in behavior come from a circular pattern, but the effects of the organizational system on the individual are greater than those of the individual on the system.
The target for renewal should be at the individual level.	The target for renewal should be at the level of roles, responsibilities, and relationships.

reorganization may change the boxes on a formal organization chart but not provide the necessary attitudes and skills to make the new structure work. A pay-for-performance system may force managers to differentiate better performers from poorer ones, but it doesn't help them internalize new standards by which to judge subordinates' performances. Nor does it teach them how to deal effectively with performance problems. Such programs cannot provide the cultural context (role models from whom to learn) that people need to develop new competencies, so ultimately they fail to create organizational change.

Similarly, training programs may target competence, but rarely do they change a company's patterns of coordination. Indeed, the excitement engendered in a good corporate training program frequently leads to increased frustration when employees get back on the job only to see their new skills go unused in an organization in which nothing else has changed. People end up seeing training as a waste of time, which undermines whatever

commitment to change a program may have roused in the first place.

When one program doesn't work, senior managers, like the CEO at U.S. Financial, often try another, instituting a rapid progression of programs. But this only exacerbates the problem. Because they are designed to cover everyone and everything, programs end up covering nobody and nothing particularly well. They are so general and standardized that they don't speak to the day-to-day realities of particular units. Buzzwords like "quality," "participation," "excellence," "empowerment," and "leadership" become a substitute for a detailed understanding of the business.

All these change programs also undermine the credibility of the change effort. Even when managers accept the potential value of a particular program for others— quality circles, for example, to solve a manufacturing problem—they may be confronted with another, more pressing business problem, such as new product development. One-size-fits-all change programs take energy *away* from efforts to solve key business problems—which explains why so many general managers don't support programs, even when they acknowledge that their underlying principles may be useful.

This is not to state that training, changes in pay systems or organizational structure, or a new corporate philosophy are always inappropriate. All can play valuable roles in supporting an integrated change effort. The problems come when such programs are used in isolation as a kind of "magic bullet" to spread organizational change rapidly through the entire corporation. At their best, change programs of this sort are irrelevant. At their worst, they actually inhibit change. By promoting skepticism and cynicism, programmatic change can inoculate companies against the real thing.

SIX STEPS TO EFFECTIVE CHANGE

Companies avoid the shortcomings of programmatic change by concentrating on "task alignment"—reorganizing employee roles, responsibilities, and relationships to solve specific business problems. Task alignment is easiest in small units—a plant, department, or business unit—where goals and tasks are clearly defined. Thus, the chief problem for corporate change is how to promote task-aligned change across many diverse units.

We saw that general managers at the business unit or plant level can achieve task alignment through a sequence of six overlapping but distinctive steps, which we call the *critical path*. This path develops a self-reinforcing cycle of commitment, coordination, and competence. The sequence of steps is important because activities appropriate at one time are often

counterproductive if started too early. Timing is everything in the management of change.

1. *Mobilize commitment to change through joint diagnosis of business problems.* As the term *task alignment* suggests, the starting point of any effective change effort is a clearly defined business problem. By helping people develop a shared diagnosis of what is wrong in an organization and what can and must be improved, a general manager mobilizes the initial commitment that is necessary to begin the change process.

Consider the case of a division we call Navigation Devices, a business unit of about 600 people set up by a large corporation to commercialize a product originally designed for the military market. When the new general manager took over, the division had been in operation for several years without ever making a profit. It had never been able to design and produce a high-quality, cost-competitive product. This was due largely to an organization in which decisions were made at the top, without proper involvement of or coordination with other functions.

The first step the new general manager took was to initiate a broad review of the business. Where the previous general manager had set strategy with the unit's marketing director alone, the new general manager included his entire management team. He also brought in outside consultants to help him and his managers function more effectively as a group.

Next, he formed a 20-person task force representing all the stakeholders in the organization—managers, engineers, production workers, and union officials. The group visited a number of successful manufacturing organizations in an attempt to identify what Navigation Devices might do to organize more effectively. One high-performance manufacturing plant in the task force's own company made a particularly strong impression. Not only did it highlight the problems at Navigation Devices, but it also offered an alternative organizational model, based on teams, that captured the group's imagination. Seeing a different way of working helped strengthen the group's commitment to change.

The Navigation Devices task force didn't learn new facts from this process of joint diagnosis; everyone already knew the unit was losing money. But the group came to see clearly the organizational roots of the unit's inability to compete and, even more important, came to share a common understanding of the problem. The group also identified a potential organizational solution: to redesign the way it worked, using ad hoc teams to integrate the organization around the competitive task.

2. *Develop a shared vision of how to organize and manage for competitiveness.* Once a core group of people is committed to a particular analysis of the problem, the general manager can lead employees toward a task-aligned vision of the organization that defines new roles and responsibilities. These new arrangements will coordinate the flow of information and work across interdependent functions at all levels of the organization. But since they do not change formal structures and systems like titles or compensation, they encounter less resistance.

At Navigation Devices, the 20-person task force became the vehicle for this second stage. The group came up with a model of the organization in which cross-functional teams would accomplish all work, particularly new product development. A

business-management team composed of the general manager and his staff would set the unit's strategic direction and review the work of lower-level teams. Business-area teams would develop plans for specific markets. Product-development teams would manage new products from initial design to production. Production-process teams composed of engineers and production workers would identify and solve quality and cost problems in the plant. Finally, engineering-process teams would examine engineering methods and equipment. The teams got to the root of the unit's problems—functional and hierarchical barriers to sharing information and solving problems.

To create a consensus around the new vision, the general manager commissioned a still larger task force of about 90 employees from different levels and functions, including union and management, to refine the vision and obtain everyone's commitment to it. On a retreat away from the workplace, the group further refined the new organizational model and drafted a values statement, which it presented later to the entire Navigation Devices workforce. The vision and the values statement made sense to Navigation Devices employees in a way many corporate mission statements never do—because it grew out of the organization's own analysis of real business problems. And it was built on a model for solving those problems that key stakeholders believed would work.

3. *Foster consensus for the new vision, competence to enact it, and cohesion to move it along.* Simply letting employees help develop a new vision is not enough to overcome resistance to change—or to foster the skills needed to make the new organization work. Not everyone can help in the design, and even those who do participate often

do not fully appreciate what renewal will require until the new organization is actually in place. This is when strong leadership from the general manager is crucial. Commitment to change is always uneven. Some managers are enthusiastic; others are neutral or even antagonistic. At Navigation Devices, the general manager used what his subordinates termed the "velvet glove." He made it clear that the division was going to encourage employee involvement and the team approach. To managers who wanted to help him, he offered support. To those who did not, he offered outplacement and counseling.

Once an organization has defined new roles and responsibilities, people need to develop the competencies to make the new setup work. Actually, the very existence of the teams with their new goals and accountabilities will force learning. The changes in roles, responsibilities, and relationships foster new skills and attitudes. Changed patterns of coordination will also increase employee participation, collaboration, and information sharing.

But management also has to provide the right supports. At Navigation Devices, six resource people—three from the corporate headquarters—worked on the change project. Each team was assigned one internal consultant, who attended every meeting, to help people be effective team members. Once employees could see exactly what kinds of new skills they needed, they asked for formal training programs to develop those skills further. Since these courses grew directly out of the employees' own experiences, they were far more focused and useful than traditional training programs.

Some people, of course, just cannot or will not change, despite all the direction and support in the world. Step 3 is the appropriate time to replace those managers who cannot function in the new organization—after they have had a chance to prove themselves. Such decisions are rarely easy, and sometimes those people who have difficulty working in a participatory organization have extremely valuable specialized skills. Replacing them early in the change process, before they have worked in the new organization, is not only unfair to individuals, it can be demoralizing to the entire organization and can disrupt the change process. People's understanding of what kind of manager and worker the new organization demands grows slowly and only from the experience of seeing some individuals succeed and others fail.

Once employees have bought into a vision of what's necessary and have some understanding of what the new organization requires, they can accept the necessity of replacing or moving people who don't make the transition to the new way of working. Sometimes people are transferred to other parts of the company where technical expertise, rather than the new competencies, is the main requirement. When no alternatives exist, sometimes they leave the company, for example, through early retirement programs. The act of replacing people can actually reinforce the organization's commitment to change by visibly demonstrating the general manager's commitment to the new way.

Some of the managers replaced at Navigation Devices were high up in the organization—for example, the vice president of operations, who oversaw the engineering and manufacturing departments. The new head of manufacturing was far more committed to change and skilled in leading a critical path change process. The result was speedier change throughout the manufacturing function.

4. *Spread revitalization to all departments without pushing it from the top.* With the new ad hoc organization for the unit in place, it is time to turn to the functional and staff departments that must interact with it. Members of teams cannot be effective unless the department from which they come is organized and managed in a way that supports their roles as full-fledged participants in team decisions. What this often means is that these departments will have to rethink their roles and authority in the organization.

At Navigation Devices, this process was seen most clearly in the engineering department. Production department managers were the most enthusiastic about the change effort; engineering managers were more hesitant. Engineering had always been king at Navigation Devices; engineers designed products to the military's specifications without much concern about whether manufacturing could easily build them or not. Once the new team structure was in place, however, engineers had to participate on product-development teams with production workers. This required them to reexamine their roles and rethink their approaches to organizing and managing their own department.

The impulse of many general managers faced with such a situation would be to force the issue—to announce, for example, that now all parts of the organization must manage by teams. The temptation to force newfound insights on the rest of the organization can be great, particularly when rapid change is needed, but it would be the same mistake that senior managers make when they try to push programmatic change throughout a company. It short-circuits the change process.

It's better to let each department "reinvent the wheel"—that is, to find its own way to the new organization. At Navigation Devices, each department was allowed to take the general concepts of co-ordination and teamwork and apply them to its particular situation. Engineering spent nearly a year agonizing over how to implement the team concept. The department conducted two surveys; held off-site meetings; and proposed, rejected, then accepted a matrix management structure before it finally got on board. Engineering's decision to move to matrix management was not surprising; but because the move was the department's own choice, people committed themselves to learning the necessary new skills and attitudes.

5. *Institutionalize revitalization through formal policies, systems, and structures.* There comes a point at which general managers have to consider how to institutionalize change so the process continues even after they've moved on to other responsibilities. Step 5 is the time: The new approach has become entrenched, the right people are in place, and the team organization is up and running. Enacting changes in structures and systems any earlier tends to backfire. Take information systems. Creating a team structure means new information requirements. Why not have the management information systems (MIS) department create new systems that cut across traditional functional and departmental lines early in the change process? The problem is that, without a well-developed understanding of information requirements, which can best be obtained by placing people on task-aligned teams, managers are likely to resist new systems as an imposition by the MIS department. Newly formed teams can often pull together enough information to get their work done without fancy new systems.

It's better to hold off until everyone understands what the team's information needs are.

What's true for information systems is even more true for other formal structures and systems. Any formal system is going to have some disadvantages; none is perfect. These imperfections can be minimized, however, once people have worked in an ad hoc team structure and learned what interdependencies are necessary. Then employees will commit to them, too.

Again, Navigation Devices is a good example. The revitalization of the unit was highly successful. Employees changed how they saw their roles and responsibilities, and became convinced that change could actually make a difference. As a result, there were dramatic improvements in value added per employee, scrap reduction, quality, customer service, gross inventory per employee, and profits. And all this happened with almost no formal changes in reporting relationships, information systems, evaluation procedures, compensation, or control systems.

When the opportunity arose, the general manager eventually did make some changes in the formal organization. For example, when he moved the vice president of operations out of the organization, he eliminated the position altogether. Engineering and manufacturing reported directly to him from that point on. For the most part, however, the changes in performance at Navigation Devices were sustained by the general manager's expectations and the new norms for behavior.

6. *Monitor and adjust strategies in response to problems in the revitalization process.* The purpose of change is to create an asset that did not exist before—a learning organization capable of adapting to a changing competitive environment. The organization has to know how to continually monitor its behavior—in effect, to learn how to learn.

Some might say that this is the general manager's responsibility. But monitoring the change process needs to be shared, just as analyzing the organization's key business problem does.

At Navigation Devices, the general manager introduced several mechanisms to allow key constituents to help monitor the revitalization. An oversight team—composed of some crucial managers, a union leader, a secretary, an engineer, and an analyst from finance—kept continual watch over the process. Regular employee attitude surveys monitored behavior patterns. Planning teams were formed and reformed in response to new challenges. All these mechanisms created a long-term capacity for continual adaptation and learning.

The six-step process provides a way to elicit renewal without imposing it. When stakeholders become committed to a vision, they are willing to accept a new pattern of management—here the ad hoc team structure—that demands changes in their behavior. As the employees discover that the new approach is more effective (which will happen only if the vision aligns with the core task), they have to grapple with personal and organizational changes they might otherwise resist. Finally, as improved coordination helps solve relevant problems, it will reinforce team behavior and produce a desire to learn new skills. This learning enhances effectiveness even further and results in an even stronger commitment to change. This mutually reinforcing cycle of improvements in commitment, coordination, and competence creates a growing sense of efficacy. It can continue as long as the ad hoc team structure is allowed to expand its role in running the business.

THE ROLE OF TOP MANAGEMENT

To change an entire corporation, the change process we have described must be applied over and over again in many plants, branches, departments, and divisions. Orchestrating this companywide change process is the first responsibility of senior management. Doing so successfully requires a delicate balance. Without explicit efforts by top management to promote conditions for change in individual units, only a few plants or divisions will attempt change, and those that do will remain isolated. The best senior manager leaders we studied held their subordinates responsible for starting a change process without specifying a particular approach.

Create a Market for Change

The most effective approach is to set demanding standards for all operations and then hold managers accountable to them. At our best-practice company, which we call General Products, senior managers developed ambitious product and operating standards. General managers unable to meet these product standards by a certain date had to scrap their products and take a sharp hit to their bottom lines. As long as managers understand that high standards are not arbitrary but are dictated by competitive forces, standards can generate enormous pressure for better performance, a key ingredient in mobilizing energy for change.

But merely increasing demands is not enough. Under pressure, most managers will seek to improve business performance by doing more of what they have always done—overmanage—rather than altering the fundamental way they organize. So, while senior managers increase demands, they should also hold managers accountable for fundamental changes in the way they use human resources.

For example, when plant managers at General Products complained about the impossibility of meeting new business standards, senior managers pointed them to the corporate organization-development department within human resources and emphasized that the plant managers would be held accountable for moving revitalization along. Thus, top management had created a demand system for help with the new way of managing, and the human resource staff could support change without appearing to push a program.

Use Successfully Revitalized Units as Organizational Models for the Entire Company

Another important strategy is to focus the company's attention on plants and divisions that have already begun experimenting with management innovations. These units become developmental laboratories for further innovation.

There are two ground rules for identifying such models. First, innovative units need support. They need the best managers to lead them, and they need adequate resources—for instance, skilled human resource people and external consultants. In the most successful companies that we studied, senior managers saw it as their responsibility to make resources available to leading-edge units. They did not leave it to the human resource function.

Second, because resources are always limited and the costs of failure high, it is crucial to identify those units with the likeliest chance of success. Successful management innovations can appear to be failures when the bottom line is devastated by environmental factors beyond the unit's control. The best models are in healthy markets.

Obviously, organizational models can serve as catalysts for change only if others are aware of their existence and are encouraged to learn from them. Many of our worst-practice companies had plants and divisions that were making substantial changes. The problem was, nobody knew about them. Corporate management had never bothered to highlight them as examples to follow. In the leading companies, visits, conferences, and educational programs facilitated learning from model units.

Develop Career Paths that Encourage Leadership Development

Without strong leaders, units cannot make the necessary organizational changes, yet the scarcest resource available for revitalizing corporations is leadership. Corporate renewal depends as much on developing effective change leaders as it does on developing effective organizations. The personal learning associated with leadership development—or the realization by higher management that a manager does not have this capacity—cannot occur in the classroom. It only happens in an organization where the teamwork, high commitment, and new competencies we have discussed are already the norm.

The only way to develop the kind of leaders a changing organization needs is to make leadership an important criterion for promotion, and then manage people's careers to develop it. At our best-practice companies, managers were moved from job to job and from organization to organization based on their learning needs, not on their position in the hierarchy. Successful leaders were assigned to units that had been targeted for change. People who needed to sharpen their leadership skills were moved into the company's model units, where those skills would be demanded and,

therefore, learned. In effect, top management used leading-edge units as hothouses to develop revitalization leaders.

But what about the top management team itself? How important is it for the CEO and his or her direct reports to practice what they preach? It is not surprising—indeed, it's predictable—that, in the early years of a corporate change effort, top managers' actions are often not consistent with their words. Such inconsistencies don't pose a major barrier to corporate change in the beginning, though consistency is obviously desirable. Senior managers can create a climate for grass-roots change without paying much attention to how they themselves operate and manage. And unit managers will tolerate this inconsistency so long as they can freely make changes in their own units in order to compete more effectively.

There comes a point, however, when addressing the inconsistencies becomes crucial. As the change process spreads, general managers in the ever-growing circle of revitalized units eventually demand changes from corporate staff groups and top management. As they discover how to manage differently in their own units, they bump up against constraints of policies and practices that corporate staff and top management have created. They also begin to see opportunities for better coordination between themselves and other parts of the company over which they have little control. At this point, corporate organization must be aligned with corporate strategy, and coordination between related but hitherto independent businesses improved for the benefit of the whole corporation.

None of the companies we studied had reached this "moment of truth." Even when corporate leaders intellectually understood the direction of change, they were just beginning to struggle with how they would change themselves and the company as a whole for a total corporate revitalization.

This last step in the process of corporate renewal is probably the most important. If the CEO and his or her management team do not ultimately apply to themselves what they have been encouraging their general managers, then the whole process can break down. The time to tackle the tough challenge of transforming companywide systems and structures comes finally at the end of the corporate change process.

At this point, senior managers must make an effort to adopt the team behavior, attitudes, and skills that they have demanded of others in earlier phases of change. Their struggle with behavior change will help sustain corporate renewal in three ways. It will promote the attitudes and behavior needed to coordinate diverse activities in the company; it will lend credibility to top management's continued espousal of change; and it will help the CEO identify and develop a successor who is capable of learning the new behaviors. Only such a manager can lead a corporation that can renew itself continually as competitive forces change.

Companies need a particular mindset for managing change: one that emphasizes process over specific content, recognizes organization change as a unit-by-unit learning process, rather than a series of programs, and acknowledges the payoffs that result from persistence over a long time as opposed to quick fixes. This mindset is difficult to maintain in an environment that presses for quarterly earnings, but we believe it is the only approach that will bring about successful renewal.

Simulation

The Merger Plan Simulation

Southern Bank Acquisition
Project File
Private & Confidential
Northern Bank

This document is an entirely fictional work, intended solely for use in an educational context. While some of its content is based on real-life data, such as names of countries and currencies, the authors do not guarantee the accuracy of any of this content and do not intend to convey any opinion whatsoever about the information that may or may not appear to be based on fact. Any similarity between the names of individuals and organisations featuring in the work and those of real-life individuals and organisations is entirely coincidental.

Source: Academic Advisor: Maurizio Zollo, Ph.D. Chaired Professor in Strategy and Corporate Responsibility, SDA Bocconi. Winner of "The Free Press Outstanding Dissertation Award" in Business Policy and Strategy (a division of the Academy of Management). This work, entitled: "Knowledge codification, process routinization and the creation of organizational capabilities: post-acquisition management in the US banking industry" forms the basis for the content of this simulation.

NORTHERN BANK—INTERNAL MEMO

TO   Chris Wycliff—Integration Manager
FROM   Jon Pettinger—CEO
DATE   16th October
SUBJECT   Southern Bank Acquisition

Dear Chris,

Following Southern Bank's acceptance of our offer, I wanted to confirm the Board's decision to give you responsibility for the integration of Southern's operations with our own over the next few months.

As you know, we have been in talks with Southern Bank since early this year, and rumours of some forthcoming regulatory changes merely accelerated the process. The main objective is a consolidation of our operations, to leverage synergy opportunities from complementary branch networks and customer bases, and strengthen our defenses to the threat from Eastern Bank, which has recently announced its merger with Western.

As we wait for regulatory and formal shareholder approval on this deal, it is essential that we establish a clear integration plan, and build consensus on it with our colleagues at Northern Bank, our shareholders, key Southern personnel, as well as relevant external "stakeholders." The deal is expected to be cleared early next January. At that time, I have promised to give the Board a finalised plan, as well as confirmation that the people I have identified as stakeholders in this acquisition are in support of it.

I have great pleasure in giving you full responsibility for this mission, to be completed by 22nd December. I am sure you will be able to judge how to obtain everyone's full support; in my view, a mixture of consultation, communication and appropriate modifications to the plan will be key. The remainder of this file contains information on the deal, a detailed profile of the two banks, and what I believe to be the key post-acquisition management decisions that need to be taken. I have also added some background information on the people you will be dealing with.

A last point—Northern's experience with recent mergers has taught us that building consensus on the integration process is a prerequisite for protecting and growing our revenue base.

The best of luck, and don't hesitate to call if you need any advice.

ACQUISITION OUTLINE

The following outline provides some basic information on the Southern Bank transaction.

BACKGROUND

Informal discussion of a potential merger started early this year, following an initial approach by Northern. The first reaction of Southern management was quite cool, but it evolved to be much more positive as nationwide M&A activity increased and rumours of a possible combination of Western Bank and Eastern Bank spread in April. The strategic logic of a possible transaction was fairly clear to both sides: it would be difficult to compete against the scale advantages and the geographic coverage of a combined Western and Eastern Bank (about twice as large as either Northern or Southern), should their merger be finalized. In addition, both Northern and Southern could clearly see numerous opportunities for significant cost savings and cross-selling activities from a combination of their two franchises. The real arguments of contention were the usual ones: the governance structure of the combined entity, the value of both franchises, the strategic approach to take in the eventual post-combination period, etc.

NEGOTIATION PROCESS

Formal negotiations started at the beginning of June, and a brief due diligence exercise was conducted in the first week of July (for Northern) and the third week of July (for Southern). The due diligence process was based on a letter of intent signed by Northern on 29th June which included a preliminary, non-binding, consideration of $1.35 billion in stock. Overall attitude was relatively friendly. The bid was uncontested; no other bank was approached or involved in the negotiation.

DATE OF SIGNATURE OF THE AGREEMENT TO MERGE

12th September

PRICE PAID

$1.5 billion in stock, based on Northern Bank share price at close of trading on 12th September.

PRE-ACQUISITION PROFILES

KEY FIGURES

	Northern	Southern
Ownership		
Public—Institutions with >5%	23%	12%
Public—Other	63%	69%
Founding Family	0%	12%
Management	14%	7%
	100%	100%
Financials (at 30th June)		
Net Interest Income	$314 m	$231 m
Non-Interest Income	$91 m	$106 m
Total Income	$405 m	$337 m
Non-Interest expenses	$239 m	$229 m
Taxes	$54 m	$23 m
Net Earnings	$112 m	$85 m
Shareholders' Equity	$850 m	$502 m
Non-performing loans (90 days)	$72 m	$68 m
Total Loan Portfolio	$6.9 bn	$5.4 bn
Total Assets	$10.4 bn	$8.6 bn
Stock Market Value (12th Sep)	$1.8 bn	$1.2 bn

QUALITATIVE ASSESSMENTS

The relative effectiveness of the following operating functions and the quality of the following resources was assessed through a benchmarking exercise with the relevant competitors ("1" = much worse, "3" = similar, "5" = much better).

	Northern	Southern
Operations (back-office)	4	2
Administration (accounting, audit)	3	2
Credit underwriting policies	4	3
Marketing & Advertising	3	4
Customer Service (i.e. tellers, phone)	3	4
Information Systems	3	2
Location/Facilities	3	4

Branch Networks

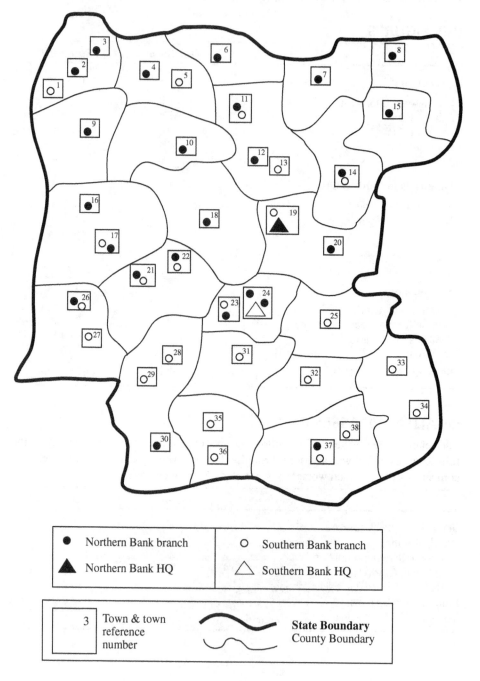

Branch List

County	Town	Northern Ref/Performance Index		Southern Ref/Performance Index	
A Worcester	01 Shelbey			S	01	2
	02 Hibbing	N	01	3		
	03 Boisevain	N	02	4		
B Montagu	04 Maple Creek	N	03	4		
	05 St Joseph				S	02	3
C Adelaide	06 White River	N	04	3		
D Esshow	07 Cobalt	N	05	2		
E Middel	08 Antigo	N	06	5		
F Rusten	09 Baraboo	N	07	5		
G Douglas	10 Randall	N	08	4		
H Jones	11 Greeley	N	09	1	S	03	3
	12 Fort Scott	N	10	2		
	13 Newport				S	04	3
I Fontein	14 Ardmore	N	11	5	S	05	4
J Scotts	15 Perryton	N	12	4		
K Suffolk	16 Hobbs	N	13	4		
	17 Pecos	N	14	5	S	06	4
L Warring	18 Deming	N	15	4		
M Tobol	19 Mesa	N	16	3	S	07	4
	20 Platte	N	17	3		
N Sutherland	21 Warren	N	18	4	S	08	5
	22 Rutland	N	19	4	S	09	4
O Enard	23 Joliette	N	20	5	S	10	4
	24 Bangor	N	21	3	S	11	5
		N	22	2		
P Trotter	25 Dayton				S	12	4
Q Strathe	26 Grangeville	N	23	3	S	13	4
	27 Klamath				S	14	4
R Cromden	28 Franklin				S	15	4
	29 Puyalop				S	16	5
	30 Bessemar	N	24	3		
S Oriol	31 Cordell				S	17	3
T Morar	32 Salt Fork				S	18	4
U Snizort	33 Leadville				S	19	4
	34 Sheridan				S	20	3
V Boulder	35 Redwing				S	21	5
	36 Harrisonburg				S	22	5
W Dee	37 Orangeton	N	25	4	S	23	4
	38 Eagle Pass				S	24	3

Performance index based on combination of profitability and last 3 yrs' growth in $ value of all retail and corporate loan applications ("1" = much worse, "3" = similar, "5" = much better)

Human Resource Practices

	Northern	Southern
Salaries	Close to industry average Fixed for each of 17 grades	Above industry average Individually negotiated
Bonus Scheme	Partly based on individual performance for most employees	Bank level profit-related bonus for management
Contracts	Fixed for each grade	Individually negotiated
Benefits		
Company car	Above grade 12	Directors
Low-interest loan	All	No
Expenses	Corporate Expense card	Reimbursed
Pensions	Voluntary contributions deducted from salary	Bank contributes 3% of annual salary to employees with more than 2 years' seniority
Holidays	20 days + public holidays	18 days + public holidays

Loan Approval Processes

	Northern	Southern
EFFECTIVENESS level of Credit underwriting policies	4	3
Loans Up To . . .	**Require Approval Of . . .**	
$100,000	Branch manager	Branch manager
$1 million	Branch manager	County manager
$5 million	County manager	Head of Corporate Banking
$50 million	Head of Corporate Banking	CFO
Primary evaluation criteria	Cashflows	Collateral
Total customer profitability evaluated?	Yes	No

IT Systems

	Northern	Southern
Computer system		
No. of servers	5	1
Server operating system	Unix	Unix
No. of PC's	408	321
Operating system	Windows XP	Windows 2000
No. of software programs		
Off-the-shelf	33	15
Custom	4	0
Performance Rating	3	2
Automated Teller Machines		
Number of locations	56	24
Performance Rating	4	3

Managers

	Northern	Southern
Total number	56	47
Management style	Participative	Directive
Average skill levels		
at HQ	4	5
in branches	3	3

Employees

	Northern	Southern
Total number	850	635
Members of BEU (Bank Employees Union)	24%	56%
Average skill levels		
At HQ	4	4
In branches	3	4

Product Portfolios

	Northern	Southern
Deposit Portfolio (by $ size)		
Current Accounts	56%	24%
Savings Accounts	44%	76%
Deposit Portfolio (profitability rating)		
Current Accounts	4	3
Savings Accounts	4	5
Loan Portfolio (by $ size)		
Commercial/corporate lending	64%	15%
Consumer/retail lending	30%	78%
Mortgage/real estate		5%
Other	6%	2%
Loan Portfolio (profitability rating)		
Commercial/corporate lending	4	4
Consumer/retail lending	3	4
Mortgage/real estate		2
Other	3	2

Each of the banks' deposit and loan 'products' corresponds to a given set of options, terms and conditions (e.g. interest rate calculation, payment period, guarantee requirements, etc..)

POST-ACQUISITION MANAGEMENT DECISIONS

The following are the 10 key decisions that make up the integration plan:

Southern Bank's branches will be . . .

RETAINED

All branches retained, no integration

CLOSED

All Southern branches present in a town with a Northern branch are closed

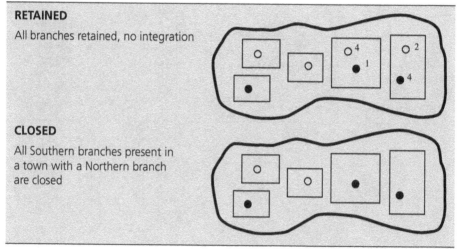

Southern Bank's branches will be . . .—*continued*

RATIONALISED

Best branches retained in each town, whether Northern or Southern; if equal, Northern branch is retained

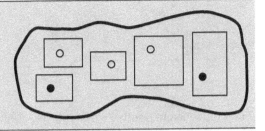

An imaginary branch network is shown here; the numbers next to the branches indicate example performance indices. Closing duplicate Southern branches is expected to reduce Southern's cost structure (non-interest expenses) by about 10%. Rationalising would cut 4% of the combined cost structure.

● Northern Bank branch
○ Southern Bank branch

Southern Bank's Human Resource Practices will be . . .

RETAINED	All practices retained, no alignment (e.g. of salaries)
REPLACED	Southern's practices replaced with Northern's

Southern Bank's Loan Approval Processes will be . . .

RETAINED	Both processes retained, no integration. Southern procedures and decisional autonomy are preserved.
LINKED	Southern's process retained but linked to Northern's. New procedures will be designed to ensure timely and effective exchange of information among the two loan processing units and to facilitate the harmonisation of the procedures in the medium/long term.
REPLACED	Southern's process replaced with Northern's. Centralisation of the loan approval process will save about 4% of the combined cost structure.

Southern Bank's IT Systems will be . . .

RETAINED	Both systems retained, no integration. The two systems will be run as autonomous units.
LINKED	Southern's system retained but linked to Northern's. A sophisticated interface will be designed to translate Southern's data outputs to formats understandable by Northern's system.
REPLACED	Southern's system replaced with Northern's. The replacement of Southern's system is estimated to save about 22% of Southern's non-interest expenses.

The Proportion of Southern's Managers Replaced will be:

0, 5, . . . , 95, 100%

Total compensation costs for the management team at Southern amount to 6% of its cost structure.

The Proportion of Southern's Employees Replaced will be:

0, 5, . . . , 95, 100%

Total compensation costs for Southern's employees account for 32% of its cost structure.

Southern Bank's Product Portfolio will be . . .

RETAINED	All products retained as part of merged bank's offering
REPLACED	Merged bank will only offer Northern's products
RATIONALISED	For each product category, 'best practice' products offered

The financial impact of product portfolio decisions is hard to quantify at this stage.

The Announcement of Replacement Decisions will be . . .

1, 2, . . . , 11, 12 weeks after the 1st January.

'Replacement' is one of our euphemisms for layoffs.

The Start Date of Implementation of Integration Decisions will be . . .

1, 2, . . . , 11, 12 weeks after the 1st January.

The Period for Implementation of Integration Decisions will be . . .

1, 2, . . . , 19, 20 weeks.

Memoranda Sent to Stakeholders

NORTHERN BANK—INTERNAL MEMORANDUM

TO   Lorenzo Stanio
            Hector Rice
            Ivan Taylor
            Carl Feinberg
            Steve Beckerman
            Tonia Yoshiro
            Elaine Bolta
FROM   Jon Pettinger
DATE   October 9

As you know, Southern Bank's Board has recently accepted our friendly offer to acquire
a controlling interest, with Northern stock. We are now waiting for agreement from
the regulator, as well as formal shareholder approval, both of which we expect by the
end of the year. All Northern and Southern employees were informed last week of this
provisional acceptance.

An acquisition raises some obvious and immediate concerns from the employees
involved, and you will all have received individually addressed letters confirming that you
will be part of the team of key managers taking this organisation forward.

Northern's acquisition experience has convinced us of the need for a consultative
approach to establishing a detailed integration plan, so I would like to take this
opportunity to introduce to you Chris Wycliff, our specialist Integration Manager, who
will be leading the integration of Southern's operations with our own over the next few
months, and more particularly, contacting you over the next few weeks in order to come
up with a plan that reflects your concerns. The plan will be 'set in stone' just before
Christmas; until that time, please use the opportunity of your discussions with Chris to
share your views on the various key decisions that need to be taken as part of the plan. I
look forward to continuing to work with you all over the coming years as part of the new
Northern Bank, and thank you in advance for your participation in this process.

NORTHERN BANK—EXTERNAL MEMORANDUM

TO   Marie Calperra—American Banking Authority
           Patrick Green—Dott Manufacturing
           Nicholas Collyn—Sergeant & Co.
           Pattie Mehrer—The Daily Post
           Hank Johnson—Sunrise Pension Fund
FROM   Jon Pettinger—CEO, Northern Bank
DATE   October 12

As you know, Southern Bank's Board has recently accepted our friendly offer to acquire a controlling interest, with Northern stock. We are now waiting for agreement from the regulator, as well as formal shareholder approval, both of which we expect by the end of the year. All Northern and Southern employees were informed last week of this provisional acceptance.

Northern's acquisition experience has convinced us of the need for a consultative approach to establishing a detailed integration plan, so I would like to take this opportunity to introduce to you Chris Wycliff, our specialist Integration Manager, who will be leading the integration of Southern's operations with our own over the next few months, and more particularly, contacting you over the next few weeks in order to come up with a plan that reflects your concerns. The plan will be 'set in stone' just before Christmas; until that time, please use the opportunity of your discussions with Chris to share your views on the various key decisions that need to be taken as part of the plan. Thank you in advance for your participation in this process.

Stakeholder Profiles

Northern Bank

Jon Pettinger
Chief Executive Officer

Jon has a BA in Finance from the University of California. Past experience includes positions as CFO and Head of Corporate Banking

---

Northern Bank

Lorenzo Stanio
Head of Retail Banking

Lorenzo's main responsibility is the profitability of the division. He spends most of his time at HQ in Mesa; there are some branches that Lorenzo has never visited! There is a quarterly meeting at HQ which all the branch managers are expected to attend though. He launched a project recently to review the effectiveness of the loan approval process.

Northern Bank

Hector Rice
HR Director

Hector is a skilled 'people' person, and has played a pro-active role in moulding Northern's HR practices to be, at least in his view, in line with both the bank's and its employees' interests. For instance, he has recently launched a training program to raise the skills of branch employees. Hector does not give much weight to project management style; it's concrete results and the views of the other people concerned by this takeover that count.

Northern Bank

Ivan Taylor
IT Director

Ivan is exploring the possibility of a corporate intranet, but it is not even at the prototype stage, and the recent upgrade to Windows XP has taken much longer than we expected. Ivan tends to focus on a very narrow range of issues in considering the merits of a proposal (he spends too much time in front of a computer screen!). For example, he is not going to pay much attention to what anyone else thinks.

Northern Bank

Carl Feinberg
Chief Financial Officer

Carl manages our investor relationships, and was instrumental in obtaining support for the acquisition from Southern's shareholders. His key attribute is his knowledge of finance and accounting, and he tends to try and interpret everything in terms of numbers; for instance, he will always look at the cost implications of a given proposal. Carl is also the kind of manager to make up his own mind when assessing a business decision.

Stakeholder Profiles—*continued*

Southern Bank

Steve Beckerman
Chief Executive Officer

Steve and I studied at college together. He was my main contact at Southern during the acquisition negotiations, and it was he in fact who suggested the idea of a merger late last year. Steve is a pragmatist, and has built his reputation as a manager who acts primarily in his shareholders' interests. He can see the woods and the trees: both the details of the plan and what his colleagues think of it will be of interest.

Southern Bank

Tonia Yoshiro
Head of Retail Banking

Tonia has recently taken on this role, having spent most of her career in the division; given the weight of the retail loan portfolio, she has considerable power at Southern. Tonia is a hands-on manager, spending most of her time in the branches; she has nevertheless been keen to delegate as much decision-making power as possible to branch managers. I don't think she is the kind of manager who will worry too much about communication style, but the views of her colleagues and clients will be given a lot of weight.

Southern Bank

Elaine Bolta
HR Director

Elaine has not been in her position long, and has not had time to change much among the HR practices inherited from her predecessor. She was not involved in the takeover discussions, but has already expressed a number of concerns about the risk of layoffs among Southern's personnel. Elaine has been criticized for the comparatively low skill levels of Southern's branch managers, but she works hard to improve the image of HR.

American Banking Authority

Marie Calperra
State Representative

Marie's primary responsibility is to enforce National Banking Laws, which define the legal framework under which Northern Bank and other commercial banks operate. A key priority is enforcing the 'no cross-subsidy' regulation, covering subsidies across corporate, retail and mortgage activities. She has hinted at forthcoming regulatory changes that will reduce hurdles to consolidation in the banking sector. Marie's team conducts an annual regulatory audit at Northern; they have been very responsive to our criticisms of current regulations governing intra-state banking restrictions. She will like an effective communication strategy in this kind of complex situation.

Stakeholder Profiles—*continued*

Dott Manufacturing

Patrick Green
CEO

Dott manufactures railway rolling stock, is a key supplier to most American railway companies, and is technically quite sophisticated. The firm is Southern's most important customer in terms of last year's $ revenue, and Southern has developed several customised products for them. Patrick is likely to want to avoid any disruption to the bank's product lines, and has given the acquisition only cautious support so far.

Sergeant & Co.

Nicholas Collyn
M&A Vice-President

Sergeant's M&A team has six full-time professionals focusing on the banking sector, and they have been instrumental in the Southern Bank transaction. This is the second Northern acquisition that Nicholas has been involved with. Nicholas is likely to have strong views on the various integration decisions that lie ahead of us; for example, he is a supporter of limited personnel shakeups.

The Daily Post

Pattie Mehrer
Editor

The Daily Post is a well-respected business-oriented daily newspaper, whose main editorial theme is deregulation, free trade and competition; it has taken a generally pro-bank line since its founding. Pattie has written a number of articles about the acquisition, some rather skeptical about our announcement of 'a merger of equals'; however, I've heard that she thinks quite highly of Northern's past acquisition performance, in terms of community impact. She will not reject layoffs outright, but there are limits.

Sunrise Pension Fund

Hank Johnson
Fund Director

The Sunrise Pension Fund holds 12% of Northern shares, pre-acquisition, and is the biggest shareholder in Northern. It has a team of internal investment analysts, with a reputation for interpreting accurately the impact on the share price of different strategic moves. The Southern Bank acquisition is the second one Hank has been involved in as Northern's main contact at Sunrise. Hank is very much in the camp of hands-on investors, who won't hesitate to throw his weight around if he perceives it to be necessary—he will not care much what anyone else thinks of your proposals, and will not want branches duplicated without a very good reason.

Case

Oticon

Building a Flexible World-Class Organization (A)

"I am 100% sure that we will try this," declared Lars Kolind, managing director of Oticon, during a 1990 speech to employees. He was referring to a radical change program, which would eventually change the structure, organizational processes, job content and careers at the then 86-year-old company. He added, "There's enough time for you to choose whether you're going to try it with us or whether you find another job."

Until the early 1980s, Oticon, a Danish high-technology company, had been the world market leader in hearing aid production. However, increasing competition and the company's inability to adapt to new technological developments had led to a loss of market share and subsequent financial difficulties. As a result, Kolind was recruited as a turnaround manager to set the organization back on the right course.

Kolind recalled:

> On New Year's Day 1990, I sat down and tried to think the unthinkable: a vision for the company of tomorrow—shaping jobs to fit the person instead of the other way around. Each person would be given more functions, and a "job"

would be developed by the individual accumulating a portfolio of functions. If people don't have anything to do, they would need to find something—or we don't need them.

Kolind knew that upsetting the status quo at Oticon by introducing a new, innovative organizational structure and new processes would be risky. Nevertheless, he was prepared to take that risk and was determined to succeed. As Kolind set out to reestablish Oticon as the leader in the hearing aid industry once again, he proclaimed:

> One thing is for sure: Oticon will change. We will create a flexible organization, where everyone realizes that the only certain thing is change.

COMPANY BACKGROUND

Oticon was founded in 1904 by Hans Demant, who was inspired to do so because his wife was hearing impaired. Determined to help her and others like her, Demant began to import hearing aids from the US. The business began to grow, and by the 1920s, sales offices were opened in Oslo, Malmö, Stockholm, Helsinki and St. Petersburg. The product range also continued to expand and by 1930, Oticon sold hearing aids, church hearing aids and hospital systems, and patient radio receivers.

During the Second World War, Oticon employed 16 people. When it became impossible to import hearing aids from the US because of the German trade

EXHIBIT 1 Main Innovations Introduced by Oticon, 1992–1996

Source: Oticon; Verona & Ravasi, 2003

Name	Year	Major Benefits of the Innovation
MultiFocus	1992	First fully automatic non-linear amplifier
PerSonic	1992	Pleasant design and surface texture, and wide color range to harmonize with facial features
Oticon 4 kids	1993	Colors and design more appealing and easy-to-wear for kids
MultiFocus Mild	1994	Same quality of sound processing, smaller size; designed for younger users
MicroFocus	1995	First programmable instrument, based on analog amplification process
DigiFocus	1996	First 100% digital hearing aid capable of improving one's ability to understand speech in noisy listening situations; winner of the Danish Industrial Design Prize, the European IT Prize and the European Design Prize

blockade, Demant started his own production in Copenhagen. Shortly thereafter, in 1946, the first true Oticon hearing aid was introduced on the market.

Oticon had become the world's leading hearing-aid manufacturer by 1979. However, in 1987, the company began losing money. The fear of being ousted by the bigger players in the hearing aid industry led the board to recruit Lars Kolind, a former mathematician, as the managing director. When Kolind arrived in 1988, he took a number of swift and decisive actions that allowed Oticon to once again become profitable. Despite the improvement in the company's performance, Kolind believed that Oticon would have to be transformed from a "command" to a "problem-solving" structure if it was to regain the number one position in the market.[1]

As a result of continuous developments in hearing instrument technology, Oticon experienced a number of revolutionary

[1] Sullivan, M. "Oticon Workers Go Walkabout." *Human Resource Management International Digest*, Vol. 6, Iss. 4, July/August 1998.

breakthroughs during the 1990s, such as MultiFocus—the first automatic hearing aid—which it developed in 1991. Four years later, the company introduced Digi-Focus on the market, which was the first fully digital hearing aid (*refer to Exhibit 1 for a description of the main innovations introduced by Oticon during the 1990s*).

Oticon's headquarters and production facilities were based in Denmark. The company's sales offices were located around the world, and its products were sold in more than 100 countries. Oticon was part of the William Demant Holding Group of international companies, which developed, manufactured and sold innovative and high-technology solutions, incorporating micro-electronics, micromechanics, wireless technology, software and audiology.

THE HEARING AID INDUSTRY

According to industry estimates, approximately 9% of the population of developed countries were believed to be hearing impaired. However, only about 10% to 25% of the hearing impaired population, depending on the country, wore a hearing aid device. Hearing aid devices consisted of several basic components: a microphone, an amplifier, a receiver and a battery for power. The microphone transformed sound into an electrical signal and sent it to the amplifier. The amplifier increased the amplitude of the electrical signal; filters and volume or tone controls could further modify the signal. The amplified signal was then transmitted to the receiver, where it was transformed into sound.[2]

The hearing aid devices market included various types of hearing aids, such as behind-the-ear (BTE), in-the-ear (ITE), in-the-canal (ITC) and completely-in-canal (CIC) models, as well as a much smaller number of body models. Both analog and digital devices were sold on the market.

BTE models accounted for about 55% of the world market, although they were once by far the most common style. Advantages of BTE models included reduced feedback and the ability to incorporate complex circuitry. Many new technologies also originated in BTE models. ITEs accounted for nearly all the remaining 45% of the market. Though these were more visible than either of the in-the-canal models, they were able to meet more severe hearing loss requirements and maintained a longer battery life.

Europe was the largest market for hearing instruments and represented 40% of the world market. The USA was the second largest market at 35%; Japan accounted for 10% and Australia represented 5%. Considerable differences existed in terms of product demand, distribution forms and growth dynamics, sometimes even between countries within the regions (*refer to* **Exhibit 2** *to view additional information about market size, demand and penetration*).

The average producer price for a hearing instrument was US$300. Experts estimated that the potential demand for devices was approximately 30 million units, hence, a total worldwide market value of roughly $9 billion.

Twenty companies had dominated 80% of the hearing aid industry during the early to mid-1990s. However, analysts expected mass consolidation in the industry through mergers and acquisitions. They also predicted that within a decade only three major players would remain.

THE NEED FOR CHANGE

During the late 1980s, Oticon slipped from first to third in the global market for hearing aids, and its book equity fell by 50% within an 18-month period. As a result, Lars Kolind laid off 15% of the workforce and subsequently took control of all investment decisions.[3] Even though Kolind's restructuring and cost-cutting returned Oticon to profitability, sales stagnated.

Kolind felt that in order to succeed in the long term, Oticon would need to transform itself into the "ultimate flexible organization" in response to what he saw as a shift from fundamentally technology-based products to fundamentally knowledge-based products. He saw little value in the mass production of conventional, low-margin, commodity-like hearing aids.

[2] Verona, G. & Ravasi, D. "Unbundling Dynamic Capabilities: An Exploratory Study of Continuous Product Innovation." *Industrial and Corporate Change*, Vol. 12, Iss. 3, June 2003.

[3] Sull, D. "After the Chainsaw." *Director*, Vol. 51, Iss. 10, May 1998.

EXHIBIT 2   Market Size, Demand and Penetration

Source: Paribas Capital Markets Group

Market	Population (millions)	Potential Market[1] (million units)	Potential Demand[2] (million units/year)
North America			
USA	275	46.8	9.4
Canada	30	5.1	1
Western Europe			
Germany	82	13.9	2.8
UK	59	10	2
France	59	10	2
Italy	58	9.9	2
Spain	40	6.8	1.4
Benelux	26	4.4	0.9
Scandinavia	19	3.2	0.6
Switzerland	7	1.2	0.2
Other Europe	70	11.9	2.4
Asia & Australia			
Japan	128	21.8	4.4
Australia/New Zealand	22	3.7	0.7
Total	**875**	**148.7**	**29.8**

[1] Assuming hearing loss incidence of 10% and that 70% of users need double hearing aids, i.e. the potential market volume is 17% of the population.
[2] Assuming technical lifetime of five years.

Instead, he considered Oticon's competitive edge to be the "fast and creative integration of all existing expertise in the field," including chip development, circuitry, anatomics and audiology.[4]

Therefore, Kolind planned to abandon Oticon's technological focus on making smaller hearing aids and focus more on developing better hearing solutions, which would allow the company to always come out on top in any hearing aid user satisfaction survey in the world.[5]

[4] Harari, O. "Open the Doors, Tell the Truth." *Management Review*, Vol. 84, Iss. 1, January 1995.
[5] LaBarre, P. "The Dis-Organization of Oticon." *Industry Week*, Vol. 234, Iss. 14, July 18, 1994.

Kolind's main strategic focus was on improving distribution, differentiating Oticon's products, and beating the global competition. He also felt that Oticon needed to reduce costs per instrument in order to earn money for future growth. The first objective was therefore to increase productivity by 30% within three years. Kolind felt that such an increase could not be achieved through employee cutbacks alone; the existing staff would need to produce 30% more. Sensing that something radical would be necessary to achieve this goal, he dismantled the company's functional departments and rebuilt Oticon as a projects-based organization.

Illustration: A Missed Opportunity

A change in the technological paradigm in the hearing aid industry was gradually taking place throughout the 1980s from "behind-the-ear" to "in-the-ear" hearing aids. Oticon's competitive advantage throughout the 1970s, however, had been miniaturization capabilities for "behind-the-ear" hearing aids. Because Oticon did not have the necessary competencies that were crucially important for the emerging "in-the-ear" hearing aids, the company did not respond appropriately to the changing landscape. In fact, many managers and developers at Oticon were convinced that "in-the-ear" hearing aids would turn out to be a commercial fiasco. Besides, they preferred to stick to their strongest technological capabilities in miniaturizing "behind-the-ear" hearing aids. Much to their dismay, the "in-the-ear" models became very successful and later dominated the market.

Source: Foss, N. "Selective Intervention and Internal Hybrids: Interpreting and Learning from the Rise and Decline of the Oticon Spaghetti Organization." *Organization Science*, Vol. 14, Iss. 3, May 2003.

THE SPAGHETTI ORGANIZATION

Kolind proclaimed that Oticon's revolutionary "dis-organization" was to begin at 8:00 on August 8, 1991. To symbolically underscore the fundamental transformation of Oticon, the headquarters moved to a completely new location north of Copenhagen. Kolind explained:

> We removed the entire formal organization. We took away all departments. We took away all managers' titles—and with them went the red tape. There were no offices and no secretaries to protect us. [. . .] In my opinion, you must change everything at once—organizational structure, culture, physical setting and the very nature of work itself. It is very dangerous to try to leap a chasm in two bounds.

In the new organization, "jobs" were reconfigured into unique and fluid combinations of functions to fit each employee's capabilities and needs. All head office employees typically performed three to five jobs, but were mostly free to decide what they did. Employees also worked in frequently shifting project teams. Anyone in the company could propose projects, although employees gravitated towards projects that interested them the most. They could even choose their working hours, vacation days and training needs, and were often encouraged to develop and include skills outside of their existing skill portfolio.

Because the new office had no walls, barriers to communication collapsed. The sharing and exploitation of knowledge was vital, which was why the company had organized itself around multidisciplinary project teams. The teams were so egalitarian and intertwined that Kolind described Oticon's organization as a "spaghetti structure."[6] Kolind and 10 managers represented the managerial team and acted as "project owners," while each of the many project teams were led by self-appointed "project managers," who recruited employees to work on their projects. All projects, however, had to be approved by the Projects and Products Committee.

[6] Harari, O. "Open the Doors, Tell the Truth." *Management Review*, Vol. 84, Iss. 1, January 1995.

Illustration: Managing the Spaghetti Organization

Three types of management jobs were defined: Project managers, competence managers and personnel managers. The project managers propelled the work forward, the specialist area managers monitored the professional quality, and the personnel managers—who were responsible for 10 to 15 employees—ensured that people were given the opportunity to contribute their utmost and develop their skills through new challenges.

Source: *Founded on Care—Oticon through 100 Years*, Oticon Foundation

---

Illustration: Where the Spaghetti Organization Failed

The Oticon model was developed against the background of Denmark's egalitarian tradition, where the individual's wishes are often subordinate to the collective, and where individual responsibility means responsibility for one's colleagues as well as oneself. The model worked at Oticon plants in [more than a dozen] other countries. However, the model failed to take root at the firm's factories in Scotland, Italy and Japan. Kolind could provide no scientifically-based reason for these failures.

Source: Sullivan, M. (1998), *Human Resource Management International Digest*, "Oticon Workers Go Walkabout," volume 6, p. 4.

Paper was also discouraged in the new organization. If someone wanted to view something on paper, they went to the mail room, where all incoming mail was scanned into a computer and then shredded. To emphasize Oticon's commitment to having a paperless office, Kolind installed a clear plastic tube that ran from the mail room, through the break room, to a trash disposal bin. While employees took their coffee break, they could see and hear shredded paper pass through the tube.

With few exceptions, anyone could access anyone else's mail, including Kolind's. His calendar was also accessible to anyone. In fact, any document—not just mail—was accessible to anyone working at Oticon. Project teams were even encouraged to tap into each other's files whenever possible. Kolind strongly believed that expertise that "flows and grows" was the key to Oticon's creativity.[7]

Staffers' only possession was their personal cart, which consisted of a drawer-less desk and a computer. Employees took their cart to wherever their teammates gathered to work on a project. Kolind remarked, "Without all thse restrictions of paper and belongings, people shift their focus from their power base and background to focus on the task, the customer, the new product."

The new organizational concept attracted much attention from the world outside, and business consultants from near and far traveled to Denmark to study Oticon. Kolind noted that almost everyone had adapted to the new way of working, and that he had been able to overcome resistance and win support by actively involving employees in the transformation process. To symbolically mark the company's commitment to change, Kolind sold all of its head office furniture to the staff in an eight-hour auction.

In the first three quarters after the spaghetti organization was established, profits fell. However, one year later, Oticon's profits doubled. After just two years, the chaotic tangle of relationships

[7] Ibid.

EXHIBIT 3   **Oticon Financial Performance: 1991–1996**
Sources: Ravasi and Verona (2000), Annual Reports of Oticon A/S and William Demant Holding A/S

	1991	1992	1993	1994	1995	1996
Net revenue (millions of Danish Krone)[1]	476.5	538.8	661.3	750.3	940.2	1,087.3
Profit margin (%)	1.8	5.8	13.1	17.9	12.4	12.8
Return on equity (%)	−1.5	7.2	37	37.9	25.9	24.3

[1] US$1 = 6 DKK in 1996

and interactions, known as the spaghetti organization, had led to increased profits, increased productivity and more innovation at Oticon.[8] (*Refer to* **Exhibit 3** *to view information on Oticon's financial performance.*)

Product development time had also been reduced by 50%. Oticon even launched a new product on the market that caught competitors completely by surprise. The innovation rate, expressed in terms of the proportion of sales due to new products, more than doubled, and by 1993, half of Oticon's sales were already accounted for by products that had been introduced in the previous two years.[9]

[8] LaBarre, P. "The Dis-Organization of Oticon." *Industry Week*, Vol. 234, Iss. 14, July 18, 1994.

[9] Verona, G. & Ravasi, D. "Unbundling Dynamic Capabilities: An Exploratory Study of Continuous Product Innovation." *Industrial and Corporate Change*, Vol. 12, Iss. 3, June 2003.

Reading

Changing the Deal While Keeping the People

Denise M. Rousseau

EXECUTIVE OVERVIEW

Companies are in danger of losing the voluntariness that makes possible much of a business's ability to compete. As whole industries undergo restructuring,

psychological contracts—those unwritten commitments made between workers and their employers—need to change in order to be kept. Service, quality, and innovation require higher contributions from people and, therefore, a new psychological contract involving commitment and trust. In high-contribution work settings, that means changing the deal while keeping the people. Changes which violate a contract or fail to substitute another effective one in its place won't do. And, even though the psychological contract is not legally binding, today's executive must know how successful firms transform it.

Source: *Academy of Management Executive,* February 1996.

This article is adapted from D. M. Rousseau, *Psychological Contracts in Organizations: Understanding Written and Unwritten Agreements* (Sage, 1995). An earlier version was presented at the International Consortium for Executive Development Research, Lausanne, Switzerland, June 1994.

Effectively changing a psychological contract depends on two things: how similar is the proposed change to the current contract? and how good is the relationship between employee and employer? Asking people to use a new work system or work a few extra hours can simply mean to modify, clarify, substitute, or expand an existing contract. However, asking people to redefine themselves—as professionals rather than job holders, customer service providers rather than technicians, or as leaders rather than middle managers—is far more complicated.

When a good-faith relationship exists, changes are more likely to be accepted as part of the existing contract, because parties are not looking for contract violations and trust creates willingness to be flexible.[1] On the other hand, when a relationship historically has been negative, changes are more likely to require more extensive overhaul in the employment relationship. In such situations, improving the employment relationship is a necessary first step in contract change.

CHANGING THE CONTRACT

There are two ways to change the psychological contract: accommodation and transformation. Accommodations modify, clarify, substitute, or expand terms within the context of the existing contract so that people feel the old deal continues despite changes. Isolated changes in performance criteria, benefit packages or work hours are frequent forms of accommodation. Because of this continuity, it is the change strategy of choice. However, to be effective, there must be a good relationship between the company and its members. Companies such as Hewlett Packard and Cummins Engine have introduced changes in employment conditions over the years that have been largely accepted by their employees based on a positive labor history.

In contrast to accommodations, transformations are radical surgery. Transformation means that new mindsets replace old ones. Contemporary contracts are changing at unprecedented rates. Shifts in job duties from individual efforts to teamwork, from short-term financial results to customer satisfaction, or moving from offering "a job for life" to "employability" necessitate the rewriting of the psychological contract. Consider, for example, the transformation of the Bell System. When divestiture was ordered by the courts in the early 1980s, the process of breaking up a highly successful, regulated business and turning it into separate competitive enterprises rewrote the deep structure of the employment contract. Employees who for generations in many cases had "bell-shaped heads," never missed a day of work, and labored loyally for a secure job and retirement began coping with the need to produce business results, and respond to market demands. A decade and a half of uncertainty, terminations, and movement of personnel from operating companies to new high-technology business units radically changed the people and their relationship to the many new organizations that the break-up created.

[1] The willingness to be flexible in a well-founded relationship has been referred to as the "zone of acceptance." Herbert A. Simon [*Administrative Behavior*, 3d ed. (New York: Macmillan, 1976)] used this term to refer to the range of duties and responsibilities in a job that employees believe to be under the discretion of their employer. So for example, whether a secretary sends a letter first class or by overnight delivery matters little to that person since both can be thought of as part of mailing correspondence. This zone of acceptance is quite elastic, being broad and open in more relational forms of employment or narrow and rigid in more transactional ones (Rousseau, 1995).

The purpose of contract transformation is the creation of a new contract that—it is hoped—engenders commitment. In some cases companies with a history of serious labor/management conflict, such as those in the steel industry, have had no choice but transformation. However, contracts resist revision, and transformation goes against the grain. Therefore, how that change is attempted determines whether change occurs—whether it degenerates into contract violation, or successfully transforms the basis of the relationship.

The fact is that individuals are open to new contract information only at certain times, a phenomenon psychologists refer to as "discontinuous information processing."[2] People often see what they expect to see, gather information only when they think they need it, and ignore a lot. Two circumstances in which people become open to new information are when they are newcomers to the organization or when a disruption occurs which they cannot ignore.

The easiest way to change a contract is to hire new people. Recruits ask a lot of questions while they are newcomers and once they start getting the answers they expect, they stop asking. Veterans may do little inquiring at all. Companies tell things to newcomers that they would never bother mentioning to an old timer. Once norms and practices are internalized, however, the newcomer is no longer new.

Significant disruptions make old mindsets tough to maintain. Several years into a major re-orientation focusing on customers, teamwork, and quality, a Xerox executive encountered a manager who mentioned that he had taken his team with him to go through a refresher training course. He asked why the course was needed given the company's sustained change efforts: "Because I never paid much attention the first time through, since I thought this thing would be gone by now; I thought it was just another ice cream flavor. But I got scared when I saw that [the new CEO] had picked it up with vigor. So we know we can't hide in the weeds anymore."[3]

Information gathering tends to be triggered by events signaling "this is the time to ask questions" such as in job interviews, or when the firm has been acquired and a new CEO from the parent company has arrived. Information is processed when there is a felt need for it, when the old information doesn't seem to work, and is otherwise pretty well ignored. The cognitive processes involved are both lazy and conservative. People do not work hard on changing contracts or any other established mindset. People work hard on fitting experiences into them. It is quite common to find newcomers and veterans working side by side holding different psychological contracts.

TRANSFORMATION STAGES

Basic principles in transformation capitalize on how employees tend to process information by seeking to unfreeze old mindsets and create new ones, a process characterized here in four stages (see Exhibit 1).

---

[2] The distinction between systematic and automatic information processing is detailed by H. Sims and D. Gioia in *The Thinking Organization* (San Francisco: Jossey-Bass, 1987).

[3] D. T. Kearns and D. A. Nadler, *Prophets in the Dark: How Xerox Re-Invented Itself and Beat Back the Japanese* (New York: Harper, 1992).

EXHIBIT 1 Transforming the Psychological Contract

Stage	Intervention

Challenging the Old Contract

• Stress	Provide new discrepant information (educate people). Why do we need to change?
• Disruption	

Preparation for Change

• Ending old contract	Involve employees in information gathering (send them out to talk with customers and benchmark successful firms).
• Reducing losses	Interpret new information (show videos of customers describing service and let employees react to it).
• Bridging to new contract	Acknowledge the end of the old contract (celebrate good features of old contract).
	Create transitional structures (cross-functional task forces to manage change).

Contract Generation

• Sensemaking	Evoke "new contract" script (have people sign on to "new company").
• Veterans become "new"	Make contract makers (managers) readily available to share information.
	Encourage active involvement in new contract creation.

Living the New Contract

• Reality checking	Be consistent in word and action (train everyone in new terms).
	Follow through (align managers, human resources practices, etc.).
	Refresh (re-emphasize the mission and new contract frequently).

STAGE 1: CHALLENGING THE OLD CONTRACT.

It takes a "good" (i.e., legitimate) reason to change a contract and keep the people. Consider the following scenarios:

> A photocopying shop has one employee who has worked in the shop for three months and earns $9 per hour. Business continues to be satisfactory, but a factory in the area has closed and unemployment has increased. Other small firms have hired reliable workers at $7 an hour to perform jobs similar to those done by the photocopy shop employee. The owner of the photocopying shop reduces the employee's wage to $7.

Is it fair for the employer to cut the employee's wage from $9 to $7 an hour? Now consider the next scenario:

> A house painter employs two assistants and pays them $9 per hour. The painter decides to change businesses and go into lawn mowing where the going wage is lower. He tells the current workers that he will keep them on if they want to work, but will only pay them $7 per hour.

Is it fair for this employer to cut the employees' wage from $9 to $7 an hour?

These two scenarios have been widely applied in training sessions with executives and consistently yield opposite answers in the vast majority of cases. When first employed, the photocopy scenario led approximately 85 percent of respondents to say it was "unfair."[4] But the reverse happens in the lawn-mowing situation where a comparable percentage of respondents indicate that cutting the wage is "fair." Each

scenario involves the same losses ($2 per hour) and each involves a change proposed by the employer. The difference is the way in which the change is framed. The frame in the house-painting scenario involves a shift in the type of business (where the labor market offers a lower wage). There is no legitimate external justification in the photocopy scenario. A core issue in the management of contract change involves how the change is framed.

The reluctance of people to endorse the actions of the photocopy shop's owner suggests a value placed on continuing contracts, especially if losses are involved ($2 per hour), unless there are legitimate reasons to do otherwise. These scenarios highlight a central issue in the success of contract transformation: effective communication of externally validated reasons for the change.

Contracts are challenged when discrepant information is available regarding their underlying assumptions. All contracts are based on certain assumptions, including the nature of the business (lawn mowing or house painting, industrial marketing or consumer sales), and good faith efforts to obtain mutual benefits. Shifts in the nature of the business, especially those not directly under organizational control, can create severe costs to either party of continuing the contract.[5] For example, at

---

[4] D. Kahneman, J. Knetsch, and R. H. Thaler, "Fairness and the Assumptions of Economics," *Journal of Business* 59: 1986, S285–S300.

[5] The slow adoption and in many cases frustrating failures of the quality of work life (QWL) movement in the United States can be attributed to a lack of any understood legitimated reasons for change in the contract. Quality of work life programs (e.g., Rushton project as described in P. S. Goodman, *Assessing Organizational Change* (New York: Wiley, 1979)) were introduced to address declining productivity. However, there is ample evidence that the threat of foreign competition—in particular from Japan—was not perceived by many managers and employees

continued

NCR, management wanted to change the way sales representatives treated customers. To help demonstrate why this change was essential, NCR videotaped major account customers complaining about service and played it to the sales representatives. At first, a few of the representatives denied that the customers had really said anything negative. This denial persisted until one person asked, "Can we see that tape again?" When the video was rerun, the reality of the customer complaints was undeniably clear.

Transformation failures are often directly attributable to failure to justify the contract change or use of insufficient or inappropriate justifications. One defense contractor downsized 10 percent of its workforce under the banner of "improved shareholder value." With great fanfare, it gave each of the more than 100 top managers in the firm a share of company stock encased in a handsome frame suitable for hanging on the walls of the executive suite. The companywide response was one of resentment, surreptitious conversations behind closed doors, and mistrust of hierarchical superiors. The message

sent touted shareholder interests, not those of the corporation generally or the organization member particularly. Unless a person is a shareholder such a message doesn't generate a lot of motivation to change.

A more effective message is that offered by Xerox in the early 1980s following its major loss of market share to Japanese competitors. The CEO, David Kearns, saw a need for greater employee involvement to foster customer responsiveness and corporate competitiveness: "It was obvious to me that we had service problems and had never addressed them . . . we dispatched a team of people to Japan. It included plant managers, financial analysts, engineers, and manufacturing specialists. . . . Our team went over everything in a thorough manner. It examined all the ingredients of cost: turnover, design time, engineering changes, manufacturing defects, overhead ratios, inventory, how many people worked for a foreman, and so forth. When it was done with its calibration, we were in for quite a shock. [One manager] remembers the results as being 'absolutely nauseating.' It wasn't a case of being out in left field. We weren't even playing the same game."[6]

Results of these analyses revealed that the Japanese carried six to eight times less inventory, had half the overhead and a near 99.5 percent quality rate on incoming parts compared to Xerox's 95 percent. Unit manufacturing cost was two-thirds that of the American firm. The product of these insights was a strategy to improve business effectiveness at Xerox with two underpinning concepts: employee involvement and external benchmarking. Commitment to Excellence and Team Xerox are titles of efforts in this strategic change.

[5] *continued*

in large companies such as General Motors and IBM. QWL efforts in the late 1970s were frequently disbanded. A turning point in organizational change efforts came with the total quality movement of the 1980s in which the popular use of benchmarking made it more likely that organization members would look at their firm's competition for information on the firm's relative health and look to other firms even in unrelated industries for best practices and innovations. In investigating the history of organizational development and change, a contracts framework suggests that it is important to ask how the change process was legitimated and whether externally anchored reasons were offered (as in the case of changing one's business from house painting to mowing lawns or from defense contractor to consumer products).

[6] Kearns and Nadler, 1992, p. 236.

Benchmarking—active monitoring of other organizations for establishing performance standards—can identify necessary new mindsets. Involvement helps people exercise these new mindsets. Challenging the contract requires creating a deep understanding of the reasons why change is necessary.

STAGE 2: PREPARATION FOR CHANGE.

The goal of this stage is to unfreeze or take apart the old contract while readying the parties for the next stage, creating the new contract. There is a three-pronged approach to effectively managing this stage: creating credible signs of change, reducing losses, and adopting transition structures to bridge to the new contract.

Credible signs of change: We really mean it this time.

Critical, undeniable events are needed for people to believe contract change is inevitable. Credible signs of change demonstrate commitment to follow through on the challenge conveyed in stage one, and create an appropriate ending for the earlier contract. Credibility involves different things in different organizations. In a family business where no one but family members have headed the company, the hiring of an outsider could provide a credible signal. In a company whose top management has changed six times in seven years, keeping the same management team on to see a change through may be the necessary signal. This credible sign of change says "this time we mean to change."

The next sign is the message that the old contract is ending. Symbolic ending of the old contract is necessary because people are strongly attached to the arrangement that must have worked well to have survived as long as it did. Some mourning for the old relationship is likely. Respecting the past is part of respecting the people who believed in the old contract. A defense contractor faced with declining markets might celebrate the success of its efforts during the Cold War and declare victory before going on to reorient its business to new markets. Before initiating a new contract, an old one needs to be completed.

Loss reduction: Losses are more painful than gains are good.

Given that any gains are not yet realized, at this stage of transformation the sense of loss exceeds gains. Major forms of loss are palpable departures from the status quo (e.g., security, status), emotional distress due to change, and the loss of certainty. Offsetting such losses involves both remedies such as training, and use of procedures that put greater information and control in the hands of people affected by the change. Loss of control and certainty typically accompanies changes, but can be offset by involving individuals in planning the changes that will affect them. When Ameritech began using downsizing through early retirement as part of its change process, employees were permitted to select their date of retirement—any day of their choosing within the calendar year—which maintained some sense of personal control and dignity.

Transition structures: When you can't get there directly from here.

Few transformations occur all at once, as is evident in the decade of change in the Bell System. Quite often they occur due to major external upheavals, which means that the full scope of the change cannot be known at the beginning and therefore changes cannot be implemented all at once. For psychological contracts to change, these transitions usually involve transitional structures—temporary practices used to promote the larger contract change effort.

Organizations that create new contracts among new hires while honoring existing ones with veterans seek to transform contracts gradually. However, the downside of such gradual transition strategies is that veterans can feel insecure about the continued benefits they obtain while newcomers may feel inequitably treated. It may be that phased-in change using two-tiered wage systems requires some form of phase-out system too, where veterans need support in learning and adjusting to new performance criteria.

Aside from phased-in changes, other transition structures can take on the form of task forces for people to look into ways of effectively introducing or managing change. Such structures are often critical in transformations because conventional communication channels are insufficient for affected individuals whose anxiety levels and information needs have skyrocketed. Having task forces that cut across several functions, areas, and levels can aid transformation planning both through the information they gather and what they share. To maintain trust, it is important to have rich information channels, conveying both bad news and any other relevant information in a timely way.

Another transitional structure is an interim contract. Change breeds uncertainty. Reactions to it may vary from overt displays of emotion and frustration to passive withdrawal—"lie low and keep your head down and you might not get shot." When past certainties are gone and nothing yet takes their place, a sort of "no guarantees" or "anything goes" type of relationship prevails, resulting in

passive vigilance where little real work gets done. A more functional transition is the creation of temporary, transaction-like contracts. When the longer term is not knowable and specific commitments cannot be made, it is useful to specify short-term objectives (e.g., project orientation) that give people a clear task and provide support to make that task a success. During this transition, managers need to remain readily available for questions and to convey whatever information they know when they know it.

STAGE 3: CONTRACT GENERATION: CREATING A NEW MINDSET.

Shotgun weddings don't create new contracts. People need to want to be a party to a contract. New commitments are needed that shift attention from the past to the future. Managers generate contract terms by conveying new expectations and commitments. Absence of commitments undercuts the contractual nature of the new arrangement, generating compliance only until a better job opportunity comes along. But when top management makes a clear statement of new terms and solicits commitment to these terms, the supplanting of one contract by another can occur. The terms Jack Welch posted on the wall at GE are an exemplar of a contract-making statement.[7] But, since even strong statements by top managers can be incomplete reflections of a new deal, employees must

[7] Described in both the 1992 GE Annual Report to Shareholders and in Robert Slater's *Get Better or Get Beaten: 31 Leadership Secrets from GE's Jack Welch* (Burr Ridge, IL: Irwin, 1994), this famous statement specifies the four scenarios for GE employees depending on whether they meet commitments and share GE values.

still inquire, observe, and monitor to understand the scope of the new contract.

During transformation, many earlier contract makers are still intact. Compensation systems and senior managers may continue sending the old contract message into the new era. Old and new contract messages have to be sorted out by employees. Getting the right message out can mean having top management, not the training department, do the training. When Jerre Stedd initiated a globally integrated manufacturing and sales strategy for Square D, he created both Vision Mission, a statement of Square D's values and goals, and Vision College, a corporation-wide program where he, his managers, and employees from all levels acted as trainers to help veterans and newcomers understand the new mission. The result was rapid dissemination and broad awareness of the new mission.

Understanding new contract terms requires employees to act like newcomers, regardless of how long they have been with the organization. New contract acceptance by veterans is aided by evoking a "new contract script"; for example, by signing a contract, recruiting for a new job within one's current company, or attending a "new employee" orientation. RR Donnelley, in the midst of a major culture shift, transferred veteran employees from its traditional core publishing business to its high-tech information services division, but required them to be treated like new employees in the process. Veterans submitted a resume, underwent interviews, testing, and a new employee orientation before actually signing a new employment contract that stressed the importance of teamwork, innovation and customer service.

Signing a new contract signifies the reader's assent to the deal, especially if the signature follows a statement that the employee has read and understands the provisions. Acceptance of new contract terms is also enhanced by having employees:

- Adopt a new frame of reference— transfer them to a new job or new organization within the same parent company.

- Actively express a choice—have them bid for a new job, fill out an application and/or participate in other recruitment-related activities.

- Convey commitment vividly and publicly—have them sign a written agreement and/or complete a new employee orientation.

- Publicly demonstrate acceptance— have them participate in training others to support the change.

- Become part of a critical mass of people with the same contract—create a contract that is widely shared and understood.

STAGE 4: LIVING THE NEW CONTRACT.

Some reality testing is part of the transformation process. People may wonder what will happen if someone reverts to the old ways. The aftermath of the U.S. Navy's Tailhook scandal with charges of harassment but few resulting convictions led to a public commitment on the part of the U.S. Navy to change the environment for its female members.

Navy women as combat pilots and aircraft carrier personnel are signs of change since these roles were previously forbidden by both custom and act of Congress. When Lieutenant Sally Fountain, 31-year-old electronic warfare officer on a radar-jamming plane, telephoned a repair office on the carrier *USS Eisenhower,* a male sailor answered and called to his boss, "Hey there is a lieutenant chick on the phone for you." Minutes later, the sailor's angry supervisor hauled the young man before Lieutenant Fountain to formally apologize.[8] Such events are part of the reality check that occurs when work roles, norms, and contract terms change. All contract makers, executives, managers, staff, and employees must be vigilant to reinforce the new contract terms so these can then become part of the taken-for-granted reality of the new contract.

Solidifying the new contract means that for a while the organization has to strive to be incredibly consistent. Until employees know with certainty that the "old deal is over," the new contract is not reality. Managers, senior executives, interviewers, co-workers, and human resource practices (e.g., performance reviews and promotions) all must be on the same page, sending consistent messages in line with the new contract. Focus groups and informal networks can help test whether the new contract is well understood. Until the new deal is taken for granted, the organization cannot afford to send mixed messages. Training all contract makers, from senior managers and recruiters to co-workers and staff, is critical to contract change. Refreshing and reinforcing that training is important to sustaining a new reality.

TOWARD CONTINUOUS CHANGE

Today's new contracts feature active, ongoing renegotiation by both employee and employer.[9] A more diverse workforce needs flexibility in working conditions, prompting employee-driven renegotiations of the contract. At the same time, a more competitive marketplace demands frequent change in the deliverables required (e.g., shorter cycle times, high quality) and the way they are produced (e.g., worldwide, customized), and drives organizations to reformulate contract terms. Sustained performance and strategic focus require psychological contracts that balance and join the interests of people and organizations.

But there is a problem. Restructurings in the 1980s led to an era of "no guarantees," an employment relationship involving no contract at all. Organizations in the throes of change over several years, downsizing frequently, and changing strategy often (which effectively means having no strategy at all) can undermine their ability to successfully manage and motivate a workforce. Though uncertainty may be necessary in the transition to a new contract more in line with competitive strategy, organizations too long in transition erode their capacity to contract. When employees don't trust their bosses, react with disbelief to would-be contract making executives, change agents, and training programs, and respond to escalating change with passivity ("keep your head down and this too shall pass"), the organization may have lost its ability to create contracts based on voluntary commitment and good faith. Restoring and protecting the capacity to contract is essential to managing contract change.

---

[8] "Navy Women Bringing New Era on Carriers," *New York Times*, February 21, 1994.

[9] New psychological contracts increasingly take the form of "balanced contracts" in which both employee and employer (and often also customer and supplier) each have performance terms to live up to and high investments in the relationship and in each other (Rousseau, 1995).

How can organizations and their members improve their ability to make and keep contracts? Acting in good faith and signaling concern for each other's interests are obviously important. But blind faith won't do. Active renegotiation of contracts over the long term requires employees to have a good understanding of the nature of the business, its strategy, market conditions, and financial indicators. Change cannot be legitimated if people don't understand the reasons for it, nor can they effectively participate in crafting appropriate new terms. The same holds true for employee-initiated changes where managers need perspective on matters outside their own experience. Improving the capacity to contract effectively involves acquiring relevant information and the skills to use it while working to make the relationship stronger.

The present and future psychological contract is increasingly a balanced one where adjustments are inevitable on both sides. The most powerful contracts of all are those that can be both changed and kept.

Ayudhya Allianz C.P.

The Turnaround

It was with a sense of relief that Wilfred (Wilf) Blackburn, CEO of Ayudhya Allianz C.P. (AACP) resumed his seat in the audience. He had just performed a duet, in the presence of 10,000 of AACP's Agents, a popular Thai song together with the country's most renowned pop singer, Bird. It was 8 December 2007, the third "AACP Day," the biggest annual agency convention in Thailand. The mood at AACP was upbeat. In a short span of three and a half years, AACP had been transformed from an unprofitable, hierarchical and demoralized organization whose very existence was at stake, to a profitable, modern and exciting company to work for (*refer to Exhibit 1 for AACP's financial performance in 2003–2007*).

Faced with the deep crisis in the summer of 2004 which could have threatened the company's existence, Wilf and his leadership team had transformed the company at a breathtaking pace. The agency compensation system was revamped, and costs were curtailed. Down went the office walls; in came flexi-time and a casual corporate uniform. Bringing in senior managers from outside the industry to replace the "old guard" revitalized the entire organization. Significant effort went into developing new insurance products, expanding distribution channels and launching bold marketing campaigns. AACP's implementation of i2s (Ideas to Success), an Allianz Global Innovation Initiative, received company-wide recognition. AACP also started to actively engage with the local community, and the once-hostile media lauded its efforts to bring about broader social change (*refer to Exhibit 2 for the timeline of change initiatives at AACP*).

Source: *This case was prepared by Professors Tatiana Zalan and Vladimir Pucik as a basis for class discussion rather than to illustrate either effective or ineffective handling of a business situation.*

EXHIBIT 1   AACP's Financial Performance, 2003–2007

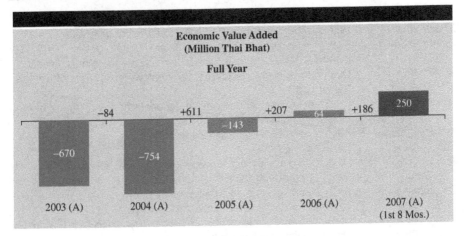

EXHIBIT 1   *continued*

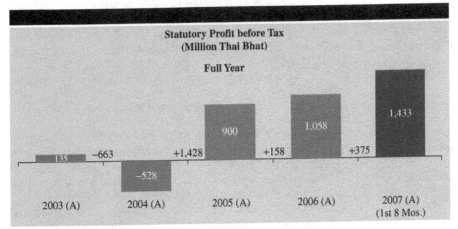

Source: AACP Presentation to IMD, 15 October 2007.

CHANGE INITIATIVES

How was this dramatic turnaround—which Wilf Blackburn described as "radical surgery"—accomplished? As he reflected on the previous three years of continuous change, Wilf observed: "We broke a lot of rules, some intentionally and some unintentionally." All in all, it was a remarkable journey.

Despite the internal upheaval in the first half of 2004, by the end of that year, AACP posted an increase of nearly half a billion baht in first-year premiums compared with 2003. Encouraged by these results,

EXHIBIT 2   Timeline of Change Initiatives at AACP, 2004–2007

Month/Year	Change Initiative
27 July 2004	Wilf Blackburn becomes the CEO and President of AACP.
October 2004	Bank of Ayudhya and CP raise its registered share capital by 1.766 billion baht to 4 billion baht for expansion and balance sheet improvement.
Nov 2004	Open floor space is introduced. Senior managers' private offices are dismantled.
Nov 2004	OneStopService customer care centre opens on the first floor of the main building on Phloen Chit Road.
January 2005	Agents' compensation system is revamped.
March 2005	Flexi-time is introduced.
August 2005	Six new products are launched to replace traditional fixed-rate products.
October 2005	Social Contribution Department is established.
December 2005	AACP Day #1 agents' convention takes place.
June 2006	AACP *Food for the Needy* project is launched.
June 2006	My Set product is relaunched, offering policyholders SET50 exposure.
April 2006	The i2S initiative is launched globally.
June 2006	AACP Pa Nong Tiew Bangkok (Take the Kids to See Bangkok) program is launched.
June 2006	World Cup 2006 convention for sales executives and 2006 World Cup Ticket contest, a regional contest for MDRT qualifiers, are launched.
July 2006	AACP Day #2: Road to Success agents' convention is held.
November 2006	AACP teams up with Tisco bank to expand the bancassurance channel.
December 2006	AACP (in conjunction with the School of Architecture and Design, KMUTT) organizes a free-of-charge AACP Animation Kids camp.
January 2007	AACP announces that it will recruit a further 10,000 sales agents by mid-2007.
January 2007	AACP and GE Capital agree to grow the bancassurance channel.
April 2007	AACP Prestige, a new loyalty program, is introduced.
June 2007	Allianz Market Winner 10/2 health insurance policy is introduced.
June 2007	AACP introduces investment-linked insurance, which gives investors the opportunity to invest in European stocks with capital guaranteed.
June 2007	AACP announces it will hold 'AACP Thailand Animation contest 2007' themed "Reducing Global Warming."
July 2007	Sunchai Larpsumphunchai, SVP for agency business, is appointed CAO.
March–June 2007	New services are launched based on customer feedback tools (such as Customer First Campaign and NPS chip boxes).
April 2007	AACP Tam Roi Prayukolabath (Follow His Majesty the King's Footsteps) program is initiated.
August 2007	AACP launches "AACP Protects Thai Families as a Tribute to His Majesty the King" project which offers free insurance to community leaders.
September 2007	A new capital-guarantee product is launched linking the investment with the stock indices from the high-growth BRIC countries.
September 2007	AACP and Bank of Ayudhya introduce the "Growing Together" initiative aimed at growing their bancassurance activities.
September 2007	AACP introduces a guaranteed insurance policy, AACP Special 5, to tap into more conservative consumers.

Source: Case writers, based on media articles and AACP internal data.

Wilf set out to regain AACP's position as Thailand's number two life insurer in 2005 (based on new premiums), and set its sales target to become the industry leader over the next two years. By mid-2006, AACP had managed to wipe out almost all of its accumulated losses of 1.6 billion baht.[1] By the end of 2007, AACP had become the top life-industry player with nearly 25% market share in first-year premiums, improved its ROE to 15% and paid out its first dividend to shareholders—the first Allianz life insurance company in Asia to do so.

REORGANIZING THE AGENCY SALES FORCE

Finding a replacement for Krisana Kritmanorote (KK), the former Chief Agency Officer who enjoyed almost "superhuman" status, was Wilf's top priority in the early days of the turnaround. In the end, Wilf made an unconventional, high-risk decision to personally manage the Agency, "stepping in the boxing ring with the agents."[2]

While Wilf spent the latter part of 2004 building the agents' trust, his tough decisions the following year put this to the test. Restructuring the agents' benefits in early 2005 by taking out all of their "fixed allowance" meant a major change in how agents got paid, and a shift of the product portfolio toward variable rate policies with lower guarantees required agents to focus on products that were not necessarily easy to sell. These initiatives were highly unpopular and several agency leaders left, including one who had managed a team of 1,500 people. In one incident Wilf was confronted by 300 angry agents, most of them dressed in military uniforms to intimidate the new CAO. Wilf's personal security became an issue and he had to move his family residence to a more protected location.

During 2005, as a result of all the changes, AACP lost a considerable number of agents. Overall, 6,000 people left, and of the Agency's original 80 General Managers (GMs), only 50 remained with the company. Many of those who left went on to join AACP's competitors at a time when AACP needed a well-trained sales force more than ever. In order to attract new agents and restore credibility with the sales force, AACP initiated monthly recruitment campaigns and readjusted agents' compensation, by tweaking elements of the new scheme in response to Agency feedback. Important morale boosters were the spectacular annual conventions for agents and their families. Conventions gave them a chance to build relationships, exchange sales techniques, listen to motivational speakers and insurance industry leaders, and enjoy entertainment by top Thai pop bands. As Wilf observed, "The agents went through intensive surgery in the first 18 months, and now they are confident that no more surgery is required."[3]

In July 2007, Sunchai Larpsumphunchai, the Senior Vice President for the agency business, succeeded Wilf as CAO to manage the 10,000-strong agency force. An excellent motivator and ardent supporter of Wilf's initiatives, Sunchai had been with AACP for five years and was well aware of the responsibility that came with his job: "I know I have power but I also know that power kills people. When you misuse your power, you lose."[4]

---

[1] "Life goes on from the touch-line." *The Nation*, 2 May 2006, p. 2B.
[2] Interview with Wilf Blackburn, CEO, 14 October 2007.
[3] Interview with Wilf Blackburn, CEO, 14 October 2007.
[4] Interview with Sunchai Larpsumphunchai, CAO, 15 October 2007.

RESTRUCTURING THE PRODUCT PORTFOLIO

As soon as he became CEO, Wilf realized that in the environment of volatile interest rates, AACP could no longer drive growth by selling potentially unprofitable products. In August 2005, the number of products was cut from 20 to 14 while the company launched six new variable rate policies. Reducing the number of products enabled sales agents to focus on more profitable offerings, but still give policyholders the flexibility to meet their life insurance needs.

Focusing on profitable, customer-focused products paid off. AACP's internal analysis showed that the product portfolio mix changed dramatically, with "value-destroying" products accounting for only 3% of the first-year premiums in 2007, in contrast to 95% in 2003 (*refer to Exhibit 3, Total company ANP, 2003–2007*). The steady rate of introduction of innovative policies continued through 2005–2007, firmly positioning AACP as a product innovator within the Thai life insurance industry. New **Customer Focus** initiatives (such as the Net Promoter Score and Prestige Service) were launched to encourage staff to provide their best service to policyholders and agents, many of them based on customer feedback.

The distribution channel mix was also rebalanced to reduce reliance on the agency. Teaming up with Tisco Bank, Standard Chartered Bank and GE Money Bank, as well as strengthening the ties with the Bank of Ayudhya, expanded the bancassurance business. As a result, the bancassurance and telesales grew faster than agency sales and in 2007 accounted for 23% and 11% of total company sales.

REBUILDING THE MANAGEMENT TEAM

Back in 2004, Wilf had realized that very few of the "old guard" senior executives

EXHIBIT 3   Total Company ANP, 2003–2007

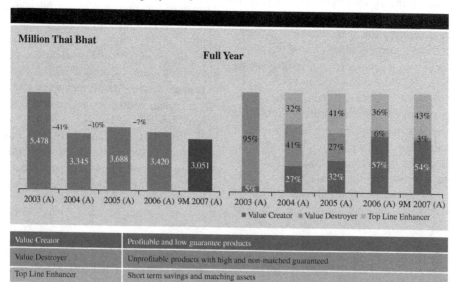

Source: AACP Presentation to IMD, 15 October, 2007.

could take up the daunting task of aligning behind his change initiatives. Within three years of the crisis, 75 people from the top four ranks (of around 100) within the company had left, including most of the expatriates. Attracting and retaining top talent in Thailand had always been a challenge, but at AACP it was exacerbated by the company's tarnished reputation. Internal promotions at the senior management level addressed only part of the problem.

In a bold move, Wilf hired eight senior executives from outside the industry. This went against the established practice in life insurance, where most of the senior management team typically had industry sales and actuarial backgrounds but, in Wilf's view, were often too short-term oriented. What he wanted was a high level of sustained commitment, fresh insights into how to serve the customer and energy to support the transformation. The new hires were mostly from consumer goods companies such as S.C. Johnson, Coca-Cola, Procter & Gamble, Federal Express and IBM. Many took their appointments as a challenge, a chance to shake up the traditional industry and an opportunity to raise the profile of life insurance as a good savings channel for people.[5]

REDESIGNING THE WORK ENVIRONMENT

When Wilf joined AACP, he had been shocked by the lack of interaction and communication at senior management level. Some managers spent almost all of their time in their offices with the door closed and barely spoke to their counterparts in other divisions. Wilf believed that this could not continue if AACP was to become the market leader in Thailand.[6]

An open office concept was a start. After hiring a professional designer to rearrange the space, Wilf set the example with his own office. When the renovation of the floor space started, he relocated from the lavish CEO quarters on the upper floor to join other employees on the first floor. "When this happened," Wilf remembered with a laugh, "they thought that I would be there only until my office got renovated; they couldn't believe I wasn't going to move!"[7] Not only did the new environment look much more attractive and friendly, the design also significantly reduced rental and electricity costs.

The dress code was also relaxed from formal business attire unsuitable for the hot and humid Bangkok climate to a more appropriate "smart casual, dress as you like" or the blue corporate T-shirt. Apart from the physical changes, the company introduced a system of flexible working hours, based on each employee's responsibilities. As part of the initiative, AACP's main office opened its doors on weekends. Both initiatives were highly unusual in the industry, and reorganizing the work environment and practices aimed at stirring up the organization were high-risk initiatives.[8] But for Wilf this was the only way to promote transparency, "accessibility" and the faster flow of information.[9]

All these changes did not sit well with the traditional Thai management culture,

---

[5] Interviews with Wachirapun Chotechoung, Chief Officer-Human Resources, and Supar Phokachaipat, Chief Officer-Corporate Affairs, both held on 15 October 2007.

[6] Interview with Wilf Blackburn, 10 January 2005, internal company document.

[7] Interview with Wilf Blackburn, CEO, 14 October 2007.

[8] Interview with Duncan Lord, General Manager, Allianz Reinsurance Branch Asia-Pacific, 15 October 2007.

[9] Kittikanya, C. "On the Rebound." *Bangkok Post*, 8 August 2005, p. B2.

where face, hierarchy and status—derived, for example, from the size of the office, a personal secretary and a private driver—were very important. Wilf had no illusion that dismantling the office walls was a high-risk decision and he was prepared for a few casualties. He did not "sell" the idea of the open-floor environment to senior managers; he simply said: "There are 24 other insurance companies in Thailand, so, if you want it so much, you can have an office with one of them."[10]

A senior AACP veteran strongly supportive of Wilf's initiatives recalled how she tried to warm up other managers on her team to the idea of having no private offices, "He [Wilf] has a modest office. So I told my staff that I cannot [oppose Wilf's idea], because I know if he can do it, then I have to do the same. After that, no one complained."[11] Following an initial period of doubt, skepticism and outright resistance, most of the staff came to embrace the new system.

REINFORCING PEOPLE MANAGEMENT

The crisis and subsequent developments had left the AACP staff demoralized and exhausted. In late 2005, staff turnover reached an unprecedented high of 32%. In a way, this was a mixed blessing, for as those without the ability to bring about business and cultural change left, so there was an opportunity to renew the employee pool. The problem was, nobody wanted to work for AACP.

In response, the company radically overhauled its performance management system, linking pay to performance against targets[12] and infusing the entire system with transparency from the highest to the lowest levels. An aggressive average variable pay component was set at 37%, allowing some employees to receive bonuses of up to 82% of their annual income. Employees who still did not have individual targets could earn a bonus based on the overall performance of the company.[13] The new system had two components: 60% to 70% of an individual's performance evaluation was based on the business objectives, while the rest—called "personal responsibility"—was linked to values that AACP wanted its employees to uphold. According to a senior executive, the new system was "very invasive and not natural for the Thai culture, but a system necessary to drive change and performance."[14] Employees ultimately embraced the benefits of the scheme and by late 2007 AACP staff turnover had decreased to the average Bangkok labor market rate of 12%.

The new target employee was young (below 30), typically Generation X, well educated, assertive, ambitious and career-driven. To attract and keep employees, Human Resources staff first needed to understand what the new employees were looking for in AACP beyond compensation (which in 2006 was reportedly above the industry average).[15] Opportunities for growth—both in terms of promotions and particularly "horizontally," via internal job

---

[10] Interview with Wilf Blackburn, CEO, 14 October 2007.
[11] Interview with Sugunya Tongchenchitt, Chief Officer-Regulatory Affairs, 15 October 2007.
[12] Employees were scored against targets, but not against each other. Target-setting (salary and bonuses) was done by a team at the beginning of the year, and new employees could renegotiate targets mid-year.
[13] Setthasiriphaiboon, P. "AACP in Career Drive." *The Nation*, 6 July 2007, p. 4B.
[14] Interview with Sally O'Hara, Chief Officer – Operations, 15 October 2007.
[15] Setthasiriphaiboon, P. "AACP in Career Drive." *The Nation*, 6 July 2007, p. 4B.

change and international assignments—came at the top of the list. Thus, in 2007, 11 employees were sent on assignments of six months to two years in either Allianz's Munich head office or Asian subsidiaries. Flexible office hours and recreational activities also made the company an attractive employer.

Effective communication had always been a weak spot at AACP. When Supar Phokachaipat, Chief Officer Corporate Affairs, assumed her role in 2005, she worked hard on streamlining and strengthening internal and external communication. Senior management meetings and face-to-face meetings with staff and agents were enhanced by technology—SMS, e-mail, notices and **Voice to You** (a combination of e-mail and SMS). The effectiveness of specific channels was measured twice a year through staff surveys. SMS and **Voice to You** proved particularly effective for agents who had little time to read e-mail.

In a short span of time, AACP was transformed from a traditional Thai company, where jobs were seen as lifelong entitlements, to an international company which rewarded talent, performance and the ability to adapt to change.

REPOSITIONING THE BRAND

In the recent past, AACP had not invested in brand-building, in part because Ayudhya Allianz C.P. was not an easy name to remember or pronounce. As a result, not many customers were aware of Allianz's ownership of AACP or that Allianz was a global industry leader. In late 2007, however, AACP committed nearly €2 million (10% of expenses) to launch a brand-building campaign to change customers' perceptions, craft a unique position and differentiate AACP from its close competitors, AIA and Thai Life.

Under the slogan "For the Rhythm of Your Life," the company challenged the traditional image of life insurance. Instead of emphasizing the negative side of life, typically associated with sickness, old age and death, AACP sought to create an entirely different brand personality—optimistic, energetic, friendly and groovy (*refer to Exhibit 4*). Short introductory commercials and floating ads on the internet, designed to create brand awareness and enhance visibility in 2007, were to be followed by a specific product- and agent-centered TV campaign in 2008. The slogan extended to all aspects of internal

EXHIBIT 4   **AACP vs. Thai Life Insurance Industry Conventions**

Industry Conventions/Given	AACP
• Negative side of life	• Positive side of life
• Sickness, Oldness, Dead	• Happy, Healthy, Enjoy life
• Oldies happy moment	• Youth happy moment
• Wish to make other's life happy	• Wish to enjoy and live their own life happily
• Protection benefit for the one we love	• Investing benefit for ourselves
• Passive, Serious, Formal, Credible	• Active, Friendly, Relax, Reliable

Source: Brand Building Campaign Presentation, 10 October 2007.

company communication, from office decoration, lifts and entrance floors to relaxation zones, and even to some unusual locations—a colorful poster in the men's toilet, depicting a young man with a musical score, urged: "Release the unhappiness, and the moment of happiness will follow."

REENGAGING THE COMMUNITY

Immediately following the 2004 crisis, AACP's corporate reputation was in tatters, and the company was frequently an object of media ridicule. Post-crisis, AACP's external communications initiatives targeted the younger generation in an attempt to improve corporate image, regain the trust of the media, build the brand and change culturally ingrained perceptions of life insurance. AACP's senior management believed passionately that they had a much broader role in Thai society than just serving the customer and the shareholders.

In early 2005, shortly after the tsunami, AACP established a Social Contribution Department to carry out a range of social projects, from educating the public about the importance of being insured to helping communities affected by natural disasters.[16] One of the major programs was the weekend tour for 150 local students from underprivileged areas to visit the historical sites of Bangkok on AACP corporate buses. Supar Phokachaipat explained that this initiative was not about selling anything to students—for the first six months, there was not even a press conference

held to cover the tours; AACP simply kept running them every weekend.[17] According to some observers, the most significant of all sweeping changes within AACP was "a climate of kindness and caring that permeate[d] all levels of the company."[18]

STEPPING UP

Allianz's internal analysis, based on financial performance data for a number of companies, showed a clear correlation between innovation and average shareholder returns.[19] Therefore, in 2006 Allianz launched the Global Innovation Initiative "i2s" (Ideas to Success) in all its affiliates in more than 70 countries, including Thailand, aiming to connect all innovation activities to the company's business strategy and generate value-creating ideas to feed the long-term pipeline. The initiative envisaged engaging all employees and agents to exploit their intellectual capital.

While historically AACP had no culture of innovation, its grassroots approach, fully supported by senior management, ensured 100% employee participation and a 30% implementation rate of innovative ideas. Some of the key tools to drive idea generation included: quarterly local innovation campaigns as well as yearly global campaigns; communication of the goals and outcomes of the program to the employees and agents to build awareness and exchange

---

[16] For example, after the tsunami AACP paid a 5 million baht premium on free life insurance for 567 families which had lost a parent in the disaster. The total sum assured was 56.7 million baht (Diadamo, E. "Ensuring Happier Lives." *Bangkok Post*, 20 December 2006, p.1).

[17] Interview with Supar Phokachaipat, Chief Officer-Corporate Affairs, 15 October, 2007.

[18] Diadamo, E. "Ensuring Happier Lives." *Bangkok Post*, 20 December 2006, p.1.

[19] Average annual shareholder returns included stock price growth and dividend income in 1990–2003. International innovation leaders (e.g., Nokia and Wal-Mart) achieved 21%, financial innovation leaders 16%, S&P 500 9% and Allianz only 7%. Source: internal company document.

ideas; and innovation training workshops, ranging from forums with innovation leaders in other industries in Thailand to creativity sessions with management.

By the end of 2007, innovation had become embedded in the company culture. This was recognized first within the region where AACP became "The Most Innovative Company in Asia" finalist in the Stevie Awards and took a sweep of Allianz's regional innovation awards. Then, in March 2008 at the annual meeting of CEOs from Allianz companies from more than 70 countries, AACP was crowned MOST INNOVATIVE entity in the Allianz Group worldwide—not a bad outcome for a company which less than four years earlier was on the edge of collapse.

Module Four

The Recipients of Change

INTRODUCTION

No one can predict the ultimate effect of the recent financial and related market crises, or the many other global economic and political forces that have set in motion so much change over the course of the first decade of the new millennium. Many of the star companies of the "new economy" have felt the same kind of squeeze others had experienced fifteen to twenty years earlier, with the massive overhaul in manufacturing, and later services, that left millions of people temporarily or long-term unemployed—receiving change in its most powerful form, at least in the individual's work life. Some people have attempted to survive as independent workers or to found their own businesses; others have attempted to forge new work arrangements within large firms; still others have clung to traditional, long-term employment systems in the (often vain) hope that their companies, or at least they personally, would be spared the upheaval. Whether or not such loyalty is becoming a quaint concept of the past, one thing is clear: The ramifications of change are profound. This module shifts the focus from designing and implementing change to what it is like to be on the receiving end. By looking squarely at the effects of change on individuals and their social arena—work environment, families, communities—we gain a better appreciation of what both companies and individuals can do to mitigate, in some way, the extremes of experiencing change.

One aim of this module, then, is to consider how change can be introduced, given an understanding of its effects. Can an organization learn from its mistakes? Its successes? Likewise, can a recipient of change in one situation use that experience positively? Or is the once-burned-twice-shy adage inevitable?

The second aim of the module is to provoke discussion of what obligations exist between employer and employee. What "right" has an organization to either demand change or superimpose it on a person or a group? Conversely, has the individual or group the right to threaten the organization's viability by refusing the change?

Finally, we examine change from the perspective of the individual's career. Until now, we have focused primarily on the impact of change in the organizational arena.

We have already seen that organizations have been profoundly affected by the forces of rapid innovation and globalization, and that flexibility and adaptability are underlying requirements for ongoing success and growth in this environment. One of the most profound outcomes of this shift has been a significant realignment in the psychological contract (see Module 3) between an organization and its individual members, who must now demonstrate the same degree of flexibility and adaptability as the organizations that they can no longer count on for lifetime employment. We take the opportunity in this module, therefore, to begin to address the individual career implications of these changes in the workplace.

CASES AND READINGS

The module opens with perhaps the best known of our Change Classics. In "Donna Dubinsky and Apple Computer, Inc. (A)," Dubinsky confronts a possible reorganization of the firm's distribution system, which she built essentially from scratch and currently manages. She is, however, in a position to influence whether or not this change will take place. What this case introduces to the subject of receiving change is reactions to the *anticipated* change—in particular, how those reactions are stirred when the change threatens someone's direct, personal contribution to the organization.

At the end of the Dubinsky session, another Apple case may be distributed, in which the same situation that Dubinsky faced is examined from someone else's perspective. This person, too, was shaken by the possible change; interestingly, both protagonists used the same phrase—"Sheer misery"—but in somewhat different ways. The reading "The Recipients of Change" accompanies the Apple case (or cases). This note introduces the *process* of reacting to change: the initial impact, the stages of coming to terms with being changed, and gradual acceptance. It also suggests some approaches for both the "changee" and the implementor that may lessen the difficulties in receiving change and shorten the process of acceptance.

The two Apple cases and the reading underscore the point that organizations that fail to appreciate the dynamics of reacting to change will, at a minimum, waste an appalling amount of time as people nurse their wounds. That is, when there is no acknowledgment, explicit or implicit, of what people are experiencing, recipients are hindered from getting through their normal, unavoidable psychological responses. Moreover, when these recipients must (or should) be carrying their everyday responsibilities as well as dealing with a potential change to those responsibilities, if there is no support for the latter, the former will surely suffer.

The next case, "Wellcome Israel (A)," introduces an executive facing a high level of uncertainty when her group's parent company, Wellcome plc, is taken over by arch-rival Glaxo. For the first time in her career, Ofra Sherman finds herself "in a situation where she [has] virtually no direct control over the outcome." Knowing she will be unable to influence decisions that will determine her future and that of her team, Sherman is cast, most unwillingly, into a potentially passive role. With the long-term outlook nowhere near as clear as it had been during her previous five years at Wellcome, Sherman must decide whether to wait for events to unfold and decisions to be handed down to her, or to take the bull by the horns and make decisions for herself and her team that might not be congruent with top management's plans for her region. She must also decide where her primary loyalties lie: with the corporation that hired her (but that may or may not retain her services once the dust from the merger settles); with her team of employees, several of whom she considers close friends; or with her own self-interest. The organizational complexities in the case provide a panoply of conflicting forces of the sort that can pull at any change recipient during such times of turbulence.

The reading that accompanies the Wellcome case, "Back to Square Zero: The Post-Corporate Career," provides insights into the problems facing Ofra Sherman—and others like her in the corporate world—who may find in the not-so-distant future that their career paths exist predominantly *outside* large organizations, or at least beyond any single one of them. Post-corporate careers sometimes involve serving—from outside—the same organizations the individuals have left (whether due to downsizing or their own initiative), but they fundamentally illustrate the kind of independence and flexibility that we have already seen to be essential to success in the twenty-first century global, networked economy. Individuals may initially find it difficult to replace the security provided by long-term organizational membership, but they can learn to derive their own secure identity from other sources, such as strengthened customer–client relationships and membership in professional or other shared-interest communities. In the concluding section of this reading, the authors offer suggestions to individuals and organizations to help them adapt to and thrive in the post-corporate career world.

With the careers discussion for background, the two cases that follow are vignettes of two victims of corporate downsizing. Emilio Kornau has built a successful career in a large, multinational company, but is unprepared when his entire department is laid off in a major restructuring. Over the next few years, Kornau finds it difficult to re-establish himself. Mark Margolis, after a number of setbacks early in his career, is hired by a major consumer products company only to be laid off a few years later. He uses his severance pay to launch a software company that he eventually sells, receiving over $10 million for his stake. The parallels and contrasts between these two cases help us understand both the individual and the situational factors inherent in being a recipient of change, and in finding a way forward.

In the Kerstin Berger (A) case, an American expatriate hired rather haphazardly into the IT area of a Swiss bank finds herself in charge of a near-impossible project without the network or support necessary to make any real progress. The change to which the expatriate, Tina Orton, has to respond is not so much corporate change as total situational change—new country, new company, new personal circumstances, new industry, new culture, new leadership style—and the challenge her colleague, Kerstin Berger, faces is how to help Tina deal with the resulting vast array of challenges in front of her.

The next segment of this module, "Broadway Brokers," is a simulation exercise. A large financial services company is preparing to notify its employees of an unprecedented, massive downsizing and is contemplating a variety of approaches it can take. These must be assessed according to importance and timing—from "Do this immediately" to "Don't do this at all." Like the Merger Plan Simulation in Module 3, this exercise entails choice and sequencing; but in this situation, the aim is not to introduce a set of changes. Rather, it is to decide how to tell thousands of people that they will lose their jobs. Of course, this is also implementing change, but to do so successfully will require drawing on a deep understanding of how change is received and how to mitigate its effects.

In the final reading in this section, "Managing to Communicate, Communicating to Manage: How Leading Companies Communicate with Employees," Mary Young and James E. Post report on how successful companies—those that have both undergone major change and been recognized for excellent internal communications—manage this perennially difficult task. The authors identify eight principles of effective corporate communications and provide examples from their research to illustrate each. Taken together, they make a convincing case that effective communication, especially when it concerns employees, is vital to any organization undergoing significant change.

The individual experience of change, of course, is not only about those on the receiving end. The personal side of change leadership—at all levels—is the subject of Module 5.

Change Classic

Donna Dubinsky and Apple Computer, Inc. (A)

At 7 A.M. on Friday, April 19, 1985, Donna Dubinsky placed an urgent phone call to her boss's boss, Bill Campbell, executive vice president for sales and marketing at Apple Computer, Inc. Dubinsky, director of distribution and sales administration, was attending a management leadership seminar located more than two hours away. Her words were crisp and to the point: "Bill, I really need to talk to you. Will you wait for me today? I'll be back at the office around five."

"Absolutely, I'll be here," Campbell replied, although he knew nothing about the purpose of her call.

Dubinsky inhaled a deep, anxious breath. She felt the time had come to "bet her Apple career" on the ultimatum she was going to deliver to Campbell at the head office in Cupertino, California.

Still, she could hardly believe it had come to this. Her first three years at Apple, from July 1981 through the fall of 1984, had been ones of continuous success with increasing authority and recognition. She had refined and formalized much of the Apple product distribution policy, and she worked closely with the six distribution centers across the country.

Unexpectedly, however, in early 1985, Steve Jobs, Apple's chairman of the board and general manager of the Macintosh Division, had proposed that the existing distribution system be dismantled and replaced by the "just-in-time" method. Jobs' proposal would not only place all of Apple's distribution activities under the supervision of the directors of manufacturing within the two product divisions, Macintosh and Apple II, but would also establish direct relationships between the dealer and the plant—essentially eliminating the need for the six distribution centers. Jobs claimed that this change would result in significant savings for the company by shrinking the product pipeline and reducing inventory, an especially attractive promise since Apple's market share was declining steadily. Dubinsky cited her experience and track record with distribution, however, and argued that the new method was infeasible. In the past four months, despite Dubinsky's criticisms, Jobs' proposal had gathered momentum and support throughout the company.

As she left the leadership seminar and drove to Cupertino for her meeting with Campbell, Dubinsky reflected on the effect this distribution proposal would have on her job and on the company. She believed that it spelled catastrophe for both and that it was time to take a stand.

DONNA DUBINSKY

Dubinsky, a Yale graduate, had worked for two years in commercial banking before entering the MBA program at the Harvard Business School. While job hunting just before her graduation, Dubinsky decided that Apple was the kind of cutting-edge technology firm that interested her, and she further decided that, despite her financial background, she wanted a position close to the customers. Apple had few MBAs at that time, and their Harvard recruiters were looking for technical backgrounds. Nevertheless, Dubinsky pushed hard for interviews and finally received an offer after pointing out that they would probably never find another Harvard MBA who wanted to work in customer service.

In July 1981, she started as customer support liaison in a department of one, reporting to Roy Weaver, the new head of the distribution, service, and support group. Over the next three years, Weaver continued to expand her responsibilities until April 1985, when she became director of distribution and sales administration with 80 employees and a $10 million budget. (This promotion had been approved in December 1984. See Table 1.) Weaver had concluded early on that the best way to retain a talented manager like Dubinsky was to continually reward and challenge her. His strategy worked so well that when Jobs himself tried to hire Dubinsky for his Macintosh introduction in 1983, she chose to stay put. Dubinsky commented:

> Roy has been the best mentor I could have asked for. He always gave me just enough rope, yet was available whenever I needed his advice and guidance. He was continually looking for opportunities to give me visibility as well as more responsibility.

Although Dubinsky rarely fought for her own career progress, she willingly and ably fought for her subordinates—her "people" as she called them—and for the Apple dealers and customers. When asked to describe her management style, Dubinsky focused primarily on her caring and honest relationships with her subordinates. One of Dubinsky's subordinates commented:

> Donna Dubinsky is very direct. She says what she thinks. And she fights for her issues. If she feels she's right and she loses her issue, she goes down

TABLE 1   **Dubinsky's Career at Apple**

July 1981	Joined firm as Customer Support Liaison.
July 1982	Became Customer Support Program Manager.
	Added first direct report and field management responsibility (six dotted-line managers).
October 1982	Added Customer Relations.
December 1982	Added Direct Sales Administration Group.
January 1984	Became distribution manager.
	Added Product Distribution Group.
	Added warehousing.
June 1984	Added Field Communications.
	Added AppleLink Operations (computerized communication with the field).
October 1984	Added Teacher Buy (special distribution project).
January 1985	Added Traffic.
	Added Developer Relations.
April 1985	Became Director, Distribution and Sales Administration (promotion approved December 1984).
	Added Forecasting.

fighting. She always presents an image of confidence. She doesn't let peer pressure sway her mind. She's not intimidated by upper management. But that's not to say that she won't change her mind.

And she'll always support a company decision even if she doesn't agree with it. That's an important quality for a "support" organization. She always has the company's interests at heart.

She's extremely intelligent. She has a great sense of humor. . . . I learned a great deal from her about taking risks and about when to really hold a hard line on an issue.

If you look at where she was three years ago and where she is now, it's phenomenal. It really is. And she can grow a lot more.

Dubinsky characterized herself as thick-skinned and nondefensive. One human resource manager commented: "Dubinsky projects a lot of confidence and conviction in her beliefs. You definitely know where she stands. She is not a political animal at all."

Commenting on her direct style and willingness to take certain risks, Dubinsky explained:

As a middle manager, I often was put in the position of making decisions beyond my authority, or at least within the gray area of unstated authority levels. In a more seasoned company, making that decision on my own could cause serious organizational repercussions. At Apple, the middle manager had to presume the boss' agreement and was comfortable that she or he was allowed to make mistakes.

Weaver, her first and longest-term supervisor, valued her clear, precise thinking; her presentation skills and voice command; and the power of her presence.

Campbell, Weaver's boss, described Dubinsky's contribution:

What we had was this unbelievable plethora of ideas in the product divisions that came down to a marketing execution funnel. We didn't have the systems in place that would enable us to execute, and Donna was the only one who understood that and who understood what we could do in terms of execution. Donna was a battler for procedure before we ever thought procedure was important.

He added, however:

But I've told her many times, "You've got to work the halls and sell your ideas. You can't expect things to happen by fiat."

COMPANY BACKGROUND

Apple's inception and meteoric rise received frequent press coverage and became well known from the time of its founding in 1976 through its entry in the Fortune 500 six years later. The easy-to-use Apple II, a home and educational computer, appeared in 1977 and, in its various enhanced forms, remained the major-selling product of the Cupertino, California-based company through 1985.

In 1983, Apple and its cofounder, Steve Jobs, lured John Sculley from his position as president of PepsiCo to take on the presidency at Apple. His challenge was to bring new organization and marketing discipline to Apple, without sacrificing creativity and spirit. He also faced IBM's 28 percent market share in 1983 as compared to Apple's 24 percent, down from 40 percent in 1981 (see Exhibit 1).

The Macintosh was introduced in early 1984 and, although its sales never

EXHIBIT 1   Apple Financial Performance and Market Share, 1980–1985

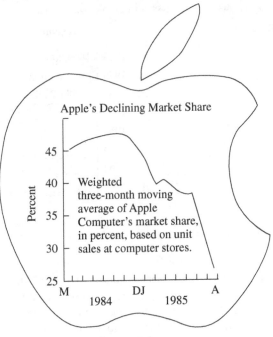

Apple's Declining Market Share

Weighted three-month moving average of Apple Computer's market share, in percent, based on unit sales at computer stores.

Source: Infocorp

continued

EXHIBIT 1   Apple Financial Performance and Market Share, 1980–1985—*continued*

Manufacturers' Share of the U.S. Personal-Computer Market,

$1,000–$5,000 Price Range

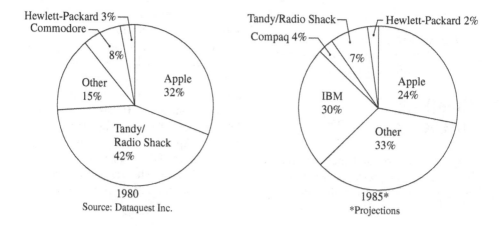

1980
Source: Dataquest Inc.

1985*
*Projections

EXHIBIT 1   Apple Financial Performance and Market Share, 1980–1985—*continued*

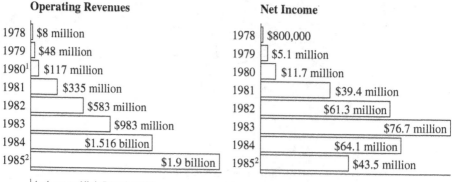

Operating Revenues

1978	$8 million
1979	$48 million
1980[1]	$117 million
1981	$335 million
1982	$583 million
1983	$983 million
1984	$1.516 billion
1985[2]	$1.9 billion

Net Income

1978	$800,000
1979	$5.1 million
1980	$11.7 million
1981	$39.4 million
1982	$61.3 million
1983	$76.7 million
1984	$64.1 million
1985[2]	$43.5 million

[1] Apple went public in December 1980
[2] Estimates

Source: Standard & Poor's Corp. *Value Line Investment Survey,* Data Research Inc., Dataquest Inc.

matched Apple's projections, they were still impressive in that first year. Although actual Mac profits were lowered by high market-entry costs, Apple II sales carried the firm through a record Christmas quarter. By 1985, however, sales failed to reach projected planning levels, causing profitability problems, since expenses had been based on the higher revenue figures. Tensions were mounting between the Apple II Division, which felt its contribution to the firm was undervalued, and the Macintosh Division, whose general manager, Jobs, saw it as the technological vanguard within Apple. Previously, Jobs had split his division off from the rest of the firm, dubbing them "pirates," whose creativity would be unfettered by rules and bureaucracy. By 1985, Jobs and Sculley were beginning to feel the strains in a hitherto remarkably close and interdependent relationship.

Apple's early rapid growth meant a constant influx of new employees. Apple attempted to create and solidify a sense of identity by developing a statement of basic values (see Exhibit 2). For a long time, organizational charts were not printed at Apple since they changed too quickly. Frequent reorganizations reflected the conflict between product organization and functional organization. When Apple began, it had only one product, and, therefore, its structure was largely functional. As new products began to develop, each team formed its own division, modeled on the original Apple, each with its own marketing, its own engineering, and so forth.

When Sculley joined the firm, he simplified its structure with a compromise format, centralizing product development and product marketing in just two divisions—the Apple II and the Macintosh—with U.S. sales and marketing services centralized in a third division. Nevertheless, this revised format still reflected a mix of functional, product, and geographic organizations. Seven divisions reported directly to Sculley (see Figure 1). He believed that a coordinated sales and marketing approach was necessary for the firm to present a clear message to dealers and to compete with IBM's highly trained sales force and other firms with larger resource bases and well-established marketing relations and procedures.

PRODUCT DISTRIBUTION AT APPLE

In January 1984, Dubinsky became U.S. distribution manager for all of Apple, with dotted-line responsibility for the six field warehouses and direct responsibility for sales administration, inventory control, and customer relations. Organizationally, she was situated within U.S. sales and marketing, although she required ongoing contact with the product divisions.

Apple's product appealed mainly to the home and educational markets whose seasonal and sometimes fickle purchasing patterns placed a strain on physical distribution. Predicting sales patterns was difficult, but it was also imperative that the product be available when requested. In addition, Dubinsky's group maintained relationships with Apple's dealers, a critical factor in the competitive battle for limited dealer shelf space; neither Apple nor any of its competitors could afford to own their dealers. Most dealers started as mom-and-pop organizations, and they were often undercapitalized, particularly given the growth in the market. Finally, since Apple's operation was primarily design and assembly (rather than fabrication), inventory and warehousing control for parts, works in process, and finished goods were potentially costly and critical to Apple's profits and responsiveness to the market.

The distribution group took all Apple products from their respective manufacturing sites (or from their ports of entry for products imported from overseas vendors) to the dealers. For example, Macintosh

EXHIBIT 2 Apple Values

Achieving our goal is important to us. But we're equally concerned with the *way* we reach it. These are the values that govern our business conduct.

Empathy for customers/users: We offer superior products that fill real needs and provide lasting value. We deal fairly with competitors and meet customers and vendors more than halfway. We are genuinely interested in solving customer problems and will not compromise our ethics or integrity in the name of profit.

Achievement/aggressiveness: We set aggressive goals and drive ourselves hard to achieve them. We recognize that this is a unique time when our product will change the way people work and live. It's an adventure, and we're in it together.

Positive social contribution: As a corporate citizen, we wish to be an economic, intellectual, and social asset in communities where we operate. But beyond that, we expect to make this world a better place to live in. We build products that extend human capability, freeing people from drudgery and helping them achieve more than they could alone.

Innovation/vision: We build our company on innovation, providing products that are new and needed. We accept the risks inherent in following our vision and work to develop leadership products which command the profit margins we strive for.

Individual performance: We expect individual commitment and performance above the standard for our industry. Only thus will we make the profits that permit us to seek our other corporate objectives. Each employee can and must make a difference; for in the final analysis, *individuals* determine the character and strength of Apple.

Team spirit: Teamwork is essential to Apple's success, for the job is too big to be done by any one person. Individuals are encouraged to interact with all levels of management, sharing ideas and suggestions to improve Apple's effectiveness and quality of life. It takes all of us to win. We support each other and share the victories and rewards together. We're enthusiastic about what we do.

Quality/excellence: We care about what we do. We build into Apple products a level of quality, performance, and value that will earn the respect and loyalty of our customers.

Individual rewards: We recognize each person's contribution to Apple's success, and we share the financial rewards that flow from high performance. We recognize also that rewards must be psychological as well as financial and strive for an atmosphere where each individual can share the adventure and excitement of working at Apple.

Good management: The attitudes of managers toward their people are of primary importance. Employees should be able to trust the motives and integrity of their supervisors. It is the responsibility of management to create a productive environment where Apple values flourish.

computers were assembled at the facility in Fremont, California. Based on monthly sales forecasts, the distribution group allocated a specific number of those computers to each of the six distribution sites: Sunnyvale, California; Irvine, California; Chicago, Illinois; Dallas, Texas; Boston, Massachusetts; and Charlotte,

FIGURE 1   **Apple organization chart, October 1984.**

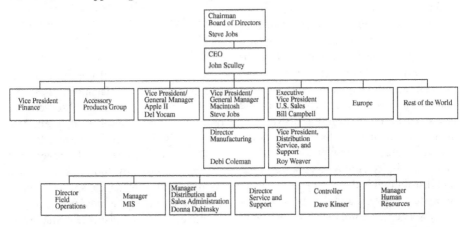

North Carolina. Each of these sites was actually a customer support center that provided warehousing, customer service, credit, repair service, order entry, and a technical group to assist dealers. Individual dealers called in orders to their area support center representative, who arranged to have the requested product sent out. Employees of the distribution group took pride in this system's efficiency and simplicity, although forecasting mistakes often caused shortages or excesses of individual products.

Planning and analysis were luxuries for product distribution as Apple grew. Dubinsky recalled:

> I might also mention what was not done: analytical overkill. One incident stands out. My boss needed to request funds from the president to build a warehouse in Boston. He showed me his notes; he merely was going to tell the president the amount of yearly lease cost. As a newly minted MBA, the idea of approaching the president without a full-blown, discounted cash flow analysis was beyond belief, so I offered to prepare one, an offer instantly accepted. After several hours of work, I produced a VisiCalc model that would

have been attacked for its simplicity by my B-School classmates, but seemed adequate under the circumstances. When my boss returned from the meeting, he told me that the president had glanced for several minutes at my neatly laid-out analysis, looked up, and asked one question; "What is the yearly lease cost?" After hearing the response he said, "OK. Let's do it." No time for analysis.

THE DISTRIBUTION CONFLICT: SEPTEMBER TO DECEMBER, 1984

The conflict over Apple's distribution strategy began in September 1984, when Dubinsky and her boss, Weaver, presented the distribution, service, and support group's 1985 business plan to the Apple executive staff for review. Both Dubinsky and Weaver had presented their plan confidently because of this group's strong performance record. The plan held no real surprises, but it did call for a long-term distribution strategy review to be conducted throughout the coming year, particularly concerning the development of additional distribution centers.

Jobs challenged the plan, however, complaining that he had not received a good explanation for the current distribution, service, and support cost levels and structure. Dubinsky and Weaver were taken aback by Jobs' criticism. Cost had never been a problem in the distribution area. In a firm that devoted most of its energy and interest to new product development, Dubinsky and Weaver were proud that distribution had never caused a delay in product delivery, and they believed that the absence of complaints was probably their highest praise. In addition, they had just shipped out goods for a record quarter by over 60 percent, without missing a beat.

A few weeks later, however, Jobs had dinner with Fred Smith, founder and CEO of Federal Express. The two dynamic entrepreneurs found much in common, and Jobs was particularly interested in Smith's discussion of IBM's just-in-time distribution of selected computer components. Jobs saw a potential for reducing costs in this process, which would eliminate the need for Apple's warehouses, carrying costs, and extensive inventory. An Apple dealer would report an order as it was placed, triggering manufacturing's immediate assembly of the requested product. Upon assembly, the product would be shipped overnight, by Federal Express, to its dealer or customer destination.

Jobs and his director of manufacturing, Debi Coleman, investigated this concept, certain that their plant could efficiently incorporate the distribution function. Jobs was proud of the Macintosh Division's fully automated manufacturing facility and confident in the ability of Coleman, a Stanford MBA who was quoted as boldly stating:

> I didn't walk into this job with all the credentials. They picked me because I will grow the fastest with it. I want to be the best in the world—there's no doubt about it.[1]

The project was all the more attractive to Jobs because Macintosh sales were down. One manager later observed, "In order to defend themselves, they [the Macintosh Division] went on the attack."

Dubinsky, however, believed the change proposed by Jobs was a mistake. As distribution manager, she was confident that she held the most pertinent perspective; and she suspected Macintosh manufacturing's motives. The flaws in a distribution plan as radical as Jobs and Coleman's seemed obvious to her:

> We were an off-the-shelf business. You've got to have inventory. The dealers couldn't stock the inventory because they didn't have the cash resources to do it, so we essentially played a role as distributor, creating a buffer for them that we could afford and that they couldn't afford. [Jobs and Coleman's idea] was a total nonrecognition of our business as far as I was concerned. It was a manufacturing/logistics/cost-control point of view that had no value in the real world.

Dubinsky was further confused by the rumored interest expressed by Sculley and the rest of the executive staff in Jobs' idea.

Weaver was similarly confused. The fall of 1984 was a difficult time for him, both personally and professionally. In particular, he felt unsure of his relationship with his new boss, Campbell. (Campbell had been personally recruited in July 1983 by Sculley from Eastman Kodak for his

---

[1] *USA Today,* August 29, 1985.

teaching ability and marketing leadership. He had previously worked at the advertising firm of J. Walter Thompson after serving six seasons as the popular head football coach at Columbia University.) Shortly after the September business plan review meeting, Campbell's responsibilities had been shifted to include Weaver's group. Weaver had previously reported directly to Sculley. The unexpected distribution issue focused on one of the areas Weaver was most proud of and threatened to remove it from his and Dubinsky's control; thus, Weaver's objections appeared to management as more defensive than well reasoned.

Both Dubinsky and Weaver had difficulty taking this new distribution idea seriously. To a certain extent they chalked it up to Jobs' penchant for "big, elegant things," like a single automated manufacturing and warehousing facility, and to Coleman's personal style. One human resources manager described Coleman as "very aggressive, very intimidating, very bright, and having little finesse." Nevertheless, responding to Jobs' challenges, Campbell and Sculley called for a strategy review and recommended improvements from the distribution group by mid-December.

Meanwhile, Dubinsky began hearing reports of an elaborate presentation, a book-length "Distribution Strategy Proposal," which Coleman and her staff were preparing. More and more people were learning about the proposal; furthermore, Dubinsky could see her boss, Weaver, growing more unsure, more certain he could not win. At one point, Weaver decided to try to talk with Sculley himself, but Weaver's boss, Campbell, discouraged him, explaining that Weaver would only appear to be defensive. Dubinsky commented:

I had always looked to Roy for advice before on how to handle any difficult situation; he always had a refreshing, honest point of view. At this point, however, he was becoming paralyzed by the situation, and I found it harder to turn to him.

As distribution was Dubinsky's responsibility, the task of preparing a strategy review fell to her. The more she heard about the presentation Coleman was preparing, the more sure Dubinsky became of her own position. She worked with Dave Kinser, controller for the distribution, service, and support group on a research project intended to defend the existing distribution system. Since this was the Christmas season—a very busy time for distribution—Dubinsky was unable to allocate an extensive number of hours or people to the project. Still, she thought, distribution was her area and she knew it best; surely her judgment and past record of effectiveness would carry more weight than Coleman's untested and radical proposal. But as the mid-December strategy review deadline set by Sculley in September drew near, Dubinsky realized that she was not prepared to defend her area against the sophisticated presentation that Coleman had reportedly prepared, and Dubinsky finally requested an extension.

THE DISTRIBUTION TASK FORCE, JANUARY–APRIL, 1985

The conflict sharpened when, unexpectedly, on a Monday evening in early January 1985, Weaver called Dubinsky at her home, the first time he had ever done so. He anxiously explained that he had just learned from Campbell that Coleman would be presenting her distribution proposal at a three-day executive meeting, scheduled for Wednesday, Thursday, and Friday of that same week. The meeting would be held off site, at Pajaro Dunes, the regular Apple retreat, and it was originally planned as an opportunity to evaluate new product developments. Only executive staff, division heads, and one engineer from each of the Apple II and Macintosh teams were supposed to attend. Dubinsky could not understand why Coleman's presentation on the distribution issue was even on the agenda, and, if this issue was to be discussed, she felt that as distribution manager, she should be the one to address the topic.

Weaver had just learned of the agenda change from Campbell, who explained that Sculley had heard Coleman's presentation recently and had asked Campbell if she could be included in the Pajaro meeting. Weaver thought Campbell should have refused since distribution fell within the authority of Campbell, Weaver, and Dubinsky, but Campbell had agreed to Sculley's request.

Weaver called that evening asking Dubinsky to drop everything and put together a counter-proposal, an overview that he would deliver at Wednesday's meeting. Dubinsky agreed and, in one day, completed a presentation that was hand-delivered to Weaver in time for the executive conference.

She learned later that Coleman's and Weaver's presentations triggered an emotional and very difficult discussion that day. The vice president for human resources, Jay Elliot, criticized the executive meeting process, pointing out that, counter to Apple values, this was an all-too-familiar instance of top management stepping around its own middle managers and engaging in top-down management. Why was Coleman presenting to Sculley instead of to Weaver, and why

was Coleman instead of Dubinsky presenting the distribution issue at Pajaro? Coming at a time when Jobs and Sculley were facing growing disagreements and when Jobs was pressuring Sculley to accept Coleman's proposal, the executive staff took this criticism to heart.

It was resolved to entrust the distribution problem to a task force composed of the parties involved and a few "neutral" individuals. The task force would report to Campbell, and, as a demonstration of its confidence and commitment to the Apple team, the executive staff pledged to accept the task force's recommendations.

The Distribution Task Force included Dubinsky, Dave Kinser (controller), and Weaver, all of the distribution service and support group; Coleman and Jim Bean, from Macintosh and Apple II manufacturing respectively, and both supporters of the just-in-time proposal; and Jay Elliot, Joe Graziano (vice president of finance), and Phil Dixon (management information systems) as the "neutral players."

Most of those at the Pajaro meeting applauded this task force solution. Campbell, who was dissatisfied and embarrassed by the presentation his group had mounted, saw it as a way to force analysis. He thought his group "hadn't done its homework" and that its presentation did not reflect a thorough reexamination of the distribution process. For Weaver, it was a kind of reprieve.

But Dubinsky was angry and disappointed:

> I didn't know why there should be a task force at all. Distribution's our job. . . .
> I couldn't get out of this mentality that what we had was working so well. The thing had never broken down. . . . Now I was supposed to go back and do this strategy, and I couldn't figure out what problem I was solving.

She had always assumed that she would continue to gather ideas from the field for suggested improvements in the existing system. But Coleman's proposal was much more than simply suggested improvements; in fact, Dubinsky thought, it was more than a new distribution system. It was a total change in distribution and manufacturing strategy, taking Apple from supply-driven to demand-driven procedures, and reducing the distribution and warehouse centers from six to zero.

The longer Dubinsky, Weaver, and Kinser thought about it, the more problems they found in Coleman's proposal. As the task force began and continued over the next four months, weekly at first and then less frequently, the members raised objections: for example, the proposal failed to consider the more than 50 percent of Apple products that were manufactured offshore; it focused only on central processing units, ignoring Apple's other products; there was no provision for customer complaints and product returns; multiple product line orders would be inconvenient for dealers who would be required to split their request between the two product divisions and their respective directors of manufacturing.

Coleman consistently stressed the point that her proposal would save money, because it got inventory out of the pipeline, thereby eliminating storage costs and inventory obsolescence. Dubinsky tried to reframe the issue, explaining that the inefficiencies were not in the warehousing and the physical distribution but rather in the forecasting process. She also pointed out discrepancies in Coleman's figures and assumptions.

The task force meetings continued to hit stalemate after stalemate: Coleman made proposals; Dubinsky raised objections. The distribution issue had taken on enormous proportions because top management had seized on it as an opportunity to demonstrate its faith in middle management decision-making ability; but middle management could reach no consensus. Campbell was frustrated because he knew that Jobs was pushing Sculley to accept Coleman's plan, and Campbell had no alternative plan from his group to offer Sculley; Weaver was weary, and Dubinsky, who had never understood why the reins had been taken from her hands in the first place and given to a task force, was beginning to consider jobs in other companies.

She also found that the meetings and counter-meetings were taking all her time; she spent less time with her own staff. The task force, in still one more attempt to find some middle ground, finally reported its agreement to Campbell that the just-in-time concept was the best direction for Apple to pursue, but it had not agreed on a feasible implementation plan. Dubinsky recalled:

> It was like a dripping faucet. There was all this pressure to agree. You wanted to agree so you found a ground to agree on. . . . But you know what? I never really believed it.

During the final task force meeting, Campbell restated this conclusion for the final time, saying: "So you all agree that this is what we should work toward?" And Dubinsky, despite herself, could not choke back her late but very definite "No." Campbell ended the meeting angrily and Dubinsky, thoroughly depressed, was ready to just walk away from it all.

THE "LEADERSHIP EXPERIENCE" SEMINAR, APRIL 17–19, 1985

In April 1985, Dubinsky was asked to attend an Apple "Leadership Experience" meeting, scheduled for three days at Pajaro Dunes for a group of 40 upper-middle managers. Its purpose was to break down barriers, to encourage communication and creativity, and to challenge participants to find new perspectives and new solutions for old problems. At this point, Dubinsky was at her emotional nadir, and, being skeptical of such programs, she went merely to be out of the office for a few days. As she put it, "I had no intention of getting anything out of it."

The program was fast paced and imaginatively designed. Many of the exercises required participants to break into preassigned small groups, and, much to Dubinsky's surprise, Coleman showed up in almost all of these groups. To Dubinsky it seemed that Coleman was using the three-day workshop to lobby for her cause, while Dubinsky herself "felt destroyed and was questioning [her] own judgment."

To Dubinsky, the whole "Leadership Experience" seemed ill-fated. She wondered how she could be self-reflective and thoughtful when she felt incapable of expressing feelings to anyone without being totally negative. How could she design an action plan for her group, as one exercise required, when she did not even know if the distribution group would still exist?

As the seminar progressed, however, Dubinsky recognized that everyone felt confused, demoralized, and critical of the company. She saw the morale problems as fallout from the Macintosh/Apple II rivalry. During one exercise, for example, participants were asked to draw pictures that reflected their perceptions of Apple. One manager drew a picture of two men (Jobs and Sculley) both trying to steer a single boat, but one man (Sculley) appeared to be totally controlled by the other. Someone else sketched a caricature of Jobs with two hats—one as operating manager

and one as chairman of the board, and he had to choose between them. A third participant drew a picture of the manager of the Apple II Division, out at sea, alone on a wind surfer, looking to see which way the wind was blowing. Dubinsky began to feel less isolated with her frustration, and she began to see the distribution issue as part of a much larger problem.

On the second day of the workshop, Sculley spoke to the group. He talked generally of Apple's goals, stressing the need for both individual contribution and team effort, likening the Apple mission to the building of a cathedral. Dubinsky raised her hand and charged that Apple employees could not build that cathedral when they were not receiving any direction from him. She was beyond caution at that point, and she proceeded to question the contradictions she heard in his speech, issue by issue. Sculley responded angrily, charging that it was Dubinsky's job to make decisions, that executive staff could not hand them out on a silver platter. Before other managers could speak to the issue, time ran out. Many people ran up to Dubinsky immediately after the session and praised her for having the nerve to say what needed to be said. But somehow Dubinsky felt as if she was "alone on the boat as it pulled out, as my friends and colleagues waved from the shore."

Later that day at lunch, Dubinsky sat beside Del Yocam, executive vice president of the Apple II Division. She respected Yocam as a manager—he was one of the few seasoned executives around—and she decided to confide in him, hoping to get a reality check on the whole distribution issue. She could no longer get such a perspective from Weaver because of his closeness to the situation. She hoped that

Yocam's distance might provide a clearer view. Dubinsky asked him whether he thought the just-in-time strategy was appropriate for Apple. Yocam responded that, from his standpoint, he could not judge; that Dubinsky was in the position to know what impact this strategy change could have on Apple; and that if she truly believed it was wrong, she had better stop it. He also added sharply that he would hold her responsible if she failed.

Something clicked in Dubinsky's head as she listened to Yocam. He was so serious, and he looked at this issue not as a turf or charter battle or as a question of who was right. He saw it as a question of Apple's fate. Dubinsky recalled:

> I truly believed the proposed distribution strategy to be so radical that it would shut the company down. Yocam's reaction really brought home to me the high stakes involved in the issue.

She had critiqued and reacted to Coleman's proposals, detail by detail, but she had gone no further. This was Thursday afternoon, April 18, 1985.

THE ULTIMATUM, APRIL 19, 1985

After her 7 A.M. call to Campbell the next day, Dubinsky awaited the completion of the Pajaro Dunes seminar before returning to Cupertino to meet with him. Driving back to the office, Dubinsky flashed upon a memorable piece of advice that she had received from one of her Harvard Business School professors almost six years earlier. He had told students that the first thing to do after graduating was to start pulling together their "go-to-hell money." Dubinsky took that to mean that she should never put herself in a situation from which she could not walk away. Dubinsky had followed that advice, and now she had her savings stored away, and no prohibitive obligations. The time had come to test her independence.

Campbell and Dubinsky met for two intense hours late that afternoon. In their meeting, Dubinsky acknowledged her previous blind spots. She asked for an additional 30 days to get her own distribution strategy presentation together. "But," she added, "distribution is my area, and I will evaluate it myself, without the interference of an outside task force."

Campbell demanded: "Why can't you defend what you're doing to others if you think it's right?" But Dubinsky snapped back that she did not have to if it was really her job. They wrestled on over this point until Dubinsky finally took her stand and delivered her ultimatum: If Campbell did not agree to her terms, she would leave Apple. Campbell promised to talk with Sculley and to let her know Monday.

Over the weekend, Dubinsky wrote her letter of resignation. On Monday morning she told Weaver about the ultimatum that she had delivered to his boss the preceding Friday. She then waited for Campbell's call.

Reading

The Recipients of Change

It's tough for people who have done real well to feel pushed out the door. Tough for the ego, like cutting out a big piece of yourself. Especially when you've been there for a while, you're rooted. . . . It's who you were, part of who you are.

The comment above was made by someone in a company that was "downsized." But as the statement indicates, the person himself was downsized in a way—losing a "big piece" of himself. This image is by no means unusual; people in the throes of change often speak in terms of being diminished. They also use words like "anger," "betrayal," and "shock"—in short, they describe dramatic emotions that rarely encompass the positive. They experience being unappreciated, anxious, and at a minimum, confused.

In contrast, much has been written about the need to embrace change with enthusiasm. We are to "foster hardiness" and be flexible; change is a challenge to confront, an adventure; we must "thrive on chaos." What accounts for this difference between actual reactions to change and what we are supposed to feel? Can this gap be bridged? Not easily.

No organization can institute change if its employees will not, at the very least, accept the change. No change will "work" if employees don't help in the effort. And

Source: This case was prepared by Professor Todd D. Jick as a basis for class discussion rather than to illustrate either effective or ineffective handling of an administrative situation. Reprinted by permission of Harvard Business School. Copyright © 1990 by the President and Fellows of Harvard College. Harvard Business School case 9-491-039.

change is not possible without people changing themselves. Any organization that believes change can take hold without considering how people will react to it is in deep delusion. Change can be "managed" externally by those who decide when it is needed and how it "should" be implemented. But it *will* be implemented only when employees accept change—and the specific change—internally.

This reading explores how people, in general, react to change; why they do so; and how they may be able to understand their reactions better. The perspective is that of the "changee," or recipient, but the ideas are helpful to change agents as well. By grasping more firmly the experience of being changed, those managing the process can gain a broader understanding of the effects—intended and unintended—of the changes they are instituting.

One point must be stressed at the outset. For some people, any interference with routine provokes strong reaction. These folks we call "set in their ways"—or worse! At the other extreme are those for whom the next mountain is always to be attacked with ferocity. These are the daredevils among us. Most people fall between these two poles, and it is with them that we are concerned. Further, the "change" we address is more than minor disruption in ways of operation; we are dealing with the kinds of change that are experienced as transformational.

REACTIONS TO CHANGE

The typical employee spends at least eight hours a day at the workplace, doing, in general, fairly regular and predictable tasks. Indeed, most companies have orientation programs that emphasize the company "culture," which implies some stability. Employees usually have some sort of job description, performance appraisals that are linked to that description, and job planning and reviews, all of which tacitly indicate that there is a quid pro quo. The employee does X, and if that is done well, on time, and so on, the employee receives Y in compensation.

In addition to this external contract, there is a psychological one: belonging to the organization, and fitting into the work and social patterns that exist in the company. There is a political dimension here as well. For those seeking advancement in the organization there are written and unwritten "rules" of the game. "The way we do things around here" is something that career-minded employees attend to.

But what happens when the rules are changed in the middle of the game, as in the following:

> So this morning we get a memo addressed to "all staff." It says the policy of year-end cash performance bonuses is discontinued. Just like that—30 percent of my salary! And after all the long hours I've put in during the last months.

What would we suppose this accountant might feel? In fact, one could argue that almost any reaction she has is normal and "justifiable." She has experienced a trauma.

The "loss" a change implies need not be as definitive as the bonus situation above. A loss can be imaginary, as, for example, what a change in job description may entail. This may be a perceived loss in turf, a perceived diminution in status, in identity, or self-meaning in general. Everything that someone has built is considered threatened: Even if the change is a promotion, people can react with anxiety; in fact, people often try to perform the new job and the old one simultaneously so as not to experience the (imaginary) loss.

For most people, the negative reaction to change is related to *control*—over their influence, their surroundings, their source of pride, and how they have grown accustomed to living and working. When these factors appear to be threatened, security is in jeopardy. Considerable energy is needed to understand, absorb, and process one's reactions. Not only do I have to deal with the change per se, I have to deal with my reactions to it! Even if the change is embraced intellectually ("things were really going bad here"), immediate acceptance is not usually forthcoming. Instead, most feel fatigued; we need *time* to adapt.

THE EVOLUTION OF CHANGE REACTIONS

Most people, of course, do adapt to change, but not before passing through some other psychological gates. Two "maps" describe the complex psychological process of passing through difficult, often conflicting, emotions. Each of these approaches emphasizes a progression through stages or phases, which occurs over time and, essentially, cannot be accelerated (Exhibit 1). To speed up the process is to risk carrying unfinished psychological "baggage" from one phase to the next.

One way to think about the reaction pattern relates to a theory based on risk

EXHIBIT 1   Frameworks to Explain Reactions to Change

Change Stages (Risk Taking)

1. *Shock.* Perceived threat, immobilization, no risk taking.
2. *Defensive retreat.* Anger, holding on, risking still unsafe.
3. *Acknowledgment.* Mourning, letting go, growing potential for risk taking.
4. *Adaptation and change.* Comfort with change, energy for risk taking.

Transition Stages

1. *Ending phase.* Letting go of the previous situation (disengagement, disidentification, disenchantment).
2. *Neutral zone.* Completing endings and building energy for beginnings (disorientation, disintegration, discovery).
3. *New beginnings.* New possibilities or alignment with a vision.

taking.[1] Change, its authors assert, requires people to perform or perceive in unfamiliar ways, which implies taking risks, particularly those associated with self-esteem—loss of face, appearing incompetent, seemingly unable or unwilling to learn, and so on. People move from discomfort with risks to acceptance, in four stages: shock, defensive retreat, acknowledgment, and adaptation and change. This can be likened to bereavement reactions.

In the *shock* phase, one is threatened by anticipated change, even denying its existence: "This isn't happening." The psychological shock resembles the physiological—people become immobilized and "shut down" to protect themselves; yet at the same time, they deny the situation is occurring. As a result of this conflict, productivity is understandably low: People feel unsafe; timid; and unable to take action, much less risks.

We move from shock to *defensive retreat* (i.e., we get mad). We simultaneously lash out at what has been done to us and hold on to accustomed ways of doing things. Thus, we are keeping a grip on the past while decrying the fact that it has changed. This conflict also precludes

taking risks, for we are uncomfortable and feel unsafe.

Eventually, we cease denying the fact of change, we *acknowledge* that we have lost something, and we mourn. The psychological dynamics include both grief and liberation. Thus, we can feel like a pawn in a game while being able to take some distance from the game, viewing it with some objectivity. At this point, experimenting with taking risks becomes possible; we begin exploring the pros and cons of the new situation. Each "risk" that succeeds builds confidence, and we are ready for the final "gate."

Ideally, most people *adapt and change* themselves. The change becomes internalized, we move on, and help others to do so; we see ourselves "before and after" the change; and, even if it's a grudging acknowledgment, we consider the change "all for the best." In some cases, people actively advocate what they recently denied.

Another approach to how people come to terms with change also is based on phases, in this case three: letting go, existing in a neutral zone, and making new beginnings.[2]

[1] Harry Woodward and Steve Bucholz, *Aftershock* (New York: John Wiley, 1987).

[2] William Bridges, "Managing Organizational Transitions," *Organizational Dynamics*, Summer 1986, pp. 24–33.

Ending and letting go means relinquishing the old prechange situation, a process that involves dramatic emotions: pain, confusion, and terror. That is, we first experience a sharp break with what has been taken for granted; included in this pain is a loss of the identity we had invested in the old situation. This situational "unplugging" and loss of identity lead to a sense of disenchantment—things fail to make sense. People feel deceived, betrayed.

Such feelings lead into a second psychological phase called a *neutral zone:* a "wilderness that lies between the past reality and the one that . . . is just around the corner." People feel adrift and confused; the previous orientation no longer exists, yet the new one seems unclear. In this period of "full of nothing," we grow increasingly unproductive and ineffective. But psychologically, the neutral period is essential for mustering the energy to go on. It is the time between ending something and beginning something else. When someone is "lost enough to find oneself" and when the past becomes put in perspective, the emotions have been experienced and dealt with and put aside—then there is "mental room" to reorient and discover the new. The third phase is the seeking out of new possibilities: *beginning* to align our actions with the change. Organizations often are tempted to push people into the "beginning" phase, not recognizing—or not accepting—the need to complete the psychological work (and it *is* work) of the two previous phases. But jumping into a flurry of "beginning-type" activity—planning, pep rallies, firing up the troops—only increases people's discomfort with change. Only if sufficient attention has been paid to letting go and dwelling in the neutral zone—only if the old has been properly buried—can the new appear. People then can draw from the past and not be mired in it; they can be eager to embrace new possibilities.

These basically optimistic theories about how people eventually embrace change, while psychologically accurate, are somewhat simplistic. Most people will work through the emotional phases they delineate; some will do so more quickly than others. But others will get stuck, often in the first stages, which encompass the most keen and jagged emotions. The catch-all word "resistance" is used to describe these people: they are destructive (internally or even externally), and they won't move forward.

People get stuck for two basic—and obvious—reasons: "Change" is not some monolithic event that has neat and tidy beginnings and ends; and people's subjective experiences of change vary considerably as a result of individual circumstance.

Thus, frameworks that presume periods of psychological sorting out while the change is being digested are somewhat flimsy in helping us deal with multiple changes. How are we to be in "defensive retreat" with one change, in the "neutral zone" with another, while adapting to a third? If these changes are also rapid-fire, a fairly common situation in these upheaving days in the political and economic arenas, it becomes clearer why some people "resist." For example, changes involving significant personal redirection, like job restructuring, often are accompanied by changes in a firm's ownership, leadership, and policies. All coming at once (or in rapid sequence), they can severely stress or even undo chief anchor points of meaning. These affect the previously agreed-upon ways of doing one's work, affiliations, skills, and self-concept. When these anchor points come under siege, most of us are likely to be immobilized and even obdurate. In a worst-case scenario, the individual going through this siege at the office is simultaneously experiencing major change at home—a divorce, for example.

People do not always easily pass through the phases described above because, notwithstanding the psychological validity of the progression of emotions, not everyone interprets "change" in the same way; thus, experiences of "change" vary. Other personality issues must be considered as well. People who are fragile emotionally will have much greater difficulty swimming through feelings of loss; they may continually see themselves as victims. Such obscuring emotions will hinder their ability to move on. Instead, they may cycle back to shock-like or defensive behavior, never breaking out of the early phases.

ORGANIZATIONAL RESPONSES

As indicated, many firms attempt to accelerate employees' adaptation to change, for understandable reasons. Employees who are preoccupied with their internal processes are less likely to be fully productive; indeed, as the description of patterns of change reveal, people in the early phases of reacting to change often are unable to do much at all. Thus, it makes good "business sense" to help people cope, with a minimum of dysfunctional consequences.

Unfortunately, from the recipient's perspective, such good intentions often are considered as controlling, even autocratic. If the change is hyped too much—too many pep rallies, too many "It's really good for you and all for the best"—those of us who feel no such thing can grow increasingly isolated and resentful. *"How*

can they say everything is rosy when I feel so miserable?"* Consider the following list of typical advice presented, in one form or another, for dealing with change:

- Keep your cool in dealing with others.

- Handle pressure smoothly and effectively.

- Respond nondefensively when others disagree with you.

- Develop creative and innovative solutions to problems.

- Be willing to take risks and try out new ideas.

- Be willing to adjust priorities to changing conditions.

- Demonstrate enthusiasm for and commitment to long-term goals.

- Be open and candid in dealing with others.

- Participate actively in the change process.

- Make clear-cut decisions as needed.

Seemingly straightforward and commonsensical, this advice is eminently rational and usually presented in good faith. But as we now understand, such directives—for that is what they are—fail to take into account that psychological needs must be addressed. Most people are aware of the wisdom of taking responsibility for dealing with change themselves; they recognize the importance of the "right attitude." Americans in particular pride themselves on pioneer spirit, challenges, adventure—the can-do philosophy.

It appears, however, that most people do not want this shoved down their throats, especially when they are first grappling with the magnitude, or their perception of it, of a change's effect on them. Rather, most of us prefer some empathy, some understanding of what we are experiencing—not just advice for getting on with it.

The next two sections explore ways in which people facing change can help themselves experience the change less painfully, and some guidelines their managers can use to help their employees (and themselves) cope with difficult parts of the change process. While these ideas are simple, even commonplace, they look at the experience of change in its totality; they acknowledge that "change" is not merely doing A on Monday and B on Tuesday. There is a transition between the two, and if that is ignored—by either the recipient or those instituting the change—full adaptation to, and embracing of, the change itself is jeopardized.

INDIVIDUAL COPING WITH CHANGE

Given the strong emotional responses that most of us feel at the onset of a change—anger, depression, and shock—and given that often these emotions are "unacceptable" either to ourselves or at the workplace, we need to console ourselves that these are indeed natural reactions. People need to give themselves permission to feel what they are feeling; change always implies a loss of some kind, and that must be mourned: a job, colleagues, a role, even one's identity as it has been wrapped up in the prechange situation. Accepting and focusing on our negative reactions is not the same as wallowing in them, of course.

It has already been pointed out that dealing with change takes energy. Even more energy is required in fighting negative reactions. Thus, to accept, at the outset, that strong emotions are part and parcel of the change process is at least to avoid wasting some energy; we are better able to reduce the added strain of constantly keeping feelings at bay. In fact, one's strength is increased by letting what is natural take its course.

A corollary to accepting strong reactions to change is patience—understanding that time is needed to come to grips with a situation, and that moving through various constellations of emotions is not done in an instant. Whereas most people experience the range of emotions described earlier, there is no timeclock that works for everyone. The adaptation process involves an unsettled and ambiguous period for most of us,[3] and, if we accept that, at the least we can function superficially—if not at our peak—until we strengthen and begin to act more meaningfully.

A major reaction to change is a feeling of losing control; what was assumed to be the norm now isn't, and we are in an unknown land. A valuable antidote to feeling powerless is to establish a sense of personal control in other areas of our lives, and avoid as much as possible taking on other efforts that sap energy. Thus, if one accepts that adapting to change will be arduous, one husbands one's resources. This means maintaining our physical well-being and nourishing our psyches.

It is no coincidence that a new field called "managing stress" has arisen during a period of major and pervasive organizational restructuring. And the recommendations that practitioners in this area make, while simple, are useful: Get enough sleep; pay attention to diet and exercise;

[3] Leonard Greenhalgh and Todd Jick, "Survivor Sense Making and Reactions to Organizational Decline," *Management Communications Quarterly* 2 (3): February 1989, pp. 305–327.

take occasional breaks at the office; relax with friends; engage in hobbies. Such efforts are not escapism or distractions from "reality." Rather, they are ways of exerting control over one's life during a period of uncertainty.

Accepting strong emotions and acknowledging the importance of patience in dealing with change are vital, but so is developing a sense of objectivity about what is happening. We do have choices in how we perceive change, and we are able to develop the capacity to see benefits, not just losses, in new situations. Coming to accept and adapt to change is in fact a process of balancing: What have I lost? What am I gaining? Different from the "look-on-the-bright-side" exhortations frequently espoused by those who ignore the powerful emotions a change can evoke, inventorying personal losses and gains is a real step toward gathering the strength to move on.

Related to such inventorying is "diversified emotional investing." The individual balances the emotional investment in essential work-related anchor points of meaning—how work is done, affiliations, skills, and self-concept in relation to the work—with emotional investments in other areas of life—family, friends, civic and religious activities. Thus, when one or more anchor points at the workplace are threatened, the person can remain steadier through the transition to adaptation.

Admittedly, such inventorying and "diversified emotional investing" are difficult when one is in the throes of strong emotions. Perhaps the best mechanism for coping with change, then, is anticipating it. No one escapes the effects of change, in the workplace or elsewhere; and those who recognize that its impact will be powerful, that the process of adaptation and change takes time, and that we all have other sources of strength, are in much better shape than those who delude themselves into thinking, "It can never happen to me."

MANAGING THE RECIPIENTS OF CHANGE

Obviously, the manager who has experienced change personally is potentially more effective in helping others work through their adaptation processes. But beyond recalling their own experiences, managers should consider three areas that are essential for easing their employees' difficulties: rethinking resistance, giving "first aid," and creating capability for change. (See Exhibit 2.)

RETHINKING RESISTANCE

Resistance to change, as mentioned earlier, is a catch-all phrase: It describes anyone who doesn't change as fast as we do, as well as people who seemingly refuse to budge. As such, resistance per se is considered an obstacle, something to be overcome at all costs. Those labeled resistant are deemed people with poor attitudes, lacking in team spirit. Not surprisingly, treating "resistance" this way serves only to intensify real resistance, thereby thwarting or at least sidetracking possibilities of change.

As the discussion of patterns of change has revealed, however, resistance is a part of the natural process of adapting to change; it is a normal response of those who have a strong vested interest in maintaining their perception of the current state and guarding themselves against loss. Why should I give up what has successfully made meaning for me? What do I get in its place? Resistance, at the outset of the change process,

EXHIBIT 2   **Strategies for Coping with Change**

Individuals

1. *Accepting feelings as natural:*

   Giving oneself permission to feel and mourn.

   Taking time to work through feelings.

   Tolerating ambiguity.

2. *Managing stress:*

   Maintaining physical well-being.

   Seeking information about the change.

   Limiting extraneous stressors.

   Taking regular breaks.

   Seeking support.

3. *Exercising responsibility:*

   Identifying options and gains.

   Learning from losses.

   Participating in the change.

   Inventorying strengths.

   Learning new skills.

   Diversifying emotional investing.

Managers

1. *Rethinking resistance:*

   As natural self-protection.

   As a positive step toward change.

   As energy to work with.

   As information critical to the change process.

   As other than a roadblock.

2. *Giving first aid:*

   Accepting emotions.

   Listening.

   Providing safety.

   Marking endings.

   Providing resources and support.

3. *Creating capability for change:*

   Making organizational support of risks clear.

   Continuing safety net.

   Emphasizing continuities, gains of change.

   Helping employees explore risks and options.

   Suspending judgment.

   Involving people in decision making.

   Encouraging teamwork.

   Providing opportunities for individual growth.

is far more complicated than "I won't." It is much more of a painful "Why should I?"

When resistance is considered a natural reaction, part of a process, it can thus be seen as a first step toward adaptation. At the very minimum, resistance denotes energy—energy that can be worked with and redirected. The strength of resistance, moreover, indicates the degree to which change has touched on something valuable

to individuals and the organization. Discovering what that valuable something is can be of important use in fashioning the change effort organizationally. One theorist puts it this way:

> First, they ["resistors"] are the ones most apt to perceive and point out real threats, if such exist, to the well-being of the system which may be the unanticipated consequences of projected changes.

Second, they are especially apt to react against any change that might reduce the integrity of the system.

Third, they are sensitive to any indication that those seeking to produce change fail to understand or identify with the core values of the system they seek to influence.

Because "resistance to change" is such an amorphous phrase, many attitudes labeled "resistant" are not that at all. Depending on the change involved, people may be required to learn new and difficult skills, for example. Their frustration in doing so may cause them to naysay the effort. Calling the naysaying resistance is a genuine error: If the effort to change is in fact being made, it should be encouraged. Further, listening to the criticism may provide clues that the training is ineffective.

There are also entirely rational reasons for resistance. By no means are all change agendas perfect, as the quote above indicates. The organization that assumes it can superimpose "change" on its employees and then labels any negative reaction "resistance" is guaranteeing that change, if it occurs at all, will hardly accomplish the purpose for which it was intended.

One of the common mistakes made by managers when they encounter resistance is to become angry, frustrated, impatient or exasperated. . . . The problem with an emotional reaction is that it increases the probability that the resistance will intensify. Remember that anger directed toward others is likely to make them afraid and angry in return.[4]

In sum, rethinking resistance to change means seeing it as a normal part of adaptation, something most of us do to protect our self-integrity. It is a potential source of energy, as well as information about the change effort and direction. Instead of assuming that all "resistance" is an obstacle, managers should look carefully to see whether real resistance is present, over time (i.e., there are always people who won't change and who will complain all the while). In general, however, going with the "resistance," not condemning it but trying to understand its sources, motives, and possible affirmative core, can open up possibilities for realizing change. Writes one expert on the subject:

Without it [resistance], we are skeptical of real change occurring. Without real questioning, skepticism, and even outright resistance, it is unlikely that the organization will successfully move on to the productive stage of learning how to make the new structure effective and useful.[5]

GIVING "FIRST AID"

Many managers find that addressing straightforward technical issues in the change effort—such as the new department layout, who gets what training—is comparatively easy. But consciously or not, they ignore the more complex and often unpredictable concerns of people being changed. The rationale can be a business one: we don't have time for that; we're here to make money. Or it can be emotional: I don't want to get involved in messy feelings; that's not my job.

For whatever reason, not allowing employees opportunities to vent feelings is overlooking a powerfully effective coping strategy. Administering emotional first aid, particularly in the early and most difficult stages of change, validates recipients in their terms and doesn't leave them in an

---

[4] Ken Hultman, *The Path of Least Resistance* (Austin, TX: Learning Concepts, 1979).

[5] Ibid.

emotional pressure cooker. We have already seen that a major coping mechanism for the individual is acknowledging that his or her reactions are natural; when this is combined with external validation, the result is profoundly effective. Indeed when management provides opportunity for grievances and frustrations to be aired constructively, employee bitterness and frustration may be diminished.

As the above implies, first aid, in its most powerful form, is simply listening. Nonjudgmental listening. The dominant attitude of the nonjudgmental listener is respect for what the individual is experiencing; this in turn is predicated on accepting that everyone needs time to absorb change, and that complicated and even contradictory emotions belong to the early stage of the process.

First aid also means providing safety by delineating expectations and establishing informal and formal rewards for those experiencing change. It also involves identifying and clarifying what is not changing—and probing to uncover why. Where do people feel they will be taking the biggest risks? It is in these areas, as we have seen, that the most powerful concerns—and resistance—lie.

Finally, first aid means providing resources to help people through their greatest difficulties—ongoing information about the change, support, and counseling where needed, particularly forums in which employees can help each other. These resources are especially critical when someone has bid farewell to the old but has yet to become attached to the new.

"Listen," "accept," and "support" may seem like simple, almost basic, advice for the manager of changees. Unfortunately, all too often these qualities are missing from the manager's tool kit for change. Such essential human interaction tends to get lost in the maze of plans, committees, and reports that typically accompany major change efforts. For the recipients to adapt fully to their new circumstances requires more than the passive response of managers, however; managers need to help changees become more capable of change.

CREATING THE CAPABILITY FOR CHANGE

Creating the capability for change is undertaken after the "bleeding" has stopped and the need for first aid lessens. The manager's dual task is to help people move into the current change and encourage them to feel confident about accepting subsequent changes.

Providing safety and rewards, a part of first aid, also is essential to creating a climate in which people will take risks. (This is similar to what good parenting is all about!) In the workplace, managers who expect their employees to change—and particularly if the change is in fact multiple changes—need to make clear how the organization is willing to support their efforts. What differentiates this effort from first aid is its continuance. First aid is *first;* it is the effort that eases the pain, but it does not cure the disease, much less help prevent its occurrence.

Safety in creating the capability for change goes deeper into risk taking. Perhaps a nonevaluative period can be declared, one in which income, rank, or other aspects of job security are put on hold, as employees test the waters. Having employees evaluate themselves vis-à-vis the change is another approach; in all cases, the more involvement people have in the changes that surround them the better. It is a fundamental tenet of participative management that employees are more likely to support what they help to create.

Cooperation, negotiation, and compromise are critical to the implementation of any change; it is difficult to *get* cooperation, negotiation, and compromise from people who are effectively ordered to change, never listened to or supported, and then faulted if they fail to change as expected.

Rewards, in creating capabilities for change, often are implicit. Consider the popularity of programs like Outward Bound. The "rewards" in these arenas are the pride of accomplishment and the cheers from one's co-participants. Encouraging employees to take similarly difficult, albeit in many cases psychological, risks means creating environments in which they can shine, not necessarily the standard rewards of money and promotion. Creative managers who truly wish their employees to grow, who recognize the difficulties inherent in the challenge of change, and who support efforts to make change are patient along the way; their reward, in turn, is the trust of their employees—and a potentially more flexible organization.

IS CONTINUOUS CHANGE "GOOD" FOR US?

I hear change is coming, and it no longer sends shivers up my spine. I have to trust it won't clobber me. There's not really anything I can do but learn to survive and help others through it.

This article has treated "change" and its effects on employees as a first-time event: The company, having done its thing for about 50 years, suddenly throws the cards in the air and everyone picks up from there. It is, of course, increasingly rare to find such situations. Most people are more or less continually facing major changes in their work environments, from the rapid fire of new technology and processes to new owners, perhaps foreign, to an increasing emphasis on change itself as essential. The ability to change rapidly and frequently seems to be a critical mechanism for survival, many argue.

Obviously, an organization that encourages constant change hardly has the time to do first aid, and all the rest; everyone is moving around, and no one—neither the changee nor the manager—has time to examine the psychological ramifications, much less get into support. Two questions need answering in the face of such constant change: Does experience with change help people cope with it better? What are the longer-term implications of constant change for individuals and organizations?

Some evidence exists that an "inoculation effect" takes hold after confronting continuous change; people do react to the same situation, when it recurs, differently. Hurricane victims, for example, exhibit a "confidence curve" as a result of repeated experiences with the phenomenon. Those who have been through a hurricane once are most stressed; they become hyperwatchful and overprepare on even the faintest signal of a hurricane warning. They become gun-shy about the prospect of another similar event. In contrast, those who have had repeated exposure to hurricanes come to view the approach of an impending storm with more equanimity.

If this analogy is transferable, then recipients—in the face of continuous change—may exhibit a learning curve. At first, they will be hypersensitive, but later they will become more "matter of fact" and psychologically more ready for change. However, we haven't enough evidence yet to be certain of this. And some fear that the opposite effects could occur, instead—that recipients will become more vulnerable, more resistant, and less equipped as more and more change unfolds. Moreover, if someone experiences constant change, has she or he ever completely dealt with the first change?

Perhaps the answer revolves around expectations. In some companies today, people are routinely moved in and out of projects and positions: It is the nature of the work requirements in that organization. But this is understood by all from the beginning. As such, employees harbor the expectation that there will be constant change. Indeed, some are attracted to the company because of that. If people know at the outset that frequent change—in positions, responsibilities, and the like—is in fact their job, we can suppose that a kind of self-selection takes place: Those who wish that kind of experience will seek out jobs in the company, and, in turn, the company will hire those who can accept that kind of mobility. With more and more companies now exhibiting continuous change, people may come to expect it and be more inured to it.

The notion of continuous change as the ideal organizational state is fairly recent, so many of its effects in the long term on individuals within such environments are not known precisely. But we all—change agents and change recipients—must develop the strength and the capability to cope with the emotions and the demands that come with this new territory. The individual and the organization share the responsibility and obligation. When both make good-faith efforts, the results can be buoying.

Case
Wellcome Israel (A)

As Ofra Sherman was explaining to the interior designer how much space she and her team would need in the new building, she thought to herself how this whole meeting might be a waste of time. She was having trouble concentrating on the carpet samples being put under her nose. She knew that by the time the new building would be completed her team might no longer be there to occupy their newly designed offices.

As the paint samples came onto the desk, she smiled as she realized how ironic it was that only 15 minutes earlier she had been in a meeting with the general manager of Promedico discussing the possible departure of herself and her team from the company. It was now April 1995. It would take some months to resolve the issues arising from Glaxo's acquisition of Wellcome, which had just occurred in March. What was she to do in the interim? How would she manage her team? Keep them motivated? What did the future hold for her?

Sherman was the general manager of Wellcome Israel, a company that technically did not exist. It was perhaps more accurate to say that she was the general manager of the U.K.-based pharmaceutical company Wellcome's operations in Israel. And now Wellcome itself was being taken over by arch-rival Glaxo.

Source: This case was written by MBA student Daniel Mueller, under the supervision of Professor Maury A. Peiperl.

Copyright © 1998 London Business School.

Under the best of circumstances, the uncertainty caused by takeovers disrupted the operation of an organization. But this situation was complicated by the involvement of a third company, Promedico. Promedico was the official Israeli representative for several drug companies, including Wellcome, whose personnel were based in Promedico's offices. And although Sherman and her team actually received their salaries from Wellcome, for historical reasons, their paychecks were issued by Promedico. Legally, were they employees of Wellcome or Promedico? The status had always been unclear, and there had never been any motivation to clarify it.

Sherman did not have the answers to any of the questions which she knew she would have to face shortly. As the merger unfolded, would she and her team be fired? Kept on? Within Glaxo? Within Promedico? What should she tell her staff to keep them motivated? For that matter, what should she tell her customers? The only thing she knew with certainty at that moment was that she did not want her office painted the awful shade of yellow she was being shown. If only the rest of her decisions over the coming tumultuous months would be so easy.

As the interior designer left her office, she thought about how she would manage her team during this transitional phase. On a personal level, she wondered what would happen to herself and her team in the wake of the acquisition and what the future would hold for the business she had just spent five years of her life building.

WELLCOME PLC

Wellcome plc was one of the main competitors in the international pharmaceutical industry. In recent years Wellcome had ranked between tenth and twentieth worldwide in revenue. Its main operations were in the U.S. and the U.K., and its headquarters were located next to Euston Station in London. It developed, manufactured, and marketed human health care products worldwide, with subsidiaries in 33 countries. In 1994, it had 17,182 employees and revenues of £2.6 billion, with a profit margin of just over 33 percent. Its products could be divided into two categories, prescription and non-prescription (over the counter) medicines, with the former representing over 85 percent of total revenues.

Wellcome had become known in the pharmaceutical industry as a specialist in antiviral drugs (although it also had several other specialties, including antibiotics and medicines targeted at the central nervous system). Viruses were complex micro-organisms, often not well understood by medical science, that were responsible for a variety of diseases, from colds to AIDS. Wellcome's stable of products covered the range, from cold and allergy medicines such as Actifed and Sudafed (sold over the counter) to Retrovir, one of the most widely prescribed treatments for AIDS. The firm's biggest revenue-producing drug for several years had been Zovirax, a treatment for herpes. Zovirax had also been approved in some countries as an over-the-counter medicine for cold sores.

Developing drugs to treat viruses was a tortuous process of theory, experimentation, publication, clinical trial, and application for regulatory approval. The total cost of launching a drug could easily exceed £100 million, and this number was also the informal hurdle for annual sales Wellcome and other companies used to determine which drugs had "made it" in the marketplace. There was usually a limited window in which such returns could be reaped, however, since competition in the industry was fierce from both new product development (meaning successful drugs could be replaced by better ones) and generics (which could take away substantial market share as soon as a drug came off patent). Zovirax patents around the world were just beginning to expire, which posed a medium-term threat to Wellcome's earnings.

In order to balance the high-risk, high-return research and development in new prescription drugs, the company had taken two other major steps: In 1994, it entered a partnership with U.S.-based Warner-Lambert, called Warner-Wellcome, to market all the two firms' over-the-counter medicines worldwide. The partnership was expected both to save costs and to expand revenues in this part of the business, which had always been a "poor cousin" to Wellcome's prescription drugs. Also, it had entered into a set of licensing agreements, region by region, to fill out its portfolio of offerings with complementary drugs from other companies and vice versa. Again, this provided added revenues and greater economies of scale at relatively low cost.

WELLCOME IN ISRAEL

Although Wellcome products had been sold in Israel for over 40 years, strictly speaking Wellcome Israel did not exist. For political reasons (Wellcome was very active in Arab countries) Israel was never mentioned in any Wellcome literature. For many years Israel was referred to as Greenland, and then it was put under Wellcome Hellas SA (see the Wellcome Hellas organizational chart in Exhibit 1). This political sensitivity led to a unique organizational structure existing in Israel, one in which reporting lines were less than clear.

Promedico Limited was an Israeli company that represented the products of several drug companies in Israel. It handled distribution, marketing, and medical registration for companies such as Pfizer and Zima (see Exhibit 2 for a corporate organization chart). In the case of Wellcome, Promedico handled only distribution and medical registration. Marketing was the responsibility of Ofra Sherman and her team (see Exhibit 3), whose salaries and expenses were paid by Wellcome Hellas, not Promedico. In the Promedico structure the Wellcome team were part of the Pharmaceutical and Diagnostics division.

EXHIBIT 1   **Wellcome Hellas SA**

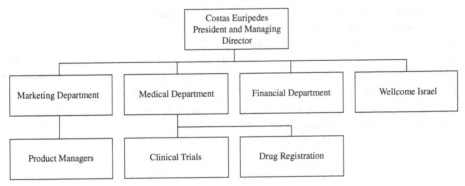

EXHIBIT 2   **Promedico**

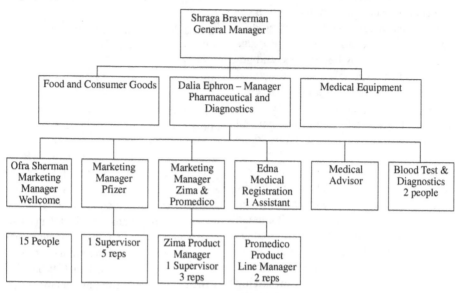

Although the costs of the Wellcome team (as they were known within Promedico) were borne by Wellcome Hellas, Promedico issued the actual paychecks every month. Promedico thus acted as a mechanism through which Wellcome could pay its people in Israel without having to put a formal structure in place.

Promedico was well paid for its services, purchasing pharmaceuticals from Wellcome and marking them up by as much as 100 percent to the end customer. Margins were high, because the cost of selling Wellcome products was limited to distribution and medical registration, since the Wellcome team was paid by Wellcome Hellas.

This strange organizational structure had served the purposes of both parties for some years. But as the size of the Wellcome team within Promedico grew, and with it the proportion of Promedico's total revenue which Wellcome accounted for, tensions began to grow as well.

There were tensions between Sherman and Promedico's management, as well as between the Wellcome team and members of other product teams within Promedico. In revenue and profit terms, the Wellcome team consistently outperformed other teams at the company. In 1994, Wellcome products accounted for approximately 50 percent of the pharmaceutical and diagnostics division's revenues. The fact that they were so successful and had more autonomy than other groups in the company (since they were paid by Wellcome Hellas) made them the focus of some jealousy.

To complicate matters, there had never been a written agreement between Wellcome plc and Promedico which outlined the terms and conditions of their relationship. It had never been clear what Wellcome would decide to do if, as had become a real possibility in the last few years, the growth in its sales in Israel began to outstrip the size of its distributor.

EXHIBIT 3   Sherman's Team

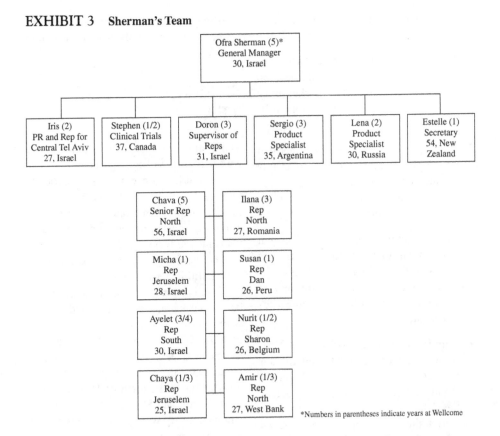

*Numbers in parentheses indicate years at Wellcome

It certainly was not clear now what role Promedico would play in the shake-out that was likely to follow the acquisition.

OFRA SHERMAN

Ofra Sherman was the manager of Wellcome Israel, where she had worked for the past five years. She had completed her bachelor's degree in Biology at the age of 25 and began working for the Wellcome team at Promedico as a medical representative. At that time the team consisted of Sherman, her boss, and two medical representatives. Sherman became Wellcome team leader after one year, as the group started to expand, and manager in 1993.

At the age of 30, Sherman was one of the youngest managing directors within Wellcome and was considered a rising star within its international division. Her team, now consisting of 15 people, had sustained tremendous growth. It generated more than two-thirds as much revenue (US$7 million) as Wellcome Hellas did with 60 people (US$10 million).

Sherman was involved in every aspect of the operation of Wellcome Israel, from how a drug should be positioned in the marketplace, to how the invitations to a medical conference should look. Her position was similar to that of an owner/manager in the sense that she had created and built the team and also controlled every aspect of its operation.

She divided her time among five activities:

1. *Managing director.* Together with her manager in Athens she would develop medium- and long-term market entry and maintenance strategies for Wellcome Israel.

2. *Product manager for Zovirax.* Sherman would give training courses about this product (one of Wellcome's biggest and most profitable) and keep up to date on all the latest clinical literature.

3. *Sales and marketing director.* Sherman would plan all promotional activities for the different drugs, including medical congresses, meetings with doctors and the activities of the Wellcome sales representatives.

4. *Training manager.* Most of the Wellcome team were relatively new in their jobs, so Sherman found herself spending much of her time on training activities. The senior members of the team were trained on a one-to-one basis. Almost every time she would meet with each of them, there was a training component to the interaction. The sales representatives, by contrast, were trained in group sessions, which concentrated, for example, on how to have a meeting with a doctor and how to present new clinical findings. Sherman ran most of these sessions.

5. *Motivator.* Sherman was also the team cheerleader. Since there was little contact with the outside Wellcome organization, and since relations with Promedico had recently been under some strain, the Wellcome Israel team sometimes felt a lack of confirmation of its mission and credit for its success. This was a need Sherman conscientiously filled, celebrating every success the team and its members had, no matter how small.

SHERMAN AND HER TEAM

The Senior Team met with Sherman once a week to discuss ongoing issues. Sherman also met at least once a week individually with each member of the team to discuss individual problems and prospects. The atmosphere was relaxed, and team members enjoyed working together.

The Senior Team had six members (see Exhibit 3 for names, tenure, titles, ages, and origin). Doron, the senior member of the team, was 31 and had worked with Sherman for three years. For 2 1/2 of those years he had worked as a sales representative. Recently he had been promoted to the position of supervisor, and he now managed the team of 10 representatives. Doron and Sherman had a close relationship; they were good friends as well as co-workers.

Iris, 27, had been with the team for two years. She was a representative responsible for central Tel Aviv and had recently been given the additional responsibility of coordinating all promotional activities. This involved organizing medical conferences to promote Wellcome's products and developing concepts for promotional gifts, which were commonly distributed to doctors. Sherman and Iris saw each other socially and were close friends.

Doron and Iris were in Sherman's inner circle. She confided in them more than in the others about Wellcome/Promedico issues and relied on them more than the others. The third member of Sherman's inner circle was Stephen, coordinator of clinical trials. Stephen was 37 and had recently immigrated to Israel from Canada. Although he had been with the team for only 6 months, Sherman had started confiding in him early on, sensing in him high levels of maturity and judgment.

The last two members of the senior team were Sergio and Lena, both product specialists. They had both started as representatives. They were the experts on their respective products and responsible for training the representatives on specific drugs and making sure they had the latest clinical information. Both had been with the team between two and three years.

There was great camaraderie among the whole Wellcome team. Most days the team would have lunch together in the lunchroom. Sherman would use this opportunity to discuss and resolve many work-related issues. It was also an opportunity for Sherman to build team spirit and find out what was going on in the field.

Sherman's office was the nerve center of the Wellcome Team. It served as file room, storage room, and meeting room. Drug samples, promotional gifts for doctors, and product files cluttered the office. It was relatively small to begin with, and the clutter made it even more so. Sherman's staff would walk in and out of the office all day, sometimes to pick something up, other times to talk to her. So informal was the atmosphere among the team that they would come in whether the door was open or closed (although it was rarely closed). The office sometimes seemed like a whirlwind, with four or five people doing different things at the same time.

PROMEDICO LIMITED

Promedico had been established in 1946 as a distribution company. It had distributed pharmaceuticals since the beginning, and over the years had added medical supplies and food and consumer products.

In 1992 new management came in and implemented a major reorganization. During 1993 and 1994 Promedico went from 70 to 200 employees (including the Wellcome Team). Of these, 68 percent were in marketing and sales, 19 percent in logistics and warehousing, and 13 percent in administration. In the same period, sales had grown only 33 percent, from US$31 million to US$40 million. Of this amount, 45 percent was from pharmaceuticals and diagnostics, 30 percent from food and consumer products, and 25 percent from medical supplies.

By the end of 1994 Promedico was a company in trouble. It had recently lost three very important lines: two consumer products and one medical supply product. The Wellcome team (only 15 people) was generating roughly 50 percent of the Pharmaceutical and Diagnostics division's revenues and a similarly disproportionate proportion of profit. In view of Glaxo's recent acquisition of Wellcome, and the fact that Glaxo already had a representative in Israel (called CTS) with distribution and medical registration capabilities, it was likely that Promedico would lose the Wellcome line. Management at Promedico were understandably doing everything in their power to prevent this eventuality.

OFRA SHERMAN AND PROMEDICO MANAGEMENT

Officially Sherman had a manager at Promedico: She was Dalia Ephron, manager of the Pharmaceutical and Diagnostics division. Ephron was Sherman's manager in name only, however, because Sherman took her orders from Costas

Euripides, manager of Wellcome Hellas in Greece. Within the Promedico hierarchy, Sherman's position was marketing manager of the Wellcome Team. Sherman's peers at Promedico envied her, partly for her success and partly for her autonomy.

Sherman did not rely on Promedico management in carrying out her day-to-day duties. She did, however, receive information from them about what was happening within Promedico and would tell them what she wanted them to know about the Wellcome team, although not directly. She knew that whatever she told them would get back to the Promedico MD. The following conversation was an example of this indirect communication:

> As the vice president of Consumer Products was passing her office door, Sherman called him in and asked him about the loss of the Nestlé line (that week Promedico had lost the representation of Nestlé products). From there, the conversation turned to pharmaceuticals:
>
> VP: Things do not look good for Promedico.
>
> OS: Both of us know what is going on but cannot say.
>
> VP: Given that both of us know, what do you think will happen?
>
> OS: I think you know what will happen.
>
> The VP smiled and left the office.

Sherman had wanted to make it clear to him that Wellcome would probably leave Promedico and to see that the message would get to the MD.

The location of Sherman's office was also significant. It was between the managing director and the manager of the Pharmaceuticals and Diagnostics division. Sherman believed that she had been given this office because of her team's importance to Promedico. The location also served as a constant reminder that she was between two companies and had to continually balance the needs of her group with the needs of Promedico.

THE ACQUISITION

Before 1986, Wellcome had been a privately held, not-for-profit enterprise. Its shares were held by the Wellcome Trust, a charitable organization set up by philanthropist Henry Wellcome nearly a century earlier. For decades, the firm operated as a charitable rather than a commercial enterprise, with the advantages of a strong public service mentality and the disadvantages of a somewhat bloated payroll and low flexibility. After the creation of Wellcome plc and an initial public share flotation of 20 percent, the Wellcome Trust (which had remained separate) had sold several further tranches of stock in the public markets. However, it had continued to hold 40 percent of the firm's shares and had made representation to the company's management that the holding was secure and would not be sold off, at least not without lengthy discussions with management beforehand. The secure status of the Trust's holding made Wellcome management and employees feel more secure than many other companies in the pharmaceutical industry, which was going through a period of consolidation that had seen many takeovers and mergers and was expecting to see many more.

It thus came as a complete surprise in January 1995 when Glaxo announced that it was making a hostile bid for control of Wellcome, which would create the world's largest pharmaceutical company, and had the support of the Wellcome Trust for the sale of its 40 percent stake. Wellcome management had heard nothing of the offer and felt that they had been betrayed. CEO John Robb asked for and received permission from the Trust to seek an alternative acquirer, but Wellcome was unable to better Glaxo's price (approximately a two-thirds premium over the prior share value) and gave up the fight in early March. Robb had agreed to stay on to help smooth the merger but resigned as soon as he had gained assurances from Glaxo's CEO, Sir Richard Sykes, that Wellcome managers would play a substantial role in merging the two companies and would have a fair chance at getting the best jobs within the new organization.

Before the acquisition, Ofra Sherman had usually spent 50 percent of her time out of the office visiting key doctors. Since the announcement, she had been spending most of her time in the office. This was necessary because several times a day she had conversations about the reorganization with someone at Wellcome Hellas or Promedico. In addition to discussions with Shraga Braverman, general manager of Promedico, and Costas Euripides, Sherman was also making use of her internal and external networks to find out as much as possible about events at Wellcome and Glaxo, and within Promedico.

When asked about the situation she was in, Sherman commented, "I have no boss, I am in the middle of nowhere."

On one side was Wellcome Hellas; on the other was Promedico. Hovering somewhere in the distance, but closing, were Glaxo and its Israeli distributor, CTS. Complicating matters was the question of whether, under Israeli law, even though Wellcome Hellas was paying their salaries, the Wellcome Team were considered Wellcome Hellas or Promedico employees.

Shraga Braverman had told Sherman not to give any information about her team's operations to anyone at Glaxo. He also told her that he would decide whether the reorganization with Glaxo would go smoothly or not and, finally, that Euripides was certain to be removed from his position at Wellcome Hellas and as a result she should no longer listen to him, taking orders only from Braverman.

Ofra Sherman was shaken by the general manager's threats. She immediately placed a call to Costas Euripides. Although she had heard from another contact at Wellcome that Euripides would be removed after the reorganization, she still needed him to help her keep Braverman from taking complete control of the situation. It was not until the next day that Euripides returned her call. She told him what Braverman had said. Furious, he told Sherman that he was her boss and that she should do nothing without his permission.

At the same time, Sherman had told her team to gather as much information about Glaxo's operations in Israel as possible. She needed to start developing a strategy for integrating her team with the Glaxo group in the event that her team did move to Glaxo.

Should she confront the Promedico management and tell them she was planning to take her team to Glaxo? Should she go to speak to the general manager of Glaxo Israel and disregard the orders of both Braverman and Euripides? Would these actions get her fired? If only she knew what Glaxo and Wellcome were planning for her and her team. But it was clear that nothing had yet been decided and that she would either have to wait or to act on very little information other than her own intuition.

All Sherman could really do at this point was develop a series of "What if?" scenarios. She needed to make sure that whatever the outcome was, she would be ready for it. What if the team stayed at Promedico? What if the team had to be integrated with Glaxo? What kind of a job would Glaxo offer her? What if they had no job for her at all? She tried to decide how she would handle each of these possibilities and what actions she would have to take.

FINDING A WAY FORWARD

This was the first time in Sherman's career that she had been involved in a situation where she had virtually no direct control over the outcome. She knew that she could do little to affect decisions that might decide her own and her team's future. The situation was very uncertain. The only certainty was that the Glaxo and Wellcome organizations were merging in all countries where they both had a presence, and Israel would be no exception.

The other variable in the equation was Promedico. The managing director of Promedico had told her that he would do everything in his power to keep the Wellcome line. And, in the event that Promedico lost the line, he claimed he would not permit Sherman or any member of her team to go to Glaxo.

To complicate matters, the former managing director of Promedico (who had been removed two years previously during the reorganization but remained as a consultant) had told Sherman the exact opposite, that she should take her team and leave Promedico immediately. Sherman suspected the former MD wanted her to do this so that he could make the current MD look bad and take control of the company again, but he had also made some

good arguments. On their own, the Wellcome team might have more power—and be able to attract more support and higher pay—than at Promedico. They were more efficient than Glaxo in Israel, making half the revenue with only one-third the people. Without Promedico in the picture, they might be able to make their own deal with Glaxo, or even approach other drug companies.

Glaxo had set June 1 as the deadline for finalizing the reorganization plans in the different countries. In theory by that date, even if Sherman did nothing, the situation would be resolved.

The result of all these events was that Ofra Sherman no longer had a clear, long-term agenda and that her short-term agenda was focused primarily on the reorganization. At the same time, she had to try to keep herself and her team motivated. The situation was particularly difficult for Sherman because she had no one to discuss it with. She could not discuss it with her subordinates or with her peers at Promedico. Although she informed her people when developments occurred, she could not discuss her personal situation with them. The one person she had thought she could confide in, the former managing director, she now felt might be biased because of his own interests. She was truly alone.

As she played with the carpet samples the interior designer had left in her office, Sherman wondered again about what she should do. Should she be patient and wait for the situation to be resolved by the respective managements? Should she be proactive and do what she felt would be in the best interests of her team? Or should she do what might be in her own best interest: not wait for the outcome, but start looking for another job now?

Reading

Back to Square Zero

The Post-Corporate Career

Maury A. Peiperl and Yehuda Baruch

The Wellcome Foundation, until 1995 one of the major independent pharmaceutical firms, was known for its positive management of employees' careers. Long-term employment, although not guaranteed, was the norm in this organization. People who performed well were usually given more responsibility as well as opportunities to move within the company, either horizontally or vertically.

Then, to everyone's surprise, the firm was bought by its rival Glaxo, creating the world's largest pharmaceutical company. Although Wellcome had previously begun its own series of limited cutbacks, the consolidation that followed brought a marked acceleration in job losses, even for those who had been performing well. For those who survived the cuts, careers looked very different.

The company's director of research and development, David Barry, was a case in point. Barry had risen through the ranks and, after a high-profile competition for the director's position, had finally been named to his post. Trevor Jones, the man he had beaten out for the job less than a year before, had left to become head of the industry's trade association. After the merger, Dr. Barry, looking at playing second fiddle in the merged R&D organization, must

Source: Reprinted from *Organizational Dynamics*, vol 25, pp. 7–22, Copyright 1997, with permission of Elsevier.

have wondered whether his rival hadn't wound up better off. Before very long, Barry himself left to form his own medical research company.

THE PROBLEM WITH ORGANIZATIONAL CAREERS

Of course, organizations have always been subject to change and cutbacks, and individuals within them subject to competition and, occasionally, layoffs. But in recent years the number of organizations whose career systems have been thrown into disarray, and the number of people affected, seems to have reached a critical mass: It is now the norm for organizations to have *no* fixed career paths, and for individuals in them to see no further than one or two years ahead, if that, in their own careers. Competence and hard work no longer guarantee continued employment. The psychological employment contract is changing. Many people who came into their organizations with an expectation of long-term career progress are finding this unmatched by reality.

Reflecting on this new situation, we pose two fundamental questions about careers inside (and outside) contemporary organizations: First, what new patterns of career development, if any, are emerging and how have they come about? Second, what can individuals do to maximize their chances of success, either as managers within organizations or as individuals outside of them? In the course of the argument, we will develop a model we call the "Post-Corporate Career" and explain its implications.

ORGANIZATIONAL CAREERS: FROM VERTICAL TO HORIZONTAL PATHS

Career expectations about long-term employment and regular promotion have their roots in the bureaucratic form of organization that started with the railroads in the nineteenth century and grew vigorously in the early and middle parts of the twentieth. The functional bureaucracy, symbolized by the well-known pyramidal organization chart, provided natural upward paths for good performers. With their many layers and the growth they typically experienced (until about 20 years ago), such organizations could reasonably offer long-term career prospects as part of their unofficial terms of employment.

People who wrote about careers during this period tended to depict them as vertical, although people might expect to cross a few functional lines on the way up. Edgar Schein's famous cone model, for example, was clearly based on a hierarchical organization. Descriptions of people working in large vertical bureaucracies tended to emphasize the extent to which the person embraced the culture of the organization, presumably in hopes of advancement through its hierarchy.

This way of working, of putting one's trust and best efforts into the organization and being rewarded for it by rising through the ranks, is still a part of the predominant business culture in many organizations, including Procter & Gamble, United Parcel Service, Wal-Mart, and Unilever, to name a few.

Of course, paths to the top are limited, and they have tended to be identified with certain functions in particular eras and industries. In the 1950s and 60s, for example, it was true that, in many companies, the senior managers always rose up through the sales ranks, gaining general management responsibility as they progressed. In the 1970s and 80s, financial and operations paths became more frequently traveled tracks as companies became preoccupied with organizational effectiveness and the cost side of the balance sheet. Before the appointment of John Reed as CEO of Citibank, for example, no one had ever made it to the top of that organization (or any other financial institution of which we are aware) by rising through operations.

Although theoretically any functional path to the top was possible, in practice only certain career tracks led to the most senior jobs. People saw where these paths were, and there was intense competition to get onto them. And although there were exceptions—the appointment of R&D director Roy Vagelos as CEO of Merck was one example—the expectation was that vertical career paths, once worn in place, would change only slowly, if at all.

That expectation began to be challenged as early as the mid-1970s, after the first oil shock sent Western economies reeling. Four factors caused organizations to shift from vertical to more horizontal career paths in which people were more likely to advance by moving sideways than by moving up. First, the economic slowdown (and others that followed) trimmed the growth that had been necessary to allow the "pyramid scheme" of vertical career paths to continue. Second, the presence of early baby-boomers in managerial roles meant that later boomers found fewer places open: It was a long time until that first bulge group would retire. Third, many firms began to respond to hard times and increased competition by taking out entire layers of organization to reduce costs. This meant, of course, that there were fewer promotional opportunities. Finally, although this was by no means a new idea, more firms began to focus on developing generalists rather than functional specialists in order to better prepare themselves for the kinds of change and instability that appeared to be the coming norm in times ahead.

To develop such generalists and to provide some kind of career path in the absence of promotions, the horizontal career path came into prominence. Cross-functional and geographic progressions of jobs became the norm. Sometimes such paths were well established (such as a two-year overseas assignment followed by a return to headquarters); others were purely opportunistic. Organizational flexibility was greater under this model of careers (which we call Model 2) than under the vertical system (Model 1). Both are depicted in Exhibit 1. The major reward was no longer promotion, but rather the increase of one's breadth and skill base. This was clearly no substitute for promotion, particularly to those who had joined expecting to attain it. But it did provide a basis for a psychological contract with new employees that still promised them growth.

With the advent of horizontal career paths, organizations could adjust to circumstances relatively quickly. If different skills and experience became important for senior management roles, they could be drawn from anywhere within the organization or developed across lines via strategic job placements for promising individuals. Multiple paths to the top were possible, and firms could focus on developing global managers: executives whose combination of skills and experience allowed them to operate effectively across borders—both geographic and organizational.

Yet for all its flexibility, the horizontal model still assumed an internal labor market—that is, it assumed most organizations would hire for the long term and fill their vacancies from within. The evidence of the last ten years has clearly shown that more and more firms have been unable or unwilling to adhere to this policy. There are fewer "jobs for life," and far more exits take place well before retirement. It seems that large organizations, having once developed vertical career paths (and then horizontal ones) for the purposes of motivating employees and providing for the future of the firm, may now be giving up on career management altogether. Put another way, it may be that careers, having existed for years predominantly within large organizations, have now started to move beyond them.

CONTEMPORARY CAREERS: LEAVING THE ORGANIZATION BEHIND

Eric Monk runs a safety testing laboratory—a small, independent concern called INTERTest Systems UK. The lab is linked in a loose network of similar labs in several countries, serving clients throughout Europe, the U.S., and Japan. By most people's estimate, Monk would be considered a successful entrepreneur. He operates a state-of-the-art plant, draws from an excellent skill base, and can claim a list of satisfied customers.

EXHIBIT 1 **Organizational Careers**
From Vertical to Horizontal Paths

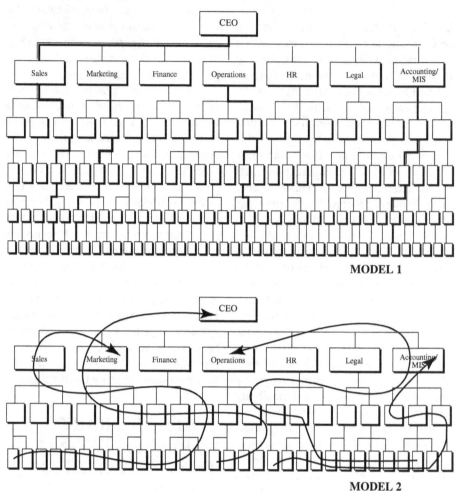

MODEL 1

MODEL 2

One customer in particular takes a great interest in the success of the lab—Digital Equipment Corporation, the global computer manufacturer that spun it off. The "entrepreneur" was in fact a career manager in this company until its outsourcing program (mandated by the U.S. headquarters) forced the sale of his unit. Not wanting to lose the expertise and service levels it had come to expect, DEC's European head office helped Monk and his colleagues move the lab off-site and set it up as their own company.

About his career change, Monk is philosophical: He would have liked to stay on at Digital but saw the opportunity inherent in the change and knew that, at least in the short term, he would be partially protected from competitive forces by the strength of that relationship. Now that he is independent, he is no longer subject to company policies, some of which had been, in his opinion, cumbersome. He sets his own hours and is free to decide the distribution of resources in his own small organization, free from constraints of headquarters or the stock market. He no longer has to make periodic trips to the U.S. and finds he has more time to spend with his family.

Much has been written recently about the changing nature of work and what it takes to succeed in the "post-corporate world." Researchers have considered the future of careers in organizations and sounded warning bells about major changes coming about through technology, ambiguity, and complexity. Big company career paths still exist, but they are no longer the principal routes to success.

Clearly there is a different model of careers now in operation (Model 3, shown in Exhibit 2). First of all, these new careers take place outside of large organizations (or across them, as in the case of turnaround experts such as IBM's Louis Gerstner). Often, this type of career develops after individuals exit such organizations, either involuntarily or by their own choice. Second, these individuals often serve the very organizations they have left, becoming trusted vendors. Exhibit 2 depicts some of the kinds of jobs taken up by those who leave large organizations; three of them include this kind of service relationship.

Third, these careers confer independence on individuals and provide them with the flexibility to respond quickly to demands and opportunities. Making all

EXHIBIT 2   Contemporary Careers
Leaving the Organization Behind

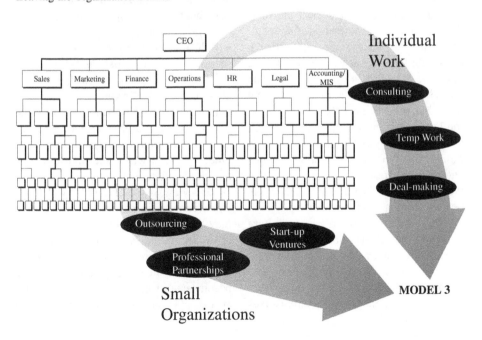

one's own choices can be extremely energizing; it is the external parallel to the elusive "total empowerment" in organizations. The rewards in such a system are no longer promotions or new postings; they are the basic individual measures of commercial success: income creation, asset growth, and the development of one's own business.

Fourth, by being removed from large organizations, the people in this new managerial career identify with their profession or industry rather than with a single company. Although this identity may have existed before, it will tend to be strengthened by the intense focus on customer service that typifies smaller organizations and by the need for detailed knowledge of industry and competitive elements required of consultants and deal makers. Long typical of professional partnerships such as accounting and law firms, the professional identity and service culture now also characterize the post-organizational career.

Finally, the new managerial career is likely to exist in a more comfortable balance with home and family, rather than at odds with them. That is, people who are in charge of their own work schedules can try to fit them in better with their personal lives. Many businesses are now run from the home or from an adjacent office. Of course, adjusting to this pattern of work is rarely easy: When the separation of home and work spheres that once dictated what was done when is removed, either can begin to encroach on the other.

Often the professional service culture demands that even more time be spent working for clients than in the large organization, and with no commute and few if any colleagues to separate them from home, some managers find themselves drawn into a quasi-permanent state of working. Says one ex-lawyer turned marketing consultant: "Because I work out of our home, I find it's nearly impossible to get away from work, or to overcome the feeling that I should always be working." When this happens in their own enterprises, however, at least managers retain control of their own schedules, and, at least in theory, can adjust them to fit their own preferences.

The last point highlights the fact that there is, of course, a negative side to these changes. Some of the problems are quite fundamental. For example, many who lose their jobs as a result of downsizing and outsourcing cannot easily continue their work outside the company's boundary. Moreover, even if this were possible, many individuals prefer membership in a large organization to total independence. Some may be better performers with a certain amount of routine rather than total flexibility; others would simply rather avoid the risks inherent in pursuing emergent, but still fuzzy, opportunities.

A more subtle problem is the way in which the post-organizational career seems to be isolating people. While working from home gives people freedom, it also cuts them off from regular contact with others. "Road warriors," people who operate entirely from automobiles, carry their business equipment (telephone, computer, and fax) with them and leave the traditional office in their dust.

One view is that the society that results from these new ways of working may be severely disabled when it comes to interpersonal communication. The consequence may turn out to be what we term an "autistic society," in which people become unaccustomed to dealing with others except in purely transactional ways—a global village of poor interpersonal communicators. In some ways, this picture represents a reversal of the progress of civilization: If the large organizations that evolved to deal with complex problems and provide for individual careers begin to decline, what are we left with but a dog-eat-dog world?

The situation in post-communist Russia, in which large state bureaucracies have crumbled—putting millions out of work—and in which numerous small organizations struggle to find a foothold but run up against economic hardship, overregulation, foreign competition, and organized crime, is a sobering vision. Although extreme, perhaps, this picture of a complete reversal of collectivism in favor of rampant individualism has its parallels in the decline of organizational careers in Western countries.

PRE-ORGANIZATIONAL CAREERS: WHAT CAME BEFORE?

Consideration of the individual aspects and the pitfalls of current careers made us think about what careers were like before the heyday of large business organizations. Mankind had centuries of experience with work between the time of the hunter-gatherers and the advent of the large industrial bureaucracy in the nineteenth century. What were careers like in this period?

Outside of such longstanding, essentially public sector organizations as the church, state, and military, pre-organizational careers consisted primarily of three types: laborers, independents, and craftsmen. Laborers made up what was essentially a contingent workforce: They worked when work was available, had no contracts of employment, and were entirely under the direction of foremen, whose discretion was total.

Independents, including farmers and merchants, were more or less self-sufficient, growing, selling, or bartering what they needed to in order to survive (although weather, war, and competition for resources could also have their effects). Their enterprises were often family-based and passed down the line from father to son.

Craftsmen, by contrast, often had clearly defined career paths: from apprentice to journeyman and, eventually, to master. Such paths were fixed, vertical, and outside work organizations. Typically, the career centered on one master's workshop and remained there until the trainee became a master himself and either succeeded his master or set up his own business. Here, too, the discretion of the master was all-important, as in this description from Dickens: "He has the power to render us happy or unhappy; to make our service light or burdensome; a pleasure or a toil."

Most pre-organizational careers could be characterized as individual, low in security, and high in risk. Except for the one or two promotions a craftsman might expect in the course of a lifetime, the major rewards were income and asset growth. People identified with their occupation rather than with any work organization and were members of strong local communities as well. Their work tended to be integrated with their home and family lives in both schedule and proximity, as families often supported the work and few people worked far from where they lived.

This early model of careers, which we call Model 0, resembles in many ways the current, post-corporate career. The independent nature of work, the pursuit of individual wealth, the integration with home and family—these are in fact many of the attributes of Model 3. The question, then, is this: Having moved beyond large corporations, are the new careers really just leading us back to the past, regressing to the pre-organizational stage (Exhibit 3)? If so, is this really the end for the development of career systems? Or is something fundamentally different now?

CAREER EVOLUTION: TWO UNDERLYING DIMENSIONS

For us, the argument that careers are moving out of organizations is compelling. We see it in the downsizing and outsourcing undertaken by companies, as well as in the entrepreneurship and independent professions being pursued by individuals. We see it in our MBA students, who have few aspirations to rise through the ranks of major corporations. But if careers have moved first into and then out of organizations over the years, has there not been a cycle that is now returning to its beginnings?

We think not. In fact, there seems to us to be one fundamental difference between the pre-organizational and post-organizational career systems we have described here, and it comes back to the basic change undergone by careers *within* organizations. Whatever limited careers existed in the pre-organizational era were essentially vertical (laborer to foreman, for example, or apprentice to journeyman), while those in the current environment are essentially horizontal, dependent as they are on movement across or out

EXHIBIT 3 **A Cycle of Careers**
Back to Square One—Or Square *Zero?*

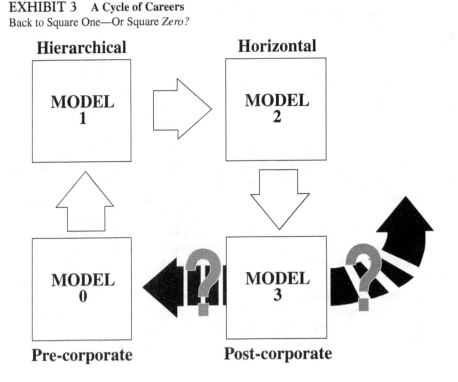

of organizations and on the subsequent selling of services to those organizations and others, through networks formed by experience and work relationships.

In considering the history of careers, therefore, we propose that there are two fundamental dimensions along which they can be categorized: organizational/individual, and vertical/horizontal. The resulting model of career evolution is shown in Exhibit 4. The development of careers has taken a clockwise direction, beginning with Model 0 and ending up with Model 3. Of course, career systems of the first three types still exist in many places, and in some of these places work well. The critical mass however, is, we believe, now firmly in Model 3.

Our concern, though, is not only to understand the historical trends in careers and how they have resulted in the present state, but more importantly, to help prepare for the future. To this end, having built the model in Exhibit 4, we must now ask, *is this it?* Are individual/horizontal careers that future? Or is there still something more? In particular, is there something beyond the individual, something that might mitigate against the dissolution of social structures considered above?

THE NEW DIMENSION: SUPPORTED GLOBAL LINKS

We believe that careers in the next century will move beyond Model 3 because this model misses out on two fundamental forces—the basic human need for

EXHIBIT 4   **Career Evolution**
Underlying Dimensions

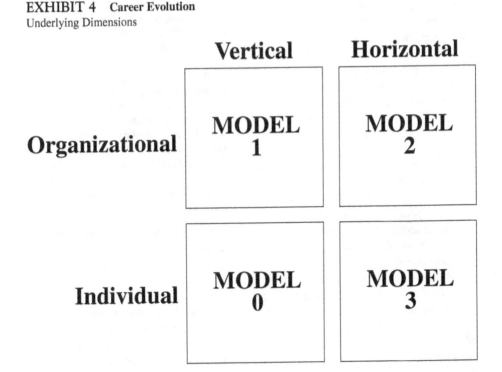

belonging and social support, and the rapid globalization of communications and services.

We expect that a new set of support structures will develop—in fact, are already developing—to take the place of the corporation in addressing the first of these forces. Moreover, we believe that the second force will not only help these structures to develop, but will itself include a powerful infrastructure that will enable careers to transcend both individuals and organizations.

SUPPORTING ELEMENTS

The need to identify with a group is a fundamental aspect of human nature. Most people inherently require contact and a social identity that refers to a set of others (the "reference set") as well as the security that a strong social base can provide. Corporations often fulfilled this role, particularly those such as IBM ("Big Blue") in computers, Kodak ("The Great Yellow Father") in photographic products, or Merrill Lynch ("Mother Merrill" to its employees) in financial services. Yet these organizations, like many others, have all faced serious economic difficulties and have cut back and restructured, ending many organizational careers in the process.

Where do individuals embarking on post-corporate careers find identification and support? Recent research gives short shrift to this question. Yet it seems reasonable to expect that, eventually, new support mechanisms will appear to fill the hole left in people's careers by the receding corporation.

We see three kinds of entities playing a role here: First, a growing number of organizations now provide a base of operations for individuals whose employment is contracted out to other organizations. These agencies, as we will call them, include temporary bureaus such as Manpower in the U.S. and U.K. and Kelly Services in the U.S.; more specialized providers such as MacTemps (computer personnel); and (more recently) a number of employee-leasing firms that take on the legal and financial aspects of employment in order to lower clients' risks and costs associated with maintaining a workforce. Although these agencies are not the users of their members' work, they can provide the members with a corporate identity and, in some cases, with regular pay and benefits, although they offer no traditional career paths.

One such organization is Staff Leasing, a Florida company that has flourished by taking over the legal employment of staff for a number of small- to medium-size businesses. Says Jules Kortenhorst, who recently completed a stint as the company's chief operating officer:

> Staff Leasing does not recruit for its clients. The hiring and firing remains with the client, the small business owner. So it's not an alternative way for people to find jobs. But a small- or medium-size business that wants to focus [on other aspects of business] can, with one signature on paper, have a comprehensive salary and benefits HR offering. The benefit for the workforce is that employees of smaller companies get access to comprehensive benefits that other small companies can't offer.

Second, a growing variety of professional bodies now offer membership and validation, sometimes in the form of formal qualifications, to practitioners of many disciplines. These have expanded beyond the traditional professions (law, medicine, clergy) and trades (which for centuries have had guilds and, later, unions) and into the realm of the new career functions.

The 1980s saw the advent, for example, of several professional associations for consultants, and even codes of conduct for them. Such organizations often play a social as well as a professional role. They can have important effects on careers by acting as gatekeepers, providers of information and counseling, or clearinghouses for talent. They even provide careers for a small minority of members, as happened for Trevor Jones in our earlier example.

Third, there is a role to be played by communities. The long decline in community well-being is now starting to be addressed, albeit in a limited number of places, because of a mix of factors. Wherever unemployment has risen sharply, there are more people staying at home in communities and therefore a greater urgency to keep the communities healthy. As cities become overcrowded and people desire to leave, many individuals and small businesses elect to return to the smaller communities from which they came, providing more of an economic base. And in both Europe and America, grass-roots movements to "promote the general welfare" beyond simply taxing individual and corporate earnings have advocated bigger contributions of time and resources to community projects.

These movements have found resonances in business, government, and academia. Where they succeed, they revitalize a basic support structure that reaches all the members of a given locality, replacing some of what they may have lost through the decline of other means of support.

GLOBALIZATION

In conjunction with the new (or rather, renewed) support structures, a new global infrastructure is emerging—one that can strengthen the first two supports (agencies and professional bodies) mentioned above by allowing them to develop more scope, and, at the same time, help the community by enabling work to return to it.

It has been an axiom of management thought and teaching for some years that business is becoming, or has become, global in scope. Industries and companies exist, it is said, not so much in local or national spheres, but in a worldwide market for goods and services. Although this view has become pervasive, we have been hesitant to fully accept it. Yet it now seems to us that several global forces have already begun to shape the careers of the future, and that anyone concerned with careers ignores these forces at their own peril.

These forces are, first, the vast increase in flows of capital, goods, and services; second, the growing number of individuals, especially recent graduates, who have lived, studied, and worked in multiple countries using multiple languages; and third, the advent of a global communications network the like of which was not imagined only a few years ago.

The increase in cross-border flows of money and the products of work is testimony to the idea that markets really are becoming global, and that competition in the future will no longer take place at a local or even a national level for any company with the means to put products in front of customers at a distance. This means that careers built on providing services to a local set of customers, and in particular to large organizations from which the service providers have recently exited, may not be sustainable in the longer term unless they have strong barriers to outside competition (such as a complex set of local regulations which they have worked out how to meet, or have helped to design). Most businesses, whether organizational or individual, will have to perform to a global standard in order to compete.

The growing number of individuals seeking and finding opportunities to study and work abroad represents a new cadre of managers with global potential. The importance of this kind of experience is emphasized in top MBA programs, a number of which now require both a second language and an overseas project in order to earn the degree. For businesses that require a worldwide presence, such people are an asset, either as employees or as service providers. Those people, therefore, who have spent their entire careers in one company or, more importantly, one country, may find they cannot compete with these broad-based, younger managers whose reference groups are essentially global. Opportunities in the new century will accrue to those whose careers reflect the global nature of business.

Finally, and perhaps most important, the sudden predominance of the Internet and the World Wide Web can bring anyone into anyone else's office. It will not be long before every working professional has a computer equipped with a camera and video card that will enable teleconferencing—which still largely takes place only in corporate communication centers—to be individually controlled and delivered.

The rush of businesses to make their products and services available on the Web simply reflects the ease, economy, and pervasiveness of this new medium for reaching potential customers and conducting transactions. At the individual level, home pages are becoming the latest means of showing one's face (and other attributes, such as qualifications and experience) to the rest of the world. This kind of network cannot help but be a source of career information, and, in fact, several Internet career forums already exist.

By some estimates, the World Wide Web is now [1997] growing at one percent *per day,* and at that rate there could be a home page for everyone in the world within four years. Such a network is both an equalizer and a separator: People who are on it are all roughly equal; they can reach and be reached by anyone. (Of course, the underlying quality of their products and services may not be the same, and this can be difficult to judge.)

People not on the network, however, will be in a handicapped class in much the same way that not having a secondary education has differentiated people since the early part of this century. Gone are the days when computers were for techies, and the Internet the province of engineers and science fiction fans. Global electronic networks are now in the process of bringing about a single market for services and labor, in much the same way that capital and goods have already globalized.

Examples of supported, globally linked careers abound. The now-familiar term "telecommuting" describes the practice of working away from the office through electronic communication (which is how this article was written, for example). A logical extension of this practice removes the office tie altogether, as has happened in the Western Isles of Scotland. Here, a small set of locals with university educations have elected to cease working (or looking for work) in the far-off cities. Instead, they have set up computers in their homes (mostly in farms and villages) to write abstracts of newspaper articles for a database publisher based thousands of miles away in San Francisco.

These are not organizational careers; the publisher has outsourced the abstracting process. But neither are they just individual careers. There is a networked community of people all doing the work, with a local coordinator also based in the Western Isles. The health of the community has been greatly enhanced, as it begins to see a way to stem the flow of its population exodus.

The "virtual organization," too, provides a new model for globally linked careers. A small software firm with which we are familiar has developers—salaried employees—who live in three different countries but link together online to critique and combine their work. Some of them also do outside work for other customers. These people's careers go beyond the individual level because they work *together,* and beyond the traditional concept of organization because the organization does not exist in a spatial sense. Managers in this enterprise ensure that linkages among members remain tight, and often combine visits to the developers with customer calls.

IMPLICATIONS FOR MANAGERS

The implications of this article will be quite different for different individuals. Those who are reading it with an eye toward managing their own careers will see ramifications markedly different from those who have their sights on devising and improving career systems in their organizations. We therefore offer some thoughts to each type of reader, under the twin headings of "supporting elements" and "globalization."

ADVICE FOR INDIVIDUALS: SUPPORTING ELEMENTS

To understand how you will fit into the workplace of the future, consider the following:

1. First, know your own abilities and preferences. If you have a low risk profile and are not comfortable with owning your own business, do everything you can to ensure you will not have to do so:

   a. Become indispensable to your organization through your knowledge, skills, and performance. This will require an in-depth understanding of the needs of the business in the short and long term, ongoing self-development to keep up with the changing state of technology and practice as they relate to those needs, and a sustained effort, likely to involve some personal sacrifices, toward maximizing results (but see item 2, below).

   b. Cultivate relationships in other organizations that could lead to your employment should your organization get into trouble. This is not the same as going for the occasional job interview in order to keep in touch with the market and your own value in it—which, if discovered by employers, is still usually seen as evidence of disloyalty. Rather, it means getting to know your suppliers and customers, for example, well enough to be aware of their needs and offering help from time to time in solving some of their problems, beyond those that might be addressed in the normal course of your work.

   c. Put aside money and resources for eventualities. This may seem a truism, but in the face of increased career uncertainty it takes on added importance and, given a long decline in saving rates (a trend that only recently has begun to reverse), would also seem to be more difficult than it once was.

   d. Consider whether there might be alternative careers you might eventually like to explore and do some groundwork to prepare for them.

This might include outside training and possibly formal qualifications, such as a part-time degree or professional certification.

2. Seek out and join the relevant professional associations for your current career. Look for ways to become active in what they are doing. Then, consider joining other organizations, such as community or vocational groups, that both hold an interest for you and can provide a support network in times of need. Start slowly if you are busy, but do start. Focusing every ounce of energy and time on your current job is a high-risk approach to your career. Many do it, but few find themselves ready when change occurs.

3. Stay in touch with friends, former colleagues, and extended family—keep your networks strong.

4. Help others through their career difficulties by counsel, referral, and emotional support. Test your own prejudices to make sure you no longer consider the loss of one's job, or working on one's own, a stigma.

ADVICE FOR INDIVIDUALS: GLOBALIZATION

In view of the emerging global infrastructure, the following actions seem prudent:

1. Get international experience, or at least visit other countries and explore their social and work environments. Take advantage of cultural sensitivity and interpersonal skills training, if available. We often take these abilities for granted, but they can improve greatly with practice, just as they can decline with disuse.

2. Learn another language, and make sure your children have the opportunity to

do so. Even if you do not expect to use it right away, the discipline and sense of achievement that come with this important skill will increase both your confidence and your marketability.

3. Get computer literate. Get on line. Get linked. There are so many ways to do this today that anyone concerned about their career has no excuse not to. Age need not be a barrier: Several of our septuagenarian relatives keep in touch with us via e-mail, and have done so for several years. Once you are on-line, explore the resources available in your career area. Try to find one or two regular forums in which you can participate and from which you will draw some benefit. It may take some exploration, and much of what you see at first may be disappointingly uninteresting or irrelevant. But continued browsing, liberal use of the "delete" key, and ever more intelligent search engines will soon make this effort well worthwhile.

ADVICE FOR MANAGERS IN ORGANIZATIONS: SUPPORTING ELEMENTS

The following actions can help employees cope with the new employment environment:

1. Offer employees a psychological contract that you will be able to keep. In the mid-1980s, People Express Airlines offered its employees a job for life—even though the company's own life in a volatile industry had only recently begun and was to end within five years. Get the psychological contract right: If your organization is better able to offer opportunities for travel and skill development than for promotion, then be explicit about this.

If you are subject to tremendous uncertainty and require great flexibility of your employees (as is the case in many organizations today), then make that clear. The successful organizations of the new century will be those whose people have control of their own work and who make decisions to align that work with the goals of the organization. To begin that relationship with a misalignment of individual and organizational expectations makes little sense.

2. If you are considering outsourcing certain tasks, look for opportunities to set up your own employees to provide those services. They know your business needs best. Establish relationships with vendors that maximize information transfer and interdependence, thereby increasing the potential for quality and responsiveness. Typically this means depending on a small number of vendors but holding them to extremely high standards.

3. Support industry trade associations and encourage your employees to participate in their activities.

4. Focus your career management practices not on elusive career tracks, but on the basics: skill development for increased performance and value, thoughtful and in-depth appraisals, and information about job opportunities within and (if appropriate) outside the firm. Offer employees counseling by managers and professionals when required, particularly when taking people out of the company.

ADVICE FOR MANAGERS IN ORGANIZATIONS: GLOBALIZATION

There are many implications for your role in this domain as well. Consider the following actions as potentially beneficial to yourself and your employees:

1. Get on line. Get linked. This can be via private, in-company networks or via Internet and World Wide Web access. Doing this has the dual advantages of providing a potential source of important information and an outlet for the company's products, while simultaneously showing employees that the organization is an enabler and a provider of links rather than a limiter of their prospects. If people are going on-line anyway, is it not better for this to happen within the organization, where some advantage might be taken of the opportunities provided, rather than outside, where they will be missed?

2. Figure out ways to let small enterprises grow within the large corporation. This goes against traditional notions of the need for control and efficiency, and wheels may indeed be reinvented. But small is beautiful, because small is flexible. We doubt whether any global organization can manage its day-to-day business better centrally than locally, no matter how good its networks. Responsiveness is the key. Large organizations that move toward the smaller organization paradigm, encouraging horizontal careers in both their internal and external labor markets, will be the ones most likely to flourish in the twenty-first century.

3. Provide lifelong learning for managers as well as links outside your organization. One recent example in our own institution is consortium programs for executive education in which five or six companies from different industries partner to provide not only classroom-based instruction but also field visits

to one another's businesses, thereby providing exposure and encouraging the transfer of ideas. Some of these programs are truly global, drawing participants from, and holding classroom sessions and visits, around the world.

THE POST-CORPORATE CAREER

Because of these two elements—support structures and global links—we believe that careers in the twenty-first century really will transcend both organizations and individuals. Rooted in identity-building professional organizations and communities and linked by global infrastructures (not only electronic networks but also the growing global transportation system), these careers will be largely, as others have put it, boundaryless. They will progress in limitless ways through countless jobs, transactions, and connections, involving ever-changing networks of people, places, and businesses.

There will be limits to the post-corporate career, of course. We do not mean to imply, for example, that all work will be done by telecommuting—far from it. But more global links mean more virtual groups and organizations, even among real physical offices. Increased air travel will mean that distances get shorter, in that more traffic leads to more options for travel. And most important, people will be exposed to more and more ways to develop and use their skills—but will be required to compete for the opportunity to do so.

Those who succeed will be those who can not only stand on their own, but can form and sustain links—links that will take them beyond existing individual and organizational models, to entirely new kinds of careers.

Selected Bibliography

Much has transpired since the time when career development was seen as a straight climb up the organizational ladder, as was described in J. E. Rosenbaum's *Career Mobility in a Corporate Hierarchy* (Orlando, FL: Academic Press, 1984). Futurist books such as Alvin Toffler's *The Third Wave* (New York: Bantam Books, 1981) and Charles Handy's *The Age of Unreason* (London: Business Books, 1989) were perhaps the first written expressions of the changing nature of the organization and careers as we used to know them.

Many of the basics in career management can be found in M. London and S. A. Stumpf, *Managing Careers* (Reading, MA: Addison Wesley, 1982), or D. T. Hall, *Careers in Organizations* (Glenview, IL: Scott Foresman, 1976) and *Career Development in Organizations* (San Francisco: Jossey-Bass, 1986). Edgar H. Schein, too, provides a conceptual framework from both individual and organizational points of view in *Career Dynamics* (Reading, MA: Addison Wesley, 1978). A more practical collection is Jeffrey Sonnenfeld's *Managing Career Systems* (Homewood, IL: Irwin, 1984). The reader may also find the *Handbook of Career Theory* (Cambridge, U.K.: Cambridge University Press, 1989), edited by M. B. Arthur, D. T. Hall and B. S. Lawrence, as well as its successor volume, the *Handbook of Career Studies* (Sage, 2007), edited by H. Gunz and M. Peiperl, to be useful.

Psychological contracts, the often tacit agreements between employers and employees setting out what each party expects to give and receive in the employment relationship, are nicely explained in Chapter 2 of Charles Handy's *Understanding Organizations,* 4th ed. (London: Penguin Books, 1993). Mismatches in psychological contracts have been enumerated by John Kotter in "The Psychological Contract: Managing the Joining-Up Process," *California Management Review* 15(3): 91–99 (1973). See also S. Robinson and D. Rousseau, "Violating the Psychological Contract: Not the Exception but the Norm," *Journal of Organizational Behavior* (1994).

For a history of the development of work organizations (in America specifically), see Alfred D. Chandler and Richard S. Tedlow, *The Coming of Managerial Capitalism* (Homewood, IL: Irwin, 1985), especially Chapter 8. Also relevant is Chandler's classic work, *The Visible Hand: The Managerial Revolution in American Business* (Cambridge, MA: Belknap Press, 1977). For a more labor-oriented approach, see *Employing Bureaucracy: Managers, Unions, and the Transformation of Work in American Industry, 1900–1945* by Sanford M. Jacoby (New York: Columbia University Press, 1985).

John Kotter's 20-year study of the careers of a group of Harvard MBAs is described in his book *The New Rules: How to Succeed in Today's Post-Corporate World* (New York: Free Press, 1995). Kotter identifies eight rules for succeeding in contemporary managerial careers.

Recent works on the changing nature of careers in organizations include a number of references to boundaryless careers. See especially the special issue (1994) of the *Journal of Organizational Behavior,* in particular the articles by M. B. Arthur and R. J. DeFillippi; M. B. Arthur; and also P. H. Mirvis and D. T. Hall. See also the article "Intelligent Enterprise, Intelligent Careers," by M. B. Arthur, P. Claman, and R. J. DeFillippi, in *Academy of Management Review* No. 4, (1995). Several books also address this topic: *The Boundaryless Career* by M. Arthur and D. Rousseau (New York: Oxford, 1996) and *The Career Is Dead: Long Live the Career* by D. T. Hall (San Francisco: Jossey-Bass, 1996).

Case

Emilio Kornau

Emilio Kornau grew up believing he would be successful. His parents had emigrated to the United Kingdom from northern Italy in 1940. His father, once a machinist in a factory near Turin, had left his homeland for political reasons, bringing his young bride to an uncertain life in the sooty tenements of Manchester, where he found work as a laborer in a steel mill. Emilio was born in Manchester in 1948, and by the time he was ten was supplementing his family's meager income by selling newspapers and delivering groceries.

The 1960s saw an improvement in the lot of the Kornau family. Emilio's father finally overcame a strong anti-immigrant (and, during and after World War II, anti-Italian) bias and became a line manager in a major British steel manufacturer. The family was able to buy a home in one of the newer Manchester suburbs, and Emilio attended one of the new "polytechnic"

Source: Prof. Maury Peiperl prepared this case for the purpose of classroom discussion, rather than to illustrate effective or ineffective handling of a career situation. Certain information in the case has been altered for reasons of confidentiality.

colleges where he obtained a diploma in electrical engineering. His parents encouraged him to seek a career in one of the computer firms that were then showing tremendous growth, and after a six-month search Emilio was hired by ICL in the summer of 1970. He was 21.

"Work hard, give to the company, and you will always have a job" his father had told him. His bosses and colleagues said the same. Emilio was an excellent engineer and a hard worker, and his efforts were gradually rewarded with more and more responsibility and seniority. Eschewing a chance to become a supervisor and manager, Emilio instead rose higher and higher on the company's technical career ladder, achieving the rank of senior engineer at the age of 39 in 1988, the youngest ever in his department to do so.

The early 1990s saw big changes in the U.K. computer industry, and the once-dominant ICL went through a series of restructurings, ending with a takeover by Fujitsu. ICL stopped making computers in the U.K. Emilio's unit was disbanded and the entire European contingent lost their jobs. The company had a history of looking after its employees, particularly the high performers, and Emilio and most of his colleagues were offered positions elsewhere in the organization. In Emilio's case, however, this would have required moving his family out of the U.K.

Emilio did not want to compound the shock of losing his job with the trauma of moving his family far from his adopted (and his wife and teenage children's native) country. Shaken but still confident of his engineering abilities, he decided to take the generous severance terms offered by the company (at 45 he was too young to take early retirement). On top of the severance, Emilio also held a substantial number of ICL shares, which he had purchased over the years through the company's employee share option purchase plan. It was a generous plan, and although Emilio was not interested in the stock market generally, he had signed up as a gesture of loyalty and confidence in the firm. He only wished, as he cleared out his office, that the price of the stock were what it had been a few years earlier.

With his severance pay as a buffer, Emilio set out to look for another job. Over the next eight months, he approached dozens of engineering firms. He soon discovered that his technical knowledge, while quite in-depth, was extremely company-specific. That is, while he knew comprehensively all the elements of the design and manufacture of the ICL products he had worked on, he had little idea of other companies' products or how they were made. Even the design software he had used was specific to his former company, and he was unfamiliar with the off-the-shelf systems used by smaller firms.

To make matters worse, his knowledge was rapidly becoming out of date. A slow decline in large manufacturing firms had been under way in the U.K. A number of start-ups had been launched in the computer hardware industry, particularly in the network area, but most of them had no need of Emilio's skills and besides, they seemed to him to have an average employee age of about 25. Furthermore, even if he could have found a job in one of these new firms, Emilio felt that it would be too risky: Many start-ups had gone under in the last recession, and he didn't want to go through losing his job again.

Emilio's friends and family were sympathetic and supportive, but because he has built his career inside a single firm, he had a very limited outside network on which to call for career advice and job opportunities. Many of his former colleagues shared information about their job market experiences, but most were in similar situations and had either retrained, moved away, or gone on unemployment.

Emilio was not happy with any of these options, but it was gradually becoming clear that there was no market for his skills. After eight months of looking, he finally applied for unemployment benefits, which he hated to do because he did not want to be a burden on the society that had offered his family the opportunity to get ahead.

After a year on the dole Emilio took a job as a driver for an airport car service. "I had to do something" he said. "I never thought I would end up like this. But there aren't any jobs out there for someone with my specific skills, and I don't want to start again at the bottom in one of the high-tech firms. At least now I have some independence; I set my own hours and I know most of my clients personally. You have to be philosophical about it; at least my family and I are healthy; we have a home of our own and enough to eat.

"Do I ever think about starting my own company? Not really. I wasn't trained for it and I don't want the hassle, the risk. Some of these guys, you see them work 20 hours a day for five years to build something and then it all goes wrong and what do they have left? Even their families are strangers after that kind of single-minded effort. No, I'll stick with driving until something better comes along."

Case

Mark Margolis

Mark Margolis grew up in Long Island, New York, the son of a businessman. From a young age he was partial to music, gadgets, and marketing. In high school he formed a band called the Canines, for which he wrote pop songs (Mark played the guitar). Taking advantage of his early interest in electronics, after high school he started a part-time business called Fix-and-Trade, repairing and trading (by mail)

Source: Prof. Maury Peiperl prepared this case for the purpose of classroom discussion, rather than to illustrate effective or ineffective handling of a career situation. Certain information in the case has been altered for reasons of confidentiality.

© 2002 by Maury Peiperl.

in used electronic equipment from around the country.

Margolis attended Hofstra University, where he majored in business. From there he joined Carter Myers, a top advertising firm. In 1978 he was admitted to Columbia Business School, where he began the MBA program in September of that year.

The first year of business school can be very tough, and by June of 1979 Margolis had accumulated enough "low-pass" credits that he was asked to leave the program. The same year, he discovered that his fiancée had been having an affair with a close friend of his. Bitterly disappointed by both events, he nonetheless resolved to make the best of a difficult situation. With one main partner and a number of advisors, he started a firm called Exposign which made computerized display equipment for conference and retail applications.

The Exposign venture went well, until Margolis found one day, to his shock, that his partner had invested two-thirds of the firm's capital in the start-up speculative venture of a relative, which promptly went bust. Exposign (and Margolis) became insolvent, and, lacking the funds to sue his partner (who himself was now bankrupt), Margolis was forced to sell out to a competitor for less than the total of the firm's liabilities.

In 1983 Margolis petitioned Columbia for readmission to the second year of the MBA program, and was allowed to return in the fall of 1984. He applied himself well and graduated in 1985. To complete his rehabilitation, Margolis secured a job with the Bestaman Company, a top consumer products company, in the prestigious Marketing Department. It was the sort of job most marketers would envy, and Margolis was happy to have "made it" after some very challenging career and life experiences.

Less than two years later, Bestaman announced a layoff in the Marketing Department, and Margolis lost his job.

He had read the signs correctly this time, however, and was prepared. Immediately after being laid off, Margolis took his severance pay and, with a colleague, Howard Harris, founded a new venture, SellSoft, to develop software for retail applications. Using his many contacts from a variety of areas, principally in marketing and retail, Margolis built the firm into a strong niche position. In 1996 the firm merged with a competitor, and shortly thereafter the combined entity was sold to a Finnish company for over $50 million in cash and stock.

Margolis pocketed $16 million from the sale of his firm. Not one to rest on his laurels, he continued to be involved with the acquiring firm, and in particular with a spinoff of SellSoft called SKUBank, a digital data bank for manufacturers and retailers, of which he remained chairman until the company folded in 2000.

Margolis also pursued his long-time dream of making a splash in the entertainment industry. Over a two-year period, he expanded his house, built a small sound stage, and launched a Web-linked TV production company called HouseToHouse.com. Concurrently, he married (at age 44), and soon after became a father. Of his new business and family ventures, he says "I'm not sure exactly how I got where I am, except to say it's been both fun and a continuous challenge. Now with another start-up and a young family, I don't know how either of them will develop, but I can guarantee I'll have my hands full for the next few years . . . and I'll have fun doing it."

Case

Kerstin Berger (A)

Kerstin Berger hung up the phone and sat quietly at her desk for a moment. She had just returned from a week-long vacation and was actually looking forward to the busy schedule of her double role as project and team leader, but she had not expected the news that her boss had just given her over the phone. He had just asked her to take over the lead of the planning project that was on everybody's mind right now. This project was very high-visibility and the leadership responsibility was much larger than on any other project she had led in the past. "Go-live" for this project was set for a month from now—the end of June 2006—and she knew that the project team was terribly behind schedule. Lastly, and most disturbingly, Berger was set to take over the project from her very close co-worker and peer, Tina Orton. Berger was aware that Orton had been struggling over the last few months, but she was still shocked to see how far it had come. Sitting at her desk, Berger reflected on the last six months, the issues that the team had had to face, but also the environment in which the planning project was supposed to be rolled out. She realized how difficult the task ahead of her was and that she would not be able to succeed unless she put herself in Orton's situation and tried to understand what had made it so impossible for her.

THE COMPANY

The planning project was set in the IT department of L-Bank, a large bank based in the Zürich area of Switzerland. L-Bank was a very successful company—its key value, employee loyalty, had played a large role in its over 100 years of existence. It was still largely owned by one family and the family's influence could be felt throughout the company. Despite the banking business being quite fast-moving, L-Bank was known for its lethargic ways and its employees' resistance to any changes. In fact, a large part of the workforce started their careers at L-Bank with an apprenticeship after high school and stayed there for their entire working life, often without their job descriptions changing much over this time. Due to some successful acquisitions and a very healthy economy, the company had been growing by double digits over the past three years, stretching the workforce to its maximum.

With this fast growth, one function that had had trouble keeping up was Human Resources (HR). The department was organized both locally and globally and the roles and responsibilities were not clearly defined. This confusion resulted in minimal involvement of any HR professionals in personnel matters such as recruiting, development and training, as well as in retaining employees. Most of these processes were run by line managers with minimal

Source: *Professor Maury Peiperl and an anonymous IMD program participant prepared this case as a basis for class discussion rather than to illustrate either effective or ineffective handling of a business situation.*

consulting from the HR department. Even escalations (formal complaint or disciplinary processes) took a lot of time to be processed by the understaffed HR functions.

The IT department within L-Bank was facing a particular challenge during this high-growth period. With many new projects coming up, everybody was extremely busy while at the same time—since IT was an "overhead" department—experiencing continuous budget cuts from the business. All L-Bank's profits were going into new business opportunities and IT had to find alternative ways to keep up. Recently, a large part of the organization had been outsourced to Spain and Poland while positions in Switzerland had been cut. This led to anxiety among the existing Swiss staff and some hostility toward any newcomers within the department, particularly foreigners.

Berger and Orton, an American, were both reporting to John Haldemann, who had recently become the head of the Informatics Services organization within L-Bank IT. The Project Management team was the last to be added to Haldemann's growing organization that already included

Procurement and Quality Assurance. The team consisted of Orton, Martin Landes (another project manager) and Berger and her team of project professionals (*refer to Exhibit 1 for Haldemann's organization*).

Project management was a relatively new discipline within L-Bank IT. The goal of the newly established organization was to change the perception of project management from a "hobby," as it was currently seen by many within the organization, into an actual job with a career track and defined qualifications. In previous years, projects in IT had been managed by IT professionals who were well trained in their specific field of knowledge but rarely implemented any project management processes or tools. Projects were always delayed and often failed without any consequences. With the pressure IT and the entire organization were now under, however, projects had to succeed. It was this realization that brought about the creation of the Project Management team, without much applause from the rest of the IT organization, most of whom did not see the reason for this team's existence while their colleagues were losing their jobs.

EXHIBIT 1   L-Bank IT Organization

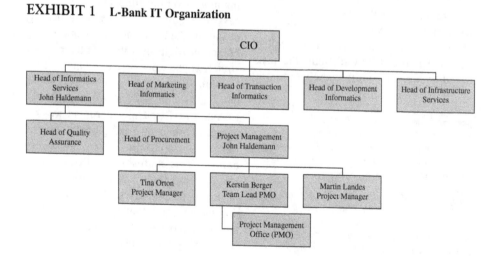

THE PLANNING PROJECT

When Orton joined the project management team in late 2005, she had found the IT organization in an unusual state. In the two years before her arrival, a new CIO had brought about numerous changes, including major reorganizations that, while yielding immediate benefits, had left the whole department somewhat shell-shocked. Many projects and very high expectations from the business departments resulted in an overstretched organization in which long hours and full commitment were a constant expectation. There was a daily competition in the open-plan office to see who was still there every night when the lights went off. Even when coming in on weekends, L-Bank's IT professionals were never alone, and with the onset of Blackberries®, 24-hour availability was expected—and lived.

Of course this environment had seen its victims. There were many stories in circulation of people who had suddenly disappeared from one day to the next and were never seen again. It was often stated that "they just couldn't take the pressure" or "they could not live up to the expectations." Others had been on leave of absence for many months and their futures in the organization were uncertain.

Adding to this pressure was the lack of an overview within the IT department of the total projects that were running at any point in time. The management team had no governance system in place to approve or decline projects before they started; as a result, small, medium and large projects were mushrooming everywhere. The planning project had been initiated in order to bring some order into this chaos. The first rollout of the project intended to implement a time recording system, through which all 2,000 employees of the IT department would input their working hours every week and allocate them to specific projects or operational tasks. This would give the management team a better overview of the hours worked and projects running. With the facts in hand, the management team could discuss and, if necessary, stop new projects coming from the business if the resources were not there to deliver them. Also, this new system would give L-Bank's IT employees a way to discuss their overtime with their supervisors. The reaction when the Planning Project had been announced to IT staff worldwide, however, was very negative. The new system was seen as an additional administrative task that would shave valuable minutes off other, very pressing tasks. Additionally, people feared that the data in the new system would be used by the management team to put tighter controls on everybody and—even worse—to detect further redundancies, resulting in further reorganizations. The resistance was massive and threatened the success of the project from its very beginning.

CAST OF CHARACTERS

John Haldemann had joined L-Bank IT in 2003 at 35 and was one of the youngest vice presidents the company had seen. Haldemann had made a career in the US military before joining a large American car manufacturer as a procurement manager. He was originally hired into L-Bank IT to head up the procurement function. The Quality Assurance and Project Management organizations were added later and Haldemann, with his expertise in procurement, had to learn not only about these different disciplines but also the very different people who worked in them. Haldemann was a big believer in stretching people to their limits, not necessarily in terms of workload, but certainly in terms of task difficulty. He often stated that he liked his people "to be able to just keep their heads above the water." He very much enjoyed the feeling of achievement and projected this onto his employees.

Kerstin Berger had joined the organization at the same time as Haldemann right after graduating from university. After several smaller roles in projects, she took on the project management team after ten months in the company. Under her supervision, the team grew from two to ten people and gained a reputation for providing junior, but highly enthusiastic, project management staff and professional services to IT projects. Highly inexperienced at the time, Berger was still finding her identity as a line manager and learned a lot from observing Haldemann's leadership approach. The ever-growing challenges and often high profile projects he assigned to her in addition to her operational role as a line manager were very motivating for her and kept her learning curve steep.

Tina Orton was forty years old and had joined L-Bank as the result of her husband's expatriate assignment in another department of the company. They had been married in their native Ohio a few months before their move to Europe and this was the first time living abroad for both of them. Through first getting married and then taking on her new assignment, Orton had moved house three times within the last few months and the many changes that had taken place in her life over the previous year were visible from her first day at work in Zürich.

Orton had never worked for a bank before. Her background was in construction project management, and while many of the same processes could be applied in construction as well as in IT projects, the environment was very different. In construction, project management planning was absolutely crucial. Plans had to be written and approved well in advance in order to ensure that the right material and the right staff were at the right place at the right time. In IT projects, however, detailed planning—while very useful—was not as common and not as essential to the success of the project. Orton herself was introverted and, while a skilled project manager and a well-liked colleague, she had often struggled to make herself heard in large teams. This problem was particularly exacerbated as she found herself in a new company within a new field and in a new country trying to manage a project team.

The process of bringing Orton on board had not been actively managed by an HR professional. On the contrary, Haldemann had heard that there was a project manager looking for a job due to her husband's expatriate assignment in the company and, because he saw the planning project come up at the same time, had decided to hire her without ever having met her in person. Afterward, Orton often mentioned that the job description had not been clear to her at the time of her recruitment. She had known she was going to be a project manager within L-Bank's IT department, but she had had no idea what that role really encompassed.

THE EARLY MONTHS (DECEMBER–APRIL)

Orton started her new assignment in early December and her first weeks in the company were spent researching what her task would actually be. With very little guidance—most people, including Haldemann, used these weeks in December to reduce their vacation days that had been building up during the year—Orton tried to outline the different parts of the planning project and the requirements and needs for such an initiative. She was asked to meet many people within the organization in order to find out more, but with nobody to steer her through an organization so complex it would take many months to understand, she felt lost. From the few conversations she did have, she came up with the following, not very motivating conclusions:

1. Implementing a time-recording project had been tried many times before within different parts and regions of the L-Bank IT organization. Every implementation so far had failed within a few months.

2. Even the IT senior management team, of which Haldemann was a member, had not found consensus around the time-recording issue and while most members agreed that such a system would indeed be needed at some point, there was general disagreement around the timing and the process of such an undertaking.

3. Some managers Orton spoke with even mentioned that the transparency that the system would bring was not necessarily a good thing for them. They wondered to what extent they would have to explain the overtime that their teams were working to their supervisors and HR and what the consequences would be for their projects.

4. The good news was that the CIO was supporting the project fully, even promising that she herself and all of her direct reports would fill out their timesheets on a weekly basis.

5. Collaboration from all IT functions and all 16 countries involved would be absolutely crucial. Orton also realized that in order to get everyone to collaborate, she would need very strong support from management and complete internal buy-in, both of which she was very far from obtaining.

With this introduction to her new role, the lack of a hand-over and particularly the lack of a job description (the case for the project was written by Orton herself after she had been hired), Orton found herself starting 2006 feeling rather demotivated. It seemed that with every step she took, she encountered another obstacle and her rather vague objectives and goals for 2006 already looked out of reach. Her biggest handicap, as it turned out, was her lack of a network. Within L-Bank IT, almost everything ran through informal connections. People were often hired and promoted because of their relationships, and decisions were taken over coffee breaks. Orton, a complete newcomer, was thus largely unable to keep up with the requirements of her role. As an introvert, she did not meet people easily and, even worse, she did not speak the local language. She also had not connected well with Haldemann during her first weeks and therefore felt uncomfortable asking him for support or even telling him of her difficulties. A strong believer in hands-off supervision, Haldemann did not interfere. He believed that as long as he did not hear anything to the contrary, Orton must feel comfortable in her assignment.

The first four months of the year were spent convincing the management team of the need for the project. It became clear very early on that the only way the project could be pushed through would be by involving a representative from every function on a cross-functional project team. Members of this team had to be appointed, but, given the lack of consensus within the management team, it was April before the last of the five functions finally appointed its project team representative. By this time, the objectives of the planning project had been changed several times, every time throwing off Orton's planning and forcing her to start from zero. The representatives from the different functions arrived at the kick-off meeting in early April having been briefed by the heads of their respective functions. It became clear during this meeting that opinions among the management team still varied since the project team members had as many different opinions regarding the overall objective of the project as there were seats at the table. In addition to the differences in opinion, there had been no alignment of the profile of the representatives, resulting in five team members varying widely in level of seniority and project management skill. Most importantly, however, interest in the project varied widely. Some functions seemed to have a vested interest in the success of the planning project, while others saw it as another chore added to their busy work life and therefore did not even bother to show up.

The first meeting was difficult for everyone involved. Because of disagreements within the team, Orton did not get through slide 5 of the 40-page presentation that she had carefully prepared. Another key difficulty crystallized in this first meeting: Orton had no track record and therefore no credibility within the organization, and the representatives assigned to work for her on the project made it clear from the beginning that they felt they knew better than she how to manage it. Orton, on the other hand, had been through too many ups and downs already to confront her team with the confidence and authority required to come to a common conclusion on that day. The meeting ended with Orton in tears due to her exhaustion and frustration, further undermining her position.

Within the wider IT organization, Orton had hardly been noticed during these four months. Her reserved and quiet manner had let her become close only with her immediate peers. To many she was only known as "that quiet woman who works so much." In fact, because of the difficulties she was experiencing with her project, Orton had become an obsessive worker. She often started her day before the building's lights were turned on at 6 in the morning and she was never home before 11 at night. Still, it was unclear to most of her colleagues what she spent her many working hours doing. The project was on hold most of the time and it seemed that her only occupation was planning and re-planning every detail of a project whose future was very much uncertain.

As her closest peer, Berger had many conversations with Orton. They met on an almost daily basis because they were running projects that were closely interlinked. However, Berger did not know how to help Orton other than providing advice and referring her to people within the organization who might be able to help. Over several months, however, Orton became increasingly wary of others who provided advice but proved unable to help. She wanted to do the project her own way and the constant feedback made it impossible for her to find herself in her role. She felt that whatever she did, it was inadequate and for every mistake, there were a dozen people pointing at her failure and providing further corrective feedback.

This allergy to others increasingly started to include Haldemann, who, Orton felt, did not support her when she needed him. Haldemann, on the other hand, did not know how to help Orton. He was used to his reports clearly communicating their issues and possible solutions. With Orton, however, if they talked at all, he received a very general "everything is terrible." By this point, Orton was so much on edge that even the smallest issue would provoke disproportionate reactions that made it even more difficult for Haldemann to assess the seriousness of the situation.

After the kick-off meeting in April, bi-weekly project team meetings were installed for the planning project and Orton would get increasingly anxious before every one of these meetings. The meetings were usually messy with the representatives waiting for some direction from Orton which she could not give because of her general state, but also the continuous lack of management support. At this time, at least the go-live date of end of June was confirmed and agreed on, although the definition of what "go-live" encompassed was still unclear. These meetings were often abruptly ended because Orton broke out in tears.

Nobody outside the project team was aware that the situation had become so emotionally straining for Orton. Only in early May did she start to show her real emotional state in front of both Berger and Haldemann. Both experienced meetings with her shouting or sobbing, but were overwhelmed by the situation and did not know how to respond. Haldemann was increasingly uncomfortable with the strong emotions displayed. He had never experienced anything like this before, and was therefore unsure how to react. Berger had repeatedly reported her concerns regarding Orton to both Haldemann and

the HR department, but her escalations had had little effect, not because of a lack of interest or concern, but because of an inability to find the right solution. Upon Berger's suggestion, Orton even met with an independent counselor, but even she did not understand the seriousness of the situation and failed to schedule regular appointments with Orton.

Finally, in a last-ditch effort Haldemann organized a meeting between Berger, Orton and himself at which Orton's workload and the state of the project were assessed, and the most pressing (and most daunting) items were divided among the three of them. This effort did seem to calm the situation somewhat but Orton continued to work late. In one meeting shortly afterward, Haldemann, who was slowly realizing the seriousness of Orton's emotional condition, warned Berger, "You will have to take over, if I have to pull the plug on this."

Toward the end of May, Orton went on a much-deserved vacation. Everyone around her hoped that a few days off would help her regain some energy and refocus her efforts toward the go-live in a few weeks. Things were to turn out very differently, however. After her vacation, Orton started her first workday very early as usual. By 7:00 when Haldemann arrived and asked her how her vacation had been, her short reply was "terrible." Upon further questioning, Orton broke into tears and told Haldemann that she could no longer do this and that she would quit. She then stormed out of the office in tears and did not return that day. It was only the next morning that Haldemann found her office completely empty, with her badge lying on her desk. The message was clear. Orton had had enough and was not coming back. It was four weeks to the go-live of the planning project.

That was when Haldemann picked up the phone to call Berger.

JH: Good morning! How was your vacation?

KB: It was very good, thank you.

JH: You will not believe what happened. Please sit down for this.

KB: I'm sitting—what's going on?

JH: Tina just quit, I think.

KB: What? You've got to be kidding—I really did think that things were going better after our meeting.

JH: So did I, but they apparently weren't. You know what's next— can you meet me later today?

KB: Yes, I know—I can be in your office in a few hours.

JH: OK. See you later.

Berger was shocked. She really did think that splitting up the responsibilities had made a difference for Orton. She was upset because she felt that she had let down a very close colleague. She was also worried because due to her many conversations with Orton she knew what she was getting herself into by taking over this project. She looked at her calendar and saw that the next project team meeting was set for the next day. "How will I ever get ready for this in 24 hours?" she thought to herself as she opened her laptop.

Simulation
Broadway Brokers

BACKGROUND

You work as a division manager for Broadway Brokers (BB), a 10,000-person firm that used to dominate its field: brokerage services for small investors. Although this has always been a competitive market, Broadway has long held the largest market share of any firm—as of 1998, this represented 22 percent of the market by customers and 30 percent by revenues. Headquartered in New York, the firm has offices in every major city in the world, with a particularly strong presence in Europe.

By 2000, however, the increase in discount brokers and Internet brokerage services caused income to fall precipitously. To meet these challenges, BB not only had to cut costs but more importantly had to re-skill to address the new products customers were demanding. Its brokers, who all had excellent interpersonal and selling skills, had to learn more high-tech skills (including helping clients to use financial software, as well as using it themselves) in order to survive. It has become increasingly clear that although these changes were taking place, BB was moving more slowly than some of its competitors, and that heavy overheads (staff numbers and offices) were threatening its profitability. You have become increasingly concerned about the pace and extent of change, and what was needed to manage the changes effectively.

Source: This simulation is based on the earlier "Apex Manufacturing," taken from William Bridges, *Managing Transitions: Making the Most of Change* (Reading, Mass.: Addison-Wesley, 1991), pp. 105–110 and reprinted in the first edition of this volume. (Updated 2009.)

You realized that the management team had to make its plans and take action.

ON THE FIRING LINE

There have been rumors of impending office consolidations and staff layoffs for some time, but only a week ago the CEO was quoted in a *Financial Times* article as saying that Broadway would be able to do its trimming by attrition alone and that he expected sales to increase significantly by the end of the year. "Our business rests on a firm base of trust and service," he said. "Customers realize this and are coming back in droves, particularly given our newly combined strengths in both the traditional and Internet businesses."

Yesterday morning you received an email from the senior vice president (SVP) of HR asking you to come to a noontime meeting in her office. When you got there, you saw a dozen of the company's most respected managers—everyone from assistant vice presidents to managing directors. The SVP told you briefly that several decisions had been made by the top management team.

First, sixteen of the company's 40 offices will be severely curtailed (shrunk by at least 75 percent) or closed, affecting approximately 3,000 staff. The situation will be complicated by several factors. Customers for the most part are linked to brokers in their local offices; these relationships will need to be preserved by moving the accounts (and many of the brokers) to other locations. The high rents and labor costs (in comparison to revenues) dictated the selection of the offices to be closed; still, it is by no means certain that customers will be willing to be moved (although for the growing proportion using the company's Internet service, this should be less of a concern).

Second, there is to be a 20 percent reduction in the level of employment at the company—2,000 jobs. All departments and offices are to make cuts, though specific targets for different groups have not yet been set. Neither have the provisions of a possible early retirement plan. It has not even been decided how many of the terminated employees will be from among the downsized or closed offices (although many will unlikely be willing to move elsewhere). Many are long-term employees whom the SVP of operations wants to keep. The employment situation is complicated by legal restrictions in a number of countries (particularly in continental Europe) where mandated payoffs for dismissals are very high.

"There are still a lot of questions," the SVP of HR said. "But you are being called together as a transition management advisory group. The top management team made the decision as to what will be necessary—downsizing and consolidation. We're asking you to help us work out *how* we should do it. Specifically, you are being asked to come up with a scenario for announcing and implementing the office cutbacks and closures and for working out a plan for handling the reductions in the workforce."

"We're going to meet together all day tomorrow," she continued, "and I want you to clear your agendas. We have to get a tentative plan back to the top management team within three days. It doesn't have to be detailed, but it does have to sketch out the issues we need to be ready to deal with and give us some ideas for dealing with them. We want it to advise us on communications, training, and any new policies or arrangements we need to have in place to get people through the transition." Then she handed out a sheet on which she had listed some of her own concerns:

Transition Management Concerns

1. Broadway has not had a layoff in the past 15 years. During most of that time it was growing.

2. The 3,000 employees from the 16 offices to be cut back or closed include some highly talented people that the organization would hate to lose.

3. There is a strong sentiment among the top management team for an across-the-board cut in employment levels ("It would be fairer"), but the HR SVP and some others share a concern that some parts of the company (including some field offices) are already dangerously lean while others are "fatter."

4. There is a perception among rank-and-file employees, particularly back office staff, that the senior managers, whose pay has always been generous, are not bearing enough of the brunt of the difficulties of the company they led to this difficult point.

5. The basic announcement of the decisions is scheduled to go out tomorrow in a memo to all employees. A copy is attached.

"We're in a tight spot," the SVP concluded. "Frankly, I'm not sure all the senior managers realize how tight it is. I'm looking to all of you to help me make the case for handling the changes as effectively as possible. And I'm looking to you to help me show that there is a way to do it, in fact, that doesn't just drop everything on the people like a bomb and then leave them to take care of their own wounded."

"I'd suggest that you go back to your offices and arrange to free up the next couple of days. Then I'd like you to look over the following list of suggestions that were made by different members of the senior management team and rate them each on a scale of 1 to 5 in terms of your degree of support."

_____ 1. Very important. Do this at once.

_____ 2. Worth doing, but may take more time. Start planning it.

_____ 3. Yes and no. Depends how it's done and what else is going on.

_____ 4. Not very important. May even be a waste of effort.

_____ 5. No! Don't do this.

"We'll compare everyone's reactions in the morning and come up with some first steps."

You have now gone back to your office, asked your assistant to postpone and cancel your meetings, and you are ready to start to work on the list of suggestions: (Write your rating, 1–5, to the left of each item on the list.)

_____ 1. Don't distribute any communications until firm plans have been made for the details of the layoffs and office closures.

_____ 2. Rewrite the memo to convey more sensitivity to the impact on the firm's employees.

_____ 3. Set up a "restructuring task force" to recommend the best way to consolidate operations and how to determine the disposition of the 3,000 employees in the affected offices.

_____ 4. Set up a "downsizing suggestion plan" through which everyone can have input into

TO: All Broadway Employees
FROM: J. T. Carpenter, President and CEO
RE: Measures Needed to Restore Profitability

In order to recover ground recently lost to competitors, who have been able to undercut our full-service products with cheap Internet-based offerings backed by rivers of free-flowing private equity, the executive team has decided to consolidate our field operations into 32 offices, down from the current 40. An additional eight offices will be substantially scaled back, losing all back office functions and much of their current office space. These consolidations will take place over the next four months.

During the same period, employment levels in the company, which have recently risen past the 10,000 mark, will be readjusted to a level around 8,000. At that level we will be able to maintain profitability if we can contain other costs. In the latter regard, all employees are asked to refrain from traveling or ordering equipment unless it has been personally approved by a member of the senior management team.

Broadway has a noble tradition, but in recent years too many of our employees have forgotten that we must make a profit for our stockholders. If, however, we can tighten our belts and do more with less, we'll not only climb back into the black, but we'll also recover the market share that slipped through our fingers when we let ourselves get too comfortable.

I will be back in touch with you when the details of the office closures and layoffs have been determined. In the meantime, I am sure that I can count on your continued hard work and loyalty.

J. T. Carpenter
President and CEO

how the downsizing will be carried out.

_____ 5. Publicize the problems that forced the changes.

_____ 6. Fire the CEO.

_____ 7. Bring in all office managers and directors for an extensive briefing. Hold a frank question-and-answer session. Don't let them leave until they are all sat-isfied that the cutbacks are the best way to handle the situation.

_____ 8. Make a video explaining the problems and the response to them. Hold meetings of all employees at each office, where the office manager takes and answers all questions.

_____ 9. Set up a dedicated internal website to give employees current, reliable information on the re-structuring.

_____ 10. Get the senior management team to agree to a one-year, 20 percent cut in their own salaries (and not to take any bonuses).

_____ 11. Order an across-the-board 20 percent budget cut throughout the company.

_____ 12. Institute a program of rewards for cost-saving suggestions from employees.

_____ 13. Plan closure ceremonies/events for the eight offices.

_____ 14. Use the time to redesign the whole business: strategy, employment, policies, and structure.

_____ 15. Get the CEO to make a public statement acknowledging the tardiness of the company's response to the realities of the marketplace.

_____ 16. Make it clear up front that the company is headed into a protracted period of change.

_____ 17. Explain the purpose, the plan, and the roles people will be playing in the announced changes.

_____ 18. Circulate an upbeat news release saying that this plan has been in the works for two years, that it isn't a sign of weakness, that its payoff will occur within six months, and so on. In all communications, accentuate the positive.

_____ 19. Allay fears by assuring employees that the changes in

the 16 offices are the only big changes that will take place.

_____ 20. Develop or find career-planning seminars to help people whose jobs are being threatened or lost because of the changes.

_____ 21. Immediately set new, higher revenue targets for the next quarter so people have something clear to shoot for and so that by aiming high, they will ensure adequate income even if they fail to reach goals.

_____ 22. Make a video in which the CEO gives a fiery "we gotta get lean and mean" speech.

_____ 23. Analyze who stands to lose what in the changes.

_____ 24. Redesign the compensation system to reward compliance with the changes.

_____ 25. Help the CEO put together a statement about organizational transition and what it does to an organization. It should be empathetic and concerned about people.

_____ 26. Set up transition monitoring teams in the 16 offices, as well as in other offices that are significantly affected by the changes.

_____ 27. Appoint a "change manager" to be responsible for seeing that the changes go smoothly.

_____ 28. Give everyone at Broadway a "We're Number One" badge.

_____ 29. Put all managers through a service quality improvement seminar.

_____ 30. Put more emphasis on U.S.-based changes than on Europe, as layoffs are less costly in the U.S.

_____ 31. Reorganize the top management team and redefine the CEO's job as that of team coordinator.

_____ 32. Give all managers a two-hour seminar on the emotional impacts of change.

_____ 33. Plan some office-wide social events in each company location—picnics, outings, dinners.

_____ 34. Launch a plan to buy one of Broadway's Internet competitors to gain market share and a strong technology group.

_____ 35. Begin to collect diversity profile information on gender, race, and nationality to help ensure that there is no disproportionate impact.

Reading

Managing to Communicate, Communicating to Manage

How Leading Companies Communicate with Employees

Mary Young and James E. Post

A study of how companies manage change uncovers eight benchmarks for effective communication.

Faced with recession, increased global competition, and restructurings, businesses are making major organizational changes to shore up productivity in every aspect of their enterprises. These practices may be beneficial for the companies, but they also can be wrenching for the companies' people. For instance, reorganizations, "rightsizings," and layoffs, common to these times, virtually ensure drops in morale and productivity. That's because they threaten jobs, business relationships, and the employees' sense of security.

How do the best companies reconcile a compelling need for organizational change with an equally compelling need, on the part of employees, for security? Our quest to answer this question led to an in-depth study of 10 leading companies. These firms, the study showed, go further than raising their employees' sense of security. They also preserve or improve productivity. And they do it with a familiar concept: communication.

These companies illustrate that organizations can convert employees' concerns into support for the major changes if they

Source: Reprinted from *Organizational Dynamics*, vol. 22, pp. 31–43, Copyright 1993, with permission of Elsevier.

effectively address employees' fears about restructuring and reorganization. On the other hand, if communication is inadequate, employees will be more resistant to change.

The overall lesson is clear: Effective managers strategically use communication to manage tough organizational changes. Before we present the results of our study, consider one striking example of this principle in action.

FEDERAL EXPRESS AND FLYING TIGER: A CASE STUDY

In December 1988, Federal Express acquired Flying Tiger Line, Inc., its rival in the international air freight business. FedEx senior managers realized that the organizations' "strategic fit" would mean little if the people in the organizations could not be convinced that the merger made sense. The FedEx credo of "People-Service-Profit" was about to be put to a highly visible test.

As Jim Perkins, senior vice president for personnel at FedEx, said, "We wanted a merger our people would be proud of, to reflect who we are as a company, our people philosophy. We wanted a merger that would bring the merged company on to the FedEx team." Employees throughout the organizations were concerned, however. Careers, loyalty, and years of trust were at stake.

FedEx management didn't waste much time addressing these concerns. In fact, some believe their communication measures were extraordinary. Less than two hours after the Dow Jones wire service announced the merger, FedEx Chairman Fred Smith and Chief Operating Officer Jim Barksdale gave an un-scripted, un-rehearsed address over the company's satellite television network—FXTV—to 35,000 employees in 800 locations. From the start, Smith and Barksdale described the move as a "merger," not an "acquisition." The phrasing had symbolic importance to people in both organizations. The choice of terminology "didn't require a lot of debate or discussion," said Carol Presley, senior vice president for marketing and corporate communications. "We wanted Flying Tiger people to feel we really did want them."

Still, FedEx employees had serious concerns. Most Flying Tiger employees, for instance, were unionized. Moreover, some had been employed by their company longer than FedEx had been in existence. To FedEx employees, therefore, joining forces with these outsiders could threaten their seniority.

Altogether, the lives—and concerns—of 70,000 people were involved. And the FedEx management team would spend what some might view as an extravagant amount of time and money to *communicate*—talk and listen—with employees. For months following the merger announcement, questions and answers traveled back and forth, up and down the organization. The means of communication included face-to-face meetings, company publications, videos, and television programs, including the daily company news broadcast, "FX Overnight."

FedEx managers considered the effort well worth the expense. In fact, assuaging the concerns proved vital to the achievement of all of the objectives that inspired the merger. Barksdale described the payoff: "Placing such an emphasis on internal communication has made us the company we are. We couldn't be anywhere near the size we are, and have the profitability or the relationship with our employees we have, if we weren't deeply into the business of communicating with people."

THE IMPORTANCE OF COMMUNICATION: AN EMERGING CONSENSUS

FedEx's efforts may seem extreme, but their approach was not unique among well-managed companies. A study by the Conference Board refers to employee communication as a "new top management priority." Faye Rice, writing in *Fortune,* concludes that "internal communication— talk back and forth within the organization, up and down the hierarchy—may well be more important to a company's success than external communications."

A Columbia University study found that 59 percent of chief executive officers (CEOs) consider frequent communication with employees important to their jobs. And 89 percent expect communication to be more important to the CEO's job in the years ahead.

The experiences of companies like FedEx, and the emerging consensus among senior executives on the importance of effective communication, underscore the need to identify and understand the strategic role of employee communication during major organizational change.

This article discusses the results of a two-year study of firms that dealt with communication needs during restructurings and reorganizations.

ABOUT THIS STUDY

Based on our reading of published accounts of many restructurings, we believed, at the start of this project, that communication processes were an important ingredient of successful change. To investigate this hypothesis, we first identified several U.S. corporations that underwent major restructuring in recent years. Then we surveyed several dozen senior human resources and employee communications managers to get the names of companies with excellent internal communications programs. The responses enabled us to identify companies with the "best practices" in diverse industries. From this list we selected 10 firms that met the dual criteria of recent organizational change and exemplary communication practices. Subsequently, we investigated the 10 companies by holding interviews, site visits, and discussions with a range of senior executives involved in the restructuring efforts.

Our purpose for the first phase of the project was to identify and compare communications practices at these organizations. To supplement the comparative analysis, we conducted a second phase: more detailed inspections of two companies undergoing major organizational restructuring. One company was involved in a reorganization and a geographic move—changes that affected 100,000 people. The other company was involved in an acquisition and in an integration of two companies.

The criteria used to identify successful management included the degree to which the changes were smooth, in the eyes of management; the amount of staff turnover; and the general tone or morale of managerial and non-managerial staff members (as reflected in employee surveys). In each of the 10 organizations, managers were able to identify quantifiable business measures (sales, profitability, revenue per employee, or other financial measures) used to track organizational performance. The comparison revealed several patterns in the way the "best practices" firms managed organizational changes.

The second-phase studies focused on two of the large "best practices" companies. The studies confirmed that certain communications practices significantly improve the ability of any senior management to make large-scale organizational changes.

EIGHT PRINCIPLES OF EFFECTIVE CORPORATE COMMUNICATIONS

During organizational changes, certain factors play roles in the effectiveness of employee communication (see Exhibit 1). Each factor alone carries weight, and also interacts with the changes in important ways.

Most important for managers: Each factor applies to a variety of industries and organizational settings. This suggests that the lessons learned from the 10 firms can be applied to many types of organizations.

1. THE CHIEF EXECUTIVE AS COMMUNICATIONS CHAMPION

The most significant factor is the CEO's leadership, including philosophical and behavioral commitments.

The CEO must be philosophically committed to the notion that communicating with employees is essential to the achievement of corporate goals. It follows that a CEO with a strong commitment, such as Smith at Federal Express, sets a different tone for the rest of the company than one who considers communication "nice, but not necessary." Executives at one firm we investigated, for instance, told us they consider employee communication "the most important managerial activity in this company." They regard it as a crucial tool for *managing* routine activities—from new product introductions to changes in the benefits policy—and for responding to extraordinary matters, such as an effort to unionize or an investigative report conducted by "60 Minutes" or "20/20."

Referring to his company's major reorganization, a senior executive commented, "We could not have done it without a very strong communication effort." At this firm, he told us, "Strategic issues are understood as communications issues." When asked about the return on the investment, the same executive said it this way:

Enormous! We can move faster, jump higher, dive deeper, and come up drier than anybody in the business. When we hang a left, everybody goes left. It gives

EXHIBIT 1   Eight Factors That Determine the Effectiveness of Employee Communications

1. The chief executive as communications champion.
2. The match between words and actions.
3. Commitment to two-way communication.
4. Emphasis on face-to-face communication.
5. Shared responsibility for employee communications.
6. The bad news/good news ratio.
7. Knowing customers, clients, and audiences.
8. The employee communication strategy.

us an enormous ability to work as a team. Other companies in our industry have yet to find that out.

Top management's attitude influences the behavior of other managers in an organization. For instance, a CEO regularly told other managers that combat experience convinced him that good communication is crucial to survival and success. Middle managers throughout his company repeated that story, describing the CEO as a "champion" for communications-oriented problem solving. That view is reinforced in the company's training manual which emphasizes the manager's role as communicator—and which was written by the CEO. In this company, more than any other we studied, the message of employee communications as a strategic weapon had been sent, received, and understood.

In addition to espousing a philosophical commitment to employee communications, the CEO must be a skilled and visible communications role model. (The CEO must walk the talk if the organization is supposed to walk the talk.) We were struck by the extent to which a number of CEOs turn their commitment into action. One, for example, spends an average of four to six hours per week talking to groups of employees—fielding their questions and actively exchanging ideas. Interestingly, this CEO is not a natural media personality. In fact, many people say he's still a bit wooden in front of television cameras, although he has improved over the years. What he does do well, however, is *communicate* often (frequently in person), display a willingness to address challenging questions, listen carefully, and respond quickly to sensitive topics. These actions appear to be much more important to his audience than flawless skills or a slick performance. As another top executive said, "People say he's a stiff son-of-a-bitch, but at least he's trying."

Besides having a philosophical commitment and serving as a role model, top management must have another attribute vital to effective communications: They must be willing to deliver key messages themselves. This task cannot be delegated, as one professional staff member explained:

> If they have a vision and they can't share it, can't make people see it, then they're not going to be effective in their job. . . . Yes, others can help, but if [leaders] can't articulate it directly themselves, nobody else can do it for them.

Or, as a veteran communications professional at another company said: "People need the icon—somebody who personifies the strategy, the change you're trying to make."

Virtually all the employee communications managers emphasized the CEO's role in the successes and limitations of their programs. Even the most senior staff people can't run the communications program by themselves. Thus the program must be championed by the top executive through words and frequent, visible action.

What happens when the CEO doesn't play a large enough role? We observed several such cases, and the result is that the communications plans have limited impact. Executives who don't understand their role or don't take action are the biggest frustration of senior communications managers. As with other areas of staff support, even a first-rate staff cannot compensate for a chief executive who is unwilling to provide visible leadership for the employee communications effort.

The chemistry between the CEO and the senior communications officer will determine the role the senior communications executive plays. At best, the officer serves as confidant, trusted adviser, "chief ear-to-the-ground," and traveling companion for the CEO. At worst, the officer's effectiveness is thwarted by indifference or disregard from the CEO. When employee communications managers recounted triumphs and failures, good years and bad, they often were referring to departures and arrivals in executive offices.

2. MATCHING ACTIONS AND WORDS

Another critical factor for effective employee communication, and one closely related to CEO support and involvement, is managerial action. Our study confirms that actions definitely speak louder than words. Too often, people told us, the implicit messages that managers send contradict the official messages as conveyed in formal communications. Consider the possible fallout if FedEx had referred to the Flying Tiger deal as a "takeover" or "acquisition" rather than as a "merger." The formal message—one of welcome, partnership, and common enterprise—could have been twisted into an "us and them" message. As one senior staff officer characterized it: "Formal communications, of and by themselves, are not how employees know their company. They know it through their supervisors and through their management."

One senior vice president described the close relationship between words and action as the critical success factor in his company's effort to restructure:

How to manage a [restructuring]? First establish a philosophy at the outset so when you run into various situations you'll at least have some frame of

reference; you'll know where you are. . . . And once you establish a philosophy, it is necessary to be consistent and not waiver, and to really just hold the line.

Without a match of values in formal channels with values in practice, employee communications may be a waste of time.

"Whether or not our bulletins and newspapers are credible anymore," noted an employee communications director who was in the middle of a massive reorganization, "is much more the result of management actions than of anything we [employee communications staff] have done."

3. COMMITMENT TO TWO-WAY COMMUNICATION

Dialogue and two-way communication have gained popularity as important elements in implementing total quality and employee involvement programs. Nevertheless, the degree to which the companies we studied were committed to this idea varied. The firm that displayed the highest commitment to two-way communication did so enthusiastically. Using interactive television broadcasts, managers at this company stage call-in meetings so employees at all locations can ask questions. Managers are trained in feedback techniques, and company publications further solicit employee comments through Q&A columns and reader-comment cards. Other techniques include reward and recognition programs for upward communications, as well as clear, swift grievance procedures.

In other firms, we found less enthusiasm behind the stated commitments. In some cases, top managers could enumerate the types of upward communication available, but lower level employees could not. In other cases, the commitment varied among managers within the same company. For example, one company used an extensive employee opinion survey to stimulate upward communication and then left employee feedback to the discretion of each manager.

An employee communications staffer remarked that if a company is serious about two-way communication, it should allocate as many resources (money, communications vehicles, and staff expertise) toward helping employees with upward communication as it does to foster downward communication. Although this comment may have been partly facetious, the point is well made.

Managers of the 10 companies agreed that they need to improve in the area of two-way communications. Even top and mid-level managers at the company with the most extensive two-way communication said they "didn't listen enough" during a recent restructuring.

Opinion or attitude surveys are one common device for listening to employees. By itself, a survey seems inadequate as a two-way communication device. But in concert with other means, it can provide valuable information. When a company has too few, or infrequently used, feedback mechanisms, it risks being blindsided by unanticipated survey results. The company may also find it has insufficient data—to interpret the results or choose among alternative "readings" of the data. It can be tempting to dismiss damning data as a blip on the screen, if the evidence is not corroborated elsewhere. And employee surveys may also serve as lightning rods for ambient ill will—even about issues the survey doesn't cover. This is most likely to happen when the employees have no other vehicles for upward communication. In such cases, survey results may be difficult to read and potentially misleading.

4. EMPHASIS ON FACE-TO-FACE COMMUNICATION

Face-to-face communication between top management and employees is a particularly useful form of two-way communication. Managers strongly endorsed it, especially for handling sensitive issues or managing large-scale changes, such as a restructuring of the organization. Many companies arrange gatherings at which employees—an entire group or a representative sample—can ask the CEO questions. The CEO may travel regularly to dispersed sites for this purpose. As a secondary benefit, the company may broadcast a Q&A meeting at one site to employees at other sites. In other companies, senior executives meet with management trainee classes at the corporate training center.

An effective ongoing practice, the face-to-face meeting plays a crucial role during times of uncertainty and change. Based on feedback from employees, one firm learned that face-to-face encounters had made a critical difference in how it managed a major acquisition. The company had sent senior management to every major installation of the acquired firm. In all, 75 percent of the acquired firm's employees had an opportunity to meet the CEO and other top officials. "We stood there for hours, until every question was answered," one participant recalled. What that gave employees, recalled another, "was the chance to take a measure of you, look you in the eye, ask some questions and see how you responded." The benefit of such give-and-take meetings, said an executive, is that they "expose you to a large group of people [many of whom] feel . . . 'I didn't ask him a question but he was there if I wanted to'. . . . You get to be seen as a person who understands what's happening, who is cognizant of feelings, who doesn't have all the answers but is willing to listen and learn, and who has a vision so that others will say, 'I'll work for that guy for a few months and see how it goes.'"

Talking face-to-face is one thing; exchanging straight talk is another, however. In the case of the acquisition, the straight talk didn't end after the first meeting with employees of the acquired firm. Afterward, the company trained 150 of its nonmanagement employees to handle nitty-gritty concerns that remained among nonmanagement employees at the acquired firm. Three- and four-person "ambassador teams" traveled to 16 cities. Although the atmosphere of the meetings was described as frosty at the outset, it usually improved as the ambassadors answered a host of questions about such issues as seniority, pay, and working conditions.

Two caveats emerge from the experiences of the 10 firms. (1) Such approaches as sending teams of managers to distant sites can be an expensive and time-consuming activity. Nevertheless, the companies we studied believed the results justified the expense. As one executive noted: "Some things you do because you believe they're right, and doing them right gives you a [long-term] financial return." (2) Face-to-face communications do not obviate the need for other communications efforts. The company that dispatched the ambassador teams also had an extensive set of communications channels, including television, videos, electronic mail, and publications. Yet other media could not substitute for in-person communication, particularly when the communication dealt with the human side of restructuring. In retrospect, people from both the acquired and acquiring organizations believed this was a critical strategy for the successful merger.

During times of crisis or major organizational changes, the best response involves multiple communications devices—pulling out all the stops—to ensure that employees understand the action. The vice president of human resources in one large company put it this way:

> *Communicate* in a timely manner, as promptly as possible. Be up front and perfectly candid, even when the news is not what people might expect. *Communicate* in as many forms as possible—writing, pictures, and other news organs, and especially people-to-people, where you provide an opportunity for people to interact and exchange ideas.

A decade ago, author/futurist John Naisbitt described the possible complementary relationship between "high-tech" and "high-touch." His point was that the more technology invades our lives, the more we seek to balance it with some humanizing counter-force. Our research findings are consistent with the essence of that "megatrend." The best practices emphasize technology, as well as "touch." The most effective employee communication programs couple a liberal and imaginative use of high technology (television and e-mail, for instance) with a high-touch strategy that involves face-to-face and personalized communications. Together these "high-tech/high-touch" approaches can reach employees on even the most sensitive matters; too little "high-touch" weakens the employee communication effort and, ultimately, the organization's capacity for change.

5. SHARED RESPONSIBILITY FOR EMPLOYEE COMMUNICATIONS

Clearly, responsibility for effective employee communications is shared, rather than centralized, in companies that have adjusted to major change. Managers and employees repeatedly stressed that every manager serves as a communication manager. "People want to hear news from their boss, not from their peers or from the grapevine," said one communications manager. This view was confirmed by employee surveys taken by several companies. When asked to rank their preferred source of company news, employees invariably cited "my supervisor" as their top choice. Yet, the more frequent sources of company news are, for many employees, "the grapevine" or "the media."

Another common communications "disconnect" occurs when messages from chief executives and communications staff get derailed by lower-level managers—through neglect, antipathy, or lukewarm support for the message. Said one employee communications veteran, "[There is] little one can achieve from a central group when you don't have some sort of agreement or buy-in at the local level."

In the end, companies need to have a clear plan that holds appropriate levels of management accountable for specific portions of the communications mission. An employee communications executive stated:

> Corporate communications should address the broad issues and the local manager should address the local issues. I don't expect the individual manager to be an expert on every subject. The 401(k) benefit programs, the company's international strategy—they shouldn't have to communicate corporate-level things and [they] aren't the best source. Your responsibility as a manager is to make sure your people get the latest information from corporate . . . and also stand up at the employee meeting and explain why they've been assigned Route 232, why Mary got promoted and they didn't.

Another company's senior employee communications director—who sees the supervisor's role as particularly important to managing change—said that top management must be responsible for conveying the "big picture," but only the supervisor can link the big picture to the work group and to the individual employee.

Some communications policies spell out the responsibilities of everyone in the organization. In one firm, managers are responsible for top-down and bottom-up communication, while non-management employees have their own responsibilities, including directives to review corporate communications and to inform supervisors of problems.

Policies also need to be bolstered with communications training, coaching, goal setting, evaluation, and reward, if they are to take root in the organization's day-to-day life. The best practice generally involves a programmatic approach that addresses needs and also improves listening, feedback (giving and receiving), and problem-solving skills and techniques. The best practice includes regular assessments by management of the effectiveness of the company's communication policies. Recall the CEO who considers communication the "single most important" management activity. In that company's employee survey, 6 out of 10 questions about employees' direct managers relate to communication. Supervisors also get evaluated at the mandatory face-to-face employee feedback sessions that follow the surveys.

Also at this company, each supervisor must identify and address communication problems as part of his or her annual performance plan. Even with this emphasis, however, the feeling is widespread that the organization is falling short. Said a communications manager: "We should be doing more to help others communicate, rather than communicating for them."

In many of the firms, including the leading firm just mentioned, people believed that managers received inadequate training, or were not held sufficiently accountable. This is despite what many see as the growing importance of communication in an era of flatter, more flexible, and quality-centered organizations. The problem in some instances is structural: The employee communications function rarely oversees the managers' related training or performance evaluation. Several communications managers suggested that companies closely link the communications function with the training and development function, perhaps by having them accountable to the same senior executive.

6. DEALING WITH BAD NEWS

A more subtle factor that affects employee communications relates to the way bad news is received by top managers, and then shared with others in the organization. "Bad news" may include service or quality failures, delays, customer complaints, or criticism from outsiders. In short, it is the antithesis of "happy news"—the cheery reporting of United Way fundraising results, retirement parties, and bowling scores—that once served as the mainstay of employee communications.

Although we did not launch a formal study of "bad-news to good-news ratios" among our 10 companies, an informal content analysis suggests it varied widely. Interestingly, the company with the highest bad-news to good-news ratio appeared to be performing very well, in terms of employee satisfaction and economic performance. It was not communicating more bad news than other companies simply because it had more problems. In fact, this was the same company whose formal communication policy held employees responsible for telling management about problems. Thus, communicating "bad news" was culturally valued and institutionally supported. Much has been written on topics of quality management, continuous improvement, and organizational learning to suggest that the free flow of information, including bad news, provides important strategic advantages. Moreover, it seems likely that when bad news is candidly reported, an environment is created in which good news is more believable.

7. CUSTOMERS, CLIENTS, AND AUDIENCES

In each of the companies we studied, the communications staff had developed a clear sense of the people they served—a "customer focus," in the words of quality management. Yet there was considerable diversity in their identification of the customers. For example, a communications director held that "top management is our customer, but employees are our audience." In contrast, the employee communications function at another firm defined its customers more broadly. Here, customers included top management, middle management, and employees. The senior executive to whom communications reports explained:

> There are messages that top management must send, but also questions employees have [that are] separate from that. The proper role of [employee communications] is to provide [for] both of those things that are important to them.
>
> We recognize that mechanics, for example, have their own set of questions [on topics] like tool box

insurance. The CEO will never want to send out a message regarding tool box insurance. But focusing on your audience, you listen to those things that are important to them.

One way to identify the internal customers is to look at the person driving the employee communications—the message-senders ("we want you to know this") or the message receivers ("this is what we need to know"). In one company we studied, the organizational structure changed and the employee communications staff began reporting to a senior marketing executive. The orientation quickly shifted. "Before, a staff member would be responsible for these communications [products] newsletters, video," a manager noted. "Now, she's responsible for these three groups of people. [It was] traumatic for the people involved, but today they would [say] it was a great move. The feedback has been so different because now they're targeting needs to an audience."

Tom Peters' concept of "keeping close to the customer" was invoked in a surprisingly large number of these companies. What does the customer want to know? When do they prefer to receive information? In what form (at home, electronic mail, graphic display) do they want to receive it? We noticed that in these companies there was a clear trend toward insisting that employee communications staff monitor their customers and audiences, and understand the organizational issues, job demands, and other communications efforts that affect the customers. At times, answering audience needs involves cut-and-dried meetings about tool box insurance issues; at other times, it means candid discussions about company performance and restructuring moves. The former is easier, the latter much more sensitive and critical to managing organizational change.

But both are important to the audience. In the best companies, communications programs serve the audience's needs and, as a result, improve the organization's capacity for dealing with change.

8. THE EMPLOYEE COMMUNICATIONS STRATEGY

Each of the previously mentioned factors involves communications and managerial processes, not products. This was surprising at first, in part because communications products—slide shows, videos, and newsletters—are frequently the focus of discussion in the communications literature. Our conclusion is that, among leading companies, employee communications is viewed as a critical management process. That is a new focus.

When viewed this way, the strategy for effective employee communications becomes much clearer and easier to understand. Five consensus ideas stand out from the data collected in our sample of leading companies:

Communicate Not Only What Is Happening, but Why and How It Is Happening.

As change occurs more frequently in organizations, and their future is less certain, employees have a need to know the rationale underlying management decisions. This need is critical to an organization's capacity for implementing change programs and derives from what has been called the "changing psychological contract" between employers and employees.

As one employee communications manager stated:

> The work force has changed. They're not looking for (news about) births and deaths. They're looking for what the

company's business direction is, how it's performing financially—they have a stake in that—because of the changing psychological contract. [This company] used to be very stable. We don't have that anymore. . . . The workforce is looking for something from management to make up the difference between what they used to have guaranteed and what they have now. One of those things is information. They consider it a right. It's not just something they feel that's nice to do. They feel that management owes them that information.

The feeling that employees are "entitled to information" is most likely to occur among the younger segments of a company's workforce, even though it is also gaining strength among older workers.

Timeliness Is Vital.

Communicate what you know, when you know it. Do not wait until every detail is resolved. Recalling mistakes made during his company's reorganization, one manager told us:

> It was quite obvious that top management was holding on to information until all the i's had been dotted and t's crossed before they would tell anybody. By the time information came out about what actually was happening, everybody had already formed an opinion about what was going on, and how it impacted everyone. . . . Their attitude was, "We resent being treated like children. We're big people. We know things change. Tell us what the current situation is and if, down the road, you have to make an adjustment to that, just tell us why you had to make the adjustment. We can work with that."

The cost of not communicating in a timely manner is disaffection, anger, and loss of trust. In a world where organizations need increasingly high levels of mutual trust among all personnel, the failure to share what you know when you know it is a prescription for trouble.

Communicate Continuously.

Communication should be continuous, particularly during periods of change or crisis. Our respondents stressed the importance of continuously sharing news, even if the news is simply that "discussions are continuing." As one veteran commented: "You have to have a steady hum, 'white noise.' A steady hum of information at least gives employees (the idea) that something's happening. Dead silence is deafening. . . . You need to keep the hum going." Moreover, in an information-rich climate, employees are more forgiving of the occasional error.

Link the "Big Picture" with the "Little Picture."

There is a consensus that truly effective communication does not occur until the employees understand how the "big picture" affects them and their jobs. Changes in the economy, among competitors in the industry, or in the company as a whole must be translated into implications for each plant, job, and employee. Often the direct supervisor or first-line manager must clarify and convince employees. As one manager explained, "Employees want that linkage between the global picture . . . and what it means to me in my job. That's the only way you can get support. You tell people what it means to them and they can buy into it." Don't tell them, and the chance of not getting a buy-in grows.

Don't Dictate the Way People Should Feel about the News.

It is insulting to tell people how they should feel about change ("This is exciting!").

Veterans of the communication wars say such efforts usually fail and often provoke antagonistic responses. It is more effective to communicate "who, what, when, where, why, and how" and then let employees draw their own conclusions.

The managers involved in this study stressed the importance of consistently applying this approach, whether times are good or bad, or normal or crisis/change-ridden. These are not emergency measures. They are elements of an ongoing, effective communications strategy.

TWO SURPRISES

Surprisingly, neither the size of the employee communications budget nor the reporting relationship emerged as a major influence on the effectiveness of employee communications.

Finances improve or constrain the ability of a communications staff to produce videos, newsletters, and other products. They do not determine the ability of the staff to serve customers, clients, and audiences. While a CEO's support might mean greater financial resources for communications, almost all respondents agreed that the hidden budget—the amount of time a CEO devotes to employee communication and the amount of training new managers receive—has far more significance than the formal budget.

One way to allocate the budget is to compare allocations to internal communication with those to external communication (public/external affairs). The firms we examined distributed much larger amounts to external communications. The closest they came to parity was a large company with multiple plant sites, where external communications had a head count of 103 people and employee communications

had 60 people. At the other extreme was an energy company, which had 95 people in public relations and which had recently assigned two staff members to employee communications.

We believe that the composition of the sample companies in this study may have led to some atypical results. We sought companies with exemplary employee communication practices, and we found several outstanding examples. For these companies, financial resources may no longer be the burning issue that determines effectiveness. For companies that are not as far along the "learning curve" of effective communication practice, budget and staff size may be greater barriers to effectiveness.

One of the most frequent questions that surfaced during the interviews concerned functional reporting relationships. Should employee communications report to the CEO, human resources, public affairs, marketing, or corporate communications? Employee communications professionals spend a lot of time considering which configuration gives the communications effort the greatest impact in the organization. Our findings, however, suggest that reporting lines have less impact on the effectiveness of employee communications than political and interpersonal relationships. Reporting to the CEO is of little advantage if the CEO is indifferent to the strategic role of communication.

CONCLUSION

Effective communication, especially when it concerns employees, is vital to any organization undergoing significant change. Affected constituencies and stakeholders need information so they can continually help the organization achieve its goal.

This study of companies considered by their peers to be leaders in effective employee communication practice has emphasized a number of key themes:

- *Employee communications is a critical management process, not a set of products.* Every company studied has broadened its definition of employee communications from the use of newsletters and videos to a vital process for promoting organizational learning, improvement, and change.

- *Effective employee communications practices should be consistent under all organizational conditions.* What works in bad times also works in good times. One of the hallmarks of these best-practices companies is their commitment to ongoing employee communication— not an emergency measure only.

- *Every manager is a communicator.* When this principle is activated, the staff's role changes from "doer" to "facilitator," and the emphasis is placed on the needs and requirements of the customers, clients, and audiences. That is the way employee communication adds real and lasting value to the modern business enterprise.

Selected Bibliography

For more on the increased importance of employee communication see Kathryn L. Troy, "Employee Communications: New Top Management Priority," Research Report No. 919 (The Conference Board, 1988); Lester Kom, "How the Next CEO Will Be Different," *Fortune,* May 22, 1989, pp. 157–161; Richard Guzzo and Katherine Klein, "HR Communication in Times of Change," in *Managing Human Resources in the Information Age,* pp. 142–166; Faye Rice, "Champions of Communication," *Fortune,* June 3, 1991, pp. 111–116.

A more extensive discussion of the impact of restructuring on employees can be found in Kim Cameron, Robert Sutton, and David Whetten, eds., *Readings in Organizational Decline* (Cambridge, MA: Ballinger, 1988); also, Anne Fisher, "The Downside of Downsizing," *Fortune,* May 23,1988, pp. 42–52; Donald Kanter and Philip Mirvis, *The Cynical Americans* (San Francisco: Jossey-Bass, 1989); Bruce Nussbaum, "The End of Corporate Loyalty?" *Business Week,* August 4,1989, pp. 42–49; and Tom Peters, *Liberation Management* (New York: Alfred A. Knopf, 1992, especially Parts II and IV).

For more on communications during restructuring, see Kim Cameron, Sarah Freeman, and Aneil Mishra, "Best Practices in White-Collar Downsizing: Managing Contradiction," *Academy of Management Executive,* 1991, pp. 57–73; Leonard Greenhalgh and Todd Jick, "Survivor Sensemaking and Reactions to Organizational Decline," *Management Communication Quarterly,* February 1989, pp. 305–327; Nancy Napier, Glen Simmons, and Kay Stratton, "Communication During a Merger: The Experience of Two Banks," *Human Resource Planning,* vol. 12, no. 2, pp. 105–122; David Bastien, "Common Patterns of Behavior and Communication in Corporate Mergers and Acquisitions," *Human Resource Management,* Spring 1987, pp. 17–33; and "Communication with Employees Following a Merger: A Longitudinal Field Experiment," *Academy of Management Journal,* March 1991, pp. 110–135.

On the importance of face-to-face communication see Roger D'Aprix, "The Oldest (And Best) Way to Communicate With Employees," *Harvard Business Review,* September–October, 1982, Reprint No. 82559; Philip Clampitt, *Communicating for Managerial Effectiveness* (Sage Publications, 1991, especially "Communicating Channels," pp. 111–145); Robert Lengel and Richard

Daft, "The Selection of Communication Media as an Executive Skill," *Academy of Management Executive,* 1988, pp. 225–232; Richard Daft, Robert Lengel, and Linda Trevino, "Message Equivocality, Media Selection, and Manager Performance: Implications for Information Systems," *MIS Quarterly,* September 1987, pp. 355–366.

On dealing with bad news, see Walter Keichell III, "How to Escape the Echo Chamber," *Fortune,* June 18, 1990, pp. 129–130; Fernando Bartolme, "Nobody Trusts the Boss Completely—Now What?" *Harvard Business Review,* March–April 1989, pp. 135–142; Edward O. Wells, "Bad News," *Inc.,* April 1991, pp. 45–49.

The final report of the research study discussed in this paper is available from the Human Resources Policy Institute, Boston University, 621 Commonwealth Avenue, Boston, MA 02215 U.S.A.

Leading Change: The Personal Side

INTRODUCTION

Just as organizational structures, practices, and careers have undergone profound transformations, so has the role of the change agent. When the term "change agent" became popular in the 1960s, it typically denoted an outside consultant, often an academic, who came into an organization to assess its need for change. Armed with the best theories of the time and charged by upper management to "fix" some specified problem, these visiting consultant(s) typically would interview workers and managers, draw up an action plan, and leave its implementation to the discretion of senior management, who were assumed to have the necessary skills.

During the 1970s, this outsider role was gradually supplemented and partially replaced by inside "consultants," usually drawn from human resources groups that focused on "people" issues, such as bettering employee–management relations and individual career development. But although it had now become an internal function, change management, led by internal change agents, was still seen as directed toward precise, rather than systemic, targets.

The experience of leading change broadened substantially as the change arena drastically expanded in the 1980s, along with the change agent's role and responsibilities. As corporate chieftains in the major industrial economies for the first time saw their firms' competitiveness eroding and heard simultaneous demands for "maximizing shareholder value," and as they embarked on new kinds of relationships—joint ventures, for example—they determined that vast changes were needed just to survive. Entire "cultures" were to be thrown out and "old" ways to be rejuvenated. This kind of change went beyond tinkering with employee policies and called for a more visible and high-powered effort. CEOs themselves—especially newly appointed ones—would frequently be called change agents.

Outside consultants were still involved; in fact, the 1980s and 1990s saw an explosion in their business, as the need for change penetrated whole sectors of the world economy and as newly founded and established consulting firms rushed in. Even consulting groups traditionally associated with other areas, such as accounting and auditing, climbed aboard the bandwagon, adding entire divisions to concentrate on "change." Moreover, unlike some of their more detached predecessors, these consultants typically guided the process of change from conception through implementation (or tried to). By the late 1990s they had become some of the largest change management firms in the industry. (One of them is featured in "The Young Change Agents," a case in this module.)

Around the turn of the millennium, however, the change consulting business became a lot tougher. First, many of the organizations that had been clients began to see managing change as a crucial skill for their own top management. Learning from their own transformations, and from a proliferation of books and training materials on quality, culture, values, and the like, these firms became better at solving their own problems, their managers (some of them former change consultants themselves) stepping up to the challenges posed by technology and the new global economy. Second, as the long economic expansion began to slow and the dot-com shakeout ensued, many firms were forced to cut back on expenses, and consultants were often the first to go.

With the advent of the true global economy and the complexities and uncertainties that beset most markets through the first decade of the twenty-first century, the experience of leading change has continued to evolve. As change effort succeeds change effort (or, more usually, as each such effort overlaps the preceding one), and as "continuous change" (a topic that we will explore in greater detail in Module 6) becomes the rallying cry for organizations, companies are experimenting with new forms of change agents. Change agents can be teams; they can be "empowered" workers; they may even play all the parts—envisioning, implementing, as well as receiving—for many times they are driving forward their own changes as well as others'.

It is this last point that is the focus of this module on the personal side of leading change: Because they are often called on to play all the change roles, change agents are the most susceptible to change themselves. Whether this susceptibility takes the form of discouragement, as we saw with Emilio Kornau in Module 4, or adventure, as will be seen in several of the ensuing cases, depends on how those finding themselves in the role of change agent come to grips with some potent issues:

Resistance. Change agents will face resistance, no matter how needed a change effort may be, and no matter how close they are to the process and the people they are dealing with; resistance can come from anywhere, even the same level as the agents themselves. The material on recipients of change in Module 4 and the Walt Disney cases in this module make this point vividly. Moreover, given the complexity of change agendas, resistance may arise from the diverse needs of multiple constituencies, all experiencing other challenges simultaneously.

Frustration. As has been made abundantly clear in the cases and readings so far, change almost always takes longer than expected, events always intrude, and the process inherently encompasses ups and downs, and, probably more frustrating, plateaus. In the middle of the process, trying to do change can feel like wading through a muddy stream against the current. It can be hard to tell whether any progress is being made, even if everyone is still heading in the right direction.

Loneliness. By the nature of their role, those leading change are "out in front," covering rough or unfamiliar terrain with little sense of whether those whom they are trying to reach are with them, straggling behind, or headed off in other directions entirely. This awareness can leave change agents with a sense of isolation from the rest of the organization. If this feeling is not acknowledged, however, it can turn, paradoxically, into a sense of elitism, widening the distance between the change agent and everyone else.

Pain. Allied to loneliness is the double-barreled problem of recognizing, first, that change agents bring change, which is rarely embraced enthusiastically, and second, that, when change involves layoffs, demotions, and wholesale firings, people are devastated. Even if the change agents are not responsible for the decision to implement such changes, they are the messengers and accordingly are blamed. Conscientious change agents in these situations feel double pain—the pain of being blamed and the pain of being aware that in some sense they "caused" the situation, if only by introducing it.

Despite this dispiriting list, the experience of leading change, alone or as part of a group, can produce near-euphoria. In the middle of a long change program described in an earlier edition of this volume, one change agent exclaimed: "[It's like] I've died and gone to heaven. I don't ever want this to end." What change agents don't want to end, typically, is the sense of gratification and excitement that can accompany a change effort. The negative emotions experienced by change agents often are interspersed with positive emotions that make for a veritable roller-coaster ride. These include the following:

Challenge. There is a real adrenaline feeling from taking on the challenges that are typically present in change efforts. Transforming all the pieces of an organization can be experienced as putting a puzzle together. Likewise, aligning all the forces necessary for a change project to succeed, and then keeping them aligned, is akin to conducting a newly formed orchestra of virtuosi and holding them all together over a long and complex musical program.

Teamwork. Since change requires collaboration, there can be a very positive affect created in working closely with others on a common challenge. New friendships and new ways of working can be the natural by-products.

Personal growth. Although loneliness may occur, there is also a strong likelihood that change agents will grow and develop their talents, skills, and resourcefulness. "Digging deep down" and utilizing a range of skills can be very revealing about one's hidden strengths. All change agents report that they learned a lot about themselves and, as one noted, "I wouldn't have given it up for the world. It definitely changed the way I look at life and business, and how I handle myself."

Gratification. Finally, despite a large number of setbacks and frustrations, many change agents find their efforts highly gratifying. Change never occurs in one step, or, to use an American football analogy, "from the long bomb." Rather, it is a series of small steps, "three yards and a cloud of dust." But those small steps can be rewarding and gratifying in and of themselves. And, as change agents step back from the dust over time, they discover that, indeed, the cumulative gains have been substantial.

The personal experience of leading change, then, is like living in a world of incompletion—constantly. As they look at their organizations, change agents almost always discover that the organization is "neither what it once was, nor what it needed to become." As change agents dwell on where the organization should be, they may experience some of the negative emotions. However, as they observe the incremental steps of progress, and as they reflect on the journey itself, more positive emotions arise. In summary, change agents live in a world of conflicting emotions—emotions felt more intensely than probably most people ever experience.

The leaders of change introduced in this module represent all levels, and their experiences illuminate the particular kinds of challenges change agents face at the top, middle, and bottom of the organization. The challenges are those increasingly associated with what might be termed dilemmas for change agents of the future. Therefore, these are people who might respond to the question "Is being a change agent a dreadfully lonely, frustrating experience, or a great adventure?" by saying, "Yes."

OVERVIEW OF CASES AND READINGS

Dennis Hightower is a top manager creating change—and yet he is still very much in the middle. In the Change Classic "Walt Disney's Dennis Hightower: Taking Charge" we first meet Hightower in June 1987. He is Disney Consumer Products' newly hired vice president for Europe. On the surface, it appears he is facing an ideal situation for a change agent. He is given a broad mandate to "do something different." He is supported in various ways by the Disney organization. His job, which is to bring a new management structure to the firm's European affiliates, has been agreed to by those directly affected by this change, and this field of change is small—only a hundred or so are employed in Europe overall. Yet, on closer examination, the situation begins to take on some complexity. Hightower is the ultimate "conflated" change agent: He must develop a vision, secure approval of it, and begin its implementation—all while he is surely experiencing great changes in his own life, and is *having* to be changed if he hopes that he will succeed.

In the succeeding case, "Dennis Hightower: Walt Disney's Transnational Manager," we revisit the situation in 1994, when Hightower is implementing transnational licensing deals with firms like Mattel, Kodak, and Coca Cola. These deals are being received differently by each of the country managers who report to Hightower. This case is an effective lens for looking at the issues that confront managers of multinational organizations. As for Dennis Hightower, his chosen management style finds him in the field much of the time. He sums up his dilemma quite neatly when he comments that "I have to have the hammer in one hand and the velvet glove on the other and know when to use which, with whom to use which, and to what extent."

Accompanying these cases is "Bob Knowling's Change Manual," which depicts a senior middle manager who has come to terms with being a change agent. In the preface to his interview with the telecommunications executive, author Noel Tichy uses these words to describe Knowling: "courageous," "gifted," "committed," "farsighted," and "for real." Although Knowling's organization exists in a rather different environment from Hightower's—the telecommunications industry has had to cope with the fallout of deregulation, just as the airline industry (which we look at in greater detail in Module 6) has—both face very similar challenges and opportunities as they implement their change programs. Knowling offers eight insights for change agents, helpful benchmarks against which to evaluate the decisions and actions of the protagonists in this text.

The next three cases describe aspiring change agents, all MBAs who, soon after completing their degrees, are attempting to make a difference in their organizations. Chew Ling Tan is a change agent "in waiting" who is about to return to her pre-MBA employer and sponsor, the Singapore Housing Development Board, with lots of energy and good ideas. Whether she will be able to make change happen, how much, and how fast, are not completely within her control—but are very much subject to her influence, and the case describes her analysis and planning in anticipation of her return. Henry Silva is very close to accepting a job in which he will be nominally in charge of changing the culture of a green energy start-up, New Power LLC, in order to "create a dynamic workplace . . . to offer an experience that can't be replicated." However, Silva is uncertain whether he is "up for" the tremendous challenges this role will entail. Susan Baskin is also returning to her previous employer, a boutique consulting firm—but in the interim, the firm has been through a disastrous merger, a precipitous decline in business, a layoff, and a major decline in morale. Baskin is returning with an explicit agenda: "to energize the firm . . . to make the company a place where I want to work." Whether she will be able to do so, and from the middle, rather than the top, is very much an open question.

This "Middle Space" is explored in an accompanying reading, "Converting Middle Powerlessness to Middle Power: A Systems Approach." The middle manager's middle position has never been simple, argues Barry Oshry, because it means being a conduit between the top and the bottom of an organization. At a time when firms have stripped their middle management ranks to the bone and simultaneously require more from those who remain—not the least of which is implementing change efforts—the author's suggestions about converting Middle Space to "potentially powerful space" are well worth considering.

We next move to the bottom of the organization and consider the case of "The Young Change Agents." This case looks at the extraordinary steps taken by three newly hired trainees who are committed to transforming Price Waterhouse (later PricewaterhouseCoopers) into a firm whose success will be measured not only by financial metrics, but by its impact on society and the global environment. As the case recounts, they realize early on that to have any hope at all of success, they need the sponsorship of a senior executive. Just as important, they are deeply *committed* to their vision: "We had nothing to lose. We were willing to risk failing."

What are the odds that such grass-roots efforts will ultimately be successful? The final reading of this module, Rosabeth Moss Kanter's "Leadership for Change: Enduring Skills for Change Masters," suggests that the young change agents may be off to a good start. Their "breakthrough idea" is challenging the prevailing organizational wisdom; they are communicating an inspiring vision and building coalitions. Kanter's conclusions about what a change leader must *be* and *do* to be successful are drawn from a clear understanding of forces for change that have been at the center of the discussions in this text—globalization and innovation—and incorporate the theme of adaptability that we have returned to again and again.

There is perhaps no more adaptable example of leading change than that of Vinesh Juglal, the South African entrepreneur whose story is the final case in this module. From extremely humble beginnings in Port Shepstone, the headstrong Juglal quits both school and home to strike out on his own as a laborer, a trader, a one-man grocery wholesaler, and eventually, in sequence, the owner of a supermarket chain, a real estate entrepreneur, and the proprietor of an institute of higher education. As his career unfolds along with the social and political future of his country, Juglal becomes, in many ways, the quintessential change agent of the developing world—a world in which, even more than in developed countries, change is the rule rather than the exception, and seeing change as a way of life is essential to success. This insight into the continuous nature of change carries us forward to Module 6, the final module of this text.

Change Classic

Walt Disney's Dennis Hightower

Taking Charge

Go out and grow the business. Do something different from what has been done in the past. Develop a strategy and bring it back to us in three months.

This was the challenge Frank Wells, president and COO of the Walt Disney Company, presented to Dennis Hightower, newly hired vice president of Disney Consumer Products for Europe, in June 1987.

THE DISNEY ORGANIZATION

Founded in 1923 by the Disney brothers, Walt and Roy, with a $500 loan, the Walt Disney Company had grown by 1987 into an entertainment industry giant with sales of nearly $3 billion. The company was involved in film and television production, theme parks, and consumer products (see Exhibit 1).

Disney struck its first consumer product licensing agreement in 1929 with the merchandising of a Mickey Mouse pencil tablet. Subsequently, the Disney Consumer Products (DCP) division was established to manage the licensing of the Walt Disney name and the company's characters, songs, music, and visual and literary properties. By 1987, the division's revenue had reached $167 million, with operating income of $97 million.

THE DISNEY ORGANIZATION IN EUROPE, 1938–1987

Soon after its inception, DCP became involved with international licensing. In

EXHIBIT 1 Walt Disney Company

Financial Performance and Business Composition

	1940	1950	1960	1970	1980
Financial Performance, 1940–1980					
Sales ($m)	2.5	7.3	46.4	167	915
Net income ($m)	(0.1)	0.7	(1.3)	22	135
Return on equity (%)	(1.7)	11.7	(6.2)	10.0	12.6
Business Composition, 1940–1980 (% of Revenue)					
Film/Television	77	74	50	41	18
Theme parks/resorts	—	—	39	49	70
Consumer products	23	26	11	10	12

Divisional Revenues and Operating Income, 1981–1987 ($m)

	1981	1983	1985	1987
Film and Television				
Sales	175	165	320	876
Operating income	35	(33)	34	131
Theme Parks				
Sales	692	1,031	1,258	1,834
Operating income	124	190	255	549
Consumer Products				
Sales	139	111	123	167
Operating income	51	57	56	97

Source: D. J. Collis and E. Holbrook, "The Walt Disney Company (A)," Harvard Business School case 388-147.

1934, Walt Disney personally visited Italy to initiate a licensing business with an Italian publisher. After the war, he hired his first country manager, for France. Over the years, the French country manager, who hired all subsequent European country managers and was credited with having essentially built Disney's European business since World War II, came to be regarded as a "living legend."

By 1987, DCP had eight wholly owned European subsidiaries that operated in 20 different markets and together employed 102 people. Each subsidiary reported individually to Barton ("Bo") Boyd, worldwide head of Disney Consumer Products, who was located at Disney's world headquarters in Burbank, California. (Disney's organization chart is presented in Exhibit 2.)

All eight country managers had spent substantial time in their positions (see Exhibit 3). The longer-tenured country managers knew the Disney family personally. Most had known Walt and his brother, Roy Disney, Sr. The Disney children were regularly sent to Europe on vacation, and

EXHIBIT 2 **Organization Chart of the Walt Disney Company, 1987**

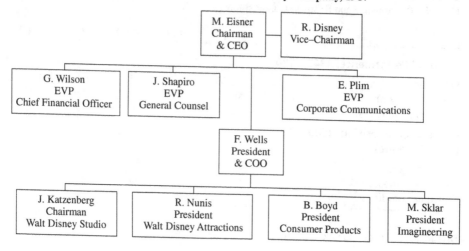

EXHIBIT 3 **Disney Consumer Products Country Managers, 1987**

Country	Age of Country Manager	No. of Years in the Role
France	70	40
Denmark	60	24
Germany	60	30
Belgium	60	35
Italy	60	26
Spain	44	16
Portugal	41	10
United Kingdom	41	15

frequently stayed in the homes of the country managers. Roy Disney, Jr., the company's current vice chairman, had "learned the business" from the French and German country managers when he became active in the company nearly three decades earlier.

Proudly independent and perceived as "senior senators," the country managers for all practical purposes *were* Disney in Europe. They had developed book and magazine publishing and a full range of merchandise licensing of apparel, toys, housewares, and stationery. The business being licensing-driven, management had made little investment in hard assets; it was a very high-margin enterprise.

The country managers operated in very different environments with diverse business compositions. The German market was much larger than the Portuguese market, for example, and whereas German and U.K. operations were historically driven by merchandise licensing, French and Italian operations were driven by book and magazine licensing. (See Exhibit 4.)

THE EUROPEAN HEADQUARTERS

Historically, Disney's market penetration in Europe had lagged behind that in

EXHIBIT 4   DCP Europe
Market Size and Performance

	Population (millions)	Per capita GNP (in US $)*	Production (m US$)		
			Merchandise	Publishing	Music
European Market, 1987					
France	55.5	15,987	155	22	18
Denmark	5.1	19,373	17	2	1
West Germany	61.2	18,183	158	15	37
Italy	57.3	13,129	114	10	6
Spain	38.7	7,499	55	6	3
Portugal	10.2	3,510	11	1	1
United Kingdom	56.8	12,533	114	22	19
Europe	**831.5**	**7,877**			

*1987 exchange rates.

Source: *European Marketing Data and Statistics*, and *National Accounts OCDE.*

$m	Merchandise Licensing	Product Line			
		Publishing	Music	Others	Total
Estimated Composition of DCP—Europe's Revenue and Income, 1987					
Revenue					
France	2.8	5.7	1.5	0.1	10.1
Denmark/Nordic countries	2.5	6.1	0.3	0.1	9.0
West Germany	4.1	4.1	0.4	0.2	8.8
Belgium	1.4	2.0	0.1	0.2	3.7
Italy	3.6	3.6	0.3	0.0	7.5
Spain	1.2	1.0	0.2	0.1	2.5
Portugal	0.4	0.3	0.1	0.0	0.8
United Kingdom	4.2	0.6	0.3	0.1	5.1
Total revenue	**20.2**	**23.4**	**3.2**	**0.8**	**47.6**
Operating revenue	**15.3**	**17.3**	**2.0**	**0.0**	**34.6**

Source: Disney Consumer Products—Europe.

the United States. But Disney management foresaw tremendous opportunities opening in Europe during the 1990s. The European Community was moving towards market harmonization and prospects for cooperation across countries were blossoming. Management expected that the 1992 opening of the EuroDisney theme park near Paris would greatly reinforce Disney's presence in Europe.

In order to take full advantage of emerging marketing opportunities, it was decided that a European headquarters for DCP would be established in Paris.

Everything concerning the eight country subsidiaries that had previously been managed by Burbank would now be run by Paris. A newly created position, vice president of DCP-Europe, would head the office. The sentiment of the country managers, who had been consulted on this decision, was that the new European head should not be a European; the notion of an American who could "relate" to the studio (as the Burbank headquarters was called) and build credibility locally was much more appealing to them.

Once the decision was made to establish the Paris office, the search firm of Russell Reynolds was hired to recruit candidates for the new European vice president job. Dennis Hightower, head of Russell Reynolds' Los Angeles office, was put in charge of the search.

RECRUITING THE RECRUITER

Boyd and Hightower spent three weeks in Europe meeting with each country manager in an effort to understand the business issues confronting them and get a sense of the kind of person who would win their confidence, respect, and trust. As they interviewed a number of prospective candidates, they became increasingly familiar with one another. "The more I traveled with Hightower," recalled Boyd, "the more I liked him." Hightower recounted the turn of events at that point:

> We were going through a very exhaustive search and had narrowed the list to six final candidates when, one Friday evening, Frank Wells invited me to Burbank for a discussion and sprang a surprise. He said, "While we think we have six good candidates, we have done some checking on you and think that

you are the person we want for the job." I was concerned with such a move since the country managers had candidly shared their points of view with me, and it would be uncomfortable for me to now go back as their boss. Frank told me that Bo had already spoken with the three senior-most country managers from France, Germany, and Italy to share the decision with them and to ask whether they anticipated any problems. The three managers had approved of the choice.

Hightower was appointed vice president of DCP-Europe in June 1987.

DENNIS HIGHTOWER

Born into a family with a rich military heritage, Dennis Hightower had joined the army in 1962 "because it offered blacks leadership opportunities that weren't available in industry at that time." Over the next eight years, he served in the army with distinction. However, upon returning from his second tour of duty to the Far East, he was ready for fresh challenges and found new fields of endeavor opening up. Industry, in particular, was becoming more receptive to minorities, so Hightower, in June 1970, resigned from the army and joined Xerox Corporation. "While working at Xerox," Hightower recalled, "I noticed that people who were doing things, who were moving things, all had MBAs." He applied for and was admitted to Harvard Business School on a fellowship.

Hightower joined McKinsey upon graduating from Harvard. Four years later, in 1978, he left McKinsey for General Electric, where he served in a strategic planning role, and later as a vice president and general manager in Mexico. In 1981, California-based Mattel hired Hightower as vice president of corporate planning. Current considerations rather than any grand plan had motivated Hightower's career moves. He summed up his advancement philosophy thus: "I have always had the confidence that, without my actively seeking them, the right opportunities will find their way to me. Other than follow a generalized desire to associate with the best, I have tried not to overmanage my career."

The next three years proved difficult, as Mattel, facing severe business problems, downsized drastically to about one-third of its 1981 size. Hightower assisted the chairman in restructuring the company, but once the restructuring was completed, the company no longer had an opening at the corporate level and he was out of a job. Family considerations drove his next job choice. "All the good opportunities were on the East Coast," he recalled. "But my family needed geographic stability for some time. They had sacrificed much in support of my career moves. I felt I owed them this one."

Hightower joined Russell Reynolds in 1984 and, two years later, became head of its Los Angeles office.

ACCEPTING THE CHALLENGE

As he contemplated his newly created job with Disney, Hightower thought wryly: "If you don't know where you are going, any road will take you there!" His task was to figure out where Disney would be in 1992, and what changes that would entail. He mused:

> These European managers have been running themselves for years. They have been very successful; it is a very profitable business for Disney. It could have been more profitable, but things were fine just the way they were.
>
> So what do I bring to the party? Not only am I an outsider, but I am also a boss they've never had before and probably don't want—no matter how much they may intellectually agree to the need for one.
>
> How am I going to develop a strategy that will unify Europe, grow the business beyond any one individual area, and introduce critical thinking and creative approaches—all in three months? Where do I begin?

Case

Dennis Hightower

Walt Disney's Transnational Manager

Dennis Hightower settled into his airplane seat on a transatlantic flight from

Source: Harvard Business School Case No. 9-395-056, Copyright 1994 by the President and Fellows of Harvard College. All rights reserved. This case was prepared by Ashish Nanda. HBS Cases are developed solely for class discussion and do not necessary illustrate effective or ineffective management.

Paris to Disney Consumer Products' worldwide head office in Burbank, California (Exhibit 1 presents revenues and operating income for Walt Disney company's three divisions). It was August 1994. Hightower was pondering over how to organize Disney Consumer Products' apparel business in Europe and the Middle East.

EXHIBIT 1   **Walt Disney Company***

Divisional Revenues and Operating Income, 1987–1994 (All figures are in $m)

	1987	1988	1989	1990	1991	1992	1993	1994
Filmed Entertainment								
Sales	876	1,149	1,588	2,250	2,594	3,115	3,673	4,793
Operating income	131	186	257	313	318	508	622	856
Theme Parks and Resorts								
Sales	1,834	2,042	2,595	2,933	2,794	3,307	3,441	3,464
Operating income	549	565	785	803	547	644	747	684
Consumer Products								
Sales	167	247	411	574	724	1,082	1,415	1,798
Operating income	97	134	187	223	230	283	355	426

*Refer to Exhibit 2 of "Walt Disney's Dennis Hightower: Taking Charge" for the 1987 organization chart of the Walt Disney Company.

CRAFTING A EUROPEAN STRATEGY

Named vice president of Disney Consumer Products–Europe in 1987, Hightower had taken charge of eight disparate country operations with a diverse composition of businesses engaged primarily in the licensing of merchandise, books, magazines, and children's music.[1]

TAKING PUBLISHING BEYOND LICENSING

Starting with Italian operations in July 1988, Hightower had begun to move beyond pure licensing into the publishing business. A country manager explained why Hightower was taking greater control of downstream operations: "As a licensor, you earn regular royalty but you are never a core business to your licensee. Your licensee will use your name to open doors with other principals, but he may invest too little time in your products. Dennis feels that the time is ripe for Disney to take greater responsibility and risk."

Over time, Disney's European publishing operations became a mosaic of licensing in the United Kingdom, Germany, and the Nordic countries, joint venturing in France and the Middle East, and vertical integration in Italy.[2]

INTEGRATING EUROPEAN OPERATIONS

In 1988, Hightower centralized European contract administration and auditing. "I told my country managers to focus on the

[1] See "Walt Disney's Dennis Hightower: Taking Charge" (Harvard Business School 395-055) for a description of DCP-Europe's evolution until 1987. The Middle East was added to Hightower's responsibilities in July 1988, when he was promoted to senior vice president in charge of Disney Consumer Products–Europe and the Middle East (DCP-EME).

[2] Because it was not yielding expected results, Disney in 1991 unwound a joint venture established in Spain in 1989 and reverted to licensing there.

revenue-production side of their business," he recalled, "and let me worry about the back office." Scale economies and elimination of redundancy yielded immediate savings.

Hightower also established marketing and creative services divisions in the regional office to offer common resources and coordinate activities of the countries and licensees. The marketing division supported merchandise licensing, the creative services division the publishing and music businesses. He began to recruit experienced MBAs from consumer products and creative companies to staff the regional office.

PAN-EUROPEAN LICENSES

With the regional office administering contracts, Hightower realized that DCP-EME could begin to enter into "mega-deals" with selected partner companies spanning multiple countries. In 1988, Hightower rolled out to the whole of Europe what had previously been a U.S.-wide deal with Mattel for toys, eliminating 68 local toy licensees in the process. Next, he negotiated with Nestlé a comprehensive deal covering food products that eliminated 57 local licensees. The Nestlé deal was subsequently rolled out worldwide. These first two deals in place, Hightower picked up the pace, negotiating broad, transnational deals with Kodak, Sega, Nintendo, Coca Cola, IBM, Johnson & Johnson, and Seiko.

Notwithstanding the accelerated growth they offered, these mega-deals garnered mixed support from the country offices. "When regional office people start talking with someone for a pan-European license," a country manager remarked, "they expect the countries to stop talking with everyone else. It takes six months to two years for their negotiations to bear fruit and, even

then, in the end they may not have any deal. Meanwhile, we are simply losing business in the countries. In any case, the mega-deal mentality of 'one size fits all,' which may work in the United States, is doomed to failure in Europe, given our diverse cultures."

Hightower was undeterred by such reservations. "I do empathize with the country managers who feel in their guts that such deals are proscribing their authority," he acknowledged, "but they need to appreciate that these deals have given them 'air cover.' The studio is leaning on all of us to reach our corporate target of 20 percent growth every year, and if pan-European deals get the whole of Europe there faster, we will take the pan-European deals route."[3]

WORLDWIDE OPERATIONS

After consolidating European Operations into a single region in 1987, worldwide head of DCP Barton K. ("Bo") Boyd had established three other regions worldwide—Asia Pacific, United States–Canada, and Latin America. Boyd took a hands-off approach toward his regional offices. "The studio has always had the philosophy of letting the operators operate," Hightower observed. "I talk with Bo three to four times a month at most."

HIGHTOWER'S MANAGEMENT APPROACH

"My role is to step back, take a global view, and evaluate tradeoffs," Hightower remarked of his role in the organization. "Once I have reached a decision, I try to

[3] Disney's worldwide head office at Burbank was called "the studio" inside the company.

make my country managers respond to my ideas in order to ensure that the entire region moves in concert. I believe not in ordering, but in persuading people to go along because they see the logic of what I want to do and how they fit into that, especially since I am leading a team of sophisticated marketing people who know their markets better than I will ever know them."

Boyd reflected on Hightower's management style:

> Dennis carefully evaluates a situation, puts a plan together spelling out what he needs to accomplish, and then sets out to attain those goals. In the process, he is very fair and honest with his troops, and they in turn are very loyal to him. This combination of strategic thinking and organizational skills gives Dennis the rare ability to lead a diverse cultural group such that they all pull together in the same direction. However, in his urge to be close to the field, Dennis travels so much that he is probably not as accessible to his subordinates as they would like him to be.

"Dennis works on the squeaky-wheel-chair theory: Get involved only when you hear a squeak," observed an executive in the regional office. "He trusts people, but they must deliver. Since he is also running all the time trying to grow business, he isn't always easily reachable. Many decisions end up getting delegated down. Having so much authority can get uncomfortable, but I guess it is part of being treated as a grownup; personally, I find it very motivating."

Hightower spent remarkable time on personnel issues. "Numbers don't get things done, people do," he remarked.

> It may not be the only concept of effective management, but it has worked for me. And there is great value in knowing who gets tweaked in what way. One of my key responsibilities is to know who to push and who to

pull back, when to push and when to pull back, and how to push and how to pull back. I use a combination of personal persuasion, and financial and nonfinancial incentives. Then, if anybody chooses to ignore me, that person does so only at considerable career risk. I have to have the hammer in one hand and the velvet glove on the other and know when to use which, with whom to use which, and to what extent.

A country manager described the management approach that Hightower had inculcated in DCP-EME:

> Dennis often remarks that we are not brain surgeons out doing our own things, but a marketing team working with a network of people. The critical requirement is that we build working partnerships with others. Talented, motivated people sometimes fail on this front because they step on each other's toes. We have had some bright but inexperienced disasters who, two years out of their MBAs, felt that they should be running Europe.

RENEWING THE ORGANIZATION

"Dennis has achieved all his plan targets," Boyd had remarked upon naming Hightower president of DCP-EME in 1991. "More important, Europe is marching to the beat of one drummer." Vertical integration had dramatically raised revenues and increased operating profits, albeit at lower margins (see Exhibit 2).

On the horizon was a host of promising opportunities and new challenges. European unification seemed to be a distant dream at best, but the demise of communism had opened new market opportunities in Eastern Europe. EuroDisney was about to open. Hightower began initiating further changes in 1992 in order

EXHIBIT 2   DCP-EME
Performance and Business Composition

	1988	1989	1990	1991	1992	1993	1994	1995e*	CAGR (%)
DCP-EME Growth Trend, 1988–1995									
Revenue ($m)	56	108	131	143	231	279	305	351	30.0
Operating income ($m)	36	58	66	68	92	101	115	142	21.7
Profitability (%)	65	53	50	48	40	36	37	40	
Human Resources									
Regional office	4	11	26	43	62	97	112	114	
Subsidiaries	124	169	186	238	282	329	354	371	

*e: expected

	Product Line				
	Merchandise Licensing	Publishing	Music	Others	Total
DCP-EME Revenue and Income, 1994† ($m)					
Revenue					
France	14.6	69.8	12.0	0.9	97.3
Germany and Eastern Europe	22.8	14.5	2.5	0.6	40.4
U.K.	16.1	3.2	2.9	0.9	23.1
Italy	6.9	93.0	5.2	0.8	105.9
Others	21.1	12.8	2.7	4.8	41.4
Total revenue	**81.5**	**193.3**	**25.3**	**8.0**	**308.1**
Operating income	**55.8**	**49.0**	**7.3**	**2.9**	**115.1**

†Refer to Exhibit 4 of "Walt Disney's Dennis Hightower: Taking Charge" for DCP-EME's revenue and income in 1987.

to build on the momentum DCP-EME had established over the past four years.

REORGANIZING THE REGIONAL OFFICE

In the space of a few months in 1992, Hightower made several organizational and personnel changes at the regional office. (Exhibit 3 presents an organization chart for DCP-EME.) Over its four-year life, the creative division at the regional office had been operating uneconomically. Rather than prune its operations,

Hightower split the division. He attracted a highly respected artist and designer from Disney U.S.A. to head creative services, which would provide central creative resources to European publishers, and he named Marie-Frances Garros, an experienced publishing industry insider who had been looking after publishing within creative services, head of the newly independent publishing division responsible for coordinating business with the country publishing operations.

Hightower moved the finance head, who had been wanting to shift into an operating role, to head the Middle East

EXHIBIT 3   DCP-EME Organization Chart, 1994

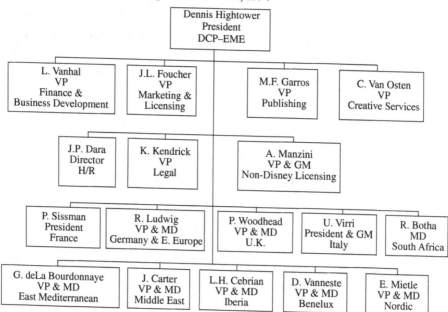

subregion, and dismissed the head of marketing, who, he observed, "had a divisive approach of pitting one country manager against another." Both positions were filled by internal promotions of European executives. One of the newly appointed division heads commented on the working atmosphere at the regional office:

> The strategies of the earlier heads weren't too bad; they just had no patience or persuasion. When I became head of my group, I was amazed by the tension that existed between the different divisions. Members of our new regional office team, who had all been understudies to the departing managers, had learned from their mistakes. We chose to operate as a more integrated group. We knew Dennis wouldn't dictate to us how to operate, but he would not be very happy otherwise.

The 22-person marketing staff at the regional office continued to lead the effort to identify and initiate pan-European contracts. The 21-person publishing group took a different approach. "We offer our country offices a central facility for quality control and coordination, and expose them to new ideas through regular meetings, newsletters, and updates," Garros explained. "Besides, we conduct monthly reviews of all the magazines in our region and send our comments to the local offices, who very much appreciate them. On most issues, we offer suggestions. When we do have to mandate something, we try to be as precise and objective as possible."

KNITTING THE COUNTRY OPERATIONS TOGETHER

Hightower believed that bringing the country operations closer together had generated enormous synergies. "One legacy that I will be proud to leave behind," he remarked, "will be of far greater interplay among the countries on a positive collegial basis than when I had arrived." An operating council established by Hightower, comprising himself, the then eight country managers, and four executives from the regional office, met every quarter, and occasionally designated special teams to look into specific issues.

In 1992, the fiercely independent U.K. country manager was replaced by an outsider. "She took a strictly British perspective," explained an executive in the U.K. subsidiary. "Whenever a pan-European deal was struck, she had to be brought into it kicking and screaming."

Even as Hightower was weaving operations together, some country managers expressed their concern at losing autonomy to the regional office. Remarked one country manager:

> I am responsible for my budgets and performance, but I have to countenance the regional office people meddling in my business, pushing needless deals, or doing country office jobs. I am not even sure whether current trends point toward harmonization of local environments in Europe. It is quite likely that people will identify even more fiercely with their local identities. Having effective local offices will continue to be critical.

EVOLVING RELATIONS WITH THE REST OF DISNEY

Hightower had been fairly successful in the ambassadorial task of building awareness of DCP-EME in Burbank. "Before Dennis, people in the studio would refer to the United States and the rest of the world,"

remarked a country manager. "Dennis has made them realize the richness, complexity, and potential of Europe."

Performance had yielded relative independence. "Chances are," reflected Hightower, "as long as we continue to deliver we'll continue to get autonomy."

Success had brought its own problems, however. Garros explained, "Some of our U.S. colleagues, whose operation is incidentally much smaller than ours, unilaterally enter worldwide agreements that can have huge consequences in our area."

LOOKING AHEAD

Looking out on the Atlantic, Hightower reflected with considerable satisfaction on his seven years with DCP-EME. He had overseen growth in the retail value of Disney business from $650 million in 1987 to $3.5 billion in 1993. Now he foresaw a number of organizational and strategic challenges.

PLANNING FOR SUCCESSION

Disney's president and COO Frank Wells died in a helicopter accident in April 1994. Three months later, Disney's chairman and CEO Michael Eisner underwent quadruple bypass heart surgery. In August, chairman of Walt Disney Studios Jeffrey Katzenberg announced that he was leaving the company. Newspapers and magazines were suddenly filled with rumors and articles debating management depth within Disney. Such speculation was particularly unsettling for a company that had for years prided itself on its stable management.

It was in this context that Hightower perceived that one of his greatest challenges in the coming years would be planning his succession. "I have been in position for several years now," he remarked. "I want to have an organization in place that allows someone from Europe to take my place. The question I am increasingly asking myself is, what should be the profile of the person who will replace me?"

REACHING FOR THE SKY

Having witnessed Disney's success in Europe, Warner Brothers had begun to move in with licensing deals and company-owned stores. Yet the Disney label continued to be extremely powerful: Of the ten most popular characters in Europe, nine belonged to Disney.

More than competitive challenges, the issue facing DCP-EME was how to maintain its frenetic pace of organizational growth as the business mix changed and the operation expanded. Business was growing at 30 percent per year in Eastern Europe, but at 11 percent in the Nordic region, in which the company enjoyed more than 90 percent market penetration. The publishing business continued to contribute 63 percent of DCP-EME's revenues, but merchandise licensing was becoming an increasingly larger part of the business (see Exhibit 2). Observed marketing head Jean Luc Foucher:

> Eisner has made a commitment to the stock market to deliver 20 percent growth per annum over any five-year period. We have to constantly reinvent our business in order to continue growing at that pace. We are a big operation, and rapid growth on such a large base is very difficult. For example, generating such growth in publishing—a mature and stable business in which we have a 70 percent share of the market—is a huge challenge. In trying to reach for the sky, we have to be careful that we

don't lose our soul by diluting our characters' images too much.

Hightower remained optimistic. "Our main lines are healthy, our structure is well established, we have a team of motivated and talented people," he remarked. "Several businesses are going in or coming out of our portfolio. Leveraging off our strengths helps us reach the 20 percent target without having to go back to Michael and ask for relief."

Besides pushing for sustained performance in existing businesses and territories, Hightower was looking at geographical expansion in Eastern Europe and the Middle East, and at growth options such as catalog selling, electronic publishing, comics syndication, and third-party licensing. However, a senior executive voiced a common concern within DCP-EME when he remarked:

> Some people at the studio say that our job is just licensing. Others see our job in a broader way, as providing entertainment products and services. How the company eventually defines the scope of our activities will determine how we grow.

THE APPAREL BUSINESS

Regional office and country subsidiary views differed on the usefulness of almost all pan-European alliances, but in no category did they diverge as much as in apparel. Apparel was the company's largest merchandise category in revenue terms, contributing more than 30 percent to the retail sales of all Disney-licensed products. "It is a business close to everyone's heart," Hightower quipped, "since everyone thinks he or she is the world's greatest fashion critic and designer."

Before Hightower's arrival, anybody could sell Disney apparel by paying the company a fee for a nonexclusive license. Distribution was spotty and product quality often shoddy. Hightower charged a regional office team to rectify this situation by developing an apparel strategy. A regional office marketing executive recalled how the team's strategy played out:

> The apparel team came up with a list of four manufacturers who could be developed into pan-European licensees. Weeding out the marginal licensees dramatically raised our designs and product quality. Europe-wide sales of apparel have gone up 24 percent since the introduction of the pan-European policy. But the four manufacturers have preferred mutual exclusivity to vigorous competition; instead of jumping into the newly opened markets, they have retreated into their home bases. Now we have several underexploited territories.

The German country manager described the consequences:

> My textile sales are down 30 percent this year. Germany has very structured retailing with big department stores and mail-order houses. It requires sustained relationship building. None of the pan-European licensees is German. As a result none of our pan-European licensees was able to win the big accounts, despite intense efforts. In contrast, Italy is made up of small retailers. None of the licensees effectively penetrated Italy. Now I am unhappy since my market is underexploited and the Italian country manager is unhappy since his market is not being served. Incidentally, apparel is not the only category in which we have been hurt by the regional office taking control over some of these issues.

These different perspectives had given Hightower pause. "Do we need to move from where we stand on this issue today?" he wondered, "and, if so, where should we be heading and by what route?"

Reading

Bob Knowling's Change Manual

Noel Tichy
University of Michigan Business School

If you're going to be a change agent, I think you come to a point where you no longer think of what you do as a change program.

The first time I really paid attention to Bob Knowling, he was working late into the night, using all his persuasive powers to overthrow the work I was doing to help transform Ameritech, the telecommunications giant based in Chicago. Twelve hours

Source: *Fast Company*, April 1997, p. 76.

later, he was standing in front of the whole executive group saying he'd been wrong.

That's when I knew he was courageous.

Over the next six months, he played a consistently constructive role in the Ameritech transformation effort—until he was assigned to set up and run the Ameritech Institute. And he resisted that. After a few months on the job, he built the internal change team that reported to the CEO and blossomed as a remarkable change agent.

That's when I knew he was gifted.

Over the next 18 months I saw him engage 30,000 Ameritech employees in community service, shift millions of dollars of Ameritech Foundation money into high-leverage community activities, practice his change skills in revitalizing the Chicago YMCA, and bring his passion to Detroit's Focus: HOPE, the country's largest inner-city manufacturing training center.

That's when I knew he was committed.

I saw him in South Africa, six weeks before Nelson Mandela's election, addressing an audience of blacks and whites—some of whom had never attended a formal talk given by a black man—describing the fundamental tenets of change.

That's when I knew he was far-sighted.

I heard him describe his upbringing to MBA students at the University of Michigan—how he was the middle child of a family of 13; how none of the first 6 made it past the ninth grade; how he was the first in his family to make it through college—and how every one of his last 6 brothers and sisters followed him into the ranks of professional employment.

That's when I knew he was for real.

He joined U S West in February 1996 as vice president, network operations. His new job is to lead more than 20,000 employees in a large-scale change effort to improve service to U S West's more than 25 million customers. Bob Knowling is a change agent's change agent, a man who's learned to align all the elements of his character so that, no matter what the setting, he leads change.

When did you finally see yourself as a full-fledged change agent?

My Road to Damascus experience was the day I woke up and realized that I had freedom: instead of worrying about my job, I only worried about never compromising my change agenda. That realization unleashes the real power of the change agent.

This goes back to 1994, when Ameritech Corp. decided to create a pool of fully dedicated internal change agents. I was selected to lead the Ameritech Institute and I was not a happy camper. I'm an operating guy. I wanted to go to the front lines. Intellectually I understood the importance of the job. But man, my heart was in the field.

In the new organization we were creating, nobody had a job. We created the institute first. Then the leadership team, with our help, picked the presidents of the units, and then the officers of those units. It was a reemployment process. I've been an athlete all my life. My new assignment as a change agent was like the owner of the Bulls telling Michael Jordan to pick the team and design the plays, and then saying, "By the way, you don't get to play."

Meanwhile at the institute I was trying to invent a model that nobody in the world of phone companies is familiar with. We benchmarked GE's Crotonville center; we looked at other best-practice change models. But it was difficult because we didn't know what we didn't know. What did it mean to be an internal consultant to the business heads? None of us could understand the authority that we'd have to drive change in the organization. We were going to put system changes in place to deal with the hearts and minds of people, while also working on real strategic issues? Yes, that sounded fun.

But it wasn't happening. We weren't being bold. We were still operating like bureaucrats. It was as if we'd been neutered. We had all of this room to play in, we had all this air cover from the chairman, but the only bold initiatives were coming from external consultants and they were getting frustrated with our change team.

Finally, one of the consultants asked me, "What are you afraid of?" I'll never forget that conversation. I said, "What do you mean?" He said, "You have great instincts, but when the chairman does something dumb, you look the other way. When a business unit leader has an operating style that is totally different from the change model, you won't call him on the carpet. Do you want a job so bad that you're willing to accept what you know is wrong?"

Man, that was heavy to wear. He finally said, "You're not free." It took some time for all that to soak in. Then I decided, "What's the worst thing that could happen to me? I could lose my job. But if I lose my job because I've developed into a world-class change agent, there ought to be about a dozen companies out there ready to pick me up."

I realized that I couldn't live in fear. Whether or not I change the company, I knew I would change myself. I'd have new skills and capabilities. I'd be a very valuable commodity.

How did that realization change the way you did your job?

What you don't know while you're having that Road-to-Damascus experience is that once you've put your toe in the water, it's not so cold. Then the confidence factor kicks in.

Once I got my freedom, I got bolder. As I got bolder, the more invaluable I became to the chairman and to the company's leaders. In fact, the CEO used to say, "If I'm not hearing from business leaders every week who want you fired because you're in their face, moving them to new levels of leadership, you're not doing your job." It became the new norm in the organization.

That experience happened at Ameritech. What brought you from Ameritech to U S West?

I started here 10 months ago on the heels of a very difficult reengineering process. When I walked in the door, the company was experiencing service performance problems in the marketplace. Many of our customers had to wait over 24 hours for us to repair their service. New service orders and activation took us an unacceptably long time to deliver.

I saw the job as an opportunity to fix a big operating system and change a culture of entitlement. Like a lot of companies that have been subject to government regulation, we didn't understand the competitive marketplace. It's not just this company. The banking, trucking, airline industries—all the industries that have been deregulated—have had to go through a major change process.

But it's even more intense in this company. We're positioned at the threshold of the future in every one of our product lines and services. So the question is, "How do you take stodgy, old, bureaucratic, entitled companies and make them competitive enterprises?"

Making that change is a challenge that even successful companies face as they age and grow. How do you get started?

For me, it begins with changing a culture of entitlement into a culture of accountability. My first week on the job it was immediately apparent that nobody had been accountable for the reengineering effort. Beyond that, no one had been accountable for meeting customer expectations or for adhering to a cost structure. It was acceptable to miss budgets. Service was in the tank, we were overspending our budgets by more than $100 million—yet people weren't losing their jobs and they still got all or some of their bonuses.

That's very much like Ameritech had been. When people failed, we moved them to human resources or sent them to international. When I got to U S West, I felt like I was walking into the same bad movie.

To get started, I used the change model I'd learned at Ameritech. First, you never announce that you're launching a change agenda. The reason is simple: Change agendas have been done to death in these companies. Everybody's completely turned off to change agendas—they dismiss them immediately as the "program of the month." In my first two days I found out all the "programs of the month" that they'd had in the last four years. If you come in and announce, "Here's the next change program," you're dead. You've just painted a target on your chest. There's a target there anyway; this just makes it bigger. So you absolutely don't announce a change initiative.

Instead you do several very high impact things in the first 30 days that are immediately distinguishable and immediately shake up the organization. From my perspective, U S West was standing on a burning platform. Unfortunately, a lot of people didn't see it that way. So I had a 30-day agenda to create a buzz in the organization, to demonstrate that something's very different.

What kinds of things did you use to create that buzz?

For example, service was in the tank. So my second day on the job I initiated a scheduled phone call involving my department heads to review service performance in all 14 states. I scheduled that call for 6 A.M. It was a literal wake-up call for the organization. It told my department heads, "You're going to serve the customer between 8 A.M. and 5 P.M., so the call happens at 6 A.M." A few days into the job I changed it, because they couldn't have the data at 6 A.M. So I moved it to noon and took away their lunch hour.

The norm is to bring people into a meeting, talk about things, but nothing ever happens. We're not going to do that. Something has to be different. Having to get your butt up at 6 A.M. to understand where your business is, that's a watershed event for an organization that's asleep.

A lot of change programs involve changing people. Did you shake up your team?

That was the next high-impact event: to make some personnel decisions within 30 days. Most lethargic organizations study things and study things and study things. It's the proverbial aim, aim, aim, aim. And never pull the trigger.

But it's not that hard to form an assessment of people within 30 days. In fact, I could tell within two weeks who the players were simply by immersing myself in the organization. I very quickly announced to my boss that I would not be attending very many meetings and I did not want to be part of conference calls. I told him, I'm putting on my combat fatigues and going to the line.

I had a constant dialog with each of my direct reports, and I touched base every day on the service call. Of course, from the service call there were follow-up coaching opportunities. Because the folks who get it, get it quick. For those who don't, you have to say, "On the service call, you didn't know your numbers, you had no idea where your organization stood, you're in the process today of disappointing 52 percent of your customers, and you have no contingency plan. Let's talk about how you run your business."

That's how I immersed myself in the organization: I touched people. And I immediately got a good sense of each person's work ethic. I could see who was strong in terms of leadership and direction. I could see if anybody had a plan. Unfortunately, few had a plan or an operating model. That's why the results were where they were.

After you'd made your assessment, what did you do?

Within 30 days, I made one varsity cut. After I fired him, I immediately met with his direct reports. You have to deal with the survivors when someone leaves. What I didn't do is to try to convince them that the firing was just. I didn't even deal with the firing. That's the open wound, so why go dig in it?

Instead, I wanted them to understand their emotions, and to get them focused on my expectations for the management team. At the end I wanted them to understand the accountability model: If we have shared expectations, then I'm not going to stand over them making sure they perform every day. My job is to make sure that they're enabled. If there's a capability problem, I'm going to work with them on their skills. If there's a problem of barriers or inadequate resources, I'm the resource granter. My job is to be the cheerleader, the developer, the coach.

Now you've got their attention. But you're dealing with an organization of

20,000 people. How did you roll out the program?

As part of my 60-day program, I decided to delayer the organization. Phone companies historically have lots of layers: You go through six levels before you get to a corporate officer. I figured we needed to have three layers of management between the technician who meets the customer and me.

Delayering was traumatic for us. When you start to delayer, you're immediately fighting an HR system that says, "You can't do that." Then you get the other departments looking over the fence, saying, "Can you believe what this idiot's doing?" All that noise makes the next department wonder, "If he's doing it there, are we next?"

The delayering was also a watershed because when you've finished, when the music stops, there are not enough chairs for everyone who's there. That's good. If you leave it to the old system, they'll take away a layer, but there will still be the same number of seats as when they started.

After the delayering, I needed to launch an organized change process. Again, I didn't announce anything. But I decided to do something called "Focus Customer." The name was critical, because it told the organization that the first thing we needed to fix was our customer performance. We'd worry about the cost structure second.

I brought the top 106 people in my organization together for three or four days to talk about our biggest business issues. No theory, no academic stuff. We didn't deal with fictitious models or case studies; we dealt with real work that they face every day. Where are our three biggest problems? They then had eight to ten weeks after the meeting to take on a significant change process, lead it, engage their people, and produce results—just like we'd practiced. I've got to tell you, it scared the bejeezus out of some of my people.

Do you consider fear a positive or negative force for change?

I don't think it's positive or negative. Fear is part of change. Once people have figured out that something very different is happening, fear permeates the organization. You can cut it with a knife. I've come to the conclusion that you cannot un-fear an organization. But I do address it. You have to tell people that if they allow fear to paralyze them, it will become a self-fulfilling prophecy: It will be their undoing because they're immobilized; they can't make decisions.

I also tell them that accountability is the best remedy for fear. If you focus on serving the customer, if you ensure that you are improving customer service, if you get after controlling costs, then you don't have anything to worry about. If you're accountable, you don't have anything to fear.

From your experience, which is more important to change first: attitudes or behaviors?

I've found that you have to be focused on results and deliverables, not attitude, expectations, or emotions. When you've got a burning platform like I've got, I don't care whether people believe it or not. Give me the results! The numbers have got to improve. Of course, there are some people who already have the right attitude; they've been waiting for this opportunity. In fact, most people said, "It's about time. Put me in, coach! Where do I sign up?"

When you come into a system that's having problems and you introduce bold initiatives, you face the challenge that there is no belief system. People don't know what they can believe in. So you have to demonstrate that everything you've said actually can happen. That is a huge challenge. Part of that 60-day agenda has to be significant movement in at least some of the areas you have to fix.

Now I got lucky because we saw tremendous improvement in the first 60 days. As a result, this organization has done some things that are being talked about in the analyst community and among the leaders of this business. They can't believe the changes. That kind of early success creates its own belief system; more people sign up, and the momentum takes off.

Let's assume that I'm not the head of a department or a division—but I still want to create change in my company. What can I do to be a change agent?

I get asked that all the time. There are eight things I tell people. The first is we all have some realm of authority that defines the sandbox in which you can play as an agent of change. A lot of people don't understand that. They think that if they're a change agent, the first thing they've got to do is work on the human resource system to give them a pay-for-performance model. They spend their time thinking, "I've got to get the HR people to cooperate." That's wrong. The place to start is with the things in your organization you already control. There's a tremendous amount you can change.

But they need to understand and accept that limitation: You're not going to revamp the reward and compensation structure, so don't make it an issue. Look within your world and find the boundaries. Then within those boundaries, go for it.

The second thing is that aspiring change agents want permission for their change agenda. I've always felt that asking for permission is asking to be told no. Don't ask permission. You know where the boundaries are. Be bold and take a few risks. Most of the time, if it nets out to the result that you wanted, you're going to be a hero not a goat.

The third thing to remember is that the system is stacked against you. Never underestimate that. Pick your battles. As a change agent, you have to pick which battle you really mean to fight, and never sacrifice the war over one little skirmish. You have to learn to think of leading change like working in an emergency room. If you go to an emergency room, the triage nurse decides who lives and who dies. The kid with a broken finger can wait for five hours while the medical team deals with a life-or-death case that's on the operating table. I faced this at Ameritech. There were 60,000 people, all potential patients. The change agent has limited resources. So you keep coming back to the question "What are the priorities?" Some people are going to have to sit in the waiting room.

Fourth, I believe that any change agent has got to have a model of change. That's what working in Ameritech gave me; it's what the Ameritech Institute was all about. Even people who barely understand the change process, who have no idea about a change model, can have a foundation if they stop and ask themselves, "What's my point of view?"

Fifth, every change agent has to deal with the political issues of change. That means they have to understand that being an effective change agent is not about being a kamikaze pilot. The few kamikaze pilots I've met since I started learning about change are genuinely stupid, bent on self-destruction. I learned a long time ago that a change agent has got to learn to stay alive. A dead change agent doesn't do anybody any good.

What's a more common political problem, and ultimately more difficult, is the issue of being seduced by the organizational opportunity and staying safe. A change agent who's looking over the hedge at the next opportunity isn't going to succeed. I don't believe change agents can stay safe. They've got to answer the question "How am I going to deal with this thing called a career and this political system?"

What I now know is, if you do this thing right, if you've got a point of view, if you are bold and free, you've become one of the most valuable people in the organization. People with those qualities can work anywhere. In a technical company like this one, give me a choice between somebody who understands bits and bytes or a change agent, and I'll take the change agent.

Sixth, you have to understand what the job of a change agent is. It's about talking about the issues that we don't want to talk about, the ones that drive the business. It's about moving people out of their comfort zones. It's also about focusing on financial performance and creating shareholder value. This is not just about the "soft stuff." Change agents who don't really understand the financial issues of the company aren't worth much.

Seventh, if you want to self-destruct as a change agent, practice the notion of "Don't do as I do, do as I say." A change agent has got to walk the talk. After all, if you're doing this work the right way, you're completely exposed. And the moment you compromise your integrity, you're rendered ineffective. That's Change Agent 101. A change agent who doesn't walk the talk? I don't think so.

Finally, if you're going to be a change agent, I think you come to a point where you no longer think of what you do as a change program. It just becomes the way you do business. I can't imagine doing any job in any corporation where I wouldn't have a change agenda.

Case

Change Agent *"In Waiting"*

INTRODUCTION

As Chew Ling Tan embarked upon her last semester at the Columbia Business School in 2009, she soaked in all the insights she could in preparation for her return to the Housing Development Board (HDB), Singapore, where she had worked since graduating from college in the 1990s. In its most recent years, HDB had been under extreme pressure to change, driven by increasing customer expectations and public scrutiny. The government agency was striving to become much more customer-focused, more efficient, and innovative in meeting the changing needs of the population it served.

Tan was eager to play a major role in helping HDB achieve its goals. Prior to being sponsored by HDB to attend Columbia, she had been the Deputy Director of an important section under the Estate Administration and Property Department (EAPD) of the HDB. She was confident that her reputation, connections, and understanding of sensitive issues, coupled with the skills learned in the MBA program, would equip her well to assume a leadership role in driving

change. Tan had begun to prepare for the return to HDB and drafted notes of a detailed plan to help achieve corporate and departmental priorities as she understood them. She was looking forward to returning and implementing key initiatives to accomplish the needed changes, and to facing head-on anticipated resistance.

BACKGROUND OF THE HOUSING DEVELOPMENT BOARD

A BRIEF HISTORY

HDB,[1] the public housing authority of Singapore, was established in February 1960. The authority had grown rapidly in size and responsibilities—from initially meeting the basic shelter needs of 6% of the population to, in 2007, providing quality homes for 81% of a 3.7 million population. Due to land scarcity, its high-rise, high density living provided an effective solution to meeting housing needs for Singapore. HDB had a comprehensive building program, under which 984,000 apartments had been completed as of March 2007. In addition to building new apartments, HDB was also involved in the pricing, marketing, sales, after-sale service and lease administration of its apartments. The organizational structure of HDB is depicted in Exhibit 1.

[1] HDB was established under a statute, and was a quasi-government body corporate funded by the Government. It is under the supervision of the Ministry of National Development, which is equivalent of the U.S. Department of Housing and Urban Development.

EXHIBIT 1   Organization Structure of HDB

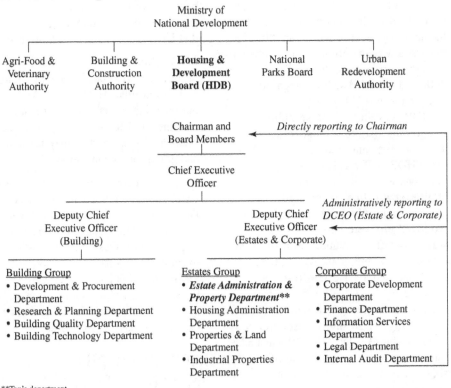

**Tan's department.

CHANGES AT THE HOUSING BOARD

Many change issues confronted HDB. Externally, the society had become more open and diverse. The profile of customers served was more affluent and vocal than before, necessitating the agency to engage its customers more often in its various policies and programs. Customers also expected to pay less for more. This was a particular challenge to HDB in the wake of rising construction costs caused by an acute building material shortage[2]

and a construction industry that was stretched in serving an overheated property market. After close to half a century of HDB developed housing, the public wanted more choices and more variety, such as public housing with a posh "private" touch.

In July 2003, HDB corporatized its technical departments[3] and shed 2,630 staff. The remaining 5,200 member staff was reorganized. Recruitment was frozen until 2007. During this period of major overhaul, the CEO was changed four

[2] At the end of 2006/2007, Indonesia imposed a sudden ban on the export of sand and granite to Singapore. Steel prices had also almost doubled since January 2007 due to a world-wide shortage.

[3] That is, architecture, engineering, surveying, project management, etc. The professional arm was corporatized to export HDB's housing expertise overseas and to allow private professionals to participate in HDB's projects.

times for various reasons.[4] The frequent CEO changes during the transitional period added to the uncertainties faced by the authority. According to Tan, "Inevitably, there was anxiety in the organization until the current CEO took office in June 2006 and provided stability regarding the direction forward."[5]

HDB was under intense public scrutiny for its manpower and other costs. This was particularly the case since 2003, when HDB staff was laid off on perceived generous terms. In many public forums, HDB's new office, completed in 2002, was mocked as the 'eighth wonder of the world.' There were allegations that HDB was over-staffed and under-worked. In addition to revamping its work processes, HDB focused its R&D efforts on new building materials to keep construction costs low. As the sole provider of public housing for so many years and with much celebrated success, HDB was under intense pressure to reinvent itself. To do so, the authority embarked on three major change initiatives:

- *Involvement of Private Developers.* In response to public demand for more choices and variety, in 2005, HDB piloted the "Design, Build and Sell Scheme" (DBSS), under which private developers designed, built, and sold new public housing units. DBSS apartments were priced by the developer on a market basis and purchasers received a fixed subsidy from HDB. Despite that the apartments were offered at a premium, the DBSS initiatives had been so well received by the public, especially by the younger generation, that HDB launched five such projects.

- *Public Outreach.* To gain greater public buy-in and support for its policies and programs, HDB embarked on outreach initiatives, such as town hall meetings and focus groups, to engage interest groups, particularly residents and grassroots organizations.

- *Improved Customer Service.* HDB also was striving to change its "service DNA." In 2005, it implemented a service system known as "Making a Great Impression on Customers" (MAGIC), to inculcate a service mindset within the organization and to share best practices. In 2007, 200 senior managers attended a motivational course to rekindle their passion for work.

BACKGROUND ON THE ESTATE ADMINISTRATION AND PROPERTY DEPARTMENT

OVERVIEW AND CHALLENGES

The Estate Administration and Property Department (EAPD) was one of the core departments in HDB, responsible for the building program, the redevelopment program, housing policies, pricing, marketing, sales, and mortgage financing for apartment purchases. Its 700-member staff was divided into six sections, each tasked with backroom or frontline work or both. Exhibit 2 depicts the EAPD organizational structure. Managers were generally in their thirties and forties, while members of the support staff were in their

---

[4] The CEO who joined in January 2002 left in December 2004 for another posting. Another CEO who joined in June 2005 left in April 2006 for political pursuits. Pending the appointment of a new CEO, there were two interim CEOs for a period of three and five months each.

[5] All quotes from an interview with Chew Ling Tan conducted on January 23, 2009.

EXHIBIT 2 Organization Structure of Estate Administration & Property Department, HDB

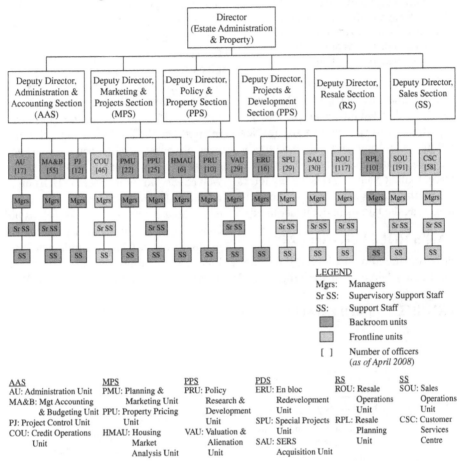

```
                        Director
                 (Estate Administration
                      & Property)
```

| Deputy Director, Administration & Accounting Section (AAS) | Deputy Director, Marketing & Projects Section (MPS) | Deputy Director, Policy & Property Section (PPS) | Deputy Director, Projects & Development Section (PPS) | Deputy Director, Resale Section (RS) | Deputy Director, Sales Section (SS) |

| AU [17] | MA&B [55] | PJ [12] | COU [46] | PMU [22] | PPU [25] | HMAU [6] | PRU [10] | VAU [29] | ERU [16] | SPU [29] | SAU [30] | ROU [117] | RPL [10] | SOU [191] | CSC [58] |

LEGEND
Mgrs: Managers
Sr SS: Supervisory Support Staff
SS: Support Staff
▇   Backroom units
▢   Frontline units
[ ]   Number of officers
        (as of April 2008)

AAS	MPS	PPS	PDS	RS	SS
AU: Administration Unit	PMU: Planning & Marketing Unit	PRU: Policy Research & Development Unit	ERU: En bloc Redevelopment Unit	ROU: Resale Operations Unit	SOU: Sales Operations Unit
MA&B: Mgt Accounting & Budgeting Unit	PPU: Property Pricing Unit		SPU: Special Projects Unit	RPL: Resale Planning Unit	CSC: Customer Services Centre
PJ: Project Control Unit	HMAU: Housing Market Analysis Unit	VAU: Valuation & Alienation Unit	SAU: SERS Acquisition Unit		
COU: Credit Operations Unit					

late forties and fifties, having served HDB for over three decades.

Tan reflected on her department's role in implementing changes needed at HDB:

The changes which HDB is undergoing are most felt by EAPD. Resources are stretched as staff members at all levels juggle their heavy workloads with change. Many established work procedures and systems need modification to cater to new business partners and schemes. Public consultation is a new ball game. Managers struggle to identify what issues to bring forward for consultation, how/who to consult, how to manage public expectations, and any possible backlash.

On the customer service front, a new service mindset needs to be ingrained, and support staff members are counted upon to deliver "magic." The results often fall short of target, and managers blame the difficulty on 'teaching old dogs new tricks.' There is a great deal of tension within the department, and also a strong sense of instability, especially among the staff who work on pricing, marketing and sales. They wonder if their jobs will be completely taken away by DBSS initiatives. We need to do more to train staff to prepare them for other kinds of work that they may need to do in the future.

While there were many challenges, Tan also felt that her department had many strengths that would foster change. The department's work ethic was strong. New training and compensation structures to facilitate change had already been set in place. Exhibit 3 summarizes the key forces facilitating change as well as the challenges, as she laid them out in her mind.

TAN'S ROLE WITHIN EAPD

Prior to attending Columbia, Tan was the Deputy Director of the Projects and Development Section in EAPD, a role in which she managed 75 officers responsible for conducting redevelopment projects to rejuvenate old housing estates. In her view, her role as Deputy Director had given her "experience in both backroom and frontline work and a keen sense of sensitive issues." Furthermore, the Director of EAPD was her mentor. Tan commented on their relationship: "He has been my boss for more than ten years and knows my work quality. Both of us are well connected throughout the HDB organization." Her prior experience and knowledge about the department, as well as her connections, made her feel confident in mapping out a Change Implementation Plan and to propose that she be designated the Change Leader in EAPD. With

EXHIBIT 3 **EAPD Force Field Analysis**

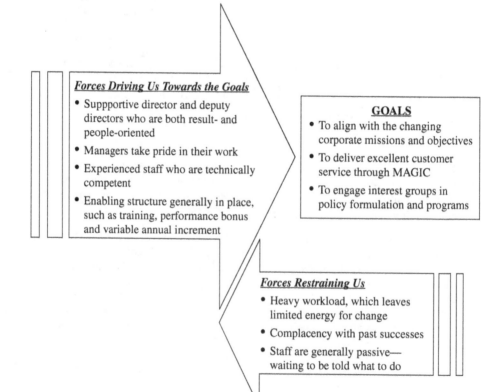

Forces Driving Us Towards the Goals
- Suppportive director and deputy directors who are both result- and people-oriented
- Managers take pride in their work
- Experienced staff who are technically competent
- Enabling structure generally in place, such as training, performance bonus and variable annual increment

GOALS
- To align with the changing corporate missions and objectives
- To deliver excellent customer service through MAGIC
- To engage interest groups in policy formulation and programs

Forces Restraining Us
- Heavy workload, which leaves limited energy for change
- Complacency with past successes
- Staff are generally passive—waiting to be told what to do

or without the title, she was dedicated to driving needed change!

CHANGE IMPLEMENTATION PLAN

Tan reflected on the changes she wanted to see implemented within EAPD. A first step was to draft a new mission statement for the department that would be consistent with HDB's new vision.[6] According to Tan, the new mission statement[7] needed to focus on the department, its human capital, and its core competencies from its successful past. Customer service excellence would be an explicit part of the statement. In developing a Change Implementation Plan, Tan's goal was to "face head-on the major changes that need to be made at HDB."

CHANGE INITIATIVES

Tan focused on three change initiatives, and commented on the importance of each one:

- *Streamlining Work Processes and Systems.* As staff is being called upon to take on new responsibilities and do things differently, it is important to streamline existing work processes to lighten their workload. This would garner the support of the departmental staff members, who are worried about increasing workload. This initiative shows that their concerns are being addressed.

---

[6] The old vision "Affordable homes, vibrant towns, cohesive communities" had been replaced by "An outstanding organization with people committed to fulfilling the aspirations for homes and communities all are proud of."
[7] The current one was "We provide affordable homeownership options; we formulate effective housing policies; we implement comprehensive redevelopment programs; we deliver quality housing services."

- *Achieving Customer Service Excellence Through Magic.* Improving customer service is a key goal for the entire HDB. While customer service initiatives are coordinated at the corporate level, we need to do our experiments at the ground level, to demonstrate successful approaches.

- *Engage Interest Groups in Policy Formulation and Programs.* Incorporating a diverse set of voices into policy formulation is a key new direction at HDB. We need to build a more progressive organization that is less top-down, but one that takes into account the perspectives of the various stakeholders.

Exhibit 4 depicts Tan's implementation plan in detail. She laid out information on roles, responsibilities and deliverables.

STRATEGIST TEAMS

The Resource Person and the Strategist Teams identified in Exhibit 4 played key roles in accomplishing the change. Each Resource Person would mentor a Strategist Team, which was responsible for proposing strategies and enabling structures to achieve the objectives of each change initiative. Tan reflected on her proposed team members:

Deputy Directors in the department need to play leadership roles as Resource People, in order to get the respect and support of lower level staff. There is a clear hierarchical structure in the organization—if change comes from above, the bottom would be more receptive.

I will also propose that promising young officers in the department play major roles in the strategy and implementation of the three initiatives. It's important that capable officers get assignments that are challenging and give them the exposure.

EXHIBIT 4   Change Implementation Plan—First Draft

Change Initiative 1: Streamline Work Processes and Systems

Objectives:	(a) To fully align work processes and systems with the new business models of outsourcing of building consultancy services and the new scheme DBSS
	(b) To cut down bureaucracies to ease workload
	(c) To share best practices for better work efficiency
Resource Person:	Deputy Director, Administration & Accounting Section (he enjoys the "cut-red-tape" stuff)
Strategist Team:	Heads of the frontline units, i.e. COU, SPU, SAU, SOU and ROU, led by Head of SOU since his unit is the largest and will be most affected by the change
Implementers:	Managers in charge of the affected work processes and systems
Recipients:	Users (i.e. EAPD staff) of the affected work processes and systems
Deliverables:	Strategist Team to ensure that all DBSS applications can be processed electronically within three months, and to deliver the following quarterly:
	(a) Reduce the processing time (measured by time-motion study) of five business processes by 20% (the number "five" is based on the involvement of five units in the strategist team); and
	(b) Replicate five best business practices in other units.

Change Initiative 2: Achieve Customer Service Excellence Through MAGIC

Objective:	To improve customer service delivery at EAPD
Resource Person:	Deputy Director, Sales Section (he oversees customer service in EAPD)
Strategist Team:	Managers in charge of frontline staff in COU, SPU, SAU, SOU, CSC and ROU, led by Head of CSC since her unit takes charge of customer service
Implementers:	Managers in charge of frontline staff
Recipients:	Frontline staff
Deliverable:	EAPD to attain the top five positions in HDB's yearly Customer Satisfaction Survey (EAPD was "below average" in the 2007 survey among the 22 service centers nationwide).

Change Initiative 3: Engage Interest Groups in Policy Formulation and Programs

Objectives:	(a) To draw up guidelines and Standard Operating Procedures on public consultation
	(b) To share experience and best practices on public consultation
Resource Person:	Deputy Director, Policy & Property Section (she is the housing policy "guru")
Strategist Team:	Heads of the relevant backroom units, i.e. PMU, PRU, ERU and RPL, led by Head of PRU since her unit, which formulates policies, requires the most varied form of public consultation

EXHIBIT 4 **Change Implementation Plan—First Draft**—*continued*

Implementers:	Heads of the relevant units (this work area requires higher signature given its sensitivity)
Recipients:	Interest groups
Deliverables:	Strategist Team to deliver the following quarterly:

    (a) Guidelines and Standard Operating Procedures on public consultation; and

    (b) Best practices (and the dos and don'ts) on public consultation.

Tan recommended that each Strategist Team meet weekly to discuss plans and report to the Change Leader every two weeks. In addition, given the fact that change proposals cut across different sections at EAPD, Tan wanted the Strategist Teams to meet biweekly with Deputy Directors whose sections would be affected, to apprise them of progress and get feedback.

TAN'S ROLE AS CHANGE LEADER

Tan developed a detailed action plan for herself personally, as depicted in Exhibit 5, to be used to achieve the proposed changes. One of her first priorities was to gain support for herself to be designated as the Change Leader responsible for galvanizing and coordinating these initiatives. In her view:

> With changes expected to cut across the various sections, it is crucial to appoint a Change Leader to drive the change and co-ordinate the efforts. I believe that I will have the support of my fellow Deputy Directors in EAPD. We are fortunate within the department that most people have a positive work ethic and want to make things better.

EXHIBIT 5 **Tan's Personal Action Plan for Change within EAPD**

Step	Schedule	Action to be Taken	Rationale
1	Week 1	Meet and seek Director's approvals to: (a) Re-craft the departmental mission statement; (b) Adopt the change implementation plan in Exhibit 4; and (c) Mandate me as the Change Leader.	• To line up political sponsorship • A new mission statement to guide the change of the departmental culture
2	 Week 2 Week 3	Meet the following officers to draft a new mission statement and review Exhibit 4, and seek their feedback: (a) All Deputy Directors; and (b) All unit heads.	
3	Week 4	Meet all the three strategist teams to review the draft mission statement and Exhibit 4.	To energize them and align them for the work

continued

EXHIBIT 5   **Tan's Personal Action Plan for Change within EAPD**—*continued*

Step	Schedule	Action to be Taken	Rationale
4	Week 4	Through the unit heads, seek the staff's feedback on the draft mission statement.	To communicate new focus and involve people
5	Fortnightly after Step 3	Meet strategist teams to review their proposals and endorse those which can be approved at my level as the Change Leader.	To push the change proposals forward
6		Give progress report to Director and Deputy Directors on the changes to be made, and seek their approval for proposals under their jurisdiction.	To give them the heads up for the impending changes, and to push more change proposals forward
7	Monthly after Step 3	Review Exhibit 4. If revision is needed, it will be communicated to Director, Deputy Directors and the strategist teams.	To ensure that the change plan stays on the right path
8	Quarterly after Step 3	Town hall meeting, to be chaired by Director, with EAPD staff. The agenda for the *first* meeting will include: (a) Explanation of the need and the urgency for change (b) Unveiling of the new departmental mission statement (c) Presentations by Strategist Teams 1 and 2 on their change plans, the rationale and the progress of change (d) Question and answer session (c) and (d) will become standard items for subsequent town hall meetings, while (a) and (b) will be repeated appropriately.	• To communicate changes and involve people • To reinforce and institutionalize change
9	Half-yearly after Step 3	Stock-take the changes made and carry out environmental scan to ensure continuous alignment with the corporate objectives.	To ensure that the change direction remains correct
10	On-going	Informal chats with the strategist team leaders/members, implementers and recipients on how they feel about the changes so far.	To check on the progress and provide early intervention if necessary
11		Celebrate success (e.g. a meal) with the strategist teams at each milestone, such as after achieving a deliverable or after a town hall meeting.	To continue to energize the teams and foster comradeship

Tan had a rapid timeline for launching her change plans. Key action items included:

- Gaining support for her designation as Change Leader.

- Crafting a new departmental mission statement and having it circulated and reviewed.

- Meeting with Strategist Teams to discuss the proposed change implementation plan, reviewing their proposals for change, and seeking approval for proposals that involved the Deputy Directors of different sections in EAPD.

- Establishing a biweekly meeting with Strategist Teams to review proposals.

- Providing Progress Reports to senior staff.

- Establishing quarterly town hall meetings with EAPD staff, to explain the urgency for change and to review change initiatives.

- Monitoring change progress continuously.

- Celebrating successes.

Tan's plans involved a great deal of communication, throughout EAPD. She commented:

> It will take a lot of communication and trust from people at all levels to make this successful. We need to be able to articulate the benefits of these change initiatives. Staff may have reservations about the extra work involved. I want to use town hall meetings to release information important to staff, such as the likely proportions of DBSS projects and internal HDB's developed projects in the future. This will give the staff a heads up and increase their receptivity towards change.

RETURNING TO HDB

While Tan knew that many challenges lay ahead, she was optimistic. She knew HDB and her own EAPD department very well, and understood how to use her connections and leverage the hierarchy to make things happen. Furthermore, she felt she had gained a new skill set from her MBA courses. In her view:

> Change is a continuous journey for EAPD, and for HDB as a whole. The repertoire of skills, knowledge and self-awareness learned at Columbia will go a long way in enabling me to navigate successfully through changes and help make EAPD and HDB stronger.

Case

Henry Silva: Aspiring Change Agent for a Start-up Company

INTRODUCTION

In his second year at Columbia Business School, Henry Silva was wrestling with a difficult decision: should he join New Power LLC, an extremely innovative company working on clean energy? Silva had worked at the company as a summer intern in product management after his first year at Columbia. His internship convinced him that the company had an amazing business plan and vision, as well as a dynamic founder who had already launched one company. At the same time, Silva felt that changes in the culture and communication at the company could increase New Power's ability to achieve its ambitious goals.

The founder of the company, Seth Perkins, agreed with Silva's vision and had offered him the job of director of special projects with the goal of creating a dynamic work environment. As Silva considered the job offer, he wondered if he would be able to transform the company in the ways it needed to change. For starters, he had no formal background in change management. And while the founders

supported his vision for change, he knew that it would be enormously difficult to be one of the company's lead change agents. Silva was debating whether he was up for the challenge.

BACKGROUND ON NEW POWER LLC

New Power LLC (NP) was a start-up that focused on clean energy technologies. Based in Seattle, Washington, the company was founded in 2006 by CEO Seth Perkins, whose first company had a successful IPO in 1999. In his first venture, Perkins had shown a keen ability to design a new business model and to envision successful new products and services.

The company's products and services focused on helping electric utilities and customers to better manage energy demand. Its "Smart Grid" technologies were increasingly viewed by policymakers as a way to help the United States reduce dependence on foreign energy supplies as well as create jobs in a time of recession. In 2009, the company's 125 employees primarily focused on technical fields, with only a few employees working in marketing, finance, and other business functions. Diverse technological professionals, including software developers, engineers, battery experts, and others, were represented on the NP team. While there were interactions between the different functional teams, typically, employees primarily interacted with others in their areas of expertise.

SILVA'S SUMMER EXPERIENCE AT NEW POWER

Silva's work experience before business school was as a product manager at an established energy company. In this role, he was at the hub of coordinating many people and a great deal of information. He enjoyed working in a culture in which he and his colleagues communicated frequently, both about work and also in social activities after office hours.

After his summer internship, Silva came away with a very positive view of NP's founder, describing him as an "absolutely amazing person with an absolutely amazing business plan. The company promises to be groundbreaking. I was fortunate to have interned there last summer." However, Silva's experience on his first day of work had left a very strong impression of the cultural aspects of the company:

> On my first day of work, I was brimming with energy. I couldn't wait to meet my coworkers, to exchange ideas, and to begin to build new friendships. But when I walked into the office, I was greeted by silence, shown to a computer in a dark and isolated corner, and told to begin my research. There was no talking, no laughter, and no sense of place or culture. Day after day, I would go to work, hoping that something would change, hoping that someone would speak!

Silva suspected that the technical nature of most employees' work might have created a more introverted culture. In addition, he felt there was a gap between the founder's vision and that of the majority of the company's staff. In Silva's view,

There is no reason this company cannot knock the socks off all the competition. The company has incredible potential and the people have amazing drive. But that potential and drive needs to be molded and directed in order to spur the company to the level of success I know it is capable of achieving.

At the end of his summer internship, Silva decided to communicate his views directly to CEO Perkins. After Perkins offered him a full-time job in product management, Silva conveyed his view that the company's key challenge and opportunity lay elsewhere—in creating a vibrant environment that fostered communication and the sharing of ideas. Silva was taken aback when Perkins "smiled and immediately revised the job offer. He asked me to become the director of special projects, and to help him create a dynamic workplace."

CHANGE ISSUES

In NP, Silva saw a company with tremendous potential, but staff that worked in silos, disconnected from each other. His approach to change at NP stemmed from his beliefs about the value of a corporate culture that involved employees. In his words:

> In a start-up company, people—developers, engineers, marketers, the sales team—are the company's most valuable asset, because they determine product quality and speed to market. In such a company, it is crucial to have a corporate culture that focuses on engaging employees. At a start-up, incentives cannot be monetary, and they can't be based on long-term job security. The way to differentiate, then, is to offer an experience that can't be replicated.

Furthermore, Silva thought it was crucial for employees to both believe in the company's vision and to shape the company's strategy:

> At NP, there is a unique opportunity to change the face of global business. But employees must believe that this is possible—they must have faith in the product. Most often, this kind of faith is built on trust in the founder, his vision, and his business sense, and results from the founder's dedication, accessibility, and ability to engage others. The NP founder and senior management team believe in the importance of management leading by example. There are no offices and the conference area is open. These steps signal that they have nothing to hide about the business and that everyone is part of the same team. This is a huge leap in the right direction. However, I believe there is still more that can be done to engage employees in the development of the company's vision and to help them grow as individuals and as part of the team.

While Silva knew that Perkins, given his previous entrepreneurial successes, had an intuitive sense of how all the aspects of the business—marketing, technology, product development—came together, he wanted to make sure that all the employees shared this understanding.

CHANGE IMPLEMENTATION PLAN

As Silva considered whether to accept the job offer with NP, he decided to map out a plan of how he would go about implementing change, should he join the company. Silva's change implementation plan set out to develop structures and processes that did not currently exist at the company. In his view, "Every initiative should serve a business or cultural purpose. In a small and informal environment, you often need formal structures and processes to make things work effectively." Key initiatives he planned to implement included:

EMPLOYEE INTERVIEWS

As a first step, Silva planned to interview a sample of employees to get their perspectives about the company: what they enjoyed and how things could better meet their needs. Interviews with managers in the company would be particularly important—to get their views about the role of culture in the company. Given the company's small size, he planned to later extend these interviews to every employee. Silva wanted to create feedback mechanisms whereby employees could participate in shaping new initiatives and learn how any previous suggestions they made had been adopted by the company.

ORIENTING NEW EMPLOYEES

Silva wanted to establish a formal orientation program for new employees. He envisioned:

- Developing an FAQ guide, informing new hires of "who's who" in the company, good information sources, and how to reach people internally

- Pairing each new hire with a "mentor" who could show them the ropes and talk candidly about the office environment

- Preparing brief bios about new hires and existing employees that would provide information on people's areas of interest; Silva's goal was to foster cross-pollination of technical information across the company.

DEVELOPING A VISION

Silva thought it was important to develop a vision statement for the company, based on its key values. The process of developing the vision statement would include substantial feedback from employees and would be an iterative process.

PERFORMANCE MANAGEMENT SYSTEM

A performance management system was one of the most important change innovations Silva wanted to introduce. In his view:

> A performance management system is the best way to get feedback to employees about performance and to enforce communication between employees and managers. It fosters fairness, transparency, and objectiveness. It is also a great source of data for the company. If everyone in the company is deficient in particular areas, the company can work on building these skills across the board.

Silva knew that a performance management system could be met with resistance:

> Some employees at NP might see the launching of a performance measurement system as indicating a faltering business, or even worse, management's unhappiness with employee effort and output. Others may see it as a roadmap for career and company success. It is important to move employees towards the latter view, and get them involved early on in the development of the measurement system, to help them to connect with the initiative and not feel as if the change was mandated from above.

Silva planned to study several different performance review systems and then develop one that would be tailored for NP. In his view, it was critically important to involve managers in the development and review of the performance system.

He envisioned using a "cascade of personal communications meetings" to introduce both the performance management system and the new vision statement. Using this process, Silva and company executives would convey to managers the importance of the new initiatives. Managers would then communicate the value and relevance of new initiatives to their direct reports. Silva said, "Because the company is still so young, I believe that the use of cascade meetings to introduce important initiatives can become a hallmark of our corporate culture, a symbol of our commitment to openness and cohesiveness."

EMPLOYEE AWARDS PROGRAM

An inexpensive but meaningful employee awards program would recognize exceptional individual contributions to NP, giving employees something to strive for. The awards would be based on the new performance measurement system, which would reflect the company's strategy and goal of stepping up both innovation and productivity.

TEAMWORK DAY

Silva planned to have a "Teamwork Day" which would feature a cross-functional teamwork assignment focusing on a real problem NP was facing. He thought this assignment would be a good way to teach new hires how to work in teams and practice negotiation and other problem-solving techniques that would be very useful in the workplace.

OFF-HOURS EVENTS

Silva planned to periodically host company off-hours events. These events would showcase all that Seattle had to offer, and would follow presentations made by employees at all levels of the organization about important projects they were conducting. The goals of these off-hours events were to enable employees to expand their knowledge of the company as well as to develop their internal social networks.

SILVA'S PERSONAL ACTION PLAN

Silva's detailed action plan, which he planned to begin implementing even before starting his new job, was a guide to help transition into his new role as a change implementor. Silva reflected on his role:

> I will be translating the vision of the company's founder into reality. As an implementor, I will be responsible for the daily tactical and operational aspects of accomplishing change and must be prepared to accept that my action—or inaction—will be a key determinant of the program's success.

Silva's action plan included the following key elements:

- Immediately: Silva would start to read books on change management and implementation and interview professionals in the field. He would identify and begin to make personal changes that would help him to be more successful in his new role.

- Month 1: Understand and analyze NP's business and how decisions were made

- Month 2: Interview employees; create a company vision and value statement

- Month 3: Roll out vision statement and performance management system;

announce off-hours events, start developing employee recognition rewards

- Month 4: Evaluate employee response to new programs; consider new enabling structures

- Month 5: Present results of initiatives to date; start developing a longer-term plan

While Silva had a plan of action going in, he was willing to adapt it if necessary to make his plans more likely to be accepted by the company. For example, he wondered if it would be too risky to roll out the performance management system in his third month on the job.

A NEW ROLE

Silva had a powerful vision of how a more dynamic and communicative culture could catapult the company to a more successful future. Yet he had many concerns as he considered whether to embark on this new role. While founder Seth Perkins agreed with his vision, he wondered if he could count on his attention and unequivocal support as he started making changes. Given that he had never worked in a role like this before, he was nervous about the level of responsibility he was about to assume. He would also need to earn the respect and enlist the cooperation of senior managers to make his initiatives a success. Henry wondered whether he would be jumping off a cliff or, alternatively, propelling the company to new heights.

Silva also thought about the personal challenges of choosing to work at New Power. A start-up company by its very nature was a high-stress, fast-paced environment—and he would have the mission of catalyzing powerful changes in the organization. He wondered how he would react if NP staff resisted his initiatives or disliked him personally for trying to transform the company. In taking on this job, Silva knew he would not win any popularity contests. The job could be incredibly exciting, yet it would also extract a high personal cost. The real question Silva asked himself was, "Am I up for this?"

Case

Susan Baskin: Aspiring Change Agent (A)

INTRODUCTION

Susan Baskin, a second-year MBA student at Columbia, enjoyed the feeling of April springtime and her last month in school before returning to the strategy consulting firm where she had previously worked. And yet, she was unsettled by her anticipated return. The firm was not the same firm she had left—it had merged with another, it was struggling with its performance, and morale was eroding. It seemed to be in need of some considerable "spring cleaning." Baskin was ambitious and talented and wanted to see the firm succeed, but many changes would need to happen. She had a plan, but would it work? And since she was by no means in charge of the firm, how would she make it happen?

Source: *Afroze Mohammed provided research and writing support for this case.*

CURRENT COMPANY SITUATION

In December, Rensight Associates, a boutique strategy consulting firm located in San Francisco, agreed to merge with JPZ Partners, a small product development company run by a group of partners with prestigious backgrounds in product development and operations management. The goal behind the merger was that JPZ could add to Rensight's customer offering by focusing on innovative approaches to new product development. The expectation was that JPZ's proprietary methodologies could be sold to Rensight customers and that the large rolodexes of JPZ's partner group would expand Rensight's customer base. The merger was heralded as an exciting entrepreneurial opportunity.

From the very start, however, the merger was controversial, and it actually led to a great deal of cultural friction and financial difficulties. Even though a few were excited about the merger, many in the firm did not see the strategic rationale for the union. This led to some early friction and the loss of two very senior and highly respected partners, both of whom were rainmakers. These partners thought the merger was a bad idea, and they joined another top tier strategy consulting firm. Although their departure caused unease, the merger went ahead. To signal a new beginning, the joint firm was given a new name, Strategic Innovation (SI). The JPZ team, mainly based in San Francisco, moved into the Rensight offices, and thus began the life of the new firm.

However, the year proved to be a very difficult one for the new firm, primarily because of weak financial performance. The former JPZ partners had several innovative new product development methodologies, but they failed to generate any revenues. By the end of the year, it became clear that the new firm was in financial difficulty. In October, 10% of the professional work force (out of a total of 300 people) was laid off, something that had only happened once in the firm's history, and on a much smaller scale.[1] Additional key senior people left the firm. When the year-end bonuses were delayed, the crisis became apparent to all staff.[2]

SI faced a series of strategic and cultural challenges. How it resolved these issues would determine the firm's future. Front and center was the core question—whether to "unravel" the merger, and in so doing, halt the tide of people leaving. In addition, the firm had to confront its immediate cash flow issues that were exacerbated by the emergent recession, when many customers were slashing their consultant budgets.

BASKIN'S RECOMMENDATIONS

Baskin was returning to the firm's San Francisco office as an engagement manager. Prior to attending CBS, she had worked in

[1] There was a small headcount reduction in the U.S. offices a few years earlier.
[2] Bonuses were to be paid out monthly to conserve cash flow in the near term.

both the firm's London and San Francisco offices and was viewed as being on the fast track. She had a very good relationship with senior partners, especially the senior partner in North America. She knew people in front and back offices throughout the firm from both work and social activities.

While at business school, she was privy to unique perspectives on the unfolding situation at the firm. Baskin spoke regularly with members of the partner group, which involved highly confidential discussions related to her decision to return. There was a very close network of the pre-MBA/pre-engagement manager level consultants. She also stayed close to the rank and file younger members of the firm. Each group had a distinct perspective about the future. The partners tended to favor a "wait and see how things work out" approach, while the younger members of the firm were increasingly frustrated and indeed had started leaving. In Baskin's mind, if the firm did not act decisively, it would die a slow death, because the best talent would bleed away.

Baskin had a plan and proposals for change which may have been on the radar screen, but had not yet been enacted. She was clear and articulate about actions for the partner group to take. Here was her thinking:

- Acknowledge openly that the merger with JPZ had failed. Partners should admit that the merger did not increase revenues, had led to the departure of key rainmaking partners, and had caused great uncertainty among staff.

- Disband the JPZ alliance in whatever way was possible and do so quickly. Partners should not worry about loss of face in making this change.

- Communicate openly and continuously with the members of the firm, sharing a simple message that "we can get back to the winning ways of the past" and that we will be "returning to our core."

- Individual partners and/or engagement managers should draw up lists of key consultants and persuade them to stay at the firm at all costs. They should continuously be in dialogue with these people to ensure that they would be on board and excited to make the firm a success.

The firm was small enough to do this on a one-to-one basis, and no time and expense should be spared. When good people leave, everyone loses hope.

- Accelerate and make decisions. Partners were far more comfortable doing analytic work with customers than with making internal people decisions. They were more comfortable in discussion than agreeing on a point of view. It was slowing change; she felt they could be making more decisions.

- Finally, and very importantly, the firm should change its name back to Rensight Associates. Though this change might cause some confusion, it would send a powerful message to the employees that "we are returning to our roots." Most clients still referred to the firm as Rensight Associates, and many did not even know that a name change had occurred. Returning to the Rensight name would be a clear signal that the merger was a bad decision and that things would return to the way they were when the firm was successful.

BASKIN'S ROLE IN DRIVING CHANGE

Baskin did not think of herself as a bystander or advisor, but wanted to be personally involved in implementing a number of the recommendations. As she said:

> I have a huge personal interest in driving change on my return. I decided to return to Rensight despite all the changes, because it has always been a company where I've loved working. I can have a big personal impact given my history at the firm. I have been through every level of the firm (with the exception of partner), and I have a good understanding of how people throughout the firm think about the current situation.
>
> I can leverage my relationships and trust specifically to help the partner group drive future changes into the lower levels of the firm, to persuade people to believe in the future and stick around, and to energize the consultant group to make the firm a great place to build a career again. This is a people business, and it is all about sharing a common goal and vision and being excited about coming to work each day. This will be the focus upon my return.

And she was specific on her entry action plan:

- I will speak to the VP of Global Talent and get assigned to her team on my return. This assignment would be in addition to my consulting responsibilities. I will work with the VP of Global Talent to put together a program of events and communications targeted at the associate and consultant groups, designed to make sure that they are fully in the loop about the future direction of the firm.

- I will organize a series of internal events that simply aim to energize the firm. On my trips to the San Francisco office this past year, I sensed a lack of energy and low morale. One should not underestimate the impact low morale has on the culture.

- I will act as a bridge between the partner-manager group and the junior members to ensure that partners really listen to feedback from the junior staff. The partners have become isolated and defensive in recent months and need to open up again. I will facilitate better communication.

All in all, she was hopeful. She wanted to succeed, and she wanted the firm to succeed. Baskin set out to return to the firm with these thoughts:

Hopefully, through hard work and by reaching out to many people in the company at different levels, I will be able to·have a big impact on renewing the culture of the firm, therefore ensuring its future success. I will be returning to this difficult situation, but am in a unique position to drive change within the organization and help it return to its previous successes. My goal upon returning is to make the company a place where I want to work. If I cannot, I will have to move on.

Reading

Converting Middle Powerlessness to Middle Power: A Systems Approach

Barry Oshry
Management Consultant

INTRODUCTION

As we unravel the pitfalls and possibilities of middle positions, it becomes clear that the "middle question" is but a piece of a larger challenge, the challenge of system literacy.

We are systems creatures; our consciousness is shaped by the nature of the system conditions in which we exist. For the most part, however, we are illiterate regarding systems: We do not see systems and we are unaware of the effects they have on our consciousness. As a consequence, we are at the mercy of system processes. Put us into certain systemic conditions, and when things go predictably

Source: An earlier version of this article was published in *National Productivity Review.*

wrong—with us or with our relationships with others—we fix the wrong things. We focus on fixing people rather than on helping people see, understand, and master the systemic conditions in which they exist.

The good news is this: We can do better. Once our focus shifts from fixing people to mastering a space, a whole other domain of strategies begins to emerge.

ARE MIDDLES OUR MODERN-DAY WITCHES AND DEMONS?

We are in the Dark Ages of organizational understanding. In the years ahead we will be mocked for the primitiveness of our beliefs just as we now look condescendingly upon those who in great earnestness hanged witches. In those dark days when things went badly, people had their witches to blame; now, when things go badly for us in our organizations, we have our demons. They had their evidence, we have ours. They hanged or burned their witches; we rotate our demons, or fire them or humiliate them or hang them out to slowly twist in the wind. Looking back on the witch burners from our "modern-day" perspective, we see how bizarre their beliefs were. When future "moderns" look back at us, what will they see?

When things go wrong in our organizations, we see demons. We point the finger at particular people—they are the ones we blame, and they are the ones we "fix" or replace or fire. Yet many of these demons are as innocent as the witches of yesteryear. You say, "Not so." All the evidence of your senses tells you that these people are in fact the culprits—and I say, "Welcome to twentieth-century witchcraft."

Proust suggests that "the voyage of discovery rests not in seeking new lands but in seeing with new eyes." Which is precisely what we need: a new set of lenses for looking at organizational behavior. With the right lenses, our demons will disappear.

THE MISSING LENS

Like you, I am a primitive person living in the Dark Ages of organization behavior. My lenses are as primitive as yours. But over the past thirty years I have had the privilege of observing many hundreds of organizations. Some of these organizations are like the ones you work in and are familiar with, others are simulations we have created for purposes of education and research. I have seen things that give me a glimmer into what is missing—the lenses we don't have.

What strikes me most about organizations is their regularity: The same scenarios keep happening again and again in the widest variety of settings—manufacturing, high technology, religious institutions, schools, community groups, government agencies, universities. The same patterns keep showing up—but rarely do people feel that they are living out a pattern. Each event seems specific to their unique organization, circumstances, and people. It matters little that all over the world many thousands of people in all varieties of organizations are having the very same experience.

The lens we are missing is a systemic one. We don't see systems; we just see people. We don't see system spaces; we see only the effects these spaces have on us. So when things go wrong, we blame what we see—the people, our demons.

THE MIDDLE SPACE

In this article we direct our attention to the Middle Space. A *Middle Space* is a space that pulls us between others. Whoever enters a Middle Space is caught between the conflicting agendas, perspectives, priorities, needs, and demands of two or more individuals or groups. Some Middle Spaces exist between contending vertical pressures (for example, supervisors between their managers and their work groups); others exist between lateral pressures (for example, a liaison between customers and producers); and many Middle Spaces have multiple contending forces vertically and laterally. Supervisors in plants and offices exist in Middle Spaces, as do department chairpersons and deans in universities, middle managers, heads of medical departments, union stewards, and people occupying the many hundreds of other positions in the widest spectrum of organizations and institutions. [In our analyses we will for the most part limit our discussion to the relatively simple Middle Space between Above and Below.] (See Exhibit 1.)

All of these are Middle Spaces. Some spaces are more Middle than others—the greater the differences between Above and Below in perspective, priorities, and needs, the more powerful the Middleness of the space.

Put people into a Middle Space and there is a story that develops with great regularity. The story varies from situation to situation, but the basic pattern is the same. It is a story of gradual disempowerment, in which reasonably healthy, confident, and competent people become transformed into anxious, tense, ineffective, and self-doubting wrecks. When this happens, we see these persons as our demons: It's too bad we're stuck with such weak and ineffective Middles; fire them or fix them or rotate them or let them swing slowly in the wind.

EXHIBIT 1   **The Middle Space—A Space That Pulls Us between Others**

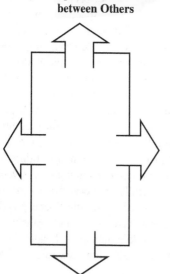

The questions is: If we look at these many different Middle stories through a systemic lens, what new understanding and what new strategies for empowerment open up for us?

THE FAMILIAR STORY OF MIDDLE DISEMPOWERMENT

Middles live in a tearing world.

It is a world in which people are pulling you in different directions;

Tops have their priorities and they expect your support;

Bottoms have their priorities—which are generally different from Tops'—and they expect your support;

Tops want you to get production out of Bottoms but you can't do that without the cooperation of Bottoms;

Bottoms want you to deliver on their needs and wants but you can't do that without the cooperation of Tops;

When Tops and Bottoms are in conflict, one or the other or both try to draw you in on their side.

You please one,

you displease the other;

you try to please both

you end up pleasing neither.[1]

Life in the Middle Space is hectic. You are always on the go. So much to do—for everyone—so little time. You spend your time working in other people's spaces and on other people's agendas. You feel squeezed. Tops are distant and remote;

[1] B. Oshry, *The Possibilities of Organization* (Power and Systems, Boston, 1992), pp. 68–69.

they're on another, less tangible wavelength, talking about strategy, planning, and organization. Meanwhile, Bottoms are looking to you for concrete direction and support, but you don't have the direction and support to give to them. You see the attitudes of Bottoms deteriorating and can't do anything about it. You feel useless, like a conduit simply carrying information back and forth. You spend your time going back and forth between Tops and Bottoms, explaining each to the other, justifying each to the other. There are lots of opportunities to let people down, and few opportunities to succeed. Tops don't seem to move your world ahead; they just give you more work and more uncertainty. You feel like a Ping-Pong ball, and Tops and Bottoms are the paddles. You are confused. (In the Middle Space, if you're not confused it means you're not paying attention. You talk to Tops and they make sense; you talk to Bottoms and they make sense too. It's hard to figure out what *you* believe.) Your actions are weak, compromises, never quite strong enough to satisfy Tops or Bottoms. Sometimes you feel important yet insignificant—as a telephone wire is important, but the real action is not with you, it's on either end of the line. You take a lot of flak from Bottoms, and never feel you can give it back (it wouldn't be managerial). For some reason you feel it's your responsibility to keep this system from flying apart, yet much of the time you feel invisible: When Tops and Bottoms are together, they talk as if you're not even there. You feel inadequate, never doing quite enough for Tops or Bottoms, never quite measuring up to the job. In time, you begin to doubt yourself: Maybe there is something wrong with you; maybe you're not smart enough or strong enough; maybe you're not as competent as you thought. And others in the organization mirror this impression. They see you as a nice person—trying hard, acting responsibly,

maybe even well-intentioned. It's just too bad you're so weak and ineffective. Well, maybe with a little more training or meditation or aerobic exercise or therapy or a better diet. . . .

Primitive, primitive! There are no demons here. This is not a personal story; it's a space story. The solution lies not in fixing people but in seeing and mastering the Middle Space. (See Exhibit 2.)

A SYSTEMIC LOOK AT HOW WE FALL INTO DISEMPOWERMENT IN MIDDLE POSITIONS

Our methods of preparing people for Middle positions are primitive. We promote them on the basis of dimensions which may be totally irrelevant to their ability to master Middleness. We train them on the technical aspects of the job. At best, we offer them leadership or supervisory training—which is Top's way of telling Middle how to handle Top's agenda, but which leaves Middle totally unprepared for the fact that Bottom has its own agenda for Middle in relation to Top.

No dean, no supervisor, no department chair, no section head should enter such a position without first understanding the dynamics of Middle positions and learning how to master the Middle Space.

There is a process that happens to us with great regularity when we enter the Middle Space, and this process lies at the heart of our disempowerment as Middles. Simply put, the process is this: We slide into the middle of *other people's* issues and conflicts and make these issues and conflicts *our own.* Once we slide into the middle, we are torn.

Objectively, even in Middle positions, we are not torn until we put ourselves into the position to be torn. Objectively, Above has its agenda for Below, and Below has

EXHIBIT 2   **From Healthy to Torn**

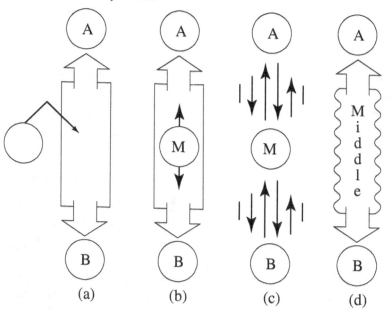

(a) A perfectly healthy, happy, and competent person about to enter the Middle Space between Above (A) and Below (B).
(b) Middle enters the space and attempts to be responsive to both A and B.
(c) Life becomes hectic.
(d) Middle becomes torn—confused, weak—and loses independence.

its agenda for Above. In that nanosecond before sliding in, Middle could be relaxedly observing, "Isn't it interesting the conflicts *they* are having *with one another*? What's it got to do with *me*?"

That moment never happens or, if it does, it is too brief. As Middles, we slide into the Middle and become torn between Above and Below. In that torn condition we feel that it is *our* responsibility, and our responsibility alone, to resolve their issues and conflicts. Our self-esteem now rests on *their* evaluations of how well we satisfy *them.* (See Exhibit 3.)

This "sliding-in" process is not a conscious choice we make. It is more like a reflex. We don't *do* it, it *happens* to us. We see a conflict *between others,* and we feel the full weight of that conflict resting on *our* shoulders.

Charlie complains to me, his supervisor, that the shower is not working. In a flash, I'm feeling that it's my fault that the shower is not working and that it's my responsibility to get it working. When I don't get it working fast enough because I can't get the approval from upstairs or because maintenance has this huge backlog, Charlie gets on my case, and I'm feeling weak and foolish and ineffective.

Louise has been called in to manage a meeting between Above and Below. This is an important meeting; Above and Below have a number of issues between them. Louise is very nervous;

EXHIBIT 3   We Slide into the Middle of Other People's Issues and Processes and Make Them Our Own.

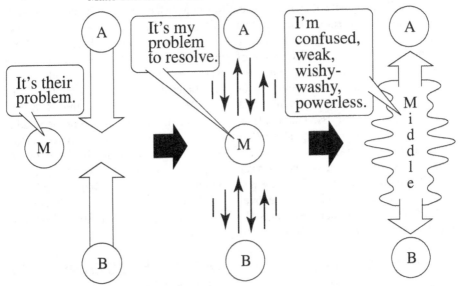

she feels that *her* success or failure rests on how well this meeting turns out.

If Charlie's supervisor and Louise had their systemic lenses on, they might see something else—a flashing sign: "Middleness—Beware of Sliding into the Middle!"—and they might pause to consider whether there might not be some more powerful way to handle this situation.

COACHING FOR MIDDLENESS: TWO STRATEGIES AND FIVE TACTICS FOR EMPOWERING YOURSELF IN THE MIDDLE

In the absence of a systemic lens, we see only specific events, specific circumstances, specific people—our demons—and we react. With a systemic lens, we see Middleness, and that seeing opens up for us new strategies and tactics for mastering the Middle Space.

STRATEGY I: DON'T SLIDE INTO THE MIDDLE OF THEIR ISSUES AND CONFLICTS AND MAKE THEM YOUR OWN.

At all times, be clear that this is not *your* problem. *They* are having an issue with one another. Do what you can to empower *them* to resolve *their* issues. Resist all efforts on their part to pull you into the Middle; the pressures can be quite strong. Understand that Above and Below don't mind at all having you feel responsible for resolving their problems.

STRATEGY II: DO NOT LOSE *YOUR* MIND.

The Middle Space is an easy place to lose your mind—*your* view, *your* thoughts, *your* perspective on what needs to happen. When we are torn, our attention is on Above and Below—what they think, what they want, what will satisfy them. In that Middle Space, however, we are in a unique position to formulate our own vision of what needs to happen. Generally it is the conflicting information that comes at us from Above and Below that confuses us and causes us great stress. That conflicting information, however, can also be the source of our unique strength. We need to seek out that information—rather than run from it. We need to allow it in and use it to formulate our unique Middle perspective.

With these two general strategies in mind, we can explore specific tactics by which we empower ourselves and others from the Middle position.

TACTIC 1: BE TOP WHEN YOU CAN, AND TAKE THE RESPONSIBILITY OF BEING TOP.

Sometimes *we* beg for trouble, and then complain when we get it. In certain situations we make ourselves Middle when we could be Top. Two Middles walk away from a meeting with Tops. One Middle says to the other, "Say, we didn't ask them if we could do (such and such). Let's go back and ask." The second Middle says, "We didn't ask, and they didn't tell us. If they don't like it, they'll tell us." The first Middle is uncomfortable with this; he wants to go back, to be in the middle, to find out what *they* want, to ask permission. The second Middle is uncomfortable with going back; she wants to go ahead, she wants to be Top, to figure out what she thinks needs to happen, to do it, and, if it turns out poorly, to ask forgiveness. (See Exhibit 4.)

TACTIC 2: BE BOTTOM WHEN YOU SHOULD.

Middles sometimes describe themselves as "sewer pipes": "Any garbage that Tops send us we simply pass along to Bottoms . . . without question." Middle passes the garbage along to Bottom;

EXHIBIT 4   **Be Top When You Can.**

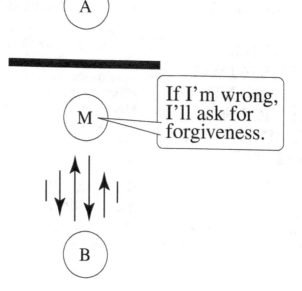

EXHIBIT 5   Be Bottom When You Should.

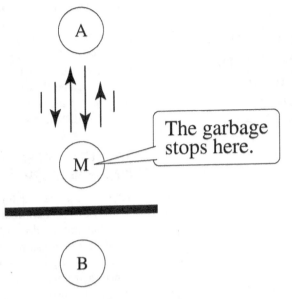

Bottom complains about the garbage; Middle justifies the garbage, explaining that it's really good stuff; Bottom still sees it as garbage and continues to complain; Middle passes these complaints along to Tops; Tops explain to Middle how the garbage really is good stuff and chastise Middle for not doing a good enough job convincing Bottoms; and on and on it goes. Middles, if they haven't lost their minds, are often in a better position than Tops to recognize garbage as garbage. Don't be just a mindless funnel. Be bottom. Work it out with Tops. The buck stops at the Top; the garbage stops in the Middle. (See Exhibit 5.)

TACTIC 3: BE COACH.

When others bring their complaints to Middles, Middles assume that it's *their* job to handle these complaints—which is precisely what it means to slide into the middle. Middles feel ashamed if they still haven't fixed some lingering complaint; they feel embarrassed to admit that all their efforts to date have failed; they feel guilty about not having got around to it; they feel weak and inadequate for not being a more powerful, more effective, more competent Middle. Why all the shame, guilt, and self-doubt, Middle? *It's not your problem.* They're the ones with the complaints. This doesn't mean that you are to be callous, unsympathetic, unfeeling; nor does it mean that you have no important role to play. People have problems. Let them know that you understand their situation, that you empathize with their condition, *and* that you are not going to solve their problem for them. That's not your job. Your job is to empower others to solve their own problems. Offer to be their coach—to work with them, to empower them so that they can do what *they* need to do to solve *their* problems. (See Exhibit 6.)

TACTIC 4: FACILITATE.

In the Middle we often find ourselves running back and forth between people, carrying messages from one to the other, explaining one to the other. We learn from

EXHIBIT 6 **Coach**

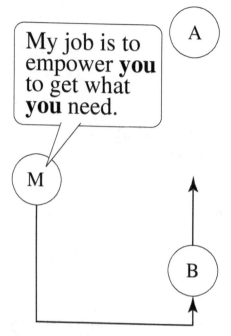

> My job is to empower **you** to get what **you** need.

the Customer what the Customer's needs are; we carry this information to the Producers; the Producers have questions, which we then bring back to the Customer; and then we carry the Customer's answers—along with a modified set of requirements—back to the Producers; and on and on it goes, sliding into the Middle. When we are in the middle of such a process, we are harried but we have a sense of the importance of our role—we are needed by both sides. When we are caught up in this process, it may never occur to us to ask: Why am *I* doing all this running? Why not step out of the middle; bring together those people who need to be together, and do whatever it takes to make their interaction with one another as productive as possible? (See Exhibit 7.)

New options open up for us when we see situations systemically. Our interactions in organizations are not simply people interacting with people—isolated events in unique circumstances. People always interact with one another in systemic spaces. When we are blind to the effects of these system forces, we invite the space to disempower us. When we see systemically, we understand the space, we know what it can do to us, and we know what challenges we face in mastering the space.

TACTIC 5: INTEGRATE WITH ONE ANOTHER.

There is another factor that relates to the power and contribution of Middles, and that has to do with the nature of Middles' relationships with one another. Middles strengthen themselves and enhance their contributions to their organizations by developing strong peer group relationships—among supervisors, among deans, among section heads, among plant managers, among department heads. Yet such relationships rarely develop. For most people the term "Middle Group" is an oxymoron—if it's a group, then it can't be Middles, and if there are Middles, it can't be a group. Middles, left to their own devices, do not become teams, they do not develop powerful and supportive relationships with one another. They generally resist all efforts at team development. This alienation from one another is a major contributor to their ineffectiveness in systems. So where does this dysfunctional alienation come from? Middles have their explanations: "I have little in common with the others." "There are a number of them I don't particularly like." "There's no potential power in this group." "We bore one another." "I'm not particularly interested in their areas." "They are my competitors so why collaborate?" "This one talks too much; that one's too emotional." It's demons all over again.

EXHIBIT 7 Facilitate

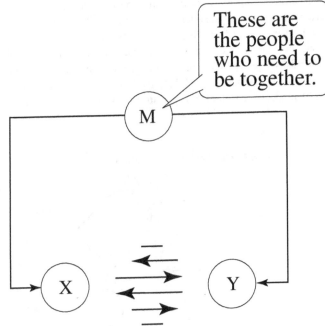

Through the systemic lens, we see a different story: Here in our Dark Ages we are oblivious to the impact different system spaces have on us. As Tops we regularly fall into territorial struggles with one another; as Bottoms we regularly experience great pressures to conform to whatever the group opinion is; as Middles we regularly become isolated and alienated from one another.[2]

The Middle Space is a diffusing space; it pulls us apart from one another and toward other individuals and groups we service or manage. We disperse. We spend our time away from one another. In that configuration our specialness becomes highlighted—our uniqueness, our separateness from one

another, our differences. In the Top group we become territorial—a collection of "Mine"s; in the Bottom group we become "We"; and in the Middle group we become a collection of "I"s. Whatever real differences exist among us become magnified. Each of us feels unique, special, different. We feel we have little in common with one another, we feel competitive with one another, we are critical of one another, we deal at the surface with one another, we are wary of one another, and we see little potential power in us as a collectivity.

There is a vicious cycle that happens to us in the Middle Space. The space pulls us apart from one another; that apartness heightens our separateness, our alienation from one another; and our alienation reinforces our staying apart—why would we want to spend time together when we have so little in common, we don't like one

[2] For further information on the predictable relationship problems that develop among Tops, among Bottoms, and among Middles, see B. Oshry, *Space Work* (Power and Systems, Boston, 1992).

another, there is no potential for power in the collective, we are competitors, and so forth? So we stay apart, which reinforces the alienation, and on and on it goes. All of which is unfortunate because that Middle Space is a potentially powerful space. There are productive relationships to be had and powerful contributions to be made. (See Exhibit 8.)

Middle peer groups are, potentially, the integrating mechanisms for their systems. They are in the best position to tie these systems together, to provide strong and informed leadership to their Bottoms or to the groups they service, and to create consistency, evenness, and fairness throughout the system.

EXHIBIT 8   **The Vicious Cycle of Middle Alienation**

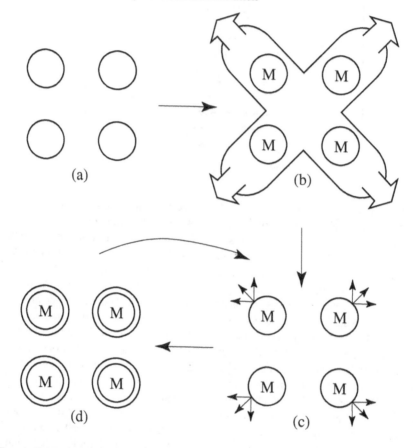

(a) Four individuals who under other circumstances might get along perfectly well with one another . . .
(b) Enter a middle space.
(c) The space pulls them apart from one another and toward the groups they service or manage.
(d) In their separateness they harden into an "I–ness" mentality which reinforces their staying apart.

Middles integrate the system by integrating with one another. Each Middle moves out, manages or services his/her part of the system and collects intelligence about what is happening there; Middles come together and share their intelligence; they move back out and then come together—moving back and forth between diffusing and integrating. Goodbye demons. Goodbye, uninformed, weak, fractionated, surpriseable, uncoordinated Middles. Through this process the Middle Space becomes the most solidly informed part of the system. Individual Middles become more knowledgeable about the total system; they become able to provide more consistent information to others; they become better able to provide guidance and direction; there is less unproductive duplication among units; there is more evenness of treatment. (See Exhibit 9.)

Middles who integrate are a potent force in their systems. They develop a powerful support network for themselves; they provide informed leadership for others; and they lighten the burden of their Tops, making it possible for Tops to do the Top work they should be doing. This is the possibility of Middle integration. When Middles are in the grip of the Middle Space, however, they do not see integration as a possibility for *them*—"Maybe it's a good idea for some people in some circumstances but not in our organization, given the situation *we're* facing, and certainly not with this particular cast of characters; we have no reason to integrate, our responsibilities are diverse, we have so little in common, we don't get along, we are too competitive . . . " and so forth.

In the absence of a systemic lens, Middles feel that they do not integrate because of how they feel about one another. When viewed systemically, the truth is seen to be just the other way around: Middles feel the way they do as a consequence of not integrating; were they to integrate they would experience one another quite differently.

EXHIBIT 9 **Middles Integrate the System by Integrating with One Another**

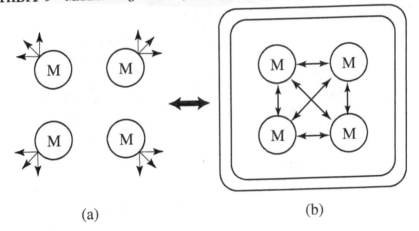

(a)

(b)

(a) Middles move back and forth between servicing, managing, and collecting intelligence about their pieces of the system, and
(b) Coming together, integrating, sharing their intelligence.

Group empowerment supports individual empowerment. Without integration, Middles face the tearing pressures of the Middle Space alone. With integration, they create an informational and emotional base that strengthens each individual Middle.

YOU DON'T KNOW WHAT YOU DON'T KNOW UNTIL YOU KNOW IT

When Middles don't integrate, they have no basis for comprehending the possibilities of empowered middleness. Middles may think that the range of possibilities is from 1 to 5, and since they're at 4, that's not so bad. Only when they integrate successfully do Middles realize that the range of possibilities was from 1 to 100, and 4 wasn't so hot after all. (See Exhibit 10.)

Middle integration creates a whole new level of possibility for Middles. From facing system pressures alone and unsupported, they become part of a powerful and supportive peer group. From being

uninformed and surpriseable, they become part of the most well-informed part of the system. From being Ping-Pong balls batted back and forth in other people's games, they become central players who create and manage their own games.

MIDDLES INTEGRATING

For example, we find a Middle group in a highly sensitive chemicals plant whose members have been integrating for over seven years. According to the Plant Manager, these Middles run the day-to-day business of the plant and do it better than he ever did. These Middles like, respect, and support one another: They have such a sense of teamwork that they have created their own summer and winter uniforms; they are respected by Above and Below as a strong and informed leadership team; they do their own hiring into the group; and they are rewarded (50 percent) for how well they individually manage their units and (50 percent) for how well they collectively integrate the system as a

EXHIBIT 10   The Range of Middle Possibilities

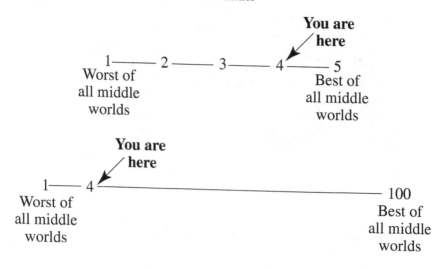

whole. Their Plant Manager is liberated by this process; rather than being mired in the details of day-to-day operations, he spends his time on "Top business"—exploration of where the industry is heading and how to prepare for the future, community relations, interaction with headquarters, integration with his peers, and so forth. Not the way it usually goes with Middles.

In another setting, we find a Middle in a software company who had been having difficulty selling top management on a project idea. The Middle brought the project to the Middle group, which had been integrating for several months. Without the knowledge or permission of senior management, the Middle group took on the project. All the necessary expertise was in that group—marketing, sales, production, finance, and human resources. They did their research meticulously; they put together a package top management could not and did not refuse. Great pride, great teamwork, great effectiveness, and significant contribution to profitability. Not the way it usually goes with Middles.

WHAT *ARE* MIDDLES GOOD FOR?

Do we really need Middles? I am asked that question regularly. The truth is: We do not need weak, uninformed, torn, confused, wishy-washy, and fractionated Middles. However, this is not the only available Middle option. Middles do have a unique perspective in organizations and special contributions to make. These can be developed only as Middles learn to see their condition systemically and learn to master the Middle Space. That mastery does not come easily. To be "a Middle who

stays out of the Middle" makes special demands on Middles. Middles may complain about their current "no-win" situation, yet, when they discover what it takes to empower themselves, they may decide they want no part of it.

There is great need for empowered Middles—Middles who act responsibly toward others; who are committed to their success; and who can deliver the information, direction, and support others need. The challenge for Middles is to do this while maintaining their own independence of thought and action. And that requires a different kind of fortitude, one that keeps Middles from being torn apart individually and collectively—preserving their boundaries rather than allowing them to be overrun; shaping situations rather than being shaped by them; standing up to both Above and Below; sometimes saying "no" or "not now" or "not this way" rather than dancing to every tune others play for them.

Middles who stay out of the middle; who empower themselves and others; who are Top when they can be; who are Bottom when they should be; who coach and who facilitate; and above all else, who integrate with one another—these are a different order of Middles. They value themselves and they bring value to their systems.

WHAT HAPPENED TO THE DEMONS?

What happened to those weak, confused, wishy-washy, fractionated, powerless Middles? They weren't sent off for therapy; they weren't replaced or fixed or fired. When Middles see and master the Middle Space, the demons—like the witches of yesteryear—simply disappear.

Case

The Young Change Agents

My experience at AIESEC helped shape my future. It is there I learned that opportunities and challenges come only to people who take up leadership roles within the organization. If you don't take on those roles, these seemingly immense challenges and opportunities just don't come your way. Once I joined a large corporate enterprise and tried to foster change, it really tested everything I had learned.

James Shaw

Young, ambitious, and idealistic, James Shaw had always been attracted to situations where he could have an impact and make a difference. As he described to an interviewer, "I only get out of bed in the morning if I know I am making a difference in the work I do. I cannot stand the idea of being one of those people who check their values in at the door in the morning and pick them up again on the way back home."

His training ground was a well-known student organization, AIESEC, but his first test in the corporate arena—at Price Waterhouse (PW; later PricewaterhouseCoopers, or PwC)—proved to be more challenging on many fronts. Nevertheless, his efforts at instigating change attracted a popular business journal to feature a story on

Source: This case was written by Nikhil Tandon, Research Associate, under the supervision of Prof. Todd Jick and Prof. Maury Peiperl, as a basis for class discussion rather than to illustrate effective or ineffective handling of an administrative situation. This case draws from the article "Fire Starters" by Bill Breen and Cheryl Dahle in the December 1999 issue of *Fast Company,* and from an interview with James Shaw.

Shaw and two of his colleagues with an eye-catching title, "Fire Starters."

THE AIESEC EXPERIENCE

Shaw, a native New Zealander and a student at Victoria University in Wellington, joined AIESEC, the world's largest student-run international student exchange and leadership development organization, during his university days. In typical AIESEC fashion, he was given responsibility immediately upon joining for recruiting, training, motivating, utilizing and retaining the organization's members. One year later, Shaw was elected president of the local committee and subsequently, president of the national office of AIESEC in New Zealand.

Shaw recalled:

The experiences from my days at AIESEC were strongly shaped by the training we gave and received at our frequent conferences. At the time I was a member, there was a very deliberate leadership program focusing on developing knowledge, skills, attitudes, and values associated with corporate social responsibility, entrepreneurship, cultural understanding, higher education, and the information society.

My experience at AIESEC over the years nurtured and validated my idealism. It built my sense of values and vision and gave me a community and network of trusted colleagues. It gave me my skills and acumen—and ridiculously high standards. Ultimately it gave me entrance into Price Waterhouse, in the form of a six-month traineeship in the London office.

JAMES SHAW AT PRICEWATERHOUSE COOPERS

Shaw joined the Learning and Education group of Price Waterhouse in February 1998, six months before the organization's merger with Coopers & Lybrand. With no specific projects planned for him during his traineeship, it was up to Shaw to keep himself constructively engaged. He did so by spending time networking within the firm and making suggestions on ways to improve processes wherever he felt improvements were needed. As a result, he built for himself a reputation for being enthusiastic, creative, and ambitious, as well as naïve, inexperienced, and unrealistic.

Shaw's circumstances at PwC, in contrast to those at AIESEC, resulted in an understandable feeling of insecurity. After all, he had moved from a position of executive leadership at AIESEC—a large global organization, where he was actively involved with the organization's global strategy, cross-cultural learning, and membership development—to being a "staff number in a database, a 'Golden Cog' in another large global organization." Shaw described his experience as

"humbling. I lost my self-confidence, the surety that I could do anything if I had the will to do it."

He recalled, "In some ways running AIESEC was more challenging than running a Big Five firm. Imagine having to develop a strategy to recruit, train, motivate, direct, and retain staff without the luxury of paying them—staff that were already studying 20 hours a week, working in bars and restaurants 20 hours a week, and hanging out with friends the rest of the time!"

Shaw was also shocked by the spending power of PwC. In his words,

The stationery budget for the 10-person Learning and Education group was substantially higher than the total operating budget of the national office of AIESEC New Zealand which supported four executive staff and sent us to national and international conferences every year. And, technologically, the world's leading professional services company felt clunky and painfully behind AIESEC which had developed an extraordinary Web-based system for knowledge management, learning, communities of interest, management information, communications and operational systems.

Although he admitted that it was not fair to compare PwC with AIESEC, as the two were very different organizations with different objectives, he felt that the student association (AIESEC) could actually teach the well-known PwC "a few tricks."

Said Shaw, "I had the Ten Commandments of Intrapreneurship from the book *Intrapreneuring* by Gifford Pinchot [Exhibit 1] framed above my desk. These served as a constant reminder to me that I was there to make a difference—and with a will anything was possible."

EXHIBIT 1   The Ten Commandments of Intrapreneurship

THE TEN COMMANDMENTS OF INTRAPRENEURSHIP

1. Come to work each day willing to be fired.
2. Circumvent any orders aimed at stopping your dream.
3. Do any job needed to make your project work, regardless of your job description.
4. Find people to help you.
5. Follow your intuition about the people you work with and work only with the best.
6. Work underground as long as you can. Publicity triggers the corporate immune system.
7. Never bet on a race unless you are running in it.
8. Remember: it is easier to ask for forgiveness than for permission.
9. Be true to your goals, but be realistic about the ways to achieve them.
10. Honor your sponsors.

Source: G. Pinchot, *Intrapreneuring* (San Francisco: Berrett-Koehler, 2000).

THE OPPORTUNITY

Keith Bell, the PwC partner responsible for both the recruitment and community affairs functions in the U.K., was also on the AIESEC international board. It was Bell who had hired Shaw and another AIESEC alum, Amy Middelburg. Bell asked Middelburg to work on three major areas:

- Supporting the international partnership between PwC and AIESEC.

- Supporting the U.K. Community Investment office.

- Secondment to an external partner—the Prince of Wales Business Leaders Forum.

These activities gave Middelburg an overview of the community affairs area. She had a lot of ideas, and increasingly hinted to Bell that a number of improvements could be made. Taking her cue, Bell asked Middelburg for a two-page list of suggestions on what the firm could do to improve in the area.

Middelburg was excited about the possibility of making a difference to a large organization like PwC and through it, to the communities that it operated in. She recruited Shaw to work with her on this project.

Recalls Shaw, "To get ourselves going our first questions were, 'How does PwC want to be seen by the community?' and 'What is the difference we want to make in the world?' We went looking for a statement of vision and values for the organization and were not satisfied with what we found."

So, instead of giving Bell a two-page list of ideas, the two worked over the weekend, working late into the night, and gave Bell a 10-page paper titled 'NewCo Values and NewCo's Value.' (NewCo was the 'nom de plume' of the new organization after the Price Waterhouse and Coopers and Lybrand merger.) The paper proposed a highly improbable notion: Post-merger, PwC would measure its business success not only by its financial goals but also by its effects on society and the global environment. In addition the company would encourage its clients to apply the same values to their business practices.

The proposal meant that the firm would have to adopt internal business practices and services for clients that, in addition to being economically viable, were also socially responsible and environmentally sound. It would mean that PwC would volunteer to be held accountable for the practices of a wide group of stakeholders—the partners of the firm, their staff, their clients, their suppliers, and the communities in which they operated.

The proposition was that if this was done, the long-term value of PwC would be significantly enhanced as the business would enjoy increased loyalty from the staff and clients, reduced risk of negative action by regulators or nongovernmental organizations, and increased operational and financial effectiveness. In addition, it would help stabilize and enhance the conditions for healthy global and national marketplaces.

The proposal made by Shaw and Middelburg was influenced by exposure to the issues of corporate social responsibility during their days at AIESEC. They had raised the issue of "sustainable development" (also called sustainability).[2]

This was a radical idea for a mammoth consulting firm with a strong accounting pedigree and a history of being relentlessly focused on the bottom line. It represented a bold and a risky leap to the leading edge of nonfinancial reporting—and to the adoption of a focus on a "triple bottom line" (economic, social, and environmental).

[2] *Sustainability* is defined as: "Meeting the needs of the present generation without compromising the ability of the future generations to meet their needs." (Brundtland Report, 1987; refer to Appendix 1.)

Bell was impressed and he forwarded the paper to the global head of branding, to the partner who had recently started the Reputation Assurance (stakeholder reporting) business line, and to the global head of HR, as well as a number of other key leaders in the firm.

Shaw and Middelburg suddenly found themselves getting a lot of attention and being invited into meetings. This attention encouraged the duo to approach other senior managers in the organization themselves. They were positively received and almost always seemed to be able to gain agreement, but never any concrete action.

Shaw said, "I was not sure if we were being patronized, but the executives we were meeting were not the type who liked to waste their time. They genuinely seemed interested in hearing our perspective. After all, in the first year after the merger, the firm had a goal of recruiting 50,000 graduates globally and they wanted to know what their target audience was thinking about their organization."[3]

GAINING SUPPORT FOR SUSTAINABILITY AS A NEW PLATFORM FOR THE BUSINESS DECISION

Middelburg could win people over with her talent for impassioned speech. Shaw said, "When it came to winning new sponsors and building the network, I credit her

[3] In the pro-employee market of the 1990's, research consistently showed that "Generation X" graduates were making employment decisions based in part on factors related to corporate social responsibility and sustainability, such as the prospective employer's organizational vision, environmental record, and employee investment.

with every big breakthrough we made in the subsequent years. She used to carry around copies of 'NewCo Values and NewCo's Value' on the off chance she met someone who could help us. She is an incredible networker."

It was at the champagne event celebrating the first day of the merger with Coopers & Lybrand on July 1, 1998, that Middelburg headed straight to Ian Brindle, head of the U.K. firm and a member of the Global Leadership Team, and asked him directly what the values of the new firm were going to be. This bold approach earned Shaw and Middelburg a follow-up conversation in Brindle's office within a week.

Following their meeting with Brindle, Shaw and Middelburg were asked if they'd be interested in joining the effort to start the Reputation Assurance group—the firm's offering on social and environmental reporting. The duo grabbed the opportunity and joined a small team incubating the service for eventual release.

Shaw recalls,

In the first year we were very excitable about every meeting we had with the various national and global executives, thinking that we could change things with the sheer power of our inspiration. There was something different about these meetings—the stakes seemed much higher because we were talking about an agenda for change rather than a short-term commercial arrangement—so we were a little nervous. However, over time we became somewhat blasé, even cynical, about meetings from which no actionable result seemed to occur. We became more astute about creating strategies for change and about what it would take.

In part the lack of action was because we were short of specific

proposals for action—we had been talking about certain principles on which to base action, organizational values, and strategic direction. This was certainly where our talent lay—not in operationalizing it. We may not have recognized that early enough, and in so doing we made it easy for people to agree with us in principle and hard for them to take any specific action.

The other major impediments Shaw and Middelburg faced in getting any concrete action were the organizational culture and the passive resistance from some of the executives they engaged with. With its long history of stability, PwC had a deep sense of risk aversion consistent with its accounting background. There was a tendency to engage in extended intellectual debate with little action—again, a product of the level and type of education of the staff, and their roles as consultants rather than executors. It was an organization where the duo's ideas were too "radical" to implement.

Said Shaw, "What we were talking about was hard to disagree with, without appearing like a 'heartless capitalist'—so executives agreed but then took no action, or agreed and then suggested actions or projects for us that would have been a diversion from our goal but were disguised as consistent with it."

Although Shaw and Middelburg characterized themselves as having "zero stature and zero credibility," with no results forthcoming, they felt that that their proposal could stand a chance if they could elicit strong executive sponsorship. They went into networking mode and finally hit the target at AIESEC's global annual conference in Stockholm, where they found a key executive sponsor, Jermyn Brooks. Brooks had been the worldwide chairman of PW prior to the merger, and post-merger (prior to his own planned retirement), he was responsible for completing the integration of the two firms globally.

Recalled Shaw, "Amy went looking for Brooks and proceeded to tell him all about our paper on values. He was intrigued, and later we ended up spending a whole afternoon sitting in his office chatting about these ideas. It was incredible—the synergy was apparent from the first moment."

Brooks suggested taking on a trainee in his office to work on the issue of sustainability. Said Shaw, "This was too good an opportunity to pass up. So rather than going through normal channels I headhunted Fabio Sgaragli, who had been the national president of AIESEC Italy and with whom I had also worked at AIESEC International in Brussels. Sgaragli was deeply talented and a real visionary. With Sgaragli in the global Chairman's office we would be able to create access to the rest of the global leadership."

FORMING A SUSTAINABILITY "SKUNK WORKS"

With the arrival of Sgaragli, the trio became a tightly knit team. Shaw and Middelburg worked with the Reputation Assurance Group and Sgaragli in Brooks' office.

Said Sgaragli, "With this kind of project, it is impossible to overestimate the importance of having a community—people who share the same values and vision as you do. These few people around you remind you in the face of overwhelming apathy or opposition that you are not crazy. Or if you are, at least a couple of other people are too."

The three found this mutual support important, especially when they all had to fit the sustainability agenda in with their "day jobs." They met over lunch and after work to plan their next steps. The group was operating "underground," with senior sponsors and supporters but no direct manager. They were a co-equal team, leading one another, but they recognized one another's distinct strengths—Middelburg the powerful communicator, Sgaragli the campaign strategist, and Shaw the developer of models and theories.

Said Middelburg, "When one of us was down, the others would pull them up. Later, it would be someone else's turn to be down. We were always there for one another. We had our own rules about how we worked: We kept one another accountable and made one another feel guilty if we hadn't delivered. But we also gave one another a break when no one else could or would." This teamwork proved to be one of their most critical assets in the time to come.

The trio concentrated their efforts on broadening the buy-in. With Brooks' help, they secured meetings with other global managing partners.

They used different strategies for making their pitch to the various partners. For some audiences, the focus was on "how to make it happen," so they advocated a couple of proposals for moving the agenda forward and asked for specific help in doing so. With others, the trio focused on how the new values would distinguish PwC from its competitors, as a strategy and recruitment differentiator.

As the three expanded their network, their reputation as a passionate and audacious team grew. Recalls Shaw, "One of the partners I used to work for said, 'James, I can't believe the access you have. I have been a partner here for 10 years, and I still haven't met Brooks.'"

GAINING MOMENTUM AT PWC; CHANGE MANAGEMENT ROLE

In mid-1999 Brooks asked Shaw, Middelburg, and Sgaragli to work on an internal project to review the implications for PwC of actively advocating sustainability and corporate social responsibility. Recalls Shaw, "Besides the tangible output—a report titled 'Money Does Grow on Trees'—our role evolved into 'change management.' I only learned it was called that after the fact, though—I was describing our activities to a senior PwC change consultant, who said, 'Oh you guys are doing change management!'"

The team's goal was to persuade the partners to endorse the concepts in "Money Does Grow on Trees" and to commit to a plan of implementation. The three did not leave anything to chance. While researching and writing the report, they created a "war room," posting on the walls a "who's who" list of the organization's leadership, their level of interest in the project, and their relationships to known allies.

To build credibility with the leadership, they signed onto the project an impressive list of outside advisers, including the legendary environmental advocate and CEO of Interface Inc., Ray Anderson, and the founding CEO of VISA International, Dee Hock. They mapped out the events that needed to happen over the next two years to make PwC an advocate for social responsibility and revised the plan monthly to account for new alliances built (or not built), and changes in the leadership structure and firm's strategy.

The team circulated the report to the managing partners of every country in the PwC network, as well as the heads of every service line and industry group.

With every report they included an invitation to join an e-mail discussion for people wanting to learn more about sustainability and build it into their operations.

They tried to replicate their own story using the AIESEC network to supply other young, idealistic trainees to internship positions with other groups and senior partners within the organization. In addition to their regular duties these interns were tasked by their sponsors with "causing as much trouble as possible" and feeding their employers with the sustainability theme.

During this time period, a leading U.S.-based business magazine (*Fast Company*) covered their story, and Shaw, Middelburg, and Sgaragli found themselves being contacted by its readers from countries as diverse as Kenya, Malaysia, Canada, and Australia. Many of these readers were PwC employees. These people were invited to join the discussion group.

The team found that, with the validation given to their project by external media, they were taken more seriously in meetings with senior executives at PwC. Shaw described this as:

the inverse of the saying "Familiarity breeds contempt." Most people are humble, even insecure, and they feel that their own words may not be taken seriously. Because they know their colleagues, they assume that the same is true of their colleagues; they don't take their colleagues' words seriously either. So, when someone with a very credible reputation comes along from outside, they take them more seriously than their own colleagues. Did we take advantage of the credibility that story gave us? Sure!

"The Trio," as the team started to be known, also made efforts to increase the familiarity of people in their new network with the language and the concepts they were using. They attended numerous external conferences and made sure that they took many executives and line staff with them. At one point Brooks even arranged for then-CEO James Schiro to co-chair a day at the Aspen Institute conference on sustainability alongside the CEO of Shell International—which led to further breakthroughs in bringing the sustainability agenda forward to board level.

The greatest challenge the team faced was in activating the network. Said Shaw:

> We were surprised that a lot of people did not demonstrate much initiative. Many people wanted to become directly involved with our team, which we did not have a budget or a capacity for. And we didn't want to drag activity to the center anyway—we wanted to support people in the lines to create change there, not become a bottleneck in the hierarchy.
>
> We did not believe that the will would come easily. The question was always, "Is the firm really willing to change?" It was a long shot, but it was a chance in a million to affect the world's leading business advisory firm. The impact would be so significant, much bigger than the firm itself.

Said Brooks, "I was hopeful but less optimistic. There were plenty of people whose noses were so far down to the level of delivering their daily targets that they regarded this as nice but basically unessential."

The team was officially adopted into the strategy group of the firm, with a particular focus on sustainability. Their goal was to get the sustainability agenda onto the management agenda of the firm. The timing seemed opportune. Moreover, the merger itself stimulated a discussion about the values of the firm and the need to recruit on a large scale a very different workforce whose values themselves might be more compatible with the sustainability agenda. The "Fire Starters" were right in the middle of this—continually chosen to voice their opinions as representatives of the "next generation of employees."

OUTCOMES

The young change agents had started a process of change in a mammoth organization. Their targets, as they characterized them, were to achieve the following tangible outcomes:

- To develop, through a rigorous stakeholder dialogue process, a set of values that was visionary and called to a purpose higher than profit alone—and to implement those values root and branch across the organization (i.e., to ensure that we were living by them).

- To start the process of "triple-bottom-line" reporting (economic, environmental, and social) to all PwC stakeholders (the partners, staff, clients, suppliers, and community) on a global level (although the team suggested a series of country-level reports in the early stages to build comfort and experience with it).

- To adopt principles of sustainability into the advice PwC was offering to clients—that is, to ensure that the recommendations they were adopting assisted them to become more sustainable organizations, not necessarily just more efficient or profitable at any cost.

- To invest in becoming the market leader in the provision of directly related sustainability services—for example, triple-bottom-line reporting, environmentally sound and socially conscious business processes, sustainability in business strategy, supply chain accountability, and ethics.

Said Shaw, "Our goals changed over time. In the first six months we were very focused on values. In time we added the concept of 'triple-bottom-line reporting,' and focused on it during the second 12 months. After those 18 months had passed we started working for Brooks directly and adopted the last two objectives, which we have focused on to this day."

Further outcomes included the following:

- PwC's new values were developed about six months after the merger by an extensive process that included the inputs of the trio, and there were three main clusters: excellence, teamwork, and leadership. There was no explicit language, however, to the effect that community and social responsibility were more important than profitability.

- PricewaterhouseCoopers took tentative first steps toward triple-bottom-line reporting. The U.K. firm created the first ever Big Five stakeholder report—an online, interactive website called "PwCTalking," which won plaudits from *Accountancy Age* and the *Financial Times* both for taking the high ground of greater transparency and for being forward-thinking in the use of new media. The trio co-developed the site with the firm's public relations team, and was responsible for most of the content—in other words, they were the internal audit team on the firm's first non-financial report. The South African firm also released a report to stakeholders, and other countries were considering the move to stakeholder reporting as well. Plans were also in place to release, for the first time, a global, organization-wide report on an annual basis.

- The new global board at PwC adopted sustainability as one of its top strategic priorities, and there was a working group responsible for advancing it on the management agenda. The Values and Sustainability team, which in addition to Middelburg and Sgaragli now included AIESEC alumni Aaron Caplan, Marco Villa, and others, directly supported the working group. Additionally, there were over 200 members in the internal sustainability e-mail discussion group, which covered more than 30 countries and included a significant cross-section of industry group leaders, country executives, service line leaders, and global executives—as well as a large number of line staff from different services and countries. Thus there was management intent, and a community of interest supporting it, but the process of bringing the principles of sustainability and corporate social responsibility into the existing client services would involve changing the thought processes of 150,000 employees—and progress was slow.

- Brooks convened, and the trio managed, a series of roundtables among different lines of service that related to sustainability (including Environmental Services, Reputation Assurance, Business Ethics, and Contractor Compliance). In addition, they networked with and supported other inter-service line initiatives. Eventually these services combined into a Sustainability Services offering. This was due in part to the trio's efforts to have the services work together, and in part to external competition (KPMG was already offering services to clients under that banner).

- There was a new executive development program in place for new junior partners and senior managers from countries where PwC wanted to have future representation on the global executive, such as Turkey, China, India, and Brazil. Future leaders from those countries were handpicked to go on a two-month development project with an NGO in another developing country, including Tajikistan, Swaziland, and India. This highly rated program was developed by Jermyn Brooks and Marco Villa to develop future leadership for the firm that not only helped to balance it culturally, but also provided leaders who had a strong grounding in sustainability concepts.

Said Sgaragli:

> The firm made enormous progress toward becoming a sustainable organization. How much of it was because of us? This is a really hard question to answer, because a number of things happened that were consistent with recommendations we made or initiatives we suggested. We will never know—and it doesn't really matter. I believe we had a strong influence on the pace and direction of change, and we continue to do so.

The most tangible sign of the progress that PwC had made on the issue of sustainability came when research on 'Selling Sustainable Success' conducted by the International Business Leaders Forum (also called the Prince of Wales International Business Leaders Forum) rated PricewaterhouseCoopers as having the most developed program for deep and wide implementation of sustainability and corporate social responsibility among its peers, which included Accenture, A. D. Little, Bain & Co., CGEY, Deloitte Touche Tohmatsu, ERM, Ernst & Young, ICF Consulting, KPMG, and MMC.

Against 13 criteria, PwC took the top position for best practice. The firm demonstrated the following progress:

Good Practice

Fully in place:

- Active senior executive championship for corporate social responsibility (CSR).

- Public statement of the values of the firm.

- Code of conduct and statement of business principles.

- An internal CSR-review team.

- NGO clients and pro bono charity work.

- Structured employee-community involvement.

- Contribution to global public policy debates.

Good Practice

Some activity getting there:

- Sensitizing employees to CSR through formal programs.

- Formal procedures for stakeholder engagement and dialogue.

- CSR-related client services.

Good Practice

In discussion:

- Financial disclosure.

- Non-financial disclosure.

- Explicit CSR emphasis in all client services.

The firm had no criteria on which it was rated as having either "unsure or mixed indications" or "little or no evidence."

EPILOGUE

Recalled Shaw:

> It is inevitable that PwC will eventually move down the same path as Shell, DuPont, and a number of other organizations struggling with the multi-decade task of becoming sustainable organizations. But because they are "smelly industries" and PwC is not, we may be taking longer to start and not be as urgent about it once we have started. Shell was galvanized by crisis—the loss of public confidence after the Ogoniland and Brent Spar incidents. We have not had our Brent Spar yet.

With the collapse of Enron in late 2001 and the ensuing scandal at its auditors Andersen, the Big Five accounting firms—of which PwC was one—came under intense public scrutiny for their commitment to transparency and accountability toward their stakeholders. PwC's new CEO Sam di Piazza committed the firm to much greater levels of public reporting, and to shedding any business lines that could cause conflicts of interest. The Big Five's "Brent Spar" had arrived.

Appendix 1

The Brundtland Report and Sustainable Development

THE BRUNDTLAND REPORT

The United Nations set up the World Commission on Environment and Development, headed by Gro Harlem Brundtland, Prime Minister of Norway, as an independent body in 1983. Its brief was to re-examine critical threats to the environment, to develop proposals to solve them, and to ensure that human progress would be sustained through development without bankrupting the resources of future generations.

In its 1987 report entitled "Our Common Future," the commission served notice that the time had come for a marriage of economy and ecology, so that governments and their people could take responsibility not just for environmental damage, but also for the policies that caused the damage. It was not too late to change those policies; but the report warned that immediate action would have to be taken. In this, perhaps the most important document on the future of the world, the urgency of changing certain policy decisions, some of which threatened the very survival of the human race, was made abundantly clear.

The report provided a key statement on sustainable development, defining it as:

> Development that meets the needs of the present without compromising the ability of future generations to meet their own needs.

It aimed at securing a global equity, redistributing resources toward poorer nations while encouraging their economic growth. The report also suggested that equity, growth, and environmental maintenance were simultaneously possible and that each country was capable of achieving its full economic potential while at the same time enhancing its resource base. It recognized that achieving this equity and sustainable growth would require technological and social change.

The report highlighted three fundamental components to sustainable development: environmental protection, economic growth, and social equity. The environment would have to be conserved and the resource base enhanced, by gradually changing the ways in which we develop and use technologies. Developing nations would have to be allowed to meet their basic needs of employment, food, energy, water, and sanitation. If this was to be done in a sustainable manner, then there was a definite need for a sustainable level of population. Economic growth would be revived and developing nations would be allowed a growth of equal quality to the developed nations.

SUSTAINABLE DEVELOPMENT

In June 1992, the Rio Earth Summit declared, "The right to development must be fulfilled so as to equitably meet developmental and environmental needs of present and future generations." Sustainable development was not just about the environment, but about the economy and society as well.

Sustainable development encouraged the conservation and preservation of natural resources and of the environment, and the management of energy, waste, and transportation. Sustainable development was based on patterns of production and consumption that could be pursued into the future without degrading the human or natural environment. It involved the equitable sharing of the benefits of economic activity across all sections of society, to enhance the well-being of humans, protect health, and alleviate poverty. For sustainable development to be successful, the attitudes of individuals as well as governments with regard to current lifestyles and the impact they had on the environment would need to change.

Appendix 2

James Shaw on Young and Powerless Change Agents

It is important to note that most well-known change initiatives, perceived as being "top-down," or led by a senior executive or the CEO, probably started at the bottom or the middle, years earlier. In our case, and in a number of cases I have stumbled across, the major change program was conceptually well developed, and "low-hanging fruit" (i.e., small and easy wins) had been picked off before the senior executives started to talk publicly about it. Young change agents often start those initiatives themselves, or are part of a small "skunk works" team sponsored by a middle manager who is leading the project. Only once they have chipped away at it for some time and created a level of comfort with the initiative on the part of the executive will the executive pick it up. So young change agents, I would say, can simply get started on their projects—the rest can come through time. However, they may have to sacrifice nights and weekends.

There is an hourglass effect at PwC, and other similar organizations. When new graduates join the organization at the bottom, they don't know what they can't do, they have nothing to lose, and they have a certain amount of arrogance to them. In other words their self-expression is wide and they aren't afraid to ask dumb questions or challenge conventions. As their careers advance, however, they become more and more concerned about what people think. They become more political, more risk averse.

Eventually they make partner and pass through the neck of the hourglass. They have achieved their main career goal and they are now "safe." But they are at the bottom of a new hierarchy—management. Their confidence and self-expression grow only as they advance up the chain of command. Eventually they reach the very top—senior executive. No longer under any real threat they feel that they can say what they want (again).

What really worked about our approach, I think, and what other junior staffers can do to create change, is to connect the top and the bottom. Both have broad horizons and similar levels of self-expression and similar values—although for different reasons. The about-to-be-retired senior executive is thinking about their legacy, while the graduate joiner has the idealism of their youth and education, untempered by bitter experience.

Working together, they can be very powerful. The senior executive is too busy to engage in detailed project work, researching, communicating, and organizing. This work the junior staffers can do with 100 percent attention, while the executive does what they do better—open doors, make introductions, speak to their peers with respect and authority. Both sets of work are important and powerful contributions. I noticed that a number of the senior executives we worked with had in fact been making pronouncements or arguments about sustainability and CSR before we even joined PwC. But it was not until we started working with them that any real progress beyond intellectual discussion was made.

Reading

Leadership for Change: Enduring Skills for Change Masters

Rosabeth Moss Kanter

"Change masters" are people who know how to conceive and lead productive and effective projects, initiatives, or ventures that bring new ideas into use. "Change" takes diverse forms: product innovations, new business enterprises, social change, turnarounds, organization culture shifts, development of new technology or work arrangements, organizational restructuring or improvement, or implementation of new business models. Yet, regardless of the type of change, generic skills are used by leaders of successful change efforts.

My research and consulting projects have led me to identify seven fundamental skills, based on work with hundreds of leaders of successful innovations—those

who guided projects inside larger organizations or started new ones. At each phase of the change process, successful leaders reflect these skills in their own actions, and they create a climate in which others can also use them.

SKILL #1: SENSING NEEDS & OPPORTUNITIES: TUNING IN TO THE ENVIRONMENT

Innovation begins with someone being aware enough to sense a new need. Of course, being "smart enough" comes from focusing time and attention on things going on in the environment around you that send signals that it's time for a change. Change masters are adept at anticipating the need for change as well as leading it. They sense new ideas or appetites emerging on the horizon—sometimes because they feel hungry themselves. The concept for eBay came from the desire of the founder's girlfriend to swap Pez dispensers. Fidelity Investments started Boston Coach because their own executives wanted a reliable car service. The idea for Citizen Schools, an after-school apprenticeship program for middle school students, came from working in a service program during the school day and seeing kids hang out on street corners afterwards;

the founders wanted something more productive for the kids they mentored.

Change masters sense problems and weaknesses before they represent full-blown threats. They see the opportunities when external forces change—new technological capabilities, industry upheavals, and regulatory shifts. And then they identify gaps between what is and what could be. They find many ways to monitor external reality. Change masters become idea scouts, attentive to early signs of discontinuity, disruption, threat, or opportunity. Vanessa Kirsch, who had already founded one successful nonprofit, spent a year traveling around the world to tune into the needs and opportunities for social change organizations; that led her to the idea for a new kind of social venture financing that became New Profit Inc. Change masters can establish listening posts—a satellite office in an up-and-coming location, an alliance with an innovative partner, investments in organizations that are creating the future. Reuters Greenhouse founder John Taysom began to see the potential of new technology when posted in Bahrain, because peculiarities of transmitting financial information (Reuters' mainstay) suggested new possibilities. Then he put himself in the middle of Silicon Valley and started tuning in. After a few strategic investments, the Reuters Greenhouse opened for business, with a philosophy that getting an inside look at a number of innovative companies would be the best way to learn about what was about to happen, not what had already been created. Partnerships and alliances not only help you accomplish particular tasks, they also provide knowledge about things happening in the world that you wouldn't see otherwise.

Max Jones, managing director of Kerry Logistics in Hong Kong, attributed his company's success as a fulfillment house to the ability to tune in: "There's a word in Cantonese with no direct translation, *jahp sahn*, that means to be forever mindful, watch the environment around you, and respond to it on the spot." Improvisational theatre begins with becoming very aware of every nuance of the context. Robin McCulloch, who founded Corporate Agility to teach improvisational techniques to business teams, proposes: "Once you have placed yourself in context, you must prepare for working in the moment. You can't react to change if you can't see it. And you can't see it if you are preoccupied and not looking for it." Sensing change is a subtle skill, and it requires firsthand contact, not distilled, packaged, secondhand information. Drs. Craig Feied and Mark Smith determined opportunities for change in the Washington Hospital Center Emergency Department by mobilizing medical students to shadow physicians and note what seemed to cost them the most time as they served patients.

Change masters are more likely to emerge in companies already open to change. I call them "pacesetters," in contrast to the "laggards" that resist anything new or different. It's a self-reinforcing cycle; those already successful at change create the circumstances that make it easier for people to sense the need for the next changes, because they have opened minds and broken through walls. Pace-setter organizations produce more need-sensors because they value curiosity and open dialogue. They encourage encounters with customers, competitors, and challengers that provide opportunities to sense needs.

For some, opportunity is triggered by customer encounters. The British

Broadcasting Corporation (BBC) invited 36 members of the "audience" who were swapping files of American, British, and international television programs over the Internet to join 360 top managers at a conference and challenge managers' beliefs about the future of broadcasting. The executives of a leading airline routinely travel in the coach cabin to talk to passengers about their experiences. At Sun Microsystems, telephone calls to the CEO from a new kind of customer triggered Doug Kaewert's change efforts. For others, the change sequence begins with challenges. Williams-Sonoma's CEO, Howard Lester, began his conversion to an Internet fan when students at Berkeley's business school challenged his biases. Nokia's CEO regularly talks to teenagers for clues to the future.

Laggards, in contrast, are much more likely than pace-setters to fall into traps that prevent tuning in to new possibilities. They avoid learning from customers, competitors, or challengers. *The customer avoidance trap* has three components: Assuming you already know what customers are thinking. Asking customers questions about past experiences, rather than about future hopes. Being content with overall positive averages, instead of getting agitated about the few minor negatives. *The competitor avoidance trap* involves another three: Making yourself feel good by concentrating on your competitors' flaws and flops, while thinking about your own successes. Imitating their practices, seeing only their mistakes, and not considering what they could do to wipe you out. Looking only at current competitors, and failing to see emerging competition that might be coming from far outside the industry. *The challenger avoidance trap* adds still other mistakes:

Talking only to people who agree with you and think exactly the same way. Enjoying that classic "benefit" of attaining a top position in a hierarchy: never again having to talk to someone who disagrees. Never meeting people who come from a different place, speak a different language, practice a different specialty, fall in a different industry, use a different set of tools, feel differently about the value of your field.

Change masters don't make these mistakes. Instead, they are never quite satisfied, even with success. One CEO's ambitious goals for her company were accompanied by constant fear about how fast the competition was moving; she kept reminding people to take nothing for granted. Mark Leckie, head of Gillette's Duracell battery business, which was based on alkaline batteries, set up an alliance with solar cell companies to ensure that Duracell could destroy its own business before somebody else did it to them. A change leader at Sun Microsystems opened meetings with a chart headlined "old-line vs. on-line": "Because Barnes and Noble screwed up, there's an Amazon.com. Because Merrill Lynch screwed up, there's an e-Trade. Because Kroger screwed up, there's a Peapod. Then I'd say, 'Sun.' You guys tell me. Who's going to put us out of business? And some people still didn't get it. They'd say, 'But we're doing great, our stock's high, everything's cool.' And we'd say, 'It was at Compaq, too.'"

When people are encouraged to tune in all the time, to be conscious of the context, and to become restlessly dissatisfied, they are less likely to be jarred by change. Mindless habitual behavior is the enemy of innovation. Change masters begin by being mindful.

SKILL #2: KALEIDOSCOPE THINKING: STIMULATING BREAKTHROUGH IDEAS

It is one thing to sense an opportunity on the horizon; an additional mental act of imagination is needed to find a creative new response to it. Change masters take all the input about needs and opportunities and use it to shake up reality a little, to get an exciting new idea of what's possible, to break through the old pattern and invent a new one.

Creativity is a lot like looking at the world through a kaleidoscope. You look at a set of elements, the same ones everyone else sees, but then reassemble those floating bits and pieces into an enticing new possibility. Innovators shake up their thinking as though their brain is a kaleidoscope, permitting an array of different patterns out of the same bits of reality. Change masters challenge prevailing wisdom. They start from the premise that there are many solutions to a problem and that by changing the angle on the kaleidoscope, new possibilities emerge. Where other people would say, "That's impossible. We've always done it this way," they see another approach. Where others see only problems, they see possibilities. Kaleidoscope thinking is a way of constructing new patterns from the fragments of data available, patterns that no one else has yet imagined, because they challenge conventional assumptions about how pieces of the organization, the marketplace, or the community fit together. A yard sale down the street? So why not a giant yard sale on the Internet? (We call

that eBay.) Often it is not reality that is fixed, it is assumptions about reality—like Williams-Sonoma executives telling e-commerce champion Patrick Connolly that their customers would never buy up-scale kitchenware on the Internet or skeptical bankers telling Gail Snowden that there was no profitable market for banking in the inner city, something that her First Community Bank proved wrong. (Every time I get on an airplane, I remember that doubters told the Wright brothers their machine would never fly.)

Innovators reframe the situation, reset the kaleidoscope on a new pattern which then becomes the convention for everyone else. Even in "me-too" changes, a leader has to shake up assumptions about existing routines. Laggard companies often claim limited capital for investment in new projects as a barrier to change. But their problem is not lack of money, it is lack of imagination.

For some companies, a search for new markets involves rethinking assumptions and challenging the pattern. Honeywell International's commercial airline unit had traditionally segmented its customers by size and type of aircraft—large airlines or regional/commuter airlines. But when managers used a kaleidoscope, they asked a different set of questions. A fresh look at the marketplace, focusing on the aircraft maintenance activity, caused a new cut through their customer base: those who regarded their own maintenance as a core competency, such as Lufthansa; those who did not want to do their own maintenance, such as Southwest Airlines; and those who were forced to do their own maintenance because of asset or union constraints, such as American Airlines. This fresh perspective led to the idea for a line of business managing aircraft maintenance.

Organizational practices can encourage kaleidoscope thinking. For example:

- *"Monday Morning Quarterbacking"* (after a dissection of each Sunday's game common in American professional football). Change masters second-guess their own successes as well as their own mistakes. Looking for root causes but also for unexpected juxtapositions of events can challenge assumptions and suggest new approaches. Continental Airlines' daily cross-functional operations meeting examines each previous day's performance, and the dialogue often identifies new areas requiring focused attention.

- *"Expeditions to Labrador"* (in honor of frozen food innovator Clarence Birdseye, who got the idea while fur-trapping in Labrador). Sending people outside the company and the industry—not just on field trips, but "far a-field trips," can shake kaleidoscopes. When John Taysom took Reuters' CEO and top executives to California in 1997 for two days of meetings with Silicon Valley entrepreneurs, complete with fast electric car rides in one company's parking lot to jar minds (as well as bodies), that was probably as strange as Labrador to many of them. But it opened minds to how the Greenhouse could trigger innovation. Indeed, there are now several consulting firms specializing in bringing European executives to visit exemplary American companies outside their industry.

- *"Blue Sky Events"* (designed to look up, beyond the horizon). Large brainstorming sessions consisting of people from a wide variety of areas allow interested outsiders to ask questions, make suggestions, and trigger new

ideas. The BBC held a number of large conferences to generate new ideas, full of entertaining exercises to stimulate new kinds of thinking.

- *"Talent Shows"* (everyone has a hidden talent). Humor, play, artistic expression, and poking fun at tradition signal that it is okay to question the status quo. Abuzz' Cool Talks were twice-monthly lunchtime talent shows that allowed people to get to know each other's out-of-work pursuits, but they also reinforced a spirit of creativity throughout the company.

SKILL #3: SETTING THE THEME: COMMUNICATING INSPIRING VISIONS

A raw idea that emerges from the kaleidoscope must be shaped into a theme that makes the idea come alive. Ideas don't launch productive changes until they become a theme around which others begin to improvise, a vision that raises aspirations.

"If you can dream it, you can do it," the saying goes. Not exactly. There is a gap between dreaming and doing that is filled by the support of others. A vision remains just a dream unless it can inspire others to follow. The third skill for mastering change is to shape ideas into a theme that makes a compelling case for the value and direction of change—especially when you are pursuing a new idea that has not yet taken shape. Successful organizations are often the hardest to sell on the need for change, despite the time and money and desire to remain on top. But they are often complacent, and their people are too comfortable to want to rise from inertia for the hard work of change. Sukyana Lahiri's analysis of a sub-set of respondents to my 2000 global corporate culture survey showed that financial service and retail companies with the highest revenues per employee (one measure of success) were more often laggards than pace-setters in terms of change. Perhaps those rich laggards thought they were already perfect, so why rock the boat by doing strange new things? Or perhaps they were running so tightly that there was no time for envisioning change.

Leaders must wake people out of inertia. They must get people excited about something they've never seen before, something that does not yet exist. The theme provides the setting for a story that has to come to life, to raise aspirations and inspire action. A vision is not just a picture of what could be; it is an appeal to our better selves, a call to become something more. It reminds us that the future does not just descend like a stage set; we construct the future from our own history, desires, and decisions. And we have to stretch our imaginations just as we take on stretch goals—Cisco CEO John Chamber's favorite kind of goal. The aspiration must be so compelling that it is worth the extra time and effort to achieve. That means an appeal also to our pragmatic selves, addressing the classic first question of "What's in it for me?" One answer might be that the hard work of change now will make life easier later. Change masters have to focus people's eyes on the prize—to get them to see the value beyond the hardship of change to the prize waiting at the end. When HongKong.com changed its business model and set a new theme, director Rudy Chan reported: "We needed to go through quite a bit of explaining. We had to tell them why. And what's in it for them in terms of career opportunities. And we needed to do that several times. It was a lot of communication."

Setting the theme involves more than a lot of communication; it's a special kind of communication, with dramatic flourishes. Inspiring visions provide a picture of the future combining poetry and prose, imagination and pragmatism, drawing on six elements:

- *Destination:* Where are we headed?

- *Dream:* What will be different because of this goal? What will our world look like then?

- *Prize:* What positive outcomes will be obtained? Who will benefit, how?

- *Target:* What deadlines or metrics make the outcomes concrete?

- *Message:* What memorable image, slogan, or headline conveys the essence of the goal?

- *First step:* What tangible step can be taken that will give reality to the goal?

These pieces of the picture are important because sometimes people just don't understand what the change leader is talking about. They nod at the words, but do not hear the music or get the meaning. Or sometimes they prefer to misunderstand. The one kind of power that is universal, held by every person in every role in every organization, is silent veto power—like the pocket veto, in which people simply put a request in their pocket and forget about it. They exercise that power by doing nothing to support or advance the change. People can ignore change by denying that it requires anything they are not already doing. Or they can disclaim any responsibility for it. Time is the most valuable commodity, and people can only put so many things on their plate. Things that are not part of their immediate goals can fall by the wayside. So unless they have a compelling reason to cooperate, they can slow down even changes ordered by the top. When Albert Ormiston, vice president for direct sales at Sun Microsystems, began to communicate the vision for a fundamentally new sales process, he reported that: "We found people that said, 'Hey, it's not my job' or 'I'm doing the best I can.' This really meant 'Take a hike, I'm not interested.'"

Words matter. The rhetoric of change can open wounds or heal them. How the vision is conveyed matters because symbols matter to people. Ormiston's project was considered mysterious and threatening to some in the direct sales force; but the way my Sun informants talked about the macho character of the sales force made me think they felt that the shift of Internet sales was a loss of manhood. The elimination of business unit CIO titles at IBM in 1997 was a loss of status and loss of face that got in the way of some of the former CIOs (newly named business information executives) embracing the bigger "One IBM" goal. They saw "re-engineering," not a journey to business leadership. Healing visions avoid blame, maintain respect for traditions, but still keep the dream and destination in clear focus.

The big picture element of a new aspiration is critical for the message even to be heard by people bogged down in daily routines. The skeptics Philip Nenon encountered at Sun Microsystems for his team's new network product were "people who were more focused on the tactical, day-to-day, status quo type of product growth," he said. Ormiston and his colleagues not only had to compete for time and attention to get his vision understood, but as leaders based outside of Boston, they had to overcome a bias against things that did not emanate from California. Only a big picture aspiration can lift people out of their own immediate tasks and make a change

effort appear central of the community— not just more work piled on by peripheral people.

A vision isn't a written goal distributed to people, like a business plan or mission statement; nor is it communicated once as an announcement of a new venture. It is embodied by the change master's personal enthusiasm, reflected in his or her passion for the cause, communicated over and over again in every encounter. If the project is viewed as just another assignment, then either it's so routine that it doesn't produce much change, or skeptics and resisters (who are already too busy) have good reasons to slow it down. So it is important for potential change leaders to make sure that their passion matches their aspiration, asking themselves questions such as:

- *Do I feel strongly about the need for this?*

- *Am I convinced that this can be accomplished?*

- *Can I convey excitement when I talk about it?*

- *Am I willing to put my credibility on the line to promise action on it?*

- *Am I committed to seeing this through, over the long haul?*

- *Am I willing to make sacrifices to see that this gets done?*

Personal passion helps the change master do whatever it takes to get started, to demonstrate the value of the vision even when others cannot yet see it. An e-commerce head of a large bank reported that: "Those of us who are believers are dedicated to what we want to do, but the others are not sure or convinced of the right path to follow, especially given the big expenses involved. . . . So I rather sneakily chunk out big projects into smaller pieces that I can approve myself." And then, the small projects produce tangible results that help others picture the goal.

SKILL #4: ENLISTING BACKERS & SUPPORTERS: GETTING BUY-IN, BUILDING COALITIONS

As every entrepreneur knows, a great idea is not enough. Even a great mandate from a powerful sponsor to "just do it" isn't enough. Potential change masters must sell the idea more widely: attract the right backers and supporters, entice investors and defenders, get buy-in from stakeholders in a position to help or harm the venture at later stages. The newer the idea, the more critical this coalition building. A great deal of the work of innovation and change is to reach deeply into, across, and outside the organization to identify key influencers and get them interested and supportive. Does the idea have financial implications? Better get buy-in from Arthur in Accounting. Will it affect company image? Involve Peggy from PR.

Coalition building requires an understanding of the politics of change and the skills of a community organizer. Instead of trying to recruit everyone at once, change masters seek the minimum number of investors necessary to launch the new venture and then to champion it when they need help later. Each successive round of buy-in brings more people and groups on board—a process that is similar for stand-alone startups and internal change.

"To make anything successful, you must work a personal network," many successful innovators repeat. Without that network of contacts, identifying the people to ask for support can be challenging. That's why change masters are often more effective when they are insiders bringing a revolutionary new perspective. A foundation of community and a base of strong relationships inside large organizations can speed the change process; people already trust each other. For independent entrepreneurs, their file of phone numbers is one of their most important early assets. For intrapraneurs and internal change agents, potential coalition members are not limited by the walls of the company; they can extend to suppliers, customers, and partners. At a large nonprofit, innovators routinely drew on key donors as backers of ventures that had not yet secured the full approval of senior management. An enterprising innovator at an investment bank made an external strategic partner her ally in convincing peers to back her vision for change. The spirit of community and a network of partners are key elements of a culture for change.

Early in the change process, leaders need the support of powerholders—those who possess resources, information, and credibility that can be invested in the venture to get it moving. Resources can include people or technology as well as funds. Information includes political intelligence and savvy as well as data or expertise. Both are important, but they are often widely available. Equally important is the intangible asset of legitimacy. Powerful, well-connected sponsors make the idea credible, open doors, speak on behalf of the change master at meetings she does not attend, and quell opposition. Early coalition members help sell others. Union City, New Jersey, school superintendent Thomas Highton used Bell Atlantic (now Verizon) for credibility with New Jersey officials when he wanted to buy an old parochial school and turn it into a technology showcase connecting home and school via the Internet.

Effective coalition building proceeds through three kinds of actions. First is *pre-selling*. The change leader speaks to many people, to gather intelligence (such as where people stand, who is likely to support or resist the idea) and to plant seeds, leaving behind a germ of an idea that can blossom and gradually become familiar. Change masters must be willing to reveal an idea or proposal before it's fully-developed, following the Rule of No Surprises. Secrecy denies you the opportunity to get feedback, and when things are sprung on people with no warning, the easiest answer is always no. Smart leaders pave the way for a good reception to new ideas by one-on-one preparation before convening people, and they avoid initiating discussions or holding meetings where people hear something they are not prepared for.

A second action is *making deals*. Having identified those likely to provide strategic support, the leader gets them to chip in ("tin-cupping," one company calls the process of "begging" for resources). This can involve some creative exchange of benefits ("horse trading"), so that supporters get something of value right away. Some change masters seek contributions beyond the amount they actually need because investment builds the commitment of other people to help them. It lets other people in on the action, even if what they are investing is minor—a little time, a little data, a staff member to serve as a liaison. This is a good pre-emptive move, because otherwise "everyone who is left out secretly wants to see you fail," a leader of a change effort in a conservative company said. But this attitude can occur even in entrepreneurial companies; Mark Ahn encountered resistors at Genentech to his new marketing methods, and he had to get existing managers to invest.

A third piece of coalition-building is *getting a sanity check*—confirming or adjusting the idea in light of reactions from backers and potential backers. Change masters want to secure the blessings of those with experience, but they also need their wisdom to ensure that "I'm not out of my mind," one said. A coalition is generally a loose network, with people chipping in various things at various levels of commitment. Sometimes, when the project is significant and controversial, the coalition can become an official advisory board. Internal boards build a set of spokespeople and cheerleaders for the initiative while reassuring others in the mainstream that their views are represented.

Throughout, change masters do not just communicate, they over-communicate—more than seems necessary through more media more times. One leader who successfully bridged silos to establish new flexible work arrangements for a large manufacturer attested to the truth of this principle: "You've got to go back over it over and over and over again. You have to present it orally, present it visually. You have to get consensus and buy in from their peers and the people above them."

Having a mandate from top management to make radical change does not guarantee that other supporters fall in line. (Remember the veto power I mentioned earlier—the ability to slow down anything by just doing nothing.) At a large manufacturer, the CEO and other officers underscored their support for a major change effort at a senior management conference, and then business unit heads seemed to conveniently forget some of the messages when they got home. Under some circumstances, being too close to the bosses could provoke backlash, and efforts to persuade colleagues could be seen as spying on them and reporting their resistance. This is a risk especially in cases in which change forces managers to give up territory. At IBM, some former business unit CIOs who lost power in the centralization of Web initiatives had little desire to cooperate with the people leading the changes, raising objections or engaging in passive resistance. Albert Ormiston commented about his direct sales prototype team: "I would say that this is not a real popular group at Sun. People that work for me say it is like being in the internal affairs department of the police."

Coalitions are fragile, especially when they contain people who look to see which way the political wind is blowing. Top management might withdraw their support if organizational opposition swells instead of declining. Thus, change masters try to widen their coalition—to move people up a continuum toward more active support, if they were neutral, and to the neutral zone if they were opponents. So to develop his direct sales effort, Ormiston focused on constant selling: "You have to really work hard on communicating that message. And then somehow you have a whole bunch of hooks in that message, where you can kind of come back and sneak up behind people to see if they really got it. The fact that I know what I want to do doesn't really cut much if I can't clearly get you to understand what I'm going to do. So—and the fact that I want to get to the end game doesn't mean much to people either. So you show them benefits, how it fits what they need. This is why it's good for you."

Support from powerholders gets the venture underway; other stakeholders help it move forward. Bringing key stakeholders into the coalition (which means active communication) avoids problems later. And stakeholder representatives can be co-opted to help sell their peers. That's how Vauxhall was able to win support from car dealers for its growing e-commerce initiatives. In 1995, Vauxhall (a General Motors subsidiary) was the first U.K. manufacturer to have a website of any sort. In September 1999, Vauxhall moved from brochureware to electronic sales completed by a dealer, and by 2000 Vauxhall had launched an exclusive range of "dotcom cars" available only over the Web, with the entire transaction online. Paul Confrey, Vauxhall's change master as manager of relationship marketing and new media, faced the same channel conflict as other manufacturers: online sales threatened offline dealers. Confrey used the franchise board of 20 dealers with which he met frequently to provide the sanity check and then to sell the idea to the rest of the 400 dealers. (The early supporters were undoubtedly flattered to get so much attention from the company and a chance to shape the initiative, despite its potential to displace them.) He did some horse trading, offering the dealers a partial commission on Internet sales in their region. He also displayed his other support, bringing in heavy-hitters, such as the company chairman, to meet with the dealers. Although about half the dealers were wary at first, eventually all of them accepted the dotcom cars and began to display computers on the showroom floors to differentiate themselves from other dealers.

Backers and supporters help avoid the risk that change agents will be viewed as mavericks to be undercut. Gail Snowden had direct backing from Bank Boston CEO Chad Gifford that could be used to ensure that staff departments couldn't turn down her requests. At "Handy Gadgets," an anonymous division of Honeywell, "Craig

Lebolt" described himself as the "Craig Lebolt one-man show." He got some help from marketing on creative ideas for a new venture, and customer service helped him refine his options. But his efforts "just flew in the face of our traditional organization. I kept hearing people say, 'That's not how it's done here.' I drove the projects with the force of my personality." His boss, "Michelle Hellman," was very helpful as a sounding board and advocate to other groups, especially "when I thought I was crazy because thirty people were against my idea," Lebolt said. Like the wise old hands that invest in new ventures, Hellman helped her associate pass the sanity check. Now he could pull the team together to get the new venture launched.

SKILL #5: DEVELOPING THE DREAM: NURTURING THE WORKING TEAM

Once a coalition of backers is in place, change masters enlist others in turning the dream into reality. Too often executives announce a plan, launch a task force, and then simply hope that people find the answers—instead of offering a dream, stretching their horizons, and encouraging people to do the same. In contrast, the areas where people feel that they are in charge of creating the future always seem to hum with communication. People cluster to help each other over rough spots. There's a team identity, maybe a team name. The team has deadlines that are considered milestones whose accomplishment can be celebrated.

Leaders now shift their role in the drama of change from lead actor to producer-director. They bring on stage the rest of the improvisational actors who take on the task of translating an idea into implementation, a promise into a prototype. There are two parts of this job: team-building and team-nurturing. The first consists of encouraging the actors to feel like a team, with ownership of the goals and a team identity that motivates performance—like a sports team that wants to win. A working team that feels deep commitment and responsibility for delivering on deadlines and promises is the best way to ensure high performance at Internet speed. The second involves care and feeding of the team as it does its work—to support the team, provide coaching and resources, and patrol the boundaries within which the team can freely operate.

"Team" is one of those over-used words, like "partner," that is part of corporate-speak even when it doesn't fit the reality of the situation. Just because a group of people has a common assignment, they are not a team unless more stringent criteria are met: a common identity, strong respect for each other as individuals, and a desire to do whatever it takes to support each other in succeeding. In short, they need to reflect the spirit of community at a micro level, with both structure (deadlines, routines, tools, disciplines) and soul (bonds among people). There is a big difference between the committees that have trouble getting anything done at sluggish laggards and the high performance teams that met impossible goals at Seagate. Both involve groups, but beyond that, there are no similarities. Committees are often convened to ensure that many people weigh in and no unpopular decisions are made, and that by definition slows down the action. Working teams, in contrast, should be designed to make sure things happen quickly. Honeywell captures this speed goal when it establishes "tiger teams."

Team-building begins with allowing a set of people to embrace the goals, not just to be told what to do by their manager—encouraging a more voluntary commitment through face-to-face relationship-building. At Abuzz, product development teams met as a large group over several days to create the plan together, with individuals making commitments to pieces of the schedule, and lots of back and forth among all team members until everyone knew what they could expect from everyone else. The result was full ownership for stringent deadlines that turned enterprise software into an Internet offering in record time. Getting everyone together from any function that might have anything to do with the solution to hear the same message at the same time has long been associated with faster product development or process implementation. Rapid prototyping and parallel development are a big part of the improvisation that produces innovation.

Team names and slogans and T-shirts and mascots symbolize identity, but these can be empty of meaning unless the team has first taken ownership of its tasks. The theme set by the leader provides a starting point, and the vision offers inspiration, but details are best left to the team to create through their own interactions among themselves and with their audiences. That approach not only confers team ownership, but allows for creative approaches. Unleashing team creativity involves intensity and focus, with brains fully engaged—a contrast with the mindlessness possible when people are just following a script. Leaders must give team members the time and the space to focus, protected from distractions. Creative effort, whether development of new knowledge or the solving of challenging problems, takes full attention on the task and excellent communication among team members so that elusive bits of not-yet-fully understood knowledge can be pinned down and shared quickly. Communication over the Web through e-mail and team rooms, with everyone looking at the same documents or drawings, can facilitate speed and seamlessness. But face-to-face communication at the beginning and at critical moments throughout the team's work is more commonly associated with success than pure virtuality. People looking each other in the eyes and talking directly to one another live and in person builds the foundation that permits virtual communication to be effective in between face-to-face meetings.

The second big job is to see to the care and feeding of the team—to be their advocate to the world around them, to get them whatever they need to get the job done. Successful teamwork is determined not just by the personalities of the people on the team or the particular process they use, but by whether or not the team is linked appropriately to the resources they need from the wider world around them, as Harvard psychologist Richard Hackman has found. Team leaders as diverse as Parkash Ahuja at Charles Schwab or Helen Yang at Sun Microsystems described meal delivery as an important act. Yang, who led the Sun-Peak project that converted Sun to run on its own systems, also secured valet parking (workers couldn't find enough legal parking spaces), stress management, and pep talks. But even more important than amenities are the best tools to do the job. Among the biggest differences between pace-setters and laggards was whether leaders helped working teams get the resources they needed.

SKILL #6: MASTERING THE DIFFICULT MIDDLES: PERSISTING AND PERSEVERING

My personal law of management, if not of life, is that *"Everything can look like a failure in the middle."* Every new idea runs into trouble before it reaches fruition, and the possibilities for trouble increase with the number of ways the venture differs from current approaches. The more innovation, the more problems. The more problems, the greater the importance of skills in getting over the difficult middles.

One of the mistakes leaders make in change processes is to launch them and leave them. There are many ways a new venture or change initiative can get derailed. These tempt people to give up, forget it, and chase the next enticing rainbow. Stop the effort too soon, and by definition it will be a failure. Stay with it through its initial hurdles, make appropriate adjustments and mid-course corrections, and you are on the way to success. Of course, if the process takes too long, you have to return to the beginning—monitor the environment again, recheck assumptions, look at the way the theme is being played out, and reset the vision. Constant monitoring is important to keep ideas on track or to redirect them if circumstances change—and they often do.

Four common problems arise in the middle of developing new products, implementing new processes, or getting new ventures off the ground.

FORECASTS FALL SHORT

You have to have a plan—but if you are doing something new and different, the plan often does not hold. Plans are based on experience and assumptions. When attempting to innovate, to do something that has never been done before, it is difficult to predict how long it will take or how much it will cost. Change leaders must be prepared to accept serious departures from plans. They must also understand that if they hope to encourage innovation it is foolish to measure people's performance according to the script. That's why improvisational theatre is so important: the team is expected to take the project in a direction that could not have been envisioned in advance. That's positive, part of the process of innovation. Projects designed to be completed on Internet time often involve a scramble. An aggressive 14-week launch time for Vauxhall's e-commerce site featuring Internet-exclusive cars meant that not all the back-end systems were ready when the front-end went live. In situations like this, leaders must secure additional resources, beg for additional time, or be even more innovative in figuring out how to work around limitations.

UNEXPECTED OBSTACLES POP UP

Everyone knows that a new path is unlikely to run straight and true, but when we actually encounter those twists and turns we often panic. Especially when attempting to make changes in a complex system, diversions are likely—and sometimes unwelcome. It's a mistake to simply stop in your tracks. Every change brings unanticipated consequences, and teams must be prepared to respond, to troubleshoot, to make adjustments, and to make their case. Although scenario planning can help identify the possible problems that can pop up, the real message is to expect the unexpected. Not only do projects hit potholes, but external events disrupt the best-laid plans—e.g., a reorganization of AlliedSignal's Specialty Films business in the middle of multiple new projects; the turnover of school superintendents in IBM's Reinventing Education projects. External events can also create new opportunities, such as the New York Times' offer to buy Abuzz just as Abuzz was in the middle of launching an enterprise software product.

Leaders must ensure that plans are not rigid, making it possible to redirect the venture around obstacles, or to mount a second project to deal with the new challenge. This kind of flexibility is apparent in pace-setter companies but not characteristic of the laggards. If success or failure of an initiative rests on rigid conformity, without the ability to explore other approaches, then the venture is doomed from the start.

MOMENTUM SLOWS

Most people get excited about things in the beginning, and everybody loves endings, especially happy endings. It's the hard work in between that demands effort and requires attention from leaders. After the excitement and anticipation of a project launch, reality sinks in. You do not have solutions to the problems you face; the multiple demands of your job are piling up; the people you have asked for information or assistance are not returning your calls. After longer-than-normal work days (and nights, in dotcoms), the team is tired. And within the team, after the initial warm glow of membership, differences among team members—in work styles or points of view—start to surface, and conflict starts to slow things down.

At Sun Microsystems, the SunPeak project to convert all of Sun's systems to its own networks almost got hurt by sagging morale. The team had a punishing

work schedule (mandated Saturdays) and a firm deadline (go-live in August 1998). Then two months from completion, vice president Helen Yang told the team that the date would slip by six weeks. "No one was thrilled to work 80 hours a week for six additional weeks," one of her sponsors recalled. To her existing morale boosters (free meals and more) she added days off July 4th and 5th ("That got the loudest cheer in our meeting," she reported), and she brought in the project's chief backers to pick up team spirit by reminding them how much more successful they would be because of the extra effort.

It is important for change leaders to revisit the team's mission, to recognize what's been accomplished and what remains, and to remember that the differences in outlook, background, and perspective that now may divide the group can ultimately provide solutions. When teams are stuck in the middle, shuffling assignments, breaking into subgroups, and trying a different tack can often break the logjam. The best morale-booster and team unifier is a successful solution.

CRITICS GET LOUDER

The final problem of middles is often the most frustrating. Even if you have built a coalition and involved key stakeholders, the critics, skeptics, and cynics will challenge you—and they will be strongest not at the beginning but in the middle of your efforts, just when the project itself is not quite ready and thus most vulnerable. It is only then that the possible impact of the change becomes clear, and those who don't like it have had time to formulate their objections and harden their positions. In the beginning, the theme is just a distant possibility, and the vision is just rhetoric. Perhaps people didn't even understand what the words meant, or what the venture would imply for their own activities, until the unfolding project made the consequences concrete. And now that it looks like the venture might succeed, the threat to those who oppose it increases.

At a number of companies, enthusiastic public commitment at the executive committee level to support a strategic change was followed by dissension once those same business unit heads found out what it would mean for their territorial sovereignty. The e-commerce team at a manufacturing company thought the opponents of a unified corporate website were converted by top management speeches and a beautiful demo at a leadership meeting in February 1999. "You might think it would be easy to get acceptance for the website from rank and file management after that demo, but that's not how it worked in reality," recalled the head of Web initiatives. "We never did really sell it. Even right before we went live no one really believed it would happen. People would tell me, 'You are never going to get it done.' But we had to keep pushing." Another observed, "The very generality of the theme leaves room for low level folks to speculate, are we really going to do this? Even now people are saying we're really not going to do this. That goes on forever." And so the same venture that was authorized and backed by powerholders and has a working team well underway remains open for discussion. A change leader reported: "One of the things that's been discouraging for me is you think you're past a certain point, and then you find, no you're not, you're revisiting that point again. Why is it? It's not just the resisters, it's sometimes even people in your own organization. You think you've got an agreement, you think you've communicated something. And then you come back later, and the whole thing is stuck again in arguments. Maybe there was just one little detail that you assumed that everybody understood that they didn't."

Critics and skeptics can be internal and external. At Sun, internal skeptics dismissed the (ultimately successful) network computer being designed by Robert Gianni's team as an old-fashioned model, a dumb design that would never work and would never be bought. Even customers doubted it would work, or grumbled about having to change networks they had just installed. Gianni is an engineer, but he had to become a salesperson, explaining the product to key customers even before they could see it in full operation.

In the middle, then, the persistence and perseverance of a change master makes the difference between success and failure. While the working team soldiers on, the change master needs to be there to fight for additional resources, remove obstacles, boost team morale, and deal with the critics. And now the real value is derived from having taken the time to create a clear and compelling vision, a strong and committed coalition of backers, and a team that feels ownership. Each of these—the vision, the supporters, and the team—helps weather the middles. With the help of coalition members and their own team, change masters can make adjustments, veer around obstacles, and push forward.

Leaders can remind people of the vision. Powerful sponsors can neutralize or remove the critics. Team members can be enlisted for the political campaign. Sun change master Robert Gianni turned his engineers into educators, teaching people at Sun about the product at big events in each major geography—how to sell it, how to understand it. Philip Nenon drew on internal and external coalition members. His unit's venture into telecom products involved a tough, evolving marketplace and customers such as Cisco with very stringent standards. When unexpected technical problems appeared, upper management supporters were brought in to help. "It's a tribute to the management team that when implementation issues came up, they did not freak out," Nenon recalled. "They got closer to it. They got directly involved and gave both the attention and support that were needed for us to execute." Having key customers in the coalition of backers also proved useful: they served as unofficial consultants. The venture found additional engineering resources, worked around obstacles, and eventually proved the value of Sun's "billion dollar bet" on this market.

Sometimes powerholders use their clout to silence the critics. The finance vice president of a manufacturing company opposed a new initiative because he would have to merge a portion of his operation with the sales group. He frustrated the change team leader by appearing to agree (after a seemingly endless set of meetings and slide presentations), and then throwing up objections or letting schedules slip. At a major meeting, the finance head was confronted by the sales vice president and embarrassed in front of his peers. With the CEO watching closely, the finance executive committed to an aggressive implementation schedule.

One leader compared leading change to pushing a boulder up a hill: it takes muscle-power and the determination to never let go, or the boulder will roll down, and you'll be crushed. To another leader of transformation, a change master is like a pest, never taking no for an answer, never letting go, following up relentlessly, staying on top of people to make sure they do what they promised. "You have to constantly come back. Someone said, 'You guys are like a bug around my head.

You're bothering me, go away.' Well, I'm not going away," he said. That kind of persistence helps turn difficult middles into successful achievements.

SKILL #7: CELEBRATING ACCOMPLISHMENT: MAKING EVERYONE A HERO

Remembering to recognize, reward, and celebrate accomplishments is the final critical leadership skill. Organizations that desire initiative and innovation thrive on celebration. Creative organizations, with their spirit of fun, are likely to celebrate everything in sight, including just the fact that it's Friday afternoon. Some are better than others at publicizing the accomplishments that give change leaders and their team members that warm glow that comes from being recognized by other members of their community. Recognition is important not only for its motivational pat on the back but for its publicity value; the whole organization and maybe the whole world now knows what is possible, who has done it, and what talents reside in the community gene pool.

Larry Kellner, president and COO of Continental Airlines, has said, "We can't go so fast that we forget to celebrate. It helps us the next time—when we ask people to go back and do it again." Continental uses DNU's (daily news updates), weekly voicemail from the CEO, and monthly publications to highlight accomplishments. Formal recognition—awards, merit badges, or medals of honor—is also a way to boost reputations, as people can list awards on their resumes. Of course, the company doesn't want to lose talent, but promising to make someone a star is a good way to attract and hold talent. That's the value of the RAVEs for employee achievements that a small growth company posts on its website and communicates at company-wide meetings.

In traditional organizations, recognition is probably the most underutilized motivational tool. There is no limit to how much recognition you can provide, and it is often free. Recognition brings the change cycle to its logical conclusion, but is also motivates people to attempt change again. So many people get involved in and contribute to changing the way an organization does things that it's important to share the credit. Change is an ongoing issue, and you can't afford to lose the talents, skills, or energies of those who can help make it happen.

THE RHYTHM OF CHANGE

The seven skills of change masters—tuning in to the environment, kaleidoscope thinking, conveying the theme through an inspiring vision, building coalitions, nurturing the working team, persisting through the difficult middles, and making heroes—correspond roughly to phases of change projects. The first two involve *generating ideas,* the next two *selling ideas,* and the final three *developing and implementing ideas.*

But this is not to suggest that there is an orderly sequence, one careful step at a time. In fast-moving industries, where innovation is improvisational theater, opportunities become themes before the need is fully documented, the actors start the play while the producer is still finding backers, and the team celebrates milestones while the ending is still undetermined.

Sometimes a set of people share responsibility, sometimes people enter after the idea has already been formulated, sometimes they hand it off to another leader to pick up. At Williams-Sonoma, Patrick Connolly shook the kaleidoscope and set the e-commerce theme, but then stood back to become a sponsor while other change agents picked up the challenge of coalition-building and team-nurturing.

Depending on the nature of the effort, projects move through these phases at different rates of speed. Some ventures gestate in the minds of innovators and then spring into being seemingly all at once, because the gestation period got everything lined up for incredible speed once the action began. (Even instant success takes time.) Others get organized quickly and then bump up against those murky middles, so time slows down again, e.g., as the go-live date is postponed, features are delayed, the national office people promise something the field offices can't yet deliver, or stakeholders intervene and must be dealt with. The successive iterations, rapid prototypes, and unexpected creative bursts that characterize e-culture mean that there are many simultaneous innovation projects, and they are likely to overlap. One is hardly finished before another is underway; change masters are often protecting still-embryonic projects from the ripples of neighboring ventures.

Certain kinds of change appear simple and fast. If you're a senior executive, you can order budget reductions, buy or sell a division, form a strategic alliance, or arrange a merger. Such "bold strokes" do produce fast change, but they do not necessarily build support for the work that follows, the work that creates the value the leader hoped to gain from the bold stroke. Bold strokes are decisions, and while decisiveness is important to move quickly (one of the lessons Pamela Thomas-Graham learned when she moved from McKinsey consultant to CNBC CEO) change is not just a decision, it is a campaign. Gillette announced an initiative to reduce stock-keeping units (SKUs), representing a proliferation of product and package variations, which was seemingly a simple business change; even so, it took nearly a year to align all the pieces, convert all the systems, commit all the stakeholders. It takes "long marches" to turn decisions into new sources of value, to produce and ultimately sustain change. Long marches can proceed at a run, but they still involve voluntary, discretionary, ongoing efforts of people throughout the community. Real change requires people to adjust their behavior, and their behavior is often beyond the control of top management. A senior executive can allocate resources for new product development or reorganize a unit, but he or she cannot order people to use their imaginations or to work collaboratively. Shaking things up with a bold stroke makes good external press (that's why some leaders like dramatic moves), but that doesn't necessarily change anyone's behavior.

Some revolutionaries make a big splash, attacking the castle head-on; there is drama and heroics, but the fortifications harden, and even if the battle is won, there is blood everywhere. Other change leaders operate by stealth, tunneling underneath the castle, taking actions that are hardly visible, until suddenly the castle collapses. Consider this contrast within the same company. One change agent talked about the fast immediate painful changes that he "muscled" through ("April 12, 1999, a day that will live in infamy")—cutting people and changing their jobs—and then the longer period of persuasion that followed (perhaps slower because the pain brought backlash). Another, however, reported a

slow seven months—identifying supporters and resisters, letting people get familiar with the change, getting the team to develop the idea a little further—and then the accelerated four months, as he started to use clout to force faster progress ("The 'golly, gee, I hope we can all work this out and still be friends' day is gone"). Leaders must sense what the context will handle and then pick the rhythm of change that appears right for their organization. But as a general tendency, starting more slowly and then accelerating for a really fast finish reduces the risk of being blindsided by obstacles or resistance. Leaders who manage by press release, making public announcements before they deliver, often have to back-peddle furiously. Better to take a little time to build the coalitions, get the buy-in, nurture the team, and then make a huge splash when there are results to celebrate.

Individuals in the audience for change respond to different rhythms, too. Some like their music fast (get it over with), others like it slow (time to get ready and get it right), and some would prefer to sit it out, hoping it goes away. Some jump on every bandwagon, others hold back no matter what. The "rule of thirds"—1/3 with you, 1/3 against you, 1/3 that can be converted—seems to fit a large number of types of change. After leading a major new initiative, a bank executive concluded: "When you move to a new business model, there are those precious few who say 'I get it, let's go.' Folks who can see the bigger picture. Then there are folks that say they get it, but they don't really mean it; they're pretending. And then there are folks that just screw themselves to the floor, don't communicate, and are thinking 'I ain't doing that.' The hardest to deal with are the people who consider what you're doing totally insignificant, so they ignore you." For some kinds of changes, he said,

"Folks just don't want to go there. The eyes glaze over. Don't want to talk about it, don't want to think about it, don't want to know about it." Change resisters often go through denial, anger, and superficial cosmetic change, before they are willing to permit deeper, systemic change.

Like community organizing, organizational change is a numbers game: a few early enthusiasts to carry the message, then a building of critical mass until even avoiders can no longer remain in denial. There are always holdouts, there is always pushback (Is she serious? Will he fold?), so maintaining the momentum for the long march makes a difference. When change masters are successful, what started as a rogue initiative—an opportunity that one person seized—becomes a real option, then the norm, and ultimately embedded everywhere. Sometimes people who think they have the assignment to create a bold stroke change discover that they must instead be organizers and shapers of initiatives already underway elsewhere. A corporate team given the goal of creating a globalization strategy for Gap Inc. found that groups within the business units were already working on the same thing. The team kaleidoscoped their thinking and shifted from seeking decisions to working with the other globalization groups to make sure that they all moved in roughly the same direction.

The most important personal traits a leader can bring to change efforts are imagination, conviction, passion, and confidence in others. Leaders must also heed political lessons:

- Position power is not enough. Personal passion and force of personality isn't enough. Other people must become believers, too. Their behavior shapes what the change turns out to be.

- Marshal data in support of change. Make the theme memorable and the vision concrete. Prototypes and test programs can be effective in demonstrating the power of change, and in building momentum.

- Endorsers and investors lend credibility and wisdom. Tap into the experience of others inside and outside the organization. Utilize relationships to get resources.

- Winning supporters can take time. Try iterative waves of coalition-building, in which many get the message and some become champions who reach out to many more.

- Seek to minimize loss and uncertainty for those who will be impacted by change. Listen to the resistors; sometimes they are telling you things you need to hear. Walk in the shoes of resistors; show them you understand them and are on their side. Co-optation of your opponents through a role in the venture can be effective. If they can't be converted, get them out of the way.

- Choose the rhythm that fits the situation. Know the audience. Know what people and the organization can handle, and push—but not too much too fast. Stretch people, but not to the breaking point.

- Persistence pays off. Stick with it. Follow up and follow through.

- Respect and recognition wins friends. Throughout the process, make all those who are part of the change look good.

Skillful leaders in receptive environments can speed up the pace of change, but they cannot avoid the hard work of convincing others to join them in mastering change.

Case

Vinesh Juglal: South African Serial Entrepreneur

Vinesh Juglal was excited and—if he stopped to think about it, which he didn't much—worried. As the previous owner (the wife of the former principal) of Durban Computer College (DCC) left the building, serial entrepreneur Vinesh wondered what it would be like to run the institution he had just bought. The education market in Africa was growing by leaps and bounds, and the ever-opportunistic Vinesh knew that buying a successful training enterprise could help him make the most of this market.

On the other hand, Vinesh was well aware that in order to grow the institution he would need another source of financing, since his current lines were tied up in his real estate and supermarket businesses. Infrastructure was not an issue, since Vinesh had most of the fixed assets he needed to grow DCC Campus. Attracting more students would happen either by lowering fees or by offering financial aid. Vinesh had heard of many sponsoring bodies, including government programs, set up for this purpose. But these sponsors tended to give grants only to non-profit entities.

Source: *Archana Raja (MBA 2007) and Professor Maury Peiperl prepared this case as a basis for class discussion rather than to illustrate either effective or ineffective handling of a business situation.*

Many questions occupied Vinesh's mind:

- What would be the best way to grow this "business"—if it could be called a business in the first place?

- Should he target the same return on investment as in his other businesses? More broadly, could he be successful using his previous, purely commercial approach?

- Who were (or should be) the stakeholders of DCC Campus? Did it make sense to think beyond the usual set of stakeholders in Vinesh's current businesses to the value to South African society of the services DCC provided? If so, how would this affect decisions about target profitability and other operational issues?

- Who would be able to take over once Vinesh retired, yet again?!

SOUTH AFRICA

The Republic of South Africa was located in the southernmost region of the African continent, with a long coastline that stretched more than 2,500 kilometres (1,550 mi) along two oceans (the Atlantic and the Indian). At 470,979 square miles (1,219,912 km^2), South Africa was the 25th-largest country in the world in 2009 and had a population of 47 million people and a GDP of USD 282.6 billion. (See Exhibit 1.)

EXHIBIT 1

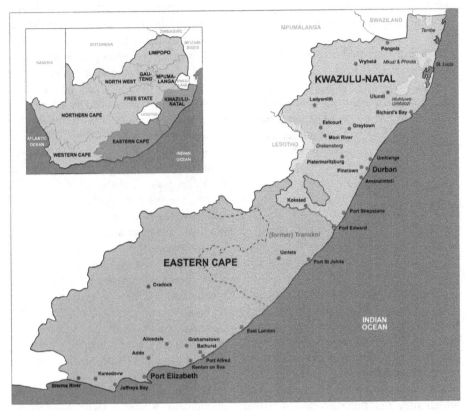

Brief history: After the British seized the Cape of Good Hope in 1806, many of the earlier Dutch settlers (the Boers) trekked north to found their own republics. The discovery of diamonds (1867) and gold (1886) spurred wealth and immigration and intensified the settlers' subjugation of the native inhabitants. The Boers resisted British encroachments, but were defeated in the Boer War (1899–1902). The resulting Union of South Africa operated under a policy of apartheid—the separate development of the races.

Apartheid: The apartheid system of racial segregation in South Africa recognized four racial groups: Black, White, Coloured and Indian. Blacks were persons of Sub-Saharan African descent. Whites were those of European ancestry. Coloured referred to those of mixed African sub-type, European and/or Malaysian/Indonesian descent. They were typically descendents of many generations who were themselves coloured. Vinesh was of the Indian race, whose parents or earlier ancestors had come from the Indian subcontinent.

Reserved townships: In South Africa, the term "township" usually referred to the (often underdeveloped) urban living areas that, under Apartheid, were reserved for non-whites (principally Blacks and Coloureds, but also working-class Indians). Townships were usually built on the periphery of towns and cities. Non-whites were evicted from areas designated as "white only" and forced to move into these townships.

It was in this environment in 1979 that Vinesh Juglal, aged 15, a high school dropout from a small town called Port Shepstone, decided to start his own business. He would go on to become one of the most successful supermarket wholesalers in the Kwazulu Natal region.

THE ANGRY TEENAGER

Vinesh's first encounter with business came through his family. Both his parents were businesspeople. As they were of Indian origin, it was impossible for them to work in white-collar jobs: Under apartheid, all clerical, managerial, and professional positions were reserved for Whites. They therefore developed expertise in the supermarket, fishery, and vegetable trades. Vinesh's parents owned a supermarket which they ran themselves. His father contracted with a team of fishermen to sell their catch in the wholesale market; he also sold fruits and vegetables to the wholesale market from the family's farms.

Like the other members of his family, Vinesh spent a significant amount of time after school and on weekends helping with the business from a young age. His parents taught him the nuances of running a supermarket, including the art of packing and bundling products, accounting for the cash, driving the produce to the wholesale market, and strategizing to bring in more sales. His parents' regimen of involving a school-going Vinesh in their businesses every weekend sparked a passion in him. He dreamt of going on to greater heights—of becoming a wholesaler. Wholesalers at that time made higher margins than shopkeepers, and there was little competition in the coloured market segment.

The young Vinesh began to get restless for an opportunity to take the next step. A student in the 8th grade, he was continually being reprimanded by a particular teacher over the level of his writing skills. One day Vinesh was so fed up with a constant taunting that he stood up and simply walked out of class. Ignoring the fact that his father was the chairman of the school committee, Vinesh decided he could not wait any longer to pursue his dream of becoming a businessman.

His parents were not at all happy with this rash decision. All of Vinesh's siblings were good students, and his parents very much wanted Vinesh to grow up to be a highly educated professional. But Vinesh had other plans. At the age of 15, he argued with the school principal and walked through the school gate, vowing never to come back.

Wandering along the shore of the Indian Ocean, Vinesh thought about his future. It did not bother him that he could not say exactly where he was going next. He only knew that he had taken the first step on his dream project. Now he had to earn the money to make it happen. He walked back into his hometown, Port Shepstone, where he took his first job as a helper at a construction site.

Upon hearing what Vinesh had done, his father became very angry. Heated arguments ensued and Vinesh soon walked out of his home as well.

Undeterred, Vinesh pursued his work. He slept on the site itself and satisfied his hunger with *megeu*, a traditional African drink made of maize and water. His hard work earned him his first 400 rand, with which he came up with his first entrepreneurial idea.

LUCK OR OPPORTUNITY?

One early morning, the still 15-year-old Vinesh walked 20 km to the house of his foreman, a white man, the 400 rand in his pocket. His mind was set on buying the foreman's Mazda buggy, with which he intended to start his first business. On reaching the house, Vinesh negotiated for three hours, after which he managed to get the buggy for 300 Rand. Using the remaining funds to purchase gas, Vinesh launched himself into the wholesale business.

Though too young to get a driving license, Vinesh knew how to drive as he had driven the vehicles used in his father's business. He began visiting the fish market at night, when there were no police to catch him, and selling fish to the Black reservation areas. Being first of the day to arrive with fresh fish, Vinesh could charge a premium. Very soon he began to accumulate significant capital. He hired a driver and started trading in vegetable produce during the day. In a year's time he had saved enough to buy himself an 8-ton truck, which he aptly named "Vinesh's pride."

Vinesh decided to focus entirely on the Transkei market, one of the largest of the reserved townships. He made it a point to work beyond the 8am-to-5pm routine of the mostly white businessmen of that area. In this way, he became the first supplier of all types of commodities in the market, which enabled him to charge a premium for both timeliness and freshness. Before long, most of the supermarket owners were buying produce from him. By the time the white sellers arrived, Vinesh had already finished selling. He had no access to credit facilities from banks like the white businessmen were receiving.

Nonetheless, his high profitability helped him buy more trucks, and soon his brother joined the business. With this increased capacity, he expanded to Port Elizabeth, again making a 100% profit on the trade of commodities.

As his business continued to grow, Vinesh was offered the chance to rent a supermarket in Transkei. He quickly understood that such an on-the-ground presence could help him trade without the high amount of travel needed in his current business model.

Vinesh opened his "Quality Supermarket" in Transkei in 1980. Besides produce trucked in from the big markets, the supermarket also stocked wholesale goods from multinationals such as Unilever, and sold them in smaller lots to nearby retailers. His choice of goods and his prompt service enabled Vinesh to grow the supermarket business quickly, and thus to gain the confidence of the MNCs. As a result, Vinesh became one of the few Indian businessmen in South Africa to receive credit facilities during the apartheid regime.

This growth in business gave him a chance to afford a franchise of "Jumbo Wholesalers" near his first shop. With this step, Vinesh broadened his range of goods yet again to include petrol and diesel. He soon opened satellite supermarkets, exploiting the still-prevailing pricing opportunity in the Transkei area. Their high quality and selection of goods, as well as long opening hours, quickly made Quality Supermarkets a popular choice among the locals.

In a year's time, Vinesh had made his first million, with the help of Jumbo and its four to five satellites. He bought his first Mercedes at age 17 and thereby regained the confidence of his father, who was finally convinced that his son had a very special business acumen.

So, at the age of 21, Vinesh Juglal decided to retire.

"RETIREMENT" TRAVELS

Somehow, Vinesh had developed the idea that he should tour different parts of the world to get a thorough understanding of how business was conducted, before starting another of his own. He was also open to conducting his existing business in other locations. He first traveled to India, but found the market there very closed. He then went to the Far East—to Malaysia and Japan—to learn how their supermarkets operated. He also "traveled" up the value chain to understand how and where produce was grown as well as how and where fast-moving consumer goods (FMCGs) sold in Japanese and Malaysian supermarkets were manufactured.

Then, heading west, Vinesh conducted similar observations in Europe and North America, gaining an even better understanding of the nuances involved in running a supermarket business. Armed with this knowledge, he returned to South Africa and resolved to re-enter the supermarket business, again in Transkei, in an area called Matata.

Vinesh's travels had given him a deeper understanding of what he had done well in his previous business, and where he might now change and expand focus in a new enterprise. He decided to enter the retail markets for both supermarket goods and hardware. His track record and his professionalism allowed him to negotiate good credit facilities with manufacturers. At the same time he carefully managed working

capital and inventory. For example, Vinesh would negotiate with wholesalers for a price to buy 100 tons, but manage to keep 99 tons in their warehouse, taking only a ton at a time to sell. With this kind of business acumen he quickly became successful yet again, founding the hardware retailer Tsolo Pack and the grocery chain Win Supermarkets.

To his businesses' trademark long opening hours, combined with flat management structures, Vinesh added two other hallmarks of successful retail operations: good customer service and careful working capital management. It was all these traits, learned partly as a child and partly on the job, that helped Vinesh realize his second commercial dream of developing a successful retail chain. Within a few years, his businesses had a monthly turnover of about 1.5 million rand.

So, at age 30, Vinesh Juglal retired again.

MOVING INTO REAL ESTATE

For his second retirement, Vinesh had a plan. He now had built up enough capital to enable him to trade in some high-value assets.

Vinesh went back to Port Shepstone to look for a likely property deal. He bought his first property for 70,000 rand and sold it for an astonishing 500,000 rand. Vinesh accomplished this by making full use of the gap in information between real estate agents.[1] By merely buying from one agent and then promoting the property to others,

---

[1] Transparency in real estate deals at that time was much lower in South Africa than in most developed countries.

he could ask for a price that bore no relation to what he had paid.

It was now the period between 1995 and 1998. Nelson Mandela had been set free and positive reforms were happening almost daily in South Africa, beginning with the fall of apartheid in 1994. Other South Africans were now able to buy into areas previously reserved for Whites. As Vinesh put it, "It was fun."

At the same time, people were still learning about the real estate market, and Vinesh knew that he could benefit by learning faster. Commercial property, he felt, had particularly strong investment potential, given the right timing. With the reforms taking place, if an investor were willing to make a bet on a piece of commercial real estate, the subsequent development and leasing might itself bring an economic boost to the surrounding area, thereby increasing the value of the original investment. Following this approach, Vinesh's second transaction gave him a profit of 1.7 million rand.

Since it still was not possible for a person sitting 100 km away from such a property to even be aware of its existence, Vinesh now began traveling the country, forming networks with property dealers, looking to acquire information about interesting deals anywhere at all in South Africa. As a result of some 30 deals over a decade, not only in South Africa but also in neighboring Swaziland, Mozambique and Botswana, Vinesh became one of the region's wealthiest investors.

In 2000, at age 36, Vinesh Juglal retired a third time.

This time he toured both within and outside the country, visiting major FMCG manufacturers, such as Lever Brothers in the UK, Coca Cola in the USA, and Shoprite in South Africa. Vinesh had always found that observing leading companies' ways of working taught him something new and inspired him to greater achievements.

THE CHANGING FACE OF SOUTH AFRICA

By now, South Africa had a new government and a rapidly developing infrastructure. There was far more power in the hands of the people. At the same time industries were becoming more organized, taking shape in line with their counterparts in the developed world. Large retailers, for example, had grown up to cover the entire country, serving all its regions and races.

Thus, even though Vinesh did make another attempt to enter the retail supermarket business, he found his success limited because of the far superior buying power of large retailers such as Shoprite and Spar. The business dynamics of South Africa were quickly changing, and Vinesh's previous success factors no longer applied to the retail industry.

As no fourth retirement therefore seemed likely, Vinesh went back into real estate instead, this time concentrating on industrial property. The new government had launched a number of policies aimed at industrialization, and investment had begun flowing into factories.

In 2004, Vinesh visited Richards Bay, on the other side of Durban from his native Port Shepstone, to familiarize himself with this newly developing area. As he was casually observing the area, he came across a real estate agent. The man showed Vinesh a 500,000-square-meter industrial plot, which he decided to buy for 100 rand per square meter. On his way home, Vinesh began making calls to his contacts around the country. Within a few hours he managed to find an investor willing to buy the plot for 150 rand per square meter. The investor happened to be an Indian who was regularly selling industrial plots to potential factory owners and other industrialists. Although he later realized he could have sold at a much better price, Vinesh never looked back. Indeed, by executing three to four deals a year for several years at an annual level of some 35 million rand, Vinesh Juglal once again became wealthy.

This time, however, Vinesh chose not to retire. Instead, he began to think about how to get involved in shaping the future of his country.

DURBAN COMPUTER COLLEGE

Throughout his days in the supermarket business, Vinesh had observed the need of Black South Africans for access to education. He firmly believed that investing in human assets was of paramount importance to his nation. He also believed this could become a lucrative business opportunity.

The opportunity presented itself to Vinesh in the form of the option to buy Durban Computer College (DCC or "DCC Campus"). The college provided higher education diplomas in the field of commerce, communication, computer science, and hospitality, and further education diplomas in secretarial studies. A professor had run this college for the past 15 years, before passing away in 2007. His wife, a doctor, had had no interest in carrying on the business, and had decided to put it up for sale. In the process, she had approached Vinesh. Believing in the potential of this deal, on both real estate as well as operational grounds, he had negotiated and bought the college and its campus.

At the same time, Vinesh knew he had no acumen for running the day-to-day operations of the business. He appointed himself CEO, but only to advise the existing management team on what DCC's philosophy should be. Vinesh believed there was an immense opportunity to expand the college to other parts of Southern Africa—Botswana and Swaziland, for example—because of the huge potential of the Black population there too, especially in the area of vocational education. Many Blacks, for a variety of reasons, failed to complete secondary school, leaving them no choice but to go to colleges such as DCC to learn specific skills in order to obtain a job.

MAKING MONEY OR GIVING BACK?

Although he saw its commercial potential clearly, Vinesh did not look at DCC with the same eyes as he had regarded his supermarket and real estate businesses. Instead, he saw an opportunity to give back to his community, and to the wider society, by providing them with quality education at a reasonable cost.

But this vision was not easy to attain. To bring a quality educational infrastructure to the Black community at a price it could afford, Vinesh knew his main challenge was to find a route to subsidize this level of education. The College struggled to break even, and the prospects of expanding to new locations, given the existing operating model, were dim. His biggest question was, "How do I see to it that

DCC sustains itself financially in order that it can meet its community goals?"

THE FAMILY MAN

In 1989, Vinesh had married an Indian woman, Neelam Kadwabai Parmar, from Gujarat, who unlike Vinesh had been educated through post-graduate level, in Chemistry. They met through Vinesh's uncle, who knew Neelam's father. Vinesh had gone to India to visit his uncle, but ended up getting married during the same visit. Vinesh and Neelam had three daughters (aged 17, 16, and 13 in 2009). All three were good students with strong all-round achievements. Vinesh attributed his children's good upbringing entirely to his wife's influence—in particular her education.

As he thought about the future of DCC, and of his own children, Vinesh noted how convinced he was that education was essential for anyone looking to succeed in the contemporary world. The irony was, of course, that Vinesh now believed no one should attempt what he himself had done. Much of his success, he reflected, seemed also to be the result of luck. But one could not trust in luck, only in one's ability to take advantage of it if and when it arrived. For much of the new South Africa, education looked like the key to doing just that: taking advantage of the great good fortune—many would say the very hard-earned good fortune—that the post-Apartheid era had brought. How, and with what goals, should Vinesh lead DCC to play its part?

Module **Six**

Continuous Change

INTRODUCTION

If there has been one clear development in the field of change management since its first heyday in the late 1980s, it has been a shift of focus from large-scale, first-order change to the second-order, more continuous variety. Where once the talk was of achieving major transformation tomorrow (albeit in order to stay in business), now it is about learning and adapting in the long term.

There are several reasons for this shift. First, many organizations have by now been through a major transformation, and found it painful enough that they committed to never having to undergo such radical surgery again. Like some of the firms described in the first few modules of this text, they became aware that the only way to perpetuate their achievements while avoiding further debilitating upheaval was to develop more flexible processes and a long-term, change-oriented culture. Second, many newer organizations, particularly those formed in the 1990s and 2000s, grew up in a climate of openness to change, with entrepreneurial cultures serving fast-moving markets. Having never experienced real stability, many of these firms were focused from day one on being nimble and on regularly reevaluating their approach.

Third, as we saw in Module 5, there are today far more people with experience leading change than there were a generation ago, and their recent experience tells them that the continued success of a change effort depends on succeeding that effort with continued change. Among the labor pool generally, there is also more acceptance of change than there was, though few believe in change for change's sake. The forces for change described in Module 1 are now widely acknowledged, and people expect to be subject to change. Still, this acceptance has taken many years to take root, and there are still industries and regions of the world in which it has yet to do so.

A related development has been the growing (though often grudging) acceptance of the need to embrace uncertainty rather than try to avoid it or design it away. The idea that we can control the world around us is in many ways the most unnatural conceit of the Industrial Age, and it is only slowly giving way (in some, but not all fields) to the idea that the most we can hope to do is influence what happens; that by understanding how our environment (commercial, natural, and social) is structured and how it evolves over time, we can be best equipped to work with it, rather than against it, to achieve our ends. Such a view takes almost as given the idea that change must be continuous.

OVERVIEW OF CASES AND READINGS

The cases and readings in this module also provide us with a final opportunity to consider the impact of globalization and information technology on organizations at the onset of the new millennium. The industries and firms chosen for inclusion here—the white goods industry, the airline industry, and industrial giant General Electric—are notable not only for their size but for the particularly profound impact these external forces have had on the way they do business.

Some of the biggest "external forces" have come from a realignment of the geo-political and global economic landscape, and to begin with, we consider how this has come about and where it is likely to lead. In the article "Seismic Shocks and Systemic Shifts," Jean-Pierre Lehmann makes a compelling case that a new kind of state capitalism, rather than free markets, is holding more and more sway in the world because of the tremendous resources now controlled by China, Russia, and the Gulf Arab states. It is a view that, while disturbing to many in the West, cannot be easily discounted and should figure prominently in any discussion of the future of change.

The first case in the module depicts a Chinese firm making the transition from traditional state-owned enterprise to modern competitive company. Notably, however, it is the approach to managing the company that shifts, not the fact of state ownership—and this case thus serves as a microcosm for much of the kind of change Lehmann describes. "Managing Performance at Haier (A)" is about how an existing company institutes not only a turnaround in performance, but also a system of continuous change and improvement. Some readers may be surprised at the methods employed by the firm—one of the most celebrated examples of Chinese business success—and may wonder what they ·mean for performance management elsewhere in the world as Haier and other firms in statist economies globalize. It is a very good question, and one that is at least partly addressed in the (B) case you will probably receive afterward.

In "Bringing Life to Organizational Change," Margaret Wheatley and Myron Kellner-Rogers point out the stark differences between machine-based approaches of change (which they suggest are the norm in modern enterprises) and approaches that look at organizations as living systems. The fundamental fact "that people need to be creatively involved in how their work gets done" drives what we often wrongly see as resistance to change. The authors offer four principles for working with change, aimed at making it a living and integrated—and more successful—process.

East and West come together in the next case, "Singapore Airlines: Continuing Service Improvement." The firm's commitment to quality was clear from the outset, when Singapore Airlines chose SQ as its two-letter airline code "to remind our people that an SQ flight is not just an ordinary flight, it's a quality flight." Management followed a policy of sticking to core competencies and expanding at a measured, organic pace. Singapore Airlines developed a unique culture that combined Eastern and Western values, and that reflected its home country's meritocratic society. Still, by the turn of the millennium, Singapore Airlines was threatened by a variety of pressures: the world-wide airline industry suffered its worst-ever recession; there was a labor shortage in Singapore; and (in yet another example of the impact of globalization on cultures and organizations) a new generation of Singaporeans was increasingly rejecting traditional Confucian values, such as respect for authority, and adopting Westernized expectations for a higher standard of living. The airline's efforts to continue its organic growth and maintain an informal, service-obsessed culture in the face of these challenges is the subject of the case.

In "Cracking the Code of Change," Michael Beer and Nitin Nohria start with a so-bering statistic: Approximately 70 percent of all change initiatives fail. From their observations of organizations over many years, they develop two archetypes of change: Theory E organizations focus on economic value in developing and implementing their change programs, whereas Theory O change focuses on organizational capability. The authors argue that a combination of these two approaches is essential to developing a sustained advantage in today's economy.

As an exemplar of the success of this approach, Beer and Nohria point to Jack Welch's tenure as CEO at General Electric—but they are careful also to point out that it took almost twenty years for this success to emerge. This odyssey is the focus in the next part of the module, beginning with the case "GE's Two-Decade Transformation: Jack Welch's Leadership." The legendary CEO's success at GE was the result of a series of initiatives, from 1981 to 2001, each of which positioned the company for success at the next stage. These are set out in sequence in the case. In the case and reading that follow, we look at two of these initiatives, from either end of the Welch era, in depth.

In the Change Classic "Nigel Andrews and General Electric Plastics (A)," we join GE in 1989, at a time when it has embarked on a highly publicized and massive change program called Workout. The case looks at a series of Workout sessions and at a decision that participants reached, which hits a major snag before it is even made operational. In working out the resolution of this problem, all the issues of managing change come into play: What is to be changed? Who is to be changed? How is this to be done? Can everyone live with the longer-term consequences?

"GE's Move to the Internet" describes how Welch embraced the Internet and, in so doing, fundamentally changed the way the $112 billion firm did business. The fact that Wall Street treated GE "as both a blue chip and an Internet company" illustrates the successful marriage of Beer and Nohria's Theories E and O. The reading enumerates GE's cultural attributes that have been essential to this success, and points out that even large firms can be nimble and responsive in the Internet economy.

What happens, though, when change-competent GE executives move to other companies? In "Get Me a CEO from GE," Ellen Kratz and Doris Burke examine how the executives hired out of GE to run other companies (and there are many) often find themselves getting stuck. It would appear that GE "alumni" often have trouble adjusting to their new organizational homes because the cultures in which they find themselves are not "conditioned to put bad news on the table and have it out."

And what is it like to follow a legend? "Bold thinking and creative energy" are what CEO Jeff Immelt is most concerned with bringing to GE in the post-Welch era, says *Business Week's* Diane Brady in "The Immelt Revolution." Were these not the hallmarks of Welch's leadership? Maybe so, but with over 300,000 people, many of whom have been in their jobs a long time, Immelt feels the company needs a continuous injection of innovation to "create the kind of infrastructure that can equip and foster an army of dreamers." To do this, in some areas he has turned the tables on the headhunters and begun to look outside the company for new talent—seemingly a very non-GE thing to do.

The module concludes with "Unlocking the Mystery of Effective Large-Scale Change." Peggy Holman is on a quest for a "unified field theory" of human systems, a model of "the world I want to live in." Her focus is squarely on learning, and on taking a systemic, ongoing, process-based view of change. Drawing on her experiences and observations, and with a tip of the hat to the work of Solomon Asch on effective dialogue, she identifies seven themes common to effective change efforts:

1. A vision of the future or an opportunity to contribute to something larger than themselves moves people to act.

2. Members of the organization or community collectively create a whole systems view.

3. Critical information is publicly available to members of the organization or community.

4. Head, heart, and spirit of the members of the organization or community are engaged.

5. The power of the individual to contribute is unleashed.

6. Knowledge and wisdom exist in the people forming the organization or community.

7. Change is a process, not an event.

To what extent have the protagonists and their change programs in the cases presented in this text met these criteria? As they (and you) continue to develop their organizations, their people, and their own careers, what should they—and more importantly, what should you—do differently?

Reading

Seismic Shocks and Systemic Shifts

The Irresistible Rise of a New State Capitalism

Jean-Pierre Lehmann

Seismic shocks in terms of financial crises on the one hand contrasted with rising financial powers on the other are shaking the world up. Systemic shifts from the state to a market economy are swinging back to a new state capitalism. For the global market economy to be sustained beyond this period of turbulence, we need to better understand what is beneath the surface of global politics, in particular the dramatic rise of the Russians, the Chinese and the Gulf Arabs.

A massive seismic shock hit the Western financial system in early 2008. Precipitated by the sub-prime mortgage crisis, American and many European financial institutions—UBS, Merrill Lynch, Citigroup, Bear Sterns, Morgan Stanley—were beaten and battered. The saviors of Western finance, the cocks ruling the current global financial roost, were primarily the Chinese, the Gulf Arabs and the Russians.

Rewind ten years. In 1998, Asia was in the throes of its own seismic financial crisis and the entire region stood condemned by Western policy makers and pundits for its unsustainable "crony capitalism." As China's capital market remained closed, it was not too adversely affected. But in the late 1990s China was also clearly not the powerful global economic actor it has become; it was still not a member of the World Trade Organization (WTO), and there were concerns about its macroeconomic stability. In 1998, China's exports amounted to some $175 billion, well behind Japan ($400 billion), Germany ($500 billion) and the US ($600 billion). In 2007, China's exports, at over $1,000 billion, surpassed those of both Japan and the US and were second only to Germany's. And by 2007, China's foreign exchange reserves were increasing by more than $1 million every minute! The following year, China's foreign exchange reserves reached a staggering $2 trillion.

In 1998, oil was hovering at $10 per barrel, with the expectation that it would continue to fall. Gulf Arab finances might have evaporated like water in the desert. Ten years later, it had reached $140. The price then dropped significantly along with the financial crisis, but the price of oil is widely expected to continue climbing in the decades ahead. Today the Gulf Cooperation Council (GCC)[1] has amassed a fortune that is measured in trillions of dollars. The total assets in the sovereign wealth funds (SWFs) of the Abu Dhabi Investment Authority alone are estimated to stand at $850 billion. The GCC with a population of less than 40 million has become a major global financial hub.

As for Russia, in 1998 its stock market, the rouble and the economy collapsed after being hit by the contagion effect of the Asian financial crisis. In 1999, at less than $200 billion, Russia's GDP had shrunk to the size of Belgium's—with one-fifteenth of Russia's population. Forecasts were being made that we should prepare for a "world without Russia."[2]

How wrong. In 2007, Russia's GDP stood at $1,250 billion, with the country having accumulated some $500 billion in foreign exchange reserves. GDP per capita has increased six-fold, from $2,000 at the beginning of this decade to $12,000 today.

THE SYSTEMIC SHIFTS

Seismic shocks have been accompanied by systemic shifts. The policy implications and the impact that these systemic shifts will have on the structure and spirit

---

[1] The membership of the GCC, established in 1981, is composed of Saudi Arabia, Bahrain, Qatar, Oman, UAE and Kuwait.

[2] Thornhill, John. "Russia: A Big Player Seeks Its Role." *Financial Times*, January 23, 2008.

of the global economy in the 21st century are enormous and at this stage unfathomable. The late 1990s were also the time when the "Washington consensus" became the global economic holy writ: The commanding heights of the economy must shift from the state to the market through combined measures of deregulation, privatization and liberalization. This was the medicine that the International Monetary Fund (IMF) forced Seoul, Jakarta, Moscow, Brasilia, Buenos Aires and many others to swallow. It was the prevalent uncompromising orthodoxy.[3]

The Washington consensus policy was strongly bolstered by academia. The 1990s witnessed a plethora of publications on the virtues and victory of the market economic system. Mainstream political scientists and economists shared the view that there was ultimately only one possible destination that nations should head for—a market economy resting on a democracy. Arriving at the destination required a combination of both political and economic reforms.

This view also dominated international policy circles. The Bush administration, especially in its first term, showed far more zeal in pushing countries to undertake political reform than economic reform. This was partly because while preaching economic reform, the main established global economic powers—US, EU and Japan—have been laggards in reforming their own economies. In fact, as the emerging economies became increasingly competitive, globalization became feared in the industrialized economies. This failure of leadership may in the decade ahead come to haunt the West.

Although doubts had been emerging about the Washington consensus for some time, the implications of the global financial crisis of 2008/9 could be seen as the great watershed. None of the "saviors" of the Western financial system and, by extension, of the global economy, could be described, with the remotest stretch of the imagination, as liberal democratic market economies. In many respects, as the first decade of the 21st century comes to a close, the West appears to be in retreat—with respect to its economic might and its economic "soft" power, both of which obviously are closely intertwined. Instead, as Jean-Louis Beffa, chairman of Saint Gobain, and Xavier Ragot, professor at the Paris School of Economics, argue, we are seeing the "end of the present standard model of financial capitalism."[4]

The new paradigm is well encapsulated in the title of a *Financial Times* article by Jeffrey Garten, former undersecretary of commerce in the Clinton administration and currently professor of international trade at Yale University: "The unsettling zeitgeist of state capitalism."[5] A new state-market paradigm is emerging—something which the nationalization of banks and other assets in the Western "capitalist" economies seems to confirm.

A NEW PARADIGM OF STATE CAPITALISM

Let's consider the rise of this new paradigm in three areas:

---

[3] For an incisive critique of the IMF's dogmatic application of a one-size-fits-all policy, see Stiglitz, Joseph E. *Globalization and Its Discontents*. London: Penguin, 2002.

[4] Beffa, Jean-Louis and Xavier Ragot. "The Fall of the Financial Model of Capitalism." *Financial Times*, February 22, 2008.
[5] Garten, Jeffrey. "The Unsettling Zeitgeist of State Capitalism." *Financial Times*, February 22, 2008.

THE NEW RUSSIAN REVOLUTION

Anders Åslund, a specialist of the Russian economy, entitled his most recent book *Russia's Capitalist Revolution*, with the central thesis encapsulated in the subtitle: *Why Market Reform Succeeded and Democracy Failed.*[6] One of the many indicators Åslund provides, to demonstrate the success of the market economic reforms, is that whereas in the late 1990s SMEs (small and medium-sized enterprises) accounted for not more than 10% of GDP, the present ratio is 50%, which corresponds to the average in "normal" market economies. The Russian economy has also become far more open; although Russia has been very ambivalent about its accession to the WTO, it is nonetheless widely expected that it will join, something that would have seemed unimaginable not that long ago. While there is a flourishing private sector—no longer limited to the Yeltsin era oligarchs—the state is nevertheless prominent by its presence and particularly so in the case of Gazprom; Gazprom is clearly more than "just" an energy company, it is also an instrument of Russian foreign policy. Russia is not returning to the Soviet economic mode, it has become in some ways a market economy; it is going through a period of transition, with the current state of affairs perhaps best described as a "market economy with Russian characteristics."

During the Soviet era, Russia had great political power, but negligible financial and commercial power. During the Yeltsin years, it lost political power and was, as we saw, an economic failure. In the early 21st century, Russia seems to be combining both political power and financial/commercial power. It has, so far, successfully resisted US attempts to bring Ukraine and Georgia into NATO, partly because of its ability to exercise powerful economic influence over its European neighbors dependent on Russian energy.

THE RISE OF CHINA

It is important to remember that the Chinese refer to the era that began with Mao's victory in October 1949 not as the Revolution, but as the Liberation—the liberation of the Chinese people from both national feudalism and foreign imperialism. In his first speech on the day of Liberation, Mao solemnly declared, "Never will China be humiliated again." In that respect, he and his successors have brilliantly succeeded. The previous century, extending from the first Opium War in 1838 to the Liberation in 1949, was one of such humiliation, degradation and decadence that any sign of insult and impending humiliation gets a very strong reaction. This in good part explains the Chinese furor over the fiasco that accompanied the Olympic torch parade in the lead-up to the 2008 Beijing Olympics.

While China regained political power under Mao, economically it remained a marginalized shambles. China's second revolution, which began in the late 1970s when, as reform leader Zheng Bijian put it, China "embraced economic globalization,"[7] paved the way for the fastest and deepest economic development the planet has ever witnessed. China's economic power is devastatingly evident and felt in the daily lives of pretty much the entire global population. The Chinese economic juggernaut has

---

[6] Åslund, Anders. *Russia's Capitalist Revolution: Why Market Reform Succeeded and Democracy Failed.* Washington, DC: Petersen Institute of International Economics, 2007.

[7] Bijian, Zheng. "China's 'Peaceful Rise' to Great Power Status." *Foreign Affairs*, September/October 2005: 20.

accounted in recent years for some 30% of global GDP growth and 60% of growth in world trade. Global prices of virtually everything respond to Chinese supply—e.g. the low prices of garments, consumer electronics, plastics, etc.—or to Chinese demand—e.g. the high prices of commodities and energy. The intertwining of the US and Chinese economies and the leverage that the latter has over the former led Niall Ferguson and Moritz Schularick to coin the term "Chimerica" to describe the state of the global economy at the time.[8] The crisis that erupted in 2008 was in certain important respects the consequences of this intensive relationship that generated eventually huge and unsustainable imbalances between the two.

China has been, since 2001, a full member of the WTO and by any measure can be considered one of the world's more open economies; it is also home to an increasing number of global corporate players. Not only does China earn the sobriquet "market economy with Chinese characteristics," but it could also be considered the progenitor of the term. The nature of the state-market relationship is captured in the subtitle of an article in the *Financial Times,* "China's champions: Why state ownership is no longer proving a dead hand."[9]

From having been virtually nowhere on the world economic map as recently as the early/mid 1990s, China's global economic clout has become formidable: While it supplies the US with both goods and loans, it is also massively present in

[8] Ferguson, Niall and Moritz Schularick. "Chimerical? Think Again." *Wall Street Journal,* February 5, 2007.
[9] Dyer, Geoff and Richard McGregor. "China's Champions: Why State Ownership Is No Longer Proving a Dead Hand." *Financial Times,* March 16, 2008.

Africa, where, in 2007, it invested more than all OECD economies combined. This economic clout will increasingly be reflected in global political clout.

While the speed of change following China's economic revolution of the late 1970s has been formidable, it can also be seen in a broad historical perspective. At the beginning of the 19th century, China accounted for 33% of world GDP. By the mid-20th century that figure had dwindled to less than 5%. Thus, one can argue that what we are seeing is China's re-emergence. The same could be said of India. The same could emphatically not be said about the GCC.

THE EMERGENCE OF THE GULF ECONOMY

The GCC economies have emerged in recent decades from virtually nothing beyond sand to a collection of prodigious financial skyscrapers. Their economic power has come from oil. Today the GCC is sitting on top of two-thirds of the known world oil reserves. Its financial power, measured in trillions of dollars, is likely to increase, as the price of oil is also likely to increase. However, while the gains from the big oil increases that occurred in the 1970s are recognized to have been largely squandered, the intention of the current generation of the region's leadership is to learn from past mistakes and to direct its massive wealth in far more strategic and long-term directions. This includes investment in education, which has been hitherto quite deficient, and in non-energy sectors, at the moment primarily in services. The region counts two of the world's fastest growing and increasingly most reputed airlines—Emirates and Qatar.

All six member states of the GCC are members of the WTO, with Saudi Arabia

the last to have joined (in December 2005). The six have undertaken a series of economic reforms, to different extents, but, once again, it would be impossible to describe any of them as "market economies" without adding the qualifying sobriquet, "with Omani, etc., characteristics." GCC global financial clout is formidable and is poised to become even more so.

IMPLICATIONS FOR BUSINESS LEADERS

How will the established Western economic powers respond to this change? Many in the regions concerned—Russians, Chinese and Gulf Arabs—see a rising tide of Western protectionism—not just the more traditional variety, but also new forms of financial protectionism. The assumption is that Russian, Chinese and Arab money, notably Sovereign Wealth Funds, will be rejected on security-related grounds and also for many other spurious reasons reflecting populist political tendencies. They bristle at what they see as perennial Western hypocrisy and double standards—for example, demanding standards of transparency from them that Western financial institutions themselves are far from upholding.

Business leaders, financiers and officials are looking at an emerging economic space extending from the Middle East to Central Asia, South Asia, Russia and East Asia. It is impossible to envisage that the Western markets and political clout will be obliterated for the foreseeable future, yet the axis described above will become, in all likelihood, the main center of growth and business development.

There are a number of lessons and imperatives that business leaders should recognize:

1. *Develop externally oriented antennae.* Are your global antennae functioning properly and are they well adjusted to the rapidly changing global landscape? As Peter Drucker stated more than half a century ago, "It is the external environment that leads." Spending excessive time perfecting internal processes may ultimately be the road to obsolescence. Externally oriented antennae must be well developed and constantly recalibrated. Ask yourself if you are watching developments closely, assessing trends and seeking to anticipate the impact they will have. Or will your insularity and myopia lead you to follow the fate of the dodo?

2. *Become savvy in global politics.* Do you understand global politics and the forces driving the policies and aspirations of the key emerging economic powers? In this global age, it is vital to recognize that the external environment that needs to be understood and reckoned with is expanding and deepening. This chapter has been limited to China, Russia and the GCC. The global mindset must also incorporate other key regions: India, Central Asia, Iran, Nigeria and other sub-Saharan African countries, Brazil, Mexico, Venezuela and other countries of Latin America. An Atlantic mindset is by definition an outmoded 20th-century mindset.

3. *Avoid simplification and generalization.* Are you one of those people who like simplicity? The 21st-century business environment will not be for you, for it must be recognized that never has the big picture been more complex. The world is emphatically not flat. It is full of peaks and precipices. Simplification is not only wrong, it is dangerous. With the new players emerging, it is vital to

understand not only their roles in the world, but also how they perceive the world and why. To give one example: As the West appears to be on the verge of war with Iran, how many Western business leaders are capable of explaining why Iranians appear to resent the West? And how many recognize the opportunities that may be lost in respect to this potentially thriving market of 70 to 80 million people? Now and for the foreseeable future, many emerging powers will be torn between the opportunities and attractions of globalism and the rising tide of nationalism.

4. *Be truly global and responsible as a leader.* Are you assuming your responsibilities as a leading global citizen? As things currently stand, the first decade of the 21st century looks like a story of missed opportunities. All efforts (including your efforts!) must be directed at ensuring responsible global business leadership to fathom a reliable compass and a robust rudder as the world economy is propelled into uncharted waters in hurricane conditions. The failure of business leaders to engage in the global economic policy process during the last decade in good part accounts for its paralysis. The manner in which the WTO Doha Development Round, launched in 2001 in the wake of 9/11, was allowed by business to become hostage to narrow atavistic interests stands as an indictment of global business leadership. By being too preoccupied with making money and focusing on the bottom line, business leaders have allowed the global economic climate to degenerate in a way that will ultimately be to the detriment of all, including the business leaders and their shareholders whose value they should be enhancing.

Clearly, the challenges facing Western companies are large. But, it should be noted that the increasing power of these emerging global players does not imply that their power is indestructible. This is far from being the case. All three have a number of key weaknesses and vulnerabilities. In the case of Russia, whatever economic power it attains, it will be enjoyed by fewer and fewer people—it is recording an average annual population *decrease* of 700,000. The reality is that all economies—established, emerging and poor—will face many daunting challenges in the decade ahead. The era of high growth–low inflation, from which the whole world benefited, is over. Inflation seems to be back, especially in food prices. While food may be—indeed should be—the biggest policy preoccupation in the immediate term, issues related to water, climate change, inequality, poverty, disease, terrorism, and so on, will not go away. If the emerging global economic players and the established economic powers can find a *modus vivendi* of cooperation based on mutual interest and mutual respect, then the world will survive. If the current trend of mutual mistrust, nationalism and confrontation continues, we could be in for a very rough period.

QUESTIONS TO ASK

- Are your global antennae functioning properly and are they well adjusted to the rapidly changing global landscape?

- Do you understand global politics and the forces driving the policies and aspirations of the key emerging economic powers?

- Are you prone to simplification and generalization?

- Are you truly global and responsible as a leader?

Case

Managing Performance at Haier (A)

From Bankrupt Collective Enterprise to the Cover of Forbes

One spring day in early 1985, anyone visiting the production facilities of Qingdao Refrigerator General Factory, a home appliance manufacturer in the northeastern Chinese city of Qingdao, would have been forgiven for thinking that company CEO Zhang Ruimin had taken leave of his senses. Just a few months after taking the helm of the company, at the age of 35, this former Qingdao city official in charge of the home appliance sector gathered all factory personnel outside the factory. There, they watched a group of co-workers implement an order from their young CEO: Destroy 76 refrigerators just off the production line.

The refrigerators being pounded to bits had been found to be defective in some way, even though some defects, such as chips in the paintwork, may have seemed minor. The workers who had assembled them were now handed the tools to destroy them. Wielding sledgehammers, the workers, plus Zhang himself, began the noisy demolition of the glistening new refrigerators—products that would have

retailed for RMB 1,560[1] each, or four times their annual salary. Some swung their hammers with tears in their eyes. Though his employees may have doubted it that day, Zhang had a very clear message: The company would no longer produce substandard products.

Since that day in 1985, Haier, with its unique performance management system, has often been heralded as a model for the transformation of an ailing socialist enterprise to a thriving multinational. The company was seen as capable not only of succeeding in China but also of competing on the world stage.

QINGDAO HAIER REFRIGERATOR

In 2007 Haier was ranked as the world's sixth largest maker of large kitchen appliances with a 4% global market share[2] (*refer to Exhibit 1*) and a particularly strong position in washing machines (#2) and refrigerators (#3). Starting from an almost hopeless position, in just over two decades Haier had managed to achieve what its peers had taken on average 95 years to accomplish.[3] Haier's story was one of a remarkable turnaround.

Source: Research Associate Donna Everatt prepared this case under the supervision of Professors Vladimir Pucik and Katherine Xin as a basis for class discussion rather than to illustrate either effective or ineffective handling of a business situation.

[1] Chinese Yuan Renminbi (RMB) = US$0.12
[2] Euromonitor, February 2008.
[3] The average age of the world's top five global players in the household electrical market was 95 years (Euromonitor, 2001).

EXHIBIT 1   **Global Ranking: Large Kitchen Appliances**
Company Shares (by Global Brand Owner) Retail Volume—% breakdown

	2001	2007
Whirlpool Corp	8.6	11.6
Electrolux AB	9.8	8.9
Bosch-Siemens Hausgeräte GmbH	5.7	6.3
LG Group	3.1	5.1
General Electric Co (GE)	5.0	4.3
Haier Group	2.5	4.0
Indesit Co SpA	–	3.2
Matsushita Electric Industrial Co Ltd	2.7	3.2
Samsung Corp	2.2	2.9
Sharp Electronics Corp	2.5	2.2
Maytag Corp	2.8	–
Merloni Elettrodomestici SpA	3.0	–

Source: Domestic Electrical Appliances: Euromonitor from trade sources/national statistics. © 2008 Euromonitor International.

In 1985 what was then the Qingdao Refrigerator General Factory had run up a debt of RMB 1.47 million—equivalent to the combined annual salaries of its nearly 3,000 employees—and was virtually bankrupt. At that time, Haier's performance was similar to that of many other local Chinese enterprises, characterized by bureaucracy and inefficiency, with little regard for cost or quality control or for customer needs.[4]

A shift in the company's fortunes came when Zhang was appointed CEO in 1985. Since then, he had turned the small loss-making refrigerator factory into a group of more than 240 plants and companies, employing over 50,000 workers. Between 1984 and 2006 Haier's revenues jumped from RMB 3.48 million to RMB 104 billion (*refer to Exhibits 2a and 2b for selected financials for its publicly listed main business—refrigerators*).

Since 2002 Haier had been recognized annually as China's most valuable brand, based on its success in "introducing market competition in the whole electric home appliance industry."[5] The company had become a source of national pride, both for its performance in the domestic markets and its increasing successes around the world. Overall exports increased to $1.7 billion in 2006 and the company's products were sold in 160 countries, in 12 of the 15 top European retailers and in all of the top 10 retail chains in North America.

Since it began exporting in the early 1990s, Haier had pursued a strategy of creating, then dominating, market niches. For example, it manufactured compact refrigerators of the kind typically found in college dorms or hotel rooms—and for which it had captured almost half the market in the US. Another niche in the

[4] One of the first rules Zhang set was, "Do not urinate on the factory floor."

[5] Annual report of the Beijing Famous-Brand Evaluation Co. Ltd., 2002.

EXHIBIT 2a   Selected Financials Qingdao Haier: Refrigerators (RMB million)

	1999	2000	2001
Turnover	3,974	4,828	11,442
Gross profit	819	870	1,903
Operating profit	346	358	955
Net profit	311	424	618
Net profit growth	(70)%	37%	46%
Gross margin	21%	18%	17%
Net margin	8%	9%	5%
Dividend yield	1.2	1.8	2.6

Source: Company information.

EXHIBIT 2b   Selected Financials Qingdao Haier (RMB million)

	2006	2007
Turnover	23,214	29,469
Gross profit	3,690	5,535
Operating profit	831	899
Net profit	638	754
Net profit growth	N/A	19%
Gross margin	16%	19%
Net margin	2.7%	2.6%
Dividend yield	1.1%	0.7%

Note: 2005 data is not comparable to that of 2006 and 2007 as China adopted new accounting standards in 2007, retrospective to 2006.
N/A = not applicable
Source: Company information.

US for Haier was electric wine cellars (refrigerators specially designed to store wine). With this niche marketing strategy, by 2008 the Haier brand held over 5% of the North American maket in refrigeration appliances.[6]

KEY SUCCESS FACTORS

A summary of Haier's key success factors included:

- *Product diversification.* Haier evolved from one refrigerator model in 1984 to 86 different product categories with over 13,000 specifications, including microwave ovens, air conditioners, small home appliances, TVs, washing machines and MP3 players.

- *Product innovation to create niche markets.* For example, in China's major cities, living space was limited, families were small[7] and energy was relatively more expensive. Haier invented a miniature washing machine as a secondary household machine to wash small loads of laundry daily in summer.

- *Marketing initiatives that emphasized product quality and market research.* In

[6] Euromonitor, February 2008.

[7] Due to China's one-child policy.

contrast to many Chinese manufacturers which competed on price, Haier sought to differentiate its products. In a recent price war in both the domestic and international appliance market, Haier actually increased its price to send a message to the market of Haier's quality and service.

- *Globalization.* By 2007 Haier had set up many overseas production bases, service and sales facilities, procurement networks and international technology alliances and joint ventures with foreign players to better penetrate international markets.

- *Innovative human resource management practices.* Haier was one of the first Chinese companies to tie salaries, and even job security, to performance. Its organizational strategies included transparency, fairness and justice.

HAIER GROUP'S MANAGEMENT PHILOSOPHIES

Zhang's management principles integrated Japanese management philosophy, American innovation and aspects of traditional Chinese culture, as well as Haier's own learning. These policies were introduced into an environment framed at the beginning by the Chinese cultural values of harmony, face, relationships and hierarchy, as well as by the management practices inherited from state-owned enterprises (SOEs). (*Refer to* **Exhibit 3** for a summary of characteristics of SOE managers.)

Zhang remarked on the importance of effective human resource management policies:

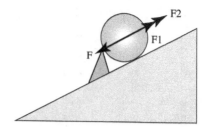

An enterprise is like a ball being pushed up a hill (F1). Under pressure of market competition and internal stress (F2), the ball needs a strong braking force (F) to prevent it from rolling back down. This braking force is the internal management infrastructure.

A SENSE OF URGENCY

Zhang explained that Haier was prepared for "moving forward in times of danger." He continued:

We are not safe in that Haier has not achieved its goal so far—a goal that is limitless. Haier has been developing for 18 years, but so far we haven't seen a day of peace and safety. The outside world is always forcing or pushing us to move forward without stopping.

This sense of urgency was heightened by internal competition as well as external. Xiwen Zhou, president of Haier University, explained:

Each Haier employee is a customer of his fellow workers. For example, Haier's Environmental Testing Laboratory must satisfy the needs of its "customers" in the Design Department by meeting deadlines and producing excellent data and useful test results. The Design Department, in turn, serves customers in the Production Department by innovative and successful designs for the manufacture of goods.

EXHIBIT 3 Characteristics of SOE Managers

Characteristics of managers in Chinese SOEs frequently mentioned in current books and articles on Chinese economy:

- Information conduits, not decision makers
- Comfortable working only in functional silos
- Risk averse/compliant
- Preference for ambiguity in oversight roles
- Averse to transparency
- Paternalistic* and coalitional (*guanxi* networks)
- Reliance on informal contacts
- Not fully appreciative of the market (incomplete buy-in)
- Professionally undereducated
- Inflexible (or constrained by unwieldy economic system).

* Chinese society was hierarchically structured based on Confucian principles of emperor over general, father over son (highly paternalistic), husband over wife, older brothers over younger brothers, for example.

Zhou used another example from a particular division:

> For example, we have 22 vacuuming technicians engaged in different divisions. They used to care only about their own job and their division. There was no communication among business divisions, and creative ideas were not shared. Now we rank them across the Group according to several indexes such as quality, cost and output. Thus everybody knows he is No. 1, No. 2 or No. 3 among the vacuuming technicians, etc., and the sense of competition instantly increases. All the workers are motivated to do better and better.

In this way, Zhang noted that "employees can begin to feel market pressures even though they are inside the organization." Further, he felt that this philosophy had helped Haier avoid two problems that had traditionally characterized Chinese organizations: hierarchy and interpersonal networks (referred to as *guanxi*),[8] or what Zhang called "speed-absorbers."

Another fundamental element of Zhang's performance management system was accountability, at all levels, at all times.

OEC: OVERALL, EVERY, CONTROL AND CLEARANCE

A guiding principle of Haier's management system was OEC: Overall, Every, and Control and Clearance. The term "overall" meant that all performance dimensions had to be considered. "Every" referred to everyone, every day and

[8] *Guanxi* refers to the Chinese cultural system of forming social—and business—relationships based on mutual obligation. In other words, "I'll help you now; you help me later."

everything. "Control and clearance" referred to Haier's end-of-work procedure each day, which stated that each employee must finish all tasks planned for that day before leaving work. Clearance was conducted through self-assessment and meeting with one's supervisors. The concept of OEC laid the groundwork for a management system that had both breadth and depth: It applied to every aspect of work, every employee, every day.

According to Mianmian Yang, the president of Haier Group:

> It is really hard to keep track of all employees every day. Since Haier started the OEC practice (i.e., a self-management system) in 1989, we have been training our employees and managers to learn how to set up, achieve and be accountable for the targets that they set for themselves every day. The targets set have to be continuously improved and stretched. We raise the bar all the time. Human beings tend to get used to the status quo. A worker must finish the task he and his supervisors set to be accomplished every day. As a manager, if you can tell the employee—with his agreement and participation—his targets, then he knows what is expected of him. Each employee should set his own challenging targets.

Once the worker knew what was expected of him, his performance was closely monitored, evaluated and rewarded.

80:20 PRINCIPLE

Under Haier's "80:20 Principle," the 20% of employees who were managers were held responsible for 80% of company results (good or bad). For example, if a worker was fined for equipment damage, he would be held responsible for 20% of the problem and his supervisor would be held responsible for 80%. This did not directly translate to a 20:80 ratio of fines, bonuses, etc. It was a slogan in Haier that communicated a clear and loud message: Managers have to have the courage and conscientiousness to assume responsibility at Haier.

RACETRACK MODEL

A key aspect of Haier's management principles was the system used for performance evaluations and promotions—and demotions—based on the concept of a racetrack. All employees were welcome to compete in work-related "races" such as job openings and promotions. But winners had to keep racing—and keep winning—to defend a title. There was no such thing as a permanent promotion. In keeping with this philosophy, every employee in the Haier Group (except the top eight senior executives) underwent frequent and transparent performance appraisals—going against the traditional Chinese culture in which "face" was extremely important.

TRACKING INDIVIDUAL PROFIT AND LOSS

Monthly measures were used to track performance, according to the revenue and profit the managers had earned for the company. A senior manager gave an example:

> Let's take the relationship between a refrigerator division director and a refrigerator production unit manager for example. If the production unit has the capacity to produce 50,000 refrigerators, the division director must provide orders for 50,000 refrigerators to the production unit, enough orders to meet its entire capacity. If you only provide orders for 45,000 refrigerators, then you, the division director, rather

than the production unit manager, must be responsible for the lack of orders for 5,000 refrigerators. That is your expense. Similarly, the division director can earn his income by achieving his target (of 50,000 refrigerators) [and if] the production unit does not meet the quality standards, or delays delivery, the division director can claim for compensation. This would be extra income for his account, as one of his normal income items would be. The claim is a cost to the production unit, but an income to the division director.

Another example was provided:

We have seven refrigerator production units altogether in our refrigerator division. They must share their best experiences to improve the lowest performer. When the average performance level is raised, the unit managers can achieve their incomes.

However, although the unit's income was attributed to the unit manager, that manager also had his own income and expenditure, accounted for in a "bankbook."

DEPOSIT BOOK[9]

Although each manager was accountable for only a small portion of the overall

[9] Haier referred to the credits employees earned with their contribution to productivity and/or innovation as income [points], recorded in a book that functioned like a bankbook, which accompanied the employee until the end of his/her career with Haier. At the same time, the employee would pay for resources used. When income was greater than expenses, it was recorded as profit (or value added). When expenses were greater than income, the employee was in debt. Thus, every employee functioned with profit/loss, as a strategic business unit. Each employee earned a salary if he/she made a "profit" (a positive contribution to the company and the unit). An employee's salary was determined by his/her bankbook.

profits, Zhang believed each one could function as a miniature company (MMC), each with his own profit and loss statement, mimicking a company's accounting records. As each MMC profited, so did the Group. Increasing revenues was similar to depositing money in a bank—the more a division profited, the more the manager accumulated in his resource bankbook. As long as a manager stayed with the company, his account existed, regardless of department or division.

Zhou explained the system:

We set basic goals for managers. Only when they meet or exceed those goals will they have money (i.e., savings) in their account, otherwise they have to pay. This is an incentive to do a better job. But this is effective for those who reach their goals first, for the goals we have set for them are merely basic ones. We give them three or five more months, and whoever reaches his goal earlier will receive more income, and the later ones do not receive any income and have to pay.

Let me give you an example. Yongshao Zhang used to be one of our purchasing agents for the logistics department. All he needed to do was buy what you wanted according to your requirements, without taking any responsibility for when these materials were used. Now we have changed the practice, and Zhang has become a purchasing manager. As a manager, he has to ensure that the steel plates he buys are the least expensive in the world and are of the best quality. Moreover, he has to provide the steel plates in time according to the demands of the business divisions, while trying not to store them in the warehouse for long, because he is charged for warehouse space. Zhang's office expenses—including water and electricity,

EXHIBIT 4   **Footprints on Factory Floor**

Source: Company information.

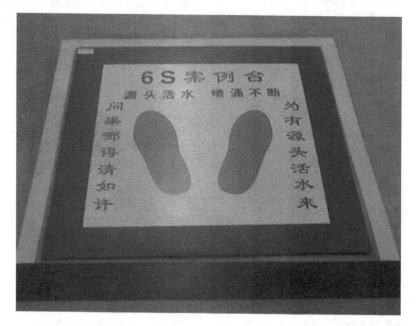

machines, customs declarations, employees' salaries—are all "paid" by him. If the steel plates have quality problems according to the feedback from the market, Zhang Yongshao is entirely responsible. Passive job performance has turned into a practice that actively drives all the units. Passive management has turned into active procedures.

MANAGING PERFORMANCE

Haier used several performance management and motivational tools. One involved a set of colored footprints on the factory floor (*refer to **Exhibit 4***). Before 1998 a pair of yellow footprints was used as a kind of warning. Every day, a poor performer would stand on the yellow footprints to "reflect." The worker was expected to share how he could improve performance the next day. Subsequently, the color was changed to green to represent encouragement. Now, a top performer—either worker or manager— would stand on the footprints and explain why he had done a good job or how he accomplished his job by being innovative and what others might learn from this. According to Zida Yu, vice president in charge of research and development promotion, "Our main purpose is to motivate our people effectively."

Another tool used to motivate workers was a board placed in the factory workshop that recorded workers' performance on a daily basis. Under a system of self-management, employees set clear goals for themselves in a brief meeting with their supervisor at the beginning of their

EXHIBIT 5   **Chart Rating Workers' Performance**

Source: Company information.

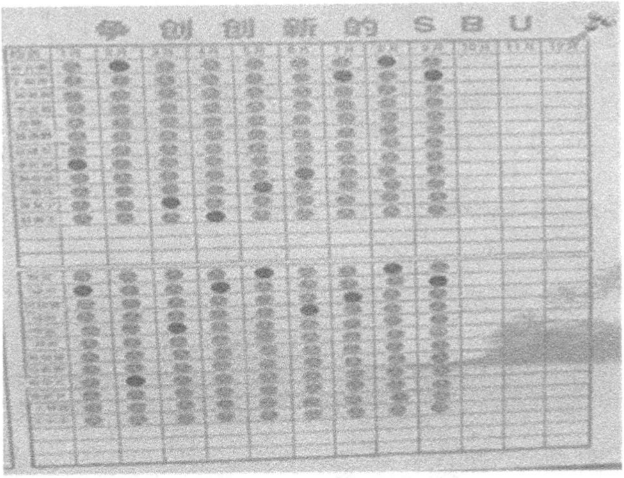

shift. At the end of the day, the employee and supervisor met again to assess how well these goals had been fulfilled. Each employee received a colored face, representing an informal grade for the day: red meant "excellent," green denoted "average" and yellow was "below average or below expectations" (*refer to Exhibit 5*).

Haier had a formal policy for managing those employees who did not meet set expectations. The lowest-performing 10% of employees were dismissed, based on a three-phase system. In the first review (either annual or quarterly), an employee who ranked in the bottom 10% was "asked to be on leave" and sent for job training at Haier's expense. If he remained in the bottom 10% during the second review, he was sent for more training—again on leave, but at his own expense. Continued performance in the bottom 10% in the third review resulted in the employee's dismissal.

The flip side of this approach was the emphasis on recognizing and rewarding successes and creativity. If an employee developed or improved a product, or suggested an efficient new procedure, the innovation carried the employee's name, and notice of it was prominently displayed.

APPRAISING MANAGERS

Although it was more challenging to evaluate the performance of managers than of workers, Haier had developed a system of review based partly on quantifiable results. For a manager responsible for domestic or overseas business development, indicators such as volume of sales and selling speed, share of local market and share of global market were used. For a division head, the number of product orders, quality, cost, time for delivery, etc. were used. And for a senior manager, strategic business unit results and profit and loss were used.

EXHIBIT 6 Managers' Performance Ranking

Source: Company information.

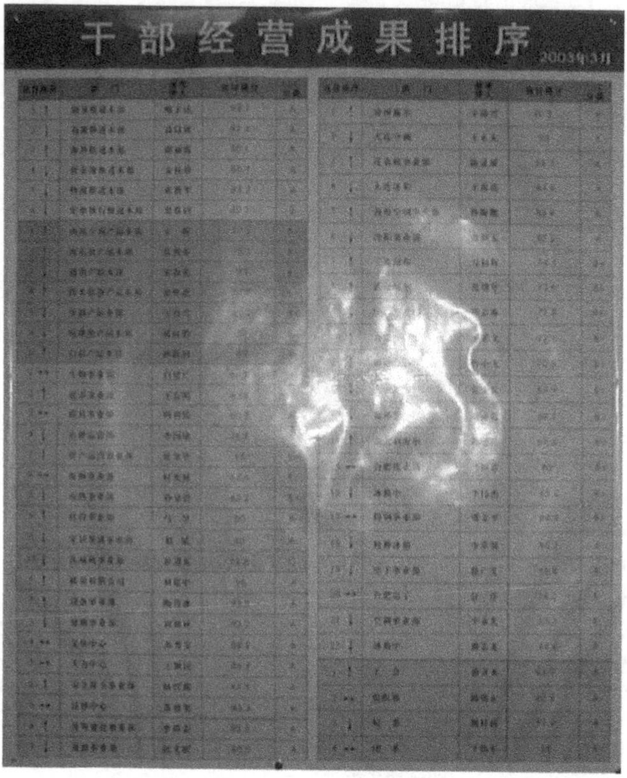

Each manager's performance was reviewed weekly. The criteria for weekly evaluation involved both achieving quantifiable goals and the degree of innovation and process improvement, for example. At the end of the month, managers received a performance grade of A, B or C. The results of this evaluation were announced at a monthly meeting for middle and upper level managers on the eighth day of the month.

The results of managers' performance ranking were openly displayed at the entrance to the company cafeteria, with a green or red arrow indicating whether their score had gone up or down that month (*refer to* **Exhibit 6**). Haier had been doing this for over 15 years. Promotions or demotions were also published in the *Haier Ren Bao.*

Haier devoted significant resources to training and development. An important part of the appraisal process also included identifying more than 80 of the mid to upper level managers in the Group. They were sent on courses at "Haier University" every Saturday morning. The classes, called Interactive Learning sessions, focused on developing an action plan and implementing improvements in operations. The grades received in these courses accounted for about 40% of each manager's performance evaluation.

DEVELOPING TALENT

When new positions opened up, Haier ensured that a wide pool of candidates competed for the position rather than promoting only from among employees of a certain position or tenure. Job rotation was critical to promote employee development and to avoid territorialism. New recruits tried out two or three different jobs before being finally assigned to a position. Later on, even when an employee performed well in a particular post, he was rotated into a new job. The average length of stay in a management position was three years (the maximum term was six years), ensuring that managers understood many different areas of the company.

At the monthly management evaluation meetings, top performers were identified, and those with the most potential were transferred into the Haier talent pool. The competitive threshold was high and selections for the talent pool were drawn from scratch every quarter, then evaluated separately for every new position. There was no philosophy of "once you're in, you're in" at Haier. However, unlike the general employee pool, the company did not have a fixed percentage of people in the talent pool that had to be eliminated.

A points system was used to assess whether a manager was achieving the performance standards to remain in the talent pool. Five points were allocated for monthly performance, five for accumulative performance, and five for current project reviews. A score of less than 10 for several months in a row would result in a transfer out of the talent pool.

DEALING WITH LOW PERFORMANCE OF MANAGERS

The pressure to perform and improve was relentless. In 2000, 13 of 58 senior managers in the headquarters in Qingdao were identified and penalized at different levels because they were not performing to ever-increasing Haier standards.

The low-performing managers were classified in three categories. If minor improvements in management performance were necessary, managers were "put on medication," which indicated that they needed to change and received training on those specific issues. More serious underperformers were referred to as "IV users" and demoted. Managers with serious performance issues were "hospitalized," and would be removed from their position.

GOING GLOBAL

Haier was among the first Chinese manufacturers to have established manufacturing bases overseas. An interesting question was whether the performance management practices that had earned Haier such success in China were transferable to other cultures as it continued with its aggressive pushes toward international expansion.

Many of Haier's performance management philosophies were considered groundbreaking not only for a Chinese company but also for any firm anywhere. How, then, could Haier's performance management systems be applied in other regions of the world?

Reading

Bringing Life to Organizational Change

Margaret J. Wheatley and Myron Kellner-Rogers

After so many years of defending ourselves against life and searching for better controls, we sit exhausted in the unyielding structures of organization we've created, wondering what happened. What happened to effectiveness, to creativity, to meaning? What happened to us? Trying to get these structures to change becomes the challenge of our lives. We draw their futures and design them into clearly better forms. We push them, we prod them. We try fear, we try enticement. We collect tools, we study techniques. We use everything we know and end up nowhere.

From *A Simpler Way*, Wheatley and Kellner-Rogers

We know that it is possible to facilitate successful organizational change. We have witnessed organizations that have changed not only in terms of a new destination—new processes, structures, performance levels—but that simultaneously have increased their capacity to deal with change generally. In these systems, after the change effort, people felt more committed to the organization, more confident of their own contributions, and more prepared to deal with change as a continuous experience.

But we'd like to start by acknowledging the more typical, and depressing, history that's accumulated around several decades of organizational change efforts. We hope that by acknowledging this dismal track record you will feel free to contemplate very different approaches.

In recent surveys, CEOs report that up to 75% of their organizational change efforts do not yield the promised results. These change efforts fail to produce what had been hoped for, yet always produce a stream of unintended and unhelpful consequences. Leaders end up managing the impact of unwanted effects rather than the planned results that didn't materialize. Instead of enjoying the fruits of a redesigned production unit, the leader must manage the hostility and broken relationships created by the redesign. Instead of glorying in the new efficiencies produced by restructuring, the leader must face a burned out and demoralized group of survivors. Instead of basking in a soaring stock price after a merger, leaders must scramble frantically to get people to work together peaceably, let alone effectively.

In the search to understand so much failure, a lot of blame gets assigned. One healthcare executive recently commented that: "We're under so much stress that all we do is look around the organization to find somebody we can shoot." (And the executive quoted is a nun!) It's become commonplace to say that people resist change, that the organization lacks the right people to move it into the future, that people no longer assume responsibility for their work, that people are too dependent, that all they do is whine.

We'd like to put a stop to all this slander and the ill will it's creating in our organizations. We strongly believe that failures at organizational change are the result of some very deep misunderstandings of who people are and what's going on inside organizations. If we can clear up these misunderstandings, effectiveness and hope can return to our experience. Successful organizational change is possible if we look at our organizational experience with new eyes.

There's something ironic about our struggles to effect change in organizations. We participate in a world where change is all there is. We sit in the midst of continuous creation, in a universe whose creativity and adaptability are beyond comprehension. Nothing is ever the same twice, really. And in our personal lives, we adapt and change all the time, and we witness this adaptability in our children, friends, colleagues. There may be more than 100 million species on earth, each of whom displays the ability to change. Yet we humans fail at our change projects and accuse one another of being incapable of dealing with change. Are we the only species that digs in its heels and resists? Or perhaps all those other creatures simply went to better training programs on "Coping with Change and Transition."

For several years, through our own work in an enormously varied range of organizations, we've learned that life is the best teacher about change. If we understand how life organizes, how the world supports its unending diversity and flexibility, we can then know how to create organizations where creativity, change, and diversity are abundant and supportive. If we shift our thinking about organizing, we can access the same change capacities that we see everywhere around us in all living beings. But learning from life's processes requires a huge shift.

It's become common these days to describe organizations as "organic." Assumedly this means we no longer think of them as machines, which was the dominant view of organizations, people, and the universe for the past three hundred years. But do current practices in organizations resemble those used by life? Do recent organizational change processes feel more alive? From what we've observed, "organic" is a new buzz word describing organizational processes that haven't changed. These processes remain fundamentally mechanistic. Nowhere is this more apparent than in how we approach organizational change.

A few years ago, we asked a group of Motorola engineers and technicians to describe how they went about changing a machine. In neat sequential steps, here's what they described:

1. Assign a manager

2. Set a goal that is bigger and better

3. Define the direct outcomes

4. Determine the measures

5. Dissect the problem

6. Redesign the machine

7. Implement the adaptation

8. Test the results

9. Assign blame

Sound familiar? Doesn't this describe most of the organizational change projects you've been involved in? We see only one real difference, which is that in organizations we skip step 8. We seldom test the results of our change efforts. We catch a glimmer of the results that are emerging (the unintended consequences) and quickly realize that they're not what we had planned for or what we sold to senior leadership. Instead of delving into what the results are—instead of *learning* from this experience—we do everything we can to get attention off the entire project. We spin off into a new project, announce yet another initiative, reassign managers and teams. Avoiding being the target of blame becomes the central activity rather than learning from what just happened. No wonder we keep failing!

Life changes its forms of organization using an entirely different process. Since human organizations are filled with living beings (we hope you agree with that statement), we believe that life's change process is also an accurate description of how change is occurring in organizations right now. This process can't be described in neat increments. It occurs in the tangled webs of relationships—the networks—that characterize all living systems. There are no simple stages or easy-to-draw causal loops. Most communication and change occur quickly but invisibly, concealed by the density of interrelationships. If organizations behave like living systems, this description of how a living system changes should feel familiar to you.

Some part of the system (the system can be anything—an organization, a community, a business unit) notices something. It might be in a memo, a chance comment, a news report. It chooses to be disturbed by this. "Chooses" is the operative word here—the freedom to be disturbed belongs to the system. No one ever tells a living system what should disturb it (even though we try all the time). If it chooses to be disturbed, it takes in the information and circulates it rapidly through its networks. As the disturbance circulates, others take it and amplify it. The information grows, changes, becomes distorted from the original, but all the time it is accumulating more and more meaning. The information may swell to such importance that the system can't deal with it in its present state. Then and only then will the system begin to change. It is forced, by the sheer meaningfulness of the information, to let go of its present beliefs, structures, patterns, values. It cannot use its past to make sense of this new information. The system must truly let go, plunging itself into a state of confusion and uncertainty that feels like chaos, a state that always feels terrible. But having fallen apart, having let go of who it has been, the system now is capable of reorganizing itself to a new mode of being. It is, finally, open to change. It begins to reorganize around new interpretations, new meaning. It re-creates itself around new understandings of what's real and what's important. It becomes different because it understands the world differently. It becomes new because it was forced to let go of the old. And like all living systems, paradoxically it has changed because it was the only way it saw to preserve itself.

If you contemplate the great difference between these two descriptions of how change occurs in a machine and in a living system, you understand what a big task awaits us. We need to better understand the processes by which a living system transforms itself, and from that understanding, rethink every change effort we undertake. We'd like to describe in more detail these processes used by life and their implications for organizational change practices.

Every living being—every microbe, every person—develops and changes because it has the freedom to create and preserve itself. The freedom to create one's self is the foundational freedom of all life. One current definition of "life" in biology is that something is alive if it is capable of producing itself. The word is auto-poiesis, from the same root as poetry. Every living being is author of its own existence, and continues to create itself through its entire life span. In the past, we've thought of freedom as a political idea, or contemplated free will as a spiritual concept. But now it appears in biology as an inalienable condition of life. Life gives to itself the freedom to become, and without that freedom to create there is no life.

In our lives together and in our organizations we must account for the fact that everyone there requires, as a condition of their being, the freedom to author their own life. Every person, overtly or covertly, struggles to preserve this freedom to self-create. If you find yourself disagreeing with this statement, think about your experiences with managing others, be they workers, children or anyone. Have you ever had the experience of giving another human being a set of detailed instructions and succeeded in having them follow them exactly, to the letter? We haven't met anyone who's had this sought after experience of complete, robot-like obedience to their directives, so we're assuming that your experience is closer to the following. You give someone clear instructions, written or verbal, and they always change it in some way, even just a little. They tweak it, reinterpret it, ignore parts of it, add their own coloration or emphasis. When we see these behaviors, if we're the manager, we feel frustrated or outraged. Why can't they follow directions? Why are they so resistant? Why are they sabotaging my good work?

But there's another interpretation possible, actually inevitable, if we look at this through the interpretive lens of living systems. We're not observing resistance or sabotage or stupidity. We're observing the fact that people need to be creatively involved in how their work gets done. We're seeing people exercising their inalienable freedom to create for themselves. They take *our* work and recreate it as *their* work. And none of us can stop anyone from this process of re-creation—of tweaking, ignoring, changing the directions—without deadening that person. The price we pay for perfect obedience is that we forfeit vitality, literally that which gives us life. We submit to another's direction only by playing dead. We end up dispirited, disaffected and lifeless. And then our superiors wonder why we turned out so badly.

You may think this is an outrageously optimistic view of what's going on in organizations, because undoubtedly you can name those around you who display no creative desires and who only want to be told what to do. But look more closely at their behavior. Is it as robot-like as it first appears? Are they truly passive, or passive aggressive (just another term for how some people assert their creativity). And what are their lives like outside of work? How complex is the private life they deal with daily?

Or look at human history. Over and over it testifies to the indomitable human spirit rising up against all forms of oppression. No matter how terrible the oppression, humans find ways to assert themselves. No system of laws or rules can hold us in constraint; no set of directions can tell us exactly how to proceed. We will always bring ourselves into the picture, we will always add our unique signature to the situation. Whether leaders call us innovative or rebellious depends on their comprehension of what's going on.

The inalienable freedom to create one's life shows up in other organizationally familiar scenes. People, like the rest of life, maintain the freedom to decide what to notice. We choose what disturbs us. It's not the volume or even the frequency of the message that gets our attention. If it's meaningful to us, we notice it. All of us have prepared a presentation, a report, a memo about a particular issue because we knew that this issue was critical. Failing to address this would have severe consequences for our group or organization. But when we presented the issue, we were greeted not with enthusiasm and gratitude, but with politeness or disinterest. The issue went nowhere. Others dropped it and moved on to what they thought was important. Most often when we have this experience, we interpret their disinterest as our failure to communicate, so we go back and rewrite the report, develop better graphics, create a jazzier presentation style. But none of this matters. Our colleagues are failing to respond because they don't share our sense that this is meaningful. This is a failure to find shared significance, not a failure to communicate. They have exercised their freedom and chosen not to be disturbed.

If we understand that this essential freedom to create one's self is operating in organizations, not only can we reinterpret behaviors in a more positive light, but we can begin to contemplate how to work with this great force rather than deal with the consequences of ignoring its existence. We'd like to highlight four critically important principles for practice.

First, when thinking about strategies for organizational change, we need to remember: **Participation is not a choice.** We have no choice but to invite people into the process of rethinking, redesigning, restructuring the organization. We

ignore people's need to participate at our own peril. If they're involved, they will create a future that already has them in it. We won't have to engage in the impossible and exhausting tasks of "selling" them the solution, getting them "to enroll," or figuring out the incentives that might bribe them into compliant behaviors. For the past fifty years a great bit of wisdom has circulated in the field of organizational behavior: People support what they create. In observing how life organizes, we would restate this maxim as: People *only* support what they create. Life insists on its freedom to participate and can never be sold on or bossed into accepting someone else's plans.

After many years of struggling with participative processes, you may hear "participation is not a choice" as a death sentence to be avoided at all costs. But we'd encourage you to think about where your time has gone in change projects generally. If they were not broadly participative—and our definition of "broad" means figuring out how to engage the whole system over time—how much of your time was spent on managing the unintended effects created by people feeling left out or ignored? How many of your efforts were directed at selling a solution that you knew no one really wanted? How much of your energy went into redesigning the redesign after the organization showed you its glaring omissions, omissions caused by their lack of involvement in the first redesign?

In our experience, enormous struggles with implementation are created every time we *deliver* changes to the organization rather than figuring out how to involve people in their creation. These struggles are far more draining and prone to failure than what we wrestle with in trying to engage an entire organization. Time and again we've seen implementation move with dramatic speed among people who have been engaged in the design of those changes.

But we all know this, don't we? We know that while people are engaged in figuring out the future, while they are engaged in the difficult and messy processes of participation, that they are simultaneously creating the conditions—new relationships, new insights, greater levels of commitment—that facilitate more rapid and complete implementation. But because participative processes seem to take longer and sometimes overwhelm us with the complexity of human interactions, many leaders grasp instead for quickly derived solutions from small groups that are then delivered to the whole organization. They keep hoping this will work—it would make life so much easier. But life won't let it work, people will always resist these impositions. Life, all of life, insists on participation. We can work with this insistence and use it to engage people's creativity and commitment, or we can keep ignoring it and spend most of our time dealing with all the negative consequences.

A second principle also derives from life's need for participation: **Life always reacts to directives, it never obeys them.** It never matters how clear or visionary or important the message is. It can only elicit reactions, not straightforward compliance. If we recognize that this principle is at work all the time in all organizations, it changes the expectations of what can be accomplished anytime we communicate. We can expect reactions that will be as varied as the individuals who hear it. Therefore, anything we say or write is only an invitation to others to become involved with us, to think with us. If we offer our work as an invitation to react, this changes our relationships with associates, subordinates, and superiors. It opens

us to the partnering relationships that life craves. Life accepts only partners, not bosses.

This principle especially affects leader behaviors. Instead of searching for the disloyal ones, or repeating and repeating the directions, she or he realizes that there is a great deal to be learned from the reactions. Each reaction reflects a different perception of what's important, and if that diversity is explored, the organization develops a richer, wiser understanding of what's going on. The capacity for learning and growth expands as concerns about loyalty or compliance recede.

As leaders begin to explore the diversity resident in even a small group of people, life asks something else of them. No two reactions will be identical; no two people or events will look the same. Leaders have to forego any desire they may have held for complete repetition or sameness, whether it be of persons or processes. Even in industries that are heavily regulated or focused on finely detailed procedures (such as nuclear power plants, hospitals, many manufacturing plants), if people only repeat the procedures mindlessly, those procedures eventually fail. Mistakes and tragedies in these environments bear witness to the effects of lifeless behaviors. But these lifeless behaviors are a predictable response to processes that demand repetition rather than personal involvement in the process. This is by no means a suggestion that we abandon procedures or standardization. But it is crucial to notice that there is no such thing as a human-proof procedure. We have to honor the fact that people always need to include themselves in how a procedure gets done. They may accomplish this by understanding the reasoning behind the procedure, or by knowing that they are sanctioned to adjust it if circumstances change. We all need to see that there is room enough for our input, for us, in how our work gets done.

And again, life doesn't give us much choice here. Even if we insist on obedience, we will never gain it for long, and we only gain it at the cost of what we wanted most, loyalty, intelligence and responsiveness.

A third principle derived from life is: **We do not see "reality." We each create our own interpretation of what's real.** We see the world through who we are, or, as expressed by the poet Michael Chitwood: "What you notice becomes your life." Since no two people are alike, no two people have exactly the same interpretation of what's going on. Yet at work and at home we act as if others see what we see and assign the same meaning as we do to events. We sit in a meeting and watch something happen and just assume that most people in that room, or at least those we trust, saw the same thing. We might even engage them in some quick conversation that seems to confirm our sense of unanimity:

"Did you see what went on in there!?"

"I know, I couldn't believe what I was seeing."

"Really!"

But if we stopped to compare further, we'd soon discover significant and useful differences in what we saw and how we interpreted the situation.

As we work with this principle, we begin to realize that arguing about who's right and who's wrong is a waste of time. If we engage with colleagues to share perceptions, if we expect and even seek out the great diversity of interpretations that exist, we learn and change. The biologist Francisco Varela redefined organizational intelligence. He said it wasn't the ability to solve problems that made an organization smart. It was the ability of its members to enter into a world whose significance they shared. If everyone in the group thinks that what is occurring is significant (even as they have different perspectives), then they don't have to convince one another. They can act—rapidly, creatively, and in concert.

Entering into a world of shared significance is only achieved, as far as we've seen, by engaging in conversations with colleagues. Not debates or oratories, but conversation that welcomes in the unique perspective of everyone there. If we remain *curious* about what someone else sees, and refrain from convincing them of our interpretation, we develop a richer view of what might be going on. And we also create collegial relations that enable us to work together with greater speed and effectiveness. When any of us feel invited in to share our perspective, we repay that respect and trust with commitment and friendship.

And a very important paradox becomes evident. We don't have to agree on an interpretation or hold identical values in order to agree on what needs to be done. We don't have to settle for the lowest common denominator, or waste hours and hours politicking for our own, decided-on-ahead-of-time solution. As we sit together and listen to so many differing perspectives, we get off our soapboxes and open to new ways of thinking. We have allowed these new perspectives to disturb us and we've changed. And surprisingly, this enables us to agree on a concerted course of action, and to support it wholeheartedly. This paradox flies in the face of how we've tried to reach group consensus, but it makes good sense from a living system's perspective. We all need to participate, and when we're offered that opportunity, we then want to work with others. We've entered into a world whose significance is shared by all of us, and because of that process we've developed a lot of energy for deciding *together* what to do next.

The fourth principle from life is the best prescription we've found for thinking about organizational change efforts. **To create better health in a living system, connect it to more of itself.** When a system is failing, or performing poorly, the solution will be discovered *within the system* if more and better connections are created. A failing system needs to start talking to itself, especially to those it didn't know were even part of itself. The value of this practice was quite evident at the beginning of the customer service revolution, when talking to customers and dealing with the information they offered became a potent method for stimulating the organization to new levels of quality. Without customer inclusion and their feedback, workers couldn't know what or how to change. Quality standards rose dramatically once customers were connected to the system.

This principle embodies a profound respect for systems. It says that they are capable of changing themselves, once they are provided with new and richer information. It says that they have a natural tendency to move toward better functioning or health. It assumes that the system already has within it most of the expertise that it needs. This principle also implies that the critical task for a leader is to increase the number, variety and strength of connections within the system. Bringing in more remote or ignored members, providing access across the system, and through those connections stimulating the creation of new information—all of these become primary tasks for fostering organizational change.

These four principles provide very clear indicators of how, within our organizations, we can work with life's natural tendency to learn and change. As we all were taught by an advertisement many years ago, we can't fool Mother Nature. If we insist on developing organizational change processes suited for machines and ignore life's imperative to participate in the creation of itself, then we can only anticipate more frequent and costly failures.

We have been careful to state principles here rather than techniques or step-by-step methods. This is in keeping with our understanding of how life organizes. The organizations that life creates are highly complex. They are filled with structures, behavioral norms, communication pathways, standards and accountabilities. But all this complexity is obtained by an organizing process that is quite simple, and that honors the individual's need to create. The complexity of a living system is the result of individuals freely deciding how best to interpret a few simple principles or patterns that are the heart of that system. These simple patterns of behavior are not negotiable and cannot be ignored. But how they get interpreted depends on the immediate circumstance and the individuals who find themselves in that circumstance. Everyone is accountable to the patterns, but everyone is free to engage their own creativity to figure out what those patterns mean. This process of organizing honors individual freedom, engages creativity and individuality, yet simultaneously achieves an orderly and coherent organization.

From such simple patterns complex organizations arise. Structures, norms, networks of communication develop from the constant interactions among system members as they interpret the patterns in changing circumstances. Individuals make decisions about how best to embody the patterns, and an organization arises. Sophisticated organizational forms appear, but always these forms materialize *from the inside out*. They are never imposed from the outside in.

In human organizations, we have spent so many years determining the details of the organization—its structures, values, communication channels, vision, standards, measures. We let experts or leaders design them, and then strategize how to get them accepted by the organization. Living systems have all these features and details, but they originate differently, from within the system. As we think of organizations as living systems, we don't need to discard our concern for such things as standards, measures, values, organizational structures, plans. We don't need to give up any of these. But we do need to change our beliefs and behaviors about where these things come from. In a living system, they are generated from within, in the course of figuring out what will work well in the current situation. In a machine where there is no intelligence or creative energy, these features are designed outside and then programmed or engineered in. We can easily discern whether we are approaching our organization as a living system or as a machine by asking: Who gets to create any aspect of the organization? We know we need structure, plans, measures, but who gets to create them? The source of authorship makes all the difference. People only support what they create.

Last year we met a junior high school principal who gave us a superb example of creating a complex and orderly system from a few simple patterns. He is responsible for eight hundred adolescents, ages twelve to fourteen. Most school administrators fear this age group and the usual junior high school is filled with rules and procedures in an attempt to police the hormone-crazed tendencies of early teens. But his junior high school operated from three rules, and three rules only.

Everyone—students, teachers, staff— knew the rules and used them to deal with all situations. The three rules are disarmingly simple: 1. Take care of yourself; 2. Take care of each other; 3. Take care of this place. (As we've thought about these rules, we've come to believe that they might be all we need to create a better world, not just a junior high school.)

Few of us would believe that you could create an orderly group of teen-agers, let alone a good learning environment, from such simple rules. But the principal told a story of just how effective these three rules were in creating a well-functioning school. A fire broke out in a closet and all 800 students had to be evacuated. They stood outside in pouring rain until it was safe to return to the building. The principal was the last in, and he reported being greeted by 800 pairs of wet shoes lined up in the lobby.

Principles define what we have decided is significant to us as a community or organization. They contain our agreements about what we will notice, what we will choose to let disturb us. In the case of these students, wet shoes and muddy floors were something they quickly noticed, something that disturbed them because they had already agreed to "take care of this place." They then acted freely to create a response that made sense to them in this unique circumstance.

In deciding on what to emphasize in this article, we knew that you required even more freedom than these students to design organizational change processes that would work best in your unique situation. Therefore we chose to give you principles to work with, principles that we have found work with life's great capacity for change. As with all principles, once they are agreed upon, they need to be taken very seriously. They are the standards to which we agree to hold ourselves accountable. But clear principles provide only standards for our efforts, they never describe the details of how to do something. They do not restrict our creativity, they simply guide our designs and create coherence among our many diverse efforts. Their clarity serves as an invitation to be creative. Think about how many *different* approaches and techniques you could create that would be congruent with the four principles we stated. How many different forms of practice could materialize as people in your organization invented change processes that honored these principles?

No two change processes need look the same. In fact this is an impossibility—no technique ever materializes in the same way twice. Nothing transfers unchanged. (If it did, you wouldn't be struggling with the issue of organizational change. You would have found what worked somewhere else and successfully imported it.) But if we hold ourselves accountable to these principles, we can create our own unique change processes confident that we are working *with* life rather than denying it. We will have been guided by these principles to create processes that take advantage of the creativity and desire to contribute that reside in the vast majority of the people in our organizations.

We'd like to invite you to experiment with this approach and these four principles. As with all good experiments, this means not only that you try something new, but that you watch what happens and learn from the results. Good experimentation is a process of constant tinkering, making little adjustments as the results come in, trying to discover what's responsible for the effects that show up. So for whatever you start in motion, we ask that you watch it carefully, involve many eyes in the observing, and tinker as you go.

One experiment you might try is to give these four principles to a project design team, either one that's just starting, or one that's trying to rescue a change process that's not working well. See what they can create as they hold themselves accountable to these principles. Encourage them to think through the implications of these principles with many others in the organization. Experiment with a design that feels congruent with the principles, and once that design is operating, observe carefully where it needs to be modified or changed. Stay with it as an experiment rather than as the perfect solution.

A second experiment can occur in every meeting, task force or event in your organization. This experiment requires a discipline of asking certain questions. Each question opens up an inquiry. We have learned that if people conscientiously ask these questions, they keep focused on critical issues such as levels of participation, commitment, and diversity of perspectives. Here are four questions we've found quite helpful:

1. Who else needs to be here?

2. What just happened?

3. Can we talk?

4. Who are we now?

The simplicity of these questions may lead you to believe they're not sufficient or important, but think about the types of inquiry they invite. Every time we ask "Who else needs to be here?" we're called to notice the system of relationships that is pertinent to the issue at hand. We're willing to be alert to who's missing, and the earlier we notice who's missing, the sooner we can include them. This question helps us move to broader participation gradually and thoughtfully, as the result of what we're learning about the issue and the organization. It's an extremely simple but powerful method for becoming good systems thinkers and organizers.

Similarly, "What just happened?" is a question that leads to learning from our experience. Since living systems always react but never obey, this question focuses us on what we might learn if we look at the reactions that just surfaced. The question moves us away from blame and instead opens us to learning a great deal about who this system is and what grabs its attention.

When we ask, "Can we talk?" we're acknowledging that others perceive the world differently from us. Imagine leaving a typical meeting where ego battles predominated. Instead of posturing, grumbling, or politicking, what if we went up to those we disagreed with and asked to talk with them. What if we were sincerely interested in trying to see the world from their perspective? Would this enable us to work together more effectively?

"Who are we now?" is a query that keeps us noticing how we are creating ourselves—not through words and position papers, but through our actions and reactions from moment to moment. All living systems spin themselves into existence because of what they choose to notice and how they choose to respond. This is also true of human organizations, so we need to acknowledge that we are constantly creating the organization through our responses. To monitor our own evolution, we need to ask this question regularly. Without such monitoring, we may be shocked to realize who we've become while we weren't watching. And for organizations that put in place a few essential patterns, like that junior high school, everyone periodically needs to review how they're doing. Are individuals and groups embodying the patterns? And are these patterns helping the organization become what people envisioned for it when the patterns were created?

But questions require us to be disciplined in asking them, a discipline we seldom practice. No matter how simple the questions, we most often rush past them. We feel compelled to act rather than to inquire. But by now, many of us in organizations want to turn away from this history of act-act-act which has led to so little learning and so much wasted energy. All other forms of life stay watchful and responsive—they learn so continuously that science writer James Gleick notes that "Life learned itself into existence." Physicist and author Fritjof Capra states that there is no distinction between living and learning, "A living system is a learning system." If we don't begin to seriously focus on learning in our organizations, there is no way we can bring them to life.

Throughout this article, we've stressed the freedom to create that all life requires. We hope that you will feel inspired to exercise your freedom and creativity to experiment with some of the ideas, principles and questions we've noted. We need each other's best thinking and most courageous experiments if we are to create a future worth wanting.

Case

Singapore Airlines

Continuing Service Improvement

A CUSTOMER'S JOURNEY

Paul Denver walked up to the Singapore Airlines Raffles Class (Business Class) check-in counter, pushing a trolley piled high with multicolored pieces of luggage. The golf clubs, scuba gear and the baby's push chair lay on top. Five-year-old Tamara ran alongside. Marsha Denver was behind, slowed down by toddler Janice who insisted on walking although she could barely stand. At the counter, the Aéroports de Paris agent in her blue uniform was speaking with a passenger, her face on a level with a soft-colored arrangement of exotic flowers.

The Denver family moved to the counter. "Good afternoon. Flying to Singapore?" In fact, their itinerary was a good deal more complicated, combining business for Paul in three Asian locations with a holiday on Bali for the family. Denver, a member of several frequent-flyer programs, had already flown Singapore Airlines and had been impressed with the quality of the service. He felt confident that the airline would solve any problems that might arise on the six-leg

trip that his wife and he were undertaking with their two small children.

SINGAPORE AIRLINES' JOURNEY

Our job is not just to fly people from A to B, but to have them enjoy the flight. We're not in the transportation business, we're in the service business. All airlines claim this, but the big difference is not in the objectives set out by management, or in the ads developed by the marketing department: it is in the delivery of service.

We have a high reputation for service and that means that when someone flies with us, they come with high expectations. Still, we want them to come away saying "Wow! That was something out of the ordinary."[1]

After years of continuing success, Singapore Airlines (SIA) had established itself as the leading carrier in terms of service. Countless awards—year after year across the 80s, 90s and in the new millennium—testified to its pre-eminence. In 2004, the *Conde Nast Traveler* magazine's Readers' Choice Awards named it the world's "best airline" for the 16th time

[1] Yap Kim Wah, SIA Senior VP, Product and Service. This information was drawn from Jochen Wirtz and Robert Johnston, "Singapore Airlines: What it takes to sustain service excellence—a senior management perspective," *Managing Service Quarterly,* Volume 13, Number 1, 2003.

in 17 consecutive years. Unlike many international airlines, SIA had retained its profitability—a significant feat in the face of SARS and the climate of terrorism that had impacted air travel. Indeed, in 2004, *Fortune* magazine had ranked SIA second in the airline category of its *World's Most Admired Companies* survey.

But SIA could not rest on its laurels. With varying degrees of success, rival carriers were emulating its preoccupation with service to lure and retain high-spending business travelers in an increasingly competitive market. Many emphasized the gourmet food, vintage wines, smiling hostesses and on-board technology that were the cornerstone of SIA's competitive advantage. Additionally, in recent years, low cost carriers (LCCs) had emerged. With a lower priced option available, delivery on SIA's service promise was even more important.

SIA saw that continuous service improvement was the only way to retain its supremacy. Its management recognized that passengers, to the extent they were still willing to pay a premium for service, expected ever more for their money—especially from SIA. Moreover, service had to progress while expansion continued—industry estimates suggested 5–8% annual increase in revenues with a 5% increase in net profit in the years after 2003. SIA planned to achieve its goals with a "three pillar" strategy of superior inflight service, the most modern fleet, and outstanding ground service.

ON BOARD: "INFLIGHT SERVICE OTHER AIRLINES TALK ABOUT"

From the 1970s on, SIA had seen superior service as its only possible source of competitive advantage. "We selected the two-letter airline code SQ to remind our people that an SQ flight is not just an ordinary flight, it's a quality flight," explained a Ground Services Senior Manager. At the outset SIA had no domestic network and a small customer base among Singapore's population of two million, few of whom could afford air travel. The Singapore government made it clear that the airline had to stand on its own feet: although a flag carrier, it would receive no subsidies.

According to a favorite piece of company lore, the first flight of SIA's predecessor, Malayan Airlines, from Singapore to a road near Ipoh in Malaysia in 1947, saw the beginning of inflight service: the pilot picked up a thermos flask of iced water from under his seat and passed it around to his five passengers. A few years later, the carrier was the first to offer free drinks and headsets, as well a choice of quality meals for economy class passengers.

> The slim, impeccably groomed flight attendant in traditional Malay costume smiled at the Denver family as they entered the aircraft and quickly glanced at their boarding cards. "Good afternoon, Mrs. Denver," she said "Let me show you to your seats."
>
> "Isn't she pretty?" Marsha whispered to Tamara. "Do you remember this dress?" She was pointing to the long-skirted sarong kebaya, a figure-hugging outfit made of flowery batik cloth. Designed by Pierre Balmain, it combined the charm of traditional Asian wear with the elegance of French haute couture. But Tamara looked uncertain. "Of course you remember!" said Marsha. "We saw it at Madame Tussaud's!"

While the face of the 'Singapore Girl' figurine was changed every 18 months, the constant attention to training had turned the real flight attendants into symbols of Asian charm, grace and hospitality. So successful was the 'Singapore Girl' advertising concept that Madame Tussaud's, the London wax museum, had chosen it as an emblem of international travel. And the outfit, on sale at most Singapore souvenir shops, was almost as popular as the 'Girls' themselves, an indication that the flight attendants were also emblems of the island-state.

But Marsha, a professional woman who believed in equal opportunities, wasn't sure that she approved of the Singapore Girl concept altogether. SIA flight attendants had to retire before they turned 35, unless promoted to a higher position: this policy would be illegal in many Western countries because of age discrimination laws.

Female flight attendants were given five-year contracts, with a maximum of three contracts, and were not taken back as cabin crew after they had given birth to a child, although they could find a ground job with the airline. Stewards were regular, not contract, employees and worked until they reached the normal retirement age in Singapore.

The young woman's gestures were graceful but precise as she advanced down the aisle with a tray of scented towels. "Would you like a hot towel, Mrs. Denver?" she asked. And to Tamara: "Be careful, you could burn your hands!" But Paul Denver was mildly annoyed when she woke him up some minutes later to offer him a glass of champagne. The flight attendant seemed to follow established procedures rather automatically, oblivious to the fact that he was asleep.

Neither of the Denvers, however, had any gripes about the smiling steward who, shortly afterwards, brought the children lots of games and small toys. After lunch (a choice of three main courses, exotic desserts, fresh fruit, fine cheeses, vintage port or a liqueur), he came back to ask whether they needed help with the baby. By then Janice was asleep—mercifully.

"THE MOST MODERN FLEET"

As Marsha Denver settled down for the 13-hour, non-stop flight to Singapore, she surveyed appreciatively the newly-fitted Raffles Class cabin with its tasteful decor and its subtle shades of purple. She was sitting on the top deck of a Boeing 747-400 'Megatop,' the fastest 747 with the largest stretched upper deck. Not quite as glamorous as the supersonic Concorde that SIA used to fly on the London-Bahrain-Singapore route in the 1970s, but nonetheless very comfortable, she thought. "No wonder Singapore Airlines comes so often on top in magazine surveys" she remarked to her husband as she activated the comfortable, 60-degree leg rest, with adjustable calf support, and stretched her legs across the 42-inch pitch.

SIA was the world's largest operator of Boeing 777 planes with 58 in operation and another 31 either on option or firm order. The 747-400, the jumbo jet's fourth generation, played a crucial role in the expansion of airlines from the Asia-Pacific region. In 2004, SIA broke its own record for the world's longest commercial flight flying from Singapore to New York City. In March 2005, SIA's passenger fleet was composed of 89 aircraft. Because it frequently brought in the latest models, the average age of SIA's aircraft was five years and four months and remained one of the industry's youngest fleets. SIA was slated to fly first the Airbus 380, one of the world's biggest planes, a super jumbo aircraft able to accommodate 500 passengers.

Flight SQ319 was equipped with SIA's inflight entertainment system (Kris World Entertainment) that included 104 TV shows, 60 movies, 85 interactive games and 12 music channels. Although tempted to use the entertainment system, Paul sighed and pulled out his laptop. Because it was not immediately visible, he asked the chief flight attendant, recognizable in her red *sarong kebaya,* where the power outlet was located. Directing Paul to the location, she also told Paul that the flight had access to high-speed internet access for a nominal fee. This way, business people could keep up to date with stock exchange or money market prices as well as work on their portable computers and transmit data to their companies or to customers on the ground without leaving their seat. An astounded Paul immediately logged on.

"OUTSTANDING SERVICE ON THE GROUND"

The holiday on Bali had been a success. The children had enjoyed the white sand at Sanur beach while their parents watched temple ceremonies and the popular *wayang kulit* Balinese shadow plays or bought batik in countless patterns and colors. The Denvers were now at Ngurah Rai airport in Denpasar, checking in for a one-day layover in Singapore on their way back to Paris. Paul Denver pointed first to a single brown leather suitcase, then to the jumble of bags and sports gear on the cart. "This one we'll need in Singapore tomorrow," he told the check-in officer. "But everything else we'd really prefer to check in through to our Paris flight." The agent replied, "I'm not sure we can do this. I'll have to ask the supervisor."

While they waited for him to return, Paul Denver gazed at the poster on the wall which declared 'Singapore Airlines Ground Services. We're with you all the way.' "We'll soon find out about that," he thought. On a previous leg, at Manila Airport, Denver had asked to have one bag sent to Singapore and checked in at the left luggage counter and the rest of his luggage sent to Denpasar. The SIA supervisor had gone to great pains to oblige, sending an e-mail to Singapore's Changi Airport to ask staff there to retrieve the bag, carry it to the security clearance area for a bomb search, and finally check it in at the left luggage office.

Attention to service "on the ground" was SIA's most ambitious pillar, dating back to the late 80s. The Outstanding Service on the Ground (OSG) campaign was launched, focusing on improving service at reservation, ticket offices and, most importantly, at each airport SIA flew to. Making customers' perception of ground service as positive as their perception of inflight service was a challenge. Typically, passengers interacted with sales or check-in staff for a few seconds or minutes, and tended to remember them only when something went wrong. And while inflight service was provided by Singapore-based staff recruited, trained, motivated and rewarded by SIA, ground service was provided by handling agents spread across 70 stations around the world. These were often direct competitors (for example, British Airways handled SIA flights at Heathrow Airport).

Each airport unit was given standards in terms of punctuality, baggage handling, speed and friendliness of check-in, efficiency of seat assignment, number of compliments and complaints from customers and professionalism in handling delays. An additional standard for Changi, the region's largest hub, was efficiency of transfers. At every airport, the station manager was held accountable for achieving these standards; awards were given to stations which did well.

The campaign inculcated three principles: 'Show You Care' through body language evidencing interest and attention, 'Dare to Care', and 'Be Service Entrepreneurs,' which meant displaying creativity to exceed customers' expectations. It involved motivational seminars, 'booster training,' reminders and reinforcement through monthly reports by country managers, a dedicated newsletter, *Higher Ground,* as well as monitoring and recognition. Posters carrying slogans such as 'Go Near, Not Away' or 'An Impossible Situation Is a Disguised Opportunity' decorated staff quarters.

INGREDIENTS OF SUCCESS

The "three pillars" all contributed to SIA's undeniable prosperity. For years the airline had topped carrier profitability tables as its pre-tax profit rose from $69 million in 1983 to $1596 million in 2004/2005, despite the company's first-ever loss; $312.3 million in the first quarter of 2003/2004. (See *Exhibit 1* for ten-year profitability trends.) Behind this

EXHIBIT 1

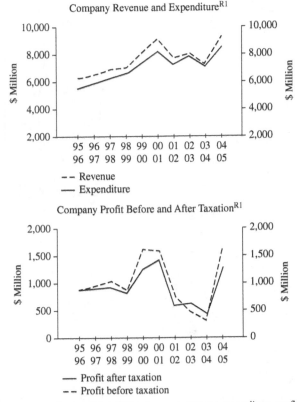

Company Revenue and Expenditure[R1]

-- Revenue
— Expenditure

Company Profit Before and After Taxation[R1]

— Profit after taxation
-- Profit before taxation

R1 *SIA cargo was corporatised on 1 July 2001. Company revenue, expenditure, profit before and after taxation in these charts for 2000-01 and prior years show the combined results of both passenger and cargo operations. The numbers for 2001-02 include cargo operations for the first three months only (April to June 2001).*

continued

EXHIBIT 1 *continued*

Ten-Year Charts

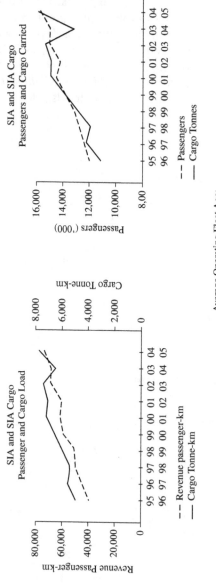

SIA and SIA Cargo
Passenger and Cargo Load

-- Revenue passenger-km
— Cargo Tonne-km

SIA and SIA Cargo
Passengers and Cargo Carried

-- Passengers
— Cargo Tonnes

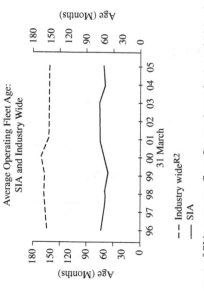

Average Operating Fleet Age:
SIA and Industry Wide

-- Industry wide R2
— SIA

Average age of SIA passenger fleet: 5 years 4 months (as at 31 March 2005)

R2   *Source: Airsoft Information Systems, Rugby, England.*

success were policies—and practices—deliberately and systematically developed by management. These included long-standing guiding principles such as long-term planning, steady growth, a diversified route network, a decision to stick to core competencies, and helping attract visitors to Singapore.

A POLICY OF STEADY ORGANIC GROWTH

Managers at SIA rejected the idea that consolidation would lead to an industry consisting of a handful of mega-carriers and a few niche players. They were nervous that SIA would grow too fast, and generally suspicious of acquisitions despite SIA's strong cash position. "Our goal is to continue to operate a successful airline," said an SIA executive. "If we have to grow to do that, we grow. But we never set out to be a mega-carrier." Because of its long-term vision, SIA did not let what one senior manager described as "the slumps and bumps in the business cycle" disrupt its investment plans. It tried to diversify its network so as not to be dependent on any one market or route, but remained focused on its core activity: aviation and its supporting services. Through the early part of the new century, SIA weathered the effects of terrorism, the impact of SARS and the rise in fuel costs—and became known as one of the most effective hedgers of oil.

"We wish to retain our individuality," said Joseph Pillay, SIA's chairman in the early 1990s, "and to expand at a measured pace that permits us to retain those essential qualities that have made SIA one of the foremost carriers in the world in terms of quality of service, depth of commitment to employees, technical prowess and financial strength."

In 2000, SIA became a member of the STAR alliance (a global network of airlines), thereby offering its customers global distribution. It reaped advantages that included sales benefits from dovetailed schedules, and savings from shared ground facilities and sales and check-in offices.

A STRONG CORPORATE CULTURE

One reason not to grow through acquisitions was to protect SIA's idiosyncratic culture, which managers saw as a hybrid of East and West reminiscent of the former colony's long-standing role as a regional crossroads. "The Singapore Girl is a cross between Western and Asian flight attendants. Typical Western service is lots of communication and talk while Asian service is shy and distanced. Our people are fairly confident and they are unique in Asia in not suffering from a language barrier when talking with international travelers, since English is Singapore's official language," remarked SIA's Personnel Director.

The importance of the Chinese Confucian ethic of filial piety and deference for hierarchy was limited. "We expect loyalty to the company and the country," said another personnel executive. "But we don't give seniority a lot of value. People move up according to performance. Singapore in general operates on meritocracy. And a lot of our operations are overseas; inevitably we imbibe a lot of Western values." However, the majority of SIA's employees were Singaporeans with shared values and concerns, and SIA's management saw the importance of this unity. "We are a cohesive group and we work together as a team with the same culture, attitudes and motivation," said one senior executive.

RECRUITMENT

The service concept required total commitment from all 'front-line' staff, whom SIA saw as its interface with passengers and greatest asset. "The only way to guarantee that customers are satisfied is by making sure that those who serve them are satisfied with their jobs and have a positive attitude," explained a senior manager. He continued, "A key element in a service-minded organization is the motivation of the employee." But years of growth presented SIA with a major challenge when it came to recruiting in Singapore's dwindling labor market. Between 1972 and 2005 the staff had grown from 6,200 to an average of 13,600. Hiring the right front-line staff was thus a major priority.

Recruitment of cabin crew in particular was highly selective. Applicants, who had to be under 25, were screened for a positive attitude towards work, good appearance and posture and language skills. To try to eliminate uncertainty, a psychological test known as the Personality Profile System was developed with outside consultants to determine the service aptitude of applicants. "Character molding and positive mental attitude are essential components of a successful cabin crew." "The Crew must anticipate passengers' needs," explained the Director of Marketing Services. "That means being attentive. This is something people must have in them to begin with; you can't change attitude. That's why SIA has the PPS test."

TRAINING

SIA continually reinforced its service emphasis with ongoing training initiatives, training about 9,000 people per year. Approximately 70% of SIA's training courses were held in-house. Training encompassed functional training and general management skills. The company had seven training schools delivering in the core functional areas of cabin crew, flight operations, commercial training, IT security, airport services training and engineering. The general management training was driven by the SIA Management Development Center.[2]

Cabin crew underwent a four-month full-time course, longer than those provided by SIA's competitors. While noting the importance of technical aspects of cabin service, one SIA executive warned crew against becoming over-dependent on procedures. "Of course we need good systems and procedures," he said. "But what has distinguished us from other airlines all these years is the human touch." The crew was taught little tricks such as memorizing the names of Raffles Class and First Class passengers at boarding, or learning to spot which flyers wanted to chat and which wanted to be left alone.

The Commercial Training department trained SIA staff and handling agents around the world. All new front-line ground staff attended an orientation program and an OSG seminar which were held in Singapore and in regional centers every three months. Within one year all new staff went to Singapore for product training. "We teach the staff that customers are our bread and butter," explained a training manager. "We say things like, 'Don't think of customers as nuisances. They are our employers.' We tell them to be customer champions."

The methods used included experiential learning such as problem-solving games, case studies of real-life situations, and role-playing, where staff were asked to

---

[2] This information was drawn from Wirtz and Johnston, 2003.

put themselves in the shoes of a frequent traveler, or a first-time flyer, or a mother with small children. There was 'rescripting,' where shy participants were told to convince themselves that they were customer champions. Training also involved brainstorming, with staff asked to think of what they could do to solve an actual problem in their station. Outdoor activities and even boot camp training were also among SIA's varied training resources. (See *Exhibit 2* for a description of an OSG course.)

In its staff training, SIA faced the seemingly contradictory challenges of achieving consistency of service with the need to be flexible in providing service. For example, SIA extensively tested and refined its service procedures before it introduced any change. Performance managers conducted research, ran time and motion studies, and assessed customer reaction in order to develop service protocols that would allow cabin crew teams of 13–14 people to deliver identically high service every time. But by the same token, SIA wanted its people to be flexible and creative so that they were able to develop solutions when an unusual situation developed. As one executive noted, "The worst thing about service delivery is when everybody just follows the book. I want them to be flexible and creative. In Singapore there is a tendency for people to be too regimented in their thinking."[3]

One recent initiative was called "Transforming Customer Service (TCS)," and involved not just cabin crew, but also engineering, flight operations, and sales support. Within the initiative, 40% of resources were allocated for training and motivating staff, 30% for reviewing

processes and procedures, and 30% for creating new product and service ideas.[4] Its goal was to help empower employees to take steps to make things better and be flexible (e.g. on-board discretion to upgrade). It was network-wide, not just in Singapore. And it was supplemented by a lot of "self improvement" training courses which, while not required, always had large enrollments.

One cabin crew director interviewed described TCS:

> TCS has led to dramatic change by giving cabin crew more flexibility. Competitors can match our equipment but they can't match "what we are" and "how we think."

LEADERSHIP DEVELOPMENT

Particular attention was paid to the 'field commanders': front-line supervisors. By motivating them and instilling leadership qualities into them, SIA believed it could facilitate the handing down of its distinctive culture to a new generation of staff. An ambitious development program for senior cabin crew was aimed at making them feel that they were part of management, and at boosting their commitment. A similar program, 'Take the Lead,' was developed for ground service supervisors. "We're training them to be OSG leaders, to play a more active role and provide better guidance to their subordinates," explained a Customer Affairs manager. "We don't want them to depend on head office. We want them to take the initiative." Being a service entrepreneur meant being assertive and resourceful, he said. "We say to them, 'There will always be opportunities for you, in your dealings with customers, to

---

[3] This information and quote were drawn from Wirtz and Johnston, 2003.

[4] "What Makes Singapore Airline a Service Champion," *Strategic Direction*, April 2003.

EXHIBIT 2   **An OSG Course**

'We are ready to give', say SATS OSG Participants

Trainee Passenger Services Agent (PSA) *Michelle Koh,* **who was in a batch of trainee PSAs from SATS to attend the Outstanding Service on the Ground Program, gives a first-person account of her experience.**

"I CARE." That is the OSG (Outstanding Service on the Ground) motto my class—Batch 140—picked up very early in the one-day program held on 8 May.

First, we chanted it as a group. Later we discovered its meaning on a more personal level when we were taught how to "stroke" each other positively to bring out the best in each person. We learned how effective positive stroking could be through an exercise in which we sent complimentary messages to one another. Initial shyness overcome, this exercise became easy and fun.

However, when asked to state our own strengths, most of us were hesitant. Yet, there was no reservation in highlighting our weaknesses. Perseverance in this exercise provided some self-discoveries.

Now that we knew ourselves a little better, we embarked on a very important project: teamwork and cooperation. I must admit, though, that I was very puzzled on seeing plastic chains, cane hoops and wooden blocks on the stage in the auditorium where our training was being held.

What had all these items to do with teamwork and cooperation? I was soon to find out. In the "centipede activity," our class was divided into two teams. With ankles shackled to one another, each team was expected to move forward and backward, and up and down a flight of stairs in the shortest time possible.

Yes, this exercise certainly called for teamwork and cooperation. When we did not move together, ankles hurt, tempers flared, and someone fell down!

One of the other exercises taught us that careful planning was necessary if we wanted to do our jobs well. This was where the hoops came in. The objective was to get each member through the hoops, without using a hoop twice and without the members coming into contact with the hoops. Sounds confusing, but we had to do it. With some planning, agility and strength, we managed.

We rounded up the day with the "Trust" activity. It entailed a participant throwing himself backward into the arms of his teammates. I remember thinking at the time that any sane person would hesitate to do this if he had the slightest doubt about the person who was to catch him. But then, at the OSG course, we were doing rather "insane" things, were we not? I held my breath and . . . my teammates caught me—a lesson in trust indeed.

At the start of the course, Instructor Clara Nai had warned us that it would not be all fun and games. She was right. It was also quite tiring, both mentally and physically. But the unanimous verdict at the end of the day was: "We are ready to give!"

establish a certain impression so that they will come back and fly SIA again.'"

STAFF RECOGNITION AND REWARD

SIA recognized staff for outstanding customer service and for good ideas, and kept them informed of company problems and plans through the glossy in-house magazine, *Outlook,* various divisional newsletters, and frequent meetings and briefings. A sizeable part of all employees' earnings, as much as three extra months of pay in a good year, came through a profit-sharing scheme. Examples of rewards included the following:

- S-I-A Staff Ideas in Action, which awarded cash prizes of up to US$9,700 for good ideas.

- Winning Ways, for cabin crew who had received a minimum of three compliment letters and no complaints over three months. One winner had received 23 letters.

- Managing Director's Awards: introduced in 1987, they recognized frontline staff who went beyond the call of duty in providing ground service. Selection criteria included both consistency in performance and outstanding acts of service (see *Exhibit 3*).

- Health for Wealth: a US$3,000 prize given out every month to a ground service employee at Changi airport to encourage all staff to stay fit. The incidence of sick leave among check-in and other ground service staff, who had to work shifts 24 hours a day, was high.

An OSG Feedback Competition tested staff's grasp of front-line issues. "Each question consisted of a scenario and three possible answers," explained a Customer Affairs Manager. "They have to think it through, maybe get together with their peers to deliberate. It encourages staff to think about these issues." The 20 winners each received a US$1,000 shopping voucher.

MONITORING CUSTOMER SATISFACTION

Much effort went into monitoring compliments and complaints from customers, which were examined at weekly meetings of SIA's Complaints and Compliments Committee. On average cabin crew received nine letters of compliment for every complaint, but ground staff, whose transactions with customers were quite different, had nearly as many criticisms as they had praise. "On board we're pouring champagne and giving out caviar," said a Ground Services' executive. "In ground service we take your money and your coupon, we check your passport." Each complaint was investigated and answered in writing. Any lessons drawn were passed on to the trainers and departments concerned and a selection of both praise and criticism was published regularly in in-house publications. By the early 1990s, ground services staff sometimes received compliments even when flights were delayed, as they were so professional in service recovery. (*Exhibit 4* has examples of both sorts of letters.)

Trends in customer satisfaction were carefully analyzed with formal customer feedback mechanisms including surveys of 10% of SIA flights, benchmarking surveys that compared SIA with other airlines, mystery shopping on competitors' flights and comments from the front-line staff.[5] An in-house Service Performance

[5] This information was drawn from Wirtz and Johnston, 2003.

EXHIBIT 3   **Managing Director's Awards: A Sample**

OUR VERY IMPORTANT EMPLOYEES AND THEIR DEEDS

Maite Losada
Cargo Supervisor, BRU
Lena Kellens
Reservations/Ticketing
Officer, BRU

Kalyan Subramanyam
Customer Services Agent,
MAA

Tadashi Yakumaru
Customer Services Officer,
NRT

Maite and Lena were on holiday when their SQ flight was diverted to AMS. Although they were on leave, they spontaneously helped their working colleagues manage the disruption. They helped passengers with their rebookings, distributed meals and newspapers on the coach to AMS, assisted passengers at AMS, and helped them with their transfer flights in SIN. They assisted layover passengers, looked after them at the hotel, and helped them with their onward flights the next day. On arrival at MEL, they again helped the passengers before catching their own flight to BNE.

Over 36 hours and over three continents, Maite and Lena displayed many OSG qualities. They went beyond the call of duty to help the affected passengers throughout the journey, they sacrificed their own time, displayed initiative and showed they cared. They truly embody the OSG spirit, "We're with you all the way."

During the year 1991/92 Kalyan received 15 written compliments. In all these cases, he repeatedly showed that he cares for our passengers. The passengers were impressed not just by his acts of assistance but also by his high standard of service and the kindness he displayed.

For example, he helped a sick and elderly passenger who was booked to fly on another airline. His selfless act for a competitor airline's passenger so impressed the passenger's relative that the relative said in his letter of compliment that he would in future travel on SIA.

Kalyan wins the award for consistently giving outstanding service to our passengers.

Tadashi received four written compliments and numerous verbal compliments in the year.

For example, Tadashi voluntarily gave a distraught passenger, who had no cash in local currency, the money he required for his airport tax. The passenger, who turned out to be a priority passenger, later wrote in to compliment Tadashi and to return the money.

In another case, a couple were delayed in arriving at the airport due to a traffic jam, and had to park their car at the terminal instead of their pre-arranged car park. Tadashi offered to drive the car to the other car park and looked after the car until they returned.

The many compliments Tadashi received were testimony of his consistent helpfulness beyond the call of duty.

EXHIBIT 4   Compliments and Complaints from Passengers

FEEDBACK EXAMPLE

CUSTOMER COMMENTS ON GROUND SERVICE . . .

✘ *". . . our flight was disabled due to mechanical problems and we were stuck in Jakarta airport without access to a telephone or a fax machine for most of the day. The ground crew in Jakarta promised to send fax messages on our behalf . . . these messages were not transmitted.*

"They attempted to arrange alternative bookings for us but . . . these arrangements were never completed. We did suggest that as the delay had caused us to miss our connection in Singapore and because it was not possible to book an alternative flight with Qantas, we should be put on the Singapore-Darwin flight on 4 July. We were told this was not possible as the flight was fully booked in economy and although business class seats were available we would only be able to upgrade if we paid the extra fare.

". . . On arriving in Singapore . . . we were given vouchers for Hotel accommodation and meals, but, although our luggage had not arrived in Singapore, were not given an allowance to purchase toiletries, etc. . . . Our luggage still had not been traced when we boarded SQ223 and we were told that it was probably still in Jakarta. When we arrived in Perth, however, we found our things had in fact been loaded. Although it was a relief to see the luggage, I find the fact that it had been loaded but not recorded on the flight manifest most disturbing.

*". . . As you can imagine the experience was most upsetting and extremely tiring. In addition, as a consequence of the missed connection we "lost" several days from a holiday which had been planned for over a year. . . ." —**R.C.P., Surrey***

✘ *". . . When we returned to San Francisco, my wife removed two of our four bags from the carrousel while I was in the rest room. At our hotel I discovered that one bag was not ours. After many phone calls, I contacted the Singapore Airline baggage person and learned that my bag was at the airport and that I had a bag of a man who was going to Honduras. I was surprised that it was not suggested that the bags would be exchanged. Having flown all night and being 76 years of age, I was quite tired after the 12-hour flight. Nevertheless, I got a taxi, returned the bag to the airport and retrieved mine. My friends tell me that in similar circumstances they have had their bags returned to them at the hotel by the airline." —**F.A.G., Texas***

continued

EXHIBIT 4   *continued*

✔ *"It was indeed our pleasure to see you last week at the Singapore Airlines counter at Brussels Airport. Our children have always traveled alone, but were never as happy as they were with your company. They were very well looked after, and also at N.Y. the ground staff was very helpful and courteous. We take this opportunity to thank you, and your Airline for the excellent service, and it's surely not for nothing that you are known as the best!*

"My husband is a non-resident Singaporean, and we are happy that you have started this service to N.Y. and hope to use it more often . . . ." —D. & P. M., New York

Index survey continuously tracked SIA service. Every quarter 18,000 passengers' ratings of 30 factors, such as eye appeal of meals or friendliness of check-in staff, were analyzed. Index movements were carefully studied for early indications of how SIA was meeting passengers' expectations. The index improved year by year.

MANAGEMENT STYLE

SIA's management made conscious efforts to delegate authority to the lowest possible level. Employees described SIA as a democratic company where the top welcomed new ideas, criticisms and decision-making from the lower echelons and encouraged them to speak out, make suggestions and generally express their opinion. "We try to keep reporting lines as short as possible," said an SIA leader. "We are not a formal Organization."

SIA tried hard to become a flat Organization, spinning off business units as soon as they were self-sustaining. "We're trying to stay small," explained one Managing Director. "We are creating many small, autonomous divisions to keep decision-making down." When a new engineering subsidiary was formed, top management pointed to several benefits, saying it would increase accountability, enhance *esprit de corps,* encourage innovation

and entrepreneurship and reap the benefits of competitive advantage in the high growth engineering maintenance business. Next on the list were computer services and cargo.

The group had a policy of management mobility, rotating managers and directors every three to five years. This prevented managers from becoming jaded and fostered team spirit, according to the Assistant Director of Personnel. "Loyalty to a function or a division is not as great. It's difficult to say, 'I'm a marketing man,' when tomorrow you may be in finance. It forces you to look at the company as a whole." Managers also moved between the airline and the various subsidiaries. In the same spirit, SIA encouraged multidivisional task forces.

SIA'S DEMANDING CUSTOMER

In Denpasar, the check-in officer at Ngurah Rai airport had returned with the SIA supervisor. "I am sorry, Sir," the supervisor said. "Our procedures require that your luggage travel to only one location. You can send it to Singapore, or to Paris but not both." His tone was courteous, but strained Paul Denver who launched into a lengthy explanation, pointing to the fact that a week earlier in Manila his request to split his luggage at check-in had been accepted quite easily. Then he realized he was wasting his time and shut up, but decided to complain in writing. His letter read as follows:

> I thought that Singapore Airlines was committed to service, in particular to improving ground service. I was pleased with check-in staff in Manila, who went out of their way to help me. This is the kind of service I expected from SIA. What I cannot understand is why your man in Denpasar was so uncooperative.

THE BUSINESS AND COMPETITIVE ENVIRONMENT WORSENS

In the post-9/11 world, air travel across the world was under siege by threats of terrorist attacks, disease, and escalating fuel costs. One industry observer noted of the industry and SIA,

> As other airlines sank into financial distress, SIA spent much of the previous year battling SARS . . . earnings and margins took a nose dive . . . and new discount entrants popped up on the radar and oil prices took flight. . . . Flying is big business but airlines are generally a bad business, one that's getting worse. In 2003, seven of the world's 16 largest airlines lost money. Their return on assets was just 3.4%, far less than the average cost of capital needed to keep this capital-intensive business going . . . cost has become the industry buzzword.[6]

Customers also began to take perks such as frequent flyer programs (FFPS)

for granted in the increasingly competitive marketplace. Finally one other menace to continued growth was corporations' decisions to slash travel costs, requiring executives to travel less, or to fly economy class.

Despite these many challenges to SIA and the industry in the early 2000 years, and an unprecedented first quarterly loss in early 2003, SIA executives remained confident that Asia's most successful airline would succeed without major cost cutting, or a merger.

In terms of strategic response, airlines roughly fell into three camps:

- The Traditionalists, who continued to raise standards, even though this meant maintaining high prices and perhaps frightening off cash-strapped customers, and who advertised heavily. The logic was simple: surveys showed that 88 per cent of business and first class travelers rated the size of their seat as their 'preferred aspect of business class travel,' and that what they feared most on long-haul routes was physical discomfort;

- Old-Style Entrepreneurs, who competed on price, even though this put at risk the perceived quality of their product and hurt revenue per seat. Their target was the budget conscious traveler;

- The Radical Entrepreneurs, who were prepared to abolish the traditional class structure of aircraft and try to sell something entirely new, offering for instance a combination of first class seats and business-class levels of service and prices.[7]

---

[6] "Turbulent Times," *The Edge Singapore,* May 16, 2005.

[7] Adapted from "A Time for Fresh Ideas," *Financial Times,* April 19, 1993.

INTERNAL PRESSURES

THE LABOR SHORTAGE IN SINGAPORE

The economic success of Singapore had at least one unwanted consequence for SIA. In the 1990s, almost all its flight attendants had been Singaporeans and Malaysians, with the only exceptions being a few nationals of Japan, Taiwan or Korea recruited for linguistic reasons. But the continued labour shortage made it increasingly difficult for the airline to recruit the home-grown attendants who had been its main marketing tool for two entire decades: in its advertising it exclusively used its own Singapore or Malaysian nationals.

SIA clearly saw that it would have to recruit beyond the borders of the tiny island-state and neighboring Malaysia. But could the 'Singapore Girl' be Thai or Indian or even Caucasian? This move would erode a key difference with Cathay Pacific, which cultivated a cosmopolitan image with multi-ethnic cabin crew fluent in a variety of languages besides English. While SIA's leadership saw some advantages in heterogeneity, they thought it made it harder to have shared values and dedication to service. "Cathay has problems with the assimilation of different nationalities: they have a hard time getting them to work as teams," said one senior manager.

THE 'YOUNG TURKS'

Traditionally SIA staff had felt a strong attachment to the company. "We're almost like Communists, we believe in a cause," joked one senior manager. "I want the company to do well. I don't see it as an employer." But the new generation, whom one executive described as 'the young Turks,' had somewhat different expectations. As the republic became more affluent, individual values tended to replace the Confucian tradition of respect for authority and some managers felt the young generation lacked dedication and a service spirit.

Young Singaporeans were better educated, more mobile and readier to challenge. While proud of working for Singapore's most prestigious employer, they also expected higher standards of living. As a result, unions were becoming more militant. "In the early years, we were like a small family," said Managing Director Cheong. "As we grow bigger, the relationship between management and unions is becoming more formalized and there's a greater degree of tension."

STRATEGIES FOR SATISFYING THE DEMANDING CUSTOMER

SIA's Marketing Director knew that competitive advantage would be tougher to retain:

> More and more airlines are trying to duplicate the causes of SIA's success. Even if the world economy picks up, the good old days are over. The industry will be fitter. Competitors are doing away with excess manpower and looking at their route structure. The bottom line is becoming more important, the aircraft more reliable, the staff more motivated. There is structural change, as well as mental change, among airline executives.

Another SIA executive spoke of the challenge to remain strong:

> SIA is changing all the time. We start off telling ourselves we must continually improve. There is no such thing as: "we have nothing more to learn." But we're not talking about changing people, we're talking about strengthening what we have. We encourage our people to look for new ways of doing things. SIA's image is strong: that is not easy to keep up unless you continue to strengthen your operations, you come up with new ways of doing things. We never will sacrifice quality. If you try to save by cutting down on what you give the customer, people feel it straight away. We won't allow cost-cutting to affect what we've built over the years. For instance, we're looking for ways to prepare the food ahead of time, but that is to give cabin crew more time to look after our passengers, not to reduce the number of crew.

The challenge for SIA was to train front-line staff to anticipate customers' needs in order to satisfy them—even before the passengers even realized they had those needs! One answer was to be flexible, explained an Inflight Services Senior Manager:

> Demand is evolving, and one of our strategies is to provide flexibility, especially in first class and business class. For instance, on long trips you can have your meals at any time you like. We encourage our people to be flexible. They have to be on the watch-out to do more things that will remain ingrained in passengers' minds, and turn any negative impression into a positive one. As long as the company continues to see itself as its main competitor, it will continue to improve and innovate.

RESPONDING TO THE CUSTOMER: TWO APPROACHES

Customer feedback was analyzed at weekly meetings of SIA's Complaints and Complaints Review Committee. Paul Denver's letter provided an interesting test of the airline's approach to continuous service improvement: one of its demanding customers was challenging it to go further. Two major views emerged at the meeting.

Approach #1; The first, underlining the importance of safety, standards and consistency, could be summarized as follows:

> First and foremost, we have considerations of security, cost and efficiency: there are lots of security regulations on the handling of luggage. Secondly, the Manila supervisor incurred a lot of expense for the company: if we were to have this as a standard procedure, it would mean tremendous costs. Thirdly, the risk of mishandling would be a lot higher. We are proud of our low rate of mishandled luggage, by far the lowest among major airlines. Passengers far prefer to have their bags with them in a normal situation. But of course we tell our staff that OSG means going beyond, finding a way to satisfy the passenger. This is a classic dilemma. I'm not saying it would be impossible to satisfy Mr. Denver, but it is a choice we'd have to make. I certainly wouldn't tell off our people in Denpasar for refusing to split the luggage. In this industry, in the final analysis the safety and security of the passenger are more important, and this means procedures. I don't want to compromise on that.

Approach #2: A second view stressed the need for staff to use their judgment and make considered decisions, rather than follow established guidelines:

We need a balance between the soft part, people's judgment, and the system of rules. We need the system of course, but only as a guide. More emphasis must now be placed on judgment, responsibility, and entrepreneurship.

At first glance, the Manila agent should be congratulated for his decision. We encourage staff, even junior staff, to take considered decisions. The Manila agent took a decision and he took responsibility for it. He went out of his way to help a passenger. The Bali agent didn't show any courage, he just played by the rules. We've been telling our people, "Go beyond the rules. We dare you to innovate." We've asked them to use their judgment. He was probably worried about giving away the 'company store.' We must show him what was missing in his thought process: if he tries to accommodate a passenger, we will support him.

I want all our people to show that they can think through a situation and make judgments on behalf of customers, whether they're traveling economy, business or first class. The pressure is on the front line. The pressure is also on us to coach and counsel. If we determine that the Bali agent did make a mistake, he should discuss the issue with his staff. In that case, we would congratulate the Manila agent, and also recommend discussion there. The issue would be mentioned in the Manila agent's annual performance review, but the Bali agent would not be penalized.

In fact, the issue is more complex. What we really need to understand is the thinking behind both decisions. What led each of them to his decision? Saying 'No' to a passenger is more difficult than saying 'Yes.' But did the Bali agent just fall back on regulations, or was there a basis for his judgment? What about the Manila agent? Did he say 'Yes' to make it easy? How did he arrive to his judgment? Front-line staff must put themselves in the customer's shoes and determine whether a request is reasonable, genuine, or whether someone is trying to take advantage of the airline. The Bali agent did not have to copy the Manila agent's decision if his conclusions were different. Consistency is to do well all the time, not consistently to say 'No,' or 'Yes'— this is what SIA is trying to inculcate.

This debate was part of a larger set of issues for SIA. Could the airline contain costs without sacrificing service? Could it grow, yet maintain its high service standards? And could it in fact further improve its already high quality of service? Meanwhile, Paul Denver awaited an answer to his letter.

Reading

Cracking the Code of Change

Michael Beer and Nitin Nohria

The New Economy has ushered in great business opportunities—and great turmoil. Not since the Industrial Revolution have the stakes of dealing with change been so high. Most traditional organizations have accepted, in theory at least, that they must either change or die. And even Internet companies such as eBay, Amazon.com, and America Online recognize that they need to manage the changes associated with rapid entrepreneurial growth. Despite some individual successes, however, change remains difficult to pull off, and few companies manage the process as well as they would like. Most of their initiatives—installing new technology, downsizing, restructuring, or trying to change corporate culture—have had low success rates. The brutal fact is that about 70 percent of all change initiatives fail.

In our experience, the reason for most of those failures is that in their rush to change their organizations, managers end up immersing themselves in an alphabet soup of initiatives. They lose focus and become mesmerized by all the advice available in print and on-line about why companies should change, what they should try to accomplish, and how they

should do it. This proliferation of recommendations often leads to muddle when change is attempted. The result is that most change efforts exert a heavy toll, both human and economic. To improve the odds of success, and to reduce the human carnage, it is imperative that executives understand the nature and process of corporate change much better. But even that is not enough. Leaders need to crack the code of change.

For more than 40 years now, we've been studying the nature of corporate change. And although every business' change initiative is unique, our research suggests there are two archetypes, or theories, of change. These archetypes are based on very different and often unconscious assumptions by senior executives—and the consultants and academics who advise them—about why and how changes should be made. Theory E is change based on economic value. Theory O is change based on organizational capability. Both are valid models; each theory of change achieves some of management's goals, either explicitly or implicitly. But each theory also has its costs—often unexpected ones.

Theory E change strategies are the ones that make all the headlines. In this "hard" approach to change, shareholder value is the only legitimate measure of corporate success. Change usually involves heavy use of economic incentives, drastic layoffs, downsizing, and restructuring. E change strategies are more common than

O change strategies among companies in the United States, where financial markets push corporate boards for rapid turnarounds. For instance, when William A. Anders was brought in as CEO of General Dynamics in 1991, his goal was to maximize economic value—however painful the remedies might be. Over the next three years, Anders reduced the workforce by 71,000 people—44,000 through the divestiture of seven businesses and 27,000 through layoffs and attrition. Anders employed common E strategies.

Managers who subscribe to Theory O believe that if they were to focus exclusively on the price of their stock, they might harm their organizations. In this "soft" approach to change, the goal is to develop corporate culture and human capability, through individual and organizational learning—the process of changing, obtaining feedback, reflecting, and making further changes. U.S. companies that adopt O strategies, as Hewlett-Packard did when its performance flagged in the 1980s, typically have strong, long-held, commitment-based psychological contracts with their employees.

Managers at these companies are likely to see the risks in breaking those contracts. Because they place a high value on employee commitment, Asian and European businesses are also more likely to adopt an O strategy to change.

Few companies subscribe to just one theory. Most companies we have studied have used a mix of both. But all too often, managers try to apply theories E and O in tandem without resolving the inherent tensions between them. This impulse to combine the strategies is directionally correct, but theories E and O are so different that it's hard to manage them simultaneously—employees distrust leaders who alternate between nurturing and cutthroat corporate behavior. Our research suggests, however, that there is a way to resolve the tension so that businesses can satisfy their shareholders while building viable institutions. Companies that effectively combine hard and soft approaches to change can reap big payoffs in profitability and productivity. Those companies are more likely to achieve a sustainable competitive advantage. They can also reduce the anxiety that grips whole societies in the face of corporate restructuring.

In this article, we will explore how one company successfully resolved the tensions between E and O strategies. But before we do that, we need to look at just how different the two theories are.

A TALE OF TWO THEORIES

To understand how sharply theories E and O differ, we can compare them along several key dimensions of corporate change: goals, leadership, focus, process, reward system, and use of consultants. (For a side-by-side comparison, see Exhibit 1, "Comparing Theories of Change.") We'll look at two companies in similar businesses that adopted almost pure forms of each archetype. Scott Paper successfully used Theory E to enhance shareholder value, while Champion International used Theory O to achieve a complete cultural transformation that increased its productivity and employee commitment. But as we will soon observe, both paper producers also discovered the limitations of sticking with only one theory of change. Let's compare the two companies' initiatives.

GOALS

When Al Dunlap assumed leadership of Scott Paper in May 1994, he immediately

EXHIBIT 1 Comparing Theories of Change

Our research has shown that all corporate transformations can be compared along the six dimensions shown here. The table outlines the differences between the E and O archetypes and illustrates what an integrated approach might look like.

Dimensions of Change	Theory E	Theory O	Theories E and O Combined
Goals	Maximize shareholder value	Develop organizational capabilities	Explicitly embrace the paradox between economic value and organizational capability
Leadership	Manage change from the top down	Encourage participation from the bottom up	Set direction from the top and engage the people below
Focus	Emphasize structure and systems	Build up corporate culture: employees' behavior and attitudes	Focus simultaneously on the hard (structures and systems) and the soft (corporate culture)
Process	Plan and establish programs	Experiment and evolve	Plan for spontaneity
Reward system	Motivate through financial incentives	Motivate through commitment—use pay as fair exchange	Use incentives to reinforce change but not to drive it
Use of consultants	Consultants analyze problems and shape solutions	Consultants support management in shaping their own solutions	Consultants are expert resources who empower employees

fired 11,000 employees and sold off several businesses. His determination to restructure the beleaguered company was almost monomaniacal. As he said in one of his speeches: "Shareholders are the number one constituency. Show me an annual report that lists six or seven constituencies, and I'll show you a mismanaged company." From a shareholder's perspective, the results of Dunlap's actions were stunning. In just 20 months, he managed to triple shareholder returns as Scott Paper's market value rose from about $3 billion in 1994 to about $9 billion by the end of 1995. The financial community applauded his efforts and hailed Scott Paper's approach to change as a model for improving shareholder returns.

Champion's reform effort couldn't have been more different. CEO Andrew

Sigler acknowledged that enhanced economic value was an appropriate target for management, but he believed that goal would be best achieved by transforming the behaviors of management, unions, and workers alike. In 1981, Sigler and other managers launched a long-term effort to restructure corporate culture around a new vision called the Champion Way, a set of values and principles designed to build up the competencies of the workforce. By improving the organization's capabilities in areas such as teamwork and communication, Sigler believed he could best increase employee productivity and thereby improve the bottom line.

LEADERSHIP

Leaders who subscribe to Theory E manage change the old-fashioned way: from the top down. They set goals with little involvement from their management teams and certainly without input from lower levels or unions. Dunlap was clearly the commander in chief at Scott Paper. The executives who survived his purges, for example, had to agree with his philosophy that shareholder value was now the company's primary objective. Nothing made clear Dunlap's leadership style better than the nickname he gloried in: "Chainsaw Al."

By contrast, participation (a Theory O trait) was the hallmark of change at Champion. Every effort was made to get all its employees emotionally committed to improving the company's performance. Teams drafted value statements, and even the industry's unions were brought into the dialogue. Employees were encouraged to identify and solve problems themselves. Change at Champion sprouted from the bottom up.

FOCUS

In E-type change, leaders typically focus immediately on streamlining the "hardware" of the organization—the structures and systems. These are the elements that can most easily be changed from the top down, yielding swift financial results. For instance, Dunlap quickly decided to outsource many of Scott Paper's corporate functions—benefits and payroll administration, almost all of its management information systems, some of its technology research, medical services, telemarketing, and security functions. An executive manager of a global merger explained the E rationale: "I have a [profit] goal of $176 million this year, and there's no time to involve others or develop organizational capability."

By contrast, Theory O's initial focus is on building up the "software" of an organization—the culture, behavior, and attitudes of employees. Throughout a decade of reforms, no employees were laid off at Champion. Rather, managers and employees were encouraged to collectively reexamine their work practices and behaviors with a goal of increasing productivity and quality. Managers were replaced if they did not conform to the new philosophy, but the overall firing freeze helped to create a culture of trust and commitment. Structural change followed once the culture changed. Indeed, by the mid-1990s, Champion had completely reorganized all its corporate functions. Once a hierarchical, functionally organized company, Champion adopted a matrix structure that empowered employee teams to focus more on customers.

PROCESS

Theory E is predicated on the view that no battle can be won without a clear, comprehensive, common plan of action that encourages internal coordination and inspires confidence among customers, suppliers, and investors. The plan lets leaders quickly motivate and mobilize their businesses; it compels them to take tough, decisive actions they presumably haven't taken in the past. The changes at Scott Paper unfolded like a military battle plan. Managers were instructed to achieve specific targets by specific dates. If they didn't adhere to Dunlap's tightly choreographed marching orders, they risked being fired.

Meanwhile, the changes at Champion were more evolutionary and emergent than planned and programmatic. When the company's decade-long reform began in 1981, there was no master blueprint. The idea was that innovative work processes, values, and culture changes in one plant would be adapted and used by other plants on their way through the corporate system. No single person, not even Sigler, was seen as the driver of change. Instead, local leaders took responsibility. Top management simply encouraged experimentation from the ground up, spread new ideas to other workers, and transferred managers of innovative units to lagging ones.

REWARD SYSTEM

The rewards for managers in E-type change programs are primarily financial. Employee compensation, for example, is linked with financial incentives, mainly stock options. Dunlap's own compensation package—which ultimately netted him more than $100 million—was tightly linked to shareholders' interests. Proponents of this system argue that financial incentives guarantee that employees' interests match stockholders' interests. Financial rewards also help top executives feel compensated for a difficult job—one in

which they are often reviled by their one-time colleagues and the larger community.

The O-style compensation systems at Champion reinforced the goals of culture change, but they didn't drive those goals. A skills-based pay system and a corporatewide gains-sharing plan were installed to draw union workers and management into a community of purpose. Financial incentives were used only as a supplement to those systems and not to push particular reforms. While Champion did offer a companywide bonus to achieve business goals in two separate years, this came late in the change process and played a minor role in actually fulfilling those goals.

USE OF CONSULTANTS

Theory E change strategies often rely heavily on external consultants. A SWAT team of Ivy League–educated MBAs, armed with an arsenal of state-of-the-art ideas, is brought in to find new ways to look at the business and manage it. The consultants can help CEOs get a fix on urgent issues and priorities. They also offer much-needed political and psychological support for CEOs who are under fire from financial markets. At Scott Paper, Dunlap engaged consultants to identify many of the painful cost-savings initiatives that he subsequently implemented.

Theory O change programs rely far less on consultants. The handful of consultants who were introduced at Champion helped managers and workers make their own business analyses and craft their own solutions. And while the consultants had their own ideas, they did not recommend any corporate program, dictate any solutions, or whip anyone into line. They simply led a process of discovery and learning that was intended to change the corporate culture in a way that could not be foreseen at the outset.

In their purest forms, both change theories clearly have their limitations. CEOs who must make difficult E-style choices understandably distance themselves from their employees to ease their own pain and guilt. Once removed from their people, these CEOs begin to see their employees as part of the problem. As time goes on, these leaders become less and less inclined to adopt O-style change strategies. They fail to invest in building the company's human resources, which inevitably hollows out the company and saps its capacity for sustained performance. At Scott Paper, for example, Dunlap trebled shareholder returns but failed to build the capabilities needed for sustained competitive advantage—commitment, coordination, communication, and creativity. In 1995, Dunlap sold Scott Paper to its longtime competitor Kimberly-Clark.

CEOs who embrace Theory O find that their loyalty and commitment to their employees can prevent them from making tough decisions. The temptation is to postpone the bitter medicine in the hopes that rising productivity will improve the business situation. But productivity gains aren't enough when fundamental structural change is required. That reality is underscored by today's global financial system, which makes corporate performance instantly transparent to large institutional shareholders whose fund managers are under enormous pressure to show good results. Consider Champion. By 1997, it had become one of the leaders in its industry based on most performance measures. Still, newly instated CEO Richard Olsen was forced to admit a tough reality: Champion shareholders had not seen a significant increase in the economic value of the company in more than a decade. Indeed, when Champion was sold recently to Finland-based UPM-Kymmene, it was acquired for a mere 1.5 times its original share value.

MANAGING THE CONTRADICTIONS

Clearly, if the objective is to build a company that can adapt, survive, and prosper over the years, Theory E strategies must somehow be combined with Theory O strategies. But unless they're carefully handled, melding E and O is likely to bring the worst of both theories and the benefits of neither. Indeed, the corporate changes we've studied that arbitrarily and haphazardly mixed E and O techniques proved destabilizing to the organizations in which they were imposed. Managers in those companies would certainly have been better off to pick either pure E or pure O strategies—with all their costs. At least one set of stakeholders would have benefited.

The obvious way to combine E and O is to sequence them. Some companies, notably General Electric, have done this quite successfully. At GE, CEO Jack Welch began his sequenced change by imposing an E-type restructuring. He demanded that all GE businesses be first or second in their industries. Any unit that failed that test would be fixed, sold off, or closed. Welch followed that up with a massive downsizing of the GE bureaucracy. Between 1981 and 1985, total employment at the corporation dropped from 412,000 to 299,000. Sixty percent of the corporate staff, mostly in planning and finance, was laid off. In this phase, GE people began to call Welch "Neutron Jack," after the fabled bomb that was designed to destroy people but leave buildings intact. Once he had wrung out the redundancies, however, Welch adopted an O strategy. In 1985, he started a series of organizational initiatives to change GE culture. He declared that the company had to become "boundaryless," and unit leaders across the corporation had to submit to being challenged by their subordinates in open forum. Feedback and open communication eventually eroded the hierarchy. Soon Welch applied the new order to GE's global businesses.

Unfortunately for companies like Champion, sequenced change is far easier if you begin, as Welch did, with Theory E. Indeed, it is highly unlikely that E would successfully follow O because of the sense of betrayal that would involve. It is hard to imagine how a draconian program of layoffs and downsizing can leave intact the psychological contract and culture a company has so patiently built up over the years. But whatever the order, one sure problem with sequencing is that it can take a very long time; at GE it has taken almost two decades. A sequenced change may also require two CEOs, carefully chosen for their contrasting styles and philosophies, which may create its own set of problems. Most turnaround managers don't survive restructuring—partly because of their own inflexibility and partly because they can't live down the distrust that their ruthlessness has earned them. In most cases, even the best-intentioned effort to rebuild trust and commitment rarely overcomes a bloody past. Welch is the exception that proves the rule.

So what should you do? How can you achieve rapid improvements in economic value while simultaneously developing an open, trusting corporate culture? Paradoxical as those goals may appear, our research shows that it is possible to apply theories E and O together. It requires great will, skill—and wisdom. But precisely because it is more difficult than mere sequencing, the simultaneous use of O and E strategies is more likely to be a source of sustainable competitive advantage.

One company that exemplifies the reconciliation of the hard and soft approaches is ASDA, the UK grocery chain that CEO Archie Norman took over in December 1991, when the retailer was nearly bankrupt. Norman laid off employees, flattened the organization, and sold off losing businesses—acts that usually spawn distrust among employees and distance executives from their people. Yet during Norman's eight-year tenure as CEO, ASDA also became famous for its atmosphere of trust and openness. It has been described by executives at Wal-Mart—itself famous for its corporate culture—as being "more like Wal-Mart than we are." Let's look at how ASDA resolved the conflicts of E and O along the six main dimensions of change.

EXPLICITLY CONFRONT THE TENSION BETWEEN E AND O GOALS

With his opening speech to ASDA's executive team—none of whom he had met—Norman indicated clearly that he intended to apply both E and O strategies in his change effort. It is doubtful that any of his listeners fully understood him at the time, but it was important that he had no conflicts about recognizing the paradox between the two strategies for change. He said as much in his maiden speech: "Our number one objective is to secure value for our shareholders and secure the trading future of the business. I am not coming in with any magical solutions. I intend to spend the next few weeks listening and forming ideas for our precise direction....We need a culture built around common ideas and goals that include listening, learning, and speed of response, from the stores upwards. [But] there will be management reorganization. My objective is to establish a clear focus on the stores, shorten lines of communication, and build one team." If there is a contradiction between building a high-involvement organization and restructuring to enhance shareholder value, Norman embraced it.

SET DIRECTION FROM THE TOP AND ENGAGE PEOPLE BELOW

From day one, Norman set strategy without expecting any participation from below. He said ASDA would adopt an everyday-low-pricing strategy, and Norman unilaterally determined that change would begin by having two experimental store formats up and running within six months. He decided to shift power from the headquarters to the stores, declaring: "I want everyone to be close to the stores. We must love the stores to death; that is our business." But even from the start, there was an O quality to Norman's leadership style. As he put it in his first speech: "First, I am forthright, and I like to argue. Second, I want to discuss issues as colleagues. I am looking for your advice and your disagreement." Norman encouraged dialogue with employees and customers through colleague and customer circles. He set up a "Tell Archie" program so that people could voice their concerns and ideas.

Making way for opposite leadership styles was also an essential ingredient to Norman's—and ASDA's—success. This was most clear in Norman's willingness to hire Allan Leighton shortly after he took over. Leighton eventually became deputy chief executive. Norman and Leighton shared the same E and O values, but they had completely different personalities and styles. Norman, cool and reserved, impressed people with the power of his mind—his intelligence and business acumen. Leighton, who is warmer and more people oriented, worked on employees' emotions with the power of his personality. As one employee told us, "People respect Archie, but they love Allan." Norman was the first to credit Leighton with having helped to create emotional commitment to the new ASDA. While it might be possible for a single individual to embrace opposite leadership styles, accepting an equal partner with a very different personality makes it easier to capitalize on those styles. Leighton certainly helped Norman reach out to the organization. Together they held quarterly meetings with store managers to hear their ideas, and they supplemented those meetings with impromptu talks.

FOCUS SIMULTANEOUSLY ON THE HARD AND SOFT SIDES OF THE ORGANIZATION

Norman's immediate actions followed both the E goal of increasing economic value and the O goal of transforming culture. On the E side, Norman focused on structure. He removed layers of hierarchy at the top of the organization, fired the financial officer who had been part of ASDA's disastrous policies, and decreed a wage freeze for everyone—management and workers alike. But from the start, the O strategy was an equal part of Norman's plan. He bought time for all this change by warning the markets that financial recovery would take three years. Norman later said that he spent 75 percent of his early months at ASDA as the company's human resource director, making the organization less hierarchical, more egalitarian, and more transparent. Both Norman and Leighton were keenly aware that they had to win hearts and minds.

As Norman put it to workers: "We need to make ASDA a great place for everyone to work."

PLAN FOR SPONTANEITY

Training programs, total-quality programs, and top-driven culture change programs played little part in ASDA's transformation. From the start, the ASDA change effort was set up to encourage experimentation and evolution. To promote learning, for example, ASDA set up an experimental store that was later expanded to three stores. It was declared a risk-free zone, meaning there would be no penalties for failure. A cross-functional task force "renewed," or redesigned, ASDA's entire retail proposition, its organization, and its managerial structure. Store managers were encouraged to experiment with store layout, employee roles, ranges of products offered, and so on. The experiments produced significant innovations in all aspects of store operations. ASDA's managers learned, for example, that they couldn't renew a store unless that store's management team was ready for new ideas. This led to an innovation called the Driving Test, which assessed whether store managers' skills in leading the change process were aligned with the intended changes. The test perfectly illustrates how E and O can come together: It bubbled up O-style from the bottom of the company, yet it bound managers in an E-type contract. Managers who failed the test were replaced.

LET INCENTIVES REINFORCE CHANGE, NOT DRIVE IT

Any synthesis of E and O must recognize that compensation is a double-edged sword. Money can focus and motivate managers, but it can also hamper teamwork, commitment, and learning. The way to resolve this dilemma is to apply Theory E incentives in an O way. Employees' high involvement is encouraged to develop their commitment to change, and variable pay is used to reward that commitment. ASDA's senior executives were compensated with stock options that were tied to the company's value. These helped attract key executives to ASDA. Unlike most E-strategy companies, however, ASDA had a stock-ownership plan for all employees. In addition, store-level employees got variable pay based on both corporate performance and their stores' records. In the end, compensation represented a fair exchange of value between the company and its individual employees. But Norman believed that compensation had not played a major role in motivating change at the company.

USE CONSULTANTS AS EXPERT RESOURCES WHO EMPOWER EMPLOYEES

Consultants can provide specialized knowledge and technical skills that the company doesn't have, particularly in the early stages of organizational change. Management's task is figuring out how to use those resources without abdicating leadership of the change effort. ASDA followed the middle ground between Theory E and Theory O. It made limited use of four consulting firms in the early stages of its transformation. The consulting firms always worked alongside management and supported its leadership of change. However, their engagement was intentionally cut short by Norman to prevent ASDA and its managers from becoming dependent on the consultants. For example, an expert in store organization was hired to support the task force assigned to renew ASDA's first

Change Theories in the New Economy

Historically, the study of change has been restricted to mature, large companies that needed to reverse their competitive declines. But the arguments we have advanced in this article also apply to entrepreneurial companies that need to manage rapid growth. Here, too, we believe that the most successful strategy for change will be one that combines theories E and O.

Just as there are two ways of changing, so there are two kinds of entrepreneurs. One group subscribes to an ideology akin to Theory E. Their primary goal is to prepare for a cash-out, such as an IPO or an acquisition by an established player. Maximizing market value before the cash-out is their sole and abiding purpose. These entrepreneurs emphasize shaping the firm's strategy, structure, and systems to build a quick, strong market presence. Mercurial leaders who drive the company using a strong top-down style are typically at the helm of such companies. They lure others to join them using high-powered incentives such as stock options. The goal is to get rich quick.

Other entrepreneurs, however, are driven by an ideology more akin to Theory O—the building of an institution. Accumulating wealth is important, but it is secondary to creating a company that is based on a deeply held set of values and that has a strong culture. These entrepreneurs are likely to subscribe to an egalitarian style that invites everyone's participation. They look to attract others who share their passion about the cause—though they certainly provide generous stock options as well. The goal in this case is to make a difference, not just to make money.

Many people fault entrepreneurs who are driven by a Theory E view of the world. But we can think of other entrepreneurs who have destroyed businesses because they were overly wrapped up in the Theory O pursuit of a higher ideal and didn't pay attention to the pragmatics of the market. Steve Jobs' venture, Next, comes to mind. Both types of entrepreneurs have to find some way of tapping the qualities of theories E and O, just as large companies do.

few experimental stores, but later stores were renewed without his involvement.

By embracing the paradox inherent in simultaneously employing E and O change theories, Norman and Leighton transformed ASDA to the advantage of its shareholders and employees. The organization went through personnel changes, unit sell-offs, and hierarchical upheaval. Yet these potentially destructive actions did not prevent ASDA's employees from committing to change and the new corporate culture because Norman and Leighton had won employees' trust by constantly listening, debating, and being willing to learn. Candid about their intentions from the outset, they balanced the tension between the two change theories.

By 1999, the company had multiplied shareholder value eightfold. The organizational capabilities built by Norman and Leighton also gave ASDA the sustainable competitive advantage that Dunlap had been unable to build at Scott Paper and that Sigler had been unable to build at Champion. While Dunlap was forced to sell a demoralized and ineffective organization to Kimberly-Clark, and while a languishing Champion was sold to UPM-Kymmene, Norman and Leighton in June

1999 found a friendly and culturally compatible suitor in Wal-Mart, which was willing to pay a substantial premium for the organizational capabilities that ASDA had so painstakingly developed.

In the end, the integration of theories E and O created major change—and major payoffs—for ASDA. Such payoffs are possible for other organizations that want to develop a sustained advantage in today's economy. But that advantage can come only from a constant willingness and ability to develop organizations for the long term combined with a constant monitoring of shareholder value—E dancing with O, in an unending minuet.

Case

GE's Two-Decade Transformation: Jack Welch's Leadership

On September 7, 2001, Jack Welch stepped down as CEO of General Electric. The sense of pride he felt about the company's performance during the previous two decades seemed justified judging by the many accolades GE was receiving. For the third consecutive year, it had not only been named *Fortune*'s "Most Admired Company in the United States," but also *Financial Times'* "Most Admired Company in the World." And, on the eve of his retirement, *Fortune* had named Welch "Manager of the Century" in recognition of his personal contribution to GE's outstanding 20-year record.

Yet while the mood at GE's 2001 annual meeting had clearly been upbeat,

Source: Harvard Business Case No. 9-399-150. Copyright © 1999 by the President and Fellows of Harvard College. Research Associate Meg Wozny prepared this case under the supervision of Professor Christopher A. Bartlett. HBS cases are developed solely as the basis for class discussion. Cases are not intended to serve as endorsements, sources of primary data, or illustrations of effective management.

some shareholders wondered whether anyone could sustain the blistering pace of change and growth characteristic of the Welch era. And specifically, many worried if any successor could generate the 23% per annum total shareholder return Welch had delivered in his two decades leading GE. It would be a tough act to follow. (See **Exhibit 1** for financial summary of Welch's era at GE.)

THE GE HERITAGE

Founded in 1878 by Thomas Edison, General Electric grew from its early focus on the generation, distribution, and use of electric power to become, a hundred years later, one of the world's leading diversified industrial companies. A century later, in addition to its core businesses in power generation, household appliances, and lighting, the company was also engaged in businesses as diverse as aircraft engines, medical systems, and diesel locomotives.

EXHIBIT 1   Selected Financial Data: General Electric and Consolidated Affiliates ($ millions)

	2000	1999	1998	1997	1996
Revenues	$129,853	$111,630	$100,469	$90,840	$79,179
Earnings from continuing operations	12,735	10,717	9,296	8,203	7,280
Loss from discontinued operations	—	—	—	—	—
Net earnings	12,735	10,717	9,296	8,203	7,280
Dividends declared	5,647	4,786	4,081	3,535	3,138
Earned on average share owners' equity	27.5%	26.8%	25.7%	25.0%	24.0%
Per share					
Net earnings	3.87	3.27	2.84	2.50	2.20
Net earnings—diluted	3.81	3.21	2.80	2.46	2.16
Dividends declared	1.71	1.47	1.25	1.08	0.95
Stock price range[1]	181.5-125.0	159.5-94.3	103.9-69	76.6-47.9	53.1-34.7
Total assets of continuing operations	437,006	405,200	335,935	304,012	272,402
Long-term borrowings	82,132	71,427	59,663	46,603	49,245
Shares outstanding—average (in thousands)	3,299,037	3,277,826	3,268,998	3,274,692	3,307,394
Employees at year end					
United States	168,000	167,000	163,000	165,000	155,000
Other countries	145,000	143,000	130,000	111,000	84,000
Discontinued operations (primarily U.S.)	—	—	—	—	—
Total employees	313,000	310,000	293,000	276,000	239,000

[1] Price unadjusted for four 2-for-1 stock splits during the period.

Long regarded as a bellwether of American management practices, GE was constantly undergoing change. In the 1930s, it was a model of the era's highly centralized, tightly controlled corporate form. By the 1950s, GE had delegated responsibility to hundreds of department managers, leading a trend towards greater decentralization. But a subsequent period of "profitless growth" in the 1960s caused the company to strengthen its corporate staffs and develop sophisticated strategic planning systems. Again, GE found itself at the leading edge of management practice.

When Reg Jones, Welch's predecessor, became CEO in 1973, he inherited the company that had just completed a major reorganization. Overlaying its 10 groups, 46 divisions, and 190 departments were 43 strategic business units designed to support the strategic planning that was so central to GE's management process. Jones raised strategic planning to an art form, and GE again became the benchmark for hundreds of companies that imitated its SBU-based structure and its sophisticated planning processes. Soon, however, Jones was unable to keep up with reviewing and approving the massive volumes of information generated by 43 strategic plans. Explaining that "the review burden had to be carried on more shoulders," in 1977 he capped

1995	1994	1993	1992	1991	1990	1986	1981
$70,028	$60,109	$55,701	$53,051	$51,283	$49,696	$36,725	$27,240
6,573	5,915	4,184	4,137	3,943	3,920	3,689	NA
—	−1,189	993	588	492	383	NA	NA
6,573	4,726	4,315	4,725	2,636	4,303	2,492	1,652
2,838	2,546	2,229	1,985	1,808	1,696	1,081	715
23.5%	18.1%	17.5%	20.9%	12.2%	20.2%	17.3%	19.1%
1.95	1.38	3.03	2.75	2.55	2.42	2.73	NA
1.93	1.37	2.52	2.75	1.51	2.42	NA	NA
0.845	0.745	1.31	1.16	1.04	0.96	1.18	NA
36.6-24	27.4-22.5	26.7-20.2	87.5-72.7	79.1-53	75.5-50	44.4-33.2	69.9-51.1
228,035	185,871	251,506	192,876	166,508	152,000	84,818	20,942
51,027	36,979	28,194	25,298	22,602	20,886	100,001	1,059
3,367,624	3,417,476	1,707,979	1,714,396	1,737,863	1,775,104	912,594	227,528
150,000	156,000	157,000	168,000	173,000	183,000	302,000	NA
72,000	60,000	59,000	58,000	62,000	62,000	71,000	NA
—	5,000	6,000	42,000	49,000	53,000	NA	NA
222,000	221,000	222,000	268,000	284,000	298,000	373,000	404,000

GE's departments, divisions, groups, and SBUs with a new organizational layer of "sectors," representing macrobusiness agglomerations such as consumer products, power systems, or technical products.

In addition to his focus on strategic planning, Jones spent a great deal of time on government relations, becoming the country's leading business statesman. During the 1970s, he was voted CEO of the Year three times by his peers, with one leading business journal dubbing him CEO of the Decade in 1979. When he retired in 1981, *The Wall Street Journal* proclaimed Jones a "management legend," adding that by handing the reins to Welch, GE had "replaced a legend with a live wire."

WELCH'S EARLY PRIORITIES: GE'S RESTRUCTURING

When the 45-year-old Welch became CEO in April 1981, the U.S. economy was in a recession. High interest rates and a strong dollar exacerbated the problem, resulting in the country's highest unemployment rates since the Depression. To leverage performance in GE's diverse portfolio of businesses, the new CEO challenged each to be "better than the best" and set in motion a series of changes that were to radically restructure the company over the next five years.

EXHIBIT 2   The Three Circle Vision for GE, 1982

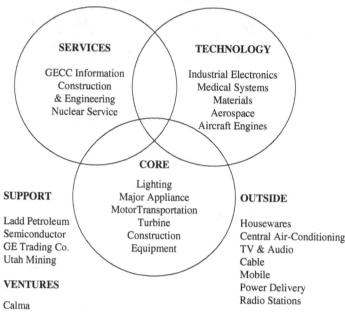

SERVICES

GECC Information
Construction
& Engineering
Nuclear Service

TECHNOLOGY

Industrial Electronics
Medical Systems
Materials
Aerospace
Aircraft Engines

CORE

Lighting
Major Appliance
MotorTransportation
Turbine
Construction
Equipment

SUPPORT

Ladd Petroleum
Semiconductor
GE Trading Co.
Utah Mining

VENTURES

Calma

OUTSIDE

Housewares
Central Air-Conditioning
TV & Audio
Cable
Mobile
Power Delivery
Radio Stations

#1 OR #2: FIX, SELL, OR CLOSE

Soon after taking charge, Welch set the standard for each business to become the #1 or #2 competitor in its industry—or to disengage. Asked whether this simple notion represented GE's strategy, Welch responded, "You can't set an overall theme or a single strategy for a corporation as broad as GE." By 1983, however, Welch had elaborated this general "#1 or #2" objective into a "three circle concept" of his vision for GE. (See **Exhibit 2**.) Businesses were categorized as core (with the priority of "reinvesting in productivity and quality"), high-technology (challenged to "stay on the leading edge" by investing in R&D), and services (required to "add outstanding people and make contiguous acquisitions"). To a question about what he hoped to build at GE, Welch replied:

A decade from now, I would like General Electric to be perceived as a unique, high-spirited, entrepreneurial enterprise . . . the most profitable, highly diversified company on earth, with world quality leadership in every one of its product lines.[1]

But as GE managers struggled to build #1 or #2 positions in a recessionary environment and under attack from global—often Japanese—competitors, Welch's admonition to "fix, sell, or close" uncompetitive businesses frequently led to the latter options. Scores of businesses were sold, including central air-conditioning, housewares, coal mining, and, eventually,

[1] "General Electric: 1984" (HBS Case No. 385-315), by Professors Francis J. Aguilar and Richard G. Hamermesh and RA Caroline Brainard. © 1985 by the President and Fellows of Harvard College.

even GE's well-known consumer electronics business. Between 1981 and 1990, GE freed up over $11 billion of capital by selling off more than 200 businesses, which had accounted for 25% of 1980 sales. In that same time frame, the company made over 370 acquisitions, investing more than $21 billion in such major purchases as Westinghouse's lighting business, Employers Reinsurance, RCA, Kidder Peabody, and Thomson/CGR, the French medical imaging company. (See **Exhibit 3**.)

Internally, Welch's insistence that GE become more "lean and agile" resulted in a highly disciplined destaffing process aimed at all large headquarters groups, including a highly symbolic 50% reduction in the 200-person strategic planning staff. Welch described his motivation:

> We don't need the questioners and checkers, the nitpickers who bog down the process.... Today, each staff person has to ask, "How do I add value? How do I make people

EXHIBIT 3   **Changes in the GE Business Portfolio**

Major Acquisitions ($21 Billion Total)	Major Divestitures ($11 Billion Total)
• Calma (CAD/CAM equipment)	• Central Air Conditioning
• Intersil (semiconductors)	• Pathfinder Mines
• Employers Reinsurance Corp.	• Broadcasting Properties (non-RCA TV & radio stations)
• Decimus (computer leasing)	• Utah International (mining)
• RCA (NBC Television, aerospace, electronics)	• Housewares (small appliances)
• Kidder, Peabody (investment banking)	• Family Financial Services
• Polaris (aircraft leasing)	• RCA Records
• Genstar (container leasing)	• Nacolah Life Insurance (RCA's)
• Thomson/CGR (medical equipment)	• Coronet Carpets (RCA's)
• Gelco (portable building leasing)	• Consumer Electronics (TV sets)
• Borg-Warner Chemicals (plastics)	• Carboloy (industrial cutting tools)
• Montgomery Ward Credit (credit cards)	• NBC Radio Networks
• Roper (appliances)	• Roper Outdoor Lawn Equipment
• Penske Leasing (truck leasing)	• GE Solid State (semiconductors)
• Financial Guaranty Insurance Co.	• Calma (CAD/CAM equipment)
• Thungsram (light bulbs)	• RCA Globcomm international telex)
• Burton Group Financial Services	• Ladd Petroleum (oil exploration & refining)
• Travelers Mortgage (mortgage services)	• RCA Columbia Home Video
• Thorn Lighting (light bulbs)	• Auto Auctions (auctions of used cars)
• Financial News Network (cable network)	
• Chase Manhattan Leasing	
• Itel Containers (container leasing)	
• Harrods/House of Fraser Credit Cards	

Source: *The Business Engine.*

on the line more effective and competitive?"[2]

As he continued to chip away at bureaucracy, Welch next scrapped GE's laborious strategic planning system—and with it, the remaining corporate planning staff. He replaced it with "real time planning" built around a five-page strategy playbook, which Welch and his 14 key business heads discussed in shirtsleeves sessions "unencumbered by staff." Each business's playbook provided simple one-page answers to five questions concerning current market dynamics, the competitors' key recent activities, the GE business response, the greatest competitive threat over the next three years, and the GE business's planned response.

The budgeting process was equally radically redefined. Rather than documenting internally focused comparisons with past performance, results were now evaluated against external competitively based criteria: Do sales show increases in market share, for example? Do margins indicate a cost advantage compared with competition?

In 1985, Welch eliminated the sector level, previously the powerful center of strategic control. (See **Exhibits 4a** and **4b**.) By reducing the number of hierarchical levels from nine to as few as four, Welch ensured that all businesses reported directly to him. He said:

> We used to have department managers, sector managers, subsector managers, unit managers, supervisors. We're driving those titles out....We used to go from the CEO to sectors to groups to businesses. Now we go from the

CEO to businesses. There is nothing else. Zero.[3]

Through downsizing, destaffing, and delayering, GE eliminated 59,290 salaried and 64,160 hourly positions between 1981 and 1988; divestiture eliminated an additional 122,700. Even when offset by the acquisitions, the number of employees at GE declined from 404,000 in 1980 to 330,000 by 1984 and 292,000 by 1989. Between 1981 and 1985, revenues increased modestly from $27.2 billion to $29.2 billion, but operating profits rose dramatically from $1.6 billion to $2.4 billion. This set the base for strong increases in both sales and earnings in the second half of the decade (see **Exhibit 5**).

This drastic restructuring in the early- and mid-1980s earned Welch the nickname "Neutron Jack," a term that gained currency even among GE managers when the CEO replaced 12 of his 14 business heads in August 1986. Welch's new "varsity team" consisted of managers with a strong commitment to the new management values, a willingness to break with the old GE culture, and most of all, an ability to take charge and bring about change. Despite his great dislike for a nickname he felt he did not deserve, Welch kept pushing the organization for more change. The further into the restructuring he got, the more convinced he became of the need for bold action:

> For me, the idea is to shun the incremental and go for the leap.... How does an institution know when the pace is about right? I hope you won't think I'm being melodramatic if I say that the institution ought to stretch itself, ought to reach, to the point where it almost comes

[2] Noel Tichy and Ram Charan, "Speed, Simplicity, Self-Confidence: An Interview with Jack Welch," *Harvard Business Review,* September–October 1989.

[3] Anon, "GE Chief Hopes to Shape Agile Giant," *Los Angeles Times,* June 1, 1988.

EXHIBIT 4a   GE Organization in 1981

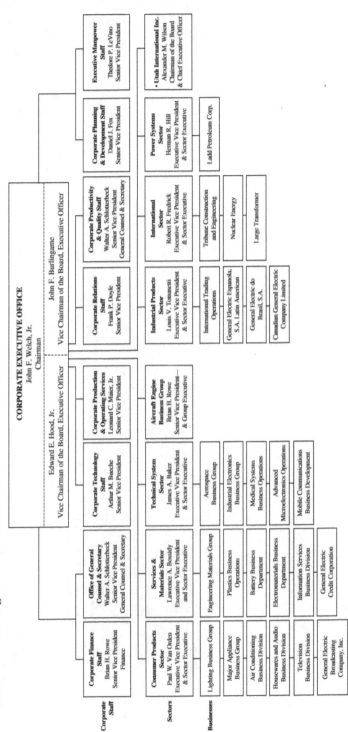

EXHIBIT 4b   GE Organization in 1992

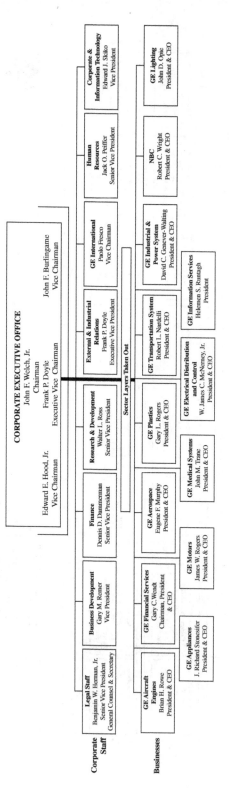

EXHIBIT 5   General Electric's Performance in Three Eras (millions of dollars)

	Borch		Jones		Welch		
	1961	1970	1971	1980	1981	1990	2000
Sales	4,666.6	8,726.7	9,557.0	24,950.0	27,240.0	52,619.0	129,853.0
Operating profit	431.8	548.9	737.0	2,243.0	2,447.0	6,616.0	19,630.0
Net earnings	238.4	328.5	510.0	1,514.0	1,652.0	4,303.0	12,735.0
ROS	5.1%	3.8%	5.3%	6.1%	6.1%	8.2%	9.8%
ROE	14.8%	12.6%	17.2%	19.5%	18.1%	19.8%	28.7%
Stock market capitalization	6,283.7	7,026.7	10,870.5	12,173.4	13,073.4	50,344.9	389,442.9
S&P 500 Stock Price							
Index—Composite	65.7	83.0	97.9	119.4	126.4	330.2	1,365.3
Employees	279,547	396,583	402,000	366,000	404,000	298,000	313,000
U.S GNP ($ billion)	523.0	982.0	1,063.0	2,626.0	2,708.0	5,524.5	9,276.4

Source: Annual Reports, Survey of Current Business, Datastream.

unglued....Remember the theory that a manager should have no more than 6 or 7 direct reports? I say the right number is closer to 10 or 15.[4]

THE LATE 1980S: SECOND STAGE OF THE ROCKET

By the late 1980s, most of GE's business restructuring was complete, but the organization was still reeling from culture shock and management exhaustion. Welch was as eager as anyone in GE to move past the "Neutron-Jack" stage and begin rebuilding the company on its more solid foundations.

THE "SOFTWARE" INITIATIVES: WORK-OUT AND BEST PRACTICES

Years after launching GE's massive restructuring effort, Welch concluded, "By mid-1988 the hardware was basically in place. We liked our businesses. Now it was time to focus on the organization's software." He also acknowledged that his priorities were shifting: "A company can boost productivity by restructuring, removing bureaucracy and downsizing, but it cannot sustain high productivity without cultural change."

In 1989, Welch articulated the management style he hoped to make GE's norm—an approach based on openness, candor, and facing reality. Simultaneously, he refined the core elements of the organizational culture he wanted to create—one characterized by speed,

simplicity, and self confidence.[5] Over the next few years, he launched two closely linked initiatives—dubbed Work-Out and Best Practices—aimed at creating the desired culture and management approach.

In late 1988, during one of Welch's regular visits to teach in the company's Management Development Institute, he engaged a group of GE managers in a particularly outspoken session about the difficulty they were having implementing change back at their operations. In a subsequent discussion with James Baughman, GE's director of management development, Welch wondered how to replicate this type of honest, energetic interaction throughout the company. His objective was to create the culture of a small company—a place where all felt engaged and everyone had voice. Together, they developed the idea of a forum where employees could not only speak their minds about how their business might be run more effectively, but also get immediate responses to their ideas and proposals. By the time their helicopter touched down at GE's headquarters, Welch and Baughman had sketched out a major change initiative they called "Work-Out"—a process designed to get unnecessary bureaucratic work out of the system while providing

---

[5] Interestingly, Welch's first attempts at articulating and communicating GE's new cultural values were awkward. For example, in 1986 he defined 10 desirable cultural "attitudes and policies" which few in GE could remember, let alone practice. Furthermore, he communicated his new organizational model as the GE Business Engine, a concept that many found depersonalizing since it seemed to depict people as inputs into a financial machine. Gradually, Welch became more comfortable articulating cultural values which he continued to refine into what he termed "GE's social architecture." Eventually his concept of The Business Engine evolved to become The Human Engine.

---

[4] Tichy and Charan, op. cit., p. 112.

a forum in which employees and their bosses could work out new ways of dealing with each other.

At Welch's request, Baughman formed a small implementation team and, with the help of two dozen outside consultants, led the company-wide program rollout. Assigned to one of GE's businesses, each consultant facilitated a series of off-site meetings patterned after the open-forum style of New England town meetings. Groups of 40 to 100 employees were invited to share views about their business and how it might be improved. The three-day sessions usually began with a talk by the unit boss, who presented a challenge and a broad agenda. Then, the boss was asked to leave, allowing employees aided by facilitators to list their problems, debate solutions, and prepare presentations. On the final day, the bosses returned and were asked to listen to their employees' analyses and recommendations. The rules of the process required managers to make instant, on-the-spot decisions about each proposal, in front of everyone, to 80% of proposals. If the manager needed more information, he or she had to charter a team to get it by an agreed-upon decision date.

Armand Lauzon, a manager at a GE Aircraft Engine factory, described to *Fortune* how he felt as his employees presented him with their suggestions in a room where they had carefully arranged the seating so his boss was behind him. "I was wringing wet within half an hour," he said. "They had 108 proposals; I had about a minute to say yes or no to each one. And I couldn't make eye contact with my boss without turning around, which would show everyone in the room I was chickenshit." In total, Lauzon supported all but eight of the 108 proposals.

By mid-1992, over 200,000 GE employees—over two-thirds of the workforce—had participated in Work-Out, although the exact number was hard to determine, since Welch insisted that none of the meetings be documented. "You're just going to end up with more bureaucracy," he said. What was clear, however, was that productivity increases, which had been growing at an average annual rate of 2% between 1981 and 1987, doubled to a 4% annual rate between 1988 and 1992.[6]

As Work-Out was getting started, Welch's relentless pursuit of ideas to increase productivity resulted in the birth of a related movement called Best Practices. In the summer of 1988, Welch gave Michael Frazier of GE's Business Development department a simple challenge: How can we learn from other companies that are achieving higher productivity growth than GE? Frazier selected nine companies, including Ford, Hewlett Packard, Xerox, and Toshiba, with different best practices to study. In addition to specific tools and practices, Frazier's team also identified several characteristics common to the successful companies: they focused more on developing effective processes than controlling individual activities; customer satisfaction was their main gauge of performance; they treated their suppliers as partners; and they emphasized the need for a constant stream of high-quality new products designed for efficient manufacturing.

On reviewing Frazier's report, Welch became an instant convert and committed to a major new training program to introduce Best Practices thinking throughout the organization, integrating it into the ongoing agenda of Work-Out teams.

---

[6] In GE, productivity was defined by the following calculation: Productivity = Real Revenue (net of price increases)/Real Costs (net of inflationary increases).

As a result of the Best Practices program, many GE managers began to realize they were managing and measuring the wrong things. (Said one, "We should have focused more on *how* things get done than on just *what* got done.") Subsequently, several units began radically revising their whole work approach. For example, the head of the corporate audit staff explained: "When I started 10 years ago, the first thing I did was count the $5,000 in the petty cash box. Today, we look at the $5 million in inventory on the floor, searching for process improvements that will bring it down."

GOING GLOBAL

During the early- and mid-1980s, internationalization had remained a back-burner issue at GE, but strong advocates of globalization such as Paolo Fresco, the Italian-born president of GE Europe, understood why Welch had to concentrate his early efforts on the rationalization of the U.S. operations. "It's very difficult to jump into the world arena if you don't have a solid base at home," said Fresco, "but once the solid base was created, we really took the jump."

The first rumblings of the emerging globalization priority came in Welch's challenges to his Corporate Executive Council meetings during 1986. Reflecting his own early experience in GE Plastics, he did not try to impose a corporate globalization strategy, preferring to let each business take responsibility for implementing a plan appropriate to its particular needs:

> When I was 29 years old I bought land in Holland and built the plants there. That was "my land" for "my business." I was never interested in the global GE, just the global Plastics business.

> The idea of a company being global is nonsense. Businesses are global, not companies.[7]

This did not mean, however, that Welch was uninvolved in his business managers' globalization plans. In 1987, he focused their attention by raising the bar on GE's well-known performance standard: from now on, "#1 or #2" was to be evaluated on world *market* position. As if to underline his seriousness, a few months later he announced a major deal with Thomson S.A., in which GE agreed to exchange its struggling consumer electronics business for the large French electronics company's medical imaging business, a business in which GE had a leading global position.

To provide continuing momentum to the internationalization effort, in 1989 Welch appointed Paolo Fresco as head of International Operations and in 1992 made him a vice-chairman and member of his four-man corporate executive office. Fresco, a key negotiator on the Thomson swap, continued to broker numerous international deals: a joint venture with German-based Robert Bosch, a partnership with Toshiba, and the acquisition of Sovac, the French consumer credit company. As Eastern Europe opened, he initiated a major thrust into the former Communist bloc, spearheaded by the purchase of a majority share in the Hungarian lighting company, Tungsram. Fresco became the locator and champion of new opportunities. "I fill vacuums," he said. "All these assignments are temporary—once they are complete, I get out of the way."

Like subsequent strategic initiatives, globalization was not a one-time effort,

[7] Robert Slater, *Jack Welch and the GE Way: Management Insights and Leadership Secrets of the Legendary CEO* (McGraw-Hill), 1998, p. 195.

EXHIBIT 6   **Growth through Globalization**

Increase in Sales Over Previous Year ($ millions)

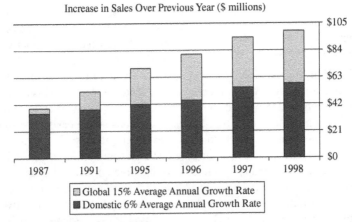

Source: GE Annual Report, 1998.

but an ongoing theme that Welch doggedly pursued over the years. Taking advantage of Europe's economic downturn, GE invested $17.5 billion in the region between 1989 and 1995, half on new plants and facilities and half to finance 50 or so acquisitions. Then, in 1995, after the Mexican peso collapsed, the company again saw the economic uncertainty as a great buying opportunity. Within six months GE had acquired 16 companies, positioning it to participate in the country's surprisingly rapid recovery. And as Asia slipped into crisis in 1997–1998, Welch urged his managers to view it as a buying opportunity rather than a problem. In Japan alone the company spent $15 billion on acquisitions in six months.

By 1998, international revenues were $42.8 billion, almost double the level just five years earlier. The company expected to do almost half its business outside the United States by 2000, compared with only 20% in 1985, the year before the first international push. More important, global revenues were growing at almost three times the rate of domestic sales. (See **Exhibit 6**.)

DEVELOPING LEADERS

While the global thrust and the new cultural initiatives were being implemented, Welch was also focusing on the huge task of realigning the skill sets—and, more important, the mindsets—of the company's 290,000 employees with GE's new strategic and organizational imperatives. Amidst the grumbling of those who felt overworked in the new demanding environment and the residual distrust left over from the layoffs of the 1980s, he recognized his challenge was nothing short of redefining the implicit contract that GE had with its employees:

Like many other large companies in the U.S., Europe and Japan, GE has had an implicit psychological contract based on perceived lifetime employment. This produced a paternal, feudal, fuzzy kind of loyalty. That kind of loyalty tends to focus people inward. But in today's environment, people's emotional energy must be focused outward on a competitive world.... The new psychological contract, if there is such a thing, is that jobs at GE are the best in the world for people willing to compete. We have the best training and development resources and an environment committed to providing opportunities for personal and professional growth.[8]

Like all GE managers, Welch grew up in an organization deeply committed to developing its people. He wanted to harness that tradition and use it to translate his broad cultural changes down to the individual level. This would mean adapting GE's well-established human resource systems to his goals. For example, for as long as he could remember, the company's top executives had committed substantial amounts of time to the rigorous management appraisal, development, and succession planning reviews known as Session C. He began using this process to help achieve his objectives, predictably adding his own intense personal style to its implementation.

Starting in April and lasting through May each year, Welch and three of his senior executives visited each of his businesses to review the progress of the company's top 3,000 executives. Welch kept particularly close tabs on the upper 500, all of whom had been appointed with his personal approval. In these multi-day meetings, Welch wanted to be exposed to high-potential managers presenting results on major projects. In an exhaustive 10- to 12-hour review in each business, Welch asked the top executive to identify the future leaders, outline planned training and development plans, and detail succession plans for all key jobs. The exercise reflected his strong belief that good people were GE's key assets and had to be managed as a company resource. "I own the

people," he told his business heads. "You just rent them."

As these reviews rolled out through GE, all professional-level employees expected honest feedback about where they were professionally, reasonable expectations about future positions they could hold, and the specific skills required to get there. Managers at every level used these discussions as the basis for coaching and developing their staff. (As a role model, Welch estimated he spent at least 70% of his time on people issues, most of that teaching and developing others.)

A strong believer in incentives, Welch also radically overhauled GE's compensation package. From a system driven by narrow-range increases in base salary supplemented by bonuses based on one's business performance, he implemented a model in which stock options became the primary component of management compensation. He expanded the number of options recipients from 300 to 30,000 and began making much more aggressive bonus awards and options allocations strongly tied to the individual's performance on the current program priority (globalization, for example, or best practices initiatives).

Through all of these human resource tools and processes, Welch's major effort was increasingly focused on creating an environment in which people could be their best. Entering the 1990s, he described his objective for GE in these terms:

> Ten years from now, we want magazines to write about GE as a place where people have the freedom to be creative, a place that brings out the best in everybody. An open, fair place where people have a sense that what they do matters, and where that sense of accomplishment is rewarded in the

---

[8] Tichy and Charan, op. cit., p. 120.

pocketbook and the soul. That will be our report card.

A key institution that Welch harnessed to bring about this cultural change was GE's Crotonville management development facility. Welch wanted to convert Crotonville from its management training focus and its role as a reward or a consolation prize for those who missed out on a promotion to a powerful engine of change in his transformation effort. In the mid-1980s, when he was cutting costs almost everywhere else, he spent $45 million on new buildings and improvements at Crotonville. He also hired some experienced academics—Jim Baughman from Harvard and Noel Tichy from Michigan—to revolutionize Crotonville's activities.

Under Welch's direct control and with his personal involvement, Crotonville's priority became to develop a generation of leaders aligned to GE's new vision and cultural norms. Increasingly, it evolved from a training center to a place where teams of managers worked together on real priority issues and decided on results-oriented action. And this led to the gradual replacement of outside faculty by GE insiders acting as discussion leaders. Leading the change was Welch, who twice a month traveled to Crotonville to teach and interact with GE employees. ("Haven't missed a session yet," he boasted in the late 1990s.) (See **Exhibit 7**.) It was during one of these sessions that the idea for Work-Out emerged, and it was at Crotonville that many of the Best Practices sessions were held.

Despite all the individual development and the corporate initiatives, not all managers were able to achieve Welch's ideal leadership profile. (See **Exhibit 8**.) Of greatest concern to the CEO were those who seemed unwilling or unable to embrace the open,

participative values he was espousing. In 1991, he addressed the problem and the seriousness of its consequences:

> In our view, leaders, whether on the shop floor or at the top of our businesses, can be characterized in at least four ways. The first is one who delivers on commitments—financial or otherwise—and shares the values of our company. His or her future is an easy call. Onward and upward. The second type of leader is one who does not meet commitments and does not share our values. Not as pleasant a call, but equally easy. The third is one who misses commitments but shares the values. He or she usually gets a second chance, preferably in a different environment.
>
> Then there's the fourth type—the most difficult for many of us to deal with. That leader delivers on commitments, makes all the numbers, but doesn't share the values we must have. This is the individual who typically forces performance out of people rather than inspires it: the autocrat, the big shot, the tyrant. Too often all of us have looked the other way and tolerated these "Type 4" managers because "they always deliver"—at least in the short term.[9]

To reinforce his intention to identify and weed out Type 4 managers, Welch began rating GE top-level managers not only on their performance against quantifiable targets but also on the extent to which they "lived" GE values. Subsequently, many of GE's 500 officers started using a similar two-dimensional grid to evaluate and coach their own direct reports. And when coaching failed, Welch was prepared to take action on the type 4s. "People are removed

[9] GE Annual Report, 1991.

EXHIBIT 7   Welch at GE's Crotonville Center

A typical note Welch sent to 30 participants to prepare for his session of GE's Executive Development Course (EDC):

Dear EDC Participants,

I'm looking forward to an exciting time with you tomorrow. I've included here a few thoughts for you to think about prior to our session:

As a group—

Situation: Tomorrow you are appointed CEO of GE.

- What would you do in first 30 days?
- Do you have a current "vision" of what to do?
- How would you go about developing one?
- Present your best shot at a vision.
- How would you go about "selling" the vision?
- What foundations would you build on?
- What current practices would you jettison?

Individually—

1. Please be prepared to describe a leadership dilemma that you have faced in the past 12 months, i.e., plant closing, work transfer, HR, buy or sell a business, etc.
2. Think about what you would recommend to accelerate the Quality drive across the company.
3. I'll be talking about "A, B & C" players. What are your thoughts on just what makes up such a player?
4. I'll also be talking about energy/energizing/edge as key characteristics of today's leaders. Do you agree? Would you broaden this? How?

   I'm looking forward to a fun time, and I know I'll leave a lot smarter than when I arrived.

—Jack

Source: *The Leadership Engine.*

EXHIBIT 8 GE Leadership Capabilities

- Create a clear, simple, reality-based, customer-focused vision and are able to communicate it straightforwardly to all constituencies.

- Understand accountability and commitment and are decisive...set and meet aggressive targets...always with unyielding integrity.

- Have the self-confidence to empower others and behave in a boundaryless fashion...believe in and are committed to Work-Out as a means of empowerment...be open to ideas from anywhere.

- Have a passion for excellence...hate bureaucracy and all the nonsense that comes with it.

- Have, or have the capacity to develop global brains and global sensitivity and are comfortable building diverse global teams.

- Stimulate and relish change...are not frightened or paralyzed by it. See change as opportunity, not just a threat.

- Have enormous energy and the ability to energize and invigorate others. Understand speed as a competitive advantage and see the total organizational benefits that can be derived from a focus on speed.

Source: 1992 Annual Report.

for having the wrong values," he insisted. "We don't even talk about the numbers."

To back up this commitment to the new leadership criteria, a few years later GE introduced a 360° feedback process. Every employee was graded by his or her manager, peers and all subordinates on a 1 to 5 scale in areas such as teambuilding, quality focus, and vision. Welch described it as a powerful tool for detecting and changing those who "smile up and kick down." Tied into the evaluation process and linked to the Session C human resource planning exercise, the 360° feedback became the means for identifying training needs, coaching opportunities, and, eventually, career planning—whether that be up, sideways, or out.

INTO THE 1990S: THE THIRD WAVE

Entering the 1990s, Welch felt that GE's new foundation had been laid. Despite the slowdown in the industrial sector in the first few years of the new decade, he was committed to the task of rebuilding the company at an even more urgent pace. The new initiatives rolled on.

BOUNDARYLESS BEHAVIOR

Moving beyond the earlier initiatives aimed at strengthening GE's individual businesses, Welch began to focus on creating what he called "integrated diversity." He articulated his vision for GE in the 1990s as a "boundaryless" company, one characterized by an "open, anti-parochial environment, friendly toward the seeking and sharing of new ideas, regardless of their origins"—in many ways an institutionalization of the openness "Work-Out" had initiated and "best practices" transfers had reinforced. Describing his barrier-free vision for GE, Welch wrote:

> The boundaryless company we envision will remove the barriers among engineering, manufacturing, marketing,

sales, and customer service; it will recognize no distinctions between domestic and foreign operations—we'll be as comfortable doing business in Budapest and Seoul as we are in Louisville and Schenectady. A boundaryless organization will ignore or erase group labels such as "management," "salaried" or "hourly," which get in the way of people working together.[10]

One of Welch's most repeated stories of how best practices could be leveraged by boundaryless behavior described how managers from Canadian GE identified a small New Zealand appliance maker, Fisher & Paykel, producing a broad range of products very efficiently in its small, low-volume plant. When the Canadians used the flexible job-shop techniques to increase productivity in their high-volume factory, the U.S. appliance business became interested. More than 200 managers and employees from the Louisville plant went to Montreal to study the accomplishments, and soon a Quick Response program had cut the U.S. production cycle in half and reduced inventory costs by 20%. Not surprisingly, GE's Appliance Park in Louisville became a "must see" destination for many other businesses, and within a year, the program had been adapted for businesses as diverse as locomotives and jet engines.

The CEO gave the abstract concept of boundarylessness teeth not only by repeating such success stories but also by emphasizing that there was no place at GE for the adherents of the old culture: "We take people who aren't boundaryless out of jobs. . . . If you're turf-oriented, self-centered, don't share with people and aren't searching for ideas, you don't

belong here," he said. He also changed the criteria for bonuses and options awards to reward idea-seeking and sharing, not just idea creation. Five years later, Welch had a list of boundarylessness success stories:

> We quickly began to learn from each other: productivity solutions from Lighting; "quick response" asset management from Appliances; transaction effectiveness from GE Capital; cost-reduction techniques from Aircraft Engines; and global account management from Plastics.[11]

One of the most impressive examples of the way ideas and expertise spread throughout GE was the company's "integration model." Developed on the lessons drawn from literally hundreds of post-acquisition reviews, the model guided the actions of managers in any part of the company responsible for integrating a newly acquired operation: from taking control of the accounts to realigning the organization, and from identifying and removing "blockers" to implementing GE tools and programs. By the late 1990s, GE's integration programs were completed in about 100 days.

STRETCH: ACHIEVING THE IMPOSSIBLE

To reinforce his rising managerial expectations, in the early 1990s Welch made a new assault on GE's cultural norms. He introduced the notion of "stretch" to set performance targets and described it as "using dreams to set business targets, with no real idea of how to get there."[12] His objective was to change the way targets were set and performance was measured

[10] GE Annual Report, 1989.

[11] GE Annual Report, 1995.
[12] GE Annual Report, 1993.

by creating an atmosphere that asked of everyone, "How good can you be?"

Stretch targets did not replace traditional forecasting and objective-setting processes. Managers still had to hit basic targets—adjusted to recognize the world as it turned out to be, not some rigid plan negotiated a year earlier. But during the budget cycle they were also required to set higher, "stretch" goals for their businesses. While managers were not held accountable for these goals, those who achieved them were rewarded with substantial bonuses or stock options. Said Welch: "Rigorous budgeting alone is nonsense. I think in terms of . . . what is the best you can do. You soon begin to see what comes out of a trusting, open environment."

Within a year of introducing the concept of stretch, Welch was reporting progress:

> We used to timidly nudge the peanut along, setting goals of moving from, say, 4.73 in inventory turns to 4.91, or from 8.53% operating margin to 8.92%; and then indulge in time-consuming high-level, bureaucratic negotiations to move the number a few hundredths one way or the other. . . . We don't do that anymore. In a boundaryless organization with a bias for speed, decimal points are a bore. They inspire or challenge no one, capture no imaginations. We're aiming at 10 inventory turns, at 15% operating margins.[13]

By the mid-1990s, stretch goals were an established part of GE's culture. A senior executive explained: "People like problem solving. They want to go to that next level. That's becoming a bigger driver for the company than Work-Out." But the introduction of stretch targets did not come without implementation difficulties. According to Steve Kerr, the head

of Crotonville, "You absolutely have to honor the don't-punish-failure concept; stretch targets become a disaster without that." Unless properly managed, he explained, stretch could easily degenerate into a justification for forcing people to work 60-hour weeks to achieve impossible goals. "It's not the number per se, especially because it's a made-up number. It's the process you're trying to stimulate. You're trying to get people to think of fundamentally better ways of performing their work."[14]

In early 1996, Welch acknowledged that GE did not meet two of its four-year corporate stretch targets: to increase operating margins from their 1991 level of 10% to 15% by 1995, and inventory turns from 5 to 10 times. However, after decades of single-digit operating margins and inventory turns of 4 or 5, GE did achieve an operating margin of 14.4% and inventory turns of almost 7 in 1995. "In stretching for these 'impossible' targets," said Welch, "we learned to do things faster than we would have going after 'doable' goals, and we have enough confidence now to set new stretch targets of at least 16% operating margin and more than 10 turns by 1998."[15]

SERVICE BUSINESSES

In 1994, Welch launched a new strategic initiative designed to reinforce one of his earliest goals: to reduce GE's dependence on its traditional industrial products. In the early 1980s, he had initiated the initial tilt towards service businesses through the acquisition of financial service companies such as Employers Reinsurance and

[13] GE Annual Report, 1993.

[14] "Stretch Goals: The Dark Side of Asking for Miracles," Interview excerpts with Steve Kerr, GE's Vice President of Leadership Development. Fortune, November 13, 1995.
[15] GE Annual Report, 1995.

Kidder, Peabody. "Nearly 60% of GE's profits now comes from services," said Welch in 1995. "Up from 16.4% in 1980. I wish it were 80%."[16]

To fulfill that wish, Welch began moving to the next stage—a push for product services. During his annual strategic reviews with senior managers, Welch began to challenge his managers "to participate in more of the food chain." While customers would always need high-quality hardware, Welch argued that GE's future challenge would be to offset slowing growth for its products by supplementing them with added-value services. Describing it as one of "the biggest growth opportunities in [GE's] history," he named a cadre of rising executives to focus on the issue. At the same time, he asked Vice Chairman Paolo Fresco to set up a Services Council through which top managers could exchange ideas.

Soon, all GE's businesses were exploring new service-based growth opportunities. The medical business, for example, developed a concept called "In Site." This involved placing diagnostic sensors and communications capability into their installed base of CT scanners, MRI equipment, and other GE medical devices. The system linked the equipment directly to GE's on-line service center, continuously diagnosing its operating condition in real time. Soon, GE was offering its remote diagnostics and other services to all medical equipment—including non-GE products.

Like other internal "best practice" service examples, the "In Site" story was shared in the Services Council, and soon online diagnostic technology was being transferred to other GE businesses. In Aircraft Engines, critical operating parameters of GE jet engines were monitored by GE Service experts while the engines were in flight, providing the company with a major value-added benefit for its customers. The same-real time diagnostic concepts were also applied in GE's power systems business, and other businesses had plans to develop remote diagnostic capability as well.

According to Welch, the opportunity for growth in product services was unlimited. With an advantage unique in the world—an installed base of some 9,000 GE commercial jet engines, 10,000 turbines, 13,000 locomotives, and 84,000 major pieces of medical diagnostic imaging equipment—he felt GE had an incredibly strong platform on which to build. Commented Lewis Edelheit, GE's senior VP for Corporate Research and Development:

> A few years ago, businesses were seen as a pyramid, with the base as the product and the other elements—services, manufacturing processes and information—resting on that base. We are now looking at turning the pyramid upside down. The product will become just one piece of the picture—the tip of that inverted pyramid. The biggest growth opportunities may come from providing services to the customer: providing the customer with ways to become more productive—and with information so valuable the customer will pay for it.[17]

By 1996, GE had built an $8 billion equipment services business, which was growing much faster than the underlying product businesses. Equally important, in Welch's view, it was changing internal

---

[16] Tim Smart, "Jack Welch's Encore," *Fortune*, October 28, 1996.

[17] Lewis Edelheit, "GE's R&D Strategy: Be Vital," *Research Technology Management*, March–April, 1998.

EXHIBIT 9   **Growth in GE's Service Businesses**

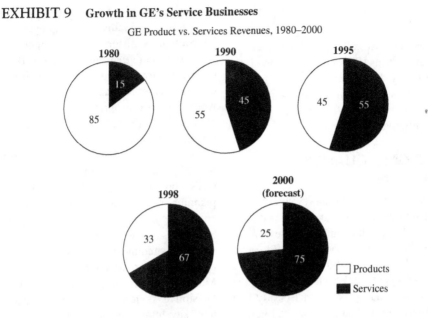

GE Product vs. Services Revenues, 1980–2000

1980 — 15 / 85

1990 — 45 / 55

1995 — 45 / 55

1998 — 33 / 67

2000 (forecast) — 25 / 75

☐ Products
■ Services

mindsets from selling products to "helping our customers to win." GE's product services were to be aimed at making customers' existing assets—power plants, locomotives, airplanes, factories, hospital equipment and the like—more productive. Yet while GE was helping its customers reduce their capital outlays, its managers were also shifting demand from low-margin products to their newer high-profit services with margins almost twice the company average.

This initiative led to a new round of acquisitions. In 1997 alone, GE made 20 service-related acquisitions and joint ventures, including a $1.5 billion acquisition of a jet engine service business and the $600 million purchase of a global power generation equipment service company. GE's radical business shift over two decades led Welch to claim, "We have changed the very nature of what we do for a living. Today, services account for two-thirds of our revenues." (See **Exhibit 9.**)

CLOSING OUT THE DECADE: RAISING THE BAR

As he entered the last half of the decade, Welch was aware that he would reach GE's mandatory retirement age in 2001. Yet his commitment to keep building GE was undiminished, despite critics who continued to question if the company could keep adding value to such a highly diversified business portfolio. In the 1995 Annual Report, he tackled the issue head on:

The hottest trend in business is the rush toward breaking up multi-business companies. The obvious question to GE, the world's largest multi-business company, was, "When are you going to do it?" The short answer is that we're not. . . . We are a company intent on getting bigger, not smaller. Our only answer to the trendy question "What do you intend to spin off?" is "Cash—and lots of it."

Despite hospitalization for triple by-pass surgery in 1995, he showed no signs of slowing down. Indeed, many felt he gained new energy in his post-operative state as the pressure for performance and new initiatives continued.

SIX SIGMA QUALITY INITIATIVE

When a 1995 company survey showed that GE employees were dissatisfied with the quality of its products and processes, Welch met with Lawrence Bossidy, an old friend who had left GE in 1991 to become CEO of AlliedSignal Inc. Welch learned how the Six Sigma quality program Bossidy had borrowed from Motorola Inc. had helped AlliedSignal dramatically improve quality, lower costs, and increase productivity. Immediately, he invited Bossidy to GE's next Corporate Executive Council meeting. His presentation of the AlliedSignal program won universal rave reviews.

After the meeting, Welch asked Gary Reiner, vice president for Business Development, to lead a quality initiative for GE. Reiner undertook a detailed study of the impact of quality programs at companies like Motorola and AlliedSignal. His analysis concluded that GE was operating at error rates ten thousand times the Six Sigma quality level of 3.4 defects per million operations. Furthermore, he estimated that the gap was costing the company between $8 billion and $12 billion a year in inefficiencies and lost productivity. On the basis of Reiner's findings, at GE's 1996 annual gathering of its 500 top managers in Boca Raton, Welch announced a goal of reaching Six Sigma quality levels company-wide by the year 2000, describing the program as "the

biggest opportunity for growth, increased profitability, and individual employee satisfaction in the history of our company."

Like all initiatives announced in Boca (services, globalization, etc.), Six Sigma quality was more than a slogan: it was a well-developed program, with a detailed plan for its implementation. Furthermore, it would be monitored throughout the year in a carefully linked series of management meetings that Welch started to refer to as GE's "operating system"—the series of planning, resource allocation, review, and communication meetings that were at the heart of its management process. The Boca initiative announcement was followed up by a first progress report at the two-day March CEC meeting; then in the April Session C reviews, Welch would check how key human resources had been deployed against the target; the July strategic review sessions would review the impact of the initiative on each business's three-year outlook; October's Officers Meeting tracked progress and showcased best practice; and the November operating plan reviews would fold the impact into the following year's forecasts. (See **Exhibit 10.**) Said Welch, "We are relentless."

Six Sigma participation was not optional, and Welch tied 40% of bonus to an individual's Six Sigma objectives. To provide managers the skills, Reiner designed a massive training of thousands of managers to create a cadre of "Green Belts," "Black Belts," and "Master Black Belts" in Six Sigma quality. "Green Belt" training took about four weeks, followed by implementation of a five-month project aimed at improving quality. Black Belts required six weeks of instruction in statistics, data analysis, and other Six Sigma tools which prepared the candidate to undertake three major quality projects that resulted in measurable performance increases.

EXHIBIT 10 The GE Management System

Core Business Processes

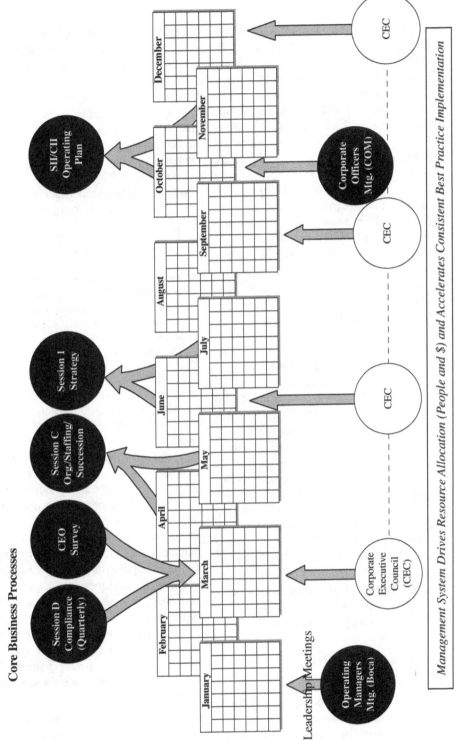

Management System Drives Resource Allocation (People and $) and Accelerates Consistent Best Practice Implementation

Master Black Belts—full-time Six Sigma instructors—mentored the Black Belt candidates through the two-year process.

At the January 1998 Boca Raton meeting, speakers from across the company and around the world presented Six Sigma best practice and achievements. Managers from Medical Systems described how Six Sigma designs produced a tenfold increase in the life of CT scanner x-ray tubes; the railcar leasing business described a 62% reduction in turnaround time at its repair shops, making it two to three times faster than its nearest rival; and a team from the plastics business described how the Six Sigma process added 300 million pounds of new capacity, equivalent to a "free plant." In all, 30,000 Six Sigma projects had been initiated in the prior year.

At the April 1999 Annual Meeting, Welch announced that in the first two years of Six Sigma, GE had invested $500 million to train the entire professional workforce of 85,000. In addition, 5,000 managers had been appointed to work on the program full-time as Black Belts and Master Black Belts, leading Welch to claim "they have begun to change the DNA of GE to one whose central strand is quality." Returns of $750 million over the investment exceeded expectations, and the company was forecasting additional returns of $1.5 billion in 1999 (see **Exhibit 11**). Clearly delighted by the program, Welch stated, "In nearly four decades with GE, I have never seen a company initiative move so willingly and so rapidly in pursuit of a big idea."

"A PLAYERS" WITH "FOUR E'S"

The closer he got to his planned retirement date, the more Welch seemed to focus on the quality of the organization he would leave to his successor. While he felt he had assembled a first-class team of leaders at the top of the company, he wanted to continue upgrading quality deep in the organization. This implied not only raising the bar on new hires but also weeding out those who did not meet GE's high standards. Modifying his earlier language of four management types, he began describing GE as a company that wanted only "A Players"—individuals with vision, leadership, energy, and courage. He described what he was trying to achieve:

> The GE leader sees this company for what it truly is: the largest petri dish of business innovation in the world. We have roughly 350 business segments. We see them as 350 laboratories whose ideas are there to be shared, learned, and spread as fast as we can. The leader sees that sharing and spreading near the top of his or her responsibilities.

"A Players" were characterized by what Welch described as the 4E's—energy ("excited by ideas and attracted to turbulence because of the opportunity it brings"), ability to energize others ("infecting everyone with their enthusiasm for an idea and having everyone dreaming the same big dreams"), edge ("the ability to make tough calls") and execution ("the consistent ability to turn vision into results").

To meet the company's need for exceptional leadership talent, Welch insisted that GE move to phase three of its globalization initiative. Beyond focusing on global markets and global sources—the earlier two phases of globalization—he urged his managers to expand their efforts in "globalizing the intellect of the company." At the same time, he urged his top management group to take strong action to upgrade the quality of their existing employees:

> We're an A-plus company. We want only A players. We can get anyone

EXHIBIT 11 **Costs and Benefits of GE's Six Sigma Program**

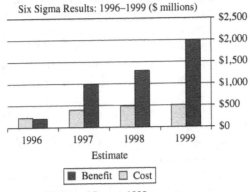

Six Sigma Results: 1996–1999 ($ millions)

Estimate

■ Benefit □ Cost

Source: GE Annual Report, 1998.

we want. Shame on any of you who aren't facing into your less-than-the-best. Take care of your best. Reward them. Promote them. Pay them well. Give them a lot of [stock] options and don't spend all that time trying to work plans to get Cs to be Bs. Move them on out early. It's a contribution.[18]

To help clarify those decisions, the company implemented a performance appraisal system that required every manager to rank each of his or her employees into one of five categories based on his or her long-term performance—the "top" 10% as 1s, the "strong" 15% as 2s, the "highly valued" 50% as 3s, the "borderline" 15% as 4s, and the "least effective" 10% as 5s.[19] Every group, even a 10-person team, had to be ranked on this so-called "vitality curve." All 1s and most 2s received stock options but anyone rated a 5 had to go. Welch elaborated on the need to weed out

poor performers: "With the 5s it's clear as a bell. I think they know it, and you know it. It's better for everyone. They go on to a new place, a new life, a new start." At the other end of the scale, Welch expected managers to take action on their top performers to develop them: "You send your top 10 on and see how many of them get into the top 10 of the whole business."

Welch knew that the nurturing and continuously upgrading the quality of management was one of the main keys to GE's success. He felt that the talent he amassed over 18 years—especially at the senior management levels—was of a significantly higher quality than in past years. "I've got all A players in the Corporate Council. It wasn't like that before. I'm really pleased about that," he said.

TOWARD RETIREMENT: ONE MORE INITIATIVE

Just when the organization felt Welch had put his final stamp on GE, at the 1999 Operating Managers' Meeting in Boca, the 64-year-old CEO introduced his fourth

---

[18] Slater, op. cit., p. 39.

[19] Eventually, the five categories were reduced to three—the top 20%, the high-performance 70%, and the bottom 10%. The practice of counseling out the bottom 10% continued under the philosophy of "improve or move."

strategic initiative—e-business.[20] Describing the impact of the Internet as "the biggest change I have ever seen," he launched a program he described as "*destroyyourbusiness.com.*" Within two months each unit had a full-time *dyb.com* team focused on the challenge of redefining its business model before someone else did. "Change means opportunity," he told them. "And this is our greatest opportunity yet."

Yet Welch also knew that GE was late to the Internet party. As he acknowledged in his address to shareholders three months after the Boca meeting, "Big companies like us were frightened by the unfamiliarity of the technology. We thought this was mysterious, Nobel Prize stuff, the province of the wild-eyed and purple haired." But the more he explored the Internet and talked to people about it, the more Welch came to believe that, through processes like Six Sigma, GE had done the really hard work of building the assets needed to support e-business—like strong brands, top ranked product reliability, great fulfillment capability, and excellent service quality. "It's much harder for a dot com startup to challenge us when they don't have the fundamentals down," he said. "They're popcorn stands without a real business or operating capabilities."

As the organization cranked up to push the new initiative through the monthly schedule of reviews that GE operating system required, Welch was impressed by early results from the *dyb.com* teams. "Digitizing the company and developing e-business models is easier—not harder—than we ever imagined," he said.

[20] The three earlier ones were globalization, services, and Six Sigma. For more detail on the implementation of GE's strategic initiatives across its business see "GE's Digital Revolution: Redefining the E in GE" (HBS 9-302-001).

But others were more sanguine. Said David Mark, a partner at McKinsey and Co., "It's going to take a decade for this to play out. I don't think it's a simple transition." If Mark was correct, building GE's e-business would be a long-term challenge for Welch's successor.

SOURCES AND REFERENCES

Byrne, John A., "Jack," *Business Week*, June 8, 1998.

Cosco, Joseph P., "General Electric Works It All Out," *Journal of Business Strategy*, May–June, 1994.

Filipczak, Bob, "CEOs Who Train," *Training*, June, 1996.

Grant, Linda, "GE: The Envelope, Please," *Fortune*, June 26, 1995.

Hodgetts, Richard M., "A Conversation with Steve Kerr, GE's Chief Learning Officer," *Organizational Dynamics*, March 22, 1996.

Kandebo, Stanley, "Engine Services Critical to GE Strategy," *Aviation Week*, February 23, 1998.

Koenig, Peter, "If Europe's Dead, Why Is GE Investing Billions There?" *Fortune*, September 9, 1996.

Lorenz, Christopher, "The Alliance-Maker," *Financial Times*, April 14, 1989.

Norman, James R., "A Very Nimble Elephant," *Forbes*, October 10, 1994.

Rifkin, Glenn, "GE: Bringing Good Leaders to Life," *Forbes*, April 8, 1996.

Tichy, Noel M. and Eli Cohen, *The Leadership Engine: How Winning*

Companies Build Leaders at Every Level (HarperBusiness, New York, 1997).

Tichy, Noel M. and Eli Cohen, "The Teaching Organization," *Training & Development*, July 1998.

Tichy, Noel M. and Stratford Sherman, *Control Your Destiny or Someone Else Will* (HarperBusiness, New York, 1994).

Tichy, Noel M. and Stratford Sherman, "Walking the Talk at GE," *Training & Development*, June 1996.

Slater, Robert, *Get Better or Get Beaten!* (McGraw-Hill, New York, 1996).

Smart, Tim, "GE's Brave New World," *Business Week*, November 8, 1993.

Stewart, Thomas A., "GE Keeps Those Ideas Coming," *Fortune*, August 12, 1991.

Change Classic

Nigel Andrews and General Electric Plastics (A)

A slight frown crossed Nigel Andrews' brow as he hung up the phone. Andrews, recently installed general manager of the Silicones business of General Electric Plastics (GEP), had just finished speaking to the chair of his division's Workout steering committee, who seemed quite agitated. Could they get together later in the day for a brief meeting, the man had inquired? When Andrews agreed, they had arranged to meet at five o'clock. Everything appeared to be going well with Workout, Andrews brooded; the first session had been a great success, and the most recently concluded session had, by all accounts, been fruitful as well. He had

been expecting the chair to call and set up a time for a debrief of this second meeting. Instead, this request for a rushed few minutes later in the day—had something gone wrong?

WORKOUT AT GE

In January 1989, GE chairman Jack Welch, with the support of his two vice chairmen, launched a major organizational transformation called Workout. Its purpose was nothing short of radical cultural change, empowering the organization to eliminate unnecessary work, tasks, and activities left over from the company's significant downsizing and structural realignment of the 1980s. The goal was to move this 300,000-person, $50 billion organization away from centralized controls, multilevel approvals, and bureaucracy toward an operation characterized by "speed, simplicity, and self-confidence."

EXHIBIT 1   **Key Roles and Responsibilities for Workout at GE Silicones**

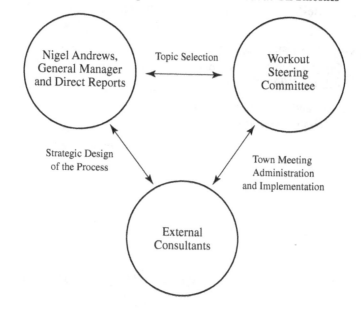

Silicones was to become the first GEP division to develop a Workout program. Three months after Welch's announcement, Andrews and his staff met with a Workout consultant to begin designing how to establish and introduce the new goals, and how the process might be implemented in "town meeting" style workshops. These two-day problem-solving sessions, made up of 50 to 75 participants, were to be used to identify bureaucratic encumbrances and devise action steps to change the way the division was operating. Another purpose was to reduce boundaries across functions.

At that initial meeting, Andrews and his staff made two decisions. First, a series of employee focus groups would help identify Workout issue opportunities. Second, a steering committee of employees, supervisors, and managers would work with Andrews' staff and the outside consultants as the "implementor" of the Workout process, and as a partner in its development (see Exhibit 1).

THE WORKOUT STEERING COMMITTEE

In May, the Silicones human resource department selected steering committee candidates, inviting people from across all functions and levels with a broad range of experience. In all, 18 people agreed to participate. At its first meeting, the committee discussed the Workout concept, how the group would interact effectively, and began planning a first Town Meeting workshop for June. This workshop was to be organized around themes that had emerged from the focus group findings. After studying the data, Andrews' staff chose two major themes, and the steering committee added one more: The three issues were reports, approvals, and meeting management.

Despite some healthy skepticism and busy schedules, the members of the steering committee met frequently. There were no manuals to guide them—this was on-the-job training. First, the group planned the actual session: It split the three major themes into specific topics, chose 60 people to invite, and broke them into eight groups to attack the topic areas. Along with such procedural decisions, the group also dealt with invitations, hotel logistics, the workshop agenda, and other administrative matters. Its final task was to schedule the first five workshops, one a month from June to October, and to lock in the calendars of Andrews and his staff.

WORKOUT I, JUNE 6–7, 1989

When Workout I convened, the eight groups set out to reduce or eliminate wasteful, time-consuming, and unnecessary reports and approval steps at GE. The turning point came during the first evening's plenary at which all the teams presented their initial recommendations. After viewing the flip charts around the room and listening to the discussion, one participant demanded: "Why are we being so cautious? These aren't bold and groundbreaking suggestions. And why are we asking 'them' to do so much? Why can't we do more ourselves?" The evening concluded with a bonfire into which participants threw all the written reports they had brought along and now thought unnecessary.

During the second day, the teams refined and expanded their recommendations and devised action plans that were bolder and more within their own control. The groups made presentations to Andrews and the manager of finance for cutting back approval steps, eliminating reports, and streamlining certain business processes.

One recommendation, in particular, seemed to unite all the participants: to make Wednesdays "meeting-free" in order to cut down the volume of meetings and increase the time devoted to "work." The presenting group asked Andrews to decide whether Wednesday or Friday should be the meeting-free day. Because customers often visited on Fridays, Andrews chose Wednesdays, starting the Wednesday after Labor Day, so people could plan accordingly. This proposal was greeted with thunderous applause, the loudest of the session.

Everyone declared Workout I a "victory," including the participants, the steering committee, the consultants, and Andrews. People left wearing buttons inscribed "Ask Me about Workout!"

WORKOUT II, JULY 18–19, 1989

Workout II followed the model of the first session. Based again on focus group findings, the steering committee chose two new themes, and Andrews' staff chose one. The steering committee then divided these issues into topics, selected new participants and teams, and set the agenda. Things were going smoothly.

Steering committee members opened the second meeting by endorsing the effort and sharing their perspectives on how Workout was faring. Over the next two days, they served as team facilitators, answering numerous questions about Workout I decisions, in particular "meeting-free Wednesdays." Toward the end of the session, as participants finalized their recommendations, the steering committee members informally began to map out the subsequent workshops. What would be the issues and who should attend? Who beyond Andrews should be sitting in to hear the recommendations? How would the union be included? But as these issues were debated, one question quickly overshadowed all others: the date for Workout IV.

Workout IV was scheduled for the Tuesday and Wednesday following Labor Day. But, given the decision to forbid meetings on Wednesdays (after Labor Day), the committee realized that this session would violate the new policy. In late May, when the schedule originally had been set, these two days had been the only back-to-back dates Andrews had available in September. Further, GE vice chairman Larry Bossidy had called Andrews June 3 to arrange a time to observe a Workout session and had selected Wednesday, September 6. His date was now locked in and could take as long as three months to reschedule.

Bossidy wasn't just interested in Workout, Andrews knew. The vice chairman—often characterized as a terse, fast-moving, bottom-line-oriented decision maker—was visiting all nine of the 13 GE divisions reporting directly to him to evaluate both Workout and business results.

Moreover, Silicones was likely to undergo particular scrutiny. The business had struggled in recent years, and, in 1988, had been rumored to be on the block.

Andrews, in his first line management position, had replaced his fired predecessor just six months before with the charge of revitalizing the business. He was anxious now to show Bossidy both the early indications of success with Workout and his progress at Silicones overall.

THE FIVE O'CLOCK MEETING

The chair of the steering committee entered Andrews' office, wearing a distracted look. He came right to the point. The committee had informally caucused, he explained, at the conclusion of Workout. The issue they now faced was one of principle, they agreed, and Andrews needed to be apprised of it immediately. He continued:

> We have to reschedule the September session. It lands on a Wednesday, and you know that's our meeting-free day. We just can't have a Workout on that day or it will kill Workout. And our own credibility is really on the line here. We have been telling everybody about this "win" and now we are going to violate it. You have to call Bossidy and tell him to come some other time. He can look us over whenever he wants but not on a Wednesday.

Reading
GE's Move to the Internet

Few managers achieved the stature of General Electric Co. CEO John F. Welch. He was not only the iconic chief of one of the most valuable companies on earth, but also the corporate world's top-ranking business professor. His compass guided the actions of countless captains of industry.

But even the captain's captain had to prove he could navigate the treacherous waters of the Internet economy. At the beginning of 1999, new-economy zealots wondered aloud whether Welch's staunch refusal to grant special equity deals for technology talent signaled that he was past his prime, a prisoner of old-economy thinking. It wouldn't be long, critics predicted, before top GE managers would flee to dot-coms offering ownership stakes that would make them instant multimillionaires.

That's when Welch had an epiphany. GE's vast resources weren't enough of a weapon to combat promises of instant wealth; he would have to place his legendary reputation on the line. So at a management meeting in Boca Raton, Florida, in January 1999, Welch outlined a sweeping Internet agenda that would leave no GE businesses untouched. He added e-business to a short list of broad initiatives—including globalization, customer service, and a quality control yardstick called Six Sigma—that each manager would be responsible for carrying out. The Internet was no longer just a new medium for buying and selling, he said; it was fundamentally changing how business operated.

A year and a half later, the critics were silent and Welch had fully vindicated himself. Many of the dot-com threats had fizzled, and GE had moved billions of dollars in sales and spending to the Internet in record time, aided largely by a corporate culture that rewarded the "stealing" of ideas among GE's 20 units and 340,000 employees. The result was new buying,

Source: Based on David Joachim's "GE's E-Biz Turnaround Proves That Big Is Back—Size Becomes an Advantage as Net Apps Multiply Like Rabbits across 20 Diverse Businesses," the leading article of "*InternetWeek* 100," originally published in *InternetWeek* 8 June 2000, with alterations by Brandon Miller under the supervision of Prof. Maury Peiperl.

selling, and manufacturing techniques that spread through the massive company in weeks, not years.

"We've become pretty good at using size to our advantage," Welch said. "Size gives you the ability to experiment, to take risks because you are not going to sink yourself. That is the only advantage of size. The small company is faster, but one wrong swing can wipe them out. They have to be right."

In other words, big is back, and no company made that point more convincingly than GE, where e-business experimentation paid off in a big way.

Private e-auctions were forcing suppliers to fight for GE's business, squeezing hundreds of millions of dollars out of purchases in 2000 alone. Full-time Internet connections were letting GE remotely monitor heavy equipment—and tell customers how they could be working more efficiently. Whole new businesses were sprouting up throughout GE, including the repackaging of homegrown technology for sale. And the money machine was pouring record sums into its own technology suppliers.

It was an e-business ecosystem that had earned GE the No. 1 spot in 2000's *InternetWeek* 100 listing of top e-businesses.

Perhaps a better sign that the strategy was working: Wall Street was treating GE as both a blue chip and an Internet company, sending the stock higher when one or the other was in style. GE's stock price doubled within a year and a half after Welch's edict was handed down.

"The key revelation is that the Internet is primarily a productivity tool, and secondarily a selling and procurement tool," said Jeanne Terrile, a financial analyst at Merrill Lynch. "They're using the Internet to eliminate paperwork and run operations a lot more efficiently."

In the middle of 2000, GE expected to slash overhead costs by as much as 50 percent—which would amount to a staggering $10 billion—in as little as two years. Some of this savings would fall to the bottom line, while some would be spent on new initiatives.

As for the technology talent war, Welch never did give in by spinning off Internet tracking stocks or showering Web experts with riches. Rather, in a corporate culture known to compensate employees almost solely based on the number of years they've worked, Welch and his high-powered recruiters created new formulas that accounted for the unique experiences of young talent. Many were placed in the same salary brackets as executives with twice the business experience.

Among the other perks: highly visible and well-financed projects, as well as direct access to Welch and chief information officer Gary Reiner.

"Before the Internet, if people with the same experience came to me and said, 'I want to work at GE, I want to be compensated like an executive, and I want to report to the CIO,' I would have said, 'We're not breathing the same air.' Now we were offering them a chance to a be a first-mover in a Fortune 5 company," said Paul Daversa, president of Resource Systems Group, a recruitment firm hired by GE to lure e-business executives following Welch's Internet address.

Daversa related one story about an executive who was torn between GE and Boo.com. Going with the hotshot fashion startup would have meant equity worth $15 million at the time.

"We're in a position to play Monday morning quarterback, but look at Boo.com now," Daversa said. The British dot-com was forced to liquidate after burning through $120 million in 12 months. The software assets sold in May 2000 for a paltry $373,000, and the rest were sold to Fashionmall.com for slightly more.

In the end, the prestige of being responsible for mapping the future of GE attracted high-ranking executives from companies such as Andersen Consulting, Bertelsmann AG, Boston Consulting Group, DHL International Ltd., PepsiCo, and Snap-on Inc.

LICENSE TO STEAL

Those executives were plugged into a $112 billion goliath whose culture had celebrated the sharing of knowledge across diverse businesses ever since it emerged from a dark period of downsizing in the late 1980s and early 1990s.

"It turns out that all the work that GE did to break down the bureaucracy and create a culture of sharing was wonderful preparation for e-commerce," said Merrill Lynch's Terrile. Drastic changes in mindset resulting from that period—such as measuring fulfillment performance based not on how well GE met its own objectives but on how well it met customer needs—"moved through GE rather quickly because each idea cuts a path that the next one can follow," Terrile said.

That included GE's efforts in e-business. Welch's rallying cry in 2000 was about the assets GE had that dot-coms didn't: a wealth of products to sell, legions of devoted customers, and the ability to deliver quality products on time. "We already have the difficult part, the 'stuff' that startups are looking for—world-leading products and technology, a century-old brand identity and a reputation," Welch said.

The next challenge was to coordinate e-business endeavors among GE's 20 far-flung units, including Appliances,

Aircraft, Capital, Lighting, Medical Systems, Plastics, Power Systems, and Transportation Systems. E-business leaders in these groups held monthly interactive teleconferences, using PC screen emulators to demonstrate new Internet applications for buying, selling, customer care, manufacturing, logistics, and fulfillment. They met in person quarterly.

"We really give great praise to those who have copied from others, as much as those who came up with the idea to begin with," said CIO Reiner. "There's been a lot of work on the culture so that people are proud to take ideas from others."

BIDDING FOR DOLLARS

One such idea was an e-auction application developed in less than three weeks by a handful of developers in the Transportation Systems business. Launched in December 1999, by the middle of 2000, it was in use at nearly all of GE's manufacturing units and was on track to handle $5 billion in GE purchasing volume by the end of 2000, Reiner said.

Auctions were conducted daily and were generally held for three hours, during which time approved suppliers bid against one another for GE's business. Purchasing managers across the company had access to an auction calendar on the Web, allowing them to post requests for quotes on production and nonproduction supplies.

GE Power Systems, which made turbines for power production, devoted about 15 percent of its purchasing activity, totaling $1 billion, to e-auctions in 2000, said Jean-Michel Ares, the unit's vice president of e-business and chief technical officer. Most of that spending was planned to be on indirect materials—products that would not be used in finished GE products—such as office supplies and computers.

The auctions exposed the $11 billion unit to a whole new set of suppliers, Ares said, and could have saved the unit as much as $150 million in 2000.

"We try to force as many items as we can into this auction model because of how much of a reduction you can get on cost," said Joseph Hogan, President of GE Medical Systems. However, auctions would generally be useful only for commodity items, such as cabling or microprocessors, that didn't require customization.

In the three months after it launched e-purchasing applications in March of 2000, for both auctions and straight purchases, the Medical Systems unit shifted 10 percent of its spending to the Internet. It was on track to move 50 percent of spending online by year's end, Hogan said, totaling hundreds of million of dollars in volume.

Aside from the competitive nature of auctions, e-purchasing "improves quality, because a lot of times invoices are wrong; specifications are wrong," Hogan said. "You do it online, and it takes a lot of the touch time and the opportunity for defects out of the system."

GE's approach to e-auctions was starkly different than most companies'. Big businesses tended to partner with dot-com companies which operated auctions as a service. "We don't see any reason to have another hand in the till," Hogan said. "Why do you want anyone to stand between you and your supplier? That's one of the advantages of being part of a big business like GE. We have our own technology."

E-BUSINESS GENESIS

As early as 1994, GE's Plastics unit was distributing technical documentation over the Web on a site called Polymerland. By 1999, Welch was praising that site as an example of what the rest of the company should emulate.

That year, Polymerland—which sold GE plastics and complementary products from 30 other vendors—handled $100 million in orders, and it was on track to tally $1.2 billion in volume in 2000, said Gerry Podesta, the $7 billion unit's general manager of e-business.

But more than just freeing up salespeople from the low-level task of taking orders, Polymerland's ability to integrate ordering systems with production and delivery systems decreased call volume 20 percent and improved on-time deliveries by 50 percent, Podesta said.

"You must have a world-class fulfillment capability to operate successfully on the Internet," Podesta said. "There is clearly a higher level of expectation on the Web than over the phone. You will lose customers on the Web if they get a late shipment."

The systems integration that made that possible led the Plastics unit to invent a metric called Span that measured how well a company was meeting customer expectations. In 2000, it was used to measure fulfillment on all Plastics orders, online and offline. It was also used by units such as GE Capital to measure how quickly mortgage applications were processed, Podesta said.

GE Plastics, which made engineered plastics used in electronics, cars, and buildings, borrowed technology from Power Systems to remotely monitor customer sites. The system, called Vendor Managed Inventory, kept track of materials in silos and would automatically submit an order when inventory got low. Similar technology was used by GE Lighting to monitor light-bulb stockpiles

at retail stores such as Wal-Mart, CIO Reiner said.

GE Plastics also pioneered customer-support tools called Wizards that, by mid-2000, were in all of GE's manufacturing businesses.

One such Wizard let product engineers select materials and colors for plastic pellets, mold a digital representation of a custom-designed product, and even get cost estimates for materials on the Web.

"A customer who is making a part—it could be a phone, a TV, a PDA, an automotive part, a blender, a vacuum cleaner—can use the site to factor out the specs and cost of parts," Podesta says.

A Wizard in use at GE Medical helped GE's salespeople and customer technicians work together to spec out and set up magnetic resonance imaging (MRI) scanning equipment in hospitals.

"Some of these pieces of equipment can be pretty complicated," Hogan said. "That information used to be in a person's head, and the only way you could get it was to make a phone call or send a fax, and someone would take a look at it and suggest what the configuration should be. Having it online allows the salesperson to ask the proper question, and it lets the customer see what the options are for that piece of equipment."

GE Power Systems launched a series of Wizards to help customers plan their need for power generators at temporary events, such as concerts and sporting events. For instance, the unit handled energy needs at the summer Olympics in Sydney, Australia.

Previously, serving temporary needs would require physical locations in every region served. But after these innovations, customers could get customer service and support over the Web, Ares said. The result: What was a $7 million business in

1999 was predicted to be a $100 million business in 2000.

DATA FOR SALE

For its part, GE Medical discovered a way to use the Internet to layer data services on top of equipment sales. The application, called iCenter, relied on a direct Web connection to equipment operating at a customer's site. It kept track of the patients examined by the equipment and fed the data back to the customer. Customers could also use the link to send questions about the operation of the equipment.

GE also analyzed the data and compared it with other customer sites and provided those comparisons to customers so they could achieve greater performance. "We can say, 'Do you know you're only 60 percent as productive as another customer using the same equipment in another part of the world? And by doing x, y and z, you can increase productivity,'" Hogan said.

Similar remote-diagnostic systems were used in GE's Aircraft and Power Systems units. The Aircraft unit even monitored jet engines in flight.

The counterpart to iCenter in Power Systems was called the Turbine Optimizer. Released in the fall of 1999, the Turbine Optimizer let customers view and analyze the performance of their turbines compared with turbines of similar capacity and in similar operating environments. GE charged additional fees for both the iCenter and Turbine Optimizer services.

New revenue streams were also a side benefit of GE Power Systems' Parts Edge site, which kept track of 3,000 parts used on turbines and replaced printed catalogs and calls to customer services centers. Benefits included reduced printing costs,

real-time updates, and reduced call volume. The quoting cycle was also reduced from two weeks to less than an hour, said Ares, the unit's CTO.

GE AS GUINEA PIG

The lessons learned by GE's manufacturing units didn't just contribute to the success of other units. They also provided valuable product-development data to GE's Global Exchange Services unit, a developer of business-to-business trading technology.

The unit, formerly the value-added network operator GE Information Services, operated a so-called Global Supplier Network extranet used exclusively by GE businesses. It also provided similar e-marketplace technology to other companies, including 60 percent of the Fortune 500, said Jan Malasek, vice president of business development.

In 2000, Global Exchange was handling 1 billion transactions per year totaling $1 trillion in volume. The unit interacted with GE's other divisions in a variety of ways. First, it treated the others as beta customers for emerging technology. It also scouted out technology developed by those divisions and repackaged it for sale.

For instance, the e-auction technology developed by GE Transportation Systems and in use across GE's manufacturing operations was enhanced into an "industrial strength" application by Global Exchange and became part of the Global Supplier Network. Indeed, most of GE's internal auctions were hosted by Global Exchange.

Global Exchange planned to take the next step in June 2000 when it began selling the auction capabilities as a service to other companies, Malasek said. It planned to port the Windows NT application to various Unix platforms, and to provide support services on top.

"We not only provide technology to GE businesses, but we're also GE's technology face to the world," Malasek said.

Of course, GE was running several other, better-known Internet operations, such as NBCi, a unit of GE's NBC broadcasting business that included e-retail site Spap.com, data storage service Xoom.com, financial site CNBC.com, small business information site AllBusiness.com, and MSNBC.com, a news service co-owned with Microsoft. The GE Capital unit also ran the GE Financial Network, a personal finance site.

EARLY-STAGE INVESTOR

GE's Internet activities weren't limited to the use and sale of technology. In 1999 GE Equity invested $1.5 billion in technology suppliers, bringing the value of the total portfolio to $5 billion, covering 250 companies. About 24 percent of that total was e-business specific.

The company planned to increase investment activity in 2000, after watching valuations rise instantly when GE announced large-volume commitments with technology suppliers. Getting in as an investor prior to such deals let GE share in the equity gains, Reiner said. "I'd say that's more than one of the motivations," he said with a laugh.

Equity investments were as much a collaboration among GE businesses as any other technology initiative. Prospects came in either through one of the manufacturing businesses, directly from GE Equity or from Reiner's office. No matter how the lead was generated, a group assembled from all three entities to evaluate the opportunity and negotiate terms, Reiner said.

All told, nearly 18 months after Welch risked his legacy to convince his troops that they needed to consume themselves with all things Internet, GE's considerable resources were put to work, and the giant battleship had turned.

As far as Reiner was concerned, GE's manufacturing operations laid an e-business foundation that it next needed to build upon in three main areas: the buy side, the make side, and the sell side. In mid-2000 Reiner predicted that all activities for the foreseeable future would be aimed at going "deeper and deeper into those three areas."

Which, if you ask Welch, would not imply that GE's work was largely done. "We're at the beginning of one of the most important revolutions in business," said Welch, who sat on the boards of NBCi and Internet incubator idealab. The Internet "will forever change the way business is done. It will change every relationship, between our businesses, between our customers, between our suppliers. Distribution channels will change. Buying practices will change. Everything will be tipped upside down. The slow become fast, the old become young. It's clear we've only just begun this transformation."

Case

Get Me a CEO from GE!

The call comes from all corners of the *Fortune* 500. But how well does the General Electric playbook travel?

Matt Espe couldn't understand. He would gather his managers for a simple operating review. But no one, it seemed, could give him a clear picture of the business. "I felt like I was trying to find the issue, and they were trying to hide it," he says. "I lost it in a few of those reviews—which would have been acceptable in the GE world."

Then Espe remembered: This wasn't General Electric, where managers are conditioned to put bad news on the table and have it out, and where he'd spent the past 22 years (finishing as chief of its lighting unit). This was IKON Office Solutions (No. 415), a $4.7 billion distributor and servicer of photocopiers and printers. And Espe was the new CEO. "You should have seen the faces around the table looking at me," he recalls. He thought to himself, "I can't do this anymore."

It was the type of thing that might play into fears—the sort that HR chief Beth Sexton had expressed to the board when she said, "I hope you don't hire some GE headbanger."

Sexton knows how things work. When a company needs a loan, it goes to a bank.

When a company needs a CEO, it goes to General Electric, which mints business leaders the way West Point mints generals. Had you visited GE ten years ago, you'd have found Bob Nardelli running transportation, Jim McNerney running international, Larry Johnston in appliances, and a pair of VPs named David Cote and Jeff Immelt. Today they run companies like Home Depot, 3M, Albertsons, Honeywell, and GE—with combined revenues of $311 billion. Before Harry Stonecipher was ousted at Boeing last month, five of the Dow 30 were headed by GEers.

Anywhere else such an outflow of talent would be cause for alarm; at GE it's just a strong graduating class. One headhunter estimates the company harbors another dozen execs of *Fortune* 500 caliber. Immelt guesses the number is double that. "I'm disappointed" to lose talent, he says, "but we march on."

Yes, GE does seem to manage. But what happens to those who march out the door? Do they bring good things to life at companies that aren't GE?

Not always. When *Fortune* compared the performance of 34 current and former GE transplants against the S&P 500, the results were perfectly split: 17 beat the S&P 500, and 17 did not. But boards dream of landing the next Larry Bossidy, who oversaw a 700% rise in AlliedSignal stock from 1991 to 1999, or a Stanley Gault, who propelled Rubbermaid to the top of *Fortune*'s Most Admired list before taking a final victory lap at Goodyear, where the stock price tripled. But not all stories are so happy: Glen Hiner's ten years at Owens Corning ended in a giant pile of asbestos. And between 2000 and 2002, longtime GE Capital chief Gary Wendt collected $53 million for not executing his turnaround plan at Conseco.

The experience of John Trani, whose seven years at toolmaker Stanley Works ended without the decisive turnaround investors wanted, may be more telling. While many saw a manager willing to make the tough calls in a toughening climate—like canceling construction of a factory in his first month on the job—others saw an imperious GE superstar. Says one former Stanley manager: "It was sort of, 'Get out of the way, boys. I know where we're going, and I'll take us there.'" (Trani's plan to reincorporate in Bermuda—abandoned after a public uproar—did little to help perceptions.) "At the end of the day," says Trani, "I think the company is in a better place."

And at the end of the day, the point holds: "Unless you get a culture that's warmly receptive to these kinds of tools," says GE human resources chief Bill Conaty, "they're not going to work."

For Matt Espe, leaving GE was something like leaving home. It's where he'd grown up and where his father, a 35-year GE veteran, had grown up before him. "I was kind of waiting for the [moment] when I would wake up at the foot of the bed sobbing, wondering, What the hell was I thinking leaving GE?" he says. It never happened. But before he stepped into IKON's corner office, he flew to Minnesota to spend a day with Jim McNerney. McNerney's transition to 3M in 2001 had set something of a standard for seamlessness. And Espe came away with two big messages: Take time

to understand the business and the team around you, and respect the culture—don't try to eradicate it.

The advice was sound, but Espe's assignments at GE had often involved blowing things up and starting over. "I fought every fiber of my GE DNA to avoid pulling the trigger on moves I thought we needed to make in the first 60 to 90 days," he says. "I told myself to wait." He enrolled in IKON University (a companywide training program) as a student and traveled the country on a listening tour. He held 35 employee roundtables and four big town halls, and visited dozens of customers. When he did make his first big move—removing a layer of bureaucracy nine months into his tenure—e-mails flooded his in-box congratulating him. "Had I made that decision the month after I got here, it wouldn't have had nearly the effect," he says.

Holding his fire also let him observe. What he saw were competent, energized people harboring enormous frustrations. Sales employees were angry with the "customer-care center" and vice versa. Everybody was mad at headquarters. Nobody was placing the blame where it belonged: on screwed-up processes. "Our best people at IKON are every bit as good as the best people at GE," says Espe. So he went ahead and introduced Six Sigma, the complex statistical discipline that GE made famous. "Once they started training and saw results, there was a wow effect," says Andrew Twadelle, who was put in charge of the effort. "Now instead of listening to whoever is the best debater, it's about what the data tells us."

Espe also profited from something he didn't observe. Jim McNerney's office had betrayed no trace of an 18-year career at GE. Espe's Malvern, Pa., office contains an IKON business-card holder, statuettes to various IKON milestones . . . and not a single GE tchotchke. "There's nothing more offensive than having someone come in and seeing a GE shrine."

But GE is always there—just less visibly. In striving to simplify IKON, which evolved out of a holding company of 450 businesses, from aerospace equipment to ice cream for dogs, Espe can't help but think of a 1996 presentation he made to Jack Welch. Espe had included a complex graph showing shifts in revenue mix. As he attempted to answer his boss's pointed questions, a look of disgust formed on Welch's face. "So what you're telling me is that it's just an awful chart," Welch said. "Maybe next time you can give us a revenue chart we can understand." Says Espe today: "Elegant sophisticated thinking doesn't have to be complex." He sees no reason, therefore, that IKON's 20-page sales order form can't be reduced to a single page. And why have 43 dispatch centers when you need only four?

His grillings can be Welch-like. At one point, Espe invited the chiefs of IKON's ten worst-performing territories to his office for questions. He had to prompt one of them who kept referring to his notes, "Let me help you. The answer I'm looking for is a number." But he's still working on softening his ways. "If all you do is come down, people shut down," he says.

To understand how GE is able to produce those armies of leaders, it's important to recognize that it isn't a jet engine company or an appliance company or even a financial services company. The real business of GE is manufacturing leaders—something it has been doing for almost as long as it's been making light bulbs. Its training center in Crotonville, N.Y., gets much of the attention (spawning imitations at the likes of Boeing and Home Depot). But at least as important

was GE's early decision to create dozens of autonomous units and rotate managers among them. "If you were the old IBM or Ford or GM or Exxon, you didn't run a true profit and loss until you were way up in your career," says Noel Tichy, a professor at the University of Michigan and the former director of Crotonville. "At GE you have all these farm leagues where you can test people."

But GE isn't a business school. "Our whole system is to educate people for the GE system," says Immelt—not any other company's. When executives leave the GE bubble, it's up to them to figure out what travels and what doesn't.

Language can be a problem. When Barry Perry (Silicones, '89) used the term "boundarylessness" in a meeting at Engelhard Corp., he was told there was no such word. When he dared bring it up again, he reframed the notion as "seamlessly integrated decentralized."

Most tend to skirt the idea of ranking employees against their peers. "I have an allergic reaction to forced ranking," says Intuit's Steve Bennett (GE Capital, '00). "I don't think employees need to know whether they're 342 or 343. They just want to know, 'Am I okay or am I in trouble?'"

As for GE's practice of giving the weakest 10% the heave-ho, Vivek Paul (Medical Systems, '99) tried it at IT outsourcing firm Wipro in Bangalore, India. The experiment lasted a year. "It went from bottom 10%, to bottom 5%, to bottom 2.5%, to 'Let's not talk about it anymore,'" he says.

Then there's Six Sigma—mysterious and dizzyingly complex. Asking employees to wrap their minds around it instantly, says Pentair CEO Randy Hogan (Power Systems, '94), would be "like asking a couch potato to run a marathon." He waited five years before testing the waters.

Mentioning GE just makes things harder. "As soon as you say it, antibodies form," says Amgen's Kevin Sharer. Albertsons CEO Larry Johnston (Appliances, '01) invoked his alma mater once too often after joining the grocer in 2001. "I wasn't trying to do it," he says. But "it's really hard after you've been someplace for your whole life."

So what tools in the GE tool kit do work?

Tenneco Automotive CEO Mark Frissora may have left GE 18 years ago, but he still remembers Jack Welch drilling it into managers' heads that they had to increase revenues and cut costs at the same time. He's done both at the parts maker, finding some quick wins by simplifying process. To provide a quote on an exhaust system, paperwork had to stop in 57 mail trays, which took an average of six months. Today it's down to 12 trays and six weeks.

Layers of bureaucracy get the same treatment. When Dan Mudd became interim CEO of troubled Fannie Mae late last year, he increased his direct reports from three people to ten. Intuit's Bennett went from eight to 20.

If Welch had one key device, it was giving GE a simple roadmap and repeating it incessantly. When Tom Tiller arrived at Polaris in 1998 from GE Silicones, the company had no roadmap to speak of. The stock was stuck in the $15 range, and the company had missed internal targets five years in a row. When he became CEO the following year, he listed the company's goals on a single sheet of paper, then plastered it on conference room walls and distributed it to employees. Virtually anytime Tiller opened his mouth—to dealers, investors, board members, or employees—the same goals came out. Today the stock

trades around $70, and the company has hit earnings 27 quarters in a row.

A tribute to Welch and the GE playbook? "I don't want you to call it a playbook," says Welch, and he's insistent on that point. Outsiders look at GE's practices—Six Sigma, Work-Out, whatever—and mistake them for philosophy. In fact, they're just tools—tools that may or may not work at a different company or a different time. If there is a GE playbook, it's this: "An absolute belief that great people build great companies," Welch says. "Getting great human resources people and making them a part of the game, not making them do the picnics and the plant newspaper, and making them flextime managers." As CEO, Welch spent more time with his human resources executive than he did with his CFO. It's a mindset that GE emigrés carry with them. When Bob Nardelli joined Home Depot in 2000, HR was "a function of last resort," he told *Fortune* in 2002, "not first resort, as it should be."

And that, ultimately, could be Espe's biggest legacy: not just to run a company but to build a house that builds people. When he first asked his marketing head for a list of people who could succeed her, she said the company would have to look outside. Two years later she could list three insiders who were on track.

Even Beth Sexton, who's occasionally teased about her "GE headbanger" comment, has come full circle on the whole GE thing. "We've been a huge beneficiary of having an executive come out of GE," she says today. Next time IKON needs a CEO, there may be plenty of homegrown headbangers to choose from. And hopefully, as one IKON exec puts it, "other companies will want to have IKON leaders come to them."

Captain-of-Industry University

GE's alumni network includes a dozen FORTUNE 500 CEOs. Here's what the class-mates are up to.

Jeff Immelt—General Electric
No. 5 "Most likely to succeed Jack Welch" (and did). GE builds a lot of leaders, but only one gets to run the place.

Bob Nardelli—Home Depot
No. 13 Did not succeed Jack Welch, but may yet succeed at America's second-largest retailer—despite a rocky beginning.

Larry Johnston—Albertsons
No. 35 He sold refrigerators at GE. Now he's filling them up. Too bad one competitor is even bigger than GE: No. 1 grocer Wal-Mart.

David Cote—Honeywell
No. 75 TRW stole him from GE Appliances. Larry Bossidy stole him from TRW. Now he runs the house that Jack couldn't buy.

Jim McNerney—3M
No. 105 A "foiled contender" no more. Sales, profits, and stock price are all up since his arrival in 2001. New identity: standard-setter.

Kevin Sharer—Amgen
No. 212 Traded a plum job in aircraft engines for . . . MCI. "A pretty stupid move," he says. Recovered nicely at the biotech leader.

Peter Cartwright—Calpine
No. 242 After 19 years in GE's nuclear power unit, he founded a company of his own in 1984. Natural gas, though. No nukes.

Christopher Kearney—SPX
No. 345 Succeeded another GE man, John Blystone, who ran the industrial conglomerate until his abrupt exit last year.

Matt Espe—IKON
No. 415 Now GE has something to remember him by: IKON's office-products-leasing business, which GE bought last year.

Mark Frissora—Tenneco Automotive
No. 453 Welch drilled it into him: Cut costs and grow sales. He's done both at the parts maker, despite its heavy load of debt.

Barry Perry—Engelhard
No. 456 Wants people and knowledge to flow freely among its four business units. Welch called it "boundarylessness."

Dan Mudd—Fannie Mae
His company's name is mud too—and is missing from this year's 500, for want of current financials. The interim boss is son of journalist Roger.

Reading

The Immelt Revolution

Diane Brady

He's turning GE's culture upside down, demanding far more risk and innovation.

Despite his air of easy-going confidence, Jeffrey R. Immelt admits to two fears: that General Electric Co. will become boring, and that his top people might act like cowards. That's right: cowards. He worries that GE's famous obsession with bottom-line results—and tendency to get rid of those who don't meet them—will make some execs shy away from taking risks that could revolutionize the company.

Immelt, 49, is clearly pushing for a cultural revolution. For the past 3 1/2 years, the GE chairman and CEO has been on a mission to transform the hard-driving, process-oriented company into one steeped in creativity and wired for growth. He wants to move GE's average organic growth rate—the increase in revenue that comes from existing operations, rather than deals and currency fluctuations—to at least 8% from about 5% over the past decade. Under his former boss, the renowned Jack Welch, the skills GE prized above all others were cost-cutting, efficiency, and dealmaking. What mattered was the continual improvement of operations, and that mindset helped make the $152 billion industrial and finance behemoth a marvel of earnings consistency. Immelt hasn't turned his back on the old

ways. But in his GE, the new imperatives are risk-taking, sophisticated marketing, and above all, innovation.

This is change born of necessity. The Welch era reached its zenith in the booming, anything-goes economy of the late 1990s. Back then, GE always seemed to beat the consensus forecasts by a penny a share—and investors felt no burning need to figure out exactly how they did it. Immelt has no such luxury. With a slower-growing domestic economy, less tolerance among investors for buying your way to growth, and more global competitors, Immelt, like many of his peers, has been forced to shift the emphasis from deals and cost-cutting to new products, services, and markets. Any other course risks a slow descent into irrelevance. "It's a different era," says Immelt, a natural salesman who still happily recounts the days when he drove around his territory in a Ford Taurus while at GE Plastics. He knows the world looks to GE as a harbinger of future trends, says Ogilvy & Mather Worldwide Chief Executive Rochelle B. Lazarus, who sits on the GE board. "He really feels GE has a responsibility to get out in front and play a leadership role."

So how, exactly, do you make a culture as ingrained as GE's sizzle with bold thinking and creative energy? To start, you banish some long-cherished traditions and beliefs. Immelt has welcomed outsiders into the highest ranks, even making one, Sir William M. Castell, a vice-chairman. That's a serious break with GE's promote-from-within past. He is pushing hard for a more global workforce that reflects the communities in which GE operates. Immelt is also encouraging his homegrown managers to become experts in their industries rather than just experts in managing. Instead of relying on execs who barely had time to position a family photo on their desk before moving on to the next executive assignment, he's diversifying the top ranks and urging his lieutenants to stay put and make a difference where they are.

Most of all, Immelt has made the need to generate blockbuster ideas more than an abstract concept. In true GE fashion, he has engineered a quantifiable and scalable process for coming up with money-making "eureka!" moments. While Welch was best known for the annual Session C meetings during which he personally evaluated the performance of GE's top several hundred managers, Immelt's highest-profile new gathering is the Commercial Council. Immelt leads the group of roughly a dozen top sales and marketing executives, including some unit heads such as GE Consumer Finance CEO David R. Nissen. The members hold phone meetings every month and meet each quarter to discuss growth strategies, think up ways to reach customers, and evaluate ideas from the senior ranks that aim to take GE out on a limb. "Jeff has launched us on a journey to become one of the best sales and marketing companies in the world," says Nissen, who describes the meetings as collegial and more experimental than other GE gatherings.

This is no free-for-all, however. Business leaders must submit at least three "Imagination Breakthrough" proposals per year that ultimately go before the council for review and discussion. The projects, which will receive billions in funding in the coming years, have to take GE into a new line of business, geographic area, or customer base. Oh, and each one has to give GE incremental growth of at least $100 million.

Such change can be scary stuff for folks steeped in Six Sigma, who were led to believe that if you made your numbers and were prepared to uproot your family every year or two, you had a shot at the top rungs. Now they're being asked to develop real prowess in areas such as creativity, strategy, and customer service that are harder to measure. They are being told to embrace risky ventures, many of which may fail. Immelt's GE can be seen as a grand experiment, still in its early days, to determine whether bold innovation can thrive in a productivity-driven company.

To inspire the fresh thinking he's looking for, Immelt is wielding the one thing that speaks loud and clear: money. The GE chief is tying executives' compensation to their ability to come up with ideas, show improved customer service, generate cash growth, and boost sales instead of simply meeting bottom-line targets. As Immelt puts it, "you're not going to stick around this place and not take bets." More concretely, 20% of 2005 bonuses will come from meeting pre-established measures of how well a business is improving its ability to meet customer needs. And while he hasn't exactly repudiated Welch's insistence that managers cull the bottom 10% of their staff, insiders say there's more flexibility, more subjectivity to the process. Risking failure is a badge of honor at GE these days.

To lay the groundwork for an organization that grows through innovation, Immelt took steps early on to rejigger the GE portfolio. He committed to sell $15 billion of less profitable businesses such as insurance, while shelling out more than $60 billion in acquisitions to dive into hot areas such as bioscience, cable and film entertainment, security, and wind power that have better growth prospects. In doing so, he pared the low-margin, slower-growth businesses like appliances or lighting, which he diplomatically calls "cash generators" instead of "losers," down to 10% of the portfolio, from 33% in 2000. Nicole M. Parent of Credit Suisse First Boston is impressed with "the way they have been able to evolve the portfolio in such a short time" and with so little disruption. "This is a company where managers will do anything to achieve their goals."

Good thing, as their back-slapping chief is now looking for "those things that grow the boundaries of this company." He's confident that the new business mix and growth incentives are already paying off. At GE's annual gathering of its top 650 executives in Boca Raton, Fla., in January, he insisted that "there's never been a better day, a better time, or a better place to be [at GE]!" Strong words in a company that stretches back 127 years to founder Thomas Edison. After an 18% jump in revenues and earnings in the fourth quarter, to $43.7 billion and $5.4 billion, respectively, Immelt predicts up to 17% earnings growth and 10% sales gains for all of 2005, with double-digit returns through 2006. While economists scratch their heads over the next quarter, Immelt is promising two years of explosive growth. No wonder Sharon Garavel, a quality leader at GE Commercial Finance says that, at Boca, "everyone was talking about a $60 stock price," or about $24 more than its current price.

That in itself may be a stretch of the imagination for now, but Immelt is trying to recast the company for decades to come.

He's spending big bucks to create the kind of infrastructure that can equip and foster an army of dreamers. That means beefing up GE's research facilities, creating something akin to a global brain trust that GE can tap to spur innovation. He has sunk $100 million into overhauling the company's research center in Niskayuna, N.Y., and forked out for cutting-edge centers in Bangalore, Shanghai, and Munich.

Globalizing research has allowed GE to get closer to overseas customers. The simple fact is that most of GE's growth will come from outside the U.S. Immelt predicts that developing countries will account for 60% of the company's growth in the next 10 years, vs. about 20% for the past decade. But he is also spreading new practices to lethargic economies such as Germany. After a 2002 meeting with German Chancellor Gerhard Schröder reinforced his notion that GE could be doing more in that country, Immelt decided to open the Munich center. As Immelt explains, "there's no place in GE where you feel more like a loser than in Germany. You have Siemens and Philips, and we haven't been that good." By July, 2004, a new center was up, and the results were immediate. According to Nani Beccalli-Falco, CEO of GE International, the company saw a 21.5% growth in German-speaking markets last year from 2003.

Now that Immelt has repositioned the portfolio and added resources, his main objective is to get more immediate growth out of the businesses he already has. That's where the Imagination Breakthroughs come in. Over the past 18 months, Immelt has agreed to invest $5 billion in 80 projects that range from creating microjet engines to overhauling the brand image of 3,000 consumer-finance locations. The hope is that the first lot will generate $25 billion in revenue by 2007—cheap, if it works, when you consider what it would cost to acquire something from the outside with that level of sales. In the next year or two, Immelt expects to have 200 such projects under way.

The pressure to produce could not be more intense. Many of the company's 307,000 workers weren't exactly hired to be part of a diverse, creative, fleet-footed army of visionaries who are acutely sensitive to customers' needs. "These guys just aren't dreamer types," says one consultant who has worked with the company. "It almost seems painful to them, like a waste of time." Even insiders who are openly euphoric about the changes under Chairman Jeff admit to feeling some fear in the depth of their guts.

"This is a big fundamental structural change, and that can be tough," says Paul T. Bossidy, CEO of GE Commercial Equipment Financing, who is reorganizing his sales force so that each person represents all of GE to particular customers. Susan P. Peters, GE's vice-president for executive development, even talks about the need for employees to "reconceptualize" themselves. "What you have been to date isn't good enough for tomorrow," she says. Ouch.

To Immelt, the best managers are great marketers and not just great operators. That's a rethinking of GE's long-held bias that winning products essentially sell themselves. Beth Comstock, who was appointed chief marketing officer three years ago with the mission of boosting the company's marketing expertise, says that when she started, a number of insiders were skittish about the new agenda: "Everyone thought, 'I've got to get into sales and marketing to be relevant in this company?'"

Well, yes. Comstock is trying to elevate the role of marketing throughout GE. She has helped develop a commercial leadership program that sends the best and brightest marketers around the organization for two intensive years, much as GE's corporate audit staff has long done on the finance side. The auditors were important to maintaining financial discipline under Welch. Now, GE has initiated new courses in marketing, as well as ones on how to spark idea generation. Some executives have also taken to holding "idea jams," where people from diverse businesses brainstorm. Within GE Energy alone, there are "growth heroes," who are held up as emblematic of where the company wants to go, a "virtual idea box" to spur brainstorming via the Web, and "Excellerator awards" for the development of ideas. The jargon may smack of classic GE, but the approach is novel. "This is about unlocking the curiosity, yet having the rigor stay intact," says Comstock.

In this era, marketing is not just a matter of producing edgier commercials or catchier slogans. It means getting outside the company to understand markets and customers. Among other things, GE's top marketing executives have spent a lot of time examining the practices of companies such as Procter & Gamble Co., which let them spend time last November in "The GYM" where strategies and issues are debated, examined, and maybe even solved. "The idea is to enhance a team's creative thinking," says P&G spokesman Terry Loftus. GE staffers also spent time at FedEx Corp., which has exceptional customer service. Welch did the same thing in benchmarking Motorola Inc. when he delved into Six Sigma, but the external focus is even stronger now.

Immelt wants his managers to lead industries rather than merely follow demand. Take the company's move to create a cleaner coal plant—another Imagination

Breakthrough—before its customers were even asking for it. GE initiated the push after acquiring ChevronTexaco Corp.'s gasification-technology business last year. Immelt and GE Energy CEO John G. Rice brought together big power customers and experts on subjects such as climate change at GE's education center in Croton-on-Hudson, N.Y., last July to debate where the industry would be in 2015. James E. Rogers, chairman and CEO of public utilities giant Cinergy Corp., was shocked to hear Immelt talk about the need to generate electricity with far fewer emissions—a touchy subject in an industry that still burns a lot of coal. "He was unafraid to articulate a point of view that his customers might not share," says Rogers, whose company burns 30 million tons of coal a year.

What convinced Rogers to partner with GE and Bechtel Corp. on a cleaner coal power plant was the prospect of having an integrated package managed by GE. Instead of forcing Rogers to license the technology and figure it out himself, GE in partnership with Bechtel will design and implement the plan, while Cinergy will provide and help develop the site. GE's promise: that the cleaner-burning plant will soon become competitive with pulverized coal and that GE will handle any hiccups in the process. "I like the way they're thinking about the future," says Rogers. "They're going to make this work."

OUTSIDERS' INFLUENCE

But there's a limit to how much Immelt can transform his own people. A key strategy—and one that amounts to a gut punch to the culture—involves bringing in more outsiders. In sales and marketing alone, GE has hired more than 1,700 new faces in the past few years, including hundreds of seasoned veterans such as David J. Slump, a former ABB Group executive who is the chief marketing officer of GE Energy. "I just didn't think outsiders would do well here," says Slump, who was surprised at the unit's openness to changing its ways, though one of the senior executives did warn him about coming off as "too intense." That said, he was also amazed at the lack of attention to marketing when he arrived—with no marketers among the senior ranks and no real sense of strategy beyond the occasional ad or product push. Slump felt needed.

Immelt is also looking for more leaders who are intensely passionate about their businesses and are experts in the details. "I want to see our people become part of their industries," he says. No one represents Immelt's vision of what a GE leader should be better than Bill Castell—who has spent his entire career in one industry and who has rarely, if ever, focused on maximizing profits. The cerebral Brit was heading up diagnostics-and-bioscience giant Amersham PLC when Immelt acquired it—after much wooing—for $10.7 billion last year. Not only did Immelt make Castell head of the new $14 billion GE Healthcare, he named him a vice-chairman of GE and located the unit's headquarters outside the U.S., in the English village of Chalfont St. Giles.

Castell is quite unlike the archetypal GE executive. He's totally immersed in his industry, a leading thinker on the future of personalized medicine who will never head up a business based on jet engines or commercial finance. Nor is he pursuing a black belt in Six Sigma or losing sleep over making his numbers. "People were surprised at first that I didn't tend to talk about the quarter," admits Castell. Yet Immelt loves him. "I want managers to have the kind of curiosity that Bill has, his passion for the industry," he says. "He understands where the market is going." This is, after all, a man known to call up his boss and wax on about an angiogenesis marker that won't hit the marketplace for 10 years. Imagine how long that conversation would have lasted with Welch.

To encourage that kind of expertise and passion in the rest of his organization, Immelt is urging people to stay in place longer to build stronger relationships with customers and markets. GE Energy's Rice—a hotshot who is emblematic of the old system, in which a great GE manager could parachute onto the scene to turn any business into gold—notes that the idea of staying put takes some adjustment. "There was always an impression in the midlevel ranks that if you weren't moving every few years, something was wrong," says Rice. He now says he likes the fact that he has been in one place for four years, because he's developing a deeper knowledge.

CULTURE SHOCK

How CEO Immelt is trying to shift the GE mindset:

PAY Link bonuses to new ideas, customer satisfaction, and sales growth, with less emphasis on bottom-line results

RISK Spend billions to fund "Imagination Breakthrough" projects that extend the boundaries of GE

EXPERTS Rotate executives less often, and bring in more outsiders to create industry experts instead of professional managers

---

SHUFFLING THE PORTFOLIO

Immelt has spent more than $60 billion to bolster GE's mix of businesses. Some new capabilities:

MEDIA CONTENT Buying Universal gave GE a rich library, film studio, cable networks, and theme parks. Bravo and Telemundo help, too.

BIOSCIENCES With Amersham, GE can bring diagnostics down to the cellular level and be a leader in personalized medicine.

SECURITY GE bought its way into fire safety and industrial security with Edwards Systems. Ion Track and InVision gave it entree into homeland security, from bomb detection to screening for narcotics.

WATER Buying Ionics and Osmonics gets GE into desalination, fluid filtration, and other water-processing services. The goal: to increase the availability of clean water around the world.

RENEWABLE ENERGY GE moved into solar and wind power and biogas with acquisitions such as Enron Wind.

Investors are still waiting to see whether GE's evangelizing chairman can truly make his company grow faster than the world around it. Even some of his fans think that GE's new momentum has more to do with the overall economy than with idea generation. Says Steve Roukis of Matrix Asset Advisors, which owns 2 million GE shares: "If you have a revolutionary decade of growth around the world, who's going to be there to capture it? GE."

Capture it? Jeff Immelt wants to shape it, drive it, make it his own. For him, reinventing GE is the only way to make his company dominate this century, much as it led the one before.

Reading

Unlocking the Mystery of Effective Large-Scale Change

Peggy Holman

I am on a quest to unlock the mystery of how to achieve lasting and positive large-scale change. I am convinced that this is the key to creating a better world.

My first experience with large-scale change was an extraordinary success. It was 1988, and I was the Software Development Manager for a cellular phone company, US WEST NewVector Group (NVG). The pace was intense, spirits ran high, and NVG was an exciting and fun place to be. After all, we were inventing a whole new industry. When the company was about three years old, our new VP of Finance took a fresh look at the numbers and made a startling discovery: we were retaining only about 48 percent of the customers who bought a mobile phone.

That meant the company had to sell two phone lines for every one we'd keep. The industry term is *churn,* the rate at which phone lines turn over.

Reducing churn became the rallying cry. A cross-functional team, on which I represented Information Technologies (IT), was formed to "solve churn." Over several months, we looked at how every aspect of the business affected this key indicator, making changes as we went. Ironically, while churn definitely dropped, we made so many changes along the way that no one knew which actions made the most difference. Later, we learned about measurement and discipline and got very good at not only getting results but also knowing what we did to achieve them. We concluded ultimately that churn was a quality issue. That was before I'd heard of total quality (TQ). Fortunately, someone in the group had heard about this idea and attracted a superb TQ consultant to join NVG. That's when things really took off.

At their first retreat company executives learned what embracing TQ would mean to them personally and to the organization. They then spent the next nine months doing site visits, reading and discussing books on quality, and creating a plan for how to proceed. A key element of that plan was to engage the top 60 people in this 2,200-person company in training every employee in quality. This meant that every director and vice president, as well as the CEO, each allocated at least eight full days over six months to prepare for and deliver several sessions of a two-day quality awareness overview. The rest of the employees got the message: This was important work.

Over the next two years, we changed the company. To an innovative, high-energy, and fun place we added knowledge, skills, and discipline that also made it profitable and produced the highest customer satisfaction and lowest churn rates in the industry for the rest of the company's existence.

WHAT MAKES FOR A SUCCESSFUL CHANGE EFFORT?

Since I clearly knew what we had done to transform this organization, I left IT and became a TQ consultant. I was shocked when my next attempt to change a company flopped badly. After I picked myself up and asked, "What happened?" I began a search for the magic formula: What is it that makes the difference between extraordinary, unimagined success and demoralizing failure? In other words:

> What does it take to achieve large-scale change, to align people to achieve some greater good in a business or in society at large?

With this question in mind I started my search for a "unified field theory" of human systems. I borrowed the name from physics. According to Stephen Hawking, "The eventual goal of science is to provide a single theory that describes the whole universe."[1] That's what I wanted to find as it applied to people. Why? So that I could, with confidence, always repeat the experience of transformation that occurred at NewVector Group.

My search led me to the field of organization development. I found several "large-group interventions," including future search, open space technology, and dialogue. The methods seemed to be distinguished by two common characteristics: They intelligently involved people in changing their workplaces and communities, and they approached change systemically.

During this period I also learned about the work of Solomon Asch, who identified conditions for effective dialogue:

- Perception of a shared world
- Perception that all are equally human
- Perception of an open dialogue[2]

Asch's conditions profoundly influenced my consulting work. I proceeded with the assumption that anything could be learned without lecture; I just had to be

---

[1] He says a lot more on the subject: "It turns out to be very difficult to devise a theory to describe the universe all in one go. Instead, we break the problem up into bits and invent a number of partial theories.... It may be that this approach is completely wrong. If everything in the universe depends on everything else in a fundamental way, it might be impossible to get close to a full solution by investigating parts of the problem in isolation." Stephen Hawking, *A Brief History of Time* (Bantam Books, 1998, pp. 10, 11).

[2] Marvin R. Weisbord et al., *Discovering Common Ground* (Berrett-Koehler, 1992, pp. 21–23).

sure Asch's conditions were present. This meant designs in which people discussed what the subject meant to them—why it was worth the time. It meant offering new communication tools that put the emphasis on inquiring into each other's beliefs rather than advocating for one's own position. Also it meant asking people to speak their heart-felt truths in front of their colleagues.

I learned that people reveled in their new-found freedom, moving from passive consumers of presentations to active learners pursuing their own paths to understanding. I discovered that the tools of dialogue enabled even the crustiest, most cynical of people to develop new understanding and appreciation for their colleagues. Many also found a deeper understanding of themselves. And I observed that when people changed, when their relationships changed, the likelihood of sustainable organizational change dramatically increased.

What remained elusive for me was *consistently* creating the conditions in which people expressed their deepest thoughts and feelings about their work. Sometimes this happened, leading to catharsis and growth. Sometimes it did not. I knew that I had part of the equation for achieving change: personal involvement, connection with a larger purpose, and a chance to be heard. But until I could be confident people would choose to speak, I knew something was still eluding me.

So I took my search for ways to achieve large-scale change into other disciplines using the keys I'd uncovered so far: high-involvement, a systemic approach, and Asch's conditions. A diverse array of possibilities emerged (see Exhibit 1, "Approaches for Achieving Large-Scale Change"). As I worked with my newly acquired knowledge, my own

practice grew more effective, and people began seeking me out when they wanted to involve people in changing their organizations. Some of this work took me out of the corporate world and into new realms: nonprofits and government. Not surprisingly, I found the setting didn't matter; whatever the work, the keys were the same.

WHAT I LEARNED

In addition to finding a wide variety of approaches that could consistently produce results, I now had data to continue my search. By identifying what these approaches had in common I thought I could learn what it takes to consistently achieve large-scale change. I found seven themes present in all the methods I researched:

A vision of the future or an opportunity to contribute to something larger than themselves moves people to act.

When people see the possibility of contributing to something larger than themselves, they act differently. The emphasis shifts from focusing on "why something can't be done" to "how can we make this happen?" There is a tangible difference in the atmosphere of organizations that have made this shift: They feel alive with possibility and excitement.

Members of the organization or community collectively create a whole systems view.

People begin to understand their system at a deeper level. They see interconnections among departments or processes or relationships. When this occurs, system members know better how to participate and therefore make commitments that

EXHIBIT 1   Approaches for Achieving Large-Scale Change

The eighteen approaches for achieving large-scale change that I've listed below are powerful testament to a revolution-in-progress that has been building since the 1960s. Each approach involves a wide array of people—not just a few "leaders"—in changing their workplaces and communities. In addition, reflecting the observation that no change happens in isolation, each approach is committed to systemic change.

The approaches derive from many disciplines. Many of the methods have their roots in organization development, while others bring rich traditions from community development; total quality; social science; system dynamics; the wisdom of indigenous cultures; and studies of intelligence, creativity, and the arts.

Hundreds of examples around the world of dramatic and sustained increases in organization and community performance now exist.[3] For example, Appreciative Inquiry was cited as the backbone of an award-winning change initiative that has unleashed the power of the front-line staff at GTE. At Brooklyn Technical High School, Real Time Strategic Change supported curriculum redesign and faculty development through a unique partnership between principal and faculty. And in Hopkinton, Massachusetts, a future search conference helped a town of 9,000 overcome a tax-limiting referendum to provide double-digit school budget increases and create partnerships with local businesses to fund libraries, technology, and teacher training.

The Methods and Their Creators

1960s

Preferred Futuring
  Ronald Lippitt and Ed Lindaman
Search Conference
  Fred Emery, Eric Trist, and Merrelyn Emery

1970s

Participative Design Workshop
  Fred Emery
SimuReal
  Donald C. Klein
Organization Workshop
  Barry Oshry

1980s

Future Search
  Marvin Weisbord and Sandra Janoff
Whole-Scale Change
  Paul D. Tolchinsky, Kathleen D.
  Dannemiller, and Dannemiller Tyson
  Associates
Technology of Participation's Participatory
Strategic Planning Process
  Institute of Cultural Affairs and The
  Ecumenica Institute

Dialogue
  David Bohm
Open Space Technology
  Harrison Owen
Gemba Kaizen
  Masaaki Imai
Appreciative Inquiry
  David L. Cooperrider, Suresh Srivastva,
  and colleagues
The Strategic Forum
  Barry Richmond

1990s

The Conference Model
  Richard H. and Emily M. Axelrod
Fast-Cycle Full-Participation
  Bill and Mary Pasmore, Alan Fitz, Bob
  Rehm, and Gary Frank
Think Like a Genius Process
  Todd Siler
Real Time Strategic Change
  Robert W. Jacobs and Frank McKeown
Whole Systems Approach
  W. A. (Bill) and Cindy Adams

---

[3] *The Change Handbook: Group Methods for Shaping the Future* (Berrett-Koehler, 1999), edited by Peggy Holman and Tom Devane, contains over twenty such stories of stellar results from high-involvement, systemic change efforts.

were previously unlikely. Because more people understand the whole system, they can make intelligent, informed contributions to substantive decisions.

Critical information is publicly available to members of the organization or community.

This is a corollary to the whole systems view. What keeps the system whole over time is a commitment to sharing information that is traditionally provided on a "need to know" basis. When people are informed of what is important to the system and how it is performing, they make more informed decisions about their own activities.

Head, heart, and spirit of the members of the organization or community are engaged.

Over the years, words such as hands or heads have become a way to count numbers of people in organizations. They reflect a focus on what is considered important: hands to do the manual work, heads to do the thinking work. These methods engage the whole person: hands for doing, heads for thinking, hearts for caring, and spirits for achieving inspired results.

The power of the individual to contribute is unleashed.

When people understand the whole system, when they see the possibility of meaningful intentions, when they feel their voice matters, they commit. While this doesn't happen every time, the potential for extraordinary accomplishments exists within each of these approaches.

Knowledge and wisdom exist in the people forming the organization or community.

This belief, that the people in the system know best is a profound shift from the days of bringing in the outside "efficiency" expert with the answer. While several of these approaches rely on new ideas, such as Gemba Kaizen's use of the concepts of just in time and total productive maintenance, not one of them presumes to have the answer. Instead, they involve people in the organization in making choices about what's best for them.

Change is a process, not an event.

While most of the practitioners describe a half-day to three-day event as their "method" for change, they are all quick to add that the sum total of a transformational effort should not be one change event. Though events can be helpful in focusing people's attention, they are only a part of the change equation. Organizations and communities also need to focus on actively supporting the plans and improvements achieved during the event. Without such ongoing support, conditions may return to what they were before the event occurred.

PUTTING THESE CHARACTERISTICS TO WORK

I could now describe what seemed to exist in successful approaches to large-scale change. And I had a wide variety of proven alternatives I could use with clients. But I wanted more. I wanted to know why these approaches worked so that I could consistently help clients achieve their highest aspirations in any situation. My next thought was to create a picture to help me understand how these characteristics related to one another. Are they all of equal importance? Are some the results of

EXHIBIT 2 Changing Assumptions

Characteristic	Old Think	New Think
Vision/purpose	Management owns	Shared ownership
Information	Need to know	Public
Contribution	I just do my job	What can I do?
Person	They just want my hands/head	I can be myself; who I am matters
Wisdom	Hire an expert	Among us, we have the knowledge and skills we need or know how to get it
System	I know my part and that's all I need to know	I understand how we fit together
Process	That was a nice event, now back to the real work	We continually learn and change together

others? Which ones provide the greatest leverage? I figured that understanding this would give me the key I was seeking.

On my way to creating this picture, I looked at what was different about the assumptions of these change approaches (see Exhibit 2, "Changing Assumptions"). After all, such things as purpose and information are just there. What facilitates transformation are the beliefs about them from which we act.

By visually describing "new think," I hoped to discover a larger message or pattern. When I was done, I realized that I had drawn a compass. It was a great reminder that change can take me anywhere; I just need to choose the destination and establish the rules of the road. My effectiveness with the compass will determine the success of the trip.

The drawing (Exhibit 3) describes a route to reliable large-scale change in organizations, communities, and society: *Systems View* and *Change Is a Process* bound the picture, affirming the importance of establishing what, who, and

how. Systemic, high-involvement change begins with two questions that help describe the system:

What is our purpose? By exploring this question both intellectually (What do we want to accomplish?) and emotionally (Why is it worth investing time and energy?), the shift to thinking systematically begins.

Who participates? Understanding the system requires knowing who is involved: who affects it, who cares about it, who holds responsibility for its health and well-being.

Having established a preliminary systems view, we can choose an approach to change that suits our needs. Culture— both current and desired—plays an important role in making that choice because how the approach deals with the current culture's assumptions will help shape its impact.

Public Information is the crossroads, the connection of the individual and the

EXHIBIT 3 The World I Want to Live In

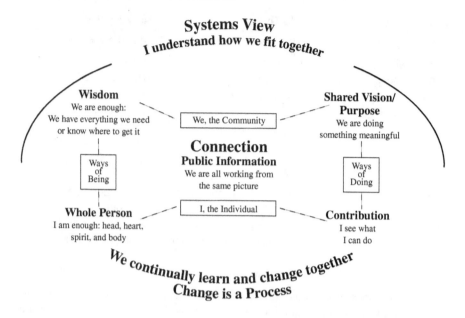

community and of being and doing. I have observed amazing results when people see a multi-faceted picture of their world for the first time. In addition, I have been struck by the central role of public information. It sustains the systems view and renews the process of learning and change. Remove it and fundamental connections are severed. I am convinced that effective communication sustains us. The illustration shows why: It ties the whole system together.

The "compass points"—*beliefs about wisdom, purpose, personal wholeness,* and *contribution*—shape culture. This is a graphic reminder that successful change depends on the attitudes we hold about our ways of being and ways of doing, individually and as a community. It is the successful weaving together of these beliefs that distinguishes the approaches that consistently succeed.

Humbled by this realization, I remain determined to understand what it takes to create the conditions where these beliefs always emerge. I am convinced it requires a shift from a mechanical (follow these steps) to an organic (support what is called forth) way of working. For me, Asch still holds the key because I see being and doing, community and individual implicit in his work. His conditions are like the magnet in the compass—unseen and utterly vital. When they are present, "new think" occurs. Indeed, after working with his conditions for several years, I believe Asch actually uncovered the conditions for trust. I speculate that as trust grows, the conditions become "normal" and form the basis of loving community.

What draws people to act from Asch's conditions? I think the conclusion of my quest lies in this answer. To continue testing this belief, I use three questions to guide my work:

- Are we spending time understanding what we collectively aspire to? (Shared world)

- Does every individual identify what is personally meaningful to them? (Equally human)

- Is there room for all voices? (Open dialogue)

I have been highly successful in increasing the energy, commitment, and effectiveness of organizations with these questions when all voices choose to speak. Consistently calling forth that choice remains the mystery in my quest.

If these questions attract you, I invite you to join my quest. You don't need to wait for a large-scale change effort to begin. The next time you have an activity or meeting to plan, ask about purpose and participation, and choose your approach to the task using the questions inspired by Asch. And let me know how it goes. Together, perhaps we can uncover a unified field theory of human systems.